Contents by Topic

Use this list as a quick reference for finding entries by topic. To search this book in more detail, see the Index.

The Business
Writer's Handbook

About the Authors

Gerald J. Alred is Professor Emeritus of English at the University of Wisconsin–Milwaukee, where he teaches courses in the Professional Writing Program. He is the author of numerous scholarly articles and several standard bibliographies on business and technical communication, and he is a founding member of the editorial board of the *Journal of Business and Technical Communication.* He is a recipient of the prestigious Jay R. Gould Award for "profound scholarly and textbook contributions to the teaching of business and technical writing."

Charles T. Brusaw served as a faculty member at NCR Corporation's Management College, where he developed and taught courses in professional writing, editing, and presentation skills for the corporation worldwide. Previously, he worked in advertising, technical writing, public relations, and curriculum development. He has been a communications consultant, an invited speaker at academic conferences, and a teacher of business writing at Sinclair Community College. He is also the author of *Soldat: Reflections of a German Soldier: 1936–1949.*

Walter E. Oliu served as Chief of the Publishing Services Branch at the U.S. Nuclear Regulatory Commission, where he managed the agency's printing, graphics, editing, and publishing programs as well as managing daily operations of the agency's public Web site. He has taught at Miami University of Ohio; Slippery Rock State University; and, as an adjunct faculty member, at Montgomery College and George Mason University.

Tenth Edition

The Business Writer's Handbook

Gerald J. Alred

Charles T. Brusaw

Walter E. Oliu

St. Martin's Press   New York

For Bedford/St. Martin's

Developmental Editor: Kate Mayhew
Production Supervisor: Samuel Jones
Marketing Manager: Molly Parke
Editorial Assistant: Regina Tavani
Project Management: Books By Design, Inc.
Copy Editor: Kathy McQueen
Indexer: Ellen Kuhl Repetto
Permissions Manager: Kalina K. Ingham
Senior Art Director: Anna Palchik
Text Design: Janis Owens, Glenna Collett
Cover Design: Billy Boardman
Cover Art: Office workers. *Photographer:* Toru Takeuchi
Composition: Achorn International, Inc.
Printing and Binding: RR Donnelley & Sons

President: Joan E. Feinberg
Editorial Director: Denise B. Wydra
Editor in Chief: Karen S. Henry
Director of Marketing: Karen R. Soeltz
Director of Production: Susan W. Brown
Associate Director, Editorial Production: Elise S. Kaiser
Manager, Publishing Services: Andrea Cava

Library of Congress Control Number: 2011933006

6   5   4   3   2   1
f   e   d   c   b   a

For information, write: Bedford/St. Martin's, 75 Arlington Street, Boston, MA 02116   (617-399-4000)

ISBN: 978-0-312-67943-9 (paperback)
ISBN: 978-1-250-00442-0 (hardcover)

Acknowledgments

Acknowledgments and copyrights are continued at the back of the book on page 592, which constitute an extension of the copyright page.

Contents

Preface

Like previous editions, the tenth edition of *The Business Writer's Handbook* is a comprehensive, easy-access guide to all aspects of business writing in the classroom and on the job. It places writing in a real-world context with quick reference to hundreds of business writing topics and scores of model documents and visuals. Anticipating the needs of today's business writers and job seekers, the tenth edition has expanded coverage of the job search, offering both students and new professionals relevant and up-to-date advice on securing a position in today's economy and quickly acclimating to the professional environment. This comprehensive reference tool is also accompanied by a robust Web site that works together with the text to offer expanded resources online, including additional model documents and tips.

Helpful Features

The ESL Tips boxes throughout the book offer special advice for multilingual writers. In addition, the Contents by Topic on the inside front cover includes a list of entries—ESL Trouble Spots—that may be of particular interest to nonnative speakers of English.

Digital Tips and Web Links boxes throughout the book direct readers to specific, related resources on the companion Web site. Digital Tips in the book suggest ways to use technology to simplify complex tasks such as writing and reviewing documents collaboratively or scheduling and conducting meetings remotely. Expanded Digital Tips on the companion Web site offer step-by-step instructions for completing each task. Web Links in the book point students to related resources on the companion Web site, such as model documents, tutorials, and links to hundreds of useful, related Web sites.

Ethics Notes throughout the text highlight the ethical concerns in today's business world and offer advice for dealing with these concerns. A thorough discussion of copyright and plagiarism clarifies what plagiarism is in the digital age and highlights the ethical aspects of using and documenting sources appropriately.

New to This Edition

As mentioned, our focus in revising the *Handbook* for this edition has been the job search. We've provided relevant advice for obtaining a job in today's economy and for navigating the technologies needed to perform that job effectively. New material advises students on how to network using professional and social media and helps them to successfully prepare for and field difficult questions in professional interviews. Updated samples in print and online and a brand-new section on completing a job-application form provide effective examples and advice for new and experienced applicants, as well as for those changing fields or handling gaps in employment. We have thoroughly updated the entry on documenting sources, providing the most up-to-date guidelines for following APA style, MLA style, and the *Chicago Manual of Style*. We have also made the following additions and improvements:

- **A new entry on adapting to new technology** helps students evaluate and learn how to use new technologies in a constantly evolving workplace context.

- **Professionalism Notes** throughout the text cover professional behavior, guidelines for online and interpersonal communication for both the workplace and the classroom, and tips on preparing for important projects and presentations.

- **A new entry on grant proposals** describes the different components, advises students on how to prepare them, and refers students to useful sites for models and writing tips.

- **Coverage of plain language** helps students communicate clearly even when the topic is complex.

- **New and revamped Digital Tips** throughout the book advise students on relevant skills, including using technologies to schedule and conduct meetings, synchronizing information across different media, and using wikis and other collaborative software to circulate and revise documents.

- **A new user-friendly Index** incorporates the terms that students use to search for help with writing problems, formatting issues, and communication advice.

- **An updated and all-encompassing Student Site for Alred Handbooks at *bedfordstmartins.com/alred*** features additional free course resources not only for the *Handbook* but also for the *Handbook of Technical Writing*, Tenth Edition and *The Business Writer's Companion*, Sixth Edition. This site allows instructors to take advantage of the texts' potential in face-to-face, online, or hybrid classes by offering lesson plans, handouts, teaching tips, and assignment ideas. For students, the Web site includes additional sample documents, useful tutorials, expanded Digital Tips, and links to hundreds of useful Web sites keyed to the *Handbook*'s main entries.

- **Now available in popular e-book formats.** Students can purchase *The Business Writer's Handbook* in popular e-book formats for computers, tablets, and e-readers. For details, visit *bedfordstmartins .com/ebooks.*

How to Use This Book

The Business Writer's Handbook is made up of alphabetically organized entries with color tabs. Within each entry, underlined cross-references such as **proposals** link readers to related entries that contain further information. Many entries present advice and guidelines in the form of convenient Writer's Checklists.

The *Handbook*'s alphabetical organization enables readers to find specific topics quickly and easily; however, readers with general questions will discover several alternate ways to find information in the book and on its companion Web site at *bedfordstmartins.com/alred.*

- **Contents by Topic.** The complete Contents by Topic on the inside front cover groups the alphabetical entries into topic categories. This topical key can help a writer focusing on a specific task or problem browse all related entries; it can also help instructors correlate the *Handbook* with standard textbooks or their own course materials.

- **Commonly Misused Words and Phrases.** The list of Commonly Misused Words and Phrases on pages 639–40 extends the Contents by Topic by listing all of the usage entries, which appear in *italics* throughout the book.

- **Model Documents and Figures by Topic.** The topically organized list of model documents and figures on the inside back cover makes it easier to browse the book's most commonly referenced sample documents and visuals to find specific examples of business writing genres.

- **Checklist of the Writing Process.** The checklist on pages xxiii–xxiv helps readers reference key entries in a sequence useful for planning and carrying out a writing project.

- **Comprehensive Index.** The new user-friendly Index lists all the topics covered in the book—including subtopics and Model Documents—within the main entries in the alphabetical arrangement.

Acknowledgments

For their invaluable comments and suggestions for this edition of *The Business Writer's Handbook*, we thank the following reviewers who responded to our questionnaire: Roberta Allen, Western Michigan

University; Katie Bliss, College of San Mateo; Claudine L. Boros, Marymount Manhattan College; Don Cunningham, Radford University; Sharon M. Gallagher, Pennsylvania State University Erie, The Behrend College; Melanie K. Hoftyzer, University of Wisconsin–Madison; Sun Huatong, Miami University; Thomas Kull, Arizona State University; Mariann Maris, University of Wisconsin–Milwaukee; Patricia McArver, The Citadel; Rolf Norgaard, University of Colorado Boulder; Jon Ramsey, University of California Santa Barbara; C. David Rota, University of Missouri–St. Louis; Sara Schaff, University of Michigan–Ann Arbor; Jennifer R. Veltsos, Minnesota State University; and Carol Venable, San Diego State University.

For their helpful reviews of the model documents, we also thank Melissa Smith, Illinois State University; Debra Danielson, California State University Fullerton; and Steve Byars, University of Southern California.

For this edition, we owe special thanks to Sally Stanton of Write Now! Consulting, for building a comprehensive and expert new entry on grant writing and for her astute review of the "proposals" section.

We thank Kim Isaacs for continuing to lend her considerable expertise to the job-search sections, as well as Lisa Parker- CPRW, Professional Résumé Presentations, who ably stepped in to update these sections at the eleventh hour.

We are indebted to Kenneth J. Cook, President, Ken Cook Co., for his ongoing support for this and earlier editions and for continued permission to reprint the exemplary company newsletter.

We especially thank Quinn Warnick, St. Edward's University, for developing the new entry "adapting to new technologies" and Richard C. Hay, Founder and CEO of the RiCH Company, for consulting on technology-related issues. Thanks also to Rachel Spilka for her work on the entry "adapting to new technologies" and to Ulrike Mueller, SAP AG, for his contributions to social networking and the entry "global communication." We appreciate the wonderfully attentive work of Ellen Kuhl Repetto, who reinvented and revitalized the Index, and of Mary Ellen Smith, who expertly amended the "documenting sources" entry. In addition, we are very much indebted to the many reviewers and contributors not named here who helped us shape the first nine editions.

We wish to thank Bedford/St. Martin's for supporting this book, especially Joan Feinberg, President, and Karen Henry, Editor in Chief. We are grateful to Andrea Cava, Manager of Publishing Services at Bedford/St. Martin's, and to Herb Nolan of Books By Design for their patience and expert guidance. We thank Regina Tavani for her organization and attention to detail. Finally, we wish to thank Kate Mayhew, our developmental editor at Bedford/St. Martin's, for her expert and patient editorial direction throughout this always challenging project.

We offer heartfelt thanks to Barbara Brusaw for her patience and time spent preparing the manuscript for the first five editions. We also gratefully acknowledge the ongoing contributions of many students and instructors at the University of Wisconsin–Milwaukee. Finally, special thanks go to Janice Alred for her many hours of help in coordination and for continuing to hold everything together.

G. J. A.
C. T. B.
W. E. O.

Five Steps to Successful Writing

Successful writing on the job is not the product of inspiration, nor is it merely the spoken word converted to print; it is the result of knowing how to structure information using both text and design to achieve an intended purpose for a clearly defined audience. The best way to ensure that your writing will succeed—whether it is in the form of a memo, a résumé, a proposal, or a Web page—is to approach writing using the following steps:

1. Preparation
2. Research
3. Organization
4. Writing
5. Revision

You will very likely need to follow those steps consciously—even self-consciously—at first. The same is true the first time you use new software, interview a candidate for a job, or chair a committee meeting. With practice, the steps become nearly automatic. That is not to suggest that writing becomes easy. It does not. However, the easiest and most efficient way to write effectively is to do it systematically.

As you master the five steps, keep in mind that they are interrelated and often overlap. For example, your readers' needs and your purpose, which you determine in step 1, will affect decisions you make in subsequent steps. You may also need to retrace steps. When you conduct research, for example, you may realize that you need to revise your initial impression of the document's purpose and audience. Similarly, when you begin to organize, you may discover the need to return to the research step to gather more information.

The time required for each step varies with different writing tasks. When writing an uncomplicated memo, for example, you might follow the first three steps (preparation, research, and organization) by simply listing the points in the order you want to cover them. In such situations, you gather and organize information mentally as you consider your purpose and audience. For a formal report, the first three steps require well-organized research, careful note-taking, and detailed outlining. For a routine e-mail message to a coworker, the first four steps merge as you type the information onto the screen. In short, the five steps expand, contract, and at times must be repeated to fit the complexity or context of the writing task.

Dividing the writing process into steps is especially useful for **collaborative writing**,* in which you typically divide work among team members, keep track of a project, and save time by not duplicating effort. When you collaborate, you can use e-mail to share text and other files, suggest improvements to each other's work, and generally keep everyone informed of your progress as you follow the steps in the writing process.

Preparation

Writing, like most professional tasks, requires solid **preparation**. In fact, adequate preparation is as important as writing a draft. In preparation for writing, your goal is to accomplish the following four major tasks:

- Establish your primary **purpose**.
- Assess your **audience** (or readers) and the **context**.
- Determine the **scope** of your coverage.
- Select the appropriate medium. See **selecting the medium**.

Establishing Your Purpose.   To establish your primary purpose, simply ask yourself what you want your readers to know, to believe, or to be able to do after they have finished reading what you have written. Be precise. Often a writer states a purpose in such broad terms that the purpose statement is almost useless. A purpose such as "to report on possible locations for a new research facility" is too general. However, "to compare the relative advantages of Paris, Singapore, and San Francisco as possible locations for a new research facility so that top management can choose the best location" is a purpose statement that can guide you throughout the writing process. In addition to your primary purpose, consider possible secondary purposes for your document. For example, a secondary purpose of the research-facilities report might be to make corporate executive readers aware of the staffing needs of the new facility so that they can ensure its smooth operation in whichever location is selected.

Assessing Your Audience and Context.   The next task is to assess your **audience**. Again, be precise and ask key questions. Who exactly is your reader? Do you have multiple readers? Who needs to see or to use the document? What are your readers' needs in relation to your subject? What are your readers' attitudes about the subject? (Are they skeptical? Supportive? Anxious? Bored?) What do your readers already know about the subject? Should you define basic terminology, or will such

---

*In this discussion, as elsewhere throughout this book, words and phrases underlined and set in an alternate typeface refer to specific alphabetical entries.

definitions merely bore, or even impede, your readers? Are you communicating with international readers and therefore dealing with issues inherent in **global communication**?

For the research-facilities report, the readers are described as "top management." Who is included in that category? Will one of the people evaluating the report be the human resources manager? If so, that person likely would be interested in the availability of qualified professionals as well as in the presence of training, housing, and perhaps even recreational facilities available to potential employees in each city. The purchasing manager would be concerned about available sources for materials needed by the facility. The marketing manager would give priority to the facility's proximity to the primary markets for its products and services and to the transportation options that are available. The chief financial officer would want to know about land and building costs and about each country's tax structure. The chief executive officer would be interested in all this information and perhaps more. As with this example, many workplace documents have audiences composed of multiple readers. You can accommodate their needs through one of a number of approaches described in the entry **audience**.

In addition to knowing the needs and interests of your readers, learn as much as you can about the context. Simply put, context is the environment or circumstances in which writers produce documents and within which readers interpret their meanings. Everything is written in a context, as illustrated in many entries and examples throughout this book. To determine the effect of context on the research-facilities report, you might ask both specific and general questions about the situation and about your readers' backgrounds: Is this the company's first new facility, or has the company chosen locations for new facilities before? Have the readers visited all three cities? Have they already seen other reports on the three cities? What is the corporate culture in which your readers work, and what are its key values? What specific factors, such as competition, finance, and regulation, are recognized as important within the organization?

ESL TIPS for Considering Audiences

In the United States, **conciseness**, **coherence**, and **clarity** characterize good writing. Make sure readers can follow your writing, and say only what is necessary to communicate your message. Of course, no writing style is inherently better than another, but to be a successful writer in

(continued)

ESL TIPS for Considering Audiences (*continued*)

> any language, you must understand the cultural values that underlie the language in which you are writing. See also <u>awkwardness</u>, <u>copyright</u>, <u>global communication</u>, <u>plagiarism</u>, <u>plain language</u>, and <u>English as a second language</u>.
>
> Throughout this book we have included ESL Tips boxes like this one with information that may be particularly helpful to nonnative speakers of English. See the Contents by Topic on the inside front cover for listings of ESL Tips and ESL Trouble Spots, entries that may be of particular help to ESL writers.

Determining the Scope.   Determining your purpose and assessing your readers and context will help you decide what to include and what not to include in your writing. Those decisions establish the scope of your writing project. If you do not clearly define the scope, you will spend needless hours on research because you will not be sure what kind of information you need or even how much. Given the purpose and audience established for the report on facility locations, the scope would include such information as land and building costs, available labor force, cultural issues, transportation options, and proximity to suppliers. However, it probably would not include the early history of the cities being considered or their climate and geological features, unless those aspects were directly related to your particular business.

Selecting the Medium.   Finally, you need to determine the most appropriate medium for communicating your message. Professionals on the job face a wide array of options—from <u>e-mail</u>, fax, voice mail, videoconferencing, and Web sites to more traditional means like <u>letters</u>, <u>memos</u>, <u>reports</u>, telephone calls, and face-to-face <u>meetings</u>.

The most important considerations in selecting the appropriate medium are the audience and the purpose of the communication. For example, if you need to collaborate with someone to solve a problem or if you need to establish rapport with someone, written exchanges could be far less efficient than a phone call or a face-to-face meeting. However, if you need precise wording or you need to provide a record of a complex message, communicate in writing. If you need to make information that is frequently revised accessible to employees at a large company, the best choice might be to place the information on the company's intranet site. If reviewers need to make handwritten comments on a proposal, you may need to provide paper copies that can be faxed, or you may use word-processing software and insert comments electronically. The comparative advantages and primary characteristics of the most typical means of communication are discussed in **selecting the medium**. See also **writing for the Web**.

Research

The only way to be sure that you can write about a complex subject is to thoroughly understand it. To do that, you must conduct adequate **research**, whether that means conducting an extensive investigation for a major proposal — through interviewing, library and Internet research, careful **note-taking**, and **documenting sources** — or simply checking a company Web site and jotting down points before you send an e-mail message to a colleague.

Methods of Research.   Researchers frequently distinguish between primary and secondary research, depending on the types of sources consulted and the method of gathering information. *Primary research* refers to the gathering of raw data compiled from interviews, direct observation, surveys, experiments, **questionnaires**, and audio and video recordings, for example. In fact, direct observation and hands-on experience are the only ways to obtain certain kinds of information, such as the behavior of people and animals, certain natural phenomena, mechanical processes, and the operation of systems and equipment. *Secondary research* refers to gathering information that has been analyzed, assessed, evaluated, compiled, or otherwise organized into accessible form. Such forms or sources include books, articles, reports, Web documents, e-mail discussions, and brochures. Use the methods most appropriate to your needs, recognizing that some projects may require several types of research and that collaborative projects may require those research tasks to be distributed among team members.

Sources of Information.   As you conduct research, numerous sources of information are available to you:

- Your own knowledge and that of your colleagues
- The knowledge of people outside your workplace, gathered through **interviewing for information**
- Internet sources, including Web sites, directories, archives, and discussion groups
- Library resources, including databases and indexes of articles as well as books and reference works
- Printed and electronic sources in the workplace, such as brochures, memos, e-mail, and Web documents

Consider all sources of information when you begin your research and use those that are appropriate and useful. The amount of research you will need to do depends on the scope of your project.

Organization

Without organization, the material gathered during your research will be incoherent to your readers. To organize information effectively, you need to determine the best way to structure your ideas; that is, you must choose a primary **method of development**.

Methods of Development.   An appropriate method of development is the writer's tool for keeping information under control and the readers' means of following the writer's presentation. As you analyze the information you have gathered, choose the method that best suits your subject, your readers' needs, and your purpose. For example, if you were writing instructions for assembling office equipment, you would naturally present the steps of the process in the order readers should perform them: the **sequential method of development**. If you were writing about the history of an organization, your account would most naturally go from the beginning to the present: the **chronological method of development**. If your subject naturally lends itself to a certain method of development, use it—do not attempt to impose another method on it.

Often you will need to combine methods of development. For example, a persuasive brochure for a charitable organization might combine a specific-to-general method of development with a **cause-and-effect method of development**. That is, you could begin with persuasive case histories of individual people in need and then move to general information about the positive effects of donations on recipients.

Outlining.   Once you have chosen a method of development, you are ready to prepare an outline. **Outlining** breaks large or complex subjects into manageable parts. It also enables you to emphasize key points by placing them in the positions of greatest importance. By structuring your thinking at an early stage, a well-developed outline ensures that your document will be complete and logically organized, allowing you to focus exclusively on writing when you begin the rough draft. An outline can be especially helpful for maintaining a collaborative writing team's focus throughout a large project. However, even a short letter or memo needs the logic and structure that an outline provides, whether the outline exists in your mind, on-screen, or on paper.

At this point, you must begin to consider **layout and design** elements that will be helpful to your readers and appropriate to your subject and purpose. For example, if **visuals** such as photographs or tables will be useful, this is a good time to think about where they may be deployed and what kinds of visual elements will be effective, especially if they need to be prepared by someone else while you are writing and revising the draft. The outline can also suggest where **headings,** **lists,** and other special design features may be useful.

Writing

When you have established your purpose, your readers' needs, and your scope, and you have completed your research and your outline, you will be well prepared to write a first draft. Expand your outline into **paragraphs,** without worrying about **grammar,** refinements of language **usage,** or **punctuation.** Writing and revising are different activities; refinements come with **revision.**

Write the rough draft, concentrating entirely on converting your outline into sentences and paragraphs. You might try writing as though you were explaining your subject to a reader sitting across from you. Do not worry about a good opening. Just start. Do not be concerned in the rough draft about exact **word choice** unless it comes quickly and easily—concentrate instead on ideas.

Even with good preparation, writing the draft remains a chore for many writers. The most effective way to get started and keep going is to use your outline as a map for your first draft. Do not wait for inspiration—you need to treat writing a draft as you would any on-the-job task. The entry **writing a draft** describes tactics used by experienced writers—discover which ones are best suited to you and your task.

Consider writing the **introduction** last because then you will know more precisely what is in the body of the draft. Your opening should announce the subject and give readers essential background information, such as the document's primary purpose. For longer documents, an introduction should serve as a frame into which readers can fit the detailed information that follows.

Finally, you will need to write a **conclusion** that ties the main ideas together and emphatically makes a final significant point. The final point may be to recommend a course of action, make a prediction or a judgment, or merely summarize your main points—the way you conclude depends on the purpose of your writing and your readers' needs.

Revision

The clearer a finished piece of writing seems to the reader, the more effort the writer has likely put into its **revision.** If you have followed the steps of the writing process to this point, you will have a rough draft that needs to be revised. Revising, however, requires a different frame of mind than does writing the draft. During revision, be eager to find and correct faults and be honest. Be hard on yourself for the benefit of your readers. Read and evaluate the draft as if you were a reader seeing it for the first time.

Check your draft for accuracy, completeness, and effectiveness in achieving your purpose and meeting your readers' needs and expectations. Trim extraneous information: Your writing should give readers exactly what they need, but it should not burden them with unnecessary information or sidetrack them into loosely related subjects.

Do not try to revise for everything at once. Read your rough draft several times, each time looking for and correcting a different set of problems or errors. Concentrate first on larger issues, such as **unity** and **coherence**; save mechanical corrections, like **spelling** and punctuation, for later **proofreading**. See also **ethics in writing**.

Finally, for important documents, consider having others review your writing and make suggestions for improvement. For collaborative writing, of course, team members must review each other's work on segments of the document as well as the final master draft. Use the Checklist of the Writing Process on pages xxiii–xxiv to guide you not only as you revise but also throughout the writing process.

WEB LINK	Style Guides and Standards

Organizations and professional associations often follow such guides as *The Chicago Manual of Style, MLA Style Manual and Guide to Scholarly Publishing*, and *United States Government Printing Office Style Manual* to ensure consistency in their publications on issues of usage, format, and documentation. Because advice in such guides often varies, some organizations set their own standards for documents. Where such standards or specific style guides are recommended or required by regulations or policies, you should follow those style guidelines. For a selected list of style guides and standards, see *bedfordstmartins.com/ alred* and select *Links for Handbook Entries.*

Checklist of the Writing Process

This checklist arranges key entries of *The Business Writer's Handbook* according to the sequence presented in Five Steps to Successful Writing, which begins on page xv. This checklist is useful both for following the steps and for diagnosing writing problems.

Preparation   412

✔ Establish your **purpose**   461

✔ Identify your **audience** or **readers**   49, 474

✔ Consider the **context**   111

✔ Determine your **scope** of coverage   519

✔ **Select the medium**   413

Research   482

✔ **Brainstorm** to determine what you already know   59

✔ Conduct **research**   482

✔ Take notes (**note-taking**)   365

✔ **Interview for information**   287

✔ Create and use **questionnaires**   463

✔ Avoid **plagiarism**   402

✔ **Document sources**   142

Organization   379

✔ Choose the best **methods of development**   346

✔ **Outline** your notes and ideas   380

✔ Develop and integrate **visuals**   573

✔ Consider **layout and design**   316

  logic errors   332

  positive writing   409

  voice   577

✔ Check for **ethics in writing**   190

  biased language   54

  copyright   113

  plagiarism   402

✔ Check for appropriate **word choice**   583

  abstract / concrete words   6

  affectation, **jargon**, and **plain language**   24, 302, 403

  clichés   82

  connotation / denotation   110

  defining terms   129

✔ Eliminate problems with **grammar**   248

Writing a Draft   584

✔ Select an appropriate **point of view**   405

✔ Adopt an appropriate **style** and **tone**   540, 557

✔ Use effective **sentence construction**   526

✔ Construct effective
  paragraphs   385

✔ Use **quotations** and
  paraphrasing   464, 390

✔ Write an **introduction**   294

✔ Write a **conclusion**   106

✔ Choose a **title**   554

Revision   511

✔ Check for **unity** and
  coherence   564, 82

  conciseness   104

  pace   385

  transition   558

✔ Check for **sentence variety**   533

  emphasis   182

  parallel structure   388

  subordination   543

✔ Check for **clarity**   80

  agreement   26

  ambiguity   34

  awkwardness   52

  case   73

  modifiers   352

  pronoun reference   431

  sentence faults   530

✔ Review mechanics and
  punctuation   460

  abbreviations   2

  capitalization   70

  contractions   113

  dates   128

  italics   300

  numbers   370

  proofreading   438

  spelling   540

The Business
Writer's Handbook

A

a / an

A and *an* are indefinite **articles** because the **noun** designated by the article is not a specific person, place, or thing but is one of a group.

▶ The insurance agent sold *a* policy.
  [This is not a specific policy but an unnamed policy.]

Use *a* before words or abbreviations beginning with a consonant or consonant sound, including *y* or *w*.

▶ The office manager resolved *a* scheduling problem.

▶ It was *a* historic event for the company.
  [*Historic* begins with the consonant *h*.]

▶ We were awarded *a* DoD contract.

▶ The year's activities are summarized in *a* one-page report.
  [*One* begins with the consonant sound "wuh."]

Use *an* before words or abbreviations beginning with a vowel or a consonant with a vowel sound.

▶ He seems *an* unlikely candidate for the job.

▶ The applicant arrived *an* hour early.
  [*Hour* begins with a silent *h*.]

▶ She bought *an* SLR digital camera.
  [*SLR* begins with a vowel sound "ess."]

Do not use unnecessary indefinite articles in a sentence.

▶ The meeting begins in *a* half *an* hour.
  [Choose one article and eliminate the other.]

See also **adjectives**.

a lot

A lot is often incorrectly written as one word (*alot*). The phrase *a lot* is informal and normally should not be used in business writing. Use *many* or *numerous* for estimates or give a specific number or amount.

► We received ~~a lot of~~ *many* e-mails supporting the new policy.

abbreviations

Abbreviations are shortened versions of words or combinations of the first letters of words (*Corp./Corporation, URL/Uniform Resource Locator*). Abbreviations, if used appropriately, can be convenient for both the reader and the writer. Like symbols, they can be important space savers in business writing.

Abbreviations that are formed by combining the initial letter of each word in a multiword term are called *initialisms*. Initialisms are pronounced as separate letters (*SEC/Securities and Exchange Commission*). Abbreviations that combine the first letter or letters of several words—and can be pronounced—are called *acronyms* (*PIN/personal identification number, LAN/local area network*).

Using Abbreviations

In business, industry, and government, specialists and those working together on particular projects often use abbreviations. The most important consideration in the use of abbreviations is whether they will be understood by your **audience**. The same abbreviation, for example, can have two different meanings (NEA stands for both the National Education Association and the National Endowment for the Arts). Like **jargon**, shortened forms are easily understood within a group of specialists; outside the group, however, shortened forms might be incomprehensible. In fact, abbreviations can be easily overused, either as an

affectation or in a misguided attempt to make writing concise, even with **instant messaging** where abbreviations are often used. Remember that **memos**, **e-mail**, or **reports** addressed to specific people may be read by other people—you must consider those secondary audiences as well. A good rule to follow is "when in doubt, spell it out."

WRITER'S CHECKLIST   Using Abbreviations

✔ Except for commonly used abbreviations (*U.S.*, *a.m.*), spell out a term to be abbreviated the first time it is used, followed by the abbreviation in parentheses. Thereafter, the abbreviation may be used alone.

✔ In long documents, repeat the full term in parentheses after the abbreviation at regular intervals to remind readers of the abbreviation's meaning, as in "Remember to submit the CAR (Capital Appropriations Request) by October 15."

✔ Do not add an additional period at the end of a sentence that ends with an abbreviation. ("The official name of the company is DataBase, Inc.")

✔ For abbreviations specific to your profession or discipline, use a style guide recommended by your professional organization or company. (See the Web Link at the end of **documenting sources**.)

✔ Write acronyms in capital letters without periods. The only exceptions are acronyms that have become accepted as common nouns, which are written in lowercase letters, such as *scuba* (*self-*contained underwater *breathing apparatus*).

✔ Generally, use periods for lowercase initialisms (*a.k.a.*, *d.b.a.*, *p.m.*) but not for uppercase ones (*GDP*, *IRA*, *UFO*). Exceptions include geographic names (*U.S.*, *U.K.*, *E.U.*) and the traditional expression of academic degrees (*B.A.*, *M.B.A.*, *Ph.D.*).

✔ Form the plural of an acronym or initialism by adding a lowercase *s*. Do not use an **apostrophe** (*CARs*, *DVDs*).

✔ Do not follow an abbreviation with a word that repeats the final term in the abbreviation (*ATM location* not *ATM machine location*).

✔ Do not make up your own abbreviations; they will confuse readers.

Forming Abbreviations

Names of Organizations.   A company may include in its name a term such as *Brothers*, *Incorporated*, *Corporation*, *Company*, or *Limited Liability Company*. If the term is abbreviated in the official company name that appears on letterhead stationery or on its Web site, use the abbreviated form: *Bros.*, *Inc.*, *Corp.*, *Co.*, or *LLC*. If the term is not abbreviated in the official name, spell it out in writing, except with addresses, footnotes, **bibliographies**, and **lists** where abbreviations may be used. Likewise, use an **ampersand** (&) only if it appears in the official company name. For names of divisions within organizations, terms such as *Department* and *Division* should be abbreviated only when space is limited (*Dept.* and *Div.*).

Measurements. Except for abbreviations that may be confused with words (*in.* for *inch* and *gal.* for *gallon*), abbreviations of measurement do not require periods (*yd* for *yard* and *qt* for *quart*). Abbreviations of units of measure are identical in the singular and plural: *1 cm* and *15 cm* (not *15 cms*). Some abbreviations can be used in combination with other symbols (°F for *degrees Fahrenheit* and *ft²* for *square feet*).

The following list includes abbreviations for the basic units of the International System of Units (SI), the metric system. This system not only is used in science but also is used in international commerce and trade.

MEASUREMENT	UNIT	ABBREVIATION
length	meter	m
mass	kilogram	kg
time	second	s
electric current	ampere	A
thermodynamic temperature	kelvin	K
amount of substance	mole	mol
luminous intensity	candela	cd

For additional definitions and background, see the National Institute of Standards and Technology Web site at *http://physics.nist.gov/cuu/Units/units.html*. For information on abbreviating dates and time, see **numbers**.

Personal Names and Titles. Personal names generally should not be abbreviated: *Thomas* (not *Thos.*) and *William* (not *Wm.*). An academic, civil, religious, or military title should be spelled out and in lowercase when it does not precede a name. ("The *captain* wanted to check the orders.") When they precede names, some titles are customarily abbreviated (*Dr. Smith, Mr. Mills, Ms. Katz*). See also **Ms. / Miss / Mrs.**

An abbreviation of a title may follow the name; however, be certain that it does not duplicate a title before the name (*Angeline Martinez, Ph.D.* or *Dr. Angeline Martinez*). When addressing **correspondence** and including names in other documents, you normally should spell out titles (*The Honorable Mary J. Holt; Professor Charles Matlin*). Traditionally, periods are used with academic degrees, although *The Chicago Manual of Style* suggests omitting these (*M.A./MA, M.B.A./MBA, Ph.D./PhD*).

Common Scholarly Abbreviations and Terms.   The following is a partial list of abbreviations commonly used in reference books and for documenting sources in research papers and reports. Other than in formal scholarly work, generally avoid such abbreviations.

anon.	anonymous
bibliog.	bibliography, bibliographer, bibliographic
ca., c.	*circa*, "about" (used with approximate dates: *ca. 1756*)
cf.	*confer*, "compare"
chap.	chapter
diss.	dissertation
ed., eds.	edited by, editor(s), edition(s)
e.g.	*exempli gratia*, "for example" (see <u>e.g. / i.e.</u>)
esp.	especially
et al.	*et alii*, "and others"
etc.	*et cetera*, "and so forth" (see <u>etc.</u>)
ff.	and the following page(s) or line(s)
GPO	Government Printing Office, Washington, D.C.
i.e.	*id est*, "that is"
MS, MSS	manuscript, manuscripts
n., nn.	note, notes (used immediately after page number: *56n., 56n.3, 56nn.3–5*)
N.B., n.b.	*nota bene*, "take notice, mark well"
n.d.	no date (of publication)
n.p.	no place (of publication); no publisher; no page
p., pp.	page, pages
proc.	proceedings
pub.	published by, publisher, publication
rev.	revised by, revised, revision; review, reviewed by (Spell out "review" where "rev." might be ambiguous.)
rpt.	reprinted by, reprint
sec., secs.	section, sections
sic	so, thus; inserted in <u>brackets</u> ([*sic*]) after a misspelled or wrongly used word in quotations
supp., suppl.	supplement
trans.	translated by, translator, translation
UP	University Press (used in MLA style, as in *Oxford UP*)
viz.	*videlicet*, "namely"
vol., vols.	volume, volumes
vs., v.	*versus*, "against" (*v.* preferred in titles of legal cases)

WEB LINK	Using Abbreviations

For links to Web sites specifying standard abbreviations and acronyms, including U.S. Postal Service abbreviations, see *bedfordstmartins.com/ alred* and select *Links for Handbook Entries.*

above

Avoid using *above* to refer to a preceding passage or **visual** because its reference is vague and often an **affectation**. The same is true of *aforesaid* and *aforementioned.* (See also **former / latter**.) To refer to something previously mentioned, repeat the **noun** or **pronoun**, or construct your **paragraph** so that your reference is obvious.

> *your travel voucher*
> ► Please complete and submit ~~the above~~ by March 1.
>   ^

absolutely

Absolutely means "definitely," "entirely," "completely," or "unquestionably." Avoid it as a redundant **intensifier** to mean "very" or "much."

> ► We are ~~absolutely~~ certain we can meet the deadline.

abstract / concrete words

Abstract words refer to general ideas, qualities, conditions, acts, or relationships — intangible things that cannot be detected by the five senses (sight, hearing, touch, taste, and smell), such as *learning, leadership,* and *technology. Concrete words* identify things that can be perceived by the five senses, such as *diploma, manager,* and *keyboard.*

Abstract words must frequently be further defined or described.

> *to develop its own customer database*
> ► The marketing team needs freedom.
>   ^

Abstract words are best used with concrete words to help make intangible concepts specific and vivid.

> ► *Transportation* [abstract] was limited to *buses* [concrete] and *commuter trains* [concrete].

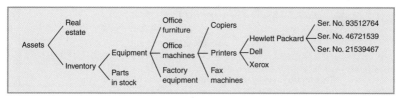

FIGURE A–1. Abstract-to-Concrete Words

The example in Figure A–1 represents seven levels of abstraction from most abstract to most concrete; the appropriate level depends on your **purpose** in writing and on the **context** in which you are using the word. See also **word choice**.

abstracts

An abstract summarizes and highlights the major points of a **formal report**, trade journal article, dissertation, or other long work. Its primary purpose is to enable readers to decide whether to read the work in full. For a discussion of how summaries differ from abstracts, see **executive summaries**.

Although abstracts, typically 200 to 250 words long, are published with the longer works they condense, they can also be published separately in periodical indexes and by abstracting services (see **research**). For this reason, an abstract must be readable apart from the original document.

Types of Abstracts

Depending on the kind of information they contain, abstracts are often classified as descriptive or informative. A *descriptive abstract* summarizes the **purpose**, **scope**, and methods used to arrive at the reported findings. It is a slightly expanded **table of contents** in sentence and paragraph form. A descriptive abstract need not be longer than several sentences. An *informative abstract* is an expanded version of the descriptive abstract. In addition to information about the purpose, scope, and research methods used, the informative abstract summarizes any results, **conclusions**, and recommendations. The informative abstract retains the **tone** and essential scope of the original work, omitting its details. The first two paragraphs of the abstract shown in Figure A–2 alone would be descriptive; with the addition of the paragraphs that

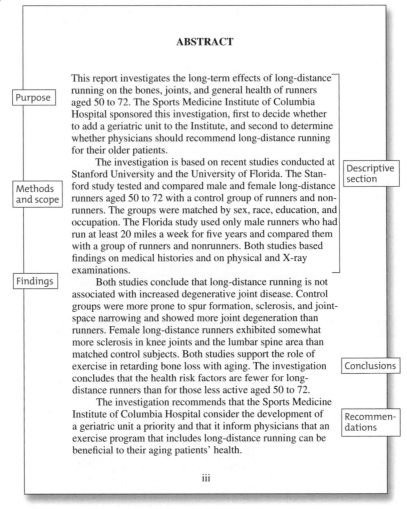

FIGURE A–2. Informative Abstract (from a Report)

detail the findings and conclusions of the report, the abstract becomes informative.

The type of abstract you should write depends on your **audience** and the organization or publication for which you are writing. Informative abstracts work best for wide audiences that need to know conclusions and recommendations; descriptive abstracts work best for compilations, such as proceedings and progress reports, that do not contain conclusions or recommendations.

Writing Strategies

Write the abstract *after* finishing the report or document. Otherwise, the abstract may not accurately reflect the longer work. Begin with a topic sentence that announces the subject and scope of your original document. Then, using the major and minor headings of your outline or table of contents to distinguish primary ideas from secondary ones, decide what material is relevant to your abstract. (See **outlining**.) Write with **clarity** and **conciseness**, eliminating unnecessary words and ideas. Do not, however, become so terse that you omit articles (*a, an, the*) and important transitional words and phrases (*however, therefore, but, next*). Write complete sentences, but avoid stringing together a group of short sentences end to end; instead, combine ideas by using **subordination** and **parallel structure**. Spell out all but the most common **abbreviations**. In a report, an abstract follows the title page and is numbered page iii.

accept / except

Accept is a **verb** meaning "consent to," "agree to take," or "admit willingly." ("I *accept* the responsibility.") *Except* is normally used as a preposition meaning "other than" or "excluding." ("We agreed on everything *except* the schedule.")

acceptance / refusal letters (for employment)

When you decide to accept a job offer, you can notify your new employer by telephone or in a meeting—but to make your decision official, you need to send an acceptance in writing. What you include in your message and whether you send a **letter** or an **e-mail** depends on your previous conversations with your new employer. See also **correspondence**. Figure A–3 shows an example of a job acceptance letter written by a graduating student with substantial experience. (See his **résumé** in Figure R–7 on page 499.)

Note that in the first paragraph of Figure A–3, the writer identifies the job he is accepting and the salary he has been offered—doing so can avoid any misunderstandings about the job or the salary. In the second paragraph, the writer details his plans for relocating and reporting

Dear Ms. Castro:

I am pleased to accept your offer of $47,500 per year as a Graphic Designer with the Natural History Museum.

After graduation, I plan to leave Pittsburgh on Tuesday, June 5. I should be able to find living accommodations and be ready to report for work on Monday, June 18. If you need to reach me prior to this date, please call me at 412-555-1212 (cell) or contact me by e-mail at jgoodman@aol.com.

I look forward to joining the marketing team and working with the excellent support staff I met during the interview.

Sincerely,

Joshua S. Goodman

Joshua S. Goodman

FIGURE A–3. Acceptance Letter (for Employment)

for work. Even if the writer discussed these arrangements during earlier conversations, he needs to confirm them, officially, in this written message. The writer concludes with a brief but enthusiastic statement that he looks forward to working for the new employer.

When you decide to reject a job offer, send a written job refusal to make that decision official, even if you have already notified the employer during a meeting or on the phone. Writing to an employer is an important goodwill gesture.

In Figure A–4, an example of a job refusal, the applicant mentions something positive about his contact with the employer and refers to the specific job offered. He indicates his serious consideration of the offer, provides a logical reason for the refusal, and concludes on a pleasant note. (See his résumé in Figure R–8 on page 500.) For further advice on handling refusals and negative messages generally, see **refusal letters**.

◀ PROFESSIONALISM NOTE Be especially tactful and courteous—the employer you are refusing has spent time and effort interviewing you and may have counted on your accepting the job. Remember, you may apply for another job at that company in the future. ▶

Dear Mr. Vallone:

I enjoyed talking with you about your opening for a manager of aerospace production at your Rockford facility, and I seriously considered your generous offer.

After giving the offer careful thought, however, I have decided to accept a management position with a research-and-development firm. I feel that the job I have chosen is better suited to my long-term goals.

I appreciate your consideration and the time you spent with me. I wish you success in filling the position.

Sincerely,

Robert Mandillo

Robert Mandillo

FIGURE A–4. Refusal Letter (for Employment)

acknowledgment letters

When a colleague or client sends you something or makes a request, you should acknowledge what was sent, respond to the request, or explain that you cannot respond to the request immediately in a short, polite note. The message shown in Figure A–5 could be sent as a **letter** or an **e-mail**. See also **correspondence**.

acronyms and initialisms

Acronyms are formed by combining the first letter or letters of several words; they are pronounced as words and written without periods (*FEMA/Federal Emergency Management Agency*). *Initialisms* are formed by combining the initial letter of each word in a multiword term; they are pronounced as separate letters (*ABC/Association for Business Communication*). See **abbreviations** for the use of acronyms and initialisms.

Dear Ms. Stein:

I received your comprehensive report today. When I finish studying it in detail, I'll send you our cost estimate for the installation of the Checkout Reporting System.

Thank you for preparing such a thorough analysis.

Regards,

Wilbur Kohn

FIGURE A–5. Acknowledgment

active voice (*see* voice)

ad hoc

Ad hoc is Latin for "for this" or "for this particular occasion." An ad hoc committee is one set up temporarily to consider a particular issue. The term has been fully assimilated into English and thus does not have to be italicized. See also **foreign words in English**.

adapt / adept / adopt

Adapt is a verb meaning "adjust to a new situation." *Adept* is an adjective meaning "highly skilled." *Adopt* is a verb meaning "take or use as one's own."

▶ The company will *adopt* a policy of finding executives who are *adept* managers and who can *adapt* to new situations.

adapting to new technologies

Technology constantly evolves and, whether you are in the classroom or in the workplace, the devices and software tools that are familiar and comfortable to you today will be out of date all too quickly. Imagine, for example, that you have spent months learning to use your employer's preferred word processing software, and just when you've finally mastered it, your employer announces that a new version of the software is being acquired. Although the new software promises more features and improved efficiency, it also promises to make much of your hard work obsolete. This entry is designed to help you cope with such a situation by providing useful approaches to working with new technologies. See also **selecting the medium**.

Technology You Need to Know

The question you should ask when faced with a new technology is "how much do I *need* to know about the specific technology or device to do my work?" That is, you must determine the *level of knowledge* you need to accomplish your goals for making effective use of a technology, new application, or device.

What you need to learn will depend on your workplace context. For many circumstances, you may need only a basic level that will enable you to accomplish specific and limited tasks, such as navigating a software program to open, modify, save, and print files. For technologies directly related to your work, however, you may need a thorough knowledge so that you can adapt the technology to many situations and can assess its effectiveness for the benefit of colleagues, clients, or others. In other cases, you may need to gain just enough knowledge to allow you to work well with technical specialists with expert knowledge and to ask the right questions.

Strategies for Learning a New Technology

Because of the flood of new technologies, it is important to develop methods for quickly mastering new technological tools to the level you need. The following are suggestions for navigating the functions and operations of devices and programs with which you are unfamiliar:

- *Experimentation.* Often, the best way to acquaint yourself with a new tool is simply to begin using it, even if you don't fully understand what the tool does or why you might want to learn it. This approach, in which you "play" with a new tool until it becomes familiar, will help you develop greater confidence with new technologies and will rarely have negative consequences. Most software programs cannot be "broken" merely by experimenting with them and doing so is good preparation for more formal learning.

- *IT staff and trusted colleagues.* Many organizations employ information technology (IT) specialists and trainers whose primary task is helping other employees use technology more effectively. Don't be afraid to call on them as you begin to use a new tool. If you can't rely on a dedicated IT staff to train you, seek out tech-savvy individuals who seem to have a high level of technological knowledge. You may be able to return the favor by sharing your expertise in another area.

- *Built-in help.* Most modern software programs come equipped with built-in tutorials and searchable help files. In the past, many help menus were less than helpful, but trends in technical documentation have led to greatly improved help files. Many built-in help documents today are thorough and written in plain, easy-to-understand language.

- *Official help manuals.* Upon acquiring a new technological tool, such as a cell phone or camera, you may be inclined to skip the instruction manual that came in the box or that is available online, but often these manuals contain a good overview of the device's features and hidden gems of information that you would otherwise miss.

- *Third-party help manuals.* Many publishers offer how-to guides for computer software and hardware. With full-color printing, plenty of photos, and a casual, friendly tone, these books attempt to simplify information that may seem overwhelming or confusing in the tool's official documentation.

- *Online tutorials.* Sometimes the easiest way to learn a new technology is by watching someone use it. Video tutorial sites such as Lynda.com offer precise, professional guidance for a fee; many amateur technology enthusiasts upload tutorials of their own to free video-sharing Web sites.

- *Careful Internet searches.* When you encounter a problem with a technological tool, chances are someone else has dealt with it before. You may find helpful advice on an Internet message board or on the Web site of the company that developed the tool. Search for the issue by using precise terminology, including the name of the tool and several additional keywords that describe your specific problem.

DIGITAL TIP

Assessing Hardware and Software

When individuals or organizations consider adopting a new technology, they need to ask a number of questions to assess the value of the technology for themselves or other organizations. For a list of such questions, see *bedfordstmartins.com/alred* and select *Digital Tips*, "Assessing Hardware and Software."

adjectives

An adjective is any word that modifies a **noun** or **pronoun**. *Descriptive adjectives* identify a quality of a noun or pronoun. *Limiting adjectives* impose boundaries on the noun or pronoun.

▶ *hot* surface [descriptive]

▶ *three* phone lines [limiting]

Limiting Adjectives

Limiting adjectives include the following categories:

- Articles (*a, an, the*)
- Demonstrative adjectives (*this, that, these, those*)
- Possessive adjectives (*my, your, his, her, its, our, their*)
- Numeral adjectives (*two, first*)
- Indefinite adjectives (*all, none, some, any*)

Articles.   Articles (*a, an, the*) are traditionally classified as adjectives because they modify nouns by either limiting them or making them more specific. See also **articles** and **English as a second language**.

Demonstrative Adjectives.   A demonstrative adjective points to the thing it modifies, specifying the object's position in space or time. *This* and *these* specify a closer position; *that* and *those* specify a more remote position.

▶ *This* report is more current than *that* report, which Human Resources distributed last month.

▶ *These* sales figures are more recent than *those* reported last week.

Demonstrative adjectives often cause problems when they modify the nouns *kind*, *type*, and *sort*. Demonstrative adjectives used with those nouns should agree with them in number.

▶ *this* kind, *these* kinds; *that* type, *those* types

Confusion often develops when the preposition *of* is added (*this kind of*, *these kinds of*) and the object of the preposition does not conform in number to the demonstrative adjective and its noun. See also **agreement** and **prepositions**.

▶ *This kind of* human resources ~~policies are~~ *policy is* standard.

▶ *These kinds of* human resources ~~policy is~~ *policies are* standard.

Avoid using demonstrative adjectives with words like *kind*, *type*, and *sort* because doing so can easily lead to vagueness. Instead, be more specific. See also **kind of / sort of**.

Possessive Adjectives. Because possessive adjectives (*my*, *your*, *his*, *her*, *its*, *our*, *their*) directly modify nouns, they function as adjectives, even though they are pronoun forms (*my* idea, *her* plans, *their* projects). See also **functional shift**.

Numeral Adjectives. Numeral adjectives identify quantity, degree, or place in a sequence. They always modify count nouns. Numeral adjectives are divided into two subclasses: cardinal and ordinal. A *cardinal adjective* expresses an exact quantity (*one* pencil, *two* computers); an *ordinal adjective* expresses degree or sequence (*first* quarter, *second* edition).

In most writing, an ordinal adjective should be spelled out if it is a single word (*tenth*) and written in figures if it is more than one word (*312th*). Ordinal numbers can also function as adverbs. ("John arrived *first*.") See also **first / firstly** and **numbers**.

Indefinite Adjectives. Indefinite adjectives do not designate anything specific about the nouns they modify (*some* CD-ROMs, *all* designers). The articles *a* and *an* are included among the indefinite adjectives (*a* chair, *an* application).

Comparison of Adjectives

Most adjectives in the positive form show the comparative form with the suffix *-er* for two items and the superlative form with the suffix *-est* for three or more items.

- ► The first report is *long*. [positive form]
- ► The second report is *longer*. [comparative form]
- ► The third report is *longest*. [superlative form]

Many two-syllable adjectives and most three-syllable adjectives are preceded by the word *more* or *most* to form the comparative or the superlative.

- ► The new media center is *more* impressive than the old one. It is the *most* impressive in the county.

A few adjectives have irregular forms of comparison (*much, more, most; little, less, least*).

Some adjectives (*round, unique, exact, accurate*), often called *absolute words*, are not logically subject to comparison. See also **equal / unique / perfect**.

Placement of Adjectives

When limiting and descriptive adjectives appear together, the limiting adjectives precede the descriptive adjectives, with the articles usually in the first position.

- ► *The ten yellow* taxis were sold at auction. [article (*The*), limiting adjective (*ten*), descriptive adjective (*yellow*)]

ESL TIPS for Using Adjectives

Do not add *-s* or *-es* to an adjective to make it plural.

- ► the *long* trip
- ► the *long* trips

Capitalize adjectives of origin (city, state, nation, continent).

- ► the *Venetian* canals
- ► the *Texas* longhorn steer
- ► the *French* government
- ► the *African* deserts

(*continued*)

ESL TIPS for Using Adjectives (*continued*)

> In English, verbs of feeling (for example, *bore, interest, surprise*) have two adjectival forms: the present participle (*-ing*) and the past participle (*-ed*). Use the present participle to describe what causes the feeling. Use the past participle to describe the person who experiences the feeling.
>
> ► We heard the *surprising* election results.
>   [The *election results* cause the feeling.]
>
> ► Only the losing candidate was *surprised* by the election results.
>   [The *candidate* experienced the feeling of surprise.]
>
> Adjectives follow nouns in English in only two cases: when the adjective functions as a subjective complement ("That project is not *finished*") and when an adjective phrase or clause modifies the noun ("The project *that was suspended temporarily*"). In all other cases, adjectives are placed before the noun.
>
> When a sentence has multiple adjectives, it is often difficult to know the right order. The guidelines illustrated in the following example would apply in most circumstances, but there are exceptions. (Normally do not use a phrase with so many stacked <u>modifiers</u>.) See also <u>articles</u>.
>
> ► The six extra-large rectangular brown cardboard take-out containers
>
>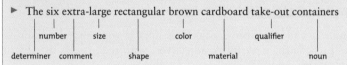

Within a sentence, adjectives may appear before the nouns they modify (the attributive position) or after the nouns they modify (the predicative position).

► *The small* jobs are given priority. [attributive position]

► The exposure is *brief*. [predicative position]

Use of Adjectives

Nouns often function as adjectives to clarify the meaning of other nouns.

► The *accident* report prompted a *product* redesign.

When adjectives modifying the same noun can be reversed and still make sense or when they can be separated by *and* or *or*, they should be separated by commas.

▸ The company seeks *bright, energetic, creative* managers.

Notice that there is no comma after *creative*. Never use a comma between a final adjective and the noun it modifies. When an adjective modifies a phrase, no comma is required.

▸ We need an *updated Web-page design*.
  [*Updated* modifies the phrase *Web-page design*.]

Writers sometimes string together a series of nouns used as adjectives to form a unit modifier, thereby creating stacked (jammed) **modifiers**, which can confuse readers. See also **word choice**.

adjustment letters

An adjustment **letter** or **e-mail** is written in response to a **complaint** and tells a customer or client what your organization intends to do about the complaint. Although sent in response to a problem, an adjustment letter actually provides an excellent opportunity to build goodwill for your organization. An effective adjustment letter, such as the examples shown in Figures A–6 and A–7, can not only repair any damage done but also restore the customer's confidence in your company.

No matter how unreasonable the complaint, the **tone** of your response should be positive and respectful. Avoid emphasizing the problem, but do take responsibility for it when appropriate. Focus your response on what you are doing to correct the problem. Settle such matters quickly and courteously, and lean toward giving the customer or client the benefit of the doubt at a reasonable cost to your organization. See also **refusal letters**.

Full Adjustments

Before granting an adjustment to a claim for which your company is at fault, first determine what happened and what you can do to satisfy the customer. Be certain that you are familiar with your company's adjustment policy—and be careful with **word choice**.

▸ We have just received your letter of May 7 about our defective gas grill.

Saying something is "defective" could be ruled in a court of law as an admission that the product is in fact defective. When you are in doubt, seek legal advice.

Grant adjustments graciously: A settlement made grudgingly will do more harm than good. Not only must you be gracious, but you must

INTERNET SERVICES CORPORATION
10876 Crispen Way
Chicago, Illinois 60601

May 11, 2012

Mr. Jason Brandon
4319 Anglewood Street
Tacoma, WA 98402

Dear Mr. Brandon:

We are sorry that your experience with our customer support help line did not go smoothly. We are eager to restore your confidence in our ability to provide dependable, high-quality service. Your next three months of Internet access will be complimentary as our sincere apology for your unpleasant experience.

Providing dependable service is what is expected of us, and when our staff doesn't provide quality service, it is easy to understand our customers' disappointment. I truly wish we had performed better in our guidance for setup and log-on procedures and that your experience had been a positive one. To prevent similar problems in the future, we plan to use your letter in training sessions with customer support personnel.

We appreciate your taking the time to write us. It helps to receive comments such as yours, and we conscientiously follow through to be sure that proper procedures are being met.

Yours truly,

Inez Carlson

Inez Carlson, Vice President
Customer Support Services

www.isc.com

FIGURE A–6. Adjustment Letter (When Company Is at Fault)

Dear Mr. Sanchez:

Enclosed is your Addison Laptop Computer, which you shipped to us on August 31.

Our technical staff reports that the laptop was damaged by exposure to high levels of humidity. You stated in your letter that you often use your laptop on a covered patio. Doing so in a high-humidity environment, as is typical in Louisiana, can result in damage to the internal circuitry of your computer—as described on page 32 of your Addison Owner's Manual.

We have replaced the damaged circuitry and thoroughly tested your laptop. To avoid similar problems, we recommend you avoid leaving your laptop exposed to high humidity for extended periods.

If you should find that the problem recurs, please call us at 800-555-0990. We will be glad to work with you to find a solution.

Sincerely,

Customer Service Department

FIGURE A–7. Partial Adjustment (Accompanying a Product)

also acknowledge the error in such a way that the customer will not lose confidence in your company. Emphasize early what the reader will consider good news.

- ▶ Enclosed is a replacement for the damaged part.
- ▶ Yes, you were incorrectly billed for the delivery.
- ▶ Please accept our apologies for the error in your account.

◀ PROFESSIONALISM NOTE If an explanation will help restore your reader's confidence, explain what caused the problem. You might point out any steps you may be taking to prevent a recurrence of the problem. Explain that customer feedback helps your firm keep the quality of its product or service high. Close pleasantly, looking forward, not back. Avoid recalling the problem in your closing (do not write, "Again, we apologize . . ."). ▶

The adjustment letter in Figure A–6, for example, begins by accepting responsibility and offers an apology for the customer's inconvenience (note the use of the pronouns *we* and *our*). The second paragraph expresses a desire to restore goodwill and describes specifically how the writer intends to make the adjustment. The third paragraph expresses appreciation to the customer for calling attention to the problem and assures him that his complaint has been taken seriously.

Partial Adjustments

You may sometimes need to grant a partial adjustment—even if a claim is not really justified—to regain the lost goodwill of a customer or client. If, for example, a customer incorrectly uses a product or service, you may need to help that person better understand the correct use of that product or service. In such a circumstance, remember that your customer or client believes that his or her claim is justified. Therefore, you should give the explanation before granting the claim—otherwise, your reader may never get to the explanation. If your explanation establishes customer responsibility, do so tactfully. Figure A–7 is an example of a partial adjustment letter. See also **correspondence**.

adverbs

An adverb modifies the action or condition expressed by a **verb**.

► The wrecking ball hit the side of the building *hard*.
  [The adverb tells *how* the wrecking ball hit the building.]

An adverb also can modify an **adjective**, another adverb, or a **clause**.

► The brochure design used *remarkably* bright colors.
  [*Remarkably* modifies the adjective *bright*.]

► The redesigned brake pad lasted *much* longer.
  [*Much* modifies the adverb *longer*.]

► *Surprisingly*, the engine failed.
  [*Surprisingly* modifies the clause *the engine failed*.]

Types of Adverbs

A simple adverb can answer one of the following questions:

Where? (adverb of place)

► Move the display *forward* slightly.

When? or *How often?* (adverb of time)

- ► Replace the thermostat *immediately*.
- ► I worked overtime *twice* this week.

How? (adverb of manner)

- ► Add the solvent *cautiously*.

How much? (adverb of degree)

- ► The *nearly* completed report was sent to the director.

An interrogative adverb can ask a question (*Where? When? Why? How?*):

- ► *How* many hours did you work last week?
- ► *Why* was the hard drive reformatted?

A conjunctive adverb can modify the clause that it introduces as well as join two independent clauses with a **semicolon**. The most common conjunctive adverbs are *however, nevertheless, moreover, therefore, further, then, consequently, besides, accordingly, also,* and *thus*.

- ► I rarely work on weekends; *however*, this weekend will be an exception.

In this example, note that a semicolon precedes and a comma follows *however*. The conjunctive adverb (*however*) introduces the independent clause (*this weekend will be an exception*) and indicates its relationship to the preceding independent clause (*I rarely work on weekends*). See also **transition**.

Comparison of Adverbs

Most one-syllable adverbs show comparison with the suffixes *-er* and *-est*.

- ► This motor runs *fast*. [positive form]
- ► This motor runs *faster* than the old one. [comparative form]
- ► This motor runs the *fastest* of the three tested. [superlative form]

Most adverbs with two or more syllables end in *-ly*, and most adverbs ending in *-ly* are compared by inserting the comparative *more* or *less* or the superlative *most* or *least* in front of them.

- ► The patient recovered *more quickly* than the staff expected.
- ► *Most surprisingly*, the engine failed during the final test phase.

A few irregular adverbs require a change in form to indicate comparison (*well, better, best; badly, worse, worst; far, farther, farthest*).

▸ The training program functions *well*.

▸ Our training program functions *better* than most others in the industry.

▸ Many consider our training program the *best* in the industry.

Placement of Adverbs

An adverb usually should be placed in front of the verb it modifies.

▸ The pilot *methodically* performed the preflight check.

An adverb may, however, follow the verb (or the verb and its object) that it modifies.

▸ The system failed *unexpectedly*.

▸ They replaced the hard drive *quickly*.

An adverb may be placed between a helping verb and a main verb.

▸ In this temperature range, the pressure will *quickly* drop.

Adverbs such as *only, nearly, almost, just*, and *hardly* should be placed immediately before the words they limit. See also **modifiers** and **only**.

affect / effect

Affect is a **verb** that means "influence." ("The decision could *affect* the company's stock value.") *Effect* can function as a **noun** that means "result" ("The decision had a positive *effect*") or as a verb that means "bring about" or "cause." However, avoid *effect* as a verb when you can replace it with a less formal word, such as *make* or *produce*.

▸ The new manager will ~~effect~~ several changes to improve morale.
               make

affectation

Affectation is the use of language that is more formal, technical, or showy than necessary to communicate information to the reader. Affectation is a widespread writing problem in the workplace because many people feel that affectation lends a degree of authority to their writing. In fact, affectation can alienate customers, clients, and colleagues because it forces readers to work harder to understand the writer's meaning.

Affected writing typically contains inappropriate abstract, highly technical, or foreign words and is often liberally sprinkled with trendy **buzzwords**.

❖ ETHICS NOTE **Jargon** and **euphemisms** can become affectation, especially if their purpose is to hide relevant facts or give a false impression of competence. See **ethics in writing**. ❖

Writers easily slip into affectation through the use of long variants — words created by adding prefixes and suffixes to simpler words (*orientate* for *orient*; *utilization* for *use*). Unnecessarily formal words (such as *penultimate* for *next to last*), created words using *-ese* (such as *managementese*), and outdated words (such as *aforesaid*) can produce affectation. (See also **above**.) Elegant variation — attempting to avoid repeating a word within a paragraph by substituting a pretentious synonym — is also a form of affectation. Either repeat the term or use a pronoun.

> ▸ The use of digital modules in the assembly process has increased
>
>   *and*
> production. ~~Modular utilization has also~~ cut costs.
>   ^

Another type of affectation is **gobbledygook**, which is wordy, roundabout writing with many legal- and technical-sounding terms (such as *wherein* and *morphing*).

Understanding the possible reasons for affectation is the first step toward avoiding it. The following are some causes of affectation.

• *Impression*. Some writers use pretentious language to try to impress the reader with fancy words instead of evidence and logic.

WEB LINK	Affected Writing Revised
For an example of regulations that are revised to eliminate various forms of affectation, see *bedfordstmartins.com/alred* and select *Model Documents Gallery*.	

- *Insecurity.* Writers who are insecure about their facts, conclusions, or arguments may try to hide behind a smoke screen of pretentious words.
- *Imitation.* Perhaps unconsciously, some writers imitate the poor writing they see around them.
- *Intimidation.* A few writers, consciously or unconsciously, try to intimidate or overwhelm their readers with words, often to protect themselves from criticism.
- *Initiation.* Writers who are new to a field often feel that one way to prove their professional expertise is to use as much technical terminology and jargon as possible.
- *Imprecision.* Writers who are having trouble being precise sometimes find that an easy solution is to use a vague, trendy, or pretentious word.

See also **clichés**, **conciseness**, **nominalizations**, and **word choice**.

affinity

Affinity refers to the attraction of two persons or things to each other. *Affinity* should not be used to mean "ability" or "aptitude."

> She has an ~~affinity~~ ^{aptitude} for problem solving.

agreement

DIRECTORY

Grammatical agreement is the correspondence in form between different elements of a sentence to indicate **number**, **person**, **gender**, and **case**.

A subject and its **verb** must agree in number.

> The *design is* acceptable.
> [The singular subject, *design*, requires the singular verb, *is*.]

▶ The new *products are* going into production soon.
[The plural subject, *products*, requires the plural verb, *are*.]

A subject and its verb must agree in person.

▶ *I am* the designer.
[The first-person singular subject, *I*, requires the first-person singular verb, *am*.]

▶ *They are* the designers.
[The third-person plural subject, *they*, requires the third-person plural verb, *are*.]

A **pronoun** and its antecedent must agree in person, number, gender, and case.

▶ The *employees* report that *they* are more efficient in the new facility.
[The third-person plural subject, *employees*, requires the third-person plural pronoun, *they*.]

▶ *Kaye McGuire* will meet with the staff on Friday, when *she* will assign duties.
[The third-person singular subject, *Kaye McGuire*, requires *she*, the third-person feminine pronoun, in the subjective case.]

See also **sentence construction**.

Subject-Verb Agreement

Subject-verb agreement is not affected by intervening **phrases** and **clauses**.

▶ *One* in twenty hard drives we receive from our suppliers *is* faulty.
[The verb, *is*, must agree in number with the subject, *one*, not *hard drives* or *suppliers*.]

The same is true when **nouns** fall between a subject and its verb.

▶ Only *one* of the emergency lights *was* functioning.
[The subject of the verb is *one*, not *lights*.]

▶ *Each* of the managers *supervises* a very large region.
[The subject of the verb is *each*, not *managers*.]

Note that *one* and *each* are normally singular.

Indefinite pronouns such as *some*, *none*, *all*, *more*, and *most* may be singular or plural, depending on whether they are used with a mass noun ("*Most* of the oil *has* been used") or with a count noun ("*Most* of the drivers *know* why they are here"). Mass nouns are singular, and count nouns are plural. Other words, such as *type*, *part*, *series*, and *portion*, take singular verbs even when they precede a phrase containing a plural noun.

▸ A *series* of meetings *was* held to develop a marketing strategy.

▸ A large *portion* of most annual reports *is* devoted to promoting the corporate image.

Modifying phrases can obscure a simple subject.

▸ The *advice* of two engineers, one lawyer, and three executives *was* obtained prior to making a commitment.
[The subject of the verb *was* is *advice*.]

Inverted word order can cause problems with agreement.

▸ From this work *have come* several important *improvements*.
[The subject of the verb is *improvements*, not *work*.]

The number of a subjective **complement** does not affect the number of the verb—the verb must always agree with the subject.

▸ The *topic* of his report *is* employee benefits.
[The subject of the sentence is *topic*, not *benefits*.]

A subject that expresses measurement, weight, mass, or total often takes a singular verb even when the subject word is plural in form. Such subjects are treated as a unit.

▸ *Four weeks is* the normal duration of the training program.

A verb following the relative pronoun *who* or *that* agrees in number with the noun to which the pronoun refers (its antecedent).

▸ This is one of those management *problems* that *require* careful analysis.
[*That* refers to *problems*.]

▸ She is one of those *employees* who *are* rarely absent.
[*Who* refers to *employees*.]

The word *number* sometimes causes confusion. When used to mean a specific number, it is singular.

▸ *The number* of committee members *was* six.

When used to mean an approximate number, it is plural.

▸ A *number* of people *were* waiting for the announcement.

Relative pronouns (*who*, *which*, *that*) may take either singular or plural verbs, depending on whether the antecedent is singular or plural. See also **who / whom**.

▶ He is a manager *who seeks* the views of others.

▶ He is one of those managers *who seek* the views of others.

Some abstract nouns are singular in meaning but plural in form: *mathematics*, *news*, *physics*, and *economics*.

▶ *News* of the merger *is* on page 4 of the *Chronicle*.

Some words, such as the plural *jeans* and *scissors*, cause special problems.

▶ The *scissors were* ordered last week.
[The subject is the plural *scissors*.]

▶ *A pair* of scissors *is* on order.
[The subject is the singular *pair*.]

A book with a plural title takes a singular verb.

▶ *Accounting Essentials is* an essential resource.

A collective noun (*committee*, *faculty*, *class*, *jury*) used as a subject takes a singular verb when the group is thought of as a unit and a plural verb when the individuals in the group are thought of separately.

▶ The *committee is* unanimous in its decision.

▶ The *committee are* returning to their offices.

A clearer way to emphasize the individuals would be to use a phrase.

▶ The *committee members are* returning to their offices.

Compound Subjects

A compound subject is composed of two or more elements joined by a **conjunction** such as *and*, *or*, *nor*, *either . . . or*, or *neither . . . nor*. Usually, when the elements are connected by *and*, the subject is plural and requires a plural verb.

▶ *Professional writing and translation are* prerequisites for this position.

One exception occurs when the elements connected by *and* form a unit or refer to the same thing. In that case, the subject is regarded as singular and takes a singular verb.

▶ *Bacon and eggs is* a high-cholesterol meal.

▶ Our greatest *challenge and business opportunity is* the Internet.

A compound subject with a singular element and a plural element joined by *or* or *nor* requires that the verb agree with the closer element.

▶ Neither the director nor the *project assistants were* available.

▶ Neither the project assistants nor the *director was* available.

If *each* or *every* modifies the elements of a compound subject, use the singular verb.

▶ *Each* manager and supervisor *has* a production goal to meet.

▶ *Every* manager and supervisor *has* a production goal to meet.

Pronoun-Antecedent Agreement

Every pronoun must have an antecedent—a noun to which it refers. See also **pronoun reference**.

▶ When *employees* are hired, *they* must review the policy manual. [The pronoun *they* refers to the antecedent *employees*.]

Gender. A pronoun must agree in gender with its antecedent.

▶ *Mr. Swivet* in the accounting department acknowledges *his* share of responsibility for the misunderstanding, just as *Ms. Barkley* in the research division must acknowledge *hers*.

Traditionally, a masculine, singular pronoun was used to agree with such indefinite antecedents as *anyone* and *person*. ("*Each* may stay or go as *he* chooses.") Because such usage ignores or excludes women, use alternatives when they are available. One solution is to use the plural. Another is to use both feminine and masculine pronouns, although that combination is clumsy when used too often.

> *All employees*   *their*   *cards*
▶ ~~Every employee~~ must sign ~~his~~ time ~~card~~.

> *or her*
▶ Every employee must sign his time card.

Do not attempt to avoid expressing gender by resorting to a plural pronoun when the antecedent is singular. You may be able to avoid the pronoun entirely.

> *a*
▶ Every employee must sign ~~their~~ time card.

Avoid gender-related stereotypes in general references, as in "the nurse . . . *she*" or "the doctor . . . *he*." What if the nurse is male or the doctor female? See also **biased language**.

Number.   A pronoun must agree with its antecedent in number. Many problems of agreement are caused by expressions that are not clear in number.

▶ Although the typical engine runs well in moderate temperatures,

   it   *stalls*
   ~~they~~ often ~~stall~~ in extreme cold.

Use singular pronouns with the antecedents *everybody* and *everyone* unless to do so would be illogical because the meaning is obviously plural. See also **everybody / everyone**.

▶ *Everyone* pulled *his or her* share of the load.

▶ *Everyone* thought my plan should be revised, and I really couldn't blame *them*.

Collective nouns may use a singular or plural pronoun, depending on the meaning.

▶ The *committee* agreed to the recommendations only after *it* had deliberated for days. [*committee* thought of as collective singular]

▶ The *committee* quit for the day and went to *their* respective homes. [*committee* thought of as plural]

Demonstrative **adjectives** sometimes cause problems with agreement of number. *This* and *that* are used with singular nouns, and *these* and *those* are used with plural nouns. Demonstrative adjectives often cause problems when they modify the nouns *kind*, *type*, and *sort*. When used with those nouns, demonstrative adjectives should agree with them in number.

▶ *this* kind, *these* kinds; *that* type, *those* types

Confusion often develops when the **preposition** *of* is added (*this kind of*, *these kinds of*) and the object of the preposition does not agree in number with the demonstrative adjective and its noun.

               plan is
▶ This kind of retirement ~~plans are~~ best.

Avoid that error by remembering to make the demonstrative adjective, the noun, and the object of the preposition—all three—agree in number. The agreement makes the sentence not only correct but also more precise. Using demonstrative adjectives with words like *kind*, *type*, and *sort* can easily lead to vagueness. See **kind of / sort of**.

Compound Antecedents.   A compound antecedent joined by *or* or *nor* is singular if both elements are singular and plural if both elements are plural.

▶ Neither the *engineer* nor the *technician* could do *his* job until *he* understood the new concept.

▶ Neither the *executives* nor the *directors* were pleased at the performance of *their* company.

When one of the antecedents connected by *or* or *nor* is singular and the other plural, the pronoun agrees with the closer antecedent.

▶ Either the *computer* or the *printers* should have *their* serial numbers registered.

▶ Either the *printers* or the *computer* should have *its* serial number registered.

A compound antecedent with its elements joined by *and* requires a plural pronoun.

▶ *Seon Ju and Juanita* took *their* layout drawings with them.

If both elements refer to the same person, however, use the singular pronoun.

▶ The noted *economist and author* departed from *her* prepared speech.

all ready / already

All ready is a two-word phrase meaning "completely prepared." *Already* is an **adverb** that means "before this time" or "previously." ("They were *all ready* to cancel the order; fortunately, we had *already* corrected the shipments.")

all right

All right means "all correct." ("The answers were *all right*.") In formal writing, it should not be used to mean "good" or "acceptable." It is always written as two words, with no hyphen; *alright* is nonstandard.

all together / altogether

All together means "all acting together" or "all in one place." ("The new employees were *all together* at the orientation.") *Altogether* means "entirely" or "completely." ("The trip was *altogether* unnecessary.")

allude / elude / refer

Allude means to make an indirect reference to something. ("The report simply *alluded* to the problem, rather than stating it explicitly.") *Elude* means to escape notice or detection. ("The discrepancy in the account *eluded* the auditor.") *Refer* is used to indicate a direct reference to something. ("She *referred* to the merger during her presentation.")

allusion / illusion

An *allusion* is an indirect reference to something not specifically mentioned. ("The report made an *allusion* to metal fatigue in the support structures.") An *illusion* is a mistaken perception or a false image. ("The manager is under the *illusion* that the reorganization will cost very little.")

allusions

An allusion is an indirect reference to something from past or current events, literature, or other familiar sources. The use of allusion promotes economical writing because it is a shorthand way of referring to a body of material in a few words or of helping to explain a new and unfamiliar process in terms of one that is familiar. In the following example, the writer sums up a description with an allusion to a well-known story. The allusion, with its implicit reference to "right standing up to might," concisely emphasizes the writer's point.

> ▶ As it currently exists, the review process involves the consumer's attorney sitting alone, usually without adequate technical assistance, faced by two or three government attorneys, two or three attorneys from CompuSystems, and large teams of experts who support the government and the corporation. The entire proceeding is reminiscent of David versus Goliath.

Be sure, of course, that your reader is familiar with the material to which you allude. Allusions should be used with restraint, especially in **international correspondence**. If overdone, allusions can lead to **affectation** or can be viewed merely as **clichés**. See also **business writing style**.

almost / most

Do not use *most* as a colloquial substitute for *almost* in your writing.

> New shipments arrive ~~most~~ *almost* every day.

also

Also is an adverb that means "additionally." ("Two 5,000-gallon tanks are on-site, and several 2,500-gallon tanks are *also* available.") *Also* should not be used as a connective in the sense of "and."

> He brought the reports, the memos, ~~also~~ *and* the director's recommendations.

Avoid opening sentences with *also*. It is a weak transitional word that suggests an afterthought rather than planned writing.

> ~~Also,~~ *In addition* he brought a cost analysis to support his proposal.

> ~~Also, he~~ *He also* brought a cost analysis to support his proposal.

ambiguity

A word or passage is ambiguous when it can be interpreted in two or more ways, yet provides the reader with no certain basis for choosing among the alternatives.

> Language is more valuable to a writer than a computer.
> [Does that mean a writer is more in need of language than a computer is? Or does it mean that language is more valuable to a writer than a computer is?]

Ambiguity can take many forms, as in ambiguous **pronoun reference**.

AMBIGUOUS   Inadequate quality-control procedures have resulted in more equipment failures. This is our most serious problem at present.
[Does *this* refer to *inadequate quality-control procedures* or to *equipment failures?*]

SPECIFIC   Inadequate quality-control procedures have resulted in more equipment failures. *These failures* are our most serious problem at present.

SPECIFIC   Inadequate quality-control procedures have resulted in more equipment failures. *Quality control* is our most serious problem at present.

Incomplete **comparison** and missing or misplaced **modifiers** (including **dangling modifiers**) cause ambiguity.

▶ Ms. Lee values rigid quality-control standards more than

does
Mr. Rosenblum.
       ^
[Complete the comparison.]

                          also
▶ He lists his hobby as cooking. He is especially fond of cocker spaniels.
                                         ^
[Add the missing modifier.]

The placement of some modifiers enables them to be interpreted in either of two ways.

▶ She volunteered *immediately* to deliver the toxic substance.

By moving the word *immediately*, the meaning can be clarified.

▶ She *immediately* volunteered to deliver the toxic substance.

▶ She volunteered to deliver the toxic substance *immediately*.

Imprecise **word choice** (including faulty **idioms**) can cause ambiguity.

                       rescinded
▶ The general manager has denied reports that the plant's recent
fuel-allocation cut will be ~~restored~~. [inappropriate word choice]
                             ^

Various forms of **awkwardness** also can cause ambiguity.

amount / number

Amount is used with things that are thought of in bulk and that cannot be counted (mass **nouns**), as in "the *amount* of electricity." *Number* is used with things that can be counted as individual items (count nouns), as in "the *number* of employees."

ampersands

The ampersand (&) is a symbol sometimes used to represent the word *and*, especially in the names of organizations (*Kirkwell & Associates*). When you are writing the name of an organization in sentences, addresses, or references, spell out the word *and* unless the ampersand appears in the organization's official name on its letterhead stationery or Web site.

and/or

And/or means that either both circumstances are possible or only one of two circumstances is possible. This term is awkward and confusing because it makes the reader stop to puzzle over your distinction.

AWKWARD   Use A *and/or* B.

IMPROVED   Use A or B or both.

annual reports

The corporate annual report is, in effect, a state-of-the-company message, which publicly traded companies are legally required to publish annually but private companies are not. Written primarily for stockholders, the report also addresses such **audiences** as bankers, the financial media, labor unions, employees, and local elected officials. An annual report usually covers the high points of the previous year's operations and finances and forecasts the coming year's operations. It may also explain the company's current direction and highlight its strengths. If weaknesses have developed or failures have occurred, the annual report may analyze them and explain the efforts being made to overcome them.

Study your company's annual reports of the past several years for content, **style**, and **format**. Then review the writing process outlined in the "Checklist of the Writing Process" on pages xxiii–xxiv and use all the steps listed there. Finally, collaborate closely with your company's (or outside contractor's) graphics, print-production, and Web staffs. Learn their file-format requirements, schedule **photographs,** and schedule milestones for producing the print and Web versions of the report. See also **business plans, collaborative writing, mission statements,** and **writing for the Web**.

Structure and Parts

Some annual reports are lavishly produced publications that present the company and its operations in glowing terms; others are spartan financial summaries that merely meet the legal requirements for annual financial reporting. Most are a combination of both. Annual reports vary greatly in organization, but they typically include five major sections:

- Financial highlights
- A statement to the stockholders or a letter from the president
- A narrative section on the company's operations
- A financial statement
- A listing of the company's board of directors and officers

Financial Highlights.   The financial highlights section is a brief review of the company's sales and earnings that usually precedes the statement to the stockholders, sometimes even appearing on the inside of the front cover. This section often compares sales and earnings for three years and typically includes the percentage of change from year to year.

Statement to Stockholders.   This section is a direct statement to stockholders from the company's president or the chair of the board of directors. It sets the stage for the rest of the report. This section should not repeat the financial facts already cited in the financial highlights; instead, it should interpret the entire year's performance, touch on plans and future directions, and give the company's explanations for any failures.

The statement to stockholders may be an in-depth review of the company's operations during the past year or a brief summary of the entire report. A brief summary of the annual report is sometimes followed by an article in question-and-answer format in which the president of the company reviews the past year's operations.

Narrative Section.   The narrative section of the annual report is normally used to present company operations and new products or developments in a positive light. Select the topics for this section carefully, making certain they are timely and meaningful and that they contribute to the primary objective of the annual report. Topics for this section might include the following:

- Major profit factors in the last year's performance
- Current market performance of existing products or services
- Prospects for increasing stock dividends
- Significant new products or services
- Productivity and profits
- The company's performance compared with that of its competition
- Outlook for next year (for the company as a whole or by divisions)
- Major acquisitions and restructuring
- Significant organizational changes
- Research and development
- Global operations and economic climate (when appropriate)
- Service and support operations
- Social responsibilities (such as environmental responsibility and community service)

Financial Statement.   At minimum, most financial statements include the following:

- A company balance sheet
- A statement of income
- Changes in financial position
- An independent auditor's statement
- Footnotes, as necessary

Most annual reports also include a comparison of financial results of the past three years. Footnotes in the financial section should be written in simple, direct language rather than in accounting terms. The auditor's statement should be limited to no more than one-third of a page.

The financial statement should be uncluttered and inviting. Although it may appear at the beginning, the middle, or the end of the report, it most often appears at the end.

Board of Directors and Company Officers.   The final part of the annual report lists the company's board of directors and their corporate affiliations. Many annual reports also include a photograph of each director, as well as a listing of the company's officers by name and title (sometimes with photographs). The officers generally include the chair of the board of directors, the president, vice presidents, secretary, treasurer, and legal counsel. Do not underestimate the importance of photographs, for they lend a human touch to what is essentially a financial report.

Preparing the Report

First interview the president of the company to determine the general direction the report is to take. Next, interview vice presidents or division heads to learn the highlights of each division's operations. Determine from them the proper emphasis to place on their divisions' performances (but stay within the general direction established by the president or chair). See **interviewing for information**.

Compose a list of primary topics, as shown here, and allot space as necessary to each division or subsidiary in order to make a number of decisions.

- Whether to show sales and earnings as a company total only or by division as well
- The contents of charts and graphs
- How lavish or spartan the report should be in appearance and cost

Tone is critical in writing and designing an annual report. The annual report should convey the image your company has established or wants to establish.

Design and Visuals.   Typography, graphics, and design communicate a message about a company as strongly as words do. Select visual elements that enhance your company's image and accurately reflect your industry. See **layout and design** and **visuals**.

Use photographs and visuals liberally, although purposefully, in the narrative section to enhance the company's image, and complement the photographs and visuals with informative and well-written captions. Choose only those photographs and illustrations that will make the maximum contribution to the report's theme. Both photographs and their captions are critical in enlivening your annual report and putting a human face on your company. Colorful photographs that are carefully composed and show action or people enjoying themselves attract favorable interest.

Charts and **graphs** enable readers to grasp numerical material quickly and easily, provided those visuals are not so complex that they defeat the purpose. Subjects that most easily lend themselves to graphs and charts, usually shown in a three-year comparison arrangement, are the following:

- Assets
- Capital expenditures
- Dividends
- Earnings (by product groups or divisions)
- Industry growth
- Inventories
- Liabilities
- Net worth
- Price trends
- Reserves
- Sales (by product groups or divisions)
- Source and disposition of funds (taxes, wages, working capital)

The following information is normally printed on the inside front and back covers of the annual report: (1) notice of the annual meeting; (2) corporate address; and (3) names of transfer agents, registrar, and stock exchange. Some annual reports use the inside front cover solely for the announcement of the annual meeting.

WRITER'S CHECKLIST   Annual Reports

✔ Review past annual reports for their content, style, and format.

✔ Review the annual reports of organizations similar to yours at Web sites, such as *www.annualreports.com*.

✔ Interview senior company officials to learn which issues they wish to highlight.

✔ Allocate topics and space to reach your company's target audiences.

✔ Adopt a writing style and layout and design consistent with your company's image.

✔ Work closely with the graphics, print-production, and Web staffs to ensure that the report is professionally designed and produced on schedule.

---

antonyms

An antonym is a word with a meaning opposite that of another word (*good/bad, wet/dry, fresh/stale*). Many pairs of words that look as if they are antonyms, such as *limit/delimit*, are not. When in doubt, consult thesauruses or **dictionaries** for antonyms as well as **synonyms**.

apostrophes

An apostrophe (') is used to show possession or to indicate the omission of letters. Sometimes it is also used to avoid confusion with certain plurals of words, letters, and **abbreviations**.

Showing Possession

An apostrophe is used with an *s* to form the possessive case of some nouns (the *report's* title). For further advice on using apostrophes to show possession, see **possessive case**.

Indicating Omission

An apostrophe is used to mark the omission of letters or **numbers** in a **contraction** or a date (*can't, I'm, I'll*; the class of *'15*).

Forming Plurals

An apostrophe can be used in forming the plurals of letters, words, or lowercase abbreviations if confusion might result from using *s* alone.

- The search program does not find *a*'s and *i*'s.
- Do not replace all *of which*'s in the document.
- *I*'s need to be distinguished from the number 1.
- Check for any c.o.d.'s.

Generally, however, add only *s* in roman (or regular) type when referring to words as words or capital letters. See also **italics**.

- Five *and*s appear in the first sentence.
- The applicants received *A*s and *B*s in their courses.

Do not use an apostrophe for plurals of abbreviations with all capital letters (*PDFs*) or a final capital letter (*ten PhDs*) or for plurals of numbers (*7s, the late 1990s*).

appendixes

An appendix, located at the end of a **formal report**, **proposal**, or other long document, supplements or clarifies the information in the body of the document. Appendixes (or *appendices*) can provide information that is too detailed or lengthy for the primary **audience** of the document.

For example, an appendix could contain such material as **maps**, statistical analysis, **résumés** of key personnel involved in a proposed project, or other documents needed by secondary readers.

A document may have more than one appendix, with each providing only one type of information. When you include more than one appendix, arrange them in the order they are mentioned in the body of the document. Begin each appendix on a new page, and identify each with a letter, starting with the letter A (*Appendix A: Sample Questionnaire*). If you have only one appendix, title it simply "Appendix." List the titles and beginning page numbers of the appendixes in the **table of contents**.

application cover letters

When applying for a job, you usually need to submit both an application letter (also referred to as a *cover letter*) and a **résumé**. Employers may ask you to submit them by standard mail, online form, fax, or **e-mail**. See also **cover letters**, **job search**, and **letters**.

The application letter is essentially a **sales letter** in which you market your skills, abilities, and knowledge. Therefore, your application letter must be persuasive. The successful application letter accomplishes four tasks: (1) it serves as your personal introduction, provoking interest in recruiters by describing how your skills can contribute to their organization, (2) it explains to a prospective employer what particular job interests you and why, (3) it convinces the reader that you are a viable candidate by highlighting specific qualifications in your résumé, and (4) it provides the opportunity to request an interview. See also **correspondence**, **interviewing for a job**, **persuasion**, and **salary negotiations**.

◀ PROFESSIONALISM NOTE It is generally a good idea to submit an application cover letter with your résumé even if the prospective employer does not specifically request one. ▶

The sample application letters shown in Figures A–8 through A–10 follow the guidelines described in this entry. In each sample, the **emphasis**, **tone**, and **style** are tailored to fit the employer's need and highlight the applicant's qualifications. Note that the letter shown in Figure A–9 matches the résumé in Figure R–7 ("Joshua S. Goodman") and the letter depicting an experienced applicant in Figure A–10 matches the résumé in Figure R–8 ("Robert Mandillo").

Opening

In the opening paragraph, provide **context** by indicating how you heard about the position and name the specific job title or area. If you have been referred to a company by an employee, a career counselor, a professor, or someone else, be sure to say so ("I understand from Mr. John Smith, Director of Operations, that your agency . . ."). Show enthusiasm by explaining why you are interested in the job and demonstrate your initiative as well as your knowledge of the organization by relating your interest to some facet of the organization. ("I am eager to continue

---

From: Marsha S. Parker <msparker@ubi.edu>
To: Patrice C. Crandal <pcrandal@abel.com>
Sent: Thursday, February 23, 2012 10:47 AM
Subject: Application for Summer Internship

Attachment: 📄 Parker_Resume.doc

Dear Ms. Crandal:

I have learned from your Web site that you are hiring undergraduates for summer internships. An internship with Abel's buyer training program interests me because I have learned that your program is one of the best in the industry.

My experience with the Alumni Relations Program and the University Center Committee demonstrates my communication and persuasive abilities as well as my understanding of compromise and negotiation. For example, in the alumni program, I persuaded both uninvolved and active alumni to become more engaged with the direction of the university. On the University Center Committee, I balanced the students' demands with the financial and structural constraints of the administration. With these skills, I can ably assist the members of your department with their summer projects.

I look forward to an interview with you at your earliest convenience. Thank you for your consideration.

Sincerely,

Marsha S. Parker

1251 Pine Street
Providence, RI 02901
401-555-9568

FIGURE A–8. Application Cover Letter Sent as E-mail (College Student Applying for an Internship)

222 Morewood Ave.
Pittsburgh, PA 15212
April 16, 2012

Ms. Judith Castro, Director
Human Resources
Natural History Museum
1201 S. Figueroa Street
Los Angeles, CA 90015

Dear Ms. Castro:

A graphic designer at Dyer/Khan, Jodi Hammel, has informed me
that you are recruiting for a graphic designer in your Marketing
Department. Your position interests me greatly because it offers me
an opportunity both to fulfill my career goals and to promote the
work of an internationally respected institution. Having participated
in substantial volunteer activities at a local public museum, I am
aware of the importance of your work.

I bring strong up-to-date academic and practical skills in multimedia tools and graphic arts production, as indicated in my
enclosed résumé. Further, I have recent project management experience at Dyer/Khan, where I was responsible for the development
of client brochures, newsletters, and posters. As project manager,
I coordinated the project time lines, budgets, and production with
clients, staff, and vendors.

My experience and contacts in the Los Angeles area media and
entertainment community should help me make use of state-of-the-
art design expertise. As you will see on my résumé, I have worked
with the leading motion picture, television, and music companies—
that experience should help me develop exciting marketing tools
museum visitors and patrons will find attractive. For example, I
helped design an upgrade of the CGI logo for Paramount Pictures
and was formally commended by the Director of Marketing.

Could we schedule a meeting at your convenience to discuss this position further? Call me any weekday morning at 412-555-1212 (cell) or
e-mail me at jgoodman@aol.com. Thank you for your consideration.

Sincerely,

Joshua S. Goodman

Joshua S. Goodman

Enclosure: Résumé

**FIGURE A–9. Application Cover Letter (Recent Graduate Applying for a Graphic
Design Job)**

Dear Ms. Smathers:

During the recent NOMAD convention in Washington, Karen Jar-
rett, Director of Operations, informed me of a possible opening at
Aerospace Technologies for a manager of new product development. My extensive background in engineering exhibit design and
management makes me an ideal candidate for the position she
described.

I have been manager of the Exhibit Design Lab at Wright-Patterson
Air Force Base for the past seven years. During that time, I received
two Congressional Commendations for models of a space station
laboratory and a docking/repair port. My experience in advanced
exhibit design would give me a special advantage in helping
develop AT's wind tunnel and aerospace models. Further, I have
just learned this week that my exhibit design presented at NOMAD
received a "Best of Show" Award.

As described on the enclosed résumé, I not only have workplace
management experience but also have recently received an MBA
from the University of Dayton. As a student in the MBA program,
I won the Luson Scholarship to complete my coursework as well
as the Jonas Outstanding Student Award.

I would be happy to discuss my qualifications in an interview at
your convenience. Please telephone me at (937) 255-4137 or e-mail
me at mand@juno.com. I look forward to talking with you.

Sincerely,

Robert Mandillo

FIGURE A–10. Application Cover Letter (Applicant with Years of Experience)

my personal and professional growth with an international firm that
specializes in creating solutions for customers, and I was impressed by
Abel's reputation in infrastructure development.")

Body

In the middle **paragraphs,** use specific examples to demonstrate that
you are qualified for the job. Limit the content by focusing on one
basic point clearly stated in the topic sentence. For example, your second paragraph might focus on educational achievements and your third

paragraph might focus on work experience. Do not just tell readers that you are qualified—*show* them by including examples and details. ("Most recently, as an intern at SJX Engineering, I assisted in the infrastructure design for a multi-million-dollar seaside resort.") Highlight a notable achievement that portrays your value and refer the reader to your enclosed résumé. Do not simply repeat information found in your résumé; rather, indicate how your talents can make valuable contributions to the company.

Closing

In the final paragraph, take the initiative. A passive approach ("I look forward to hearing from you") is likely to produce a passive reaction on the employer's part. Request an interview and consider mentioning that you intend to follow up. This approach will provoke a need for action in the reviewer—for example, the need to pass this application to the hiring authority. Additionally, your initiative will portray your sincere interest in the opportunity. Let the reader know how to reach you by including your phone number or e-mail address. End with a statement of goodwill, even if only a "thank you."

Proofread your letter *carefully*. Research shows that if employers notice even one spelling, grammatical, or mechanical error, they often eliminate candidates from consideration immediately. Such errors give employers the impression that you lack attention to detail or basic writing skills or that you are careless in the way you present yourself professionally. See also **proofreading**.

appositives

An appositive is a **noun** or noun **phrase** that follows and amplifies another noun or noun phrase. It has the same grammatical function as the noun it complements.

- ▶ George Thomas, *the noted economist*, summarized the president's speech in a confidential memo.

- ▶ The noted economist *George Thomas* summarized the president's speech in a confidential memo.

For detailed information on the use of **commas** with appositives, see **restrictive and nonrestrictive elements**.

If you are in doubt about the case of an appositive, check it by substituting the appositive for the noun it modifies. See also **pronouns**.

> My boss gave the two of us, Jim and *~~I~~* ^me^, the day off.
> [You would not say, "My boss gave *I* the day off."]

articles

Articles (*a, an, the*) function as **adjectives** because they modify the items they designate by either limiting them or making them more specific. Articles may be indefinite or definite.

The indefinite articles, *a* and *an*, denote an unspecified item.

> *A* package was delivered yesterday. [*not* a specific package]

The choice between *a* and *an* depends on the sound rather than on the letter following the article, as described in the entry **a / an**.

The definite article, *the*, denotes a particular item.

> *The* package was delivered yesterday. [*one* specific package]

Do not omit all articles from your writing in an attempt to be concise. Including articles costs nothing; eliminating them makes reading more difficult. (See also **telegraphic style**.) However, do not overdo it. An article can be superfluous.

> I'll meet you in *a* half *an* hour.
> [Choose one article and eliminate the other.]

Do not capitalize articles in titles except when they are the first word ("*The Economist* reviewed *Winning the Talent Wars*").

ESL TIPS for Using Articles

Whether to use a definite or an indefinite article is determined by what you can safely assume about your audience's knowledge. In each of these sentences, you can safely assume that the reader can clearly identify the noun. Therefore, use a definite article.

> *The* sun rises in the east.
> [The Earth has only one *sun*.]

> Did you know that yesterday was *the* coldest day of the year so far?
> [The modified noun refers to *yesterday*.]

(continued)

ESL TIPS for Using Articles (*continued*)

> *The* man who left his briefcase in the conference room was in a hurry. [The relative phrase *who left his briefcase in the conference room* restricts and, therefore, identifies the meaning of *man*.]

In the following sentence, however, you cannot assume that the reader can clearly identify the noun.

> *A* package is on the way. [It is impossible to identify specifically what package is meant.]

A more important question for some nonnative speakers of English is when *not* to use articles. These generalizations will help. Do not use articles with the following:

> Singular proper nouns
> > Utah, Main Street, Harvard University, Mount Hood
>
> Plural nonspecific count nouns (when making generalizations)
> > Helicopters are the new choice of transportation for the rich and famous.
>
> Singular mass nouns
> > She loves coffee.
>
> Plural count nouns used as complements
> > Those women are physicians.

See also **English as a second language**.

as / because / since

As, because, and *since* are commonly used to mean "because." To express cause, *because* is the strongest and most specific connective; *because* is unequivocal in stating a causal relationship. ("*Because* she did not have an MBA, she was not offered the job.")

Since is a weak substitute for *because* as a connective to express cause. However, *since* is an appropriate connective when the emphasis is on circumstance, condition, or time rather than on cause and effect. ("*Since* it went public, the company has earned a profit every year.")

As is the least definite connective to indicate cause; avoid using it for that purpose. See also **subordination**.

Avoid colloquial, nonstandard, or wordy phrases sometimes used instead of *as, because,* or *since.* See also **as much as / more than**, **as such**, **as well as**, **conciseness**, and **due to / because of**.

PHRASE	REPLACE WITH
being as, being that	because, since
inasmuch as, insofar as	since, because
on account of	because
on the grounds of/that	because
due to the fact that	because, since

as much as / more than

The phrases *as much as* and *more than* are sometimes incorrectly combined, especially when intervening phrases delay the completion of the phrase.

> ► The auditors had as much, if not more, influence in planning the
>   *as*   *, if not more*
>   program than the accountants.

as such

The phrase *as such* is seldom useful and should be omitted.

> ► Patients, as such, should be partners in their treatment decisions.

as well as

Do not use *as well as* with *both*. The two expressions have similar meanings; use one or the other and adjust the verb as needed.

>   *and*   *are*
> ► Both General Motors as well as Ford is marketing hybrid vehicles.
> ► Both General Motors as well as Ford is marketing hybrid vehicles.

audience

Considering the needs of your audience is crucial to achieving your **purpose**. When you are writing to a specific reader, for example, you may find it useful to visualize a reader sitting across from you as you write. (See **correspondence**.) Likewise, when writing to an audience composed of relatively homogeneous readers, you might create an image of a composite reader and write for *that* reader. In such cases, using the **"you" viewpoint** and an appropriate **tone** will help you meet the needs of your readers as well as achieve an effective **business writing style**. For meeting the needs of an audience composed of listeners, see **presentations**.

Analyzing Your Audience's Needs

The first step in analyzing your audience is to determine the readers' needs relative to your purpose and goals. Ask key questions during **preparation**.

- Who specifically is your reader? Do you have multiple readers? Who needs to see or use the document?

- What do your readers already know about your subject? What are your readers' attitudes about the subject? (Skeptical? Supportive? Anxious? Bored?)

- What particular information about your readers (experience, training, and work habits, for example) might help you write at the appropriate level of detail? (See **scope**.)

- What does the **context** suggest about meeting the readers' expectations for content or **layout and design**?

- Do you need to adapt your message for international readers? If so, see **global communication**, **global graphics**, and **international correspondence**.

In the workplace, your readers are usually less familiar with the subject than you are. You have to be careful, therefore, when writing on a topic that is unique to your area of specialization. Be sensitive to the needs of those whose training or experience lies in other areas; provide definitions of nonstandard terms and explanations of principles that you, as a specialist, take for granted. See also **defining terms**.

Writing for Multiple Audiences

For documents aimed at multiple audiences with different needs, consider segmenting the document for different groups of readers: an executive summary for top managers, an appendix with detailed data for technical specialists, and the body for those readers who need to make decisions based on a detailed discussion. See also **formal reports** and **proposals**.

When you have multiple audiences with various needs but cannot segment your document, first determine your primary or most important readers—such as those who will make decisions based on the document—and be sure to meet their needs. Then, meet the needs of secondary readers, such as those who need only some of the document's contents, as long as you do not sacrifice the needs of your primary readers. See also **persuasion** and "Five Steps to Successful Writing" on page xv.

augment / supplement

Augment means to increase or magnify in size, degree, or effect. ("Our retirees can *augment* their incomes through consulting.") *Supplement* means to add something to make up for a deficiency. ("This patient should *supplement* his diet with vitamins.")

average / median / mean

The *average* (or arithmetic *mean*) is determined by adding two or more quantities and dividing the sum by the number of items totaled. For example, if one report is 10 pages, another is 30 pages, and a third is 20 pages, their *average* length is 20 pages. It is incorrect to say that "each report averages 20 pages" because each report is a specific length.

> The three reports average
> ► ~~Each report averages~~ 20 pages.
>   ^

The *median* is the middle number in a sequence of numbers. For example, the *median* of the series 1, 3, 4, 7, 8 is 4.

awhile / a while

The **adverb** *awhile* means "for a short time." The **preposition** *for* should not precede *awhile* because *for* is inherent in the meaning of *awhile*. The two-word noun **phrase** *a while* means "a period of time."

> ► Wait ~~for~~ *awhile* before sending the e-mail.

>   a while
> ► Wait for ~~awhile~~ before sending the e-mail.
>   ^

awkwardness

Any writing that strikes readers as awkward—that is, as forced or unnatural—impedes their understanding. The following checklist and the entries indicated will help you smooth out most awkward passages.

WRITER'S CHECKLIST   Eliminating Awkwardness

✔ Strive for <u>clarity</u> and <u>coherence</u> during <u>revision</u>.

✔ Check for <u>organization</u> to ensure your writing develops logically.

✔ Keep <u>sentence construction</u> as direct and simple as possible.

✔ Use <u>subordination</u> appropriately and avoid needless <u>repetition</u>.

✔ Correct any <u>logic errors</u> within your sentences.

✔ Revise for <u>conciseness</u> and avoid <u>expletives</u> where possible.

✔ Use the active <u>voice</u> unless you have a justifiable reason to use the passive voice.

✔ Eliminate jammed or misplaced <u>modifiers</u> and, for particularly awkward constructions, apply the tactics in <u>garbled sentences</u>.

B

bad / badly

Bad is the **adjective** form that follows such linking **verbs** as *feel* and *look*. ("We don't want to look *bad* at the meeting.") *Badly* is an **adverb**. ("The shipment was *badly* damaged.") To say "I feel *badly*" would mean, literally, that your sense of touch is impaired. See also **good / well**.

balance / remainder

One meaning of *balance* is "a state of equilibrium"; another meaning is "the amount of money in a bank account after deposits and withdrawals have been credited and debited." *Remainder*, in all applications, means "what is left over."

be sure to

The **phrase** *be sure and* is colloquial and unidiomatic when used for *be sure to*. See also **idioms**.

► When you sign the contract, be sure ~~and~~ keep a copy.
 ^{to}

beside / besides

Besides, meaning "in addition to" or "other than," should be carefully distinguished from *beside*, meaning "next to" or "apart from." ("*Besides* two of us from Marketing, three people from Production stood *beside* the president during the ceremony.")

between / among

Between is normally used to relate two items or persons. ("Preferred stock offers a middle ground *between* bonds and common stock.") *Among*

B

is used to relate more than two. ("The subcontracting was distributed *among* three firms.") *Amongst* is a variant, chiefly British spelling.

between you and me

The expression *between you and I* is incorrect. Because the **pronouns** are **objects** of the **preposition** *between*, the objective form of the personal pronoun (*me*) must be used. See also **case**.

> ► Between you and $\overset{me}{\underset{\wedge}{I}}$, Joan should be promoted.

bi- / semi-

When used with periods of time, *bi-* means "two" or "every two," as in *bimonthly*, which means "once in two months." When used with periods of time, *semi-* means "half of" or "occurring twice within a period of time." *Semimonthly* means "twice a month." Both *bi-* and *semi-* normally are joined with the following element without a space or **hyphen**.

biannual / biennial

In conventional usage, *biannual* means "twice during the year," and *biennial* means "every other year." See also **bi- / semi-**.

biased language

Biased language refers to words and expressions that offend because they make inappropriate assumptions or stereotypes about gender, ethnicity, physical or mental disability, age, or sexual orientation. Biased language, which is often used unintentionally, can defeat your **purpose** by damaging your credibility.

◀ PROFESSIONALISM NOTE The easiest way to avoid bias is simply not to mention differences among people unless the differences are relevant to the discussion. Keep current with accepted usage and, if you are unsure of the appropriateness of an expression or the tone of a passage, have several colleagues review the material and give you their assessments. ▶

Sexist Language

Sexist language can be an outgrowth of sexism, the arbitrary stereo-typing of men and women—it can breed and reinforce inequality. To avoid sexism in your writing, treat men and women equally and use nonsexist occupational descriptions.

INSTEAD OF	CONSIDER
chairman, chairwoman	chair, chairperson
foreman	supervisor, manager
man-hours	staff hours, worker hours
policeman, policewoman	police officer
salesman, saleswoman	salesperson

Use parallel terms to describe men and women.

INSTEAD OF	USE
ladies and men	ladies and gentlemen, women and men
man and wife	husband and wife
Ms. Jones and Bernard Weiss	Ms. Jones and Mr. Weiss, Mary Jones and Bernard Weiss

One common way of handling **pronoun references** that could apply equally to a man or a woman is the use of the expression *his or her*. To avoid this awkward usage, try rewriting the sentence in the plural. See also *he / she*.

▶ ~~Every employee~~ should submit ~~his or her~~ expense ~~report~~ by Monday.
  All employees · *their* · *reports*

Another solution is to omit pronouns completely if they are not essential to the meaning of the sentence.

▶ Every employee should submit ~~his or her~~ *an* expense report by Monday.

Other Types of Biased Language

Identifying people by racial, ethnic, or religious categories is simply not relevant in most workplace writing. Telling readers that an accountant is Native American or an attorney is Jewish almost never conveys useful information.

Consider how you refer to people with disabilities. If you refer to "a disabled employee," you imply that the part (*disabled*) is as significant as the whole (*employee*). Use "an employee with a disability" instead. Similarly, the preferred usage is "a person who uses a wheelchair" rather than "a wheelchair-bound person," an expression that inappropriately equates the wheelchair with the person. Likewise, references to a person's age can be inappropriate, as in expressions like "middle-aged manager" or "young Web designer." See also **ethics in writing**.

bibliographies

A bibliography is an alphabetical list of books, articles, Web sources, and other works that have been consulted in preparing a document or that are useful for reference purposes. A bibliography provides a convenient alphabetical listing of sources in a standardized form for readers interested in getting further information on the topic or in assessing the scope of the **research**.

Whereas a list of references or works cited refers to works actually cited in the text, a bibliography also includes works consulted for general background information. For information on using various citation styles, see **documenting sources**.

Entries in a bibliography are listed alphabetically by the author's last name. If an author is unknown, the entry is alphabetized by the first word in the title (other than *A, An,* or *The*). Entries also can be arranged by subject and then ordered alphabetically within those categories.

An annotated bibliography includes complete bibliographic information about a work (author, title, place of publication, publisher, and publication date) followed by a brief description or evaluation of what the work contains. The following is an annotation of a book on style and format:

> Sabin, William A. *The Gregg Reference Manual: A Manual of Style, Grammar, Usage, and Formatting.* 11th ed. New York: McGraw Hill, 2011.
>
> > The eleventh edition of this standard 736-page office guide "is intended for anyone who writes, edits, or prepares material for distribution or publication" (p. xiii). The book includes a section titled "How to Look Things Up," which provides a reference to the *GRM* Web site. Part 1, "Grammar, Usage, and Style," contains 11 sections on topics such as punctuation, abbreviations, spelling, and usage. Part 2, "Techniques and Formats," contains seven sections on such topics as proofreading, correspondence (letters, memos, and e-mail), and other elements of manuscript preparation. Part 3, "References," includes two appendixes that cover grammatical terms and pronunciation problems and a reference to additional appendixes at www.gregg.com that treat rules for alphabetic filing and a glossary of computer terms.

blogs and forums

A *blog* (from *Web log*) is a Web-based journal in which an individual or group of "bloggers" can post entries (displayed from the most recent to the earliest posting) that document experiences, express opinions, provide information, and respond to other bloggers on subjects of mutual interest. Although blogs may allow readers to post comments, a *forum* typically fosters a wider "conversation" in which contributors can not only respond to the posts of others but also begin new topics or discussion threads. Blogs and forums may overlap or combine features. If your Web site features a blog or forum, keep it current in order to build an **audience** and to maintain the credibility of your site.

Organizational Uses

Organizations create blogs and forums to help meet such goals as attracting and retaining clients or customers, promoting goodwill, obtaining valuable feedback on their products and services, and even developing a sense of community among their customers and employees. Blogs and forums can be both external and internal.

External sites are publicly available on the Internet both for an organization's customers or clients and for executives, spokespeople, or employees to share their views. Blogs and forums can help to build loyalty for a company because customers can make a direct connection with an organization's representatives or can exchange current information that may not be available in published documents and on Web sites. *Internal sites* are usually created for an organization's employees and can be accessed only through its intranet. Internal blogs may serve as interactive **newsletters** that help build a sense of community within an organization. See also **writing for the Web**.

Writing Style

Write blog or forum entries in an informal, conversational **style** that uses **contractions**, first **person**, and active **voice**.

BLOG POSTING	Check out the latest concept for our new dashboards— we've added enough space to hold your Starbucks coffee and your iPod by moving the air ducts to. . . . Tell us what you think. [Blog posting could be a paragraph or more.]
FORUM POSTING	I'm new, but I'm surprised no one's discussed the issue of repair costs. Have I missed something? [Forum postings tend to be more brief than blogs.]

Keep your sentences and paragraphs concise. Use bulleted <u>lists,</u> <u>italics,</u> and other <u>layout and design</u> elements, such as boldface and white space if possible. Doing so can help readers scan the postings or text to find information that is interesting or relevant to them. Keep headlines short and direct to catch attention and increase the visual appeal and readability. Where helpful, provide links to other sites and resources that participants might find useful. When blogs expand or forums become popular, you may need to organize them using *categories* (links to discussion topics) or *tags* (searchable labels for postings).

WEB LINK	Developing Blogs and Forums
Google Blogger (www.blogger.com) and Google Groups (groups.google .com) provide help in finding and developing blogs and forums. For more examples of blogs and forums, see *bedfordstmartins.com/alred* and select *Links for Handbook Entries*.	

❖ ETHICS NOTE Because organizations expect employees to assume full responsibility for the content they post on a company blog or forum, you must maintain high ethical standards.

- Do not post information that is confidential, proprietary, or sensitive to your employer.
- Do not attack competitors or use abusive language toward other participants while making strong points on topics.
- Do not post content that is profane, libelous, or harassing, or that violates the privacy of others. See also <u>biased language</u>.
- Obtain permission before using any material that is protected by <u>copyright</u>, and identify sources for <u>quotations</u>. See also <u>plagiarism</u>. ❖

both . . . and

Statements using the *both . . . and* construction should always be balanced grammatically and logically. See also **parallel structure**.

▶ To succeed in management, you must be able *both* to develop
  to master
  writing skills *and* ~~mastering~~ presentation skills.
  ^

brackets

The primary use of brackets ([ ]) is to enclose a word or words inserted by the writer or editor into a quotation.

▶ The text stated, "Hypertext systems can be categorized as either modest [not modifiable] or robust [modifiable]."

Brackets are used to set off a parenthetical item within parentheses.

▶ We must credit Emanuel Foose (and his brother Emilio [1932–2002]) for founding the institute.

Brackets are also used to insert the Latin word *sic*, indicating that a writer has quoted material exactly as it appears in the original, even though it contains a misspelled or wrongly used word. See also scholarly **abbreviations** and **quotations**.

▶ The contract states, "Tinted windows will be installed to protect against son [*sic*] damage."

brainstorming

Brainstorming, a form of free association used to generate ideas about a topic, can be done individually or in groups. Brainstorming can stimulate creative thinking and reveal fresh perspectives and new connections. When brainstorming alone, jot down as many random ideas as you can think of about the topic. When working in a group, designate a person to note ideas the group suggests. Do not stop to analyze ideas or hold back looking for only the "best" ideas; just note everything that comes to mind. After compiling a list of initial ideas, ask *what, when, who, where, how,* and *why* for each idea, then list additional details that those questions bring to mind. When you run out of ideas, analyze each one you recorded, discarding those that are redundant. Then group the remaining items in the most logical order, based on your **purpose** and the needs of the **audience** to create a tentative **outline** of the document. Although the outline will be sketchy and incomplete, it will show where further brainstorming or research is needed and provide a framework for any new details that additional research yields. (See **outlining**.)

Many writers find a technique called *clustering* (also called *mind mapping*), as shown in Figure B–1, helpful in recording and organizing ideas created during a brainstorming session. To cluster, begin with a blank sheet of paper or a flip chart. Think of a key term that best characterizes your topic and put it in a circle at the center of the paper. Figure B–1

B

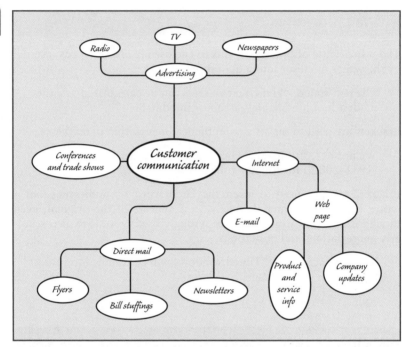

FIGURE B–1. Cluster Map from a Brainstorming Session

shows brainstorming about the best way to communicate with custom-ers, so that topic could be "Customer communication." Then think of subtopics most closely related to the main topic. In Figure B–1, the main topic ("Customer communication") might lead to such subtopics as "Ad-vertising," "Internet," and "Direct mail." Draw circles or boxes around the subtopics, connecting each to the center circle, like spokes to a wheel hub. Repeat the exercise for each subtopic. In Figure B–1, for example, the subtopic "Internet" could stimulate additional subtopics such as "E-mail" and "Web page." Continue the process until you exhaust all possible ideas. The resulting "map" will show clusters of terms grouped around the central concept from which you can create a topic outline.

brochures

Brochures are printed publications that promote the products and ser-vices offered by a business or that promote the image of a business or an organization by providing information important to a target **audience**. The goal of a brochure is to inform or to persuade or to do both. See also **persuasion** and **promotional writing**.

Types of Brochures

The two major types of brochures are sales brochures and informational brochures. *Sales brochures* are created specifically to sell a company's products and services. For example, a brochure for a consulting company would describe its seminars or specific services. *Informational brochures* are created to inform and to educate the reader as well as to promote goodwill and to raise the profile of an organization. A psychological counseling clinic, for example, might create a brochure describing how to recognize depression in teenagers.

Designing the Brochure

Before you begin to write, determine the specific **purpose** of the brochure—to provide information about a service? to sell a product? You must also identify your target audience—general reader? expert? potential or existing client? Understanding your purpose, audience, and **context** is essential to creating content and a design that will be both appropriate and persuasive to your target audience. To help you develop an effective design and to stimulate your thinking, gather sample brochures for products or services similar to yours.

Cover Panel.　The main goal of the cover panel is to gain the audience's attention. It should clearly identify the organization or product being promoted and provide a carefully selected visual image or headline geared toward the interest of the audience. Keep the amount of text to a minimum—for example, a statement about the organization's mission and success or a brief promotional quotation from a satisfied customer. Figure B–2 shows the cover panel of a brochure produced by the National Cancer Institute, which hopes to attract health-care professionals to an online course on conducting clinical trials in their practices. The cover photo features a health-care professional who appears to be counseling a patient; the text briefly defines the course, provides a Web address, and identifies the sponsoring organization.

First Inside Panel.　The first inside panel of a brochure should again identify the organization and attract the reader with headlines and brief, readable content, such as that used in advertising. The first inside panel of the National Cancer Institute brochure uses boldface **headings** to highlight brief descriptions of the course and those participants who may benefit.

Subsequent Panels.　Subsequent panels should describe the product or service with the reader's needs in mind, clearly stating the benefits and solutions to problems that your product or service offers. Include relevant and accurate supporting facts and **visuals**, such as **photographs** and cutaway **drawings**. You might further establish credibility with a brief company or product history or with a list of current clients or

B

testimonials. Use subheadings and bulleted **lists** to break up the text and highlight key points. In the final panel, be clear about the action you want the reader to take, such as calling to order the product or visiting a Web site for more information. In Figure B–3, the second inside panel describes the course objectives and tells readers how to register.

Design Style and Unity. Develop a style that unifies and complements the content of your brochure, and use it consistently throughout. For example, a brochure for a cruise line would feature many attractive photos of passengers and scenery. A brochure related to a serious medical subject, as in Figures B–2 and B–3, might use images of professionals in workplace settings. See also **layout and design**.

Incorporating Cancer Clinical Trials into Your Practice

A Web-based tutorial for health care professionals

http://cme.cancer.gov

U.S. DEPARTMENT OF HEALTH AND HUMAN SERVICES
National Institutes of Health • **National Cancer Institute**

FIGURE B–2. Brochure (Cover Panel)

WRITER'S CHECKLIST Designing a Brochure

- ✔ Collect other brochures to stimulate your thinking as you consider the goals, content, and design for your brochure.
- ✔ Create a rough sketch that maps out the content of each panel to help you select visuals, color schemes, and the number of panels.
- ✔ Experiment with margins, spacing, and the arrangement and amount of text on each panel; make appropriate changes to content or length and allow adequate white space for readability.
- ✔ Experiment with fonts and formatting, such as enlarging the first letter of the first word in a paragraph, but do not overuse unusual fonts or alternative styles, such as running type vertically.

What is "Incorporating Cancer Clinical Trials Into Your Practice?"

It's a free Web-based tutorial for health care professionals that emphasizes the importance of participating in cancer clinical trials, either through patient referral or becoming a clinical trials investigator.

The course begins with a brief overview of cancer clinical trials and explains ways one can become involved in clinical trials. It continues with practical information and guidance for professionals interested in referring patients to, or conducting, clinical trials.

Participants will hear from experienced clinicians about some of the issues they have faced and how these issues were addressed.

Who should take this course?

The course is designed for health care professionals who are new to the clinical trials process, including oncologists, family physicians, internists, nurses, and other clinical staff. Specifically, it is for those clinicians that are referring patients to cancer clinical trials for the first time, and clinical research staff who are new to conducting clinical trials in their practices.

What are the course objectives?

At the end of the course, participants should be able to:

- Describe the role of clinical research in advancing cancer care
- Explain how clinical trials are conducted
- Describe the sponsorship of clinical trials
- Demonstrate how to locate clinical trials
- Understand how clinical trial sites are set up, staffed, and funded
- Make successful patient referrals to clinical trials
- Know how a physician may become a cancer clinical trials investigator
- Understand regulatory, record keeping, and reporting requirements in conducting clinical trials
- Identify key issues in communication among the patient, referring clinician, and clinical trials investigator

To register for this course, go to **http://cme.cancer.gov**, where you will be given further instructions.

Participants may receive continuing medical education (CME) credits or contact hours for course completion.

FIGURE B–3. Brochure (Inside Panels of Brochure in Figure B–2)

WRITER'S CHECKLIST   **Designing a Brochure** (*continued*)

✔ Consider color choices: black and white, which is cheaper than color, can be effective; in some circumstances, however, color is a must.

✔ Evaluate the impact of the design with your content. Have you adequately considered the needs of your audience?

✔ Consider using a professional printer and high-quality paper, depending on your budget and the scale of your project.

B

WEB LINK	Sample Brochures

For links to Web sites with sample brochures, see *bedfordstmartins.com/ alred* and select *Links for Handbook Entries*.

bulleted lists (*see* lists)

business plans

A business plan is a **proposal** that allows potential supporters to evaluate ideas for a new business venture. Business plans are written primarily for bankers and other outside funders or consultants and sometimes for internal **audiences** (mostly senior management). Usually readers are targeted to provide funding, resources, cooperation, or, in the context of a large corporation, permission and financial support to run a division in a certain way.

Purposes and Audience

A business plan can fulfill a single **purpose** or several purposes. The most common include the following:

- *To persuade potential investors or lenders to finance a business venture.* A comprehensive business plan allows investors to review objectively the company's assumptions, facts, and future outlook.

- *To allow reviewers (usually senior management) within a company to assess the profitability and goals of a new, internal business venture.* These readers typically want to evaluate economic forecasts and determine future profitability of the new venture and perhaps to provide creative direction.

Before you write a business plan, identify and analyze your audience. The purposes of a business plan can differ dramatically, depending on which audience you are trying to convince. If you are addressing a banker, the central purpose of the business plan is to obtain funding for the new venture; to accomplish that, you need to demonstrate credibility by documenting a solid history of financial success. If you are addressing senior management, the central purpose is to demonstrate how the venture is likely to add value to the company. See also **persuasion**.

When you are writing a business plan, find out which issues are of most interest to your audience and respond directly to those issues. If you are writing a plan for multiple audiences with diverse interests and needs, be comprehensive in addressing all interests and needs in your plan.

Format, Length, and Sections

B

Because the audiences and purposes of business plans vary, the lengths and designs of the plans vary as well. Business plans can be as brief as one page, but typically they run between four and ten pages. Whether they are short or long depends on the audience, the purpose, and the nature and complexity of the proposed business ideas.

The contents and sections will vary from one company to the next, but many plans (like **formal reports**) include a title page, a **table of contents**, and an **executive summary**. Most plans cover the following topic areas in subsequent sections: company description and strategy, market analysis and strategy, marketing plan, financial analysis, and supporting documents.

Company Description and Strategy

The first section of a business plan typically describes the company's functions, products, and services; its overall strategy in a vision or **mission statement**; its goals and milestones; and its management team and its key members.

Business Description.   A business plan should begin with a concise but complete description of the type of organization, its products, and its services, as well as a brief mention of the company's place in the market.

- Identify the company's legal name and status.
- Explain exactly what the company does.
- Define the percentage and growth opportunity of each product or service and describe the customer base.
- Describe current products or services and what makes them unique and competitive.
- Mention products and services in development.

You can use this section to develop a description of the company's competitive advantage and cost versus benefits of its current and anticipated expenses.

Vision and Mission Statements.   Vision and mission statements can be the same; however, they often are written separately and serve different purposes. Vision statements broadly describe the perceived future of the company, and mission statements usually summarize the purpose of the business. Vision and mission statements may vary in length from one sentence to multiple pages. When combined, a mission statement usually precedes a vision statement.

Goals and Milestones. State short-term as well as long-term goals, with a timetable showing when the company expects to achieve specific milestones. Be realistic, especially when defining and setting short-term goals. Identify in specific, measurable terms what the company can reasonably achieve within a specified time frame.

Management and Key Team Members. Identify all members of management. Describe their strengths, including any experiences or skills that particularly contribute to the business or to a specific venture.

Identify those who will work closely with management, such as accountants, lawyers, insurance agents, and partners. Briefly describe their backgrounds and qualifications. If you are proposing that new positions be added to the company, mention that in the plan and describe basic elements of a human resources policy such as working hours, wages, vacation time, and sick leave. You can include **résumés** of candidates for the new positions in **appendixes**, along with other supporting documents.

Market Analysis and Strategy

Perhaps most important, the business plan needs to define and analyze the market and the competitive climate in which the writer proposes to launch the business venture. Once you have demonstrated a solid understanding of the market, describe the new venture or the new product or service and propose your strategy for launching the new venture and managing it over time to contribute to overall profits.

This section of the business plan also needs to identify and analyze the major competitors and examine how the company will address the competition to ensure that its products and services will make a strong entry into the marketplace. See also **research**.

Marketing Plan

Provide a specific plan for advertising and promoting products or services. Indicate the specific actions the company will take to achieve its sales and promotional objectives. This section often is written by a marketing director and includes discussions of promotional strategies and costs in different market channels, as well as sales projections for each market segment. See also **collaborative writing**.

Financial Analysis

In one or more subsections, present the company's financial plan and financial statements, especially if the business plan's purpose is to obtain venture capital. Provide historical information about financial status as well as projections about the company's financial growth. Identify both strengths and weaknesses, including new opportunities for growth, areas where the company can control costs, and ways of restructuring to make the company more efficient. Predict problems and describe the company's strategy to prevent or minimize their effects. These sections often benefit from strategically placed **graphs** and **tables**.

Provide complete and detailed financial statements (perhaps in an appendix). Bankers and other investors typically want to see a balance sheet, profit-and-loss statements, a three-year cash-flow projection, and source and use-of-funds statements. Until the business venture is up and running, the company might be able to provide only projections of profit-and-loss statements or balance sheets. Also describe the company's liability and property insurance. Make estimates of calculations conservative by using slightly low or low-end sales and margin figures and by slightly overstating expected costs.

Supporting Documents

In appendixes, provide résumés of key members of management and any other supporting information that demonstrates the company's potential and management's credibility. Other documents might include positive reviews of a new product, service, or venture, or positive articles about the company from industry or the popular press. Finally, you could provide copies of contracts with impressive clients (with the clients' permission) or information that would demonstrate relationships between the company and such clients.

WRITER'S CHECKLIST   Preparing Business Plans

✔ Identify and analyze the audience for your business plan and tailor your writing accordingly.

✔ Determine your purpose, such as convincing potential investors to finance a business venture or allowing senior management to assess the profitability and goals of a new business venture.

✔ Update and revise the plan regularly.

WEB LINK	Sample Business Plans

Business Resource Software, Inc., and Palo Alto Software, Inc., makers of business software, offer numerous sample business plans online. See *bedfordstmartins.com/alred* and select *Links for Handbook Entries*.

B business writing style

Business writing has evolved from a very formal and elaborate **style** to one that is more personal and direct. Business writing today legitimately varies from the conversational style you might use in a note sent by **instant messaging** to the formal, legalistic style found in contracts. In most **e-mails**, **letters**, and **memos**, a style between those two extremes generally is appropriate. (See **correspondence**.) Writing that is too formal can alienate readers. (See **audience**.) But an inappropriate attempt to be casual and informal may strike readers as insincere and unprofessional, especially to clients or those you do not know well.

> *Dear*
> ► H̶e̶y̶ Jane~~,~~/
>
> *Your proposal arrived today, and it looks good.*
> J̶u̶s̶t̶ g̶o̶t̶ y̶o̶u̶r̶ p̶r̶o̶p̶o̶s̶a̶l̶.̶ I̶t̶'̶s̶ a̶w̶e̶s̶o̶m̶e̶!̶

The use of personal **pronouns** is important in letters and memos. In fact, one way you can make your business writing persuasive is through the use of the **"you" viewpoint**, which often (but not always) uses the pronoun *you* to place the readers' interest foremost.

❖ ETHICS NOTE Be careful when you use the pronoun *we* in a business letter that is written on company stationery because it commits your company to what you have written. In general, when a statement is your opinion, use *I*; when it is company policy, use *we*. Do not refer to yourself in the third person by using *one* or *the writer*. It is perfectly natural and appropriate to refer to yourself as *I* and to the reader as *you*. In a **report**, however, you may be writing to more than one reader and may not necessarily want to refer to collective readers as *you*. See also **ethics in writing**, **persuasion**, and **point of view**. ❖

The best writers strive to write in a style that is so clear that their message cannot be misunderstood. In fact, you cannot be persuasive without being clear. One way to achieve **clarity**, especially during **revision**, is to eliminate overuse of the passive **voice**, which plagues most poor business writing. Although the passive voice is sometimes necessary, often it not only makes your writing dull but also is ambiguous, indirect, or overly impersonal.

You can also achieve clarity with **conciseness**. Proceed cautiously here, however, because business writing should not be an endless series of short, choppy sentences that are blunt or deliver too little information to be helpful to the reader. (See also **sentence variety** and **telegraphic style**.) Appropriate and effective **word choice** is also essential to clarity. Finally, the careful use of **punctuation** can promote clarity. See also "Five Steps to Successful Writing" (page xv).

buzzwords

Buzzwords are words or phrases that suddenly become popular and, because of an intense period of overuse, lose their freshness and preciseness. They may become popular through their association with technology, popular culture, or even sports. See also **jargon**.

► interface [as a <u>**verb**</u>]	win-win	F2F meeting
impact [as a verb]	24/7	data dump
cyberslackers	dot-com	action items

Obviously, the words in this example are appropriate when used in the right **context**.

► We must establish an *interface* between the computer and the satellite hardware.
[*Interface* is appropriately used as a **noun**.]

When writers needlessly shift from the normal function of a word, however, they often create a buzzword that is imprecise.

        cooperate
► We must ~~interface~~ with the Human Resources Department.

[*Interface* is inappropriately used as a verb; *cooperate* is more precise.]

We include such words in our vocabulary because they *seem* to give force and vitality to our language. Actually, buzzwords often sound like an **affectation** in business writing. See also **word choice**.

WEB LINK	Buzzwords
Former newspaper editor John Walston offers BuzzWhack, a lighthearted Web site "dedicated to demystifying buzzwords." See *bedfordstmartins .com/alred* and select *Links for Handbook Entries*.	

C

can / may

In writing, *can* refers to capability ("I *can* have the project finished today"). *May* refers to possibility ("I *may* be in Boston on Monday") or permission ("*May* I leave early?").

cannot

Cannot is one word.

                cannot
▶ We ~~can not~~ meet the deadline specified in the contract.

capital / capitol

Capital refers either to financial assets or to the city that hosts the government of a state or a nation. *Capitol* refers to the building in which a state or national legislature meets. *Capitol* is often written with a small *c* when it refers to a state building, but it is always capitalized when it refers to the home of the U.S. Congress in Washington, D.C.

capitalization

The use of capital, or uppercase, letters is determined by custom. Capital letters are used to call attention to certain words, such as proper **nouns** and the first word of a sentence. Use capital letters carefully because they can affect a word's meaning (march / March, china / China) and because a spell checker would fail to identify such an error.

C

Proper Nouns

Capitalize proper nouns that name specific persons, places, or things (Pat Wilde, Peru, Business Writing 205, Microsoft). Proper nouns that form other **parts of speech** are often capitalized (Keynesian economics, Boolean function, Balkanize), but you should check a current **dictionary**.

Common Nouns

Common nouns name general classes or categories of people, places, things, concepts, or qualities rather than specific ones and are not capitalized (person, country, business writing class, company).

First Words

The first letter of the first word in a sentence is always capitalized. ("Of the plans submitted, ours is best.") The first word after a **colon** is capitalized when the colon introduces two or more sentences (independent **clauses**) or if the colon precedes a statement requiring special emphasis.

▶ The meeting will address only one issue: What is the firm's role in environmental protection?

If a subordinate element follows the colon or if the thought is closely related, use a lowercase letter following the colon.

▶ We kept working for one reason: the approaching deadline.

The first word of a complete sentence in **quotation marks** is capitalized.

▶ Peter Drucker said, "The most important thing in communication is to hear what isn't being said."

The first word in the salutation (Dear Mr. Smith:) and complimentary close (Sincerely yours,) are capitalized, as are the names of the recipients. See also **letters**.

Specific Groups

Capitalize the names of ethnic groups, religions, and nationalities (Native American, Christianity, Mongolian). Do not capitalize the names of social and economic groups (middle class, unemployed).

Specific Places

Capitalize the names of all political divisions (Ward Six, Chicago, Cook County, Illinois) and geographic divisions (Europe, Asia, North America, the Middle East). Do not capitalize geographic features unless they are part of a proper name.

▶ The mountains in some areas, such as the *Great Smoky Mountains*, make radio transmission difficult.

The words *north*, *south*, *east*, and *west* are capitalized when they refer to sections of the country. They are not capitalized when they refer to directions.

▶ I may relocate further *west*, but my family will remain in the *South*.

Specific Institutions, Events, Concepts

Capitalize the names of institutions, organizations, and associations (U.S. Department of Health and Human Services). An organization usually capitalizes the names of its internal divisions and departments (Aeronautics Division, Human Resources Department). Types of organizations are not capitalized unless they are part of an official name (a business communication association; Association for Business Communication). Capitalize historical events (the Great Depression of the 1930s). Capitalize words that designate holidays, specific periods of time, months, or days of the week (Labor Day, the Renaissance, January, Monday). Do not capitalize seasons of the year (spring, summer, autumn, winter).

Titles of Works

Capitalize the initial letters of the first, last, and major words in the title of a book, an article, a play, or a film. Do not capitalize **articles** (*a*, *an*, *the*), coordinating **conjunctions** (*and*, *but*), or **prepositions** unless they begin or end the title (*The Lives of a Cell*). Capitalize prepositions within **titles** when they contain five or more letters (*Between*, *Within*, *Until*, *After*), unless you are following a style that recommends otherwise. The same rules apply to the subject lines of **e-mails** or **memos**.

Professional and Personal Titles

Titles preceding proper names are capitalized (Ms. Berger, Senator Lieberman). Appositives following proper names normally are not capitalized (Joseph Lieberman, *senator* from Connecticut). However, the word *president* is often capitalized when it refers to the chief executive of a national government. See **appositives**.

Job titles used with personal names are capitalized (Ho-shik Kim, *Division Manager*). Job titles used without personal names are not capitalized. (The *division manager* will meet us tomorrow.) Use capital letters to designate family relationships only when they occur before a name (my uncle, Uncle Fred).

Abbreviations and Letters

Capitalize **abbreviations** if the words they stand for would be capitalized, such as MBA. (Master of Business Administration). Capitalize letters that serve as names or indicate shapes (vitamin B, T-square, U-turn, I-beam).

Miscellaneous Capitalizations

The first word of a complete sentence enclosed in **dashes**, **brackets**, or **parentheses** is not capitalized when it appears as part of another sentence.

▶ We must improve our safety record this year (accidents last year were up 10 percent).

Certain units, such as parts and chapters of books and rooms in buildings, when specifically identified by number, are capitalized (Chapter 5, Ch. 5; Room 72, Rm. 72). Minor divisions within such units are not capitalized unless they begin a sentence (page 11, verse 14, seat 12).

case

Grammatical case indicates the functional relationship of a **noun** or a **pronoun** to the other words in a sentence. Nouns change form only in the possessive case; pronouns may show change for the subjective, the objective, or the possessive case.

The case of a noun or pronoun is always determined by its function in a **phrase, clause**, or sentence. If it is the subject of a phrase, clause, or sentence, it is in the subjective case; if it is an **object** in a phrase, clause, or sentence, it is in the objective case; if it reflects possession or ownership and modifies a noun, it is in the possessive case. Figure C–1 is a

SINGULAR	SUBJECTIVE	OBJECTIVE	POSSESSIVE
First person	I	me	my, mine
Second person	you	you	your, yours
Third person	he, she, it	him, her, it	his, her, hers, its

PLURAL	SUBJECTIVE	OBJECTIVE	POSSESSIVE
First person	we	us	our, ours
Second person	you	you	your, yours
Third person	they	them	their, theirs

FIGURE C–1. Pronoun-Case Chart

table of pronouns in the subjective, objective, and possessive cases. See also **sentence construction**.

The subjective case can indicate the person or thing acting ("*He* sued the vendor"), the person or thing acted upon ("*He* was sued by the vendor"), or the topic of description ("*He* is the vendor"). The objective case can indicate the thing acted on ("The vendor sued *him*") or the person or thing acting but in the objective position ("The vendor was sued by *him*"). (See also **voice**.) The possessive case indicates the person or thing owning or possessing something ("It was *his* company"). See also **modifiers**.

Subjective Case

A pronoun is in the subjective case (also called *nominative case*) when it represents the person or thing acting or is the receiver of the action even though it is in the subject position.

► *I* wrote a proposal.

► *I* was praised for my proposal writing.

A linking **verb** links a pronoun to its antecedent to show that they identify the same thing. Because they represent the same thing, the pronoun is in the subjective case even when it follows the verb, which makes it a subjective complement.

► *He* is the head of the Quality Control Group. [subject]

► The head of the Quality Control Group is *he*. [subjective complement]

The subjective case is used after the words *than* and *as* because of the understood (although unstated) portion of the clauses in which those words appear.

- ▸ George is as good a designer as *I* [am].
- ▸ Our subsidiary can do the job better than *we* [can].

Objective Case

A pronoun is in the objective case (also called the *accusative case*) when it indicates the person or thing receiving the action that is expressed by a verb in the active voice.

- ▸ They selected *me* to attend the conference.

Pronouns that follow action verbs (which excludes all forms of the verb *be*) must be in the objective case. Do not be confused by an additional name.

- ▸ The company promoted *me* in July.
- ▸ The company promoted John and *me* in July.

A pronoun is in the objective case when it is the object of a gerund or **preposition** or the subject of an infinitive.

- ▸ Between *you* and *me*, his facts are questionable. [objects of a preposition]
- ▸ Many of *us* attended the conference. [object of a preposition]
- ▸ Training *him* was the best thing I could have done. [object of a gerund]
- ▸ We asked *them* to return the deposit. [subject of an infinitive]

English does not differentiate between direct objects and indirect objects; both require the objective form of the pronoun. See also **complements**.

- ▸ The interviewer seemed to like *me*. [direct object]
- ▸ They wrote *me* a letter. [indirect object]

Possessive Case

A noun or pronoun is in the possessive case when it represents a person, place, or thing that possesses something. To make a singular noun possessive, add *'s* (the *manufacturer's* robotic inventory system). With plural nouns that end in s, show the possessive by placing an apostrophe after the s that forms the plural (a *managers'* meeting). For other guidelines, see **possessive case**.

Appositives

An **appositive** is a noun or noun phrase that follows and amplifies another noun or noun phrase. Because it has the same grammatical function as the noun it complements, an appositive should be in the same case as the noun with which it is in apposition.

▶ Two auditors, Jim Knight and *I*, were asked to review the books. [subjective case]

▶ The group leader selected two members to represent the department—Mohan Pathak and *me*. [objective case]

Determining the Case of Pronouns

One test to determine the proper case of a pronoun is to try it with some transitive verb such as *resembled* or *hit*. If the pronoun would logically precede the verb, use the subjective case; if it would logically follow the verb, use the objective case.

▶ *She* [*He, They*] resembled her father. [subjective case]

▶ Angela resembled *him* [*her, them*]. [objective case]

In the following example, try omitting the noun to determine the case of the pronoun.

> SENTENCE (*We / Us*) pilots fly our own airplanes.
>
> INCORRECT *Us* fly our own airplanes.
> [This incorrect usage is obviously wrong.]
>
> CORRECT *We* fly our own airplanes.
> [This correct usage sounds right.]

To determine the case of a pronoun that follows *as* or *than*, mentally add the words that are omitted but understood.

▶ The other sales representative is not paid as well as *she* [is paid]. [You would not write, "*Her* is paid."]

▶ His partner was better informed than *he* [was informed]. [You would not write, "*Him* was informed."]

If pronouns in compound constructions cause problems, test them singly to determine the proper case.

> SENTENCE (*We / Us*) and the clients are going to lunch.
>
> CORRECT *We* are going to lunch.
> [You would not write, "*Us* are going to lunch."]

For advice on when to use *who* and *whom*, see **who / whom**.

cause-and-effect method of development

The cause-and-effect **method of development** is a common strategy to explain why something happened or why you think something will happen. The goal of the cause-and-effect method of development is to make as plausible as possible the relationship between a situation and either its cause or its effect. The conclusions you draw about the relationships should be based on evidence you have gathered. Like all methods, this one is often used in combination with others. If you were examining a problem with multiple causes, for example, you might combine cause-and-effect with **order-of-importance method of development** as you examine each cause and its effect.

Evaluating Evidence

Because not all evidence you gather will be of equal value, keep in mind the following guidelines:

- *Your facts and arguments should be relevant to your topic.* Be careful not to draw a conclusion that your evidence does not lead to or support. You may have researched some statistics, for example, showing that an increasing number of Americans are licensed to fly small airplanes. You cannot use that information as evidence for a decrease in new car sales in the United States—the evidence does not lead to that conclusion.

- *Your evidence should be adequate.* Incomplete evidence can lead to false conclusions.

  ▶ Driver-training classes do not help prevent auto accidents. Two people I know who completed driver-training classes were involved in accidents.

  A thorough investigation of the usefulness of driver-training classes in keeping down the accident rate would require more than one or two examples. It would require a systematic comparison of the driving records for a representative sample of drivers who had completed driver training and those who had not.

- *Your evidence should be representative.* If you conduct a survey to obtain your evidence, do not solicit responses only from individuals or groups whose views are identical to yours; be sure you obtain responses from a diverse population.

- *Your evidence should be demonstrable.* Two events that occur close to each other in time or place may or may not be causally related. For example, that new traffic signs were placed at an intersection and the next day an accident occurred does not necessarily prove that the signs caused the accident. You must demonstrate the relationship between the two events with pertinent facts and arguments. See **logic errors**.

Linking Causes to Effects

To show a true relationship between a cause and an effect, you must demonstrate that the existence of the one *requires* the existence of the other. It is often difficult to establish beyond any doubt that one event was the cause of another event. More often, a result will have more than one cause. As you research a subject, your task is to determine which cause or causes are most plausible.

When several probable causes are equally valid, report your findings accordingly, as in the following excerpt from an article on the use of an energy-saving device called a furnace-vent damper. The damper is a metal plate that fits inside the flue or vent pipe of a natural-gas or fuel-oil furnace to allow poisonous gases to escape up the flue. Tests run on several dampers showed a number of probable causes for their malfunctioning.

> ▶ One damper was sold without proper installation instructions, and another was wired incorrectly. Two of the units had slow-opening dampers (15 seconds) that prevented the [furnace] burner from firing. And one damper jammed when exposed to a simulated fuel temperature of more than 700 degrees.
> —Don DeBat, "Save Energy but Save Your Life, Too," *Family Safety*

The investigator located more than one cause of damper malfunctions and reported on them. Without such a thorough account, recommendations to prevent malfunctions would be based on incomplete evidence.

center on

Use the phrase *center on* in writing, not *center around*. ("Our discussions should *center on* hiring practices.") Often the idea intended by *center on* is better expressed by other words.

> ▶ The hearings on computer security ~~centered on~~ access codes.
>   *dealt with*

chronological method of development

The chronological **method of development** arranges the events under discussion in sequential order, as in Figure C–2, emphasizing time as it

C

The Rack
Interoffice Memorandum

To: Joanna Sanchez, Vice President for Marketing

From: Larry Brown, Manager, Downtown Branch   *LB*

Date: September 19, 2011

Subject: Reducing Shoplifting at the Downtown Store

Over the past year, my staff and I have taken a number of measures to reduce the amount of shoplifting in the downtown store. As you know, we have spent much time, effort, and money on the problem, which we hope will be alleviated during the Christmas shopping season. Let me recap the specific steps we have taken.

Task Force
We formed a task force of salespeople, buyers, managers, and executive staff to recommend ways of curtailing shoplifting and methods of implementing our recommendations. We met four times during January and twice in March to reach our final recommendations.

Mark IV Surveillance System
In April, we installed a Mark IV System, which uses closed-circuit TV cameras at each exit. The cameras, which are linked with our security office, are capable of tapping signals from all exits simultaneously. The task force felt the Mark IV System might be useful in detecting a pattern of specific individuals entering and leaving the store. This system, which became operational on April 20, has been very helpful in reducing the number of thefts.

Employee Training
During May and June, we held employee workshops on detecting shoplifters. Security, Inc., a consulting firm, led the workshops and provided not only lectures and tips on spotting shoplifters but also demonstrations of common techniques shoplifters use to divert store personnel. All those who attended thought the workshops were quite helpful.

Other Steps Taken
Because the task force determined that certain items were particularly vulnerable to shoplifters, we decided in July to restructure some of the display areas. Our purpose was to make those areas less isolated from the view of clerks and other store personnel. The remodeling, most of which was relatively minor, was completed over the summer months.

For the fall and holiday sales, we have hired extra uniformed security guards. The guards from Security, Inc., should be able to deter first-time shoplifters, although we know that this step will not eliminate the problem altogether.

We believe the steps we have taken will substantially reduce our losses from theft. Of course, after we have reviewed the figures at the end of the year, the task force will meet again in January to assess the success of the methods we have used. If you need more details, please let me know.

FIGURE C–2. Chronological Method of Development

begins with the first event and continues chronologically to the last. **Trip reports**, **instructions**, work schedules, some **minutes of meetings**, and certain **trouble reports** are among the types of writing in which information is organized chronologically. Chronological order is typically used in **narration**.

In the memo shown in Figure C–2, a retail store manager describes the steps taken over a one-year period to reduce shoplifting at his store. After providing important background information, the writer presents the steps taken in chronological order.

cite / sight / site

Cite means "acknowledge" or "quote an authority." ("The speaker *cited* several famous economists.") *Sight* is the ability to see. ("He feared that he might lose his *sight*.") *Site* is a plot of land (a construction *site*) or the place where something is located (a Web *site*).

clarity

Clarity is essential to effective communication with your **readers**. You cannot achieve your **purpose** or a goal like **persuasion** without clarity. Many factors contribute to clarity, just as many other elements can defeat it.

A logical **method of development** and an outline will help you avoid presenting your reader with a jumble of isolated thoughts. A method of development and an outline that puts your thoughts into a logical, meaningful sequence brings **coherence** as well as **unity** to your writing. Clear **transition** contributes to clarity by providing the smooth flow that enables the reader to connect your thoughts with one another without conscious effort. See also **outlining**.

Proper **emphasis** and **subordination** are mandatory if you want to achieve clarity. If you do not use those two complementary techniques wisely, all your clauses and sentences will appear to be of equal importance. Your reader will only be able to guess which are most important, which are least important, and which fall somewhere in between. The **pace** at which you present your ideas is also important to clarity; if the pace is not carefully adjusted to both the topic and the reader, your writing will appear cluttered and unclear.

Point of view establishes through whose eyes or from what vantage point the reader views the subject. A consistent point of view is essential to clarity; if you inappropriately switch from the first person to the third person in midsentence, you are certain to confuse your reader.

Precise **word choice** contributes to clarity and helps eliminate **ambiguity** and **awkwardness**. **Vague words**, **clichés**, poor use of **idiom**, and inappropriate **usage** detract from clarity. That **conciseness** is a requirement of clearly written communication should be evident to anyone who has ever attempted to decipher an insurance policy or a legal contract. For the sake of clarity, remove unnecessary words from your writing. See also **plain English**.

clauses

A clause is a group of words that contains a subject and a predicate and that functions as a sentence or as part of a sentence. (See **sentence construction**.) Every subject-predicate word group in a sentence is a clause, and every sentence must contain at least one independent clause; otherwise, it is a **sentence fragment**.

A clause that could stand alone as a simple sentence is an *independent clause*. (*"The scaffolding fell* when the rope broke.") A clause that could not stand alone if the rest of the sentence were deleted is a *dependent* (or *subordinate*) *clause*. ("I was at the St. Louis branch *when the decision was made*.")

Dependent (or subordinate) clauses are useful in making the relationship between thoughts clearer and more succinct than if the ideas were presented in a series of simple sentences or compound sentences.

FRAGMENTED   The recycling facility is located between Millville and Darrtown. Both villages use it.
[The two thoughts are of approximately equal importance.]

SUBORDINATED   The recycling facility, *which is located between Millville and Darrtown*, is used by both villages.
[One thought is subordinated to the other.]

Subordinate clauses are especially effective for expressing thoughts that describe or explain another statement. Too much **subordination**, however, can be confusing and foster wordiness. See also **conciseness**.

▶ He selected instructors whose classes ~~had a slant that was~~ ^{were} specifically designed for ~~students who intended to go into accounting.~~ ^{accounting students.}

A clause can be connected with the rest of its sentence by a coordinating **conjunction**, a subordinating conjunction, a relative **pronoun**, or a conjunctive **adverb**.

- It was 500 miles to the facility, *so* we made arrangements to fly. [coordinating conjunction]
- Drivers will need to be alert *because* snow may cause hazardous conditions near the entrance to the warehouse. [subordinating conjunction]
- Robert M. Fano was the scientist *who* developed the earliest multiple-access computer system at MIT. [relative pronoun]
- We arrived in the evening; *nevertheless*, we began the tour of the facility. [conjunctive adverb]

clichés

Clichés are expressions that have been used for so long they are no longer fresh but come to mind easily because they are so familiar. Clichés are often wordy as well as vague and can be confusing, especially to speakers of **English as a second language**. A better, more direct word or phrase is given for each of the following clichés.

INSTEAD OF	USE
all over the map	scattered, unfocused
the game plan	strategy, schedule
last but not least	last, finally

Some writers use clichés in a misguided attempt to appear casual or spontaneous, just as other writers try to impress readers with **buzzwords**. Although clichés may come to mind easily while you are **writing a draft**, eliminate them during **revision**. See also **affectation**, **conciseness**, and **international correspondence**.

coherence

Writing is coherent when the relationships among ideas are clear to readers. The major components of coherent writing are a logical sequence of related ideas and clear transitions between these ideas. See also **clarity** and **organization**.

Presenting ideas in a logical sequence is the most important requirement in achieving coherence. The key to achieving a logical sequence is the use of a good outline. (See **outlining**.) An outline forces you to establish a beginning, a middle, and an end. That structure contributes greatly to coherence by enabling you to experiment with sequences and lay out the most direct route to your **purpose** without digressing.

Thoughtful **transition** is also essential; without it, your writing cannot achieve the smooth flow from sentence to sentence and **paragraph** to paragraph that results in coherence.

Check your draft carefully for coherence during **revision**. If possible, have someone else review your draft for how well it expresses the relationships between ideas. See also **unity**.

collaborative writing

Collaborative writing occurs when two or more writers work together to produce a single document for which they share responsibility and decision-making authority. Collaborative writing teams are formed when (1) the size of a project or the time constraints imposed on it require collaboration, (2) the project involves multiple areas of expertise, or (3) the project requires the melding of divergent views into a single perspective that is acceptable to the whole team or to another group. Many types of collaborations are possible, from the collaboration of a primary writer with a variety of contributors and reviewers to a highly interactive collaboration in which everyone on a team plays a relatively equal role in shaping the document.

DIGITAL TIP

Using Collaborative Software

Collaborative writing software helps teams of students, employees, researchers, and others work together on a common writing task whether they are in the same office or in different countries. Modern word processors and collaborative systems like wikis permit team members to draft, review, edit, and comment on their collective work. These systems also make it easy to conduct live chat sessions for brainstorming ideas, share documents with new collaborators, track changes from one version of a document to the next, alert collaborators when a document is altered, and export documents for offline editing. For a list of software programs that support collaborative writing and tips for using these programs effectively, go to *bedfordstmartins.com/alred* and select *Digital Tips*, "Reviewing Collaborative Documents," "Using Collaborative Software," or "Using Wikis for Collaborative Work."

Tasks of the Collaborative Writing Team

C

The collaborating team strives to achieve a compatible working relationship by dividing the work in a way that uses each writer's expertise and experience to its advantage. The team should also designate a coordinator who will guide the team members' activities, organize the project, and ensure **coherence** and consistency within the document. The coordinator's duties can be determined by mutual agreement or, if the team often works together, assigned on a rotating basis.

Planning.   The team conceptualizes the document to be produced as the members collectively identify the **audience**, **purpose**, **context**, and **scope** of the project. See also **meetings** and "Five Steps to Successful Writing" (page 000).

At this stage, the team establishes a project plan that may include guidelines for communication among team members, version control (naming, dating, and managing document drafts), review procedures, and writing **style** standards that team members are expected to follow. The plan includes a schedule with due dates for completing initial research tasks, outlines, drafts, reviews, revisions, and the final document.

◀ PROFESSIONALISM NOTE Deadlines must be met because team members rely on each other and one missed deadline can delay the entire project. A missed project deadline can result in a lost opportunity or, in the case of **grant proposals**, disqualify an application. Individual writers must adjust their schedules and focus on their own writing process to finish drafts and meet the deadline. See "Five Steps to Successful Writing" (page xv). ▶

Research and Writing.   The team next completes initial **research** tasks, elicits comments from team members, creates a broad outline of the document (see **outlining**), and assigns writing tasks to individual team members, based on their expertise and the outline. Depending on the project, each team member further researches an assigned segment of the document, expands and develops the broad outline, and produces a draft from a detailed outline. See also **writing a draft**.

Reviewing.   Keeping the audience's needs and the document's purpose in mind, each team member critically yet diplomatically reviews the other team members' drafts, from the overall **organization** to the **clarity** of each **paragraph**, and offers advice to help improve the writer's work. Team members can easily solicit feedback by sharing electronic files. Tracking and commenting features allow the reviewer to show the suggested changes without deleting the original text.

Revising. In this final stage, individual writers evaluate their colleagues' reviews and accept, reject, or build on their suggestions. Then, the team coordinator can consolidate all drafts into a final master copy and maintain and evaluate it for consistency and coherence. See also **revision**.

◀ PROFESSIONALISM NOTE As you collaborate, be ready to tolerate some disharmony, but temper it with mutual respect. Team members may not agree on every subject, and differing perspectives can easily lead to conflict, ranging from mild differences over minor points to major showdowns. However, creative differences resolved respectfully can energize the team and, in fact, strengthen a finished document by compelling writers to reexamine assumptions and issues in unanticipated ways. See also **listening**. ▶

WRITER'S CHECKLIST   Writing Collaboratively

- ✔ Designate one person as the team coordinator.
- ✔ Identify the audience, purpose, context, and scope of the project.
- ✔ Create a project plan, including a schedule and standards.
- ✔ Create a working outline of the document.
- ✔ Assign sections or tasks to each team member.
- ✔ Research and write drafts of each document section.
- ✔ Follow the schedule: due dates for drafts, revisions, and final versions.
- ✔ Use the agreed-upon standards for style and format.
- ✔ Exchange sections for team member reviews.
- ✔ Revise sections as needed.
- ✔ Meet the established deadlines.

---

collection letters

Collection letters serve two purposes: (1) collecting an overdue bill and (2) preserving the customer relationship. In some states, collection letters may be prepared by attorneys because certain language and state laws must be followed to demand payment. See also **correspondence** and **letters**.

Most companies use a series of collection letters like the series shown in Figures C–3 through C–5, in which the letters become increasingly demanding and urgent. All letters should be courteous and show a genuine interest in the customer as well as concern for whatever problems may be preventing prompt payment. See also **"you" viewpoint**.

ABBOTT OFFICE PRODUCTS, INC.

P.O. Box 544
Detroit, MI 48206
Phone: (313) 567-1221
Fax: (313) 567-2112

August 29, 2011

Mr. Thomas Holland
Holland Shoes
1661 East Madison Boulevard
Garfield, AL 36613

Dear Mr. Holland:

With the new school year about to begin, your shoe store must be busier than ever as students purchase their back-to-school footwear. Perhaps in the rush of business you've overlooked paying your account of $1,200, which is now 60 days overdue.

Enclosed is our fall sales list. When you send in your check for your outstanding account, why not send in your next order and take advantage of these special prices.

Sincerely,

Henry Bliss

Henry Bliss
Sales Manager

Enclosure: Fall Sales List

www.abbott.com

FIGURE C–3. First-Stage Collection Letter

Dear Mr. Holland:

We are concerned that we have not heard from you about your overdue account of $1,200 even though we have written three times in the past 90 days. Because you have always been one of our best customers, we have to wonder if some special circumstances have caused the delay. If so, please feel free to discuss the matter with us.

By sending us a check today, you can preserve your excellent credit record. Because you have always paid your account promptly in the past, we are sure that you will want to settle this balance now. If your balance is more than you can pay at present, we will be happy to work out mutually satisfactory payment arrangements.

Please use the enclosed envelope to send in your check, or call (800) 526-1945 to discuss your account.

Sincerely,

FIGURE C–4. Second-Stage Collection Letter

Dear Mr. Holland:

Your account in the amount of $1,200 is now 180 days overdue. You have already received a generous extension of time and, in fairness to our other customers, we cannot permit a further delay in payment.

Because you have not responded to any of our letters, we must turn your account over to our attorney for collection if we do not receive payment immediately. Such action, of course, will damage your previously fine credit rating.

Why not avoid this unpleasant situation by sending your check in the enclosed return envelope within 10 days or by calling (800) 526-1945 to discuss payment.

Sincerely,

FIGURE C–5. Third-Stage Collection Letter

C

The first stage consists of reminders stamped on the invoice ("overdue"), form letters, or brief personal notes. These early reminders should maintain a friendly **tone** that emphasizes the customer's good credit record until now. As in the example of a first-stage collection letter in Figure C–3, you might suggest that nonpayment may be a result of a simple oversight.

In the second stage, your tone should be firmer and more direct than in the first stage, but it should never be rude, sarcastic, or threatening. Ask directly for payment, and inquire whether some circumstances are preventing payment. Perhaps suggest an installment payment plan if you are able to offer one. Mention the importance of good credit and remind the customer that he or she has always received good value from you. Make it easy to respond by offering a toll-free telephone number or an e-mail address or a Web address where the customer can pay with a credit card. Notice how the second-stage letter in Figure C–4 is more direct than the first letter (but it is no less polite) and includes a return envelope for payment.

Third-stage collection letters reflect a sense of urgency because the customer has not responded to your previous letters. Although your tone should remain courteous, make your demand for payment explicit, as shown in Figure C–5. Point out how reasonable you have been and urge the customer to pay at once to avoid a collection service or legal action.

colons

The colon (:) is a mark of introduction that alerts readers to the close connection between the preceding statement and what follows.

Colons in Sentences

A colon links independent **clauses** to words, **phrases**, clauses, or lists that identify, rename, explain, emphasize, amplify, or illustrate the sentence that precedes the colon.

▶ Two topics will be discussed: *the new accounting system and the new bookkeeping procedures.* [phrases that identify]

▶ Only one thing will satisfy Mr. Sturgess: *our finished report.* [appositive (renaming) phrase for **emphasis**]

▶ Any organization is confronted with two separate, though related, information problems: *It must maintain an effective internal communication system and an effective external communication system.* [clause to amplify and explain]

► Heart patients should make key lifestyle changes: *stop smoking, exercise regularly, eat a low-fat diet, and reduce stress.* [list to identify and illustrate]

Colons with Salutations, Titles, Citations, and Numbers

A colon follows the salutation in business **letters**, even when the salutation refers to a person by first name.

► Dear Professor Jeffers: *or* Dear Georgia:

Colons separate titles from subtitles and separate references to sections of works in citations. See also **documenting sources**.

► " 'We Regret to Inform You': Toward a New Theory of Negative Messages"

► Genesis 10:16 [chapter 10, verse 16]

Colons separate numbers in time references and indicate numerical ratios.

► 9:30 a.m. [9 hours and 30 minutes]

► The cement is mixed with water and sand at 5:3:1.
[The colon is read as the word *to*.]

Punctuation and Capitalization with Colons

A colon always goes outside **quotation marks**.

► This was the real meaning of the manager's "suggestion": Cooperation within our department must improve.

As this example shows, the first word after a colon may be capitalized if the statement following the colon is a complete sentence and functions as a formal statement or question. If the element following the colon is subordinate, however, use a lowercase letter to begin that element. See also **capitalization**.

► We have only one way to stay within our present budget: to reduce expenditures for research and development.

Unnecessary Colons

Do not place a colon between a **verb** and its **objects**.

► Three fluids that clean pipettes are / water, alcohol, and acetone.

C

Likewise, do not use a colon between a **preposition** and its object.

▶ I may be transferred to/Tucson, Boston, or Miami.

Do not insert a colon after *including*, *such as*, or *for example* to introduce a simple list.

▶ Office computers should not be used for activities such as/ personal e-mail, Web surfing, Internet shopping, and playing computer games.

One common exception is made when a verb or preposition is followed by a stacked **list**; however, it may be possible to introduce the list with a complete sentence instead.

    The following companies   **:**
▶ ~~Companies that~~ produce computers ~~include~~:

Apple	HP	Dell
Gateway	IBM	Sony

comma splice

A comma splice is a grammatical error in which two independent **clauses** are joined by only a **comma**.

    INCORRECT   It was 500 miles to the facility, we arranged to fly.

A comma splice can be corrected in several ways.

1. Substitute a **semicolon**, a semicolon and a conjunctive **adverb**, or a comma and a coordinating **conjunction**.

    ▶ It was 500 miles to the facility; we arranged to fly. [semicolon]

    ▶ It was 500 miles to the facility; *therefore*, we arranged to fly. [adverb]

    ▶ It was 500 miles to the facility, *so* we arranged to fly. [conjunction]

2. Create two sentences.

    ▶ It was 500 miles to the facility. *We* arranged to fly.

3. Subordinate one clause to the other. (See **subordination**.)

    ▶ *Because it was 500 miles to the facility*, we arranged to fly.

See also **sentence construction** and **sentence faults**.

commas

C

Like all **punctuation,** the comma (,) helps **readers** understand the writer's meaning and prevents **ambiguity.** Notice how the comma helps make the meaning clear in the second example.

AMBIGUOUS   To be successful managers with MBAs must continue their education.

CLEAR   To be successful, managers with MBAs must continue their education.
[The comma makes clear where the main part of the sentence begins.]

Do not follow the old myth that you should insert a comma wherever you would pause if you were speaking. Although you would pause wherever you encounter a comma, you should not insert a comma wherever you might pause. Effective use of commas depends on an understanding of **sentence construction**.

Linking Independent Clauses

Use a comma before a coordinating **conjunction** (*and*, *but*, *or*, *nor*, and sometimes *so*, *yet*, and *for*) that links independent **clauses**.

▶ The new microwave disinfection system was delivered, *but* the installation will require an additional week.

However, if two independent clauses are short and closely related—and there is no danger of confusing the reader—the comma may be omitted. Both of the following examples are correct.

▶ The cable snapped and the power failed.

▶ The cable snapped, and the power failed.

Enclosing Elements

Commas are used to enclose nonessential information in nonrestrictive clauses, phrases, and parenthetical elements. See also **restrictive and nonrestrictive elements**.

- ► Our new factory, *which began operations last month*, should add 25 percent to total output. [nonrestrictive clause]

- ► The accountant, *working quickly and efficiently*, finished early. [nonrestrictive phrase]

- ► We can, *of course*, expect their lawyer to call us. [parenthetical element]

Yes and *no* are set off by commas in such uses as the following:

- ► I agree with you, *yes*.

- ► *No*, I do not think we can finish by the deadline.

A **direct address** should be enclosed in commas.

- ► You will note, *Jeff*, that the budget figure matches our estimate.

An **appositive** phrase (which re-identifies another expression in the sentence) is enclosed in commas.

- ► Our company, *NT Insurance Group*, won several awards last year.

Interrupting parenthetical and transitional words or phrases are usually set off with commas. See also **transition**.

- ► The report, *therefore*, needs to be revised.

Commas are omitted when the word or phrase does not interrupt the continuity of thought.

- ► I *therefore* recommend that we begin construction.

For other means of punctuating parenthetical elements, see **dashes** and **parentheses**.

Introducing Elements

Clauses and Phrases.   Generally, place a comma after an introductory clause or phrase, especially if it is long, to identify where the introductory element ends and the main part of the sentence begins.

- ► *Because we have not yet reached our hiring goals for the Sales Division,* we recommend the development of an aggressive recruiting program.

A long modifying phrase that precedes the main clause should always be followed by a comma.

► *During the first series of field-performance tests at our Colorado proving ground,* the new engine failed to meet our expectations.

When an introductory phrase is short and closely related to the main clause, the comma may be omitted.

► *In two seconds* a 5°C temperature rise occurs in the test tube.

A comma should always follow an absolute phrase, which modifies the whole sentence.

► *The presentation completed,* we returned to our offices.

Words and Quotations.   Certain types of introductory words are followed by a comma. One example is a transitional word or phrase (*however, in addition*) that connects the preceding clause or sentence with the thought that follows.

► *Furthermore,* we should include college job fairs in our recruiting plans, provided our budget is approved.

► *For example,* this change will make us more competitive in the global marketplace.

When an **adverb** closely modifies the **verb** or the entire sentence, it should not be followed by a comma.

► *Perhaps* we can still solve the turnover problem. *Certainly* we should try.
[*Perhaps* and *certainly* closely modify each statement.]

A proper **noun** used in an introductory direct address is followed by a comma, as is an **interjection** (such as *oh, well, why, indeed, yes,* and *no*).

► *Nancy,* enclosed is the article you asked me to review. [direct address]

► *Indeed,* I will ensure that your request is forwarded. [interjection]

Use a comma to separate a direct **quotation** from its introduction.

► Morton and Lucia White *said,* "People live in cities but dream of the countryside."

Do not use a comma when giving an indirect quotation.

► Morton and Lucia White *said that* people dream of the countryside, even though they live in cities.

Separating Items in a Series

Although the comma before the last item in a series is sometimes omitted, it is generally clearer to include it.

► Random House, Bantam, Doubleday, and Dell were individual publishing companies. [Without the final comma, "Doubleday and Dell" might refer to one company or two.]

Phrases and clauses in coordinate series are also punctuated with commas.

► Plants absorb noxious gases, act as receptors of dirt particles, and cleanse the air of other impurities.

When phrases or clauses in a series contain commas, use **semicolons** rather than commas to separate the items.

► Among those present were John Howard, President of the Howard Paper Company; Thomas Martin, CEO of AIR Recycling, Inc.; and Larry Stanley, President of Northland Papers.

When **adjectives** modifying the same noun can be reversed and make sense, or when they can be separated by *and* or *or*, they should be separated by commas.

► The aircraft featured a *modern, sleek, swept-wing* design.

When an adjective modifies a phrase, no comma is required.

► She was investigating the *damaged inventory-control system.* [The adjective *damaged* modifies the phrase *inventory-control system.*]

Never separate a final adjective from its noun.

► He is a conscientious, honest, reliable/worker.

Clarifying and Contrasting

Use a comma to separate two contrasting thoughts or ideas.

► The project was finished on time, but not within the budget.

Use a comma after an independent clause that is only loosely related to the dependent clause that follows it or that could be misread without the comma.

► I should be able to finish the plan by July, even though I lost time because of illness.

Showing Omissions

A comma sometimes replaces a verb in certain elliptical constructions.

▶ Some were punctual; *others, late.*
[The comma replaces *were.*]

It is better, however, to avoid such constructions in business writing.

Using with Numbers and Names

Commas are conventionally used to separate distinct items. Use commas between the elements of an address written on the same line (but not between the state and the ZIP Code).

▶ Kristen James, 4119 Mill Road, Dayton, Ohio 45401

A full date that is written in month-day-year format uses a comma preceding and following the year.

▶ November 30, 2025, is the payoff date.

Do not use commas for dates in the day-month-year format, which is used in many parts of the world and by the U.S. military. See also **international correspondence**.

▶ Note that 30 November 2025 is the payoff date.

Do not use commas when showing only the month and year or month and day in a **date**.

▶ The target date of May 2015 is optimistic, so I would like to meet on March 4 to discuss our options.

Use commas to separate the elements of Arabic numbers.

▶ 1,528,200 feet

However, because many countries use the comma as the decimal marker, use spaces or periods rather than commas in international documents.

▶ 1.528.200 meters *or* 1 528 200 meters

A comma may be substituted for the colon in the salutation of a personal **letter** or **e-mail**. Do not, however, use a comma in the salutation of a business letter or e-mail, even if you use the person's first name.

▶ Dear Marie, [personal letter or e-mail]
▶ Dear Marie: [business letter or e-mail]

Use commas to separate the elements of geographic names.

▶ Toronto, Ontario, Canada

Use a comma to separate names that are reversed (*Smith, Alvin*) and commas with professional **abbreviations**.

▶ Jim Rogers Jr., M.D., chaired the conference.
[*Jr.* or *Sr.* does not require a comma.]

Using with Other Punctuation

Conjunctive adverbs (*however, nevertheless, consequently, for example, on the other hand*) that join independent clauses are preceded by a **semicolon** and followed by a comma. Such adverbs function both as **modifiers** and as connectives.

▶ The idea is good; *however,* our budget is not sufficient.

As shown earlier in this entry, use semicolons rather than commas to separate items in a series when the items themselves contain commas.

When a comma should follow a phrase or clause that ends with words in parentheses, the comma always appears outside the closing parenthesis.

▶ Although we left late (at 7:30 p.m.), we arrived in time for the key-note address.

Commas always go inside **quotation marks**.

▶ The status display indicates "*ready,*" but the unit requires an additional warm-up period.

Except with abbreviations, a comma should not be used with a dash, an **exclamation mark**, a **period**, or a **question mark**.

▶ "Have you finished the project?/" she asked.

Avoiding Unnecessary Commas

A number of common writing errors involve placing commas where they do not belong. As stated earlier, such errors often occur because writers assume that a pause in a sentence should be indicated by a comma.

Do not place a comma between a subject and verb or between a verb and its **object**.

▶ The location of our booth at this year's conference/made attracting visitors difficult.

► She has often said/that one company's failure is another's opportunity.

Do not use a comma between the elements of a compound subject or compound predicate consisting of only two elements.

► The director of the design department/and the supervisor of the quality-control section were opposed to the new schedules.

► The design director listed five major objections/and asked that the new schedule be reconsidered.

Do not include a comma after a coordinating conjunction such as *and* or *but*.

► The chairperson formally adjourned the meeting, but/the members of the committee continued to argue.

Do not place a comma before the first item or after the last item of a series.

► The new products we are considering include/calculators, scanners, and cameras.

► It was a fast, simple, inexpensive/process.

Do not use a comma to separate a prepositional phrase from the rest of the sentence unnecessarily.

► We discussed the final report/on the new project.

compare / contrast

When you *compare* things, you point out similarities or both similarities and differences. ("He *compared* the two brands before making his choice.") When you *contrast* things, you point out only the differences. ("Their speaking styles *contrasted* sharply.") In either case, you compare or contrast only things that are part of a common category.

When *compare* is used to establish a general similarity, it is followed by *to*. ("He *compared* our receiving the grant *to* winning a marathon.") When *compare* is used to indicate a close examination of similarities or differences, it is followed by *with*. ("We *compared* the features of the new copier *with* those of the current one.")

Contrast is normally followed by *with*. ("The new policy *contrasts* sharply *with* the earlier one.") When the **noun** form of *contrast* is used, one speaks of the *contrast between* two things or of one thing being *in contrast to* the other.

► There is a sharp *contrast between* the old and new policies.

► The new policy is *in* sharp *contrast to* the earlier one.

comparison

When you are making a comparison, be sure that both or all of the elements being compared are clearly evident to your **reader**.

than the Nicom 2 software
► The Nicom 3 software is better.

The things being compared must be of the same kind.

a   briefcase
► A hard-side briefcase offers more protection than fabric.

Be sure to point out the parallels or differences between the things being compared. Do not assume your reader will know what you mean.

it is from
► Washington is farther from Boston than Philadelphia.

A double comparison in the same sentence requires that the first comparison be completed before the second one is stated.

► The discovery of electricity was one of the great ~~if not the greatest~~
, if not the greatest
scientific discoveries in history.

Do not attempt to compare things that are not comparable.

► Agricultural experts advise that ~~storage space is reduced by~~
requires 40 percent less storage space than
~~40 percent compared with~~ baled hay.   *loose hay requires*

[*Storage space* is not comparable to *baled hay*.]

comparison method of development

As a **method of development**, comparison points out similarities and differences between the elements of your subject. The comparison method of development can help **readers** understand a difficult or an unfamiliar subject by relating it to a simpler or more familiar one.

You must first determine the basis for the **comparison**. For example, if you were comparing bids from contractors for a remodeling project at your company, you most likely would compare such factors as price, previous experience, personnel qualifications, availability at a time convenient for you, and completion date. Once you have determined the basis or bases for comparison, you can determine the most effective way to structure your comparison: whole by whole or part by part.

In the *whole-by-whole method,* all the relevant characteristics of one item are examined before all the relevant characteristics of the next item. The description of typical woodworking glues in Figure C–6 is organized according to the whole-by-whole method. It describes each type of glue and all its characteristics before moving to the next one. This description would be useful for those readers who wish to learn about all types of wood glues.

If your **purpose** is to help readers consider the various characteristics of all the glues, the information might be arranged according to the *part-by-part method of comparison,* as in Figure C–7, in which the

> *White glue* is the most useful all-purpose adhesive for light construction, but it cannot be used on projects that will be exposed to moisture, high temperature, or great stress. Wood that is being joined with white glue must remain in a clamp until the glue dries, which takes about 30 minutes.
>
> *Aliphatic resin glue* has a stronger and more moisture-resistant bond than white glue. It must be used at temperatures above 50°F. The wood should be clamped for about 30 minutes. . . .
>
> *Plastic resin glue* is the strongest of the common wood adhesives. It is highly moisture resistant, though not completely waterproof. Sold in powdered form, this glue must be mixed with water and used at temperatures above 70°F. It is slow setting, and the joint should be clamped for four to six hours. . . .
>
> *Contact cement* is a very strong adhesive that bonds so quickly it must be used with great care. It is ideal for mounting sheets of plastic laminate on wood. It is also useful for attaching strips of veneer to the edges of plywood. Because this adhesive bonds immediately when two pieces are pressed together, clamping is not necessary, but the parts to be joined must be carefully aligned before being placed together. Most brands are flammable, and the fumes can be harmful if inhaled. To meet current safety standards, this type of glue must be used in a well-ventilated area, away from flames or heat.

FIGURE C–6. Whole-by-Whole Method of Comparison

C

Woodworking adhesives are rated primarily according to their bonding strength, moisture resistance, and setting time.

Bonding strength is categorized as very strong, moderately strong, or adequate for use with little stress. Contact cement and plastic resin glue bond very strongly, while aliphatic resin glue bonds moderately strongly. White glue provides a bond least resistant to stress.

The *moisture resistance* of woodworking glues is rated as high, moderate, or low. Plastic resin glue and contact cement are highly moisture resistant, aliphatic resin glue is moderately moisture resistant, and white glue is least moisture resistant.

Setting time for the glues varies from an immediate bond to a four-to-six-hour bond. Contact cement bonds immediately and requires no clamping. Because the bond is immediate, surfaces being joined must be carefully aligned before being placed together. White glue and aliphatic resin glue set in 30 minutes; both require clamping to secure the bond. Plastic resin, the strongest wood glue, sets in four to six hours and also requires clamping.

FIGURE C–7. Part-by-Part Method of Comparison

relevant features of the items are compared one by one. The part-by-part method could accommodate further comparison—such as temperature ranges, special warnings, and common use, in this case.

Comparisons can also be made effectively with the use of **tables**, as shown in Figure C–8. The advantage of a table is that it provides a quick reference, allowing readers to see and compare all the information at once. The disadvantage is that a table cannot convey as much related detailed information as a narrative description.

	White Glue	Aliphatic Resin Glue	Plastic Resin Glue	Contact Cement
Bonding Strength	Low	Moderate	High	High
Moisture Resistance	Low	Moderate	High	High
Setting Time	Thirty minutes	Thirty minutes	Four to six hours	Bonds on contact
Common Uses	Light construction	General purpose	General purpose	Laminate and veneer to wood

FIGURE C–8. Comparison Using a Table to Illustrate Key Differences

complaint letters

A complaint **letter** (or **e-mail**) describes a problem that the writer requests the recipient to solve. The **tone** of a complaint letter or e-mail is important; the most effective ones do not sound complaining. If your message is shrill and belligerent, you may not be taken seriously. Assume that the recipient will be conscientious in correcting the problem. However, anticipate reader reactions or rebuttals. See **audience**.

▶ I reviewed my user manual's "safe operating guidelines" carefully before I installed the device.
[This assures readers you followed instructions.]

Without such explanations, readers may be tempted to dismiss your complaint. Figure C–9 shows a complaint letter that details a billing problem. Although the circumstances and severity of the problem may vary, effective complaint letters generally follow this pattern:

1. Identify the problem or faulty item(s) and include relevant invoice numbers, part names, and dates. Include a copy of the receipt, bill, or contract, and keep the original for your records.
2. Explain logically, clearly, and specifically what went wrong, especially for a problem with a service. (Avoid guessing why you *think* some problem occurred.)
3. State what you expect the reader to do to solve the problem.

Subject: ST3 Diagnostic Scanners

On July 11, I ordered nine ST3 Diagnostic Scanners (order # ST3-1179R). The scanners were ordered from your customer Web site.

On August 3, I received seven HL monitors from your parts warehouse in Newark, New Jersey. I immediately returned those monitors with a note indicating that a mistake had been made. However, not only have I failed to receive the ST3 scanners that I ordered, but I have also been billed repeatedly for the seven monitors.

I have enclosed a copy of my confirmation e-mail, the shipping form, and the most recent bill. If you cannot send me the scanners I ordered by September 15, please cancel my order.

Sincerely,

FIGURE C–9. Complaint Letter

Begin by checking to see if the company's Web site provides instructions for submitting a complaint. Otherwise, for large organizations, you may address your complaint to Customer Service. In smaller organizations, you might write to a vice president in charge of sales or service, or directly to the owner. As a last resort, you may find that sending copies of a complaint letter to more than one person in the company will get faster results. See also **adjustment letters** and **refusal letters**.

complement / compliment

Complement means "anything that completes a whole" (see also **complements**). It is used as either a **noun** or a **verb**.

▶ A *complement* of four employees would bring our staff up to its normal level. [noun]

▶ The two programs *complement* one another perfectly. [verb]

Compliment means "praise." It too is used as either a noun or a verb.

▶ The manager's *compliment* boosted staff morale. [noun]

▶ The manager *complimented* the staff on its efficient job. [verb]

complements

A complement is a word, **phrase**, or **clause** used in the predicate of a sentence to complete the meaning of the sentence.

▶ Pilots fly *airplanes*. [word]

▶ To invest is *to risk losses*. [phrase]

▶ John knew *that he would be late*. [clause]

Four types of complements are generally recognized: direct **object**, indirect object, objective complement, and subjective complement. See also **sentence construction**.

A *direct object* is a **noun** or noun equivalent that receives the action of a transitive **verb**; it answers the question *What?* or *Whom?* after the verb.

▶ I designed *a Web site*. [noun phrase]

▶ I like *to work*. [verbal]

► I like *it*. [pronoun]

► I like *what I saw*. [noun clause]

An *indirect object* is a noun or noun equivalent that occurs with a direct object after certain kinds of transitive verbs such as *give*, *wish*, *cause*, and *tell*. It answers the question *To whom or what?* or *For whom or what?*

► We should buy the *office* a *scanner*.
[*Scanner* is the direct object, and *office* is the indirect object.]

An *objective complement* completes the meaning of a sentence by revealing something about the object of its transitive verb. An objective complement may be either a noun or an **adjective**.

► They call him *a genius*. [noun phrase]

► We painted the building *white*. [adjective]

A *subjective complement*, which follows a linking verb rather than a transitive verb, describes the subject. A subjective complement may be either a noun or an adjective.

► His sister is *a consultant*. [noun phrase follows linking verb *is*]

► His brother is *ill*. [adjective follows linking verb *is*]

compose / constitute / comprise

Compose and *constitute* both mean "make up the whole." The parts *compose* or *constitute* the whole. ("The nine offices *compose* the division. Unethical activities *constitute* cause for dismissal.") *Comprise* means "include," "contain," or "consist of." The whole *comprises* the parts. ("The division *comprises* nine offices.")

compound words

A compound word is made from two or more words that function as a single concept. A compound may be hyphenated, written as one word, or written as separate words.

► high-energy   nevertheless   post office
  low-level   online   blood pressure

C

If you are not certain whether a compound word should use a **hyphen**, check a dictionary.

Be careful to distinguish between compound words (*greenhouse*) and words that simply appear together but do not constitute compound words (*green house*). For plurals of compound words, generally add *s* to the last letter (*bookcases* and *Web sites*). However, when the first word of the compound is more important to its meaning than the last, the first word takes the *s* (*editors in chief*). Possessives are formed by adding *'s* to the end of the compound word (the *editor in chief's* desk, the *pipeline's* diameter, the *post office's* hours). See also **possessive case**.

conciseness

Conciseness means that extraneous words, **phrases**, **clauses**, and sentences have been removed from writing without sacrificing **clarity** or appropriate detail. Conciseness is not a synonym for brevity; a long **report** may be concise, while its **abstract** may be brief and concise. Conciseness is always desirable, but brevity may or may not be desirable in a given passage, depending on the writer's **purpose**. Although concise sentences are not guaranteed to be effective, wordy sentences always sacrifice some of their readability and **coherence**.

Causes of Wordiness

Modifiers that repeat an idea implicit or present in the word being modified contribute to wordiness by being redundant. See also **reason is [because]**.

basic essentials	*completely* finished
final outcome	*present* status

Coordinated synonyms that merely repeat each other contribute to wordiness.

each and every	*basic and fundamental*
finally and for good	*first and foremost*

Excess qualification also contributes to wordiness.

perfectly clear	*completely* accurate

Expletives, relative **pronouns**, and relative **adjectives**, although they have legitimate purposes, often result in wordiness.

WORDY   *There are* [expletive] many Web designers *who* [relative pronoun] are planning to attend the conference, at which [relative adjective] time we should meet.

CONCISE   Many Web designers plan to attend the conference scheduled for May 13–15.

Circumlocution (a long, indirect way of expressing things) is a leading cause of wordiness. See also **gobbledygook.**

WORDY   The payment to which a subcontractor is entitled should be made promptly so that in the event of a subsequent contractual dispute we, as general contractors, may not be held in default of our contract by virtue of nonpayment.

CONCISE   Pay subcontractors promptly. Then, if a contractual dispute occurs, we cannot be held in default of our contract because of nonpayment.

When conciseness is overdone, writing can become choppy and ambiguous. (See also **telegraphic style.**) Too much conciseness can produce a style that is not only too brief but also too blunt, especially in **correspondence.**

WRITER'S CHECKLIST   Achieving Conciseness

Wordiness is understandable when you are **writing a draft,** but it should not survive **revision.**

✔ Use **subordination** to achieve conciseness.

> *five-page*
> • The financial report was carefully documented, and it covered five-pages.

✔ Avoid **affectation** by using simple words and phrases.

WORDY   It is the policy of the company to provide Internet access to enable employees to conduct the online communication necessary to discharge their responsibilities; such should not be utilized for personal communications or nonbusiness activities.

CONCISE   Employee Internet access should be used only for appropriate company business.

✔ Eliminate redundancy.

WORDY   Postinstallation testing, which is offered to all our customers at no further cost to them whatsoever, is available with each Line Scan System One purchased from this company.

(*continued*)

C

> CONCISE   Free postinstallation testing is offered with each Line
> Scan System One.

✔ Change the passive **voice** to the **active voice** and the indicative **mood**
to the imperative mood whenever possible.

> WORDY   Bar codes normally are used when an order is intended
> to be displayed on a monitor, and inventory numbers
> normally are used when an order is to be placed with
> the manufacturer.
>
> CONCISE   Use bar codes to display the order on a monitor, and
> use inventory numbers to place the order with the
> manufacturer.

✔ Eliminate or replace wordy introductory phrases or pretentious
words and phrases (*in the case of, it may be said that, it appears that,
needless to say*).

REPLACE	WITH
in order to, with a view to	to
due to the fact that, for the reason that, owing to the fact that, the reason for	because
by means of, by using, in connection with, through the use of	by, with
at this time, at this point in time, at present, at the present	now, currently

✔ Do not overuse **intensifiers**, such as *very, more, most, best, quite,
great, really,* and *especially*. Instead provide specific and useful
details.

✔ Use the search-and-replace command to find and revise wordy expressions, including *to be* and unnecessary helping **verbs** such as *will*.

conclusions

The conclusion of a document ties the main ideas together and can
clinch a final significant point. This final point may, for example, make
a prediction or offer a judgment, summarize key findings, or recommend a course of action. Figure C–10 is a conclusion from a proposal
to reduce health-care costs by increasing employee fitness through

C

Conclusion and Recommendation

Summa-
rizes key
points

Enrolling employees in the corporate program at AeroFitness would allow them to receive a one-month free trial
membership. Those interested in continuing could then join
the club and receive a 30 percent discount on the $1,200
annual fee and pay only half of the one-time membership fee
of $500. The other half of the membership fee ($250) would
be paid for by ABO. If employees leave the company, they
would have the option of purchasing ABO's share of the
membership to continue at AeroFitness or selling their half
of the membership to another ABO employee wishing to join
AeroFitness.

Points to
benefits

Club membership allows employees at all five ABO warehouses to participate in the program. The more employees
who participate, the greater the long-term savings in ABO's
health-care costs. Overall, implementing this program will
help ABO, Inc., reduce its health-care costs while building stronger employee relations by offering employees a
desirable benefit. If this proposal is adopted, I have some additional thoughts about publicizing the program to encourage
employee participation that I would be pleased to share.

Makes a
recommen-
dation

I recommend, therefore, that ABO, Inc., participate in the
corporate membership program at AeroFitness Clubs, Inc.,
by subsidizing employee memberships. Offering this benefit
to employees will demonstrate ABO's commitment to the
importance of a healthy workforce.

FIGURE C–10. Conclusion

health-club subsidies. Notice that it makes a recommendation, summarizes key points, and points out several benefits of implementing the
recommendation.

The way you conclude depends on your **purpose**, the needs of your
audience, and the **context**. For example, a lengthy sales **proposal** might
conclude persuasively with a summary of the proposal's salient points
and the company's relevant strengths. The following examples are typical concluding strategies.

RECOMMENDATION

Our findings suggest that you need to alter your marketing to adjust to the changing demographics for your products.

C

SUMMARY
As this report describes, we would attract more recent graduates with the following strategies:

1. Establish our presence on social-networking sites to reach more college students before they graduate.
2. Increase our advertising in local student newspapers and our attendance at college career fairs.
3. Expand our local co-op program and establish more internships.

JUDGMENT
Based on the scope and degree of the storm's damage, the current construction code for roofing on light industrial facilities is inadequate.

IMPLICATION
Although our estimate calls for a substantially higher budget than in the three previous years, we believe that it is reasonable given our planned expansion.

PREDICTION
Although I have exceeded my original estimate for equipment, I have reduced my labor costs; therefore, I will easily stay within the original bid.

The concluding statement may merely present ideas for consideration, may call for action, or may deliberately provoke thought.

IDEAS FOR CONSIDERATION
The new prices become effective the first of the year. Price adjustments are routine for the company, but some of your customers will not consider them acceptable. Please bear in mind the needs of both your customers and the company as you implement these price adjustments.

CALL FOR ACTION
Please send us a check for $250 now if you wish to keep your account active. If you have not responded to our previous letters because of some special hardship, I will be glad to work out a solution with you.

THOUGHT-PROVOKING STATEMENT
Can we continue to accept the losses incurred by inefficiency? Or should we take the necessary steps to control it now?

Be especially careful not to introduce a new topic when you conclude. A conclusion should always relate to and reinforce the ideas presented earlier in your writing. Moreover, the conclusion must be consistent with what the **introduction** promised the report would examine (its purpose) and how it would do so (its method).

For guidance about the location of the conclusion section in a report, see **formal reports**. For letter and other short closings, see **correspondence** and entries on specific types of documents throughout this book.

conjunctions

A conjunction connects words, **phrases**, or **clauses** and can also indicate the relationship between the elements it connects.

A *coordinating conjunction* joins two sentence elements that have identical functions. The coordinating conjunctions are *and*, *but*, *or*, *for*, *nor*, *yet*, and *so*.

▶ Nature *and* technology affect petroleum prices. [joins two **nouns**]

▶ To hear *and* to listen are two different things. [joins two phrases]

▶ I would like to include the survey, *but* that would make the report too long. [joins two clauses]

Coordinating conjunctions in the titles of books, articles, plays, and movies should not be capitalized unless they are the first or last word in the title.

▶ Our library contains *Consulting and Financial Independence* as well as *So You Want to Improve Your Bottom Line?*

Occasionally, a conjunction may begin a sentence; in fact, conjunctions can be strong transitional words and at times can provide **emphasis**. See also **transition**.

▶ I realize that the project is more difficult than expected and that you have encountered staffing problems. *But* we must meet our deadline.

Correlative conjunctions are used in pairs. The correlative conjunctions are *either . . . or*, *neither . . . nor*, *not only . . . but also*, *both . . . and*, and *whether . . . or*.

▶ The auditor will arrive *either* on Wednesday *or* on Thursday.

A *subordinating conjunction* connects sentence elements of different relative importance, normally independent and dependent clauses. Frequently used subordinating conjunctions are *so, although, after, because, if, where, than, since, as, unless, before, that, though,* and *when.*

► I left the office *after* I had finished the report.

A *conjunctive adverb* functions as a conjunction because it joins two independent clauses. The most common conjunctive **adverbs** are *however, moreover, therefore, further, then, consequently, besides, accordingly, also,* and *thus.*

► The engine performed well in the laboratory; *however,* it failed under road conditions.

connotation / denotation

The *denotations* of a word are its literal meanings, as defined in a dictionary. The *connotations* of a word are its meanings and associations beyond its literal definitions. For example, the denotations of *Hollywood* are "a district of Los Angeles" and "the U.S. movie industry as a whole"; its connotations for many are "glamour, opulence, and superficiality."

Often words have particular connotations for **audiences** within professional groups and organizations. Choose words with both the most accurate denotations and the most appropriate connotations for the **context**. See also **defining terms** and **word choice**.

consensus

Because *consensus* means "harmony of opinion" among most of those in a group, the phrases *consensus of opinion* and *general consensus* defeat **conciseness**. The word *consensus* can be used to refer only to a group, never to one or two people.

► The ~~general~~ consensus ~~of opinion~~ among investors is that the Board of Directors should be replaced.

context

Context is the environment or circumstances in which writers produce documents and within which readers interpret the meanings of those documents. Everything is written in a context, as illustrated in many entries and examples throughout this book. This entry considers the significance of context for workplace writing and suggests how you can be aware of it as you write. See also **audience**.

The context for any document, such as a **proposal** or **report**, is determined by interrelated events or circumstances both inside and outside an organization.* For example, when you write a proposal to fund a project within your company, the economic condition of that company is part of the context that will determine how your proposal is received. If the company has recently laid off a dozen employees, its management may not be inclined to approve a proposal to expand its operations — regardless of how well the proposal is written.

When you correspond with someone, the events that prompted you to write shape the context of the message and will affect what you say and how you say it. If you write to a customer in response to a complaint, for example, the **tone** and approach of your message will be determined by the context — what you find when you investigate the issue. Is your company fully or partly at fault? Has the customer incorrectly used a product? contributed to a problem? (See also **adjustment letters**.) If you write **instructions** for office staff who must use high-volume document-processing equipment, other questions will reveal the context. What are the lighting and other physical conditions near the equipment? Will these physical conditions affect the **layout and design** of the instructions? What potential safety issues might the users encounter?

Assessing Context

Each time you write, the context needs to be clearly in your mind so that your document will achieve its **purpose**. The following questions are starting points to help you become aware of the context, how it will influence your approach and your readers' interpretation of what you have written, and how it will affect the decisions you need to make during the writing process. See also "Five Steps to Successful Writing" on page xv.

---

*For a detailed illustration of specific documents that have been affected by factors within particular contexts, see Linda Driskill, "Understanding the Writing Context in Organizations," in *Central Works in Technical Communication*, ed. Johndan Johnson-Eilola and Stuart A. Selber (New York: Oxford University Press, 2004), 55–69.

C

- What is your professional relationship with your readers, and how might that affect the tone, **style**, and **scope** of your writing? What is "the story" behind the immediate reason you are writing; that is, what series of events or perhaps previous documents led to your need to write?

- What is the preferred medium of your readers? See also **selecting the medium**.

- What specific factors (such as competition, finance, and regulation) are recognized within your organization or department as important?

- What is the corporate culture in which your readers work, and what are the key values that you might find in its mission statement?

- What are the professional relationships among the specific readers who will receive the document?

- What current events within or outside an organization or a department may influence how readers interpret your writing?

- What national cultural differences might affect your readers' expectations or interpretations of the document? See also **global communication**.

As these questions suggest, context is specific each time you write and often involves, for example, the history of a specific organization or your past dealings with individual readers.

Signaling Context

Because context is so important, remind your reader in some way of the context for your writing, as in the following opening for a cover message to a proposal.

▶ During our meeting last week on improving quality, you mentioned that we have previously required usability testing only for documents going to high-profile clients because of the costs involved. The idea occurred to me that we might try less-extensive usability testing for many of our other clients. Because you asked for suggestions, I have proposed in the attached document a method of limited usability testing for a broad range of clients in order to improve overall quality while keeping costs at a minimum.

Of course, as described in **introductions**, providing context for a reader may require only a brief background statement or short reminders.

▶ Several weeks ago, a financial adviser noticed a recurring problem in the software developed by Datacom Systems. Specifically, error messages repeatedly appeared when, in fact, no specific trouble . . .

▶ Jane, as I promised in my e-mail yesterday, I've attached the personnel budget estimates for the next fiscal year.

As the last example suggests, provide context for attachments that you
send with **e-mail**.

C

continual / continuous

Continual implies "happening over and over" or "frequently repeated."
("Writing well requires *continual* practice.") *Continuous* implies "occurring without interruption" or "unbroken." ("The *continuous* roar
of the machinery was deafening.")

contractions

A contraction is a shortened spelling of a word or phrase with an **apostrophe** substituting for the missing letter or letters (*cannot / can't; have
not / haven't; will not / won't; it is / it's*). Contractions are often used
in speech and informal writing; they are generally not appropriate in
reports, **proposals**, and formal **correspondence**. See also **business writing style**.

copyright

Copyright establishes legal protection for literary, dramatic, musical,
artistic, and other intellectual works in printed or electronic form; it
gives the copyright owner exclusive rights to reproduce, distribute, perform, or display a work. Copyright protects all original works from the
moment of their creation, regardless of whether they are published or
contain a notice of copyright (©).

❖ ETHICS NOTE If you plan to reproduce copyrighted material in your
own publication or on your Web site, you must obtain permission from
the copyright holder. To do otherwise is a violation of U.S. law. ❖

Permissions

To seek permission to reproduce copyrighted material, you must write
to the copyright holder. In some cases, it is the author; in other cases,
it is the editor or publisher of the work. For Web sites, read the site's
"terms-of-use" information (if available) and e-mail your request to

C

the appropriate party. State specifically which portion of the work you wish to reproduce and how you plan to use it. The copyright holder has the right to charge a fee and specify conditions and limits of use.

Exceptions

Some print and Web material—including text, **visuals**, and other digital forms—may be reproduced without permission, as described in the following list. The rules governing copyright can be complex, so it is prudent to check carefully the copyright status of anything you plan to reproduce.

- *Educational material.* A small amount of material from a copyrighted source may be used for educational purposes (such as classroom handouts) without permission or payment as long as the use satisfies the "fair-use" criteria, as described at the U.S. Copyright Office Web site, *www.copyright.gov*.

- *Company boilerplate.* Employees often borrow material freely from in-house manuals, reports, and other company documents to save time and ensure consistency. Using such "boilerplate" or "repurposed" material is not a copyright violation because the company is considered the author of works prepared by its employees on the job. See also **repurposing**.

- *Public domain material.* Works created by or for the U.S. government and not classified or otherwise protected are in the public domain—that is, they are not copyrighted. The same is true for older written works when their copyright has lapsed or never existed. Be aware that some works in the public domain may include "value-added" features, such as introductions, visuals, and indexes, that are copyrighted separately from the original work.

- *Copyleft Web material.* Some public access Web sites, such as Wikipedia, follow the "copyleft" principle and grant permission to freely copy, distribute, or modify material.*

❖ ETHICS NOTE Even when you use material that may be reproduced or published without permission, you must nonetheless give appropriate credit to the source from which the material is taken, as described in **documenting sources** and **plagiarism**. ❖

---

* "Copyleft" is a play on the word *copyright* and is the effort to free materials from many of the restrictions of copyright. See *http://en.wikipedia.org/wiki/Copyleft*.

WEB LINK	Alternative Forms of Copyright

The emergence of the Internet has greatly changed the face of copyright, creating an illusion of universal access to online material when permission is often required to alter or use it in any way. Alternative forms of copyright — like those offered by Creative Commons — allow users to freely incorporate specific content into their documents and to license thier own original content. See *bedfordstmartins.com/alred* and select *Links for Handbook Entries.*

correspondence

DIRECTORY

Correspondence in the workplace—whether through **e-mail**, **letters**, **memos**, or another medium—requires many of the steps that are described in "Five Steps to Successful Writing" (page xv). As you prepare even a simple e-mail, for example, you might study previous messages (**research**) and then list or arrange the points you wish to cover (**organization**) in an order that is logical for your readers. See also **selecting the medium**.

Corresponding with others in the workplace also requires that you focus on both establishing or maintaining a positive working relationship with your **readers** and conveying a professional image of yourself and your organization. See also **audience**.

Audience and Writing Style

Effective correspondence uses an appropriate conversational **style**. To achieve that style, imagine your reader sitting across from you and write to the reader as if you were talking face to face. Take into account your reader's needs and feelings. Ask yourself, "How might I feel if I received this letter or e-mail?" and then tailor your message accordingly. Remember, an impersonal and unfriendly message to a customer or client can tarnish the image of you and your business, but a thoughtful and sincere one can enhance it.

Whether you use a formal or an informal writing style depends entirely on your reader and your **purpose**. You might use an informal (or a casual) style, for example, with a colleague you know well and a formal (or restrained) style with a client you do not know.

> CASUAL   It worked! The new process is better than we had dreamed.
>
> RESTRAINED   You will be pleased to know that the new process is more effective than we expected.

You will probably find yourself using the restrained style more frequently than the casual style. Remember that an overdone attempt to sound casual or friendly can sound insincere. However, do not adopt so formal a style that your writing reads like a legal contract. **Affectation** not only will irritate and baffle readers but also can waste time and produce costly errors.

> AFFECTED   Per yesterday's e-mail, we no longer possess an original copy of the brochure requested. Please be advised that a PDF copy is attached herewith to this e-mail.
>
> IMPROVED   We are out of original copies of the brochure we discussed yesterday, so I am attaching a PDF copy to this e-mail.

The improved version is not only clearer and less stuffy but also more concise. See also **business writing style** and **conciseness**.

Goodwill and the "You" Viewpoint

Write concisely, but do not be so blunt that you risk losing the reader's goodwill. Responding to a vague written request with "Your request was unclear" or "I don't understand" could offend your reader. Instead, establish goodwill to encourage your reader to provide the information you need.

> ▶ I will be glad to help, but I need additional information to locate the report you requested. Specifically, can you give me the report's title, release date, or number?

Although this version is a bit longer, it is more tactful and will elicit a helpful response. See also **telegraphic style**.

You can also build goodwill by emphasizing the reader's needs or benefits. Suppose you received a refund request from a customer who forgot to include the receipt with the request. In a response to that customer, you might write the following:

WEAK We must receive the sales receipt before we can process a refund.
[The writer's needs are emphasized: "*We* must."]

If you consider how to keep the customer's goodwill, you could word the request this way:

IMPROVED Please send the sales receipt so that we can process your refund.
[Although polite, the sentence focuses on the writer's needs: "so that *we* can process."]

You can put the reader's needs and interests foremost by writing from the reader's perspective. Often, doing so means using the words *you* and *your* rather than *we*, *our*, *I*, and *mine*—a technique called the **"you" viewpoint**. Consider the following revision:

EFFECTIVE So that you can receive your refund promptly, please mail or fax the sales receipt.
[The reader's needs are emphasized with *you* and *your*.]

This revision stresses the reader's benefit and interest. By emphasizing the reader's needs, the writer will be more likely to accomplish the purpose: to get the reader to act. See also **positive writing**.

If overdone, however, goodwill and the "you" viewpoint can produce writing that is fawning and insincere. Messages that are full of excessive praise and inflated language may be ignored—or even resented—by the reader.

EXCESSIVE PRAISE You are just the kind of astute client that deserves the finest service that we can offer—and you deserve our best deal. Understanding how carefully you make decisions, I know you'll think about the advantages of using our consulting service.

REASONABLE From our earlier correspondence, I understand your need for reliable service. We strive to give all our priority clients our full attention, and after you have reviewed our proposal I am confident you will appreciate our "five-star" consulting option.

C

Use the following guidelines to achieve a <u>tone</u> that builds goodwill with your recipients.

✔ Be respectful, not demanding.

> DEMANDING Submit your answer in one week.
>
> RESPECTFUL I would appreciate your answer within one week.

✔ Be modest, not arrogant.

> ARROGANT My attached report is thorough, and I'm sure that you won't be able to continue without it.
>
> MODEST The attached report contains details of the refinancing options that I hope you will find useful.

✔ Be polite, not sarcastic.

> SARCASTIC I just now received the shipment we ordered six months ago. I'm sending it back—we can't use it now. Thanks a lot!
>
> POLITE I am returning the shipment we ordered on March 12. Unfortunately, it arrived too late for us to be able to use it.

✔ Be positive and tactful, not negative and condescending.

> NEGATIVE Your complaint about our prices is way off target. Our prices are definitely not any higher than those of our competitors.
>
> TACTFUL Thank you for your suggestion concerning our prices. We believe, however, that our prices are comparable to or lower than those of our competitors.

Good-News and Bad-News Patterns

Although the relative directness of correspondence may vary, it is generally more effective to present good news directly and bad news indirectly, especially if the stakes are high.* This principle is based on the fact that readers form their impressions and attitudes very early and that you as the writer may want to subordinate the bad news to reasons that make the bad news understandable. Further, if you are writing

---

*Gerald J. Alred, "'We Regret to Inform You': Toward a New Theory of Negative Messages," in *Studies in Technical Communication*, ed. Brenda R. Sims (Denton: University of North Texas and NCTE, 1993), 17–36.

international correspondence, consider that far more cultures are generally indirect in business messages than are direct.

Consider the thoughtlessness of the direct rejection in Figure C–11. Although the message is concise and uses the pronouns *you* and *your*, the writer does not consider how the recipient is likely to feel as she reads the rejection. Its pattern is (1) the bad news, (2) an explanation, and (3) the closing.

Dear Ms. Mauer:

Your application for the position of Records Administrator at Southtown Dental Center has been rejected. We have found someone more qualified than you.

Sincerely,

FIGURE C–11. A Poor Bad-News Message

A better general pattern for bad news is (1) an opening that provides **context** (often called a "buffer"), (2) an explanation, (3) the bad news, and (4) a goodwill closing. (See also **refusal letters**.) The opening introduces the subject and establishes a professional tone, as in Figure C–12. The body provides an explanation by reviewing the facts that make the bad news understandable. Although bad news is never pleasant, information that either puts the bad news in perspective or makes it seem reasonable promotes not only understanding but also goodwill between the writer and the reader. The closing should reinforce a positive relationship through goodwill or helpful information. The courteous rejection shown in Figure C–12 carries the same disappointing news as does the letter in Figure C–11, but the writer is careful to thank the reader for her time and effort, explain why she was not accepted for the job, and offer her encouragement.

This pattern can also be used in relatively short e-mail messages and memos. Consider the unintended secondary message the following notice conveys:

WEAK It has been decided that the office will be open the day after Thanksgiving.

"It has been decided" not only sounds impersonal but also communicates an authoritarian, management-versus-employee tone. The passive voice also suggests that the decision-maker does not want to say "I have decided" and thus accept responsibility. One solution is to remove the first part of the sentence.

C

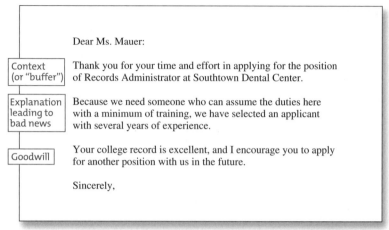

Dear Ms. Mauer:

Context (or "buffer")
Thank you for your time and effort in applying for the position of Records Administrator at Southtown Dental Center.

Explanation leading to bad news
Because we need someone who can assume the duties here with a minimum of training, we have selected an applicant with several years of experience.

Goodwill
Your college record is excellent, and I encourage you to apply for another position with us in the future.

Sincerely,

FIGURE C–12. A Courteous Bad-News Message

> **IMPROVED**   The office will be open the day after Thanksgiving.

The best solution, however, would be to suggest both that there is a good reason for the decision and that employees are privy to (if not a part of) the decision-making process.

> **EFFECTIVE**   Because we must meet the December 15 deadline for submitting the Bradley Foundation proposal, the office will be open the day after Thanksgiving.

By describing the context of the bad news first (the need to meet the deadline), the writer focuses on the reasoning behind the decision to work. Employees may not necessarily like the message, but they will at least understand that the decision is not arbitrary and is tied to an important deadline.

Presenting good news is, of course, easier. Present good news in your opening. By doing so, you increase the likelihood that the reader will pay careful attention to details, and you achieve goodwill from the start. The pattern for good-news messages should be (1) a good-news opening, (2) an explanation of facts, and (3) a goodwill closing. Figure C–13 is an example of an effective good-news message.

Openings and Closings

Although methods of development vary, the opening of any correspondence should identify the subject and often the main point of the message.

> ▶ Attached is the final installation report, which I hope you can review by Monday, December 12. You will notice that the report includes . . .

C

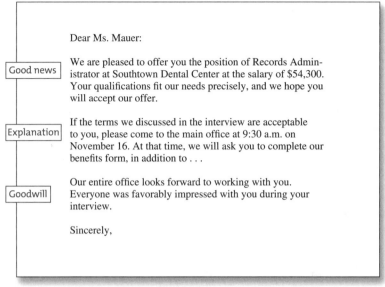

Dear Ms. Mauer:

Good news

We are pleased to offer you the position of Records Administrator at Southtown Dental Center at the salary of $54,300. Your qualifications fit our needs precisely, and we hope you will accept our offer.

Explanation

If the terms we discussed in the interview are acceptable to you, please come to the main office at 9:30 a.m. on November 16. At that time, we will ask you to complete our benefits form, in addition to . . .

Goodwill

Our entire office looks forward to working with you. Everyone was favorably impressed with you during your interview.

Sincerely,

FIGURE C–13. A Good-News Message

When your reader is not familiar with the subject or with the background of a problem, you may provide an introductory paragraph before stating the main point of the message. Doing so is especially important in correspondence that will serve as a record of crucial information. Generally, longer or complex subjects benefit most from more thorough **introductions**. However, even when you are writing a short message about a familiar subject, remind readers of the context. In the following example, words that provide context are shown in *italics*.

▶ *As Maria Lopez recommended,* I reviewed the office reorganization plan. I like most of the features; however, . . .

Do not state the main point first when (1) readers are likely to be highly skeptical or (2) key readers, such as managers or clients, may disagree with your position. In those cases, a more persuasive tactic is to state the problem or issue first, then present the specific points supporting your final recommendation, as discussed in the earlier section on bad-news messages. See also **persuasion**.

Your closing can accomplish many important tasks, such as building positive relationships with readers, encouraging colleagues and employees, and letting recipients know what you will do or what you expect of them.

▶ I will discuss the problem with the marketing consultant and let you know by Wednesday what we are able to change.

Routine statements are sometimes unavoidable. ("If you have further questions, please let me know.") However, try to make your closing work for you by providing specific prompts to which the reader can respond. See also **conclusions**.

▶ Thanks again for the report, and let me know if you want me to send you a copy of the test results.

Clarity and Emphasis

A clear message is one that is adequately developed and emphasizes your main points. The following example illustrates how adequate development is crucial to the **clarity** of your message.

VAGUE   Be more careful on the loading dock.

DEVELOPED   To prevent accidents on the loading dock, follow these procedures:

            1. Check . . . [followed by specific details]

            2. Load only . . .

            3. Replace . . .

Although the first version is concise, it is not as clear and specific as the "developed" revision. Do not assume your readers will know what you mean: vague messages are easily misinterpreted.

Lists.   Vertically stacked words, **phrases**, and other items with numbers or bullets can effectively highlight such information as steps in sequence, materials or parts needed, key or concluding points, and recommendations. As described in the entry **lists**, make sure you provide context. Be careful not to overuse lists—a message that consists almost entirely of lists is difficult to understand because it forces readers to connect separate and disjointed items. Further, lists lose their effectiveness when they are overused.

Headings.   **Headings** are particularly useful because they call attention to main topics, divide material into manageable segments, and signal a shift in topic. Readers can scan the headings and read only the section or sections appropriate to their needs.

Subject Lines.   Subject lines for e-mails, memos, and some letters announce the topic and focus of the correspondence. Because they also aid filing and later retrieval, they must be specific and accurate.

VAGUE	Subject: Tuition Reimbursement
VAGUE	Subject: Time-Management Seminar
SPECIFIC	Subject: Tuition Reimbursement for Time-Management Seminar

C

Capitalize all major words in a subject line except articles, prepositions, and conjunctions with fewer than five letters (unless they are the first or last words). Remember that the subject line should not substitute for an opening that provides context for the message. See also **titles**.

WRITER'S CHECKLIST   Correspondence and Accuracy

✔ Begin by establishing your purpose, analyzing your reader's needs, determining your **scope**, and considering the context.

✔ Prepare an outline, even if it is only a list of points to be covered in the order you want to cover them. (See **outlining**.)

✔ Write the first draft. (See **writing a draft**.)

✔ Allow for a cooling-off period prior to **revision** or seek a colleague's advice, especially for correspondence that addresses a problem.

✔ Revise the draft, checking for key problems in clarity and **coherence**.

✔ Use the appropriate or standard format, for example as in **letters** and **memos**.

✔ Check for accuracy: Make sure that all facts, figures, and dates are correct.

✔ Use effective **proofreading** techniques to check your **punctuation**, **grammar**, **spelling**, and appropriate **usage**.

✔ Consider who should receive a copy of the message and in what order the names or e-mail addresses should be listed (alphabetize if rank does not apply).

✔ Remember that when you sign a letter or send a message, you are accepting responsibility for it.

---

cover letters (or transmittals)

A cover **letter**, **memo**, or **e-mail** accompanies a document (such as a **proposal**), an electronic file, or other material. It identifies an item that is being sent, the person to whom it is being sent, the reason that it is being sent, and any content that should be highlighted for **readers**. (See **purpose**.) A cover letter provides a permanent record for both the

C

Dear Mr. Hammersmith:

Attached is the report estimating our energy needs for the year as requested by John Brenan, Vice President, on September 5.

The report is a result of several meetings with the manager of plant operations and her staff and an extensive survey of all our employees. The survey was delayed by the transfer of key staff in Building A. We believe, however, that the report will provide the information you need in order to furnish us with a cost estimate for the installation of your Mark II Energy Saving System.

We would like to thank Diana Biel of ESI for her assistance in preparing the survey. If you need any more information, please let me know.

Sincerely,

FIGURE C–14.   Cover Message

writer and the reader. For cover letters to **résumés**, see **application cover letters**.

The example in Figure C–14 is concise, but it also includes details such as how the information for the **report** was gathered.

credible / creditable

Something is *credible* if it is believable. ("The statistics in this report are *credible*.") Something is *creditable* if it is worthy of praise or credit. ("The accountant did a *creditable* job.")

criteria / criterion

Criterion is a singular **noun** meaning "an established standard for judging or testing." *Criteria* and *criterions* are both acceptable plural forms of *criterion*, but *criteria* is generally preferred.

critique

A *critique* is a written or an oral evaluation of something. Avoid using *critique* as a **verb** meaning "criticize."

▶ Please ~~critique~~ his job description.
    prepare a   *of*

D

dangling modifiers

Phrases that do not clearly and logically refer to the correct **noun** or **pronoun** are called *dangling modifiers*. Dangling modifiers usually appear at the beginning of a sentence as an introductory **phrase**.

DANGLING *While eating lunch*, the computer malfunctioned.
[*Who* was eating lunch?]

CORRECT While *I* was eating lunch, the computer malfunctioned.

Dangling modifiers can appear at the end of the sentence as well.

DANGLING The program gains efficiency *by eliminating the superfluous instructions.*
[*Who* eliminates the superfluous instructions?]

CORRECT The program gains efficiency *when you* eliminate the superfluous instructions.

To correct a dangling modifier, add the appropriate subject to either the dangling modifier or the main **clause**.

DANGLING After finishing the research, the proposal was easy to write.
[The appropriate subject is *I*, but it is not stated in either the dangling phrase or the main clause.]

CORRECT After *I* finished the research, the proposal was easy to write.
[The pronoun *I* is now the subject of an introductory clause.]

CORRECT After finishing the research, *I* found the proposal easy to write.
[The pronoun *I* is now the subject of the main clause.]

For a discussion of misplaced modifiers, see **modifiers**.

dashes

The dash (—) can perform all the punctuation duties of linking, separating, and enclosing. The dash, sometimes indicated by two consecutive **hyphens**, can also indicate the omission of letters. ("Mr. A— admitted his error.")

D

Use the dash cautiously to indicate more **emphasis**, informality, or abruptness than the other punctuation marks would show. A dash can emphasize a sharp turn in thought.

> ► The project will end May 13—unless we receive additional funding.

A dash can indicate an emphatic pause.

> ► The project will begin—after we are under contract.

Sometimes, to emphasize contrast, a dash is used with *but*.

> ► We completed the survey quickly—*but* the results were not accurate.

A dash can be used before a final summarizing statement or before repetition that has the effect of an afterthought.

> ► It was hot near the heat-treating ovens—steaming hot.

Such a statement may also complete the meaning of the **clause** preceding the dash.

> ► We try to write as we speak—or so we believe.

Dashes set off parenthetical elements more sharply and emphatically than **commas**. Unlike dashes, **parentheses** tend to deemphasize what they enclose. Compare the following sentences:

> ► Only one person—the president—can authorize such activity.
>
> ► Only one person, the president, can authorize such activity.
>
> ► Only one person (the president) can authorize such activity.

Dashes can be used to set off parenthetical elements that contain commas.

> ► Three of the applicants—John Evans, Rosalita Fontiana, and Kyong-Shik Choi—seem well qualified for the job.

The first word after a dash is capitalized only if it is a proper **noun**.

data

In formal and scholarly writing, *data* is generally used as a plural, with *datum* as the singular form. In much informal writing, however, *data* is considered a collective singular **noun**. Base your **usage** on whether your readers should consider the data as a single collection or as a group of individual facts. Whatever you decide, be sure that your **pronouns** and **verbs** agree in number, as in the following.

▶ These *data are* persuasive. *They indicate* a need for additional research questions. [formal]

▶ The attached *data is* confidential. *It is* the result of a survey of employee records. [less formal]

See also **agreement** and **English, varieties of**.

dates

In the United States, full dates are generally written in the month-day-year format, with a comma preceding and following the year.

▶ November 30, 2025, is the payoff date.

Do not use **commas** in the day-month-year format, which is used in many parts of the world and by the U.S. military.

▶ Note that 30 November 2025 is the payoff date.

No commas are used when showing only the month-year or month-day in a date.

▶ The target date of May 2015 is optimistic, so I would like to meet on March 4 to discuss our options.

When writing days of the month without the year, use the cardinal number ("March 4") rather than the ordinal number ("March 4th"). Of course, in speech or **presentations**, use the ordinal number ("March fourth").

Avoid the strictly numerical form for dates (11/6/15) because the date is not always immediately clear, especially in **international correspondence**. In many countries, 11/6/15 means June 11, 2015, rather than November 6, 2015. Writing out the name of the month makes the entire date immediately clear to all readers.

Centuries often cause confusion with **numbers** because their spelled-out forms, which are not capitalized, do not correspond with their numeral designations. The twentieth century, for example, is the 1900s: 1900–1999.

When the century is written as a **noun,** do not use a **hyphen**.

▶ During the twentieth century, technology transformed business practices.

When the centuries are written as **adjectives,** however, use hyphens.

▶ Twenty-first-century technology relies on dependable power sources.

de facto / de jure

De facto means that something exists or is a fact and therefore is accepted for practical purposes. *De jure* means that something legally exists.

▶ The law states that no signs should be erected along Highway 127. Store owners have disregarded that law, and many signs exist along Highway 127. The presence of the signs along Highway 127 is *de facto* but not *de jure*—their presence is "a fact," but it is not "lawful."

Limit the use of Latin and legal terms because they can easily become an **affectation**.

defective / deficient

If something is *defective*, it is faulty. ("The wiring was *defective*.") If something is *deficient*, it is lacking or is incomplete in an essential component. ("The company was found to be *deficient* in meeting its legal obligations.")

defining terms

Defining key terms and concepts is often essential for **clarity**. Terms can be defined either formally or informally, depending on your **purpose**, your **audience**, and the **context**.

A *formal definition* is a form of classification. You define a term by placing it in a category and then identifying the features that distinguish it from other members of the same category.

TERM	CATEGORY	DISTINGUISHING FEATURES
An *auction* is	a public sale	in which property passes to the highest bidder through successively increased offers.

An *informal definition* explains a term by giving a more familiar word or phrase as a **synonym**.

▶ Plants have a *symbiotic*, or *mutually beneficial*, relationship with certain kinds of bacteria.

State definitions positively; focus on what the term *is* rather than on what it is not.

NEGATIVE   In a legal transaction, *real property* is not personal property.

POSITIVE   *Real property* is legal terminology for the right or interest a person has in land and the permanent structures on that land.

For a discussion of when negative definitions are appropriate, see **definition method of development**.

Avoid circular definitions, which merely restate the term to be defined and therefore fail to clarify it.

CIRCULAR   *Spontaneous combustion* is fire that begins spontaneously.

REVISED   *Spontaneous combustion* is the self-ignition of a flammable material through a chemical reaction.

In addition, avoid "is when" and "is where" definitions. Such definitions fail to include the category and are too indirect.

> a binding agreement between two or more parties.
▶ A *contract* is ~~when two or more parties agree to something.~~
  ^

definite / definitive

Definite and *definitive* both apply to what is precisely defined, but *definitive* more often refers to what is complete and authoritative. ("Once we receive a *definite* proposal, our attorney can provide a *definitive* legal opinion.")

definition method of development

Definition is often essential to **clarity** and accuracy. Although **defining terms** may be sufficient, sometimes definitions need to be expanded through (1) extended definition, (2) definition by analogy, (3) definition by cause, (4) definition by components, (5) definition by exploration of origin, and (6) negative definition. See also **methods of development**.

D

Extended Definition

When you need more than a simple definition to explain an idea, use an extended definition, which explores a number of qualities of the item being defined. How an extended definition is developed depends on your **audience** and on the complexity of the subject. Readers familiar with a topic might be able to handle a long, fairly complex definition, whereas readers less familiar with a topic might require simpler language and more basic information.

The easiest way to give an extended definition is with specific examples. Examples give readers easy-to-picture details that help them see and thus understand the term being defined.

▶ Form, which is the shape of landscape features, can best be represented both by small-scale features, such as *trees* and *shrubs*, and by large-scale elements, such as *mountains* and *mountain ranges*.

Definition by Analogy

Another useful way to define a difficult concept, especially when you are writing for nonspecialists, is to use an analogy. An analogy can help the reader understand an unfamiliar term by showing its similarities with a more familiar term. In the following description of management by objective, notice how the writer develops an analogy to make a point.

▶ Management by objective has been quite popular, but the key to its success is carefully selecting objectives. Think, for example, of a golfer who wishes to improve by hitting the ball farther. Every decision the golfer makes is governed by that goal—hitting the ball as far as possible. The golfer would then be managing his or her game by objective. However, the golfer is shortsighted because golf is as much a game of accuracy as it is of hitting balls for distance. Some of the decisions the golfer makes to hit the ball farther, therefore, might well be counterproductive to achieving the larger goal of obtaining the lowest possible score. In the same way, when a company decides to use a management-by-objective strategy, it must be certain that the objective is appropriate for achieving the desired results.

D

Definition by Cause

Some terms are best defined by an explanation of their causes, as the following explanation of the term *stagflation* illustrates.

▶ Traditional economic theory says that a decline in business activity and employment causes the rate of inflation to decrease. However, in the 1970s, because of massive increases in energy prices, the economy stagnated while higher energy prices worked their way into the cost of virtually everything, and the currency inflated. To describe that condition, economist Paul Samuelson coined the term *stagflation*.

Definition by Components

Sometimes a formal definition of a concept can be made simpler by breaking the concept into its component parts. In the following example, the formal definition of *fire* is given in the first paragraph, and the component parts are given in the second.

FORMAL
DEFINITION

Fire is the visible heat energy released from the rapid oxidation of a fuel. A substance is "on fire" when the release of heat energy from the oxidation process reaches visible light levels.

COMPONENT
PARTS

The classic fire triangle illustrates the elements necessary to create fire: *oxygen*, *heat*, and *burnable material* (*fuel*). Air provides sufficient oxygen for combustion; the intensity of the heat needed to start a fire depends on the characteristics of the burnable material. A burnable substance is one that will sustain combustion after an initial application of heat to start the combustion.

Definition by Exploration of Origin

Under certain circumstances, the meaning of a term can be clarified and made easier to remember by an exploration of its origin. Medical terms, because of their sometimes unfamiliar Greek and Latin roots, benefit especially from an explanation of this type. Tracing the derivation of a word also can be useful when you want to explain why a word has favorable or unfavorable associations, particularly if your goal is to influence your reader's attitude toward an idea or activity. See also **persuasion**.

▶ Efforts to influence legislation generally fall under the head of *lobbying*, a term that once referred to people who prowled the lobbies of houses of government, buttonholing lawmakers and trying to get them to take certain positions. Lobbying today is all of this, and much more, too. It is a respected—and necessary—activity. It tells the legislator which way the winds of public opinion are blowing, and it helps inform [legislators] of the implications of certain bills, debates, and resolutions [that they must face].

—Bill Vogt, *How to Build a Better Outdoors*

Negative Definition

In some cases, it is useful to point out what something is *not* to clarify what it is. A negative definition is effective only when the reader is familiar with the item with which the defined item is contrasted. If you say "*x* is not *y*," your readers must understand the meaning of *y* for the explanation to make sense. In a crane operator's manual, for instance, a negative definition is used to show that, for safety reasons, a hydraulic crane cannot be operated in the same manner as a lattice boom crane.

▶ A hydraulic crane is *not* like a lattice boom crane [a friction machine] in one very important way. In most cases, the safe lifting capacity of a lattice boom crane is based on the *weight needed to tip the machine*. Therefore, operators of friction machines sometimes depend on signs that the machine might tip to warn them of impending danger. This practice is very dangerous with a hydraulic crane. . . .

—*Operator's Manual* (Model W-180), Harnischfeger Corporation

description

The key to effective description is the accurate presentation of details, whether for simple or complex descriptions. In Figure D–1, notice that the simple description contained in the purchase order includes five specific details (in addition to the part number) structured logically.

Complex descriptions, of course, involve more details. In describing a mechanical device, for example, describe the whole device and its function before giving a detailed description of how each part works. The description should conclude with an explanation of how each part contributes to the functioning of the whole.

In descriptions intended for readers who are unfamiliar with the topic, details are crucial. For such an **audience**, show or demonstrate

D

PURCHASE ORDER

PART NO.	DESCRIPTION	QUANTITY
IW 8421	Infectious-waste bags, 12″ × 14″, heavy-gauge polyethylene, red double closures with self-sealing adhesive strips	5 boxes containing 200 bags per box

FIGURE D–1. Simple Description

Protect Windows and Doors

Protecting windows and doors is one of the most effective actions you can take to reduce your risk of wind damage. High winds and windborne debris can easily break unprotected windows and cause doors to fail. Once wind enters a building, the likelihood of severe structural damage increases, and the contents of the building will be exposed to the elements. The most reliable method of protecting windows and doors is installing permanent storm shutters. Alternatives include using temporary plywood covers, replacing existing glass with impact-resistant glass, and covering existing glass with a protective film.

Permanent storm shutters are usually made of aluminum or steel and are attached to a

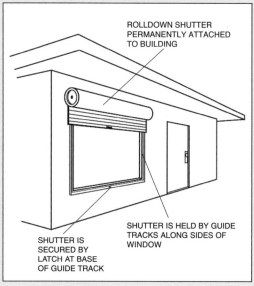

building in such a way that they can be closed quickly before a storm arrives. One type is the "rolldown" shutter (as shown above), which is contained in a housing mounted above the window and lowered when necessary. Manually and motor-operated models are available.

FIGURE D–2. Illustrated Description. *Source*: Federal Emergency Management Agency, www.fema.gov.

(as opposed to "tell") primarily through the use of images and details. Notice the use of color, shapes, and images in the following description of a company's headquarters. The writer assumes that the reader knows such terms as *colonial design* and *haiku fountain*.

> ► Their company's headquarters, which reminded me of a rural college campus, are located north of the city in a 90-acre lush green wooded area. The complex consists of five three-story buildings of red-brick colonial design. The buildings are spaced about 50 feet apart and are built in a U-shape surrounding a reflection pool that frames a striking haiku fountain.

You can also use analogy, as described in **figures of speech**, to explain unfamiliar concepts in terms of familiar ones, such as "U-shape" in the previous example.

Visuals can be powerful aids in descriptive writing, especially when they show features too intricate to explain completely in words. The example in Figure D–2 illustrates a storm-shutter installation that small businesses can use to protect windows from windborne debris damage. Note that the description concentrates on the types of shutters available and their function. The illustration, with call-outs highlighting important features, largely eliminates the need for extensive written details to describe their relationship to one another and their function.

design (*see* layout and design)

despite / in spite of

Although there is no literal difference between *despite* and *in spite of*, *despite* suggests an effort to avoid blame.

> ► *Despite* our best efforts, the plan failed.
> [We are not to blame for the failure.]

> ► *In spite of* our best efforts, the plan failed.
> [We did everything possible, but failure overcame us.]

Despite and *in spite of* (both meaning "notwithstanding") should not be blended into *despite of*.

> ► ~~Despite of~~ our best efforts, the plan failed.
>   *In spite of*

dictionaries

D

Dictionaries give more than just information about the meanings of words. They often provide words' etymologies (origins and history), forms, pronunciations, **spellings**, uses as **idioms**, and functions as **parts of speech**. For certain words, a dictionary lists **synonyms** and may also provide illustrations, if appropriate, such as tables, maps, photographs, and drawings.

WEB LINK	Online Dictionaries
Dictionaries available on the Web often include a human-voice pronunciation of words and thesaurus links. For a list of current online dictionaries, see *bedfordstmartins.com/alred* and select *Links for Handbook Entries*.	

Abridged Dictionaries

Abridged or desk dictionaries contain words commonly used in schools and offices. There is no single "best" dictionary, but you should choose the most recent edition with upward of 200,000 entries. The following are reputable dictionaries:

The American Heritage College Dictionary, 4th ed., with downloadable version, 2010

Microsoft Encarta World English Dictionary, free online edition at *uk.encarta.msn.com/encnet/features/dictionary/dictionaryhome.aspx*

Unabridged Dictionaries

Unabridged dictionaries provide complete and authoritative linguistic information. Because the size and cost of the printed, CD, and online subscription versions are impractical for many individual users, libraries make available these important reference sources.

- *The Oxford English Dictionary* is the standard historical dictionary of the English language. It includes over 500,000 words and gives the chronological developments of over 240,000 words, providing numerous examples of uses and sources. It is available online at *www.oed.com*.
- Merriam Webster offers monthly and annual access to its unabridged dictionary, which features 476,000 definitions, at *www.merriam-webster.com*.

ESL Dictionaries

English-as-a-second-language (ESL) dictionaries are more helpful to the nonnative speaker than are regular English dictionaries or bilingual dictionaries. The pronunciation symbols in ESL dictionaries are based on the international phonetic alphabet rather than on English phonetic systems, and useful grammatical information is included in both the entries and special grammar sections. In addition, the definitions usually are easier to understand than those in regular English dictionaries; for example, a regular English dictionary defines *opaque* as "impervious to the passage of light," while an ESL dictionary defines the word as "not allowing light to pass through." The definitions in ESL dictionaries also are usually more thorough than those in bilingual dictionaries. For example, a bilingual dictionary might indicate that *obstacle* and *blockade* are synonymous — but not indicate that only *obstacle* can be used for abstract meanings. ("Lack of money can be an *obstacle* [not a *blockade*] to a college education.")

The following dictionaries and references provide helpful information for nonnative speakers of English:

> *Longman English Dictionaries* at *http://longmanusahome.com/ dictionaries*
>
> *Oxford American Wordpower Dictionary for Learners of English* at *www.oup.com*

Subject Dictionaries

For the meanings of words too specialized for a general dictionary, a subject dictionary is useful. Subject dictionaries define terms used in a particular field, such as business, geography, architecture, or consumer affairs. Definitions in subject dictionaries are generally more detailed and comprehensive than those found in general dictionaries, but they are written in language that can be understood by nonspecialists. One well-known example is *Black's Law Dictionary* (West).

differ from / differ with

Differ from suggests that two things are not alike. ("Our earlier proposal *differs from* the current one.") *Differ with* indicates disagreement between persons. ("The architect *differed with* the contractor on the proposed site.")

different from / different than

In formal writing, the preposition *from* is used with *different*. ("The product I received is *different from* the one I ordered.") *Different than* is used when it is followed by a clause. ("The actual cost was *different than* we estimated in our proposal.")

direct address

Direct address refers to a sentence or phrase in which the person being spoken or written to is explicitly named. It is often used in **presentations** and in **e-mail** messages. Notice that the person's name in a direct address is set off by **commas**.

► *John*, call me as soon as you arrive at the airport.

► Call me, *John*, as soon as you arrive at the airport.

discreet / discrete

Discreet means "having or showing prudent or careful behavior." ("Because the matter was personal, he asked Bob to be *discreet*.") *Discrete* means something is "separate, distinct, or individual." ("Plans for the corporate headquarters include five *discrete* buildings.")

disinterested / uninterested

Disinterested means "impartial, objective, unbiased."

► Like good judges, researchers should be passionately interested in the problems they tackle but completely *disinterested* when they seek to solve those problems.

Uninterested means simply "not interested."

► Despite Asha's enthusiasm, her manager remained *uninterested* in the project.

division-and-classification method of development

An effective **method of development** for a complex subject is either to divide it into manageable parts and then discuss each part separately (division) or to classify (or group) individual parts into appropriate categories and discuss each category separately (classification). See also **instructions** and **process explanation**.

Division

You might use division to describe a physical object, such as the parts of a copy machine; to examine an organization, such as a company; or to explain the components of a system, such as the Internet. The emphasis in division as a method of development is on breaking down a complex whole into a number of like units—it is easier to consider smaller units and to examine the relationship of each to the other than to attempt to discuss the whole. The basis for division depends, of course, on your subject and your **purpose**.

If you were a financial planner describing the types of mutual funds available to your investors, you could divide the variety available into three broad categories: money-market funds, bond funds, and stock funds. Such division would be accurate, but it would be only a first-level grouping of a complex whole. The three broad categories could, in turn, be subdivided into additional groups based on investment strategy, as follows:

Money-market funds
- Taxable money market
- Tax-exempt money market

Bond funds
- Taxable bonds
- Tax-exempt bonds
- Balanced (mix of stocks and bonds)

Stock funds
- Balanced
- Equity income
- Domestic growth
- Growth and income
- International growth
- Small capitalization
- Aggressive growth
- Specialized

Specialized stock funds could be further subdivided as follows:

Specialized funds
- Communications
- Energy
- Health services
- Technology

- Environmental services
- Financial services
- Gold
- Utilities
- Worldwide capital goods

Classification

The process of classification is the grouping of a number of units (such as people, objects, or ideas) into related categories. Consider the following list:

triangular file	steel tape ruler	needle-nose pliers
vise	pipe wrench	keyhole saw
mallet	tin snips	C-clamps
rasp	hacksaw	plane
glass cutter	ball-peen hammer	steel square
spring clamp	claw hammer	utility knife
crescent wrench	folding extension ruler	slip-joint pliers
crosscut saw	tack hammer	utility scissors

To group the items in the list, you would first determine what they have in common. The most obvious characteristic they share is that they all belong in a carpenter's tool chest. With that observation as a starting point, you can begin to group the tools into related categories. Pipe wrenches belong with slip-joint pliers because both tools grip objects. The rasp and the plane belong with the triangular file because all three tools smooth rough surfaces. By applying this kind of thinking to all the items in the list, you can group (classify) the tools according to function (Figure D–3).

To classify a subject, you must first sort the individual items into the largest number of comparable groups. For explaining the functions of carpentry tools, the classifications (or groups) in Figure D–3 (smoothing, hammering, measuring, gripping, and cutting) are excellent. For recommending which tools a new homeowner should buy first, however, those classifications are not helpful—each group contains tools that a new homeowner might want to purchase right away. To give homeowners advice on purchasing tools, you probably would classify the types of repairs they most likely will have to do (plumbing, painting, etc.). That classification could serve as a guide to tool purchase.

Once you have established the basis for the classification, apply it consistently, putting each item in only one category. For example, it might seem logical to classify needle-nose pliers as both a tool that cuts and a tool that grips because most needle-nose pliers have a small section for cutting wires. However, the primary function of needle-nose pliers is to grip. So listing them only under "tools that grip" would be consistent with the basis used for listing the other tools.

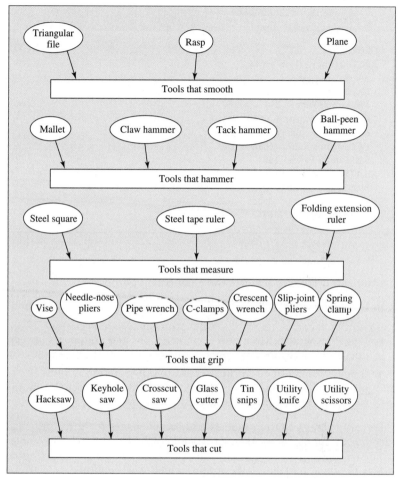

FIGURE D–3. Classification (Tools Placed into Categories)

WEB LINK	Sample of Division and Classification
For an example of an outline using division and classification with the resulting document, see *bedfordstmartins.com/alred* and select *Links for Handbook Entries*.	

documenting sources

D

Documenting sources achieves three important purposes:

- It allows readers to locate and consult the sources used and to find further information on the subject.

- It enables writers to support their assertions and arguments in such documents as **proposals**, **reports**, and trade journal articles.

- It helps writers to give proper credit to others and thus avoid **plagiarism** by identifying the sources of facts, ideas, **visuals**, **quotations**, and paraphrases. See also **paraphrasing**.

This entry shows citation models and sample pages for three principal documentation systems: APA, *CMS*, and MLA. The following examples compare these three styles for citing a book by one author: *Capital Ideas Evolving* by Peter L. Bernstein, which was published in 2007 by Wiley in Hoboken, New Jersey.

- The American Psychological Association (APA) system of citation is often used in the social sciences. It is referred to as an author-date method of documentation because parenthetical in-text citations and a reference list (at the end of the paper) in APA style emphasize the author(s) and date of publication so that the currency of the research is clear.

APA IN-TEXT CITATION

(Author's Last Name, Year)

(Bernstein, 2007)

APA REFERENCES ENTRY

Author's Last Name, Initials. (Year). *Title in italics*. City, State (abbreviated) or Country of Publication: Publisher.

Bernstein, P. L. (2007). *Capital ideas evolving*. Hoboken, NJ: Wiley.

- The *Chicago Manual of Style* (*CMS*) is widely used in publishing and various academic specialties. It presents two systems of documentation: the notes and bibliography system and the author-date system. This entry shows the notes and bibliography system, which uses the more traditional footnotes (at the bottom of the page) or endnotes (at the end of the document) and a bibliography.

CMS FOOTNOTES/ENDNOTES

CMS advocates use of full (all works cited) or selected (most important works cited) bibliographies to help readers review and locate sources cited in the text. If you are not required to provide a full bibliography citing all sources used in a text, you may instead provide a complete footnote for each work cited:

Footnote number. Author's First Name Last Name, *Title in Italics* (Place of Publication: Publisher, Date of Publication), Pages.

1. Peter L. Bernstein, *Capital Ideas Evolving* (Hoboken, NJ: Wiley, 2007), 22–23.

If you include a full bibliography, use a shortened footnote, as the reader can refer to the bibliography for publication details:

Footnote number. Author's Last Name, *Title in Italics*, Pages.

1. Bernstein, *Capital Ideas Evolving*, 22–23.

CMS BIBLIOGRAPHY ENTRY

Author's Last Name, First Name. *Title in Italics*. Place of Publication: Publisher, Date of Publication.

Bernstein, Peter L. *Capital Ideas Evolving*. Hoboken, NJ: Wiley, 2007.

- The Modern Language Association (MLA) system is used in literature and the humanities. The MLA style uses parenthetical in-text citations and a list of works cited and places greater importance on the pages on which cited information can be found than on the publication date.

MLA IN-TEXT CITATION

(Author's Last Name Page Number)

(Bernstein 162)

D

APA

MLA WORKS-CITED ENTRY

Author's Last Name, First Name. *Title Italicized*. City of Publication: Publisher, Date of Publication. Medium of Publication.

Bernstein, Peter L. *Capital Ideas Evolving*. Hoboken: Wiley, 2007. Print.

These systems are described in full detail in the following style manuals:

American Psychological Association. *Publication Manual of the American Psychological Association*. 6th ed. Washington, DC: APA, 2010. See also *www.apastyle.org*.

The Chicago Manual of Style. 16th ed. Chicago: University of Chicago Press, 2010. See also *www.chicagomanualofstyle.org*.

MLA Handbook for Writers of Research Papers. 7th ed. New York: Modern Language Association of America, 2009. See also *www.mla .org/style*.

For additional bibliographic advice and documentation models for types of sources not included in this entry, consult these style manuals or those listed in "Web Link: Other Style Manuals and Documentation Systems" on page 169. See also **bibliographies** and **research**.

APA Documentation

APA In-Text Citations.   Within the text of a paper, APA parenthetical documentation gives a brief citation—in parentheses—of the author, year of publication, and a page number for a direct quotation or if it helps locate a passage in a lengthy document.

▶ Technology has the potential to produce a transformational impact on human life that will enable the human brain to reach beyond its current limitations (Kurzweil, 2006).

▶ According to Kurzweil (2006), we will witness a "pace of technological change that will be so rapid, its impact so deep, that human life will be irreversibly transformed" (p. 7).

When APA parenthetical citations are needed midsentence, place them after the closing quotation marks and continue with the rest of the sentence.

▶ In short "the Singularity" (Kurzweil, 2006, p. 9) is a blending of human biology and technology that will help us develop beyond our human limitations.

If the APA parenthetical citation follows a block quotation, place it after the final punctuation mark.

► . . . a close collaboration with the nursing staff and the hospital bed safety committee is essential. (Jackson, 2008)

When a work has two authors, cite both names joined by an ampersand: (Hinduja & Nguyen, 2008). For the first citation of a work with three through five authors, include all names. For subsequent citations and for works with six or more authors, include only the last name of the first author followed by *et al.* (not italicized and with a period after *al.*). When two or more works by different authors are cited in the same parentheses, list the citations alphabetically and use semicolons to separate them: (Hinduja & Nguyen, 2008; Townsend, 2007).

APA Documentation Models. In reference lists, APA requires that the first word of book and article titles be capitalized and all subsequent words be lowercased. Exceptions include the first word after a colon or dash and proper nouns.

PRINTED BOOKS
Single Author

Taleb, N. N. (2007). *The black swan: The impact of the highly improbable.* New York, NY: Random House.

Multiple Authors

Jones, E., Haenfler, R., & Johnson, B. (2007). *Better world handbook: Small changes that make a big difference.* Gabriola Island, British Columbia, Canada: New Society.

Multiple Books by Same Author

List the works in chronological order, beginning with the earliest.

Orman, S. (2005). *The money book for the young, fabulous & broke.* New York, NY: Riverhead.

Orman, S. (2007). *Women & money: Owning the power to control your destiny.* New York, NY: Spiegel & Grau.

Corporate Author

J. K. Lasser Institute. (2009). *J. K. Lasser's your income tax 2010: For preparing your 2009 tax return.* New York, NY: Wiley.

Edition Other Than First

Kouzes, J. M., & Posner, B. Z. (2007). *The leadership challenge* (4th ed.). New York, NY: Wiley.

D

APA

Multivolume Work

Standard and Poor. (2010). *Standard and Poor's register of corpora-tions, directors, and executives* (Vols. 1–2). New York, NY: Standard and Poor.

Work in an Edited Collection

Sen, A. (2007). Education and standards of living. In R. Curren (Ed.), *Philosophy of education: An anthology* (pp. 95–101). Malden, MA: Blackwell.

Encyclopedia or Dictionary Entry

Gibbard, B. G. (2007). Particle detector. In *World Book encyclopedia* (Vol. 15, pp. 202–203). Chicago, IL: World Book.

ARTICLES IN PRINTED PERIODICALS
Magazine Article

McGirt, E. (2007, November). Facebook opens up. *Fast Company*, 54–89.

Journal Article

Valentine, S., & Fleischman, G. (2008). Ethics programs, perceived corporate social responsibility and job satisfaction. *Journal of Business Ethics, 77,* 159–172.

Newspaper Article

Chazan, G. (2007, November 29). Can wind power find footing in the deep? *The Wall Street Journal*, p. B1.

Article with an Unknown Author

All the right moves for 2008. (2007, December). *Money*, 96–102.

ELECTRONIC SOURCES

The APA recommends that, at minimum, references to online sources should provide an author (whenever possible), the date of publication or update (use "(n.d.)" if no date is available), the title of the article, and retrieval information, such as an address (URL or DOI*) that links directly to the document or section. Include the retrieval date only if the content could change. (The retrieval date is not necessary for content with a fixed publication date, such as a journal article.) On the rare occasion that you need to cite multiple pages of a Web site (or the entire site), provide a URL that links to the site's homepage. No periods follow URLs.

---

*A digital object identifier (DOI) is the character string used to identify an elctronic file.

Entire Web Site

Association for Business Communication. (2008). Retrieved from
http://www.businesscommunication.org

Online Book

Use this form for books made available online or for e-books.

Sowell, T. (2010). *Basic economics: A common sense guide to the economy* (4th ed.). Retrieved from http://books.google.com/books

Short Work from a Web Site, with an Author

Calore, M. (2010, October 7). Personalize your map with a custom
map marker. Retrieved from http://www.webmonkey
.com/2010/10/personalize-your-map-with-a-custom-map
-marker

Short Work from a Web Site, with a Corporate or an Organizational Author

General Motors. (2010). Company profile. Retrieved from http://www
.gm.com/corporate/about/company.jsp

Short Work from a Web Site, with an Unknown Author

Timeline: Alaska pipeline chronology. (2006, April 4). *American Experience*. Retrieved from http://www.pbs.org/wgbh/amex/pipeline/
timeline/index.html

Article or Other Work from a Database

Gaston, N., & Kishi, T. (2007). Part-time workers doing full-time work
in Japan. *Journal of the Japanese and International Economies, 21,*
434–454. doi:10.1016/j.jjie.2006.04.001

Article in an Online Periodical, Not Available in Print

Scherzer, L. (2007, December 6). Clearing emotional hurdles leads
to more profits [Online exclusive]. *SmartMoney*. Retrieved
from http://www.smartmoney.com/theproshop/index
.cfm?story=20071206

Article Posted on a Wiki

Hispanic marketing resources. (2007, September 10). Retrieved
December 9, 2010, from http://www.library.ohiou.edu/subjects/
bizwiki/index.php/Latino_Marketing

E-mail Message

E-mail messages are not cited in an APA reference list. They can
be cited in the text as follows: "According to J. D. Kahl (personal
communication, October 2, 2011), Web pages need to reflect. . . ."

D

APA

Online Posting (Lists, Forums, Discussion Boards)

Harris, S. (2007, December 5). Camera manual comments [Online forum comment]. Retrieved from http://www.techwr-l.com/archives/0712/techwhirl-0712-00071.html

Blog Entry

Brynko, B. (2009, November 30). Weathering turbulent times [Web log post]. Retrieved from http://www.infotodayblog.com/2009/11/30/weathering-turbulent-times

Publication on CD-ROM

Tapscott, D., & Williams, A. D. (2007). *Wikinomics: How mass collaboration changes everything* [CD-ROM]. Old Saybrook, CT: Tantor.

MULTIMEDIA SOURCES (Electronic and Print)

Include a description of the source in brackets (DVD, Audio podcast, etc.) after the title.

Film, Video, or Podcast

Fripp, P. (Host), & Jeffreys, M. (Director). (2007). *Super sales presentations: How to captivate your prospects in a distracted, preoccupied world* [DVD]. Waterford, MI: Seminars on DVD.

Iowa Public Television. (2007, December 12). National debt impact on national security [Video file]. Retrieved from http://www.youtube.com/watch?v=hW1UCvqWY2E

Radio or Television Program

Gardner, S. (Reporter), & Vigeland, T. (Host). (2007, December 5). Plug-in hybrids need more juice. *Marketplace* [Audio podcast]. Los Angeles, CA: American Public Media. Retrieved from http://marketplace.publicradio.org/display/web/2007/12/05/plug_in_cars

Dobbs, L. (Host). (2007, November 7). Yahoo! and China. *Lou Dobbs Tonight* [Television broadcast]. Washington, DC: CNN.

OTHER SOURCES

Visual from Secondary Source

The APA recommends citing the source in which the visual (table or figure) appeared, without mentioning the visual specifically in the reference list. The in-text citation should include a source line (Source: author's last name, year, page number) placed directly below the visual. See also **visuals** and Ethics Note on page 169.

Published Interview

Pitney, J. (2008, January). Q & A [Interview]. *Automobile, 22*(1), 66.

Personal Communications

Personal communications such as lectures, letters, interviews, and e-mail messages are generally not cited in an APA reference list. They can be cited in the text as follows: "According to J. D. Kahl (personal communication, October 2, 2011), Web pages need to reflect. . . ."

D

APA

Brochure or Pamphlet

Library of Congress, U.S. Copyright Office. (2010). *Copyright basics* [Brochure]. Washington, DC: Government Printing Office.

Government Document

U.S. Department of Labor, Bureau of Labor Statistics. (2007). *Highlights of women's earnings in 2006* (Report No. 1000). Washington, DC: Department of Labor.

Report

Ditch, W. (2007). *XML-based office document standards*. Bristol, England: Higher Education Funding Council for England.

Unpublished Data

Kavsan, G., & Hersom, P. (2008). [Oregon small business statistics, by county]. Unpublished raw data.

APA Sample Pages

Short-
ened
title and
page
number.

ETHICS CASES   14

    This report examines the nature and disposition of the 3,458 ethics

cases handled companywide by CGF's ethics officers and managers

during 2011. The purpose of such reports is to provide the Ethics and

One-inch
margins.
Text
double-
spaced.

Business Conduct Committee with the information necessary for as-

sessing the effectiveness of the first year of CGF's Ethics Program

(Davis, Marks, & Tegge, 2008). According to Matthias Jonas (2008),

recommendations are given for consideration "in planning for the sec-

ond year of the Ethics Program" (p. 152).

    The Office of Ethics and Business Conduct was created to ad-

minister the Ethics Program. The director of the Office of Ethics and

Business Conduct, along with seven ethics officers throughout CGF,

was given the responsibility for the following objectives, as described

by Rossouw (2001):

Long quote
indented
one-half
inch,
double-
spaced,
without
quotation
marks.

    Communicate the values, standards, and goals of CGF's

Program to employees. Provide companywide channels for

employee education and guidance in resolving ethics concerns.

Implement companywide programs in ethics awareness and

recognition. Employee accessibility to ethics information and

guidance is the immediate goal of the Office of Business Con-

duct in its first year. (p. 1543)

    The purpose of the Ethics Program, established by the Committee, is to

"promote ethical business conduct through open communication and

In-text
citation
gives
name,
date,
and
page
number.

compliance with company ethics standards" (Jonas, 2010, p. 89). To

accomplish this purpose, any ethics policy must ensure confidentiality

and anonymity for employees who raise genuine ethics concerns.

The procedure developed at CGF guarantees that employees can

FIGURE D–4. APA Sample Page from Report

ETHICS CASES   21

References

Heading centered.

D

APA

First word of title capitalized and subsequent words lowercased.

Davis, W. C., Marks, R., & Tegge, D. (2008). *Working in the*
    system: Five new management principles. New York,
    NY: St. Martin's Press.

Jonas, M. (2008). The Internet and ethical communication:
    Toward a new paradigm. *Journal of Ethics and*
    Communication, 32, 147–177.

List alphabetized by authors' last names and doublespaced.

Jonas, M. (2010). Ethics in organizational communication:
    A review of the literature. *Journal of Ethics and*
    Communication, 29, 79–99.

National Science Foundation. (2011). *Conflicts of interest and*
    standards of ethical conduct. Arlington, VA: Author.

Rossouw, G. J. (2001). Business ethics in South Africa.
    Journal of Business Ethics, 16, 1539–1547.

Schipper, F. (2011). Transparency and integrity: Contrary
    concepts? In K. Homann, P. Koslowski, & C. Luetge
    (Eds.), *Globalisation and business ethics* (pp.
    101–118). Burlington, VT: Ashgate.

Hanging-indent style used for entries.

Smith, T. (Reporter), & Lehrer, J. (Host). (2010). *NewsHour*
    business ethics anthology [DVD]. Encino, CA:
    Business Training Media.

FIGURE D–5. APA Sample List of References

CMS Documentation

CMS *Footnotes and Endnotes.* The CMS footnote and endnote citations give superscript numerals within the text that correspond to numbered footnotes (appearing at the bottom of the page where referenced) or endnotes (listed on a separate page at the end of the paper). The CMS recommends footnotes for ease of reference. If you have numerous long footnotes that are difficult to fit on their respective pages, consider using endnotes.

Place superscript numbers at the end of the quotation or sentence after the punctuation marks. Indent the first line of the footnote or endnote entry five spaces (1/2 inch). Use the number corresponding to the text, but do not make it superscript. Include the author's name (first name first), title, publication information (enclosed in parentheses), and page number(s), all separated by commas.

▶ In Latin America, there was a close correlation between the economic declines and torture, such as the torture inflicted by the Pinochet regime.[4]

▶ 4. Naomi Klein, *Shock Doctrine: The Rise of Disaster Capitalism* (New York: Metropolitan, 2007), 7.

If the bibliography contains all the works cited in the notes, you may abbreviate the note citations to eliminate duplication of information. The same is true for subsequent note citations already cited in full. Use the author's last name, a shortened version of the title, and the page number.

▶ 4. Klein, *Shock Doctrine*, 232.

CMS *Documentation Models**

PRINTED BOOKS
Single Author

1. Nassim Nicholas Taleb, *The Black Swan: The Impact of the Highly Improbable* (New York: Random House, 2007), 29.

Taleb, Nassim Nicholas. *The Black Swan: The Impact of the Highly Improbable*. New York: Random House, 2007.

Two or Three Authors

2. Ellis Jones, Ross Haenfler, and Brett Johnson, *Better World Handbook: Small Changes That Make a Big Difference* (Gabriola Island, BC: New Society, 2007), 120.

*Examples are shown for both footnotes and bibliographic entries.

Jones, Ellis, Ross Haenfler, and Brett Johnson. *Better World Handbook: Small Changes That Make a Big Difference*. Gabriola Island, BC: New Society, 2007.

Four or More Authors

3. Bruce Jefferson et al., *Urban Water Recycling: Techniques and Applications* (Burlington, MA: Butterworth-Heinemann, 2008), 277.

Jefferson, Bruce, Paul Jeffrey, Claire Diaper, and James Crook. *Urban Water Recycling: Techniques and Applications*. Burlington, MA: Butterworth-Heinemann, 2008.

Multiple Books by Same Author

In the bibliography, list the works alphabetically by title.

4. Suze Orman, *Women & Money: Owning the Power to Control Your Destiny* (New York: Spiegel & Grau, 2007), 54.

5. Suze Orman, *The Money Book for the Young, Fabulous & Broke* (New York: Riverhead, 2005), 212.

Orman, Suze. *The Money Book for the Young, Fabulous & Broke*. New York: Riverhead, 2005.

——. *Women & Money: Owning the Power to Control Your Destiny*. New York: Spiegel & Grau, 2007.

Corporate Author

6. J. K. Lasser Institute, *J. K. Lasser's Your Income Tax 2010: For Preparing Your 2009 Tax Return* (New York: Wiley, 2009), 65.

J. K. Lasser Institute. *J. K. Lasser's Your Income Tax 2010: For Preparing Your 2009 Tax Return*. New York: Wiley, 2009.

Edition Other Than First

7. James M. Kourzes and Barry Z. Posner, *The Leadership Challenge*, 4th ed. (New York: Wiley, 2007), 17.

Kouzes, James M., and Barry Z. Posner. *The Leadership Challenge*. 4th ed. New York: Wiley, 2007.

Multivolume Work

8. Standard and Poor, *Standard and Poor's Register of Corporations, Directors, and Executives* (New York: Standard and Poor, 2010), 2:128.

Standard and Poor. *Standard and Poor's Register of Corporations, Directors, and Executives*. 2 vols. New York: Standard and Poor, 2010.

Work in an Edited Collection

9. Amartya Sen, "Education and Standards of Living," in *Philosophy of Education: An Anthology*, ed. Randall Curren (Malden, MA: Blackwell, 2007), 98.

Sen, Amartya. "Education and Standards of Living." In *Philosophy of Education: An Anthology*, edited by Randall Curren, 95–101. Malden, MA: Blackwell, 2007.

Encyclopedia or Dictionary Entry

10. *World Book Encyclopedia*, 2007 ed., s.v. "particle detector."

Well-known reference books, such as encyclopedias and dictionaries, are not included in the bibliography.

ARTICLES IN PRINTED PERIODICALS

Magazine Article

11. Ellen McGirt, "Facebook Opens Up," *Fast Company*, November 2007, 66.

McGirt, Ellen. "Facebook Opens Up." *Fast Company*, November 2007, 54–89.

Journal Article

12. Sean Valentine and Gary Fleischman, "Ethics Programs, Perceived Corporate Social Responsibility and Job Satisfaction," *Journal of Business Ethics* 77, no. 1 (2008): 166.

Valentine, Sean, and Gary Fleischman. "Ethics Programs, Perceived Corporate Social Responsibility and Job Satisfaction." *Journal of Business Ethics* 77, no. 1 (2008): 159–72.

Newspaper Article

13. Guy Chazan, "Can Wind Power Find Footing in the Deep?," *Wall Street Journal*, November 29, 2007, sec. B.

Chazan, Guy. "Can Wind Power Find Footing in the Deep?" *Wall Street Journal*, November 29, 2007, sec. B.

Article with an Unknown Author

14. "All the Right Moves for 2008," *Money*, December 2007, 101.

"All the Right Moves for 2008." *Money*, December 2007, 96–102.

ELECTRONIC SOURCES

The *CMS* recommends that references to online sources should provide the author's name (if there is one), the title or description of the site, the name of any sponsoring organization, the date of publication or modification, and an address (URL) that links directly to the site or site section. Use a DOI (digital object identifier) instead of a URL if one is available. Italicize the title of a Web site only if it is an online book, periodical, or blog. Use quotation marks for titles of articles, pages, or sections of a Web site. Include the access date only if there is no publication date or date of modification.

Entire Web Site

15. Association for Business Communication, accessed October 25, 2010, http://www.businesscommunication.org.

Association for Business Communication. Accessed October 25, 2010. http://www.businesscommunication.org.

Online Book

16. Thomas Sowell, *Basic Economics: A Common Sense Guide to the Economy*, 4th ed. (New York: Basic Books, 2010), 125, http://books .google.com/books.

Sowell, Thomas. *Basic Economics: A Common Sense Guide to the Economy*. 4th ed. New York: Basic Books, 2010. http://books .google.com/books.

Short Work from a Web Site, with an Author

17. Michael Calore, "Personalize Your Map with a Custom Map Marker," Webmonkey, October 7, 2010, http://www.webmonkey .com/2010/10/personalize-your-map-with-a-custom-map-marker.

Calore, Michael. "Personalize Your Map with a Custom Map Marker." Webmonkey. October 7, 2010. http://www.webmonkey.com/ 2010/10/personalize-your-map-with-a-custom-map-marker.

Short Work from a Web Site, with a Corporate or an Organizational Author

18. General Motors, "Company Profile," accessed November 13, 2010, http://www.gm.com/corporate/about/company.jsp.

General Motors. "Company Profile." Accessed November 13, 2010. http://www.gm.com/corporate/about/company.jsp.

Short Work from a Web Site, with an Unknown Author

19. "Timeline: Alaska Pipeline Chronology," American Experience, last modified April 4, 2006, http://www.pbs.org/wgbh/amex/ pipeline/timeline/index.html.

"Timeline: Alaska Pipeline Chronology." American Experience. Last modified April 4, 2006. http://www.pbs.org/wgbh/amex/pipeline/timeline/index.html.

Article or Other Work from a Database

20. Noel Gaston and Tomoka Kishi, "Part-time Workers Doing Full-time Work in Japan," *Journal of the Japanese and International Economies* 21, no. 4 (2007): 441, doi:10.1016/j.jjie.2006.04.001.

Gaston, Noel, and Tomoka Kishi. "Part-time Workers Doing Full-time Work in Japan." *Journal of the Japanese and International Economies* 21, no. 4 (2007): 435–54. doi:10.1016/j.jjie.2006.04.001.

Article in an Online Periodical

21. Lisa Scherzer, "Clearing Emotional Hurdles Leads to More Profits," *SmartMoney*, December 6, 2007, http://www.smartmoney.com/theproshop/index.cfm?story=20071206.

Scherzer, Lisa. "Clearing Emotional Hurdles Leads to More Profits." *SmartMoney*, December 6, 2007. http://www.smartmoney.com/theproshop/index.cfm?story=20071206.

Article Posted on a Wiki

22. "Hispanic Marketing Resources," The Biz Wiki, last modified September 10, 2007, accessed October 23, 2010, http://www.library.ohiou.edu/subjects/bizwiki/index.php/Latino_Marketing.

Postings to wikis are cited in text but are not included in the bibliography.

E-mail Message and Other Personal Communications

23. Ari Kalil, "Customer Satisfaction Survey," e-mail message to author, January 12, 2010.

E-mail messages and other personal communications, such as letters and conversations, received by an author are usually cited in text; they are generally not included in bibliographies.

Online Posting (Lists, Forums, Discussion Boards)

24. Sandy Harris to TECHWR-L discussion list, December 5, 2007, http://www.techwr-l.com/techwhirl.

Online postings to e-mail lists, online forums, and discussion boards are cited in text; they are generally not included in bibliographies.

Blog Entry

Put the title of the blog entry in quotation marks followed by the name of the blog in italics. Include "(blog)" after the name if the word "blog" is not part of the name of the blog.

25. Barbara Brynko, "Weathering Turbulent Times." *Infotoday Blog*, http://www.infotodayblog.com/2009/11/30/weathering -turbulent-times.

Brynko, Barbara. "Weathering Turbulent Times." *Infotoday Blog*. http://www.infotodayblog.com/2009/11/30/weathering -turbulent-times.

MULTIMEDIA SOURCES (Print and Electronic)
Film, Video, or Podcast

26. *Super Sales Presentations: How to Captivate Your Prospects in a Distracted, Preoccupied World*, hosted by Patricia Fripp, directed by Michael Jeffreys (Waterford, MI: Seminars on DVD, 2007), DVD.

Super Sales Presentations: How to Captivate Your Prospects in a Distracted, Preoccupied World. Hosted by Patricia Fripp. Directed by Michael Jeffreys. Waterford, MI: Seminars on DVD, 2007. DVD.

27. "National Debt Impact on National Security," Iowa Public Television, December 12, 2007, http://www.youtube.com/ watch?v=hW1UCvqWY2E.

Iowa Public Television. "National Debt Impact on National Security." December 12, 2007. http://www.youtube.com/ watch?v=hW1UCvqWY2E.

Radio or Television Program

28. Sarah Gardner, "Plug-in Hybrids Need More Juice," *Marketplace*, American Public Media, podcast audio, December 5, 2007, http://marketplace.publicradio.org/display/web/2007/12/05/plug _in_car.

Gardner, Sarah. "Plug-in Hybrids Need More Juice." *Marketplace*. American Public Media. Podcast audio. December 5, 2007. http:// marketplace.publicradio.org/display/web/2007/12/05/plug_in _car.

29. "Yahoo! and China," *Lou Dobbs Tonight*, CNN, November 7, 2007.

"Yahoo! and China." *Lou Dobbs Tonight*. CNN. November 7, 2007.

D

CMS

OTHER SOURCES
Visual from a Secondary Source

The *CMS* classifies visuals as tables and illustrations (illustrations, or figures, include paintings, photographs, drawings, maps, and charts). If a table or an illustration is under **copyright,** follow the citation requirements of the copyright owner. If a table or an illustration is not under copyright, cite the artist or author (if available), title of work, and publication details in the source line, placed directly below the visual. A separate footnote is not needed. See also **visuals.**

Source: Reproduced by permission of the publisher from Jo Mackiewicz, "Compliments and Criticisms in Book Reviews about Business Communication," *Journal of Business and Technical Communication* 21, no. 2 (2007): 205, table 7, © 2007 by SAGE Publications.

Source: "Global Warming Effects" [map], *National Geographic,* n.d., http://green.nationalgeographic.com/environment/ global-warming/gw-impacts-interactive.html?fs=plasma .nationalgeographic.com (accessed January 22, 2010).

Include a full citation in the bibliography.

Mackiewicz, Jo. "Compliments and Criticisms in Book Reviews about Business Communication." *Journal of Business and Technical Communication* 21, no. 2 (2007): 205, table 7.

"Global Warming Effects." Map. *National Geographic,* n.d. http:// green.nationalgeographic.com/environment/global-warming/ gw-impacts-interactive.html?fs=plasma.nationalgeographic.com (accessed January 22, 2010).

See also Ethics Note on page 169.

Published Interview

30. Jack Pitney, "Q & A," interview, *Automobile,* January 2008, 66.

Pitney, Jack. "Q & A." Interview. *Automobile,* January 2008, 66.

Personal Interview

31. Mahmood Sariolgholam, interview by author, January 29, 2010, Berkeley, CA.

Sariolgholam, Mahmood. Interview by author. January 29, 2010. Berkeley, CA.

Personal Letter

32. Monica Pascatore, letter to author, April 10, 2010.

Personal letters should rarely be listed in a bibliography.

Brochure or Pamphlet

33. Library of Congress, U.S. Copyright Office, *Copyright Basics* (Washington, DC: GPO, 2007), 4.

Library of Congress. U.S. Copyright Office. *Copyright Basics.* Washington, DC: GPO, 2007.

Government Document

34. U.S. Department of Labor, Bureau of Labor Statistics, *Highlights of Women's Earnings in 2006* (Washington, DC: GPO, 2007), 17.

U.S. Department of Labor, Bureau of Labor Statistics. *Highlights of Women's Earnings in 2006.* Washington, DC: GPO, 2007.

Report

35. Walter Ditch, *XML-Based Office Document Standards* (Bristol, UK: Higher Education Funding Council for England, 2007), 86–116.

Ditch, Walter. *XML-Based Office Document Standards.* Bristol, UK: Higher Education Funding Council for England, 2007.

CMS *Sample Pages*

D

CMS

Author's last name (optional) and page number.

Litzinger 14

This report examines the nature and disposition of the 3,458 ethics

One-inch margins. Text double-spaced.

cases handled companywide by CGF's ethics officers and managers during 2011. The purpose of such reports is to provide the Ethics and Business Conduct Committee with the information necessary for assessing the effectiveness of the first year of CGF's Ethics Program.[1] According to Matthias Jonas, recommendations are given for consideration "in planning for the second year of the Ethics Program."[2]

The Office of Ethics and Business Conduct was created to administer the Ethics Program. The director of the Office of Ethics and Business Conduct was given the responsibility for the following objectives, as described by Rossouw:

Long quote indented, set in smaller font size, without quotation marks.

Communicate the values, standards, and goals of CGF's Program to employees. Provide companywide channels for employee education and guidance in resolving ethics concerns. Implement companywide programs in ethics awareness and recognition. Employee accessibility to ethics information and guidance is the immediate goal of the Office of Business Conduct in its first year.[3]

The purpose of the Ethics Program, according to Jonas, is to "promote ethical business conduct through open communication and compliance with company ethics standards."[4] To accomplish this

Raised superscripts in text correspond to footnotes or endnotes. First line of each entry indents five spaces.

1. W. C. Davis, Roland Marks, and Diane Tegge, *Working in the System: Five New Management Principles* (New York: St. Martin's, 2008), 142.
2. Matthias Jonas, "The Internet and Ethical Communication: Toward a New Paradigm," *Journal of Ethics and Communication* 32 (Fall 2008): 152.
3. George J. Rossouw, "Business Ethics in South Africa," *Journal of Business Ethics* 16, no. 14 (2001): 1543.
4. Matthias Jonas, "Ethics in Organizational Communication: A Review of the Literature," *Journal of Ethics and Communication* 29 (Summer 2010): 89.

FIGURE D–6. *CMS* Sample Page from Report

Litzinger 21

Bibliography Heading centered.

List alphabetized by authors' last names and double-spaced.

Davis, W. C., Roland Marks, and Diane Tegge. *Working in the*
     System: Five New Management Principles. New York:
     St. Martin's, 2008.

International Business Ethics Institute. Accessed January 14,
     2010. http://www.business-ethics.org/.

Jonas, Matthias. "Ethics in Organizational Communication: A
     Review of the Literature." *Journal of Ethics and Com-*
     munication 29 (Summer 2010): 79–99.

Hanging-indent style used for entries.

———. "The Internet and Ethical Communication: Toward a
     New Paradigm." *Journal of Ethics and Communication*
     32 (Fall 2008): 147–77.

National Science Foundation. *Conflicts of Interest and Stan-*
     dards of Ethical Conduct. NSE Manual No. 15. Arling-
     ton, VA: National Science Foundation, 2011.

Rossouw, George J. "Business Ethics in South Africa." *Jour-*
     nal of Business Ethics 16, no. 14 (2001): 1539–47.

Sariolgholam, Mahmood. Interview by author. January 29,
     2010. Berkeley, CA.

Schipper, Fritz. "Transparency and Integrity: Contrary Con-
     cepts?" In *Globalisation and Business Ethics*, edited by
     Karl Homann, Peter Koslowski, and Christoph Luetge,
     101–18. Burlington, VT: Ashgate, 2011.

Smith, Terrence. "Legislating Ethics." *NewsHour Business*
     Ethics Anthology. DVD. Hosted by Jim Lehrer. Encino,
     CA: Business Training Media, 2010.

FIGURE D–7. *CMS* Sample Bibliography

MLA Documentation

MLA In-Text Citations. The MLA parenthetical citation within the text of a paper gives a brief citation—in parentheses—of the author and relevant page numbers, separated only by a space.

D

MLA

> ▶ Achieving results is one thing while maintaining results is another because "like marathon runners, companies hit a performance wall" (Studer 3).

If the author is cited in the text, include only the page number(s) in parentheses.

> ▶ As Studer writes, the poor performance of a few employees will ultimately affect the performance—and the morale—of all the employees (8).

When citing Web sites where no author or page reference is available, provide a short title of the work—in parentheses.

> ▶ In 1810, Peter Durand invented the can, which was later used to provide soldiers and explorers canned rations and ultimately "saved legions from sure starvation" ("Forgotten Inventors").

If the parenthetical citation refers to a long, indented quotation, place it outside the punctuation of the last sentence.

> ▶ . . . a close collaboration with the nursing staff and the hospital bed safety committee is essential. (Jackson 208)

If no author is named or if you are using more than one work by the same author, give a shortened version of the title in the parenthetical citation, unless you name the title in the text (a "signal phrase"). A citation for Quint Studer's book *Results That Last: Hardwiring Behaviors That Will Take Your Company to the Top* would appear as (Studer, *Results* 93).

MLA Documentation Models

PRINTED BOOKS
Single Author

Taleb, Nassim Nicholas. *The Black Swan: The Impact of the Highly Improbable.* New York: Random, 2007. Print.

Multiple Authors

Jones, Ellis, Ross Haenfler, and Brett Johnson. *Better World Handbook: Small Changes That Make a Big Difference.* Gabriola Island: New Society, 2007. Print.

Multiple Books by Same Author

List the works in alphabetical order by title.

Orman, Suze. *The Money Book for the Young, Fabulous and Broke.* New
York: Riverhead, 2005. Print.

———. *Women and Money: Owning the Power to Control Your Destiny.*
New York: Spiegel, 2007. Print.

D

MLA

Corporate Author

J. K. Lasser Institute. *J. K. Lasser's Your Income Tax 2010: For Preparing
Your 2009 Tax Return.* New York: Wiley, 2009. Print.

Edition Other Than First

Kouzes, James M., and Barry Z. Posner. *The Leadership Challenge.*
4th ed. New York: Wiley, 2007. Print.

Multivolume Work

Standard and Poor. *Standard and Poor's Register of Corporations,
Directors, and Executives.* Vol. 1. New York: Standard and Poor,
2010. Print.

Work in an Edited Collection

Sen, Amartya. "Education and Standards of Living." *Philosophy of
Education: An Anthology.* Ed. Randall Curren. Malden: Blackwell,
2007. 95-101. Print.

Encyclopedia or Dictionary Entry

Gibbard, Bruce G. "Particle Detector." *World Book Encyclopedia.* 2007.
Print.

ARTICLES IN PRINTED PERIODICALS (*See also* Electronic Sources)
Magazine Article

McGirt, Ellen. "Facebook Opens Up." *Fast Company* Nov. 2007: 54-89.
Print.

Journal Article

Valentine, Sean, and Gary Fleischman. "Ethics Programs, Perceived
Corporate Social Responsibility, and Job Satisfaction." *Journal of
Business Ethics* 77.1 (2008): 159-72. Print.

Newspaper Article

Chazan, Guy. "Can Wind Power Find Footing in the Deep?" *Wall Street
Journal* 29 Nov. 2007: B1+. Print.

Article with an Unknown Author

"All the Right Moves for 2008." *Money* Dec. 2007: 96-102. Print.

ELECTRONIC SOURCES

The MLA recommends that, at minimum, references to online sources provide the author's name (whenever possible), a title for the article (in quotation marks), the title of the Web site (italicized), the name of the publisher or sponsor of the Web site, the publication date (posted or updated), the medium (Web), and the date of access.

Entire Web Site

Association for Business Communication. Assn. for Business Communication, 2008. Web. 18 Mar. 2008.

Online Book

Sowell, Thomas. *Basic Economics: A Common Sense Guide to the Economy.* 4th ed. New York: Basic, 2010. *Google Book Search.* Web. 12 Oct. 2010.

Short Work from a Web Site, with an Author

Calore, Michael. "Personalize Your Map with a Custom Map Marker." *Webmonkey.* Condé Nast Digital, 7 Oct. 2010. Web. 18 Oct. 2010.

Short Work from a Web Site, with a Corporate or an Organizational Author

General Motors. "Company Profile." *General Motors.* General Motors Co., 2010. Web. 8 Nov. 2010.

Short Work from a Web Site, with an Unknown Author

"Timeline: Alaska Pipeline Chronology." *American Experience.* WGBH, 4 Apr. 2006. Web. 22 Mar. 2010.

Article or Other Work from a Database

Gaston, Noel, and Tomoka Kishi. "Part-time Workers Doing Full-time Work in Japan." *Journal of the Japanese and International Economies* 21.4 (2007): 435-54. *Business Source Premier.* Web. 25 Oct. 2010.

Article in an Online Periodical

Scherzer, Lisa. "Clearing Emotional Hurdles Leads to More Profits." *SmartMoney.* Dow Jones, 6 Dec. 2007. Web. 25 Oct. 2010.

Article Posted on a Wiki

"Hispanic Marketing Resources." *Biz Wiki.* Ohio U. Lib., 10 Sept. 2007. Web. 9 Dec. 2010.

E-mail Message

Kalil, Ari. "Customer Satisfaction Survey." Message to the author. 12 Jan. 2010. E-mail.

Online Posting (Lists, Forums, Discussion Boards)

Harris, Sandy. "Camera Manual Comments." *TECHWR-L*. N.p., 5 Dec. 2007. Web. 8 Feb. 2010.

Blog Entry

Ojala, Marydee. "EPA Comes to SLA." *Infotoday Blog*. Information Today, 7 June 2007. Web. 12 Sept. 2010.

Publication on CD-ROM

Tapscott, Don, and Anthony D. Williams. *Wikinomics: How Mass Collaboration Changes Everything*. Old Saybrook: Tantor, 2007. CD-ROM.

MULTIMEDIA SOURCES (Print and Electronic)
Film, Video, or Podcast

Super Sales Presentations: How to Captivate Your Prospects in a Distracted, Preoccupied World. Dir. Michael Jeffreys. Perf. Patricia Fripp. Waterford: Seminars on DVD, 2007. DVD.

Iowa Public Television. "National Debt Impact on National Security." *YouTube*. 12 Dec. 2007. Web. 13 Oct. 2010.

Radio or Television Program

Treat a program that you listen to or view online as a short work from a Web site.

Gardner, Sarah. "Plug-in Hybrids Need More Juice." *Marketplace*. Host Tess Vigeland. Amer. Public Media, 5 Dec. 2007. Web. 11 Feb. 2010.

"Yahoo! and China." *Lou Dobbs Tonight*. Host Lou Dobbs. CNN. 7 Nov. 2007. Television.

Television Interview

Khazaee, Mohammad. Interview by Charlie Rose. *Charlie Rose Show*. PBS. WNET, New York. 6 Dec. 2007. Television.

OTHER SOURCES
Visual from a Secondary Source

Tables and figures (graphs, charts, maps, photographs, and drawings) are classified as visuals in MLA style. Cite the artist or author (if available), title of visual (italicized), type of visual, the original publication date (if available), and the institution where it is located (if applicable). Follow with identifying information about the medium (Print, Web, Television, CD, Film, etc.) in which the visual appeared. The in-text citation should include a source line placed directly below the visual, as shown in the following example. See also **visuals**.

Jo Mackiewicz, "Compliments and Criticisms in Book Reviews about Business Communication." *Journal of Business and Technical Communication* 21.2 (2007): 205. Print.

Mackiewicz, Jo. "Criticism Mitigation Strategies." Chart. *Journal of Business and Technical Communication* 21.2 (2007): 205. Print.

"Global Warming Effects." Map. *National Geographic*. Natl. Geographic Soc., n.d. Web. 22 Sept. 2010.

See also Ethics Note on page 169.

Interview

Pitney, Jack. "Q & A." *Automobile* Jan. 2008: 66. Print.

Personal Interview

Andersen, Elizabeth. Personal interview. 29 Nov. 2007.

Personal Letter

Pascatore, Monica. Letter to the author. 10 Apr. 2008.

Brochure or Pamphlet

Library of Congress. US Copyright Office. *Copyright Basics*. Washington: GPO, 2010. Print.

Government Document

United States. Dept. of Labor. Bureau of Labor Statistics. *Highlights of Women's Earnings in 2006*. Rept. No. 1000. Washington: GPO, 2007. Print.

Report

Ditch, Walter. *XML-Based Office Document Standards*. Bristol, Eng.: Higher Educ. Funding Council for England, 2007. Print.

Lecture or Speech

Nicholas, Ilene M., Demarest Hall, Hobart and William Smith Colls., Geneva. 3 May 2008. Lecture.

Yaden, Ryan. "Evolving Architecture around the Globe." Boston Soc. of Architects Lecture Ser. Boston Public Lib. 28 May 2008. Lecture.

MLA Sample Pages

Author's last name and page number.

Litzinger 14

This report examines the nature and disposition of the 3,458 ethics cases handled companywide by CGF's ethics officers and managers during 2011. The purpose of such reports is to provide the Ethics

One-inch margins. Text double-spaced.

and Business Conduct Committee with the information necessary for assessing the effectiveness of the first year of CGF's Ethics Program (Davis, Marks, and Tegge 142). According to Matthias Jonas, recommendations are given for consideration "in planning for the second year of the Ethics Program" ("Internet" 152).

The Office of Ethics and Business Conduct was created to administer the Ethics Program. The director of the Office of Ethics and Business Conduct, along with seven ethics officers throughout CGF, was given the responsibility for the following objectives, as described by Rossouw:

Long quote indented one inch (or 10 spaces), double-spaced, without quotation marks.

> Communicate the values, standards, and goals of CGF's Program to employees. Provide companywide channels for employee education and guidance in resolving ethics concerns. Implement companywide programs in ethics awareness and recognition. Employee accessibility to ethics information and guidance is the immediate goal of the Office of Business Conduct in its first year. (1543)

The purpose of the Ethics Program, according to Jonas, is to "promote ethical business conduct through open communication and compliance with company ethics standards" ("Ethics" 89). To accomplish this purpose, any ethics policy must ensure confidentiality for anyone

In-text citations give author name and page number. Title used when multiple works by same author cited.

FIGURE D–8. MLA Sample Page from Report

Litzinger 21

Heading centered.

Works Cited

Davis, W. C., Roland Marks, and Diane Tegge. *Working in the*

System: Five New Management Principles. New York:

St. Martin's, 2008. Print.

International Business Ethics Institute. Intl. Business Ethics Inst.,

1994-2008. Web. 14 Jan. 2010.

Jonas, Matthias. "Ethics in Organizational Communication:

A Review of the Literature." *Journal of Ethics and*

Communication 29 (2010): 79-99. Print.

---. "The Internet and Ethical Communication: Toward a New

Paradigm." *Journal of Ethics and Communication* 32 (2008):

147-77. Print.

Rossouw, George J. "Business Ethics in South Africa." *Journal of*

Business Ethics 16.14 (2001): 1539-47. Print.

Sariolgholam, Mahmood. Personal interview. 29 Jan. 2012.

Schipper, Fritz. "Transparency and Integrity: Contrary Concepts?"

Globalisation and Business Ethics. Ed. Karl Homann, Peter

Koslowski, and Christoph Luetge. Burlington: Ashgate, 2011.

101-18. Print.

Smith, Terrence. "Legislating Ethics." *NewsHour Business Ethics*

Anthology. Host Jim Lehrer. DVD. Encino: Business

Training Media, 2010. DVD.

United States. Natl. Science Foundation. *Conflicts of Interest*

and Standards of Ethical Conduct. NSF Manual No. 15.

Arlington: Natl. Science Foundation, 2011. Print.

List alphabetized by authors' last names or title and double-spaced.

Hanging-indent style used for entries.

FIGURE D–9. MLA Sample List of Works Cited

❖ ETHICS NOTE Visuals under copyright require permission from copyright owners before they can be reproduced. Contact the publisher to find out what needs permission, how best to obtain it, and what information copyright owners require in source lines and reference entries. Source lines almost always require mention of permission from the copyright owner to reproduce. ❖

D

WEB LINK	Other Style Manuals and Documentation Systems

Many professional societies, publishing companies, and other organizations publish manuals that prescribe bibliographic reference formats for their publications or for publications in their fields. For example, the American Medical Association (AMA) publishes the *American Medical Association Manual of Style*. For links to style manuals and other documentation resources, see *bedfordstmartins.com/alred* and select *Links for Handbook Entries*.

double negatives

A double negative is the use of an additional negative word to reinforce an expression that is already negative. In writing and speech, avoid such constructions.

> UNCLEAR   We don't have none.
> [This sentence literally means that we have some.]
>
> CLEAR   We have none.

Barely, *hardly*, and *scarcely* cause problems because writers sometimes do not recognize that those words are already negative.

▶ The corporate policy ~~doesn't~~ hardly cover ^s the problem.

Not unfriendly, *not without*, and similar constructions are not double negatives because in such constructions two negatives are meant to suggest the gray area between negative and positive meanings. Be careful how you use such constructions; they can be confusing to the reader and should be used only if they serve a purpose.

▶ He is *not unfriendly*.
  [He is neither hostile nor friendly.]

▶ It is *not without* regret that I offer my resignation.
  [I have mixed feelings rather than only regret.]

The correlative **conjunctions** *neither* and *nor* may appear together in a clause without creating a double negative, so long as the writer does not attempt to use the word *not* in the same clause.

▶ It was ~~not,~~ *neither,* as a matter of fact, ~~neither~~ his duty nor his desire to dismiss the employee.

▶ It was not, as a matter of fact, ~~neither~~ *either* his duty ~~nor~~ *or* his desire to dismiss the employee.

▶ She ~~did not~~ neither ~~care~~ *cared* about nor ~~notice~~ *noticed* the error.

Negative forms are full of traps that often entice writers into **logic errors,** as illustrated in the following example:

ILLOGICAL   The book reveals *nothing* that has *not* already been published in some form, but some of it is, I believe, relatively unknown.

In this sentence, "some of it" logically can refer only to "*nothing* that has *not* already been published." The sentence can be corrected by stating the idea in more **positive writing.**

LOGICAL   Everything in the book has been published in some form, but some of it is, I believe, relatively unknown.

drawings

A drawing can depict an object's appearance and illustrate the steps in procedures or **instructions.** It can emphasize the significant parts or functions of a device or product, omit what is not significant, and focus on details or relationships that a **photograph** cannot reveal. Think about your need for drawings during your **preparation** and **research.** Include them in your outline, indicating approximately where each should be placed ("drawing of . . ." enclosed in brackets). For advice on integrating drawings into your text, see **outlining** and **visuals.**

The types of drawings discussed in this entry are conventional line drawings, exploded-view drawings, cutaway drawings, and clip-art images.

A conventional line drawing is appropriate if your **audience** needs an overview of a series of steps or an understanding of an object's appearance or construction, as in Figure D–10.

D

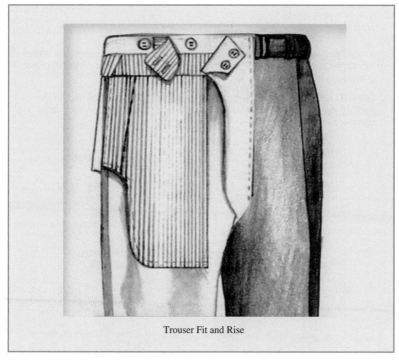

Trouser Fit and Rise

FIGURE D–10. Conventional Line Drawing Showing Custom Features

An exploded-view drawing, like that in Figure D–11, can be useful when you need to show the proper sequence in which parts fit together or to show the details of individual parts. Figure D–11 shows owners of a Xerox machine how to safely unpack the machine and its key parts.

A cutaway drawing, like the one in Figure D–12, can be useful when you need to show the internal parts of a device or structure and illustrate their relationship to the whole.

If you need only general-interest images to illustrate **newsletters** and **brochures** or to create **presentation** slides, use noncopyrighted clip-art drawings from your word-processing program or from thousands of noncopyrighted Web and library sources.

❖ ETHICS NOTE Do not use drawings from copyrighted sources without permission and proper documentation, including from the Web—the same copyright laws that apply to printed material also apply to Web-based graphics. See also **copyright**, **documenting sources**, and **plagiarism**. ❖

Installation

As you unpack the WorkCentre, familiarize yourself with its contents. After the WorkCentre is installed, and the Ready Indicator is lit, the WorkCentre is ready to make copies.

IMPORTANT: Save the carton and packing materials. They should be used to repack the WorkCentre if it has to be shipped for servicing or in case you move.

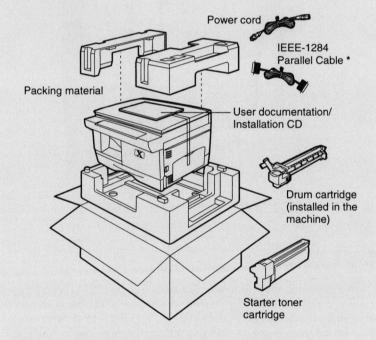

Power cord

IEEE-1284
Parallel Cable *

Packing material

User documentation/
Installation CD

Drum cartridge
(installed in the
machine)

Starter toner
cartridge

* Note: To ensure reliability of the WorkCentre, use the IEEE-1284 compliant parallel cable that is supplied with the machine. Only cables labeled "IEEE-1284" can be used with your WorkCentre.

FIGURE D–11. Exploded-View Drawing

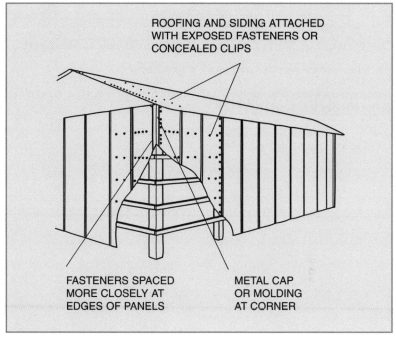

ROOFING AND SIDING ATTACHED
WITH EXPOSED FASTENERS OR
CONCEALED CLIPS

D

FASTENERS SPACED
MORE CLOSELY AT
EDGES OF PANELS

METAL CAP
OR MOLDING
AT CORNER

FIGURE D–12. Cutaway Drawing

WRITER'S CHECKLIST   Creating and Using Drawings

✔ Seek the help of graphics specialists for drawings that require a high degree of accuracy and precision.

✔ Show equipment and other objects from the point of view of the person who will use them.

✔ When illustrating a subsystem, show its relationship to the larger system of which it is a part.

✔ Draw the parts of an object in proportion to one another and identify any parts that are enlarged or reduced.

✔ When a sequence of drawings is used to illustrate a process, arrange them from left to right or from top to bottom on the page.

✔ Label parts in the drawing so that the text references to them are clear and consistent.

✔ Depending on the complexity of what is shown, label the parts themselves, as in Figure D–11, or use a key, as in Figure G–11 on page 259.

due to / because of

Due to (meaning "caused by") is acceptable following a linking **verb**.

▶ His absence was *due to* a work-related injury.

Due to is not acceptable, however, when it is used with a nonlinking verb to replace *because of*.

▶ He left work ~~due to~~ illness.
        because of

E

each

When *each* is used as a subject, it takes a singular **verb** or **pronoun**. ("*Each* of the reports *is* to be submitted ten weeks after *it* is assigned.") When *each* refers to a plural subject, it takes a plural verb or pronoun. ("The reports *each have* company logos on *their* title pages.") See also **agreement** and **conciseness**.

economic / economical

Economic refers to the production, development, and management of material wealth. ("Tax rates have an *economic* impact on communities.") *Economical* simply means "not wasteful or extravagant." ("Employees should be as *economical* as possible in their equipment purchases.")

editing (*see both* revision *and* proofreading)

e.g. / i.e.

The abbreviation *e.g.* stands for the Latin *exempli gratia*, meaning "for example"; *i.e.* stands for the Latin *id est*, meaning "that is." Because the English expressions (*for example* and *that is*) are clear to all **readers**, avoid the Latin *e.g.* and *i.e.* **abbreviations** except to save space in notes and **visuals**. If you must use *i.e.* or *e.g.*, do not italicize either and punctuate them as follows. If *i.e.* or *e.g.* connects two independent clauses, a **semicolon** should precede it and a **comma** should follow it.

> ▶ The conference reflected international viewpoints; *e.g.*, speakers included Germans, Italians, Japanese, Chinese, and Americans.

If *i.e.* or *e.g.* connects a **noun** and an **appositive**, a comma should precede it and follow it.

▶ The conference included speakers from five countries, *i.e.*, Germany, Italy, Japan, China, and the United States.

ellipses

An ellipsis is the omission of words from quoted material; it is indicated by three spaced **periods** called *ellipsis points* (. . .). When you use ellipsis points, omit original punctuation marks, unless they are necessary for **clarity** or the omitted material comes at the end of a quoted sentence.

ORIGINAL TEXT	"Promotional material sometimes carries a fee, particularly in high-volume distribution to schools, although prices for these publications are much lower than the development costs when all factors are considered."
WITH OMISSION AND ELLIPSIS POINTS	"Promotional material sometimes carries a fee . . . although prices for these publications are much lower than the development costs. . . ."

Notice in the preceding example that the final period is retained and what remains of the quotation is grammatically complete. When the omitted part of the quotation is preceded by a period, retain the period and add the three ellipsis points after it, as in the following example.

ORIGINAL TEXT	"Of the 172 major ethics cases reported, 57 percent were found to involve unsubstantiated concerns. Misinformation was the cause of unfounded concerns of misconduct in 72 cases. Forty-four cases, or 26 percent of the total cases reported, involved incidents partly substantiated by ethics officers as serious misconduct."
WITH OMISSION AND ELLIPSIS POINTS	"Of the 172 major ethics cases reported, 57 percent were found to involve unsubstantiated concerns. . . . Forty-four cases, or 26 percent of the total cases reported, involved incidents partly substantiated by ethics officers as serious misconduct."

Do not use ellipsis points when the beginning of a quoted sentence is omitted. Notice in the following example that the comma is dropped to prevent a grammatical error. See also **quotations**.

▶ The ethics report states that "26 percent of the total cases reported involved incidents partly substantiated by ethics officers as serious misconduct."

e-mail

E

E-mail (or *email*) functions in the workplace as a medium to exchange information and share electronic files with colleagues, clients, and customers. Although e-mail messages may take the form of informal notes, you should follow the writing strategy and style described in **correspondence** because e-mail messages often function as business **letters** to those outside organizations and **memos** to those within organizations. Of course, memos and letters can also be attached to e-mails. This entry reviews topics that are specifically related to the medium of e-mail. See also **selecting the medium**.

Review and Confidentiality

E-mail is such a quick and easy way to communicate that you need to avoid the temptation of sending a first draft without revision. As with all correspondence, your message should include all crucial details and be free of grammatical or factual errors, ambiguities, or unintended implications. See **proofreading** and **spelling**.

Keep in mind that e-mail can be easily forwarded and that e-mail messages are never truly deleted. Most companies back up and save all their e-mail messages and are legally entitled to monitor e-mail use. Companies can be compelled, depending on circumstances, to provide e-mail and **instant messaging** logs in a court of law. Consider the content of all your messages in the light of these possibilities, and carefully review your text before you click "Send."

◀ PROFESSIONALISM NOTE Be especially careful when sending messages to superiors in your organization or to people outside the organization. Spending extra time reviewing your e-mail before you click "Send" can save you the embarrassment of misunderstandings caused by a carelessly written message. One helpful strategy is to write the draft and revise your e-mail before filling in the "To" line with the address of your recipient. Be careful as well to observe the rules of netiquette (Inter*net* + *etiquette*) in the *Writer's Checklist* that follows. ▶

E

✔ Review your organization's policy regarding the appropriate use of e-mail.

✔ Maintain a high level of professionalism in your use of e-mail.

- Do not forward jokes or *spam*, discuss office gossip, or use <u>biased language</u>.

- Do not send *flames* (e-mails that contain abusive, obscene, or derogatory language) to attack someone. See also <u>blogs and forums</u>.

- Do not use clever or hobby-related e-mail usernames (sushilover@ domain.com); professionals and companies often base them on personal names (msmith@domain.com).

✔ Provide a subject line that describes the topic and focus of your message (as described on pages 122–23) to help recipients manage their e-mail.

✔ Adapt forwarded messages: revise the subject line to reflect the current content and cut irrelevant previous text, based on your <u>purpose</u> and <u>context</u>.

✔ Use the "cc:" (courtesy copy) address line thoughtfully to keep others informed and follow your organization's practice or protocol for copying messages to others.

✔ Include a cover message for all e-mail messages with attachments ("Attached is a copy of my budget proposal for your review. . . .").

✔ Send a "courtesy response" informing someone when you need a few days or longer to reply to a request.

✔ Do not write in ALL UPPERCASE LETTERS or in all lowercase letters.

✔ Avoid abbreviations (BTW for *by the way*, for example) used in personal e-mail, chat rooms, and <u>text messaging</u>.

✔ Do not use emoticons (keyboard characters used for conveying emotions) in business and professional e-mail.

✔ Always sign the e-mail or use a signature block (see Figure E–1 on page 181) or both; doing so not only is polite but also avoids possible confusion.

❖ ETHICS NOTE The blind-copy (*bcc:*) function allows writers to send copies of an e-mail message to someone without the primary receiver's knowledge. For printed letters and memos, the bcc: notation serves the same function and thus appears only on the copy, not on the original.* The blind-copy function may be used ethically for e-mails to protect the privacy of the e-mail addresses for a large group of recipients. Use the bcc: notation with great care. Sending sensitive or confidential information to a third party without the original recipient's knowledge is unethical, as is the use of a blind copy to play office politics. ❖

E

Design Considerations

Most e-mail programs allow you to use typographical features, such as various fonts and bullets. These options, however, may display unpredictably with some e-mail systems and settings of clients and customers outside your organization. In such circumstances, set your e-mail preferences to send messages in "plain text" and consider using alternative highlighting devices. For example, capital letters or asterisks, used sparingly, can substitute for boldface, italics, and underlines as **emphasis**.

If you find that you need many special characters or design elements, consider preparing a document that you attach to an e-mail. Doing so will allow you to use formatted elements, such as bulleted **lists** and **tables** that do not transmit well in e-mail messages. Keep in mind the following additional design considerations when sending e-mail:

- Use short paragraphs to avoid dense blocks of text.
- Provide a brief paragraph overview at the top of messages that run longer than a screen of text.
- Place your response to someone else's message at the beginning (or top) of the e-mail window so that recipients can see your response immediately.

---

*The abbreviation "bcc:" originally referred to the term *blind carbon copy* when copies of letters could only be produced on a typewriter using carbon paper. The bcc: notation (*bcc: Dr. Brenda Shelton*) was separately typed on only the copied pages. Even though technology changed, the abbreviation bcc: was retained but is often defined as "blind courtesy copy."

E

DIGITAL TIP

Sharing Electronic Files

Large attachments to e-mails can slow the transmission speed of messages and clutter the in-boxes of your recipients. When you need to send large attachments or a collection of several attachments, consider an alternative: using one of the many free online services designed for archiving and sharing files. After uploading a file to a specialized Web site, you will be given a URL that you can share via e-mail, allowing your recipients to download the file at their convenience. Although these tools shouldn't be used for sensitive documents, they work well in most situations. For a list of tools to help you share large files, go to *bedfordstmartins.com/alred* and select *Digital Tips*, "Sharing Electronic Files."

Salutations, Closings, and Signature Blocks

An e-mail can function as a letter, memo, or personal note; therefore, you must adapt your salutation and complimentary closing to your **audience**. Unless your employer requires specific formats, use the following guidelines:

- When e-mail functions as a traditional letter, use the standard letter salutation (*Dear Ms. Tucker:* or *Dear Docuform Customer:*) and closing (*Sincerely,* or *Best wishes,*).

- When you send e-mail to individuals or small groups inside an organization, you may wish to adopt a more personal greeting (*Dear Andy,* or *Dear Project Colleagues,*).

- When e-mail functions as a personal note to a friend or close colleague, you can use an informal greeting or only a first name (*Hi Mike,* or *Hello Jenny,* or *Bill,*) and a closing (*Take care,* or *Best,*).

Be aware that, in some cultures, business correspondents do not use first names as freely as do American correspondents. See **international correspondence**.

Because e-mail does not provide letterhead with standard addresses and contact information, many companies and individual writers include signature blocks (also called *signatures*) at the bottom of their messages. Signature blocks, which writers can set to appear on every e-mail they send, supply information that company letterhead usually provides as well as appropriate links to Web sites. If your organization requires a certain format, adhere to that standard. The pattern shown in Figure E–1 is typical. For signature blocks, consider as well the following guidelines:

```
======================================
```
Daniel J. Vasquez, Benefits Manager   ←   Name and Title
Human Resources Department   ←   Department or Division
Fencon Insurance Corporation   ←   Company Name
P.O. Box 5413   Salinas, CA 93962   ←   Mailing Address
Off: 888-719-6620 Fax: 888-719-5500   ←   Phone and Fax
Web: www.fencon.com   ←   Web Address
```
======================================
```

FIGURE E–1. E-mail Signature Block

- Keep line length to 60 characters or fewer to avoid unpredictable line wraps.
- Test your signature block in plain-text e-mail systems to verify your format.
- Use highlighting cues, such as **hyphens**, equal signs, and white space, to separate the signature from the message.
- Avoid using quotations, aphorisms, proverbs, or other sayings from popular culture, religion, or poetry in professional signatures.

WRITER'S CHECKLIST   Managing Your E-mail and Reducing Overload

Given the high volume of e-mail in business, you need to manage your e-mail strategically.*

✔ Avoid becoming involved in an e-mail exchange if a phone call or meeting would be more efficient.

✔ Consider whether an e-mail message could prompt an unnecessary response from the recipient and make clear to the recipient whether you expect a response.

✔ Send a copy ("cc:") of an e-mail only when the person copied needs or wants the information.

✔ Review all messages on a subject before responding to avoid dealing with issues that are no longer relevant.

✔ Set priorities for reading e-mail by skimming sender names and subject lines as well as where you appear in a "cc:" address line.

✔ Check e-mail addresses before sending an e-mail and keep your addresses current.

(continued)

---

*For understanding the causes of e-mail overload, see Gail Fann Thomas and Cynthia L. King, "Reconceptualizing E-mail Overload," *Journal of Business and Technical Communication* 20, no. 3 (July 2006): 252–87.

E

Managing Your E-mail and Reducing Overload
(continued)

✔ Check your in-box regularly and try to clear it by the end of each day.

✔ Create e-mail folders using key topics and personal names to file messages.

✔ Copy yourself or save sent copies of important e-mail messages in your folders.

✔ Use the search command to find particular subjects and personal names.

✔ Print copies of messages or attachments that you need for meetings, files, or similar purposes.

emphasis

Emphasis is the principle of stressing the most important ideas in your writing. You can achieve emphasis through one or more of the following techniques: position, climactic order, sentence length, sentence type, active **voice**, **repetition**, **intensifiers**, direct statements, long **dashes**, and typographical devices.

Achieving Emphasis

Position.   Place the idea in a conspicuous position. The first and last words of a sentence, **paragraph**, or document stand out in readers' minds.

▶ Moon craters are important to understanding the earth's history because they reflect geological history.

The term *moon craters* is emphasized because it appears at the beginning of the sentence and *geological history* because it is at the end of the sentence. See also **subordination**.

Climactic Order.   List the ideas or facts within a sentence in sequence from least to most important, as in the following example. See also **lists**.

▶ The hostile takeover of the company will result in some employees being relocated to different cities, some being downgraded, and some being let go.

Sentence Length.   Vary sentence length strategically. A short sentence that follows a long sentence or a series of long sentences stands out in the reader's mind, as in the short sentence ("We must cut costs.") that ends the following paragraph. See **sentence construction**.

▶ We have already reviewed the problem the accounting department has experienced during the past year. We could continue to examine the causes of our problems and point an accusing finger at all the culprits beyond our control, but in the end it all leads to one simple conclusion. We must cut costs.

Sentence Type.   Vary sentences by the strategic use of a compound sentence, a complex sentence, or a simple sentence. See **sentence variety**.

▶ The report submitted by the committee was carefully illustrated, and it covered five pages of single-spaced copy.
[This compound sentence carries no special emphasis; it contains two coordinate independent clauses.]

▶ The committee's report, which was carefully illustrated, covered five pages of single-spaced copy.
[This complex sentence emphasizes the size of the report.]

▶ The carefully illustrated report submitted by the committee covered five pages of single-spaced copy.
[This simple sentence emphasizes that the report was carefully illustrated.]

Active Voice.   Use the active voice to emphasize the performer of an action: Make the performer the subject of the **verb**.

▶ Our department designed the new system.
[This sentence emphasizes *our department*, which is the performer and the subject of the verb, *designed*.]

Repetition.   Repeat key terms, as in the use of the word *remains* and the phrase *come and go* in the following sentence.

▶ Similarly, atoms *come and go* in a molecule, but the molecule *remains*; molecules *come and go* in a cell, but the cell *remains*; cells *come and go* in a body, but the body *remains*; persons *come and go* in an organization, but the organization *remains*.
—Kenneth Boulding, *Beyond Economics*

Intensifiers.   Although you can use intensifiers (*most, much, very*) for emphasis, this technique is so easily abused that it should be used with caution.

▶ The final proposal is *much* more persuasive than the first one.
[The intensifier *much* emphasizes the contrast.]

Direct Statements. Use direct statements, such as "most important," "foremost," or someone's name in a **direct address**.

▶ Most important, keep in mind that everything you do affects the company's bottom line.

▶ John, I believe we should rethink our plans.

Long Dashes. Use a dash to call attention to a particular word or statement.

▶ The job will be done—after we are under contract.

Typographical Devices. Use *italics*, **bold type**, <u>underlining</u>, and CAPITAL LETTERS—but use them sparingly because overuse can create visual clutter and cause readers to ignore truly important information. See also **capitalization**, **italics**, and **layout and design**.

English as a second language

DIRECTORY

Learning to write well in a second language takes a great deal of effort and practice. The most effective way to improve your command of written English is to read widely beyond the reports and professional articles your job requires, such as magazines, newspapers, articles, novels, biographies, and any other writing that interests you. In addition, listen carefully to native speakers on television, on radio, and in person. Do not hesitate to consult a native speaker of English, especially for important writing tasks, such as **e-mails**, **memos**, and **reports**. Focus on those particular areas of English that give you trouble. This entry covers several areas often confusing to nonnative speakers and writers of English. See also **global communication**.

Count and Mass Nouns

Count nouns refer to things that can be counted (*tables, pencils, projects, employees*). *Mass nouns* (also called *noncount nouns*) identify things that cannot be counted (*electricity, air, loyalty, information*).

This distinction can be confusing with words like *electricity* and *water*. Although we can count kilowatt-hours of electricity and bottles of water, counting becomes inappropriate when we use the words *electricity* and *water* in a general sense, as in "*Water* is an essential resource." Following is a list of typical mass **nouns**.

anger	education	money	technology
biology	equipment	news	transportation
business	furniture	oil	waste
clothing	health	precision	weather
coffee	honesty	research	work

The distinction between whether something can or cannot be counted determines the form of the noun to use (singular or plural), the kind of **article** that precedes it (*a, an, the*, or no article), and the kind of limiting **adjective** it requires (such as *fewer* or *less* and *much* or *many*). (See also **fewer / less**.) Notice that count and mass nouns are always common nouns, not proper nouns, such as the names of people.

Articles and Modifiers

The general rule is that every count noun must be preceded by an article (*a, an, the*), a demonstrative adjective (*this, that, these, those*), a possessive adjective (*my, your, her, his, its, their*), or some expression of quantity (such as *one, two, several, many, a few, a lot of, some, no*). The article, adjective, or expression of quantity appears either directly in front of the noun or in front of the whole noun phrase.

► Beth read *a* report last week. [article]

► *Those* reports Beth read were long. [demonstrative adjective]

► *Their* report was long. [possessive adjective]

► *Some* reports Beth read were long. [indefinite adjective]

The articles *a* and *an* are used with count nouns that refer to one item of the whole class of like items.

► Matthew has *a* pen.
[Matthew could have any pen.]

The article *the* is used with nouns that refer to a specific item that both the reader and the writer can identify.

► Matthew has *the* pen.
[Matthew has a specific pen that is known to both the reader and the writer.]

When making generalizations with count nouns, writers can either use *a* or *an* with a singular count noun or use no article with a plural count noun. Consider the following generalization using an article.

► *An* egg is a good source of protein. [any egg, all eggs, eggs in general]

However, the following generalization uses a plural count noun with no article.

► *Eggs* are good sources of protein. [any egg, all eggs, eggs in general]

When you are making a generalization with a mass noun, do not use an article in front of the mass noun.

► *Sugar* is bad for your teeth.

Gerunds and Infinitives

Nonnative writers of English are often puzzled by which form of a **verbal** (a **verb** used as another part of speech) to use when it functions as the direct object of a verb—or a **complement**. No structural rule exists for distinguishing between the use of an infinitive and a gerund as the object of a verb. Any specific verb may take an infinitive as its object, others may take a gerund, and yet others take either an infinitive or a gerund. At times, even the base form of the verb is used.

► He enjoys *working*. [gerund as a complement]

► She promised *to fulfill* her part of the contract. [infinitive as a complement]

► The president had the manager *assign* her staff to another project. [basic verb form as a complement]

To make such distinctions accurately, rely on what you hear native speakers use or what you read. You might also consult a reference book for ESL students.

Adjective Clauses

Because of the variety of ways adjective clauses are constructed in different languages, they can be particularly troublesome for nonnative writers of English. The following guidelines will help you form adjective clauses correctly.

Place an adjective clause directly after the noun it modifies.

who is standing across the room   •
► The tall woman is a vice president of the company ~~who is standing across the room.~~

The adjective clause *who is standing across the room* modifies *woman*, not *company*, and thus comes directly after *woman*.

Avoid using a relative pronoun with another pronoun in an adjective clause.

► The man who ~~he~~ sits at that desk is my boss.

Present Perfect Verb Tense

In general, use the present perfect **tense** to refer to events completed in the past that have some implication for the present.

PRESENT PERFECT   She *has performed* the experiment three times.
[She might perform it again.]

When a specific time is mentioned, however, use the simple past.

SIMPLE PAST   I *wrote* the letter yesterday morning.
[The action, *wrote*, does not affect the present.]

Use the present perfect with a *since* or *for* phrase to describe actions that began in the past and continue in the present.

► This company *has been* in business *for* seventeen years.

► This company *has been* in business *since* 1990.

Present Progressive Verb Tense

The present progressive tense is especially difficult for those whose native language does not use this tense. The present progressive tense is used to describe some action or condition that is ongoing (or in progress) in the present and may continue into the future.

PRESENT   I *am searching* for an error in the document.
PROGRESSIVE   [The search is occurring now and may continue.]

In contrast, the simple present tense more often relates to habitual actions.

SIMPLE PRESENT   I *search* for errors in my documents.
[I regularly search for errors, but I am not necessarily searching now.]

See ESL Tips for Using the Progressive Form in the entry **tense**.

ESL Entries

Most entries in this handbook may interest writers of English as a second language; however, the specific entries listed in the Contents by Topic under ESL Tips address issues that often cause problems.

WEB LINK	English as a Second Language

For Web sites and electronic grammar exercises intended for speakers of English as a second language, see *bedfordstmartins.com/alred* and select *Links for Handbook Entries* and *Exercise Central*.

English, varieties of

Written English includes two broad categories: standard and nonstandard. Standard English is used in business, industry, government, education, and all professions. It has rigorous and precise criteria for capitalization, punctuation, spelling, and usage. Nonstandard English does not conform to such criteria; it is often regional in origin, or it reflects the special usages of a particular ethnic or social group. As a result, although nonstandard English may be vigorous and colorful, its usefulness as a means of communication is limited to certain contexts and to people already familiar and comfortable with it in those contexts. It rarely appears in printed material except for special effect. Nonstandard English is characterized by inexact or inconsistent **capitalization**, **punctuation**, **spelling**, diction, and **usage** choices.

Colloquial English

Colloquial English is spoken English or writing that uses words and expressions common to casual conversation. ("We need to get him up to speed.") Colloquial English is appropriate to some kinds of writing (personal letters, notes, some **e-mail**) but not to most workplace writing.

Dialectal English

Dialectal English is a social or regional variety of the language that is comprehensible to people of that social group or region but may be incomprehensible to outsiders. Dialect, which is usually nonstandard English, involves distinct **word choice**, grammatical forms, and pronunciations. For example, residents of southern Louisiana who descended from French colonists speak a dialect often referred to as Cajun.

Localisms

A localism is a regional wording or phrasing. For example, a large sandwich on a long split roll is known in various regions of the United States as a *submarine, hero, hoagie, grinder, poor boy*, and *torpedo*. Such words normally should be avoided in workplace writing because not all readers will be familiar with the local meanings.

Slang

Slang is an informal vocabulary composed of **figures of speech** and colorful words used in humorous or extravagant ways. There is no objective test for slang, and many standard words are given slang applications. For instance, slang may be a familiar word used in a new way (*chill* meaning "relax") or it may be a new word (*wonk* meaning "someone who works or studies excessively").

Most slang is short-lived and has meaning only for a narrow **audience**. Sometimes, however, slang becomes standard because the word fills a legitimate need. *Skyscraper* and *date* (as in "go on a date"), for example, were once considered slang expressions. Nevertheless, although slang may be valid in informal and personal writing or fiction, it generally should be avoided in workplace writing. See also **jargon** and **business writing style**.

equal / unique / perfect

Logically, *equal* (meaning "having the same quantity or value as another"), *unique* (meaning "one of a kind"), and *perfect* (meaning "a state of highest excellence") are words with absolute meanings and therefore should not be compared. However, colloquial usage of *more* and *most* as **modifiers** of *equal, unique*, and *perfect* is so common that an absolute prohibition on such use is impossible.

▶ Our system is more unique [*or* more perfect] than theirs.

Some writers try to overcome the problem by using *more nearly* (*more nearly equal, more nearly unique, more nearly perfect*). When clarity and preciseness are critical, the use of comparative degrees with *equal, unique*, and *perfect* can be misleading. It is best to avoid using comparative degrees with absolute terms. See also **comparison**.

MISLEADING Ours is a *more equal* percentage split than theirs.

PRECISE Our percentage split is 51–49; theirs is 54–46.

etc.

Etc. is an abbreviation for the Latin *et cetera,* meaning "and others" or "and so on." Therefore, do not use the redundant phrase *and etc.* Likewise, do not use *etc.* at the end of a series introduced by the phrases *such as* and *for example*—those phrases already indicate unnamed items of the same category. Use *etc.* with a logical progression and when at least two items are named. Do not italicize *etc.*

▶ The sorting machine processes coins (~~for example~~ pennies, nickels, ~~and~~ etc.), and then packages them for redistribution.

Otherwise, avoid *etc.* because the reader may not be able to infer what other items a list might include.

VAGUE He will bring note pads, paper clips, etc., to the trade show.

CLEAR He will bring note pads, paper clips, and other office supplies to the trade show.

ethics in writing

Ethics refers to the choices we make that affect others for good or ill. Ethical issues are inherent in writing and speaking because what we write and say can influence others. Further, how we express ideas affects our audience's perceptions of us and our organization's ethical stance. See also **audience.**

❖ ETHICS NOTE Obviously, no book can describe how to act ethically in every situation, but this entry describes some typical ethical lapses to watch for during **revision.*** In other entries throughout this book, ethical issues are highlighted using the symbols surrounding this paragraph. ❖

Avoid language that attempts to evade responsibility. Some writers use the passive **voice** because they hope to avoid responsibility or to

---

*Adapted from Brenda R. Sims, "Linking Ethics and Language in the Technical Communication Classroom," *Technical Communication Quarterly* 2, no. 3 (Summer 1993): 285–99.

obscure an issue: "It has been decided" (*Who* has decided?) or "Several mistakes were made" (*Who* made them?).

Avoid deceptive language. Do not use words with more than one meaning to circumvent the truth. Consider the company document that stated, "A nominal charge will be assessed for using our facilities." When clients objected that the charge was actually very high, the writer pointed out that the word *nominal* means "the named amount" as well as "very small." In that situation, clients had a strong case in charging that the company was attempting to be deceptive. Various **abstract words**, technical and legal **jargon**, and **euphemisms** are unethical when they are used to mislead readers or to hide a serious or dangerous situation, even though technical or legal experts could interpret those words or terms as accurate. See also **word choice**.

Do not de-emphasize or suppress important information. Not including information that a reader would want to have, such as potential safety hazards or hidden costs for which a customer might be responsible, is unethical and possibly illegal. Likewise, do not hide information in dense paragraphs of **gobbledygook** with small type and little white space, as is common in credit-card contracts. Use **layout and design** features such as type size, bullets, **lists**, and footnotes to highlight information that is important to readers.

Do not mislead with partial or self-serving information. For example, avoid the temptation to highlight a feature or service that readers would find attractive but that is available only with some product models or at extra cost. (See also **logic errors** and **positive writing**.) Readers could justifiably object that you have given them a false impression to sell them a product or service, especially if you also deemphasize the extra cost or other special conditions.

In general, treat others—individuals, companies, groups—with fairness and with respect. Avoid language that is biased, racist, or sexist or that perpetuates stereotypes. See also **biased language**.

Finally, be aware that both **plagiarism** and violations of **copyright** not only are unethical but also can have serious professional and legal consequences for you in the classroom and on the job.

WRITER'S CHECKLIST   Writing Ethically

Ask yourself the following questions:

✔ *Am I willing to take responsibility, publicly and privately, for what I have written?* Make sure you can stand behind what you have written.

✔ *Is the document or message honest and truthful?* Scrutinize findings and conclusions carefully. Make sure that the data support them.

(continued)

E

WRITER'S CHECKLIST   **Writing Ethically** *(continued)*

✔ *Am I acting in my employer's, my client's, the public's, or my own best long-term interest?* Have an impartial and appropriate outsider review and comment on what you have written.

✔ *Does the document or message violate anyone's rights?* If information is confidential and you have serious concerns, consider a review by the company's legal staff or an attorney.

✔ *Am I ethically consistent in my writing?* Apply consistently the principles outlined here and those you have assimilated throughout your life to meet this standard.

✔ *What if everybody acted or communicated in this way?* If you were the intended reader, consider whether the message would be acceptable and respectful.

If the answers to these questions do not come easily, consider asking a trusted colleague to review and comment on what you have written.

---

euphemisms

A euphemism is an inoffensive substitute for a word or phrase that could be distasteful, offensive, or too blunt: *passed away* for *died*; *previously owned* or *preowned* for *used*; *lay off* or *restructure* for *fire* or *terminate* employees. Used judiciously, euphemisms can help you avoid embarrassing or offending someone.

❖ ETHICS NOTE Euphemisms can also hide the facts of a situation (*incident* or *event* for *accident*) or be a form of **affectation** if used carelessly. Avoid them especially in **international correspondence** and other forms of **global communication** where their meanings could be not only confusing but also misleading. See also **ethics in writing**. ❖

---

everybody / everyone

Both *everybody* and *everyone* are usually considered singular and take singular **verbs** and **pronouns**.

▶ *Everyone* here *leaves* at 4:30 p.m.

▶ *Everybody* at the meeting presented *his or her* individual assessment.

However, the meaning can be obviously plural.

▶ *Everyone* thought the plan should be rejected, and I really couldn't blame *them*.

Although normally written as one word, write it as two words if you wish to emphasize each individual in a group. ("*Every one* of the team members contributed to this discovery.") See also **agreement**.

E

exclamation marks

The exclamation mark (!) indicates strong feeling, urgency, elation, or surprise ("Hurry!" "Great!" "Wow!"). (See also **interjections**.) However, it cannot make an argument more convincing, lend force to a weak statement, or call attention to an intended irony.

An exclamation mark can be used after a whole sentence or an element of a sentence.

▶ This meeting—please note it well!—concerns our budget deficit.

When used with **quotation marks**, the exclamation mark goes outside, unless what is quoted is an exclamation.

▶ The paramedic shouted, "Don't touch the victim!" The bystander then, according to a witness, "jumped like a kangaroo"!

In **instructions**, the exclamation mark is often used in cautions and warnings ("Danger!" "Stop!"). See also **emphasis**.

executive summaries

An executive summary consolidates the principal points of a **formal report** or other long document. Executive summaries differ from **abstracts** in that **readers** scan abstracts to decide whether to read the work in full. However, an executive summary may be the only section of a longer work read by many readers, so it must accurately and concisely represent the original document. It should restate the document's **purpose**, **scope**, methods, findings, **conclusions**, and recommendations, as well as summarize how results were obtained or the reasons for the recommendations. Executive summaries tend to be about 10 percent of the length of the documents they summarize and generally follow the same sequence.

Write the executive summary so that it can be read independently of the report or proposal. Executive summaries may occasionally include a figure, table, or footnote—if that information is essential to the summary. However, do not refer by number to figures, tables, or references contained elsewhere in the document. See Figure F–6 (pages 219–20), which is an executive summary of a report on the disposition of ethics cases in an aircraft corporation.

E

| **WRITER'S CHECKLIST**   Writing Executive Summaries |

✔ Write the executive summary after you have completed the original document.

✔ Avoid or define terminology that may not be familiar to your intended **audience**.

✔ Spell out all uncommon symbols and **abbreviations**.

✔ Make the summary concise, but do not omit transitional words and phrases (*however, moreover, therefore, for example, next*).

✔ Include only information discussed in the original document.

✔ Place the executive summary at the very beginning of the body of the report, as described in **formal reports**.

expletives

An expletive is a word that fills the position of another word, phrase, or clause. *It* and *there* are common expletives.

▶ *It* is certain that he will be promoted.

In the example, the expletive *it* occupies the position of subject in place of the real subject, *that he will be promoted*. Expletives are sometimes necessary to avoid **awkwardness**, but they are commonly overused, and most sentences can be better stated without them.

> Many   were
▶ ~~There were many~~ files lost when we converted to the new server.

In addition to its grammatical use, the word *expletive* means a profane exclamation or oath.

explicit / implicit

An *explicit* statement is one expressed directly, with precision and clarity.

> ► He gave us *explicit* directions to the Wausau facility.

An *implicit* meaning is one that is not directly expressed.

> ► Although the CEO did not mention the lawsuit directly, the company's commitment to ethical practices was *implicit* in her speech.

exposition

Exposition, or *expository writing*, informs **readers** by presenting facts and ideas in direct and concise language; it usually relies less on colorful or figurative language than writing meant to be expressive or persuasive. Expository writing attempts to explain to readers what the subject is, how it works, and how it relates to something else. Exposition is aimed at the readers' understanding rather than at their imagination or emotions; it is a sharing of the writer's knowledge. Exposition aims to provide accurate, complete information and to analyze it for the readers. See also **audience**.

Because it is the most effective form of discourse for explaining difficult subjects, exposition is widely used in **reports, memos,** and other types of business writing. To use exposition effectively, you must have a thorough knowledge of your subject. As with all writing, how much of that knowledge you convey depends on the reader's needs and your **purpose**.

F

fact

Expressions containing the word *fact* ("due to the *fact* that," "except for the *fact* that," "as a matter of *fact*," or "because of the *fact* that") are often wordy substitutes for more accurate terms.

> *Because*
> ► ~~Due to the fact that~~ the sales force has a high turnover rate, sales
> have declined.

Do not use the word *fact* to refer to matters of judgment or opinion.

> *In my opinion,*
> ► ~~It is a fact that~~ sales are poor in the Midwest because of insufficient
> market research.

The word *fact* is, of course, valid when facts are what is meant.

> ► Our tests uncovered numerous facts to support your conclusion.

See also **conciseness** and **logic errors**.

FAQs (Frequently Asked Questions)

An FAQ is a **list** of questions, paired with their answers, that readers will likely ask about products, services, or other information presented on a Web site or in customer-oriented documents. By presenting commonly sought information in one place, FAQs save readers from searching through an entire Web site or document to find what they need.

A good FAQ list can help create a positive impression with customers or clients because the writer is acknowledging that their time is valuable. An FAQ list also helps a company spend less time answering phone calls and **e-mail** questions by anticipating customer needs and providing important information in a simple, a logical, and an organized format. However, an FAQ list is not a substitute for solving problems with a product or service.

❖ ETHICS NOTE If customers are experiencing numerous problems because of a product design or programming flaw, you need to work with
your company's product developers to correct the problem rather than
try to avoid addressing the problem by hiding it within an FAQ. ❖

Questions to Include

Develop the list of questions and their answers by brainstorming with
colleagues who regularly are in contact with customers. If customers
frequently ask about company stock information and request **annual
reports**, for example, your FAQ list could include the question "How
do I obtain a copy of your latest annual report?" This question can
be followed with a brief answer that includes the Web address where
the annual report can be downloaded or the name, phone number, and
e-mail address of the person who distributes the annual reports. See
also **writing for the Web**.

Organization

Organize the list so that readers can find the information they need
quickly and easily. List your questions in decreasing **order of importance** for your readers so that they can obtain the most important information first. If you have a number of questions that are related to a
specific topic, such as investor relations, product returns, or completing forms, group them into categories and identify each category with a
heading, such as "Investor Relations," "Shipping," and "Forms." You
may also want to create a **table of contents** at the top of the FAQ page
so that readers can quickly find the topics relevant to their interests.

Study other FAQs for products or services similar to yours. Analyze
these FAQs to help you in your approach and organization: Can you
find answers quickly, or do you need to scroll through many pages to
find them? Are the questions with their answers separated into logical
categories or listed in random order? Is it easy to differentiate the question from the answer? Do the answers provide too little or too much
information?*

Placement

The location of your FAQ list should enable readers to find answers
quickly. For Web sites, an FAQ page is usually linked from the homepage either in a directory or with a text link for easy access. In small

*For examples of FAQs, search with QueryCAT at *www.querycat.com*, which offers
the "largest database of frequently asked questions."

printed documents, such as **brochures**, FAQs are usually highlighted and placed after the standard information in the body of the document.

F

WRITER'S CHECKLIST   Developing an FAQ

✔ *Focus on your reader.* Write your questions and answers from a "**you**" **viewpoint** and with a positive, conversational **tone**.

✔ *Separate long FAQ lists.* Group related questions under topic **headings**. For long online FAQs, consider listing only questions and include links to separate pages, each containing an individual question and answer.

✔ *Distinguish questions from answers.* Use boldface for questions and use white space to separate questions from answers. Use sparingly multiple colors, **italics**, or other formatting styles that can make the list difficult to read.

✔ *Keep questions and answers concise.* If a question has a long answer, add a link to a separate Web page or refer to an appropriate page number in a printed document.

✔ *Keep the list updated.* Review and update FAQs at least monthly — or more frequently if your content changes often.

✔ *Give readers the opportunity to weigh in.* Provide an e-mail link for existing and possible customers to submit questions they would like to see added to the FAQ list.

---

fax (*see* selecting the medium)

feasibility reports

When organizations consider a new project—developing a new product or service, expanding a customer base, purchasing equipment, or moving operations—they first try to determine the project's chances for success. A feasibility report presents evidence about the practicality of a proposed project based on specific criteria. It answers such questions as the following: Is new construction or development necessary? Is sufficient staff available? What are the costs? Is funding available? What are the legal ramifications? Based on the findings of this analysis, the report offers logical conclusions and recommends whether the project should be carried out. When feasibility reports stress specific steps that should be taken as a result of a study of a problem or an issue, they are often referred to as *recommendation reports*. In the condensed feasibility report shown in Figure F–1, a consultant conducts a study to determine how to upgrade a company's computer system and Internet capability.

Before beginning to write a feasibility report, analyze the needs of the **audience** as well as the **context** and **purpose** of the study. Then write a purpose statement, such as "The purpose of this study is to determine

Introduction
The purpose of this report is to determine which of two proposed options would best enable Darnell Business Forms Corporation to upgrade its file servers and its Internet capacity to meet its increasing data and communication needs. . . .

Background.   In October 2010, the Information Development Group put the MACRON System into operation. Since then, the volume of processing transactions has increased fivefold (from 1,000 to 5,000 updates per day). This increase has severely impaired system response time; in fact, average response time has increased from 10 seconds to 120 seconds. Further, our new Web-based client-services system has increased exponentially the demand for processing speed and access capacity.

Scope.   We have investigated two alternative solutions to provide increased processing capacity: (1) purchase of an additional Aurora processor to supplement the one in operation and (2) purchase of an Icardo 60 with expandable peripherals to replace the Aurora processor currently in operation. The two alternatives are evaluated here, according to both cost and expanded capacity for future operations.

Additional Aurora Processor
Purchasing a second Aurora processor would require increased annual maintenance costs, salary for a second computer specialist, increased energy costs, and a one-time construction cost for necessary remodeling and installing Internet connections.

Annual maintenance costs	$35,000
Annual costs for computer specialist	75,000
Annual increased energy costs	7,500
Total annual operating costs	$117,500
Construction cost (one-time)	50,000
Total first-year costs	$167,500

The installation and operation of another Aurora processor are expected to produce savings in system reliability and readiness.

FIGURE F–1. Feasibility Report

F

System Reliability. An additional Aurora would reduce current downtime periods from four to two per week. Downtime recovery averages 30 minutes and affects 40 users. Assuming that 50 percent of users require system access at a given time, we determined that the following reliability savings would result:

2 downtimes × 0.5 hours × 40 users × 50% × $50/hour overtime × 52 weeks = $52,000 annual savings.

[The feasibility report would also discuss the second option— purchase of the Icardo 60 and its long-term savings.]

Conclusion
A comparison of costs for both systems indicates that the Icardo 60 would cost $2,200 more in first-year costs.

	Aurora	Icardo 60
Net additional operating costs	$56,300	$84,000
One-time construction costs	50,000	24,500
First-year total	$106,300	$108,500

Installation of an additional Aurora processor would permit the present information-processing systems to operate relatively smoothly and efficiently. It would not, however, provide the expanded processing capacity that the Icardo 60 processor would for implementing new subsystems required to increase processing speed and Internet access.

Recommendation
The Icardo 60 processor should be purchased because of the long-term savings and because its additional capacity and flexibility will allow for greater expansion in the future.

3

FIGURE F–1. Feasibility Report (*continued*)

the feasibility of expanding our Pacific Rim operations," to guide you or a collaborative team. See also **brainstorming** and **collaborative writing**.

Report Sections

Every feasibility report should contain an **introduction**, a body, a **conclusion**, and a recommendation. See also **proposals** and **formal reports**.

Introduction.   The introduction states the purpose of the report, describes the circumstances that led to the report, and includes any pertinent background information. It may also discuss the **scope** of the report, any procedures or methods used in the analysis of alternatives, and any limitations of the study.

Body.   The body of the report presents a detailed review of the alternatives for achieving the goals of the project. Examine each option according to specific criteria, such as cost and financing, availability of staff, and other relevant requirements, identifying the subsections with **headings** to guide readers.

Conclusion.   The conclusion interprets the available options and leads to one option as the best or most feasible.

Recommendation.   The recommendation section clearly presents the writer's (or team's) opinion on which alternative best meets the criteria as summarized in the conclusion.

WEB LINK	Feasibility Reports
For links to full feasibility reports, see *bedfordstmartins.com/alred* and select *Links for Handbook Entries.*	

few / a few

In certain contexts, *few* carries more negative overtones than does the phrase *a few*.

NEGATIVE   The report offers *few* helpful ideas.
POSITIVE   The report offers *a few* helpful ideas.

fewer / less

Fewer refers to items that can be counted (count **nouns**). ("*Fewer* employees retired than we expected.") *Less* refers to mass quantities or amounts (mass nouns). ("We had *less* rain this year than forecasts predicted.") See also **English as a second language**.

figuratively / literally

Literally means "actually" and is often confused with *figuratively*, which means "metaphorically." To say that someone "*literally* turned green with envy" would mean that the person actually changed color.

▶ In the winner's circle the jockey was, *figuratively* speaking, ten feet tall.

▶ When he said, "Let's bury our competitors," he did not mean it *literally*.

Avoid the use of *literally* to reinforce the importance of something.

▶ She was ~~literally~~ the best of the applicants.

See also **intensifiers**.

figures of speech

A figure of speech is an imaginative expression that often compares two things that are basically not alike but have at least one thing in common. For example, if a device is cone-shaped and has an opening at the narrow end, you might say that it looks like a volcano.

Figures of speech can clarify the unfamiliar by relating a new concept to one with which readers are familiar. In that respect, they help establish understanding between the specialist and the nonspecialist. (See **audience**.) Figures of speech can help translate the abstract into the concrete; in the process of doing so, they can also make writing more colorful and graphic. (See also **abstract / concrete words**.) A figure of speech must make sense, however, to achieve the desired effect.

ILLOGICAL   Without the fuel of tax incentives, our economic engine would operate less efficiently.
[An engine would not operate at all without fuel.]

Figures of speech also must be consistent to be effective.

▶ We must get our sales program *back on course*, and we are counting on you to ~~carry the ball.~~ *steer the effort.*

A figure of speech should not overshadow the point the writer is trying to make. In addition, it is better to use no figure of speech at all than to use a trite one. A surprise that comes "like a bolt out of the blue" seems stale and not much of a surprise. See also **clichés**.

Types of Figures of Speech

Analogies are comparisons that show the ways in which two objects or concepts are similar, often used to make one of them easier to understand. The following example explains a computer search technique by comparing it to the use of keywords in a dictionary.

> ► The search technique used in *indexed sequential processing* is similar to a search technique you might use to find the page on which a particular word is located in a dictionary. You might scan the keywords located at the top of each dictionary page that identify the first and last words on each page until you find the keywords that encompass the word you seek. Indexed sequential processing works the same way with computer files.

Hyperboles are gross exaggerations used to achieve an effect or **emphasis**.

> ► We were dead after working all night on the grant proposal.

Litotes are understatements, for emphasis or effect, achieved by denying the opposite of the point you are making.

> ► Over 1,600 pages is no small size for a book.

Metaphors are figures of speech that point out similarities between two things by treating them as though they were the same thing.

> ► The astronaut's *umbilical cord* carries life-sustaining oxygen for spacewalking.

Metonyms are figures of speech that use one aspect of a thing to represent it, such as *the blue* for the sky and *wheels* for a car.

> ► The economist predicted a decrease in *hard-hat* jobs.

Personification is a figure of speech that attributes human characteristics to nonhuman things or abstract ideas. We might refer, for example, to the *birth* of a planet or apply emotions to machines.

> ► She said that she was frustrated with the *stubborn* security system.

Similes are direct comparisons of two essentially unlike things, linking them with the word *like* or *as*.

> ► Reconstructing the plane's fuselage following the accident was *like piecing together a jigsaw puzzle.*

Avoid figures of speech in **global communication** and **international correspondence** because people in other cultures may translate figures of speech literally and be confused by their meanings.

fine

When used in expressions such as "I feel *fine*" or "a *fine* day," *fine* is colloquial and, like the word *nice*, is often too vague for business writing. Use the word *fine* to mean "refined," "delicate," or "pure."

F

- ▶ A *fine* film of oil covered the surface of the water.
- ▶ *Fine* crystal is made in Austria.
- ▶ The Court made a *fine* distinction between the two statutes.

first / firstly

First and *firstly* are both adverbs. Avoid *firstly* in favor of *first*, which sounds less stiff than *firstly*. The same is true of other ordinal **numbers**, such as *second*, *third*, and so on.

flowcharts

A flowchart is a diagram using symbols, words, or pictures to show the stages of a process in sequence from beginning to end. A flowchart provides an overview of a process and allows the **reader** to identify its essential steps quickly and easily. Flowcharts can take several forms. The steps might be represented by labeled blocks, as shown in Figure F–2; pictorial symbols, as shown in Figure F–3; or ISO (International Organization for Standardization) symbols, as shown in Figure F–4.

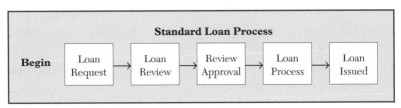

FIGURE F–2. Flowchart Using Labeled Blocks

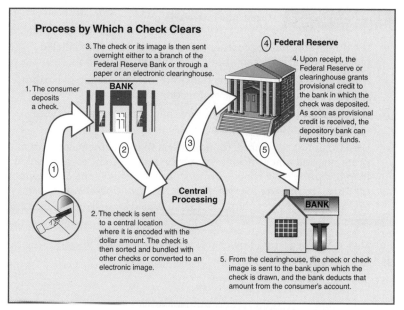

FIGURE F–3. Flowchart Using Pictorial Symbols

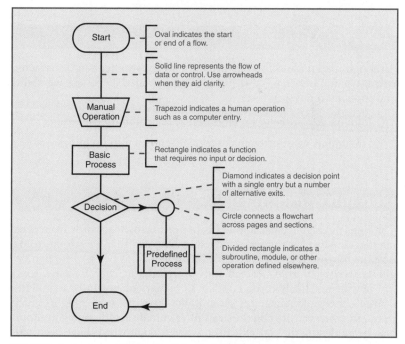

FIGURE F–4. Common ISO Flowchart Symbols (with Annotations)

WRITER'S CHECKLIST   Creating Flowcharts

✔ Label each step in the process or identify each step with labeled blocks, pictorial representations, or standardized symbols.

✔ Follow the standard flow directions: left to right and top to bottom. Indicate any nonstandard flow directions with arrows.

✔ Include a key (or call-outs) if the flowchart contains symbols your **audience** may not understand.

✔ Use standardized symbols for flowcharts that document computer programs and other information-processing procedures, as detailed in *Information Processing — Documentation Symbols and Conventions for Data, Program and System Flowcharts, Program Network Charts, and System Resources Charts*, ISO 5807-1985 (E).

For advice on integrating flowcharts into your text, see **visuals**. See also **global graphics**.

footnotes (*see* documenting sources)

forceful / forcible

Although *forceful* and *forcible* are both **adjectives** meaning "characterized by or full of force," *forceful* is usually limited to persuasive ability and *forcible* to physical force.

▶ John made a *forceful* presentation at the committee meeting.

▶ Firefighters must often make *forcible* entries into buildings.

foreign words in English

The English language has a long history of borrowing words from other languages. Most borrowing occurred so long ago that we seldom recognize the borrowed terms (also called *loan words*) as being of foreign origin (*kindergarten* from German, *animal* from Latin, *church* from Greek).

Words not likely to be familiar to **readers** or not fully assimilated into the English language are set in **italics** (*sine qua non, coup de grâce, in res, in camera*). Most dictionaries offer guidance, although you should also be guided by the **context**. Even when foreign words have been fully assimilated, they often retain their diacritical marks (*cliché, résumé, vis-à-vis*). As foreign words are absorbed into English, their plural forms give way to English plurals (*agenda* becomes *agendas* and *formulae* becomes *formulas*).

Generally, foreign expressions should be used only if they serve a real need. (See also **e.g. / i.e.** and **etc.**) The overuse of foreign words in an attempt to impress your reader or achieve elegance is **affectation**. Effective communication can be accomplished only if your readers understand what you write. So choose foreign expressions only when they make an idea clearer or when there is no English substitute (*Schadenfreude* for "pleasure taken from someone else's misfortune").

foreword / forward

Although the pronunciation is the same, the spellings and meanings of these two words are quite different. The word *foreword* is a **noun** meaning "introductory statement at the beginning of a book or other work."

▶ The director wrote a *foreword* for the report.

The word *forward* is an **adjective** or **adverb** meaning "at or toward the front."

▶ Sliding the throttle to the *forward* position [adjective] will cause the boat to move *forward*. [adverb]

form letters

A form letter is a type of **correspondence** (including **e-mail**) in which the identical message is sent to more than one person; only the name and address of the recipient differ from letter to letter. The recipients' names and addresses are stored in a database and merged with the text of the letter. The letters are then e-mailed or printed and mailed to the individuals addressed.

When to Use Form Letters

Form letters are ideal for simultaneously reaching hundreds or thousands of customers, clients, or employees with announcements and other information. In fact, **sales letters** are usually mass-produced as form letters. Form letters are also useful for situations that occur regularly, such as responses to inquiries, standard orders, acknowledgments of orders, and early-stage **collection letters**. (See also **acknowledgment letters** and **inquiries and responses**.) Of course, if a particular situation calls for a more individual response (such as an **adjustment letter** in response to a complaint), a form letter is not the best choice. Most people resent obviously impersonal treatment when they believe they deserve individual attention.

◀ PROFESSIONALISM NOTE For routine circumstances, an undisguised form letter results in a more positive response than a form letter that masquerades as a personal message. Few customers object to form letters for recurring circumstances, especially if the information is clear and the **tone** is positive. For example, a computer company may send purchasers a brief form letter or e-mail to let them know their orders have been shipped and when to expect delivery. ▶

Writing Form Letters

By using the principles of correspondence and the **"you" viewpoint**, you can produce a form letter tailored to your potential **audience** and to your **purpose**. Even though your readers know they are reading a form letter, you should give each reader the feeling that the letter fits his or her situation. Avoid broadcasting that the message is a form.

BROADCAST   Whether you live in Maine or California, you can visit our Web site or call our 24-hour customer help number. [This sentence announces that it is aimed at a wide audience.]

PERSONAL   If you have a question about your MAX-PC and cannot find the answer in the User's Guide, visit our Web site or get 24-hour personal assistance at our customer help number.
[This sentence seems aimed more at the individual reader.]

Form letters that do not need to be disguised often use a "headline lead" to replace the standard salutation, as shown in Figure F–5. By "talking" directly to the reader, you can make form letters less stiff and impersonal. Some form letters can be personalized by adding a typed or handwritten postscript.

Repurposing Form Letters

Paragraphs from previously used form letters can be combined with newly written paragraphs that are tailored to fit a specific **context**. Repurposed paragraphs are ideal for use in recurring circumstances that

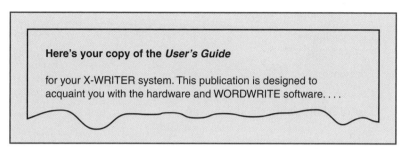

Here's your copy of the *User's Guide*

for your X-WRITER system. This publication is designed to acquaint you with the hardware and WORDWRITE software. . . .

FIGURE F–5. Headline Lead

require more personal and varied responses than form letters provide. (See **repurposing**.) They are useful, for example, when you wish either to adapt parts of the letter for particular readers or to construct sets of letters from standardized parts, as in **application cover letters**, **reference letters**, **refusal letters**, and some **memos**. Be sure to provide adequate **transition** and proofread carefully.

formal reports

Formal reports are usually written accounts of major projects that require substantial **research**, and they often involve more than one writer. See also **collaborative writing**.

Most formal reports are divided into three primary parts—front matter, body, and back matter—each of which contains a number of elements. The number and arrangement of the elements may vary depending on the subject, the length of the report, and the kinds of material covered. Many organizations have a preferred style for formal reports and furnish guidelines for report writers to follow. If you are not required to follow a specific style, use the **format** recommended in this entry. The following list includes most of the elements a formal report might contain, in the order they typically appear. (The items shown with page numbers appear in the sample formal report on pages 215–31.) Often, a **cover letter** or **memo** precedes the front matter and identifies the report by title, the person or persons to whom it is sent, the reason it was written, the **scope**, and any information that the **audience** considers important, as shown on page 215.

FRONT MATTER
Title Page (216)
Abstract (217)

F

DIGITAL TIP

Creating Styles and Templates

Most word-processing programs enable you to create templates that automate the visual appearance of text elements such as headings, paragraphs, and lists throughout a document. Once you specify your styles, save the template and use it each time you create a formal report. For step-by-step instructions, go to *bedfordstmartins.com/alred* and select *Digital Tips*, "Creating Styles and Templates."

Front Matter

The front matter serves several functions: It explains the writer's **purpose,** describes the **scope** and type of information in the report, and lists where specific information is covered in the report. Not all formal reports include every element of front matter described here. A title page and table of contents are usually mandatory, but the scope of the report and its **context** as well as the intended audience determine whether the other elements are included.

Title Page. Although the formats of title pages may vary, they often include the following items:

- *The full title of the report.* The title describes the topic, scope, and purpose of the report, as discussed in **titles**.
- *The name of the writer(s), principal investigator(s), or compiler(s).* Sometimes contributors identify themselves by their job title in the organization or by their tasks in contributing to the report (*Olivia Jones, Principal Investigator*).
- *The date or dates of the report.* For one-time reports, the date shown is the date the report is distributed. For reports issued periodically (monthly, quarterly, or yearly), the subtitle shows the period that the report covers and the distribution date is shown elsewhere on the title page, as shown in Figure F–6 on page 216.
- *The name of the organization for which the writer(s) works.*
- *The name of the organization to which the report is being submitted.* This information is included if the report is written for a customer or client.

The title page should not be numbered, as in the example on page 216, but it is considered page i. The back of the title page, which is left blank and unnumbered, is considered page ii, and the abstract falls on page iii. The body of the report begins with Arabic number 1, and a new chapter or large section typically begins on a new right-hand (odd-numbered) page. Reports with printing on only one side of each sheet can be numbered consecutively regardless of where new sections begin. Center page numbers at the bottom of each page throughout the report.

Abstract. An **abstract**, which normally follows the title page, highlights the major points of the report, as shown on page 217, enabling readers to decide whether to read the report.

Table of Contents. A **table of contents** lists all the major sections or **headings** of the report in their order of appearance, as shown on page 218, along with their page numbers.

List of Figures. All **visuals** contained in the report—**drawings, photographs, maps,** charts, and **graphs**—are labeled as figures. When a report contains more than five figures, list them, along with their page numbers, in a separate section, beginning on a new page immediately following the table of contents. Number figures consecutively with Arabic numbers.

List of Tables. When a report contains more than five **tables**, list them, along with their titles and page numbers, in a separate section immediately following the list of figures (if there is one). Number tables consecutively with Arabic numbers.

Foreword. A foreword is an optional introductory statement about a formal report or publication that is written by someone other than the author(s). The foreword author is usually an authority in the field or an executive of the organization sponsoring the report. That author's name and affiliation appear at the end of the foreword, along with the date it was written. The foreword generally provides background information about the publication's significance and places it in the context of other works in the field. The foreword precedes the preface when a work has both.

Preface. The preface, another type of optional introductory statement, is written by the author(s) of the formal report. It may announce the work's purpose, scope, and context (including any special circumstances leading to the work). A preface may also specify the audience for a work, contain acknowledgments of those who helped in its preparation, and cite permission obtained for the use of copyrighted works. See also **copyright**.

List of Abbreviations and Symbols. When the report uses numerous **abbreviations** and symbols that readers may not be able to interpret, the front matter may include a section that lists symbols and abbreviations with their meanings.

Body

The body is the section of the report that provides context for the report, describes in detail the methods and procedures used to generate the report, demonstrates how results were obtained, describes the results, draws conclusions, and, if appropriate, makes recommendations.

Executive Summary. The body of the report begins with the **executive summary**, which provides a more complete overview of the report than an abstract does. See an example on pages 219–20 and review the entry cross-referenced above.

Introduction. The **introduction** gives readers any general information, such as the report's purpose, scope, and context necessary to understand the detailed information in the rest of the report (see pages 221–23).

Text. The text of the body presents, as appropriate, the details of how the topic was investigated, how a problem was solved, what alternatives were explored, and how the best choice among them was selected. This information is enhanced by the use of visuals, tables, and references that both clarify the text and persuade the reader. See also **persuasion.**

F

Conclusions. The **conclusions** section pulls together the results of the research and interprets the findings of the report, as shown on pages 229–30.

Recommendations. Recommendations, which are sometimes combined with the conclusions, state what course of action should be taken based on the earlier arguments and conclusions of the study, as are shown on page 230.

Explanatory Notes. Occasionally, reports contain notes that amplify terms or points for some readers that might be a distraction for others. If such notes are not included as footnotes on the page where the term or point appears, they may appear in a "Notes" section at the end of the report.

References (or Works Cited). A list of references or works cited appears in a separate section if the report refers to or quotes directly from printed or online research sources. If your employer has a preferred reference style, follow it; otherwise, use one of the guidelines provided in the entry **documenting sources.** For a relatively short report, place a reference or works-cited section at the end of the body of the report, as shown on page 231. For a report with a number of sections or chapters, place a reference or works-cited section at the end of each major section or chapter. In either case, title the reference or works-cited section as such and begin it on a new page. If a particular reference appears in more than one section or chapter, repeat it in full in each appropriate reference section.

❖ ETHICS NOTE Always identify the sources of any facts, ideas, **quotations,** and paraphrases you include in a report. Even if unintentional, **plagiarism** is unethical and may result in formal academic misconduct charges in a college course. On the job, it can result in legal action or even dismissal. ❖

Back Matter

The back matter of a formal report contains supplementary material, such as where to find additional information about the topic (bibliography), and expands on certain subjects (appendixes). Other back-matter elements define special terms (glossary) and provide information on how to easily locate information in the report (index). For very large formal reports, back-matter sections may be individually numbered (Appendix A, Appendix B).

F

Appendixes. An **appendix** clarifies or supplements the report with information that is too detailed or lengthy for the primary audience but is relevant to secondary audiences.

Bibliography. A **bibliography** lists alphabetically all the sources that were consulted to prepare the report—not just those cited—and suggests additional resources that readers might want to consult.

Glossary. A **glossary** is an alphabetical list of specialized terms used in the report and their definitions.

Index. An index is an alphabetical list of all the major topics and subtopics discussed in the report. It cites the page numbers where discussion of each topic can be found and allows readers to find information on topics quickly and easily. The index is always the final section of a report. See also **indexing**.

Sample Formal Report

Figure F–6 shows the typical sections of a formal report. Keep in mind that the number and arrangement of the elements vary, depending on the context, especially the requirements of an organization or a client.

CGF Aircraft Corporation _CGF_
Memo

To: Members of the Ethics and Business Conduct
          Committee
From: Susan Litzinger, Director of Ethics and Business _SL_
          Conduct
Date: March 5, 2012
Subject: Reported Ethics Cases, 2011

Enclosed is "Reported Ethics Cases: Annual Report, 2011."   Identifies
This report, required by CGF Policy CGF-EP-01, contains a   topic
review of the ethics cases handled by CGF ethics officers and
managers during 2011, the first year of our Ethics Program.

The ethics cases reported are analyzed according to two categories: (1) major ethics cases, or those potentially involving   Briefly sum-
serious violations of company policy or illegal conduct, and   marizes
(2) minor ethics cases, or those that do not involve serious   content
policy violations or illegal conduct. The report also examines
the mode of contact in all of the reported cases and the disposition of the substantiated major ethics cases.

It is my hope that this report will provide the Committee with
the information needed to assess the effectiveness of the first
year of CGF's Ethics Program and to plan for the coming year.
Please let me know if you have any questions about this report   Offers
or if you need any further information. I may be reached at   contact
(555) 211-2121 and by e-mail at sl@cgf.com.   information

Enc.

FIGURE F–6. Formal Report (Cover Memo). Reprinted and adapted by permission of Susan Litzinger, a student at Pennsylvania State University, Altoona.

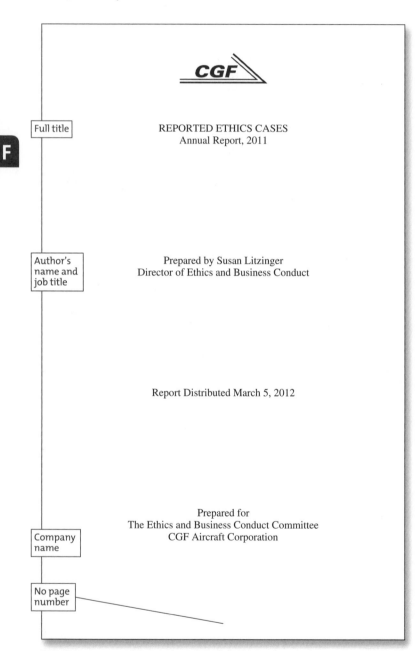

FIGURE F–6. Formal Report (*continued*) (Title Page)

Reported Ethics Cases — 2011

Adapted from MLA style to fit context

ABSTRACT

This report examines the nature and disposition of 3,458 ethics cases handled companywide by CGF Aircraft Corporation's ethics officers and managers during 2011. The purpose of this annual report is to provide the Ethics and Business Conduct Committee with the information necessary for assessing the effectiveness of the Ethics Program's first year of operation. Records maintained by ethics officers and managers of all contacts were compiled and categorized into two main types: (1) major ethics cases, or cases involving serious violations of company policies or illegal conduct, and (2) minor ethics cases, or cases not involving serious policy violations or illegal conduct. This report provides examples of the types of cases handled in each category and analyzes the disposition of 30 substantiated major ethics cases. Recommendations for planning for the second year of the Ethics Program are (1) continuing the channels of communication now available in the Ethics Program, (2) increasing financial and technical support for the Ethics Hotline, (3) disseminating the annual ethics report in some form to employees to ensure employee awareness of the company's commitment to uphold its Ethics Policies and Procedures, and (4) implementing some measure of recognition for ethical behavior to promote and reward ethical conduct.

Summarizes purpose

Methods and scope

Conclusions and recommendations

Lowercase Roman numerals used on front-matter pages

iii

FIGURE F–6. Formal Report (*continued*) (Abstract)

Reported Ethics Cases — 2011

Uniform heading styles	**TABLE OF CONTENTS**

Indented subheads

Page number for each entry

iv

FIGURE F–6. Formal Report (*continued*) (Table of Contents)

Reported Ethics Cases—2011

EXECUTIVE SUMMARY

This report examines the nature and disposition of the 3,458
ethics cases handled by the CGF Aircraft Corporation's ethics
officers and managers during 2011. The purpose of this report
is to provide CGF's Ethics and Business Conduct Committee
with the information necessary for assessing the effectiveness
of the first year of the company's Ethics Program.

States purpose

Effective January 1, 2011, the Ethics and Business Conduct
Committee (the Committee) implemented a policy and procedures for the administration of CGF's new Ethics Program. The
purpose of the Ethics Program, established by the Committee, is
to "promote ethical business conduct through open communication and compliance with company ethics standards." The Office
of Ethics and Business Conduct was created to administer the
Ethics Program. The director of the Office of Ethics and Business
Conduct, along with seven ethics officers throughout the corporation, was given the responsibility for the following objectives:

Provides background information

- Communicate the values and standards for CGF's Ethics
  Program to employees.

- Inform employees about company policies regarding
  ethical business conduct.

- Establish companywide channels for employees to obtain
  information and guidance in resolving ethics concerns.

- Implement companywide ethics-awareness and education
  programs.

Employee accessibility to ethics information and guidance was
available through managers, ethics officers, and an ethics hotline.

Major ethics cases were defined as those situations potentially
involving serious violations of company policies or illegal
conduct. Examples of major ethics cases included cover-up of
defective workmanship or use of defective parts in products;
discrimination in hiring and promotion; involvement in monetary or other kickbacks; sexual harassment; disclosure of proprietary or company information; theft; and use of corporate
Internet resources for inappropriate purposes, such as conducting personal business, gambling, or access to pornography.

Describes scope

1

FIGURE F–6. Formal Report (*continued*) (Executive Summary)

F

Reported Ethics Cases—2011

Minor ethics cases were defined as including all reported concerns not classified as major ethics cases. Minor ethics cases were classified as informational queries from employees, situations involving coworkers, and situations involving management.

Summarizes conclusions

The effectiveness of CGF's Ethics Program during the first year of implementation is most evidenced by (1) the active participation of employees in the program and the 3,458 contacts employees made regarding ethics concerns through the various channels available to them and (2) the action taken in the cases reported by employees, particularly the disposition of the 30 substantiated major ethics cases. Disseminating information about the disposition of ethics cases, particularly information about the severe disciplinary actions taken in major ethics violations, sends a message to employees that unethical or illegal conduct will not be tolerated.

Includes recommen-dations

Based on these conclusions, recommendations for planning the second year of the Ethics Program are (1) continuing the channels of communication now available in the Ethics Program, (2) increasing financial and technical support for the Ethics Hotline, the most highly used mode of contact in the ethics cases reported in 2011, (3) disseminating this report in some form to employees to ensure their awareness of CGF's commitment to uphold its Ethics Policies and Procedures, and (4) implementing some measure of recognition for ethical behavior, such as an "Ethics Employee of the Month" award to promote and reward ethical conduct.

Executive summary is about 10 percent of report length

2

FIGURE F–6. Formal Report (*continued*) (Executive Summary)

Reported Ethics Cases—2011

INTRODUCTION

This report examines the nature and disposition of the 3,458 ethics cases handled companywide by CGF's ethics officers and managers during 2011. The purpose of this report is to provide the Ethics and Business Conduct Committee with the information necessary for assessing the effectiveness of the first year of CGF's Ethics Program. Recommendations are given for the Committee's consideration in planning for the second year of the Ethics Program.

Opening states purpose

Ethics and Business Conduct Policies and Procedures

Effective January 1, 2011, the Ethics and Business Conduct Committee (the Committee) implemented Policy CGF-EP-01 and Procedure CGF-EP-02 for the administration of CGF's new Ethics Program. The purpose of the Ethics Program, established by the Committee, is to "promote ethical business conduct through open communication and compliance with company ethics standards" (CGF, "Ethics and Conduct").

Subheads signal shifts in topic

The Office of Ethics and Business Conduct was created to administer the Ethics Program. The director of the Office of Ethics and Business Conduct, along with seven ethics officers throughout CGF, was given the responsibility for the following objectives:

- Communicate the values, standards, and goals of CGF's Ethics Program to employees.
- Inform employees about company ethics policies.
- Provide companywide channels for employee education and guidance in resolving ethics concerns.
- Implement companywide programs in ethics awareness, education, and recognition.
- Ensure confidentiality in all ethics matters.

List identifies key points

Employee accessibility to ethics information and guidance became the immediate and key goal of the Office of Ethics and Business Conduct in its first year of operation. The following channels for contact were set in motion during 2011:

3

FIGURE F–6. Formal Report *(continued)* (Introduction)

F

Reported Ethics Cases—2011

- Managers throughout CGF received intensive ethics training; in all ethics situations, employees were encouraged to go to their managers as the first point of contact.

- Ethics officers were available directly to employees through face-to-face or telephone contact, to managers, to callers using the Ethics Hotline, and by e-mail.

- The Ethics Hotline was available to all employees, 24 hours a day, seven days a week, to anonymously report ethics concerns.

Confidentiality Issues
CGF's Ethics Policy ensures confidentiality and anonymity for employees who raise genuine ethics concerns. Procedure CGF-EP-02 guarantees appropriate discipline, up to and including dismissal, for retaliation or retribution against any employee who properly reports any genuine ethics concern.

Documentation of Ethics Cases
The following requirements were established by the director of the Office of Ethics and Business Conduct as uniform guidelines for the documentation by managers and ethics officers of all reported ethics cases:

- Name, position, and department of individual initiating contact, if available

- Date and time of contact

Includes detailed methods

- Name, position, and department of contact person

- Category of ethics case

- Mode of contact

- Resolution

Managers and ethics officers entered the required information in each reported ethics case into an ACCESS database file, enabling efficient retrieval and analysis of the data.

4

FIGURE F–6. Formal Report (*continued*) (Introduction)

Reported Ethics Cases — 2011

Major/Minor Category Definition and Examples
Major ethics cases were defined as those situations potentially
involving serious violations of company policies or illegal
conduct. Procedure CGF-EP-02 requires notification of the
Internal Audit and the Law departments in serious ethics cases.
The staffs of the Internal Audit and the Law departments
assume primary responsibility for managing major ethics cases
and for working with the employees, ethics officers, and
managers involved in each case.

Examples of situations categorized as major ethics cases:

- Cover-up of defective workmanship or use of defective
  parts in products

- Discrimination in hiring and promotion

- Involvement in monetary or other kickbacks from
  customers for preferred orders

Organized by
decreasing
order of
importance

- Sexual harassment

- Disclosure of proprietary customer or company
  information

- Theft

- Use of corporate Internet resources for inappropriate
  purposes, such as conducting private business, gambling,
  or gaining access to pornography

Minor ethics cases were defined as including all reported
concerns not classified as major ethics cases. Minor ethics
cases were classified as follows:

- Informational queries from employees

- Situations involving coworkers

- Situations involving management

5

FIGURE F–6. Formal Report (*continued*) (Introduction)

Reported Ethics Cases — 2011

ANALYSIS OF REPORTED ETHICS CASES

Reported Ethics Cases, by Major/Minor Category

CGF ethics officers and managers companywide handled a total of 3,458 ethics situations during 2011. Of these cases, only 172, or 5 percent, involved reported concerns of a serious enough nature to be classified as major ethics cases (see Fig. 1). Major ethics cases were defined as those situations potentially involving serious violations of company policy or illegal conduct.

Text introduces figure

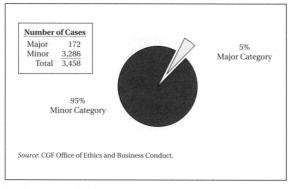

Number of Cases	
Major	172
Minor	3,286
Total	3,458

5%
Major Category

95%
Minor Category

Source: CGF Office of Ethics and Business Conduct.

Number and title identify figure

Fig. 1.   Reported ethics cases, by major/minor category in 2011.

Major Ethics Cases

Of the 172 major ethics cases reported during 2011, 57 percent, upon investigation, were found to involve unsubstantiated concerns. Incomplete information or misinformation most frequently was discovered to be the cause of the unfounded concerns of misconduct in 98 cases. Forty-four cases, or 26 percent of the total cases reported, involved incidents partly substantiated by ethics officers as serious misconduct;

6

FIGURE F–6. Formal Report (*continued*) (Body)

F

Reported Ethics Cases—2011

however, these cases were discovered to also involve inaccurate information or unfounded issues of misconduct.

Only 17 percent of the total number of major ethics cases, or 30 cases, were substantiated as major ethics situations involving serious ethical misconduct or illegal conduct (CGF, "2011 Ethics Hotline Results") (see Fig. 2).

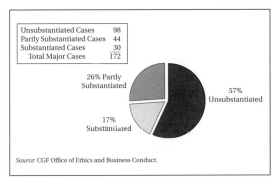

Unsubstantiated Cases	98
Partly Substantiated Cases	44
Substantiated Cases	30
Total Major Cases	172

26% Partly Substantiated

57% Unsubstantiated

17% Substantiated

Source: CGF Office of Ethics and Business Conduct.

Identifies source of information

Fig. 2.   Major ethics cases in 2011.

Of the 30 substantiated major ethics cases, seven remain under investigation at this time, and two cases are currently in litigation. Disposition of the remainder of the 30 substantiated reported ethics cases included severe disciplinary action in five cases: the dismissal of two employees and the demotion of three employees. Seven employees were given written warnings, and nine employees received verbal warnings (see Fig. 3).

FIGURE F–6. Formal Report (*continued*) (Body)

F

Reported Ethics Cases — 2011

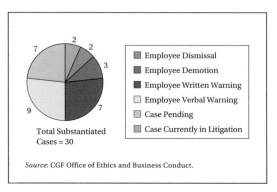

Total Substantiated
Cases = 30

- Employee Dismissal
- Employee Demotion
- Employee Written Warning
- Employee Verbal Warning
- Case Pending
- Case Currently in Litigation

Source: CGF Office of Ethics and Business Conduct.

Fig. 3. Disposition of substantiated major ethics cases in 2011.

Minor Ethics Cases
Minor ethics cases included those that did not involve serious violations of company policy or illegal conduct. During 2011, ethics officers and company managers handled 3,286 such cases. Minor ethics cases were further classified as follows:

Reports
findings
in detail

- Informational queries from employees
- Situations involving coworkers
- Situations involving management

As might be expected during the initial year of the Ethics Program implementation, the majority of contacts made by employees were informational, involving questions about the new policies and procedures. These informational contacts comprised 65 percent of all contacts of a minor nature and numbered 2,148. Employees made 989 contacts regarding ethics concerns involving coworkers and 149 contacts regarding ethics concerns involving management (see Fig. 4).

8

FIGURE F–6. Formal Report (*continued*) (Body)

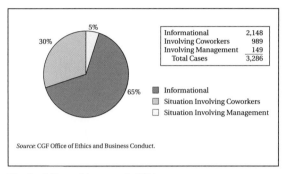

Reported Ethics Cases — 2011

Informational	2,148
Involving Coworkers	989
Involving Management	149
Total Cases	3,286

■ Informational
▨ Situation Involving Coworkers
☐ Situation Involving Management

Source: CGF Office of Ethics and Business Conduct.

Fig. 4.   Minor ethics cases in 2011.

Mode of Contact
The effectiveness of the Ethics Program rested on the dissemination of information to employees and the provision of accessible channels through which employees could gain information, report concerns, and obtain guidance. Employees were encouraged to first go to their managers with any ethical concerns, because those managers would have the most direct knowledge of the immediate circumstances and individuals involved.

> Assesses findings

Other channels were put into operation, however, for any instance in which an employee did not feel able to go to his or her manager. The ethics officers companywide were available to employees through telephone conversations, face-to-face meetings, and e-mail contact. Ethics officers also served as contact points for managers in need of support and assistance in handling the ethics concerns reported to them by their subordinates.

The Ethics Hotline became operational in mid-January 2011 and offered employees assurance of anonymity and confidentiality. The Ethics Hotline was accessible to all employees on a 24-hour, 7-day basis. Ethics officers companywide took responsibility on a rotational basis for handling calls reported through the hotline.

9

FIGURE F–6. Formal Report (*continued*) (Body)

F

Reported Ethics Cases — 2011

In summary, ethics information and guidance were available to all employees during 2011 through the following channels:

- Employee to manager
- Employee telephone, face-to-face, and e-mail contact with ethics officer
- Manager to ethics officer
- Employee Hotline

Bulleted lists help organize and summarize information

The mode of contact in the 3,458 reported ethics cases was as follows (see Fig. 5):

- In 19 percent of the reported cases, or 657, employees went to managers with concerns.
- In 9 percent of the reported cases, or 311, employees contacted an ethics officer.
- In 5 percent of the reported cases, or 173, managers sought assistance from ethics officers.
- In 67 percent of the reported cases, or 2,317, contacts were made through the Ethics Hotline.

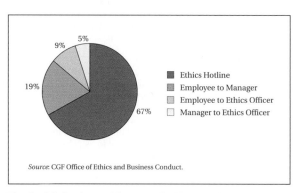

Source: CGF Office of Ethics and Business Conduct.

Fig. 5.   Mode of contact in reported ethics cases in 2011.

10

FIGURE F–6. Formal Report (*continued*) (Body)

Reported Ethics Cases — 2011

CONCLUSIONS AND RECOMMENDATIONS

The effectiveness of CGF's Ethics Program during the first
year of implementation is most evidenced by (1) the active participation of employees in the program and the 3,458 contacts
employees made regarding ethics concerns through the various channels available to them, and (2) the action taken in the
cases reported by employees, particularly the disposition of the
30 substantiated major ethics cases.

> *Pulls together findings*

One of the 12 steps to building a successful Ethics Program
identified by Frank Navran in *Workforce* magazine is an ethics
communication strategy. Navran explains that such a strategy
is crucial in ensuring

> *Uses sources for support*

> that employees have the information they need in a timely
> and usable fashion and that the organization is encour-
> aging employee communication regarding the values,
> standards and the conduct of the organization and its
> members. (119)

The 3,458 contacts by employees during 2011 attest to the accessibility and effectiveness of the communication channels
that exist in CGF's Ethics Program.

An equally important step in building a successful ethics program is listed by Navran as "Measurements and Rewards,"
which he explains as follows:

> In most organizations, employees know what's important
> by virtue of what the organization measures and rewards.
> If ethical conduct is assessed and rewarded, and if unethi-
> cal conduct is identified and dissuaded, employees will
> believe that the organization's principals mean it when
> they say the values and code of ethics are important.
> (121)

> *Long quotation in MLA style*

Disseminating information about the disposition of ethics
cases, particularly information about the severe disciplinary
actions taken in major ethics violations, sends a message to
employees that unethical or illegal conduct will not be tolerated. Making public such actions taken in cases of ethical misconduct provides "a golden opportunity to make other
employees aware that the behavior is unacceptable and why"
(Ferrell, Fraedrich, and Ferrell 129).

> *Interprets findings*

11

FIGURE F–6. Formal Report (*continued*) (Conclusions and Recommendations)

F

Reported Ethics Cases — 2011

With these two points in mind, I offer the following recommendations for consideration for plans for the Ethics Program's second year:

Recommends specific steps

- Continuation of the channels of communication now available in the Ethics Program

- Increased financial and technical support for the Ethics Hotline, the most highly used mode of contact in the reported ethics cases in 2011

- Dissemination of this report in some form to employees to ensure employees' awareness of CGF's commitment to uphold its Ethics Policy and Procedures

- Implementation of some measure of recognition for ethical behavior, such as an "Ethics Employee of the Month," to promote and reward ethical conduct

To ensure that employees see the value of their continued participation in the Ethics Program, feedback is essential. The information in this annual review, in some form, should be provided to employees. Knowing that the concerns they reported were taken seriously and resulted in appropriate action by Ethics Program administrators would reinforce employee involvement in the program. While the negative consequences of ethical misconduct contained in this report send a powerful message, a means of communicating the *positive* rewards of ethical conduct at CGF should be implemented. Various options for recognition of employees exemplifying ethical conduct should be considered and approved. See MLogs, "Create and Evaluate a Code of Conduct," *Business Ethics Forum.* Management Logs, 12 Sept. 2006. Web. 19 Jan. 2010.

Links recommendations to company goal

Continuation of the Ethics Program's successful 2011 operations, with the implementation of the above recommendations, should ensure the continued pursuit of the Ethics Program's purpose: "to promote a positive work environment that encourages open communication regarding ethics and compliance issues and concerns."

12

FIGURE F–6. Formal Report (*continued*) (Conclusions and Recommendations)

Reported Ethics Cases — 2011

WORKS CITED

CGF. "Ethics and Conduct at CGF Aircraft Corporation." *CGF Aircraft Corporation*. CGF, 1 Jan. 2010. Web. 11 Feb. 2011.

---. "2011 Ethics Hotline Investigation Results." *CGF Aircraft Corporation*. CGF, 15 Jan. 2012. Web. 11 Feb. 2012.

Ferrell, O. C., John Fraedrich, and Linda Ferrell. *Business Ethics: Ethical Decision Making and Cases*. 7th ed. Boston: Houghton Mifflin, 2008. Print.

Navran, Frank. "12 Steps to Building a Best-Practices Ethics Program." *Workforce* 76.9 (1997): 117-22. Web. 10 Sept. 2009.

Section begins on a new page

This report uses MLA style

F

13

FIGURE F–6. Formal Report (*continued*) (Works Cited)

format

Format refers to both the organization of information in a document and the physical arrangement of information on the page.

In one sense, format refers to the conventions that govern the scope and placement of information in such job-related writing as **formal reports**, **proposals**, and various types of **correspondence**. For example, in formal reports, the **table of contents** precedes the preface but follows the title page and the **abstract**. Likewise, although variations exist, parts of **letters** — such as inside address, salutation, and complimentary closing — are arranged in standard patterns. See also **e-mail** and **memos**.

Format also refers to the general physical appearance of a finished document, whether printed or electronic. See also **layout and design** and **writing for the Web**.

former / latter

Former and *latter* should be used to refer to only two items in a sentence or paragraph.

▶ The president and his aide emerged from the conference, the *former* looking nervous and the *latter* looking glum.

Because these terms make the reader look to previous material to identify the reference, however, they complicate reading and are best avoided.

forms

Forms allow you to gather information from respondents in a standardized print or online design that makes it easy for you to tabulate the responses and evaluate the information. See Figures F–7 and F–8 for two examples of forms.

❖ ETHICS NOTE Information gathered on forms can be sensitive or personal, so make sure to present questions in a way that is not invasive or illegal. Unless otherwise indicated on the form, the person filling out the form should have the expectation of confidentiality. If you are concerned about issues of confidentiality or legality, check your organization's policy or in a classroom seek your instructor's advice. ❖

104-M S A
**Section 125 Flexible Spending Account
(FSA) Claim Form**

Form title

Employee Name: _____

Social Security Number: _____-_____-_____

Writing
lines

Name of Employer: _____

Employee Signature: _____

Complete section below for medical, dental, or vision reimbursement

Instructions

CLAIM TYPE I: MEDICAL CARE ACCOUNT

Amount of Expense Incurred: $_____

Dates of Services: From: _____   To: _____

Complete section below for reimbursement of care for your dependent provided by a child-care facility, an adult dependent-care center, or a caretaker

Instructions

CLAIM TYPE II: DEPENDENT-CARE ACCOUNT

Amount of Expense Incurred: $_____

Name of Dependent-Care Provider: _____

Provider Social Security or Federal ID Number: _____-___-_____

Mail or fax form with documentation to:
Specialized Benefit Services, Inc.
P.O. Box 498
Framingham, MA 01702
Fax: (508) 877-1182

Mailing and
contact
information

For additional claim forms: www.sbsclaims.com

FIGURE F–7. Form (for a Medical Claim)

FIGURE F–8. Online Form with Typical Components

Preparing a Form

An effective form makes it easy for one person to supply information and for another person to retrieve, record, and interpret that information. Ideally, a form should be self-explanatory to someone seeing it for the first time. When preparing a form, determine the kind of information you are seeking and arrange the questions in a logical order. To ensure the usability of the form, test it with people from your target **audience** or others before publishing the final version. See also **questionnaires**.

Choosing Online or Paper. Many organizations provide their forms not only on paper and as downloadable documents but also as interactive online forms. Forms especially well suited for online use include job applications, conference or seminar registrations, and order forms. Online forms standardize respondents' interfaces and link to databases that tabulate and interpret data. An online form can be programmed to ensure that all necessary fields are completed correctly before the form can be successfully submitted. Using online forms can eliminate the problems associated with distributing and collecting forms. However, using online forms can be difficult for people with limited computer literacy or access, so consider your audience carefully before opting to collect your responses online. See also **writing for the Web**.

Writing Instructions. Place instructions at the beginning of the form or at the beginning of each section of the form and use **headings** or other design elements, such as the boldface type and text boxes in Figure F–7, to focus the readers' attention. When necessary, place instructions for distributing the copies of multiple-copy forms at the bottom of each page of the form. Instructions for submitting printed forms should be clearly indicated, as in Figure F–7. For printed forms, include space for a signature and a date. At the end of online forms, include a "submit" button that is programmed to record the data and to open a new page or send a confirming e-mail informing respondents that their responses have been successfully submitted.

F

Choosing Response Types.   Forms should ask questions in ways that are best suited to the types of data you hope to collect. The two main types are open-ended questions and closed-ended questions.

- *Open-ended questions* allow respondents to answer questions in their own words. Such questions are most appropriate if you wish to elicit responses you may not have anticipated (as in a complaint form) or if there are too many possible answers to use a multiple-choice format. However, the responses to open-ended questions can be difficult to tabulate and analyze.

- *Closed-ended questions* provide a list of options from which the respondent can select, limiting the range of possible responses. When you want to make sure you receive a standardized, easy-to-tabulate response, use any of the types of closed-ended questions that follow:
  - *Multiple choice*: Choose one (or sometimes more than one) response from a preset list of options.
  - *Ranked choice*: Rank items according to preference, such as selecting vacation days or choosing job assignments.
  - *Forced choice*: Choose between two preset options, such as yes / no or male / female.

Wording Questions.   Questions are normally presented as short phrases or labels. Keep them brief, specific, and to the point; avoid unnecessary repetition by combining related information under an explanatory heading.

WORDY   What make of car (or vehicle) do you drive? _____
What year was it manufactured? _____
What model is it? _____
What is the body style? _____

CONCISE   Vehicle Information
Make _____ Year _____
Model _____ Body Style _____

If a requested date is other than the date on which the form is being filled out, the label should read, for example, "Effective date" or "Date issued," rather than simply "Date." As in all writing, put yourself in your reader's place and imagine what sort of requests would be clear.

Sequencing Entries.   The main portion of the form includes the entries that are required to obtain the necessary data. Arrange entries in an order that will be the most logical to the person filling out the form.

- Sequence entries to fit the subject matter. For instance, a form requesting reimbursement for travel expenses would logically be organized chronologically from the first day of the week (or month) to the last day of the appropriate period.

- If the response to one item is based on the response to another item, be sure the items appear in the correct order.

- Group requests for related information together whenever possible.

- For ease of reading, arrange entries from left to right and from top to bottom.

Designing a Form

At the top of the form, clearly indicate preliminary information, such as the name of your organization, the title of your form, and any reference number. You can design computer-generated forms specific to your needs with form-design software, word-processing software, or markup languages (such as HTML or XML). However you prepare the final version of a form, pay particular attention to design details, especially to the placement of entry lines, labels, and the amount of space allowed for responses.

Entry Lines and Fields.   A print form can be designed so that the person filling it out provides information on a writing line, in a writing block, or in square boxes. A *writing line* is simply a rule with a caption, such as the line for "Employee Name" shown in Figure F–7. A *writing block* is essentially the same as a writing line, except that each entry is enclosed in a ruled block, as shown in Figure F–9, making it unlikely for the respondent to associate a caption with the wrong line.

When it is possible to anticipate all likely responses, you can make the form easy to fill out by writing the question on the form, supplying a labeled box for each anticipated answer, and asking the respondent to check the appropriate boxes. Such a design also makes it easy to tabulate the data. Be sure your questions are both simple and specific.

▶ Would your department order another X2L Copier? Yes ☐ No ☐

NAME			TELEPHONE	
STREET ADDRESS				
CITY		STATE	ZIP CODE	

FIGURE F–9. Writing Block for a Form

For online forms, these functions are accomplished with form fields such as text boxes, option (or *radio*) buttons, drop-down menus, lists, and checkboxes, which can be aligned using table cells or grouping. Each form field should have a label prompting users to type information or to select from a list of options. Labels for text boxes, drop-down menus, and lists should be positioned to the left; labels for radio buttons and checkboxes should be positioned to the right. Be sure as well to indicate required form fields. See Figure F–8 for an example of spacing and alignment in an online form.*

Spacing.   Provide enough space to enable the person filling out the form to enter the requested information. Insufficient writing or typing space makes it difficult for people to respond, resulting in responses that are hard to read, abbreviated, or incomplete. Reading responses that are too tightly spaced or that snake around the side of the form can cause errors when tabulating or interpreting data.

fragments (*see* sentence fragments)

functional shift

Many words shift easily from one **part of speech** to another, depending on how they are used. When they do, the process is called a *functional shift,* or a shift in function.

---

*For up-to-date information on designing online forms, see *www.stcsig.org/ usability/topics/forms.html.*

► It takes ten minutes to *walk* from the sales office to the accounting department. However, the long *walk* reduces efficiency.
[*Walk* shifts from **verb** to **noun**.]

► I talk to the Chicago office on the *phone* every day. He was concerned about the office *phone* expenses. He will *phone* the home office from London.
[*Phone* shifts from noun to **adjective** to verb.]

► *After* we discuss the project, we will begin work. *After* lengthy discussions, we began work. The partners worked well together forever *after*.
[*After* shifts from **conjunction** to **preposition** to **adverb**.]

Jargon is often the result of functional shifts. In hospitals, for example, an *attending physician* is often referred to simply as the "attending" (a shift from an adjective to a noun). Likewise, in nuclear plant construction, a *reactor containment building* is called a "containment" (a shift from an adjective to a noun). Do not shift the function of a word indiscriminately merely to shorten a phrase or an expression. See also **affectation**, **audience**, and **conciseness**.

G

garbled sentences

A garbled sentence is one that is so tangled with structural and grammatical problems that it cannot be repaired. Garbled sentences often result from an attempt to squeeze too many ideas into one sentence.

> ▶ My job objectives are accomplished by my having a diversified background which enables me to operate effectively and efficiently, consisting of a degree in computer science, along with twelve years of experience, including three years in Staff Engineering-Packaging sets a foundation for a strong background in areas of analyzing problems and assessing economical and reasonable solutions.

Do not try to patch such a sentence; rather, analyze the ideas it contains, list them in a logical sequence, and then construct one or more entirely new sentences. An analysis of the preceding example yields the following five ideas:

- My job requires that I analyze problems to find economical and workable solutions.
- My diversified background helps me accomplish my job.
- I have a computer-science degree.
- I have twelve years of job experience.
- Three of these years have been in Staff Engineering-Packaging.

Using those five ideas—together with **parallel structure**, **sentence variety**, **subordination**, and **transition**—the writer might have described the job as follows:

> ▶ My job requires that I analyze problems to find economical and workable solutions. Both my education and experience help me achieve this goal. Specifically, I have a computer-science degree and twelve years of job experience, three of which have been in the Staff Engineering-Packaging Department.

See also **clarity**, **mixed constructions**, and **sentence construction**.

gender

In English grammar, *gender* refers to the classification of **nouns** and **pronouns** as masculine, feminine, and neuter. The gender of most words can be identified only by the choice of the appropriate pronoun (*he, she, it*). Only these pronouns and a select few nouns (*man / woman, buck / doe*) or noun forms (*heir / heiress*) reflect gender. Many such nouns have been replaced by single terms that apply to both sexes. See also **biased language** and **he / she**.

Gender is important to writers because they must be sure that nouns and pronouns within a grammatical construction agree in gender. A pronoun, for example, must agree with its noun antecedent in gender. We refer to a woman as *she* or *her*, not as *it*; to a man as *he* or *him*, not as *it*; to a building as *it*, not as *he* or *she*. See also **agreement**.

G

ESL TIP for Assigning Gender

The English language has an almost complete lack of gender distinctions. That can be confusing for a nonnative speaker of English whose native language may assign gender. In the few cases in which English does make a gender distinction, there is a close connection between the assigning of gender and the sex of the subject. The few instances in which gender distinctions are made in English are summarized as follows:

Subject pronouns	he / she
Object pronouns	him / her
Possessive adjectives	his / her(s)
Some nouns	king / queen, boy / girl, bull / cow, among others

When a noun, such as *doctor*, can refer to a person of either sex, you need to know the sex of the person to whom the noun refers to determine the gender-appropriate pronoun.

▶ The doctor gave *her* patients advice.
  [Doctor is female.]

▶ The doctor gave *his* patients advice.
  [Doctor is male.]

When the sex of the noun antecedent is unknown, be sure to follow the guidelines for nonsexist writing in the entry **biased language**. (*Note:* Some English speakers refer to vehicles and countries as *she*, but contemporary usage favors *it*.)

general and specific methods of development

General and specific **methods of development** organize information either from general points to specific details (Figure G–1) or from specific details to a general conclusion (Figure G–2). As with all methods of development, rarely does a writer rely on only one method throughout a document. Most documents blend methods and use combinations of methods.

General to Specific

The general-to-specific method of development is especially useful for teaching **readers** about something with which they are not familiar because you can begin with generally known information and lead to new and increasingly specific details. This method can also be used to support a general statement with facts or examples that validate the

---

Subject: Expanding Our Supplier Base for Computer Chips

Based on the information presented at the supply meeting on April 12, we recommend that the company initiate relationships with computer-chip manufacturers. Several events make such an action necessary.   **General statement**

    Our current supplier, Datacom, is experiencing growing pains and is having difficulty shipping the product on time. Specifically, we can expect a reduction of between 800 and 1,000 units per month for the remainder of this fiscal year. The number of units should stabilize at 15,000 units per month thereafter.   **Supporting information**

    Domestic demand for our computers continues to grow. Demand during the current fiscal year is up 500,000 units over the last fiscal year. Our sales projections for the next five years show that demand should peak next year at about 830,000 units given the consumer demand, which will increase exponentially.   **Specific details**

    Finally, our expansion into the Czech Republic and Kazakhstan markets will require additional shipments of at least 175,000 units per quarter for the remainder of this fiscal year. Sales Department projections put global computer sales at double that rate, or 350,000 units per fiscal year, for the next five years.

FIGURE G–1. General-to-Specific Method of Development

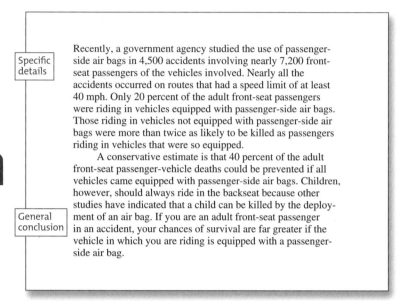

Specific details

Recently, a government agency studied the use of passenger-side air bags in 4,500 accidents involving nearly 7,200 front-seat passengers of the vehicles involved. Nearly all the accidents occurred on routes that had a speed limit of at least 40 mph. Only 20 percent of the adult front-seat passengers were riding in vehicles equipped with passenger-side air bags. Those riding in vehicles not equipped with passenger-side air bags were more than twice as likely to be killed as passengers riding in vehicles that were so equipped.

General conclusion

A conservative estimate is that 40 percent of the adult front-seat passenger-vehicle deaths could be prevented if all vehicles came equipped with passenger-side air bags. Children, however, should always ride in the backseat because other studies have indicated that a child can be killed by the deployment of an air bag. If you are an adult front-seat passenger in an accident, your chances of survival are far greater if the vehicle in which you are riding is equipped with a passenger-side air bag.

FIGURE G–2. Specific-to-General Method of Development

statement. For example, if you begin your writing with the general statement "Companies that diversify are more successful than those that do not," you could follow that statement with examples and statistics that prove to the reader that companies that diversify are, in fact, more successful than companies that do not.

A memo or short report organized entirely in a general-to-specific sequence discusses only one point. All other information in the document supports the general statement, as illustrated in Figure G–1 from a memo about locating additional computer-chip suppliers.

Specific to General

Specific-to-general development is especially useful when you wish to persuade skeptical readers of a general principle with an accumulation of specific details and evidence that reach a logical **conclusion**. It carefully builds its case, often with examples and analogies in addition to facts or statistics, and it does not actually make its point until the end. (See also **order-of-importance method of development**.) Figure G–2 is an example of the specific-to-general method of development.

global communication

The prevalence of global communication technology and international markets means that the ability to communicate with **audiences** from varied cultural backgrounds is essential. The audiences for such communications include clients and customers as well as business partners and colleagues.

Many entries in this book, such as **meetings** and **résumés**, are based on U.S. cultural patterns. The treatment of such topics might be very different in other cultures where leadership styles, persuasive strategies, and even legal constraints differ. As illustrated in **international correspondence**, organizational patterns, forms of courtesy, and ideas about efficiency can vary significantly from culture to culture. What might be seen as direct and efficient in the United States could be considered blunt and even impolite in other cultures. The reasons behind these differing ways of viewing communication are complex. Researchers have found various ways to measure cultural differences through such concepts as the importance of saving face, perceptions of time, and individual versus group orientation.

Anthropologist Edward T. Hall, a pioneer in cross-cultural research, developed the concept of "contexting" to assess the predominant communication style of a culture.* By contexting, Hall means how much or how little an individual assumes another person understands about a subject under discussion. In very low-context communication, the participants assume they share little knowledge and must communicate in great detail; thus, thorough documentation is important—written agreements (contracts) are expected, and rules are explicitly defined.

In high-context communication, the participants assume they understand the **context** and thus depend on shared history (context) to communicate with each other. Thus, communications such as written contracts are not so important, while communication that relies on personal relationships and shared history is paramount. Of course, no culture is entirely high or low context; rather, these concepts can help you communicate more effectively with those in a particular culture.

WRITER'S CHECKLIST   Communicating Globally

✔ Discuss the differing cultures within your company or region to reinforce the idea that people can interpret verbal and nonverbal communications differently.

(continued)

*Edward T. Hall and Mildred Reed Hall, *Understanding Cultural Differences: Germans, French and Americans* (Boston: Intercultural Press, 1990).

WRITER'S CHECKLIST   **Communicating Globally** *(continued)*

✔ Invite global and intercultural communication experts to speak at your workplace. Companies in your area may have employees who could be resources for cultural discussions.

✔ Understand that the key to effective communication with global audiences is recognizing that cultural differences, despite the challenges they may present, offer opportunities for growth for both you and your organization.

✔ Consult with someone from your intended audience's culture. Many phrases, gestures, and visual elements are so subtle that only someone who is very familiar with the culture can explain the effect they may have on others from that culture. See also **global graphics**.

G

WEB LINK	**Intercultural Resources**

Intercultural Press publishes "books and training materials that help professionals, businesspeople, travelers, and scholars understand the meaning and diversity of culture." (See *www.interculturalpress.com*.) For other resources for global communication, see *bedfordstmartins .com/alred* and select *Links for Handbook Entries*.

---

global graphics

In a global business and technological environment, **graphs** and other **visuals** require the same careful attention that is given to other aspects of **global communication**. The complex cultural connotations of visuals challenge writers to think beyond their own experience when they are aiming for audiences outside their own culture.

Symbols, images, and even colors are not free from cultural associations—they depend on **context**, and context is culturally determined. For instance, in North America, a red cross is commonly used as a symbol for first aid or a hospital. In Muslim countries, however, a cross (red or otherwise) represents Christianity, whereas a crescent (usually green) signifies first aid or a hospital. A manual for use in Honduras could indicate "caution" by using a picture of a person touching a finger below the eye. In France, however, using that gesture would mean "You can't fool me."

Figure G–3 shows two different graphics depicting weight lifters. The drawing at the left may be appropriate for U.S. audiences and others. However, that image would be highly inappropriate in many cultures

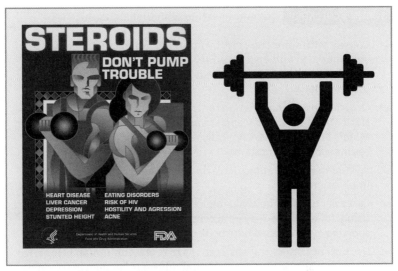

FIGURE G–3. Graphics for U.S. (left) and Global (right) Audiences

where the image of a partially clothed man and woman in close proximity would be contrary to deeply held cultural beliefs and even laws about the public depiction of men and women. The drawing at the right, however, depicts a weight lifter by using a neutral icon that avoids the connotations associated with more realistic images of people. These examples suggest why the International Organization for Standardization (ISO) established agreed-upon symbols, such as those shown in Figure G–4, designed for public signs, guidebooks, and manuals.

◀ PROFESSIONALISM NOTE Careful attention to the connotations that visual elements may have for a global **audience** makes translations easier, prevents embarrassment, and earns respect for a company and its products and services. See also **connotation / denotation**. ▶

FIGURE G–4. International Organization for Standardization (ISO) Symbols

WRITER'S CHECKLIST   Communicating with Global Graphics

✔ Consult with someone or test your use of graphics with people from your intended audience's country who understand the effect that visual elements will have on readers or listeners. See also **presentations**.

✔ Organize visual information for the intended audience. For example, North Americans read visuals from left to right in clockwise rotation. Middle Eastern readers typically read visuals from right to left in counterclockwise rotation.

✔ Be sure that the graphics have no unintended political or religious implications.

✔ Carefully consider how you depict people in visuals. Nudity in advertising, for example, may be acceptable in some cultures, but in others showing even isolated bare body parts can alienate audiences.

✔ Use outlines or neutral abstractions to represent human beings. For example, use stick figures and avoid representing men and women.

✔ Examine how you display body positions in signs and visuals. Body positioning can carry unintended cultural meanings very different from your own. For example, some Middle Eastern cultures regard the display of the soles of one's shoes to be disrespectful and offensive.

✔ Choose neutral colors (or those you know are appropriate) for your graphics; generally, black-and-white and gray-and-white illustrations work well. Colors can be problematic. For example, in North America, Europe, and Japan, red indicates danger. In China, however, red symbolizes good fortune and joy.

✔ Check your use of punctuation marks, which are as language specific as symbols. For example, in North America, the question mark generally represents the need for information or the help function in a computer manual or program. In many countries, that symbol has no meaning at all.

✔ Create simple visuals and use consistent labels for all visual items. In most cultures, simple shapes with fewer elements are easier to read.

glossaries

A glossary is an alphabetical list of definitions of specialized terms used in a **formal report**, a manual, or other long document. You may want to include a glossary if some readers in your **audience** are not familiar with specialized or technical terms you use.

Keep glossary entries concise and be sure they are written in language that all your readers can understand.

▶ *Amortize*: To write off an expenditure by prorating it over a specific period of time.

Arrange the terms alphabetically, with each entry beginning on a new line. The definitions then follow the terms, dictionary style. In a formal report, the glossary begins on a new page and appears after the appendix(es) and bibliography.

Including a glossary does not relieve you of the responsibility of **defining terms** that your reader will not know when those terms are first mentioned in the text.

gobbledygook

Gobbledygook is writing that suffers from an overdose of traits guaranteed to make it stuffy, pretentious, and wordy. Such traits include the overuse of big and mostly **abstract words**, **affectation** (especially long variants), **buzzwords**, **clichés**, **euphemisms**, inappropriate **jargon**, stacked **modifiers**, and **vague words**. Gobbledygook is writing that attempts to sound official (officialese), legal (legalese), or scientific. Consider the following statement from an auto-repair release form.

LEGALESE   I hereby authorize the above repair work to be done along with the necessary material and hereby grant you and/or your employees permission to operate the car or truck herein described on streets, highways, or elsewhere for the purpose of testing and/or inspection. An express mechanic's lien is hereby acknowledged on above car or truck to secure the amount of repairs thereto.

DIRECT   You have my permission to do the repair work listed on this work order and to use the necessary material. You may drive my vehicle to test its performance. I understand that you will keep my vehicle until I have paid for all repairs.

See also **clarity**, **conciseness**, **plain language**, and **word choice**.

good / well

Good is an **adjective**, and *well* is an **adverb**.

ADJECTIVE   Janet presented a *good* plan.

ADVERB   She presented the plan *well*.

Well also can be used as an adjective to describe health (a *well* child, *wellness* programs). See also **bad / badly**.

G

grammar

Grammar is the systematic description of the way words work together to form a coherent language. In that sense, it is an explanation of the structure of a language. However, grammar is popularly taken to mean the set of rules that governs how a language ought to be spoken and written. In that sense, it refers to the **usage** conventions of a language.

Those two meanings of grammar—how the language functions and how it ought to function—are easily confused. To clarify the distinction, consider the expression *ain't*. Unless used intentionally to add colloquial flavor, *ain't* is unacceptable because its use is considered nonstandard. Yet taken strictly as a **part of speech**, the term functions perfectly well as a verb. Whether it appears in a declarative sentence ("I ain't going") or an interrogative sentence ("Ain't I going?"), it conforms to the normal pattern for all verbs in the English language. Although readers may not approve of its use, they cannot argue that it is ungrammatical in such sentences.

To achieve **clarity**, you need to know both grammar (as a description of the way words work together) and the conventions of usage. Knowing the conventions of usage helps you select the appropriate over the inappropriate word or expression. (See also **word choice**.) A knowledge of grammar helps you diagnose and correct problems arising from how words and phrases function in relation to one another. For example, knowing that certain words and phrases function to modify other words and phrases gives you a basis for correcting those **modifiers** that are not doing their job. Understanding **dangling modifiers** helps you avoid or correct a construction that obscures the intended meaning. In short, an understanding of grammar and its special terminology is valuable chiefly because it enables you to recognize and correct problems so that you can communicate clearly and precisely. For a complete list of grammar entries, see the Contents by Topic on the inside front cover.

WEB LINK	Getting Help with Grammar

For helpful Web sites and grammar exercises, see *bedfordstmartins* *.com/alred* and select *Links for Handbook Entries* and *Exercise Central.*

grant proposals

Grant proposals are written to nonprofit and government organizations to request the approval of and funding for projects that solve a problem or fulfill a need. A scientist, for example, may write a grant to the National Institutes of Health to request a specific sum of money to study a new cancer therapy or the executive director of Habitat for Humanity may write a grant to a local government requesting funding to purchase supplies to construct new housing for disadvantaged families in the area.

The advice in the entry **proposals** for assessing audience and purpose, writing persuasively, maintaining **ethics in writing**, and managing a project within a tight deadline applies as well to writing grant proposals. This entry focuses on the particular needs of grant writers.

WEB LINK	Sample Grant Proposals

For samples of full grant proposals, see *bedfordstmartins.com/ alred* and select *Model Documents Gallery.*

Granting organizations typically post opportunities, along with detailed application guidelines, on their Web sites and specify their requirements for the format and content of proposals. Most federal and state government grants are now submitted electronically, and various sections may have imposed word or character limits that are enforced electronically. When preparing a nonelectronic proposal, always organize its elements in the exact order described or required in the request for proposals (RFP) or in the grant maker's guidelines. Although application guidelines and processes may differ from one organization to another, grant proposals generally require the following sections at a minimum:

- Cover letter
- Title page
- Application form
- Introduction / summary

- Literature review (if needed)
- Project narrative
  - *Project description*
  - *Project outcomes*
  - *Budget narrative*
  - *Task schedule*
- Organization description
- Conclusion
- Attachments (appendixes)

Cover Letter

Usually one page long, the **cover letter** should identify who you are and your affiliation. It should specify the grant that you are applying for, summarize the proposed project, and include the amount of funding you are requesting.

Title Page

On a single page, show the **title** of the project, names of project staff and their affiliations, date submitted, and the name of the recipient's organization. This page serves as the cover of the grant proposal.

Application Form

Particularly in electronic grant applications, an application form may replace the cover letter and title page. This form may be one or more pages and may require you to check boxes, fill in blanks, or insert brief descriptions or other information into text boxes or blank spaces. A word or character limit (typically 250–400 words) may be imposed or enforced. An official signature (or its electronic equivalent) is often required. This section may request detailed information about the applicant organization, such as staff or board of directors' demographic composition or its human resources policies.

Introduction / Summary

The **introduction** is your proposal at a glance—it briefly describes (within a given limit) the problem to be solved and projects the expected outcomes of your grant proposal. If substantial **research** is involved, you may also describe your proposed research methods (interviews, questionnaires, videotapes, observations, etc.) in a separate paragraph. See also **abstracts**.

Literature Review

The literature review lists the relevant research sources you consulted in preparing your proposal. Also called a *References* or *Works Cited* section, it allows reviewers of your proposal to assess your familiarity with current research in the field. Is your research up to date? Thorough? Pertinent? Be selective: include only relevant journal articles, books, interviews, broadcasts, **blogs / forums**, and other sources. In nonresearch proposals (those not based on secondary or formal research) a limited number of citations are frequently included in text within the project narrative or as footnotes or endnotes.

G

Project Narrative

The heart of the proposal, the project narrative describes in detail the scope of work, expected outcomes, list of tasks, project activity schedule from start to finish, and estimated cost. Be specific and thorough.

Project Description.   The project description includes an overview of the project and details of how the research project or program will be conducted (its methodology). In nonresearch proposals, include a succinct *statement of need*—also called a *case statement*—which presents the facts and evidence that support the need for the project. The information presented can come from authorities in the field, as well as from your agency's own experience or research. A logical and persuasive statement of need demonstrates that your company or nonprofit organization sufficiently understands the situation and is therefore capable of addressing it satisfactorily. Clearly indicate why or how your solution improves on existing or previous ones, and cite evidence to support this. Emphasize the benefits of the proposed activities for the grant maker's intended constituency or target population and why your solution to the problem or plan to fulfill the need should be approved. Most RFPs and grant-maker guidelines provide a list of specific questions for applicants to answer or required topics that must be persuasively addressed in this section.

Project Outcomes.   Having described the preparations and justification for the program, the grant writer must describe the outcomes or deliverables of the proposal—what the funding organization can expect as a result of the time, labor, and financial support it has invested in the program. Outcomes are stated as quantifiable objectives—improvements in reading scores, volume of carbon emission reductions, aerobic fitness measures, and so on. Grant proposals, especially those solicited by government agencies, also must provide detailed plans for collecting, analyzing, and interpreting data to evaluate the success or failure of the research or program in achieving the stated outcomes.*

Budget Narrative.   Next, include a budget-narrative section that provides a detailed listing of costs for personnel, equipment, building renovations, and other grant-related expenses. This information must be clear, accurate, and in a format easily grasped by those evaluating the data (usually in a **table**). Many grant makers, including government agencies, require that specified budget forms be used. If your proposal is approved, you are being entrusted with funds belonging to someone else and you are accountable for them. Your cost estimates may also be subject to changes over which you have no control, such as price increases for equipment, software, or consulting assistance. The project may also require ongoing funding following completion of the grant's tasks. Either estimate such costs or note that they will appear in a Future Funding or Sustainability section.

Task Schedule.   Next, prepare a schedule of tasks that need to be performed to implement the program or complete the project. Arrange them as bulleted points in sequence from first to last with due dates for each, or present them in a table or perhaps in a Gantt chart as described in **graphs**.

Organization Description

The organization description may follow the Introduction or it may be placed just prior to the Conclusion, depending on RFP requirements or grant-maker guidelines. Describe the applicant organization briefly in terms of mission, history, qualifications, and credibility (significant, related accomplishments), taking care to include all information requested in the RFP or grant guidelines. Grant makers consider not only the merits of the proposed program or research but also your organization's standing in the community and similar accomplishments.

Conclusion

This brief wrap-up section emphasizes the benefits or advantages of your project. This section affords you one more opportunity to give the funding organization a reason why your proposal merits its support. Emphasize the benefits of the research, program, or other activities for the grant

---

*Many grant writers find the system called SMART useful. The SMART system assists writers in setting feasible performance goals and means of measuring success. It is described at www.yale.edu/hronline/focus/goal.html, www.ala.org/ala/mgrps/divs/acrl/about/sections/is/projpubs/smartobjectives/index.cfm, and http://writenow consulting .com.

maker's intended constituency or target population. Finally, express your appreciation for the opportunity to submit the proposal and close with a statement of your willingness to provide further information.

Attachments (Appendixes)

Funding organizations request supporting information, such as nonprofit-status documentation, copies of legal documents (for example, articles of incorporation or bylaws), or lists of information that you may need to design and compose yourself. Provide a comprehensive list of attachments and clearly label each item to guide the grant reviewer in evaluating the proposal package. See also **appendixes**.

G

WRITER'S CHECKLIST   **Writing Grant Proposals**

✔ Analyze the granting organization's RFP or guidelines carefully to best formulate your request to match its funding interests and priorities.

✔ Review the descriptions of proposal contexts, strategies, and types in the **proposals** entry.

✔ Respond to every question or address every topic requested.

✔ Strive for **conciseness** in the narrative without sacrificing **clarity** — make every word count.

✔ Emphasize the benefits of your proposal to the granting organization and its constituents.

✔ Follow all instructions meticulously because failure to include requested information or to observe format requirements may be grounds for rejection or lack of review.

WEB LINK	Resources for Preparing Grant Proposals
For useful Web sources for preparing grant proposals, go to *bedfordstmartins.com/alred* and select *Links for Handbook Entries*.	

graphs

A graph presents numerical or quantitative data in visual form and offers several advantages over presenting data within the text or in **tables**. Trends, movements, distributions, comparisons, and cycles are more readily apparent in graphs than they are in tables. However, although graphs present data in a more comprehensible form than tables do, they are less precise. For that reason, some **audiences** may need graphs to be accompanied by tables that give exact data. The types of graphs described in this entry include line graphs, bar graphs, pie graphs, and picture graphs. For advice on integrating graphs within text, see **visuals**; for information about using presentation graphics, see **presentations**.

G

Line Graphs

A line graph shows the relationship between two variables or sets of numbers by plotting points in relation to two axes drawn at right angles (Figure G–5). The vertical axis usually represents amounts, and the horizontal axis usually represents increments of time. Line graphs that portray more than one set of variables (double-line graphs) allow for comparisons between two sets of data for the same period of time. You can emphasize the difference between the two lines by shading the space between them, as shown in Figure G–5.

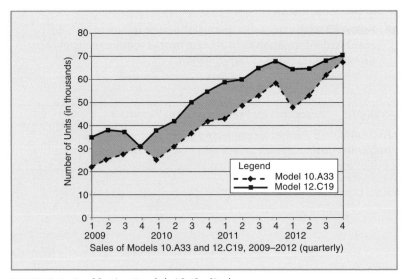

FIGURE G–5. Double-Line Graph (with Shading)

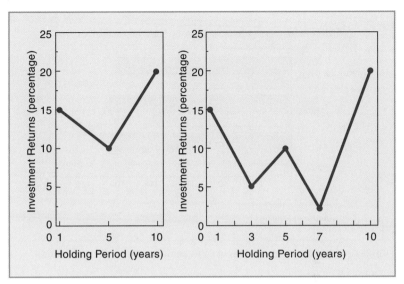

FIGURE G–6. Distorted (left) and Distortion-Free (right) Expressions of Data

❖ ETHICS NOTE Be especially careful to proportion the vertical and horizontal scales so that they give a precise presentation of the data that is free of visual distortion. To do otherwise is not only inaccurate but potentially unethical. (See **ethics in writing**.) In Figure G–6, the graph at the left gives the appearance of a slight decline followed by a steady increase in investment returns because the scale is compressed, with some years selectively omitted. The graph at the right represents the trend more accurately because the years are evenly distributed without omissions. ❖

Bar Graphs

Bar graphs consist of horizontal or vertical bars of equal width, scaled in length to represent some quantity. They are commonly used to show (1) quantities of the same item at different times, (2) quantities of different items at the same time, and (3) quantities of the different parts of an item that make up a whole (in which case, the segments of the bar graph must total 100 percent). The horizontal bar graph in Figure G–7 shows the quantities of different items for the same period of time.

Bar graphs can also show the different portions of an item that make up the whole, as shown in Figure G–8. Such a bar graph is divided according to the appropriate proportions of the subcomponents of the item. This type of graph, also called a *column graph* when constructed

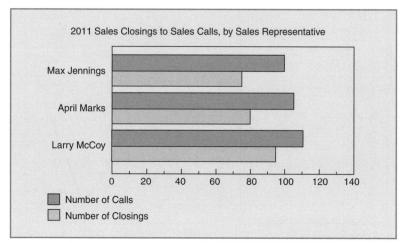

FIGURE G–7. Bar Graph (Quantities of Different Items During a Fixed Period)

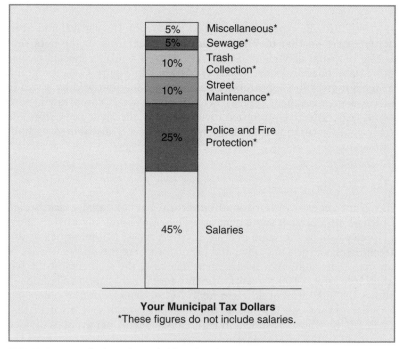

FIGURE G–8. Bar (Column) Graph (Showing the Parts That Make Up the Whole)

vertically, can indicate multiple items. Where such items represent parts of a whole, as in Figure G–8, the segments in the bar graph must total 100 percent. Note that in addition to labels, each subdivision of a bar graph must be marked clearly by color, shading, or crosshatching, with a key or labels that identify the subdivisions represented. Be aware that three-dimensional graphs can make sections seem larger than the amounts they represent.

A Gantt chart is a type of horizontal bar graph designed to plan and track the status of projects from beginning to end.* As shown in Figure G–9, the horizontal axis represents the length of a project divided into time increments—days, weeks, or months. The timeline usually runs across the top of the chart. The vertical axis represents the individual tasks that make up the project and can include a second column listing the staff responsible for each task. The horizontal bars in the body of the chart identify each task and show its beginning and end dates. Gantt charts are often prepared with spreadsheet or project-management software. See also **collaborative writing**.

WEB LINK	Resources for Preparing Gantt Charts
For useful Web sources for preparing Gantt charts, go to *bedfordstmartins.com/alred* and select *Links for Handbook Entries* or *Try a Tutorial on Web Design*.	

Pie Graphs

A pie graph presents data as wedge-shaped sections of a circle. The circle equals 100 percent, or the whole, of some quantity, and the wedges represent how the whole is divided. Many times, the data shown in a bar graph could also be depicted in a pie graph. For example, Figure G–8 shows percentages of a whole in a bar-graph form. Figure G–10 shows the same data converted into a pie graph, dividing "Your Municipal Tax Dollars" into wedge-shaped sections that represent percentages with salaries emphasized. Pie graphs provide a quicker way of presenting information that can be shown in a table with a more-detailed breakdown of the same information often accompanies a pie graph.

Picture Graphs

Picture graphs are modified bar graphs that use pictorial symbols of the item portrayed. Each symbol corresponds to a specified quantity of the item, as shown in Figure G–11. Note that for precision and clarity, the picture graph includes the total quantity following the symbols.

*The Gantt chart was developed as a production control tool in 1917 by Henry L. Gantt, an American engineer and social scientist.

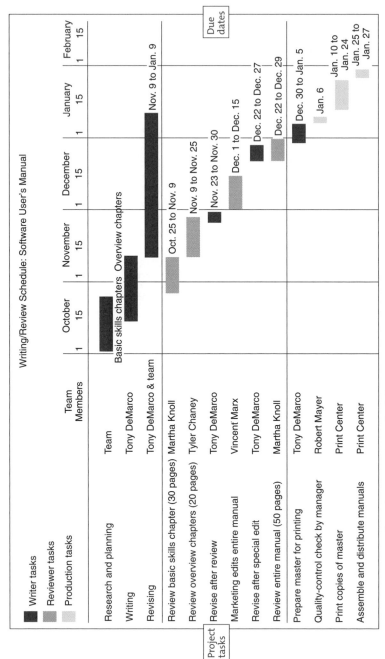

FIGURE G–9. Gantt Chart Showing Project Schedule

G

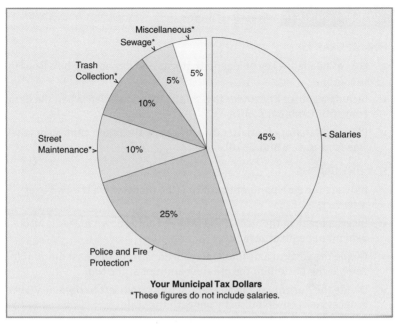

FIGURE G–10. Pie Graph (Showing Percentages of the Whole)

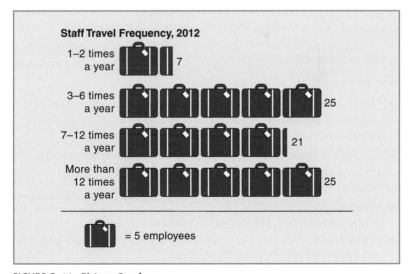

FIGURE G–11. Picture Graph

G

Creating Graphs

FOR ALL GRAPHS

✔ Use, as needed, a key or legend that lists and defines symbols (see Figure G–5).

✔ Include a source line under the graph at the lower left when the data come from another source.

✔ Place explanatory footnotes directly below the figure caption or label (see Figures G–8 and G–10).

FOR LINE GRAPHS

✔ Indicate the zero point of the graph (the point where the two axes intersect).

✔ Insert a break in the scale if the range of data shown makes it inconvenient to begin at zero.

✔ Divide the vertical axis into equal portions, from the least amount (or zero) at the bottom to the greatest amount at the top.

✔ Divide the horizontal axis into equal units from left to right. If a label is necessary, center it directly beneath the scale.

✔ Make all lettering read horizontally if possible, although the caption or label for the vertical axis is usually positioned vertically (see Figure G–5).

FOR BAR GRAPHS

✔ Differentiate among the types of data each bar or part of a bar represents by color, shading, or crosshatching.

✔ Avoid three-dimensional graphs when they make bars seem larger than the amounts they represent.

FOR PIE GRAPHS

✔ Make sure that the complete circle is equivalent to 100 percent.

✔ Sequence the wedges clockwise from largest to smallest, beginning at the 12 o'clock position, whenever possible.

✔ Limit the number of items in the pie graph to avoid clutter and to ensure that the slices are thick enough to be clear.

✔ Give each wedge a distinctive color, pattern, shade, or texture.

✔ Label each wedge with its percentage value and keep all call-outs (labels that identify the wedges) horizontal.

✔ Detach a slice, as shown in Figure G–10, if you wish to draw attention to a particular segment of the pie graph.

WRITER'S CHECKLIST   **Creating Graphs** (*continued*)

FOR PICTURE GRAPHS

✔ Use picture graphs to add interest to <u>**presentations**</u> and documents (such as <u>**newsletters**</u>) that are aimed at wide audiences.

✔ Choose symbols that are easily recognizable. See also <u>**global graphics**</u>.

✔ Let each symbol represent the same number of units.

✔ Indicate larger quantities by using more symbols, instead of larger symbols, because relative sizes are difficult to judge accurately.

✔ Indicate the total quantity following the symbols, as shown in Figure G–11.

G

H

he / she

The use of either *he* or *she* to refer to both sexes excludes half of the population. (See also **biased language**.) To avoid this problem, you could use the phrases *he or she* and *his or her*. ("Whoever is appointed will find *his or her* task difficult.") However, *he or she* and *his or her* are clumsy when used repeatedly, as are *he/she* and similar constructions. One solution is to reword the sentence to use a plural **pronoun**; if you do, change the **nouns** or other pronouns to match the plural form.

>   *Administrators*   *their jobs*   *they understand*
> ~~The administrator~~ cannot do ~~his or her~~ job until ~~he or she under-stands~~ the organization's culture.

In other cases, you may be able to avoid using a pronoun altogether.

>   *an*
> Everyone must submit ~~his or her~~ expense report by Monday.

Of course, a pronoun cannot always be omitted without changing the meaning of a sentence.

Another solution is to omit troublesome pronouns by using the imperative **mood**.

>   *Submit all*   *s*
> ~~Everyone must submit his or her~~ expense report by Monday.

headers and footers

A *header* in a **formal report** or other document appears at the top of each page, and a *footer* appears at the bottom of each page. Although the information included in headers and footers varies greatly from one organization to the next, the header and footer shown in Figure H–1 are fairly typical.

Headers or footers should include at least the page number but may also include the document title, the topic (or subtopic) of a section, the

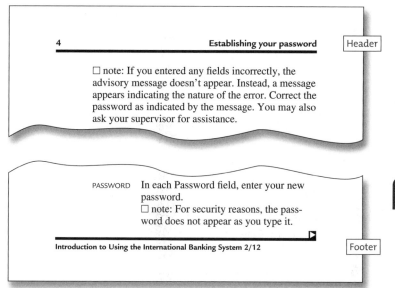

FIGURE H–1. Header and Footer

date of the document, the names of the author or recipients, and other identifying information to help **readers** keep track of where they are in the document. Keep your headers and footers concise because too much information in them can create visual clutter. For examples of headers used in correspondence, see **letters** and **memos**. See also **layout and design**.

headings

Headings (also called *heads*) are titles or subtitles that highlight the main topics and signal topic changes within the body of a document. Headings help **readers** find information and divide the material into comprehensible segments. A **formal report** or **proposal** may need several levels of headings (as shown in Figure H–2) to indicate major divisions, subdivisions, and even smaller units. If possible, avoid using more than four levels of headings. See also **layout and design**.

Headings typically represent the major topics of a document. In a short document, you can use the major divisions of your outline as headings; in a longer document, you may need to use both major and minor divisions.

First-level head	**DISTRIBUTION CENTER LOCATION REPORT**

The committee initially considered 30 possible locations for the proposed new distribution center. Of these, 20 were eliminated almost immediately for one reason or another (unfavorable zoning regulations, inadequate transportation infrastructure, etc.). Of the remaining ten locations, the committee selected for intensive study the three that seemed most promising: Chicago, Minneapolis, and Salt Lake City. We have now visited these three cities, and our observations and recommendations follow.

Second-level head	**CHICAGO**

Of the three cities, Chicago presently seems to the committee to offer the greatest advantages, although we wish to examine these more carefully before making a final recommendation.

Third-level head	**Selected Location**

Though not at the geographic center of the United States, Chicago is the demographic center to more than three-quarters of the U.S. population. It is within easy reach of our corporate headquarters in New York. And it is close to several of our most important suppliers of components and raw materials—those, for example, in Columbus, Detroit, and St. Louis. Several factors were considered essential to the location, although some may not have had as great an impact on the selection. . . .

Fourth-level head	*Air Transportation.* Chicago has two major airports (O'Hare

and Midway) and is contemplating building a third. Both domestic and international air-cargo service are available. . . .

Sea Transportation. Except during the winter months when the Great Lakes are frozen, Chicago is an international seaport. . . .

Rail Transportation. Chicago is served by the following major railroads. . . .

FIGURE H–2. Headings Used in a Document

General Heading Style

No one format for headings is correct. Often an organization settles on a standard format, which everyone in that organization follows. Sometimes a client for whom a report or proposal is being prepared requires a particular format. In the absence of specific guidelines, follow the system illustrated in Figure H–2.

Decimal Numbering System

The decimal numbering system uses a combination of numbers and decimal points to differentiate among levels of headings. Some documents, such as **policies and procedures**, benefit from the decimal numbering system for ease of cross-referencing sections. The following example shows the correspondence between different levels of headings and the decimal numbers used:

1. FIRST-LEVEL HEADING
   1.1 Second-level heading
   1.2 Second-level heading
       1.2.1 Third-level heading
       1.2.2 Third-level heading
             1.2.2.1 Fourth-level heading
             1.2.2.2 Fourth-level heading
   1.3 Second-level heading
2. FIRST-LEVEL HEADING

Although decimal headings are indented in an outline or a **table of contents**, they are flush with the left margins when they function as headings in the body of a report. Every heading starts on a new line, with an extra line of space above and below the heading.

WRITER'S CHECKLIST   **Using Headings**

✔ Use headings to signal a new topic. Use a lower-level heading to indicate a new subtopic within the larger topic.

✔ Make headings concise but specific enough to be informative, as in Figure H–2.

✔ Avoid too many or too few headings or levels of headings; too many clutter a document, and too few fail to provide recognizable structure.

✔ Ensure that headings at the same level are of relatively equal importance and have **parallel structure**.

✔ Subdivide sections only as needed; when you do, try to subdivide them into at least two lower-level headings.

✔ Do not leave a heading as the final line of a page. If two lines of text cannot fit below a heading, start the section at the top of the next page.

✔ Do not allow a heading to substitute for discussion; the text should read as if the heading were not there.

hyphens

H

The hyphen (-) is used primarily for linking and separating words and parts of words. The hyphen often improves the **clarity** of writing. The hyphen is sometimes confused with the **dash**, which is longer and has many other functions.

Hyphens with Compound Words

Some **compound words** are formed with hyphens (*able-bodied, over-the-counter*). Hyphens are also used with multiword **numbers** from twenty-one through ninety-nine and fractions when they are written out (*three-quarters*). Most current **dictionaries** indicate whether compound words are hyphenated, written as one word, or written as separate words.

Hyphens with Modifiers

Two- and three-word **modifiers** that express a single thought are hyphenated when they precede a **noun**.

▶ It was a *well-written* report.

However, a modifying phrase is not hyphenated when it follows the noun it modifies.

▶ The report was *well written*.

If each of the words can modify the noun without the aid of the other modifying word or words, do not use a hyphen (a *new laser* printer). If the first word is an **adverb** ending in *-ly*, do not use a hyphen (a *privately held* company). A hyphen is always used as part of a letter or number modifier (*A-frame house, 22-inch screen*).

In a series of unit modifiers that all have the same term following the hyphen, the term following the hyphen need not be repeated throughout the series; for greater smoothness and brevity, use the term only at the end of the series.

► The third-, fourth-, and fifth-floor laboratories were inspected.

Hyphens with Prefixes and Suffixes

A hyphen is used with a **prefix** when the root word is a proper noun (*pre-Columbian, anti-American, post-Newtonian*). A hyphen may be used when the prefix ends and the root word begins with the same vowel (*re-enter, anti-inflammatory*). A hyphen is used when *ex-* means "former" (*ex-president, ex-spouse*). A hyphen may be used to emphasize a prefix. ("He is *anti-change.*") The **suffix** *-elect* is hyphenated (*president-elect*).

Hyphens and Clarity

The presence or absence of a hyphen can alter the meaning of a sentence.

AMBIGUOUS   We need a biological waste management system.

That sentence could mean one of two things: (1) We need a system to manage "biological waste," or (2) We need a "biological" system to manage waste.

CLEAR   We need a *biological-waste* management system. [1]

CLEAR   We need a biological *waste-management* system. [2]

To avoid confusion, some words and modifiers should always be hyphenated. *Re-cover* does not mean the same thing as *recover*, for example; the same is true of *re-sign* and *resign* and *un-ionized* and *unionized*.

Other Uses of the Hyphen

Hyphens are used between letters showing how a word is spelled.

► In his e-mail, he misspelled *believed* as b-e-l-e-i-v-e-d.

A hyphen can stand for *to* or *through* between letters and numbers (*pages 44-46, the Detroit-Toledo Expressway, A-L and M-Z*).
   Hyphens are commonly used in telephone numbers (*800-555-1212*), Web addresses (*computer-parts.com*), file names (*report-09.doc*), and similar number/symbol combinations. See also **dates**.

WRITER'S CHECKLIST	Using Hyphens to Divide Words

✔ Do not divide one-syllable words.

✔ Divide words at syllable breaks, which you can determine with a dictionary.

✔ Do not divide a word if only one letter would remain at the end of a line or if fewer than three letters would start a new line.

✔ Do not divide a word at the end of a page; carry the word over to the next page.

✔ If a word already has a hyphen in its spelling, divide the word at the existing hyphen.

✔ Do not use a hyphen to break a URL or an e-mail address at the end of a line because it may confuse readers who could assume that the hyphen is part of the address.

H

I

idioms

An idiom is a group of words that has a special meaning apart from its literal meaning. Someone who "runs for office" in the United States, for example, need not be an athlete. The same candidate would "stand for office" in the United Kingdom. Because such expressions are specific to a culture, nonnative speakers must memorize them.

Idioms are often constructed with **prepositions** that follow **adjectives** (*similar to*), **nouns** (*need for*), and **verbs** (*approve of*). Some idioms can change meaning slightly with the preposition used, as in *agree to* ("consent") and *agree with* ("in accord"). The following are typical idioms that give nonnative speakers trouble.

call off [cancel]	hand in [submit]
call on [visit a client]	hand out [distribute]
cross out [draw a line through]	keep on [continue]
drop in on [visit unexpectedly]	look up [research a subject]
figure out [solve a problem]	put off [postpone]
find out [discover information]	run into [meet by chance]
get through with [finish]	run out of [deplete supply]
give up [quit]	watch out for [be careful]

Idioms often provide helpful shortcuts. In fact, they can make writing more natural and lively. Avoid them, however, if your writing is to be translated into another language or read in other English-speaking countries. Because no language system can fully explain such usages, a reader must check **dictionaries** or usage guides to interpret the meaning of idioms. See also **English as a second language** and **international correspondence**.

WEB LINK	Prepositional Idioms
For links to helpful lists of common pairings of prepositions with nouns, verbs, and adjectives, see *bedfordstmartins.com/alred* and select *Links for Handbook Entries*.	

illegal / illicit

If something is *illegal*, it is prohibited by law. If something is *illicit*, it is prohibited by either law or custom. *Illicit* behavior may or may not be *illegal*, but it does violate social convention or moral codes and therefore usually has a clandestine or immoral **connotation**. ("The employee's *illicit* sexual behavior caused a scandal, but the company's attorney concluded that no *illegal* acts were committed.")

illustrations (*see* visuals)

imply / infer

If you *imply* something, you hint at or suggest it. ("Her e-mail *implied* that the project would be delayed.") If you *infer* something, you reach a conclusion based on evidence or interpretation. ("The manager *inferred* from the e-mail that the project would be delayed.")

in / into

In means "inside of"; *into* implies movement from the outside to the inside. ("We were *in* a meeting when the intern brought copies of the contract *into* the conference room.")

in order to

Most often, *in order to* is a meaningless filler phrase that is dropped into a sentence without thought. See also **conciseness**.

▶ ~~In order to~~ improve our profit margin, we must increase our client

> To

base.

However, the phrase *in order to* is sometimes essential to the meaning of a sentence.

▶ If the vertical scale of a graph line would not normally show the zero point, use a horizontal break in the graph *in order to* include the zero point.

In order to also helps control the **pace** of a sentence, even when it is not essential to the meaning of the sentence.

▶ The committee must know the estimated costs *in order to* evaluate the feasibility of the project.

in terms of

When used to indicate a shift from one kind of language or terminology to another, the phrase *in terms of* can be useful.

▶ *In terms of* gross sales, the year has been relatively successful; however, *in terms of* net income, it has been discouraging.

When simply dropped into a sentence because it easily comes to mind, *in terms of* is meaningless **affectation**. See also **conciseness**.

▶ She was thinking ~~in terms~~ of subcontracting much of the work.

indexing

An index is an alphabetical list of all the major topics and sometimes subtopics in a written work. It cites the pages where each topic can be found and allows **readers** to find information on particular topics quickly and easily, as shown in Figure I–1. The index always comes at the very end of the work. Many Web sites also provide linked subject indexes to the content of the sites.

The key to compiling a useful index is selectivity. Instead of listing every possible reference to a topic, select references to passages where the topic is discussed fully or where a significant point is made about it. For index entries like those in Figure I–1, choose key terms that best represent a topic. Key terms are those words or phrases that a reader would most likely look for in an index. For example, the key terms in a reference to the development of legislation about environmental impact statements would probably be *legislation* and *environmental impact statement*, not *development*. In selecting terms for index entries, use chapter or section titles only if they include such key terms. For index entries on **tables** and **visuals,** use the words from their titles that will function as key terms a reader might seek. Create alphabetical Web-site indexes from links to topics in subsites throughout the larger site.

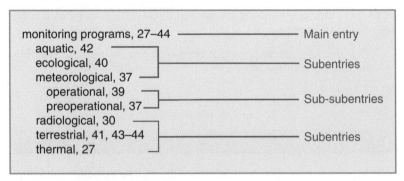

FIGURE I–1. Index Entry (with Main Entry, Subentries, and Sub-subentries)

DIGITAL TIP

Creating an Index

You can make your long documents more reader-friendly by adding an index. Most word-processing programs include tools that provide a quick and efficient way to create an alphabetical subject index of your document. The index generated by your word-processing software will still need careful review, but using the software to create the first draft can save time. If you need to index a highly complex document, you may want to consider specialized indexing software designed for use by professional indexers and publishers. For a list of indexing tools and instructions on creating a standard index, go to *bedfordstmartins.com/alred* and select *Digital Tips*, "Creating an Index."

indiscreet / indiscrete

Indiscreet means "lacking in prudence or sound judgment." ("His public discussion of the proposed merger was *indiscreet*.") *Indiscrete* means "not divided or divisible into parts." ("The separate departments, once combined, become *indiscrete*.") See also **discreet / discrete**.

inquiries and responses

The purpose of writing inquiry **letters** or **e-mail** messages is to obtain responses to requests or specific questions, as in Figure I–2, which shows a college student's request for information from an official at a

Dear Ms. Metcalf:

I am an architecture student at the University of Dayton, and I am working with a team of students to design an energy-efficient house for a class project. I am writing to request information on heating systems based on the specifications of our design. To meet our deadline, we would appreciate any information you could provide by November 16.

The house we are designing contains 2,000 square feet of living space (17,600 cubic feet) and meets all the requirements in your brochure "Insulating for Efficiency." We need the following information, based on the southern Ohio climate:

- The proper-size heat pump for such a home.
- The wattage of the supplemental electrical heating units required.
- The estimated power consumption and rates for those units for one year.

We will be happy to send you our preliminary design report. If you have questions or suggestions, contact me at kparsons@fly.ud.edu or call 513-229-4598.

Thank you for your help.

FIGURE I–2. Inquiry

power company. Inquiries may benefit either the reader (as in requests for information about a product that a company has advertised) or the writer (as in the student's inquiry in Figure I–2). Inquiries that primarily benefit the writer require the use of **persuasion** and special consideration of the needs of your **audience**. See also **correspondence**.

Writing Inquiries

Inquiries need to be specific, clear, and concise in order to receive a prompt, helpful reply.

- Phrase your request so that the reader will immediately know the type of information you are seeking, why you need it, and how you will use it.
- If possible, present questions in a numbered or bulleted **list** to make it easy for your reader to respond to them.
- Keep the number of questions to a minimum to improve your chances of receiving a prompt response.

- Offer some inducement for the reader to respond, such as promising to share the results of what you are doing. See also **"you" viewpoint**.
- Promise to keep responses confidential, when appropriate.
- Provide a date by which you need a response.

In the closing, thank the reader for taking the time to respond. In addition, make it convenient for the recipient to respond by providing your contact information, such as a phone number or an e-mail address, as shown in Figure I–2.

Responding to Inquiries

When you receive an inquiry, determine whether you have both the information and the authority to respond. If you are the right person in your organization to respond and you understand your organization's policy about the issue, answer as promptly as you can, and be sure to answer every inquiry or question asked, as shown in Figure I–3. How

---

Dear Ms. Parsons:

Jane Metcalf forwarded to me your October 12 inquiry about the house that your architecture team is designing. I can estimate the heating requirements of a typical home of 17,600 cubic feet as follows:

- For such a home, we would generally recommend a heat pump capable of delivering 40,000 BTUs, such as our model AL-42 (17 kilowatts).
- With the AL-42's efficiency, you don't need supplemental heating units.
- Depending on usage, the AL-42 unit averages between 1,000 and 1,500 kilowatt-hours from December through March. To determine the current rate for such usage, check with Dayton Power and Light Company.

I can give you an answer that would apply specifically to your house based on its particular design (such as number of stories, windows, and entrances). If you send me more details, I will be happy to provide more precise figures for your interesting project.

Sincerely,

FIGURE I–3. Response to an Inquiry

long and how detailed your response should be depends on the nature of the question and the information the writer provides.

If you have received an inquiry that you feel you cannot answer, find out who can and forward the inquiry to that person. Notify the writer that you have forwarded the inquiry. The person who replies to a forwarded inquiry should state in the first paragraph of the response who has forwarded the original inquiry, as shown in Figure I–3.

inside / inside of

In the phrase *inside of*, the word *of* is redundant and should be omitted.

▶ The switch is just inside ~~of~~ the door.

Using *inside of* to mean "in less time than" is colloquial and should be avoided in writing.

▶ They were finished ~~inside of~~ an hour.
　　　　　　　　　　in less than

instant messaging

Instant messaging (IM) is a text-based communications medium that fills a niche between the telephone and **e-mail**. It allows both real-time communications, like a phone call, and the transfer of text or other files, like an e-mail. It is especially useful to those who are working at sites without access to e-mail. See also **selecting the medium**.

To set up routine IM exchanges, add to your contact list the user names of those with whom you regularly exchange messages. Choose a screen name that your colleagues will recognize. If you use IM routinely as part of your job, create an "away" message that signals when you are not available for IM interactions.

When writing instant messages, keep them simple and to the point, covering only one subject in each message to prevent confusion and inappropriate responses. Because screen space is often limited and speed is essential, many who send instant messages use abbreviations and shortened spellings ("u" for "you"). Be sure that your **reader** will understand such abbreviations; when in doubt, avoid them.*

---

*Many online sites, such as *www.netlingo.com*, define IM and other such abbreviations.

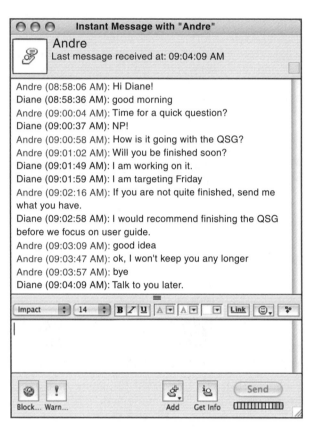

FIGURE I–4. Instant-Message Exchange

In Figure I–4, the manager of a software development company in Maine ("Diane") is exchanging instant messages with a business partner in the Netherlands ("Andre"). Notice that the correspondents use an informal style that includes personal and professional abbreviations with which both are familiar ("NP" for "no problem"; and "QSG" for Quick Start Guide). These messages demonstrate how IM can not only help people exchange information quickly but also build rapport among distant colleagues and team members. The exchange also demonstrates why IM is not generally appropriate for many complex messages or for more formal circumstances, such as when establishing new professional relationships.

❖ ETHICS NOTE Be sure to follow your employer's IM policies, such as any limitations on sending personal messages during work hours or requirements concerning confidentiality. If no specific policy exists, assume that personal use of IM is not appropriate in your workplace. ❖

Instant Messaging Privacy and Security

✔ Restrict contact lists on professional IM accounts to business associates to avoid inadvertently sending a personal message to an associate.

✔ Learn the options, capabilities, and security limitations of your IM system and set the preferences that best suit your use of the system.

✔ Be especially alert to the possibilities of virus infections and security risks with messages, attachments, and contact lists.

✔ Save significant IM exchanges (or logs) for your future reference.

✔ Be aware that instant messages can be saved by your recipients and may be archived by your employer. (See the Professionalism Note on page 177.)

✔ Do not use professional IM for office gossip or inappropriate exchanges.

instructions

Business writers often prepare many kinds of instructions for coworkers. (See also **policies and procedures**.) Instructions that are clear and easy to follow can build goodwill because they help **readers** complete tasks efficiently and prevent miscommunication. To write effective instructions, you must thoroughly understand the process or system you are describing. Finally, keep in mind that the most effective instructions often combine written elements and visual elements that reinforce each other. See also **process explanation**.

Writing Instructions

Consider your audience's level of knowledge. If all your readers have good backgrounds in the topic, you can use fairly specialized terms. If that is not the case, use **plain language** or include a **glossary** for specialized terms that you cannot avoid. See also **audience**.

Clear and easy-to-follow instructions are written as commands in the imperative **mood**, active **voice**, and (whenever possible) present **tense**.

> ▸ *Sign the*   •
>   ~~The~~ insurance request ~~will be signed by the employee.~~
>   ^   ^

Although **conciseness** is important in instructions, **clarity** is essential. You can make sentences shorter by leaving out some **articles** (*a*, *an, the*), some **pronouns** (*you, this, these*), and some **verbs**, but such sentences may result in **telegraphic style** and be harder to understand. For example, the first version of the following instruction for submitting a medical claim is confusing.

CONFUSING   Submit claim negotiated to HR with statement from attending.

CLEAR   Submit the claim to be negotiated to the Human Resources Office with the statement of the attending physician who prescribed the treatment.

One good way to make instructions easy to follow is to divide them into short, simple steps in their proper sequence. Steps can be organized with words (*first, next, finally*) that indicate time or sequence.

▶ *First*, determine the problem the customer is having with the computer. *Next*, observe the system in operation. *At that time*, question the operator until you are sure that the problem has been explained completely. *Then* analyze the problem and make any necessary adjustments.

You can also use numbers, as in the following:

▶ 1. Open the top cover and remove the toner cartridge.

2. Use the green handle to lift the paper access plate.

3. Slowly and carefully pull the paper out of the printer.

Consider using the numbered- or bulleted-list feature of your word-processing software to create sequenced steps. See **lists**.

Plan ahead for your reader. If the instructions in step 2 will affect a process in step 9, say so in step 2. Sometimes your instructions have to make clear that two operations must be performed simultaneously. Either state that fact in an **introduction** to the specific instructions or include both operations in one step.

CONFUSING   1. Hold down the CONTROL key.
2. Press the RETURN key before releasing the CONTROL key.

CLEAR   1. While holding down the CONTROL key, press the RETURN key.

Alert your readers to any potentially hazardous materials (or actions) before they reach the step for which the material is needed.

If your instructions involve many steps, break them into stages, each with a separate heading so that each stage begins again with step 1. Using **headings** as dividers is especially important if your reader is likely to be performing the operation as he or she reads the instructions.

Illustrating Instructions

Illustrations should be developed together with the text, especially for complex instructions that benefit from **visuals** that foster **clarity** and conciseness. Such visuals as **drawings**, **flowcharts**, **maps**, and **photographs** enable your reader to identify relationships more easily than do long explanations.

Consider the **layout and design** of your instructions to most effectively integrate visuals. Highlight important visuals as well as text by making them stand out from the surrounding text. Consider using boxes and boldface or distinctive headings. Experiment with font style, size, and color to determine which devices are most effective.

The instructions in Figure I–5 on page 280 guide the reader through the steps of streaking a saucer-sized disk of material (called *agar*) used to grow bacteria colonies. The purpose is to thin out the original specimen (the *moculum*) so that the bacteria will grow in small, isolated colonies. This section could be part of other larger instructional documents for which streaking is only one step among others.

Finally, to test the accuracy and clarity of your instructions, ask someone who is not familiar with the task to follow your directions. A first-time user can spot missing steps or point out passages that should be worded more clearly.

WRITER'S CHECKLIST   Writing Instructions

✔ Use the imperative mood and the active voice.

✔ Use short sentences and simple present tense as much as possible.

✔ Avoid **jargon** that your readers might not know, including undefined **abbreviations**.

✔ Do not use elegant variation (two different words for the same thing). See also **affectation**.

✔ Eliminate any **ambiguity**.

✔ Use effective visuals and highlighting devices.

✔ Test your instructions by having someone else follow them while you observe.

STREAKING AN AGAR PLATE

Distribute the inoculum over the surface of the agar in the following manner:

1. Beginning at one edge of the saucer, thin the inoculum by streaking back and forth over the same area several times, sweeping across the agar surface until approximately one-quarter of the surface has been covered. *Sterilize the loop in an open flame.*
2. Streak at right angles to the originally inoculated area, carrying the inoculum out from the streaked areas onto the sterile surface with only the first stroke of the wire. Cover half of the remaining sterile agar surface. *Sterilize the loop.*
3. Repeat as described in Step 2, covering the remaining sterile agar surface.

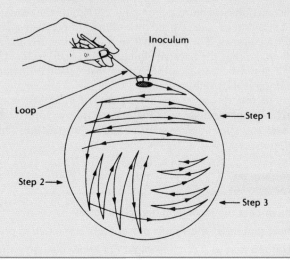

FIGURE I–5. Illustrated Instructions

insure / ensure / assure

Insure, ensure, and *assure* all mean "make secure or certain." *Assure* refers to people, and it alone has the connotation of setting a person's mind at rest. ("I *assure* you that the promotional material will arrive on time.") *Ensure* and *insure* mean "make secure from harm." Only *insure* is widely used in the sense of guaranteeing the value of life or property.

▶ We need all the data to *ensure* the success of the project.

▶ We should *insure* the contents of the warehouse.

intensifiers

Intensifiers are **adverbs** that **emphasize** degree, such as *very*, *quite*, *rather*, *such*, and *too*. Although intensifiers serve a legitimate and necessary function, unnecessary intensifiers can weaken your writing. Eliminate those that do not make an obvious contribution or replace them with specific details.

▶ The team learned the very good news that it had been awarded a
$10,000
~~rather substantial monetary~~ prize for its design.
        ^

Some words (such as *perfect*, *impossible*, and *final*) do not logically permit intensification because, by definition, they do not allow degrees of comparison. Although **usage** often ignores that logical restriction, avoid such comparisons in business writing. See also **adjectives**, **conciseness**, and **equal / unique / perfect**.

interface

An *interface* is a surface that provides a common boundary between two bodies or areas. The bodies or areas may be physical ("the *interface* of a tire and pavement") or conceptual ("the *interface* of mathematics and economics"). Do not use *interface* as a substitute for the verbs *cooperate*, *interact*, or even *work*. See also **affectation** and **buzzwords**.

interjections

An interjection is a word or phrase standing alone or inserted into a sentence to exclaim or to command attention. Grammatically, it has no connection to the sentence. An interjection can be strong (*Hey! Ouch! Wow!*) or mild (*oh*, *well*, *indeed*). A strong interjection is followed by an **exclamation mark**.

▶ *Wow!* Profits more than doubled last quarter.

A weak interjection is followed by a **comma**.

▶ *Well,* we need to rethink the proposal.

An interjection inserted into a sentence usually requires a comma before it and after it.

▶ We must, *indeed*, rethink the proposal.

Because they get their main expressive force from sound, interjections are more common in speech than in writing. Use them sparingly.

international correspondence

Business **correspondence** varies among national cultures. Organizational patterns, persuasive strategies, forms of courtesy, formality, and ideas about efficiency differ from country to country. For example, in the United States, direct, concise correspondence usually demonstrates courtesy by not wasting the reader's time. In many other countries, however, such directness and brevity may seem rude to **readers**, suggesting that the writer is dismissive or lacking in manners. (See **audience** and **tone**.) Likewise, where a U.S. writer might consider one brief **letter** or **e-mail** sufficient to communicate a request, a writer in another country may expect an exchange of three or four longer letters to pave the way for action.

Cultural Differences in Correspondence

When you read correspondence from businesspeople in other cultures or countries, be alert to differences in such features as customary expressions, openings, and closings. Japanese business writers, for example, traditionally use indirect openings that reflect on the season, compliment the reader's success, or offer hopes for the reader's continued prosperity. Consider deeper issues as well, such as how writers from other cultures express bad news. Japanese writers traditionally express negative messages, such as **refusal letters**, indirectly to avoid embarrassing the recipient. Such cultural differences are often based on perceptions of time, face-saving, and traditions. The features and communication styles of specific national cultures are complex; the entry **global communication** provides information and resources for cross-cultural study. See also **global graphics**.

Cross-Cultural Examples

Figures I–6 and I–7 are a draft and a final version of a letter written by an American businessman to a Japanese businessman. The opening and closing of the draft in Figure I–6 do not include enough of the politeness strategies that are important in Japanese culture, and the informal

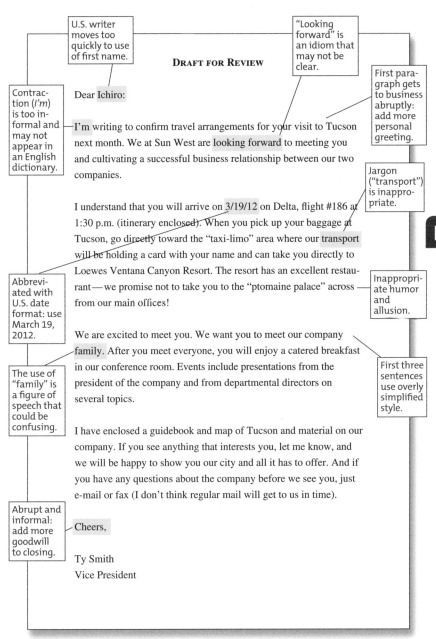

DRAFT FOR REVIEW

U.S. writer moves too quickly to use of first name.

"Looking forward" is an idiom that may not be clear.

First paragraph gets to business abruptly: add more personal greeting.

Contraction (*I'm*) is too informal and may not appear in an English dictionary.

Dear Ichiro:

I'm writing to confirm travel arrangements for your visit to Tucson next month. We at Sun West are looking forward to meeting you and cultivating a successful business relationship between our two companies.

I understand that you will arrive on 3/19/12 on Delta, flight #186 at 1:30 p.m. (itinerary enclosed). When you pick up your baggage at Tucson, go directly toward the "taxi-limo" area where our transport will be holding a card with your name and can take you directly to Loewes Ventana Canyon Resort. The resort has an excellent restaurant—we promise not to take you to the "ptomaine palace" across from our main offices!

We are excited to meet you. We want you to meet our company family. After you meet everyone, you will enjoy a catered breakfast in our conference room. Events include presentations from the president of the company and from departmental directors on several topics.

I have enclosed a guidebook and map of Tucson and material on our company. If you see anything that interests you, let me know, and we will be happy to show you our city and all it has to offer. And if you have any questions about the company before we see you, just e-mail or fax (I don't think regular mail will get to us in time).

Cheers,

Ty Smith
Vice President

Jargon ("transport") is inappropriate.

Abbreviated with U.S. date format: use March 19, 2012.

Inappropriate humor and allusion.

The use of "family" is a figure of speech that could be confusing.

First three sentences use overly simplified style.

Abrupt and informal: add more goodwill to closing.

FIGURE I–6. Inappropriate International Correspondence (Draft Marked for Revision)

Sun West Corporation, Inc.

2565 North Armadillo
Tucson, AZ 85719
Phone: (602) 555-6677
Fax: (602) 555-6678   sunwest.com

March 5, 2012

Ichiro Katsumi
Investment Director
Toshiba Investment Company
1-29-10 Ichiban-cho
Tokyo 105, Japan

Dear Mr. Katsumi:

I hope that you and your family are well and prospering in the new year. We at Sun West Corporation are very pleased that you will be coming to visit us in Tucson this month. It will be a pleasure to meet you, and we are very gratified and honored that you are interested in investing in our company.

So that we can ensure that your stay will be pleasurable, we have taken care of all of your travel arrangements. You will

- Depart Narita–New Tokyo International Airport on Delta Airlines flight #75 at 1700 on March 19, 2012.
- Arrive at Los Angeles International Airport at 1050 local time and depart for Tucson on Delta flight #186 at 1205.
- Arrive at Tucson International Airport at 1330 local time on March 19.
- Depart Tucson International Airport on Delta flight #123 at 1845 on March 26.
- Arrive in Salt Lake City, Utah, at 1040 and depart on Delta flight #34 at 1115.
- Arrive in Portland, Oregon, at 1210 local time and depart on Delta flight #254 at 1305.
- Arrive in Tokyo at 1505 local time on March 27.

If you need additional information about your travel plans or information on Sun West Corporation, please call, fax, or e-mail me directly at tsmith@sunwest.com. That way, we will receive your message in time to make the appropriate changes or additions.

FIGURE I–7. Appropriate International Correspondence

Mr. Ichiro Katsumi   2   March 5, 2012

After you arrive in Tucson, a chauffeur from Skyline Limousines will be waiting for you at Gate 12. He or she will be carrying a card with your name, will help you collect your luggage from the baggage claim area, and will then drive you to the Loewes Ventana Canyon Resort. This resort is one of the most prestigious in Tucson, with spectacular desert views, high-quality amenities, and one of the best golf courses in the city. The next day, the chauffeur will be back at the Ventana at 0900 to drive you to Sun West Corporation.

We at Sun West Corporation are very excited to meet you and introduce you to all the staff members of our hardworking and growing company. After you meet everyone, you will enjoy a catered breakfast in our conference room. At that time, you will receive a schedule of events planned for the remainder of your trip. Events include presentations from the president of the company and from departmental directors on

- The history of Sun West Corporation
- The uniqueness of our products and current success in the marketplace
- Demographic information and the benefits of being located in Tucson
- The potential for considerable profits for both our companies with your company's investment

We encourage you to read through the enclosed guidebook and map of Tucson. In addition to events planned at Sun West Corporation, you will find many natural wonders and historical sites to see in Tucson and in Arizona in general. If you see any particular event or place that you would like to visit, please let us know. We will be happy to show you our city and all it has to offer.

Again, we are very honored that you will be visiting us, and we look forward to a successful business relationship between our two companies.

Sincerely,

Ty Smith

Ty Smith
Vice President

Enclosures (2)

FIGURE I–7. Appropriate International Correspondence (*continued*)

salutation inappropriately uses the recipient's first name (*Dear Ichiro:*). This draft also contains **idioms** (*looking forward*, *company family*), **jargon** (*transport will be holding*), **contractions** (*I'm*, *don't*), informal language (*just e-mail or fax*, *Cheers*), and humor and allusion (*"ptomaine palace" across from our main offices*).

Compare that letter to the one in Figure I–7, which is written in language that is courteous, literal, and specific. This revised letter begins with concern about the recipient's family and prosperity because that opening honors traditional Japanese patterns in business correspondence. The letter is free of slang, idioms, and jargon. The sentences are shorter than in the draft; in addition, bulleted lists break up the paragraphs, contractions are avoided, months are spelled out, and 24-hour-clock time is used.

When writing for international readers, rethink the ingrained habits that define how you express yourself, learn as much as you can about the cultural expectations of others, and focus on politeness strategies that demonstrate your respect for readers. Doing so will help you achieve **clarity** and mutual understanding with international readers.

WEB LINK	Google's International Directory

Google's International Business and Trade Directory provides an excellent starting point for searching the Web for information related to customs, communication, and international standards. See *bedfordstmartins.com/alred* and select *Links for Handbook Entries*.

WRITER'S CHECKLIST   **Writing International Correspondence**

✔ Observe the guidelines for courtesy, such as those in the *Writer's Checklist: Using Tone to Build Goodwill* in **correspondence** on page 118.

✔ Write clear and complete sentences: Unusual word order or rambling sentences will frustrate and confuse readers. See **garbled sentences**.

✔ Avoid an overly simplified style that may offend or any **affectation** that may confuse the reader. See also **English as a second language**.

✔ Avoid humor, irony, and sarcasm; they are easily misunderstood outside their cultural **context**.

✔ Do not use idioms, jargon, slang expressions, unusual **figures of speech**, or **allusions** to events or attitudes particular to American life.

✔ Consider whether necessary technical terminology can be found in abbreviated English-language dictionaries; if it cannot, carefully define such terminology.

WRITER'S CHECKLIST   Writing International Correspondence (*continued*)

✔ Do not use contractions or <u>abbreviations</u> that may not be clear to international readers.

✔ Avoid inappropriate informality, such as using first names too quickly.

✔ Write out <u>dates</u>, whether in the month-day-year style (*June 11, 2012* not *6/11/12*) used in the United States or the day-month-year style (*11 June 2012* not *11/6/12*) used in many other parts of the world.

✔ Specify time zones or refer to international standards, such as Greenwich Mean Time (GMT) or Coordinated Universal Time (UTC).

✔ Use international measurement standards, such as the metric system (*18°C, 14 cm, 45 kg*) where possible.

✔ Ask someone from your intended audience's culture or with appropriate expertise to review your draft before you complete your final <u>proofreading</u>.

interviewing for information

Interviewing others who have knowledge of your subject is often an essential method of <u>research</u> in business writing. The process of interviewing for information includes determining the proper person to interview, preparing for the interview, conducting the interview, and expanding your notes soon after the interview.

Determining the Proper Person to Interview

Many times, your subject or <u>purpose</u> logically points to the proper person to interview for information. For example, if you were writing about using the Web to market a software-development business, you would want to interview someone with extensive experience in Web marketing as well as someone who has built a successful business developing software. The following sources can help you determine the appropriate person to interview: (1) workplace colleagues or faculty in appropriate academic departments; (2) local chapters of professional societies; (3) information from "Contact" or "About Us" links at company or organization Web sites; and (4) targeted Internet searches, such as using relevant domains (.edu, .gov, and .org).

Preparing for the Interview

Before the interview, learn as much as possible about the person you are going to interview and the organization for which he or she works.

◀ PROFESSIONALISM NOTE When you contact the prospective interviewee, explain who you are, why you would like an interview, the subject and purpose of the interview, and generally how much time it will take. You should also ask permission if you plan to record the interview and let your interviewee know that you will allow him or her to review your draft. ▶

After you have made the appointment, prepare a list of questions to ask your interviewee. Avoid vague, general questions. A question such as "Do you think the Web would be useful for you?" is too general to elicit useful information. It is more helpful to ask specific but open-ended questions, such as the following: "Many physicians in your specialty are using the Web to answer routine patient questions. How might providing such information on your Web site affect your relationship with your patients?"

Conducting the Interview

Arrive promptly for the interview and be prepared to guide the discussion. During the interview, take only memory-jogging notes that will help you recall the conversation later; do not ask your interviewee to slow down so that you can take detailed notes. As the interview is reaching a close, take a few minutes to skim your notes and ask the interviewee to clarify anything that is ambiguous.

WRITER'S CHECKLIST   Interviewing Successfully

✔ Be pleasant but purposeful. You are there to get information, so don't be timid about asking leading questions on the subject.

✔ Use the list of questions you have prepared, starting with the less-complex and less-difficult aspects of the topic to get the conversation started, and then going on to the more-challenging aspects.

✔ Let your interviewee do most of the talking. Remember that the interviewee is the expert. See also <u>listening</u>.

✔ Be objective. Don't offer your opinions on the subject. You are there to get information, not to debate.

✔ Ask additional questions as they arise.

✔ Don't get sidetracked. If the interviewee strays too far from the subject, ask a specific question to direct the conversation back on track.

✔ If you use an audiocassette or a digital voice recorder, do not let it lure you into relaxing so that you neglect to ask crucial questions.

✔ After thanking the interviewee, ask permission to contact him or her again to clarify a point or two as you complete your interview notes.

✔ A day or two after the interview, thank the interviewee in a brief letter or message.

Expanding Your Notes Soon After the Interview

Immediately after leaving the interview, use your memory-jogging notes to help you mentally review the interview and expand those notes. Do not postpone this step. No matter how good your memory is, you will forget some important points if you do not complete this step at once. See also **note-taking**.

Interviewing by Phone or E-mail

When an interviewee is not available for a face-to-face meeting, consider a telephone interview. Most of the principles for conducting face-to-face interviews apply to phone interviews; be aware, however, that phone calls do not offer the important nonverbal cues of face-to-face meetings. Further, taking notes can be challenging while speaking on a phone, although a phone headset or a high-quality speakerphone can alleviate that problem.

As an alternative to a face-to-face or phone interview, consider an **e-mail** interview. Such an "interview," however, lacks the spontaneity and the immediacy of an in-person or a phone conversation. If e-mail is the only option, the interviewing principles in this entry can help you obtain useful responses. Before you send any questions, make sure that your contact is willing to participate and respond to follow-up requests for clarification. As a courtesy, give the respondent a general idea of the number of questions you plan to ask and the level of detail you expect. When you send the questions, ask for a reasonable deadline from the interviewee ("Would you be able to send your response by . . . ?").

interviewing for a job

Job interviews can take place in person, by phone, or by teleconference. They may last 30 minutes, an hour, or several hours. Sometimes an initial job interview is followed by a series of additional interviews that can last a half or full day. Often just one or two people conduct the interview, but on occasion a group or panel of four or more attend. The job interview allows a potential employer to observe and evaluate your character traits (such as personality, confidence, and communication style) with the credentials and experience from your **résumé** and **application cover letter** serving as background. Because it is impossible to know exactly what to expect, it is important that you be well prepared. See also **job search**.

Before the Interview

The interview facilitates a two-way communication process. It presents you with an opportunity to ask questions of your potential employer. Before the interview, learn everything you can about the organization by answering for yourself such questions as the following:

- What kind of organization (profit, nonprofit, government) is it?
- What are the mission, goals, and objectives of the organization?
- What types of services or products does the company provide?
- Does the company operate locally, regionally, or internationally?
- Is the company privately owned or employee owned?
- How many employees are there?
- Is the company a subsidiary of a larger operation?
- How long has the company been in business?
- Where will I fit in? Does there appear to be opportunity for advancement?

You can obtain information from current employees, the Internet, the company's publications, or the business section of back issues of local newspapers. The company's Web site may help you learn about the company's size, sales volume, product line, credit rating, branch locations, subsidiary companies, new products and services, building programs, and similar information. You may also conduct **research** using a company's annual reports and other publications, such as *Moody's Industrials, Dun and Bradstreet, Standard and Poor's*, and *Thomas' Register*, as well as other business reference sources a librarian might suggest. Ask your interviewer about what you cannot find through your own research. Doing so demonstrates your interest and allows you to learn more about your potential employer.

Try to anticipate the questions your interviewer might ask and rehearse your answers in advance. Be sure you understand a question before answering it and avoid responding too quickly with a rehearsed reply. Be prepared to respond in a natural and relaxed manner, taking care not to provide unnecessary details. Interviewers typically ask the following questions:

- What are your short-term and long-term occupational goals?
- Where do you see yourself five years from now?
- What are your major strengths and weaknesses?
- Do you work better with others or alone?
- What academic or career accomplishment are you particularly proud of? Describe it.
- Why are you leaving your current job?

- May we contact your previous employer?
- Why do you want to work for this organization?
- Why should I hire you?
- What salary and benefits do you expect?

Rather than such straightforward questions, some employers use behavioral interviews that focus on asking the candidate to provide examples or respond to hypothetical situations. Interviewers who use behavior-based questions are looking for specific examples from your experience. Prepare for the behavioral interview by recollecting challenging situations or problems that you successfully resolved. Examples of behavior-based questions include the following:

- Tell me about a time when you experienced conflict while on a team.
- If I were your boss and you disagreed with a decision I made, what would you do?
- How have you used your leadership skills to bring about change?
- Tell me about a time when you failed and what you learned from the experience.

Difficult Questions

Questions that seem personal, appear to breach legal ethics, or otherwise make you uncomfortable not only can be hard to answer but also can quickly erode the confidence you worked so hard to build throughout the preparation phase. Remaining composed and remembering that the employer's objective is simply to determine whether you are the best candidate for the position will help you respond appropriately to difficult questions. Be brief, concise, and truthful in your answers. Common questions that may broach sensitive subjects may include the following:

- Have you ever experienced a layoff or been terminated?
- Why did you stay with previous employers on average for just a year?
- Why do you have such a large gap of employment between these dates?

◀ PROFESSIONALISM NOTE Plan to arrive 10 to 15 minutes early to the interview; never be late. Always bring extra copies of your résumé, a writing instrument, a note pad, samples of your work or portfolio (if applicable), and a list of references and contact information. Turn off any electronic devices prior to your arrival. If you are asked to complete an application form, read it carefully before you write and proofread it when you are finished. The form provides a written record for company files and indicates to the company how well you follow directions and complete a task. ▶

During the Interview

The interview actually begins when you arrive. Be polite to other employees you meet. What you wear and how you act make a first impression. In general, dress simply and conservatively, avoid extremes in fragrance and cosmetics, and be well groomed.

Behavior. After introductions, thank the interviewer for his or her time, express your pleasure at meeting him or her, and remain standing until you are offered a seat. Sit up straight (good posture suggests self-assurance), maintain eye contact with the interviewer, and try to appear relaxed and confident. During the interview, use nervous energy to your advantage by channeling it into the alertness that you will need to listen and respond effectively. Do not attempt to take extensive notes, use a laptop computer, or use a cell phone during the interview. You can jot down a few facts, but keep your focus on the interviewer. See also **listening**.

Responses. When you answer questions, do not ramble or stray from the subject. Say only what you must to answer each question properly and then stop, but avoid giving just yes or no answers—they usually do not allow the interviewer to learn enough about you. Some interviewers allow a silence to fall just to see how you will react. The burden of conducting the interview is the interviewer's, not yours—and he or she may interpret your rush to fill a void in the conversation as a sign of insecurity. If such a silence makes you uncomfortable, be ready to ask an intelligent question about the company.

If the interviewer overlooks important points, bring them up. Let the interviewer mention salary first. Doing so yourself may indicate that you are more interested in the money than in the work. Make sure, however, that you are aware of prevailing salaries and benefits in your field or geographic region. See **salary negotiations**.

Interviewers look for a degree of self-confidence and an applicant's understanding of the field, as well as genuine interest in the field, the company, and the job. Ask questions to communicate your interest in the job and the company. Interviewers respond favorably to applicants who can communicate and present themselves well.

Conclusion. At the conclusion of the interview, thank the interviewer for his or her time. Be sure to make note of each interviewer's name. Reiterate your interest in the position and try to get an idea of when the company expects to make a final decision. Reaffirm friendly contact with a firm handshake.

After the Interview

After you leave the interview, jot down the pertinent information you obtained, as it may be helpful in comparing job offers. As soon as possible following a job interview, send the interviewer(s) a note of thanks in a brief **letter** or **e-mail**. Such notes often include the following:

- Your thanks for the interview and to individuals or groups that gave you special help or attention during the interview
- The name of the specific job for which you interviewed
- Your impression of the opportunity
- Your confidence that you can perform the job well
- An offer to provide further information or to answer further questions

Figure I–8 shows a typical example of follow-up correspondence.

Dear Mr. Vallone:

Thank you for the opportunity to interview for the Director of Project Management position with you and your Health System directors, Mr. Sylvan Smith and Ms. Annie Rowan. I enjoyed our discussion, and the interview provided me with a clear picture of the company's operation, as well as the vision embraced by your directors for the continued success of corporate goals and objectives.

I left the interview feeling enthusiastic about the scope of the position, as well as the opportunity to lead and direct the Information Management initiatives of one of the largest health-care systems in the United States.

I remain very interested in continuing my career advancement with West End Health, and I look forward to a positive decision in reference to my candidacy. If you have any further questions, please contact me at (312) 346-9384.

Sincerely,

Elaine Treadwell

FIGURE I–8. Follow-up Correspondence

If you are offered a job you want, accept the offer verbally and write a brief letter of acceptance as soon as possible—certainly within a week. If you do not want the job, write a refusal letter or e-mail, as described in **acceptance / refusal letters**.

introductions

Every document must have either an opening or an introduction. An opening usually simply focuses the reader's attention on your topic and then proceeds to the body of your document. A formal introduction, however, sets the stage by providing necessary information to understand the discussion that follows in the body. In general, **correspondence** and routine **reports** need only an opening; more-complex reports and other longer documents need an introduction. Introductions are required for such documents as **formal reports** and major **proposals**. For a discussion of comparable sections for Web sites, see **writing for the Web**. See also **conclusions**.

Routine Openings

When your **audience** is familiar with your topic or if what you are writing is brief or routine, then a simple opening will provide adequate **context,** as shown in the following examples.

LETTER

Dear Mr. Ignatowski:

You will be happy to know that we have corrected the error in your bank balance. The new balance shows . . .

MEMO

To date, 18 of the 20 specimens your department submitted for analysis have been examined. Our preliminary analysis indicates . . .

E-MAIL

Jane, as I promised in my e-mail yesterday, I've attached the human resources budget estimates for fiscal year 2015.

Opening Strategies

Opening strategies are aimed at focusing the readers' attention and motivating them to read the entire document.

Objective.   In reporting on a project, you might open with a statement of the project's objective so that the readers have a basis for judging the results.

► The primary goal of this project was to develop new techniques to solve the problem of waste disposal. Our first step was to investigate . . .

Problem Statement.   One way to give readers the perspective of your report is to present a brief account of the problem that led to the study or project being reported.

► Several weeks ago a manager noticed a recurring problem in the software developed by Datacom Systems. Specifically, error messages repeatedly appeared when, in fact, no specific trouble. . . . After an extensive investigation, we found that Datacom Systems . . .

For proposals or formal reports, of course, problem statements may be more elaborate and a part of the full-scale introduction, which is discussed later in this entry.

Scope.   You may want to present the **scope** of your document in your opening. By providing the parameters of your material, the limitations of the subject, or the amount of detail to be presented, you enable your readers to determine whether they want or need to read your document.

► This pamphlet provides a review of the requirements for obtaining a private pilot's license. It is not intended as a textbook to prepare you for the examination itself; rather, it outlines the steps you need to take and the costs involved.

Background.   The background or history of a subject may be interesting and lend perspective and insight to a subject. Consider the following example from a newsletter describing the process of oil drilling:

> ▶ From the bamboo poles the Chinese used when the pyramids were young to today's giant rigs drilling in deep water, there has been considerable progress in the search for oil. But whether in ancient China or a modern city, underwater or on a mountaintop, the objective of drilling has always been the same—to manufacture a hole in the ground, inch by inch.

Summary.   You can provide a summary opening by describing in abbreviated form the results, conclusions, or recommendations of your article or report. Be concise: Do not begin a summary by writing "This report summarizes. . . ."

CHANGE	This report summarizes the advantages offered by the photon as a means of examining the structural features of the atom.
TO	As a means of examining the structure of the atom, the photon offers several advantages.

Interesting Detail.   Often an interesting detail will attract the readers' attention and pique their curiosity. Readers of an **annual report** for a manufacturer of telescopes and scientific instruments, for example, may be persuaded to invest if they believe that the company is developing innovative, cutting-edge products.

> ▶ The rings of Saturn have puzzled astronomers ever since they were discovered by Galileo in 1610 using the first telescope. Recently, even more rings have been discovered. . . .
> Our company's Scientific Instrument Division designs and manufactures research-quality, computer-controlled telescopes that promise to solve the puzzles of Saturn's rings by enabling scientists to use multicolor differential photometry to determine the rings' origins and compositions.

Definition.   Although a definition can be useful as an opening, do not define something with which your audience is familiar or provide a definition that is obviously a contrived opening (such as "Webster defines *technology* as . . ."). A definition should be used as an opening only if it offers insight into what follows.

> ▶ *Risk* is often a loosely defined term. In this report, risk refers to a qualitative combination of the probability of an event and the severity of the consequences of that event. In fact, . . .

Anecdote.   An anecdote can be used to attract and build interest in a subject that may otherwise be mundane; however, this strategy is best suited to longer documents and **presentations**.

▶ In his poem "The Calf Path" (1895), Sam Walter Foss tells of a wandering, wobbly calf trying to find its way home at night through the lonesome woods. It made a crooked path, which was taken up the next day by a lone dog. Then "a bellwether sheep pursued the trail over vale and steep, drawing behind him the flock, too, as all good bellwethers do." This forest path became a country lane that bent and turned and turned again. The lane became a village street, and at last the main street of a flourishing city. The poet ends by saying, "A hundred thousand men were led by a calf near three centuries dead."

Many companies today follow a "calf path" because they react to events rather than planning. . . .

Quotation.   Occasionally, you can use a quotation to stimulate interest in your subject. To be effective, however, the quotation must be pertinent—not some loosely related remark selected from a book of quotations.

▶ Richard Smith, founder of PCS Corporation, recently said, "I believe that managers need to be more 'people smart' than ever before. The management style of today involves much more than just managing the operations of a department—it requires understanding the personalities that comprise a corporation." His statement represents a growing feeling among corporate leaders that . . .

Forecast.   Sometimes you can use a forecast of a new development or trend to gain the audience's attention and interest.

▶ In the not-too-distant future, we may be able to use a handheld medical diagnostic device similar to those in science fiction to assess the physical condition of accident victims. This project and others are now being developed at The Seldi Group, Inc.

Persuasive Hook.   Although all opening strategies contain persuasive elements, the hook uses **persuasion** most overtly. A **brochure** touting the newest innovation in tax-preparation software might address readers as follows:

▶ Welcome to the newest way to do your taxes! TaxPro EZ ends the headache of last-minute tax preparation with its unique Web-Link feature.

Full-Scale Introductions

The purpose of a full-scale introduction is to give readers enough general information about the subject to enable them to understand the details in the body of the document. (See Figure F–6, pages 221–22.) An introduction should accomplish any or all of the following:

- *State the subject.* Provide background information, such as definition, history, or theory, to provide context for your readers.

- *State the purpose.* Make your readers aware of why the document exists and whether the material provides a new perspective or clarifies an existing perspective.

- *State the scope.* Tell readers the amount of detail you plan to cover.

- *Preview the development of the subject.* Especially in a longer document, outline how you plan to develop the subject. Providing such information allows readers to anticipate how the subject will be presented and helps them evaluate your conclusions or recommendations.

Consider writing an opening or introduction last. Many writers find that it is only after they have drafted the body of the document do they have a full enough perspective on the subject to introduce it adequately.

investigative reports

An investigative **report** offers a precise analysis of a workplace problem or an issue in response to a need for information. The investigative report shown in Figure I–9, for example, evaluates whether a company should adopt a program called "Basic English" to train and prepare documentation for non–English-speaking readers.

Open an investigative report with a statement of its primary and any secondary **purposes**, then define the **scope** of your investigation. If the report includes a survey of opinions, for example, indicate the number of people surveyed and other identifying information, such as income categories and occupations. (See also **questionnaires**.) Include any information that is pertinent in defining the extent of the investigation. Then report your findings and discuss their significance with your **conclusions**.

Sometimes the person requesting the investigative report may need to make recommendations as a result of your findings. In that case, the report may be referred to as a *recommendation report*. See also **feasibility reports** and **trouble reports**.

Memo

To: Noreen Rinaldo, Training Manager

From: Charles Lapinski, Senior Instructor   *CL*

Date: February 6, 2012

Subject: Adler's Basic English Program

As requested, I have investigated Adler Medical Instruments' (AMI's) Basic English Program to determine whether we might adopt a similar program.

The purpose of AMI's program is to teach medical technologists outside the United States who do not speak or read English to understand procedures written in a special 800-word vocabulary called *Basic English*. This program eliminates the need for AMI to translate its documentation into a number of different languages. The Basic English Program does not attempt to teach the medical technologists to be fluent in English but, rather, to recognize the 800 basic words that appear in Adler's documentation.

Course Analysis

The course teaches technologists a basic medical vocabulary in English; it does not provide training in medical terminology. Students must already know, in their own language, the meaning of medical vocabulary (e.g., the meaning of the word *hemostat*). Students must also have basic knowledge of their specialty, must be able to identify a part in an illustrated parts book, must have used AMI products for at least one year, and must be able to read and write in their own language.

Students are given an instruction manual, an illustrated book of equipment with parts and their English names, and pocket references containing the 800 words of the Basic English vocabulary plus the English names of parts. Students can write the corresponding word in their language beside the English word and then use the pocket reference as a bilingual dictionary. The course consists of 30 two-hour lessons, each lesson introducing approximately 27 words. No effort is made to teach pronunciation; the course teaches only recognition of the 800 words.

Course Success

The 800-word vocabulary enables the writers of documentation to provide medical technologists with any information that might be required because the subject areas are strictly limited to usage, troubleshooting, safety, and operation of AMI medical equipment. All nonessential words (*apple, father, mountain,* and so on) are eliminated, as are most synonyms (for example, *under* appears, but *beneath* does not).

Conclusions and Recommendations

AMI's program appears to be quite successful, and a similar approach could also be appropriate for us. I see two possible ways in which we could use some or all of the elements of AMI's program: (1) in the preparation of our student manuals or (2) as AMI uses the program.

I think it would be unnecessary to use the Basic English methods in the preparation of manuals for *all* of our students. Most of our students are English speakers to whom an unrestricted vocabulary presents no problem.

As for our initiating a program similar to AMI's, we could create our own version of the Basic English vocabulary and write our instructional materials in it. Because our product lines are much broader than AMI's, however, we would need to create illustrated parts books for each of the different product lines.

FIGURE I–9. Investigative Report

italics

Italics is a style of type used to denote **emphasis** and to distinguish foreign expressions, book titles, and certain other elements. *This sentence is printed in italics.* Italic type is often signaled by underlining in manuscripts submitted for typesetting or where italic font is not available. You may need to italicize words that require special emphasis in a sentence. ("Contrary to projections, sales have *not* improved.") Do not overuse italics for emphasis, however. ("*This* will hurt *you* more than *me*.")

Foreign Words and Phrases

Foreign words and phrases are italicized: *bonjour, guten tag,* the sign said "*Se habla español.*" Foreign words that have been fully assimilated into English need not be italicized: cliché, etiquette, vis-à-vis, de facto, résumé. When in doubt about whether to italicize a word, consult a current dictionary. See also **foreign words in English**.

Titles

Italicize the **titles** of separately published documents, such as books, periodicals, newspapers, pamphlets, brochures, legal cases, movies, and television programs.

▶ The book *Turning Workplace Conflicts into Collaboration* was reviewed in the *New York Times*.

Abbreviations of such titles are italicized if their spelled-out forms would be italicized.

▶ The *NYT* is one of the nation's oldest newspapers.

Italicize the titles of compact discs, videotapes, plays, long poems, paintings, sculptures, and long musical works.

CD-ROM	*Computer Security Tutorial on CD-ROM*
PLAY	Arthur Miller's *Death of a Salesman*
LONG POEM	T. S. Eliot's *The Wasteland*
MUSICAL WORK	Gershwin's *Porgy and Bess*

Use **quotation marks** for parts of publications, such as chapters of books and articles or sections within periodicals.

Proper Names

The names of ships, trains, and aircraft (but not the companies or governments that own them) are italicized: U.S. aircraft carrier *Indepen-*

dence, Amtrak's passenger train *Coast Starlight*. Craft that are known by model or serial designations are not italicized: DC-7, Boeing 747.

Words, Letters, and Figures

Words, letters, and figures discussed as such are italicized.

▶ The word *inflammable* is often misinterpreted.

▶ The *S* and *6* keys on my keyboard do not function.

Subheads

Subheads in a report are sometimes italicized.

▶ *Training Managers.* We are leading the way in developing first-line managers who not only are professionally competent but . . .

See also **headings** and **layout and design**.

its / it's

Its is a possessive **pronoun** and does not use an **apostrophe**. *It's* is a **contraction** of *it is*.

▶ *It's* important that the sales department meet *its* quota.

See also **expletives** and **possessive case**.

J

jargon

Jargon is a specialized slang that is unique to an occupational or a professional group. For example, "the *attending*" is slang used by medical professionals to refer to "the attending physician" in a hospital. Jargon is at first understood only by insiders; over time, it may become known more widely and become a **buzzword**. If all your readers are members of a particular occupational group, jargon may provide an efficient means of communicating. However, if you have any doubt that your entire **audience** is part of such a group, avoid using jargon. See also **affectation**, **functional shift**, **gobbledygook**, and **plain language**.

job descriptions

Most large companies and many small ones use formal job descriptions to specify the duties of and requirements for many of the jobs in the firm.* Job descriptions fulfill several important functions: They provide information on which equitable salary scales can be based, they help management determine whether all functions within a company are adequately supported, and they let both prospective and current employees know exactly what is expected of them. Together, all the job descriptions in a firm present a picture of the organization's structure.

Although job-description formats vary from organization to organization, they commonly contain the following sections:

- The *accountability section* identifies, by title only, the person to whom the employee reports.
- The *scope of responsibilities* section provides an overview of the primary and secondary functions of the job and states, if applicable, who reports to the employee.
- The *specific duties* section gives a detailed account of the particular duties of the job as concisely as possible.

---

*Job descriptions are sometimes called *position descriptions*, a term also used for formal announcements of openings for professional or administrative positions.

- The *personal requirements* section lists the required or preferred education, training, experience, and licensing for the job.

The job description shown in Figure J–1 is typical. It never mentions the person holding the job described; it focuses, instead, on the job and the qualifications required to fill the position.

PUBLICATIONS MANAGER
GCW Systems

Accountability

Reports directly to the Vice President, Advertising and Public Relations.

Scope of Responsibilities

The Publications Manager plans, coordinates, and supervises the design and development of sales brochures, advertisements, Web sites, and customer manuals required to support the sale, installation, and maintenance of company products and services. The manager is responsible for the administration of the Publications Department. The supervisor of customer publications, the supervisor of internal publications, and the division Webmaster report to the Publications Manager.

Specific Duties

- Directs an organization currently comprising 20 people, including supervisors, writers, designers, and production staff
- Screens, selects, and hires qualified applicants for the department
- Prepares a formal orientation program to familiarize trainees with the production of printed materials
- Evaluates the performance of and determines the salary adjustments for all department employees
- Plans documentation to support new and existing products
- Subcontracts publications and acts as a purchasing agent when needed
- Offers editorial advice to supervisors
- Develops and manages an annual budget for the Publications Department
- Recommends new and appropriate uses for the department within the company

Requirements

- B.A. in professional writing or equivalent
- Minimum of three years' professional writing experience and a general knowledge of design and current production software
- Minimum of two years' management experience and a knowledge of the general principles of management
- Strong interpersonal skills

FIGURE J–1. Job Description

✔ Before attempting to write your job description, list all the different tasks you do in a week or a month. Otherwise, you will almost certainly leave out some of your duties.

✔ Focus on content. Remember that you are describing your job, not yourself.

✔ List your duties in decreasing order of importance. Knowing how your various duties rank in importance makes it easier to set valid job qualifications.

✔ Begin each statement of a duty with a <u>verb</u> and be specific. Write "Orient new staff members to the department" rather than "New staff orientation."

✔ Review existing job descriptions that are considered well written.

J

job search

Whether you are applying for your first job or want to change careers entirely, begin by assessing your knowledge, skills, interests, and abilities, perhaps through **brainstorming**. Next, consider your career goals and values.* For instance, do you prefer working independently or collaboratively? Do you enjoy public settings? Do you like meeting people? How important are career stability and location? What would you most like to be doing in the immediate future? In two years? In five years?

Once you have narrowed your goals and identified a professional area that is right for you, consider the following sources to locate the job you want. Of course, do not rely on any one source exclusively.

- Networking and informational interviews
- Campus career services
- Web resources
- Job advertisements
- Trade and professional journal listings
- Employment agencies (private, temporary, government)
- Internships
- Direct inquiries

*A good source for stimulating your thinking is the most recent edition of *What Color Is Your Parachute? A Practical Manual for Job-Hunters & Career-Changers* by Richard Nelson Bolles, published by Ten Speed Press.

Keep a file during your job search of dated job ads, copies of **application cover letters** and résumés, and the names of important contacts. This collection can serve as a future resource and reminder.

Personal Brand and Branding

Branding is the art of associating your value as an individual with your name, service, product, business, and ability to interact with society. By learning how to manage other people and their perceptions of "your brand," you will naturally establish the unique value that sets you apart from the competition.

As you establish your business and working relationships, incorporate the principal components of your brand, including first impressions, demeanor, accomplishments, and the value you place on relationships with others, into every interaction. The following tips will help you to establish a foundation for personal and professional branding:

- *Performance, service, and reputation.* Determine the type of service or product you intend to provide to your employer, clients, or customers. Identify your goals and always deliver the service or product as promised, in a professional manner. The consistently professional and successful execution of service is the reason you will prevail over the competition.
- *Marketing strategy.* Look for opportunities to make yourself visible. In addition to the most common advertising outlets (newspapers, magazines, and professional organizations), online and social-media resources provide valuable benefits and will help you get your information out on the World Wide Web in just moments. Be sure to project a consistent and unified branding message across all media outlets.
- *Networking.* Never underestimate the power of networking. Daily routines provide often-overlooked opportunities for maintaining contacts, and it is important to continue actively networking, even after you are steadily employed. You can establish valuable contacts by volunteering within the local community or assisting others when you have nothing to gain by doing so. For your business, provide free workshops, schedule product demonstrations, or distribute promotional materials to support business growth. On an individual level, you can simply serve as a reference for a colleague who recently became unemployed.

Networking and Informational Interviews

Networking involves communicating with people who might provide useful advice or may know of potential jobs in your interest areas. They may include people already working in your chosen field, contacts in professional organizations, professors, family members, or friends. Discussion groups and professional networking sites, such as *LinkedIn* .*com*, can be helpful in this process. Use your personal and professional contacts to expand your network. Most career professionals estimate that networking fills between 60 and 80 percent of all open positions.

Informational interviews are appointments you schedule with working professionals who can give you "insider" views of an occupation or industry. These brief meetings (usually 20 to 30 minutes) also offer you the opportunity to learn about employment trends as well as leads for employment opportunities. Because you ask the questions, these interviews allow you to participate in an interview situation that is less stressful than the job interview itself. To make the most of informational interviews, prepare carefully and review both **interviewing for information** and **interviewing for a job**.

Campus Career Services

A visit to a college career-development center is another good way to begin your job search. Government, business, and industry recruiters often visit campus career offices to interview prospective employees; recruiters also keep career counselors aware of their companies' current employment needs and submit **job descriptions** to them. Not only can career counselors help you select a career, but they can also put you in touch with the best and most-current resources—identifying where to begin your search and saving you time. Career-development centers often hold workshops on résumé preparation and offer other job-finding resources on their Web sites.

Web Resources

In addition to offering professional-networking sites mentioned earlier, the Web can enhance your job search in a number of ways. First, you can consult sites that give advice about careers, job seeking, and résumé preparation. Second, you can learn about businesses and organizations that may hire employees in your area by visiting their Web sites. Such sites often list job openings, provide instructions for applicants, and offer other information, such as employee benefits. Third, you can learn about jobs in your field and post your résumé for prospective employers at a variety of privately owned or government-sponsored, online employment databases. Another benefit of using online resources to screen for opportunity lies in the ability to gather all the information required to help you make well-informed decisions as you take charge of your career path. For instance, among the many resources found at CareerOneStop (sponsored by the U.S. Department of Labor), a job seeker can research salary ranges for a particular region or career field.

This tool is particularly valuable when you are moving to a new location, considering a career transition, or determining a valid range for negotiating compensation packages. Fourth, you can post your résumé at your personal Web site. Although posting your résumé at an employment database will undoubtedly attract more potential employers, including your résumé at your own site has benefits. For example, you might provide a link to your site in e-mail correspondence or provide your Web site URL in an inquiry letter to a prospective employer. If you use a personal Web site, however, it should contain only material that would be of professional interest to prospective employers, such as examples of your work, awards, and other items that portray your value as a candidate to a prospective employer.

Social Media

A quick search of the Internet reveals that there are thousands of social communities, service providers, and professional organizations online. These resources, commonly referred to as social media, offer a broad range of services, networking included. Perhaps the most valuable aspect of social media is the opportunity to make instantaneous connections both on an individual level with like-minded enthusiasts and with a large target audience, no matter what your goals may be.

Understand that any comments, personal or professional profiles, résumés, associations you participate in, or connections you make using social media build the foundation of your personal brand through perceptions or observations of the reader. Regularly review your profile on any social-media Web sites you use for controversial content, and monitor the activity of your connections. How you present yourself in public forums and the "company you keep" online reflects on your professionalism.

◀ PROFESSIONALISM NOTE Surveys show that employers peruse *LinkedIn .com* and search engines like Google before recruiting candidates. Carefully consider the material that you post online when using social and professional media resources such as *LinkedIn.com*, MySpace, Facebook, Twitter, and YouTube. A good rule of thumb is to only share online what you would comfortably share with the office. Investigate and activate each site's privacy settings to ensure that you maintain a professional image online. ▶

WEB LINK	Finding a Job
For job-hunting tips, sample documents, and links to the sites mentioned in this entry, see *bedfordstmartins.com/alred* and select *Finding an Internship or Job* and *Links for Handbook Entries*.	

Job Advertisements

Many employers advertise jobs in the classified sections of newspapers. Because job listings can differ, search in both the printed and Web editions of local and big-city newspapers under *employment* or *job market*. Use the search options they provide or the general strategies for database searches discussed in the entry **research**.

A human-relations specialist interested in training, for example, might find the specialty listed under "Human Resources" or "Consulting Services." Depending on a company's or government agency's needs, the listing could be even more specific, such as "Software Education Specialist" or "Learning and Development Coordinator."

As you read the ads, take notes on salary ranges, job locations, job duties and responsibilities, and even the terminology used in the ads to describe the work.

WEB LINK	O*NET Online
Knowledge of keywords and key expressions that are generally used to describe a particular type of work can be helpful when you prepare your résumé and letters of application. O*NET Online is a valuable resource for obtaining relevant words, information, and descriptions for hundreds of occupational fields and job titles. For more information on the O*NET database and a link to the site, see *bedfordstmartins.com/alred* and select *Links for Handbook Entries*.	

Trade and Professional Journal Listings

In many industries, associations publish periodicals of interest to people working in the industry. Such periodicals (print and online) often contain job listings. To learn about the trade or professional associations for your occupation, consult resources on the Web, such as Google's Directory of Professional Organizations or online resources offered by your library or campus career office. You may also consult the following references at a library: *Encyclopedia of Associations* and *Encyclopedia of Business Information Sources*.

Employment Agencies (Private, Temporary, Government)

Private employment agencies are profit-making organizations that are in business to help people find jobs—for a fee. Reputable agencies provide you with job leads, help you organize your job search, and supply information on companies doing the hiring. A staffing agency or temporary placement agency could match you with an appropriate temporary or permanent job in your field. Temporary work for an organization for which you might want to work permanently is an excellent way to build your network while continuing your job search.

Choose an employment or a temporary-placement agency carefully. Some are well established and reputable; others are not. Check with your local Better Business Bureau and your college career office before you sign an agreement with a private employment agency. Further, be sure you understand who is paying the agency's fee. Often the employer pays the agency's fee; however, if you have to pay, make sure you know exactly how much. As with any written agreement, read the fine print carefully.

Local, state, and federal government agencies also offer many free or low-cost employment services. Locate local government agencies in telephone and Web directories under the name of your city, county, or state. For information on occupational trends, see the *Occupational Outlook Handbook* at *www.bls.gov/oco*, and for information on jobs with the federal government, see the U.S. Office of Personnel Management at *www.opm.gov*, or USAJOBS, the federal government's official jobs site at *www.usajobs.gov*. See also **salary negotiations**.

Internships

As you evaluate job options, consider taking an internship or entry-level position often lasting from six weeks to an entire semester (if not longer). An internship provides you with the chance to gain experience in a field through a variety of career opportunities. It enables you to

- Try a position without making a permanent commitment.
- Explore a field to clarify your career goals while getting on-the-job experience.
- Develop skills and gain experience in a new field or industry.
- Evaluate a prospective employer or firm.
- Acquire a mentor in the workplace.
- Benefit from networking contacts for future job opportunities.
- Gain access to professional references.
- Become eligible for a job offer based on an employer's satisfaction with your work.

To locate internship opportunities, begin with your campus career-development office. Such offices usually post internship opportunities at their Web site, but you can also make appointments with counselors or take advantage of walk-in hours.

Direct Inquiries

If you would like to work for a particular firm, write or call to ask whether it has any openings for people with your qualifications. Normally, you can contact the department head, the director of human resources, or both; for a small firm, however, write to the head of the firm. Such contacts work best if you have networked as described earlier in this entry.

WEB LINK	Direct-Inquiry Application Cover Letters
For an example of a direct-inquiry application cover letter — also called a "cold" application cover letter — see *bedfordstmartins.com/alred* and select *Model Documents Gallery*.	

Completing a Job or an Internship Application

The job application is often a key element to securing a job or an internship and provides you with the opportunity to portray personal assets that meet a specific job's requirements and to provide employers with a clear picture of your background and skill set. Job applications typically reflect the standard candidate information that companies require in order to consider you for a position. Forms used by employers, recruiters, institutions, and job-search sites can be found at the actual place of business or online at the company Web site. The job application may be required initially or later in the hiring process. Some employers may require just the job application, while others may require the job application, résumé, and application cover letter. In some cases, you will be required to complete the job application online—often within a time limit—and in others, you can download a form to complete at your leisure and send back to the employer via mail, fax, or attached to an e-mail.

When filling out the job application, ensure that every blank is completed—your application should be neat and easy to read. See Figure J–2, "Sections from a Job-Application Form," for guidance. Follow all directions carefully; if a particular area does not apply to you, indicate that it is not applicable by writing *N/A* in the empty space. This strategy signifies to the employer that you have thoroughly read the form and taken note of every requirement. Do not volunteer more information than the employer is asking for on the application. If you do not complete all entries or if you miss the application deadline, it is likely you will not be considered for the position.

WEB LINK	Sample Job Application
To view the full sample job application shown in Figure J–2, see *bedfordstmartins.com/alred* and select *Model Documents Gallery*.	

Employment Application

Employer Name: *ACME Tech Support–Internship Department*   **Announcement / Job Number:** *ATS-11096*

Position Title: *Computer Support Technician Candidate*   **Current Date:** *JAN/03/2012*

PERSONAL INFORMATION

Social Security Number: *404-256-0776*

Name (Last, First, Middle)		Cell Phone Number
Duffy, John W.		*404-522-7765*
Home Address	Mailing Address	Home Phone Number

EMPLOYMENT HISTORY / WORK EXPERIENCE—Begin with Most Recent Employer

Dates From–To (MMM/DD/YYYY)	Company Name	Address, City, State, Zip
JUL/04/2011 – DEC/28/2012	*Computer Service Mart*	*1234 E. HWY 1, Atlanta, GA 30301*

Job Title and Responsibilities, Skills, Attributes — *Customer Service Representative. Received more than 150 incoming calls daily, and responded to more than 100 online contacts; documented customer concerns; routed calls to appropriate department (over 15 in-house, and 10 corporate); established rapport with customers and department representatives; used five different automated data-management systems to track service initiatives; supervised and trained four employees; promoted twice in a nine-month period; filled Computer Tech position when required.*

Reason for Leaving:	Salary or Hourly Wage:	Supervisor's Name	Telephone Number
Relocation	*$29,550 per year*	*Mr. Alfred Smith*	*404-506-1298*
Dates From–To (MMM/DD/YYYY)	Company Name		Address, City, State, Zip

LEGAL

Have you ever filed for bankruptcy?	☐ YES ☒ NO

MILITARY HISTORY—Complete a Separate Entry for Each Branch of Service

Dates From–To (MMM/DD/YYYY)	Branch of Service	Last Duty Station
MAY/07/2003 – MAY/20/2011	*U.S. Army*	*Ft. Army, SC*

Occupational Skill, Description of Responsibilities — *Communications Specialist. Sustained communication assets and provided continuity in phone service, Internet service, and secure satellite connections to organizations in both tactical and garrison operating environments. Supervised and trained 10 subordinates, prepared performance evaluations and scheduled continuing education, compiled weekly/monthly equipment status reports, traveled worldwide supporting unit operations in three different continents and more than 10 countries.*

FIGURE J–2. Sections from a Job-Application Form (*continued*)

EDUCATION / TRAINING—Include Technical/Academic Achievements/Correspondence and Military Courses

Have you obtained a high school diploma or GED certificate?				☒ YES ☐ NO	
Type School	Institution Name & Location	Diploma/ Degree	Major	Date/Year	GPA
College/University	University of Maryland, College Park, MD	B.S.	Bus Mgmt	Projected 2013	3.4

PROFESSIONAL CERTIFICATIONS / LICENSES

Type of License or Certificate	Awarded by:	Registration or Certificate No.	Expiration Date (MMM/DD/YYYY)
Commercial Driver's License	State of Maryland	S87233597	NOV/07/2014
Type of License or Certificate	Awarded by:	Registration or Certificate No.	Expiration Date (MMM/DD/YYYY)
Notary Public	State of Georgia	752-09-330027	N/A

OTHER SPECIAL SKILLS—List Other Specific Skills You Have to Offer for This Job Opening

Web Page Design and Hosting (Summer Internship, Programming Department, IBM, 2009).
Computer Maintenance / Repair Technician (Freelance Consultant, Community Research Department, 2009–2011).
Unit Communications / Networking Technician (Additional Duty, U.S. Army, 2007).
Typing Evaluation (Department of Labor Skills Assessment Division, 2011).
Bilingual (Fluent; Speak, read, and write Spanish and English).
Culturally Diverse (Traveled to three continents and visited more than 10 countries; firsthand experience in overcoming communication barriers).

REFERENCES—Provide Three Professional References (Persons Not Related to You)

Name, Job Title	Mailing Address	E-mail Address	Day Telephone	May We Contact?
Dr. J.R. Howard, Professor	222 Hartford Street Atlanta, GA 30201	j.r.howard@gnet.com	404-522-9732	☒ YES ☐ NO

I, *John Duffy* , certify that the information provided on this application is true and accurate to the best of (printed name)
my knowledge.

Signature *John Duffy*   Date *1/3/12*

FIGURE J–2. Sections from a Job-Application Form (*continued*)

❖ ETHICS NOTE Providing false information in your job application can be cause for dismissal and will reflect poorly on your character. Be honest and keep in mind that if you are wrong for a position and lie to obtain it, the employer can just as easily discover this after you are hired. ❖

WRITER'S CHECKLIST   Completing a Job Application

✔ Read the entire application before you begin to fill it out.

✔ Follow all directions carefully. (This includes adhering to small details like date format, as these indicate how well you follow directions.)

✔ Always list a job title for the "Position Seeking" entry. A busy employer rarely has time to determine where you will best fit into the organization; applications with entries such as "any" or "open" will receive less consideration.

✔ Provide all requested information and complete irrelevant entries with *N/A*.

✔ Proofread the job application for errors or blank entries before submitting it.

✔ List the most-recent information (employer or education) first, working backward in time.

✔ When the application asks for your salary requirements, indicate "open," "negotiable," or a range commensurate with the industry and region.

✔ If the application asks why you left a previous employer, refrain from using negative phrases ("personal reasons," "fired," "illness," or "quit"). Positive phrases like "relocation," "seeking a new challenge," or "career advancement" will help you get to the interview stage, where you can address direct inquiries about a situation. See also **interviewing for a job**.

✔ References should be those who can speak to your professionalism, character, or work ethic. Be sure to ask permission before listing their names and contact information.

✔ Do not forget to sign and date the application.

❖ ETHICS NOTE When faced with questions that are sensitive or illegal (such as those about age, sex, disabilities, health, marital status, children, race, and criminal activity), you must carefully consider your response. If the question does not seem to raise a problem, you can choose to answer it. If you feel the question is inappropriate, you can respond with *N/A* or another response (such as a line through the blank); this will indicate that you have read the content.

Understanding that many employers conduct background checks on candidates to protect their interests will help you determine the validity of a question. For example, a banking institution might be very concerned about a candidate's credit history, current debts, or bankruptcy status, or a government organization might be concerned about citizenship or ties to foreign countries. ❖

J

K

kind of / sort of

The phrases *kind of* and *sort of* should be used only to refer to a class or type of things.

▶ We require a special *kind of* training to ensure employee safety.

Do not use *kind of* or *sort of* to mean "rather," "somewhat," or "somehow." That usage can lead to vagueness; it is better to be specific.

VAGUE   It was *kind of* a bad year for the company.

SPECIFIC   The company's profits fell 10 percent last year.

know-how

The informal term *know-how*, meaning "special competence or knowledge," should be avoided in formal writing <u>style</u>.

                                      skill.
▶ The applicant has impressive marketing ~~know-how.~~

L

lay / lie

Lay is a transitive **verb**—a verb that requires a direct object to complete its meaning—that means "place" or "put."

▶ We will *lay* the foundation one section at a time.

The past-tense form of *lay* is *laid*.

▶ We *laid* the first section of the foundation last month.

The perfect-tense form of *lay* is also *laid*.

▶ Since June, we *have laid* all but two sections of the foundation.

Lay is frequently confused with *lie*, which is an intransitive verb—a verb that does not require an object to complete its meaning—that means "recline" or "remain."

▶ A person in shock should *lie* down with legs slightly elevated.

The past-tense form of *lie* is *lay* (not *lied*). This form causes the confusion between *lie* and *lay*.

▶ The injured employee *lay* still for approximately five minutes.

The perfect-tense form of *lie* is *lain*.

▶ The injured employee *had lain* still for five minutes before the EMTs arrived.

layout and design

DIRECTORY

The layout and design of a document can make even the most complex information accessible and give **readers** a favorable impression of the writer and the organization. To accomplish those goals, a design should help readers find information easily; offer a simple and uncluttered presentation; and highlight structure, hierarchy, and order. The design must also fit the **purpose** of the document and its **context**. For example, if clients are paying a high price for consulting services, they may expect a sophisticated, polished design; if employees inside an organization expect management to be frugal, they may accept—even expect—an economical and standard company design. See also **audience**.

Effective design is based on visual simplicity and harmony and can be achieved with careful selection of typography, page-design elements, and appropriate **visuals**, as well as thoughtful layout of text and visual components on a page.

Typography

Typography refers to the style and arrangement of type on a page. A complete set of all the letters, numbers, and symbols available in one typeface (or style) is called a *font*. The letters in a typeface have a number of distinctive characteristics, as shown in Figure L–1.

Typeface and Type Size.   For most on-the-job writing, select a typeface primarily for its legibility. Avoid typefaces that make text difficult to

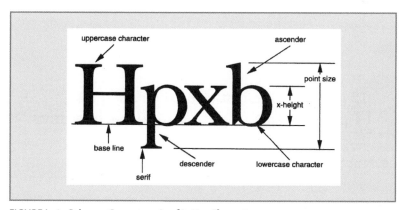

FIGURE L–1. Primary Components of Letter Characters

read or that may distract readers. Instead, choose popular typefaces with which readers are familiar, such as Times Roman, Garamond, or Gill Sans. Avoid using more than two typefaces in the text of a document. For certain documents, however, such as **newsletters**, you may wish to use distinctively different typefaces for contrast among various elements such as headlines, **headings**, inset **quotations**, and sidebars. Experiment before making final decisions, keeping in mind your audience.

One way typefaces are characterized is by the presence or absence of serifs. Serif typefaces have projections, as shown in Figure L–1; sans serif styles do not. (*Sans* is French for "without.") The text of this book is set in Sabon, a serif typeface. Although sans serif type has a modern look, serif type is easier to read, especially in the smaller sizes. Sans serif, however, works well for headings (like the entry titles in this book) and for Web sites and other documents read on-screen.

Ideal font sizes for the main text of paper documents range from 10 to 12 points.* However, for some elements or documents, you may wish to select typeface sizes that are smaller (as in footnotes) or larger (as in headlines for **brochures**). See Figure L–2 for a comparison of type sizes in a serif typeface. Your readers and the distance from which they will read a document should help determine type size. For example, **instructions** that will rest on a table at which the reader stands require a larger typeface than a document that will be read up close. For **presentations** and **writing for the Web**, preview your document to see the effectiveness of your choice of point sizes and typefaces.

Type Style and Emphasis.   One method of achieving emphasis through typography is to use capital letters. HOWEVER, LONG STRETCHES OF ALL UPPERCASE LETTERS ARE DIFFICULT TO READ. (See

---

6 pt. This size might be used for dating a source.

8 pt. This size might be used for footnotes.

10 pt. This size might be used for figure captions.

12 pt. This size might be used for main text.

14 pt. This size might be used for headings.

FIGURE L–2. Type Sizes (6- to 14-Point Type)

*A *point* is a unit of type size equal to 0.01384 inch, or approximately $^1/_{72}$ of an inch.

also **e-mail**.) Use all uppercase letters only in short spans, such as in headings. Likewise, use italics sparingly because *continuous italic type reduces legibility and thus slows readers.* Of course, **italics** are useful if your aim is to slow readers, as in cautions and warnings. **Boldface**, used in moderation, may be the best cuing device because it is visually different yet retains the customary shapes of letters and numbers.

Page-Design Elements

Thoughtfully used design elements can provide not only emphasis but also visual logic within a document by highlighting organization. Consistency and moderation are important—use the same technique to highlight a particular feature throughout your document and be careful not to overuse any single technique. The following typical elements can be used to make your document accessible and effective: justification, headings, **headers and footers**, **lists**, columns, white space, and color. Some of these elements are illustrated in Figure F–6 on pages 215–31.

Justification.   Left-justified (ragged-right) margins are generally easier to read than full-justified margins, especially for text using wide margins on $8\frac{1}{2} \times 11''$ pages. Left justification is also better if full justification causes your word-processing or desktop-publishing software to insert irregular spaces between words, producing unwanted white space or unevenness in blocks of text. Full-justified text is more appropriate for publications aimed at a broad audience that expects a more formal, polished appearance. Full justification is also useful with narrow, multiple-column formats because the spaces between the columns (called *alleys*) need the definition that full justification provides.

Headings.   Headings reveal the organization of a document and help readers decide which sections they need to read. You should provide typographic contrast between headings and the body text with either a different typeface or a different style (**bold**, *italic*, CAPS, and so on). Headings are often effective in boldface or in a sans serif typeface that contrasts with a body text in a serif typeface.

Headers and Footers.   A header in a report, letter, or other document appears at the top of each page (as in this book), and a footer appears at the bottom of each page. Document pages may have headers or footers (or both) that include such elements as the topic or subtopic of a section, an identifying number, the date the document was written, the page number, and the document name. Keep your headers and footers concise because too much information in them can create visual clutter. However—at a minimum—a multipage document should include the

L

page number in a header or footer. For more information on adding page numbers and laying out a page, see "Web Link: Designing Documents" on page 321. Headers are also important in **letters** and **memos**.

Lists.   Vertically stacked words, phrases, and other items with numbers or bullets can effectively highlight such information as steps in sequence, materials or parts needed, key or concluding points, and recommendations. For further detail, see **lists**.

Columns.   As you design pages, consider how columns may improve the readability of your document. A single-column format works well with larger typefaces, double-spacing, and left-justified margins. For smaller typefaces and single-spaced lines, the two-column structure keeps text columns narrow enough so that readers need not scan back and forth across the width of the entire page for every line. Avoid widows and orphans: a *widow* is a single word carried over to the top of a column or page; an *orphan* is a word on a line by itself at the end of a column.

White Space.   White space visually frames information and breaks it into manageable chunks. For example, white space between paragraphs helps readers see the information in each paragraph as a unit. White space between sections can also serve as a visual cue to signal that one section is ending and another is beginning.

Color.   Color and screening (shaded areas on a page) can distinguish one part of a document from another or unify a series of documents. They can set off sections within a document, highlight examples, or emphasize warnings. In **tables**, screening can highlight column titles or sets of data to which you want to draw the reader's attention.

Visuals

Readers notice visuals before they notice text, and they notice larger visuals before they notice smaller ones. Thus, the size of an illustration suggests its relative importance. For newsletter articles and publications aimed at wide audiences, consider especially the proportion of the visual to the text. Magazine designers often use the three-fifths rule: Page layout is more dramatic and appealing when the major element (**photograph**, **drawing**, or other visual) occupies three-fifths rather than one-half the available space. The same principle can be used to enhance the visual appeal of a **report**.

Visuals can be gathered in one place (for example, at the end of a report), but placing them in the text closer to their accompanying explanations makes them more effective. Illustrations in the text also provide visual relief. For advice on the placement of visuals, see the *Writer's Checklist: Creating and Integrating Visuals* on pages 576–77.

Icons. Icons are pictorial representations used to describe such concepts as computer files, programs, or commands. Commonly used icons on the Web include the national flags to symbolize different language versions of a document. To be effective, icons must be simple and easily recognized without accompanying text. For using icons that are culturally appropriate, see **global graphics**.

Captions. Captions are titles that highlight or describe visuals, such as photographs. Captions often appear below figures and above tables; they may be aligned with the visual to the left or they may be centered.

Rules. Rules are vertical or horizontal lines used to enclose material in a box or to divide one area of the page from another. For example, rules and boxes set off visuals from surrounding explanations or highlight warning statements from the steps in instructions.

Page Layout and Thumbnails

Page layout involves combining typography, design elements, and visuals on a page to make a coherent whole. The flexibility of your design is affected by your design software, your method of printing the document, your budget, and whether your employer or client requires you to use a template.

Before you spend time positioning actual text and visuals on a page, especially for documents such as brochures, you may want to create a thumbnail sketch, in which blocks of simulated text and visuals indicate the placement of elements. You can go further by roughly assembling all the thumbnail pages to show the size, shape, form, and general style of a large document. Such a mock-up, called a *dummy*, allows you to see how a finished document will look.

WEB LINK	Designing Documents

Word-processing and desktop-publishing programs offer many options for improving the layout-and-design elements of your document. For a tutorial on these options, see *bedfordstmartins.com/alred* and select *Try a tutorial*, "On designing documents with a word processor." For step-by-step instructions for setting margins, alignment, columns, and other design elements, select *Digital Tips*, "Laying Out a Page" and "Creating Styles and Templates."

lend / loan

Both *lend* and *loan* can be used as **verbs**, but *lend* is more common. ("You can *lend* [or *loan*] them the money if you wish.") Unlike *lend*, *loan* can be a **noun**. ("The bank approved our *loan*.")

letters

Business letters—normally written for those outside an organization—are often the most appropriate choice for formal communications with professional associates or customers. Letters may be especially effective for those people who receive a high volume of **e-mail** and other electronic messages. Letters printed on organizational letterhead communicate formality, respect, and authority. See **correspondence** for advice on writing strategy and style. See also **selecting the medium**.

Although word-processing software includes templates for formatting business letters, the templates may not provide the appropriate dimensions and elements you need. The following sections offer specific advice on formatting and related etiquette for business letters.*

Common Letter Styles

If your employer requires a particular format, use it. Otherwise, follow the guidelines provided here, and review the examples shown in Figures L–3 and L–4.

The two most common formats for business letters are the full-block style shown in Figure L–3 and the modified-block style shown in Figure L–4. In the *full-block style*, the entire letter is aligned at the left margin. In the *modified-block style*, the return address, date, and complimentary closing begin at the center of the page and the other elements are aligned at the left margin. All other letter styles are variations of the full-block and modified-block styles.

To achieve a professional appearance, center the letter on the page vertically and horizontally. Although one-inch margins are the default standard in many word-processing programs, it is more important to establish a picture frame of blank space surrounding the page of text. When you use organizational letterhead stationery, consider the bottom of the letterhead as the top edge of the paper. The right margin should be

---

*For additional details on letter formats and design, you may wish to consult a guide such as *The Gregg Reference Manual*, 11th ed., by William A. Sabin (New York: McGraw-Hill, 2010).

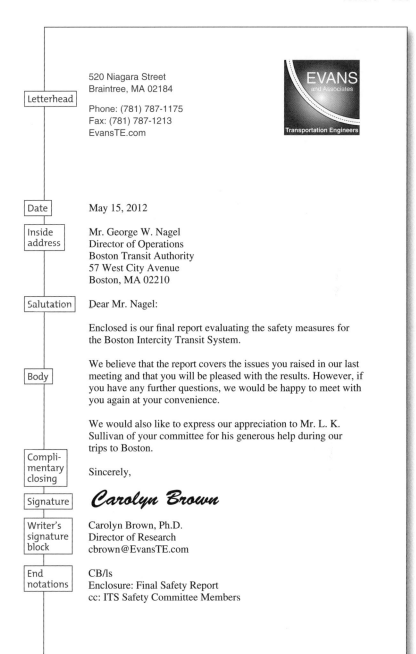

Letterhead

520 Niagara Street
Braintree, MA 02184

Phone: (781) 787-1175
Fax: (781) 787-1213
EvansTE.com

EVANS
and Associates

Transportation Engineers

Date

May 15, 2012

Inside address

Mr. George W. Nagel
Director of Operations
Boston Transit Authority
57 West City Avenue
Boston, MA 02210

Salutation

Dear Mr. Nagel:

Enclosed is our final report evaluating the safety measures for the Boston Intercity Transit System.

Body

We believe that the report covers the issues you raised in our last meeting and that you will be pleased with the results. However, if you have any further questions, we would be happy to meet with you again at your convenience.

We would also like to express our appreciation to Mr. L. K. Sullivan of your committee for his generous help during our trips to Boston.

Complimentary closing

Sincerely,

Signature

Carolyn Brown

Writer's signature block

Carolyn Brown, Ph.D.
Director of Research
cbrown@EvansTE.com

End notations

CB/ls
Enclosure: Final Safety Report
cc: ITS Safety Committee Members

FIGURE L–3. Full-Block-Style Letter (with Letterhead)

	---- Center
Heading from center to right	3814 Oak Lane Dedham, MA 02180 December 10, 2012
Inside address	Dr. Carolyn Brown Director of Research Evans and Associates Transportation Engineers 520 Niagara Street Braintree, MA 02184
Salutation	Dear Dr. Brown:
Body	Thank you very much for allowing me to tour your testing facilities. The information I gained from the tour will be of great help to me in preparing the report for my class at Marshall Institute. The tour has also given me some insight into the work I may eventually do as a laboratory technician. I especially appreciated the time and effort Vikram Singh spent in showing me your facilities. His comments and advice were most helpful. Again, thank you.

Sincerely,

Complimentary closing aligned with heading

Signature

Leslie Warden

Leslie Warden
781-555-1212

Writer's signature block

End notation   cc: Vikram Singh

L

FIGURE L–4. Modified-Block-Style Letter (without Letterhead)

approximately as wide as the left margin. To give a fuller appearance to very short letters, increase both margins to about an inch and a half. Use your full-page or print-preview feature to check for proportion.

Heading

Unless you are using letterhead stationery, place your full return address and the date in the heading. Because your name appears at the end of the letter, it need not be included in the heading. Spell out words such as *street, avenue, first,* and *west* rather than abbreviating them. You may either spell out the name of the state in full or use the standard Postal Service abbreviation available at *usps.com.* The date usually goes directly beneath the last line of the return address. Do not abbreviate the name of the month. Begin the heading about two inches from the top of the page. If you are using letterhead that gives the company address, enter only the date, three lines below the last line of the letterhead.

Inside Address

Include the recipient's full name, title, and address in the inside address, two to six lines below the date, depending on the length of the letter. The inside address should be aligned with the left margin, and the left margin should be at least one inch wide.

Salutation

Place the salutation, or *greeting,* two lines below the inside address and align it with the left margin. In most business letters, the salutation contains the recipient's personal title (such as *Mr., Ms., Dr.*) and last name, followed by a colon. If you are on a first-name basis with the recipient, use only the first name in the salutation.

Address women as *Ms.* unless they have expressed a preference for *Miss* or *Mrs.* However, professional titles (such as *Professor, Senator, Major*) take precedence over *Ms.* and similar courtesy titles.

When a person's first name could refer to either a woman or a man, one solution is to use both the first and last names in the salutation (*Dear Pat Smith:*). Avoid "To Whom It May Concern" because it is impersonal and dated.

For multiple recipients, the following salutations are appropriate:

► Dear Professor Allen and Dr. Rivera: [two recipients]

► Dear Ms. Becham, Ms. Moore, and Mr. Stein: [three recipients]

► Dear Colleagues: [*Members,* or other suitable collective term]

Subject Line

An optional element in a letter is a subject line, which should follow the salutation. Insert one blank line above and one blank line below the subject line. The subject line in a letter functions as it does for other correspondence as an aid in focusing the topic and filing the letter. (For information on creating subject lines, see pages 122–23 of **correspondence**.)

Subject lines are especially useful if you are writing to a large company and do not know the name or title of the recipient. In such cases, you may address a letter to an appropriate department or identify the subject in a subject line and use no salutation.

> ► National Medical Supply Group
> 501 West National Avenue
> Minneapolis, MN 55407
>
> *Attention: Customer Service Department*
>
> *Subject: Defective Cardio-100 Stethoscopes*
>
> I am returning six stethoscopes with damaged diaphragms that . . .

In other circumstances in which you do not know the recipient's name, use a title appropriate to the **context** of the letter, such as *Dear Customer* or *Dear IT Professional.*

Body

The body of the letter should begin two lines below the salutation (or any element that precedes the body, such as a subject or an attention line). Single-space within and double-space between paragraphs, as shown in Figures L–3 and L–4. To provide a fuller appearance to a very short letter, you can increase the side margins or increase the font size. You can also insert extra space above the inside address, the writer's signature block, and the initials of the person typing the letter—but do not exceed twice the recommended space for each of these elements.

Complimentary Closing

Type the complimentary closing two spaces below the body. Use a standard expression such as *Sincerely, Sincerely yours,* or *Yours truly.* (If the recipient is a friend as well as a business associate, you can use a less-formal closing such as *Best wishes* or *Best regards* or, simply, *Best.*) Capitalize only the initial letter of the first word, and follow the expression with a comma.

Writer's Signature Block

Type your full name four lines below and aligned with the complimentary closing. On the next line include your business title, if appropriate. The following lines may contain your individual contact information, such as a telephone number or an e-mail address, if not included in the letterhead or the body of your letter. Sign the letter in the space between the complimentary closing and your name.

End Notations

Business letters sometimes require additional information that is placed at the left margin, two spaces below the typed name and title of the writer in a long letter, four spaces below in a short letter.

Reference initials show the letter writer's initials in capital letters, followed by a slash mark (or colon), and then the initials of the person typing the letter in lowercase letters, as shown in Figure L–3. When the writer is also the person typing the letter, no initials are needed.

Enclosure notations indicate that the writer is sending material along with the letter (an invoice, an article, and so on). Note that you should mention the enclosure in the body of the letter. Enclosure notations may take several forms:

► Enclosure: Final Safety Report

► Enclosures (2)

► Enc. *or* Encs.

Copy notation ("cc:") tells the reader that a copy of the letter is being sent to the named recipient(s) (see Figure L–3). Use a blind-copy notation ("bcc:") when you do not want the addressee to know that a copy is being sent to someone else. A blind-copy notation appears only on the copy, not on the original ("bcc: Dr. Brenda Shelton"). See the Ethics Note in **e-mail** on page 179.

Continuing Pages

If a letter requires a second page (or, in rare cases, more), always carry at least two lines of the body text over to that page. Use plain (nonletterhead) paper of quality equivalent to that of the letterhead stationery for the second page. It should have a header with the recipient's name, the page number, and the date. Place the header in the upper left-hand corner or across the page, as shown in Figure L–5.

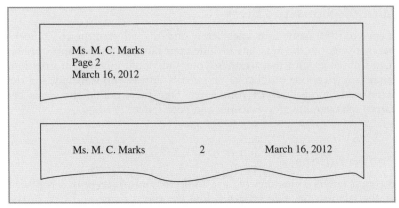

FIGURE L–5. Alternative Headers for the Second Page of a Letter

like / as

To avoid confusion between *like* and *as*, remember that *like* is a **preposition** and *as* (or *as if*) is a **conjunction**. Use *like* with a **noun** or **pronoun** that is not followed by a **verb**.

▶ The supervisor still behaves *like* a novice.

Use *as* before **clauses**, which contain verbs.

▶ He responded *as* we expected he would.

▶ The presentation seemed *as if* it would never end.

Like and *as* are used in **comparisons**: *Like* is used in constructions that omit the verb, and *as* is used when the verb is retained.

▶ He adapted to the new system *like* a duck to water.

▶ He adapted to the new system *as* a duck adapts to water.

listening

Effective listening enables the listener to understand the directions of an instructor, the message in a speaker's **presentation**, the goals of a manager, and the needs and wants of customers. Above all, it lays the foundation for productive communication.

Fallacies About Listening

Most people assume that because they can hear, they know how to listen. In fact, *hearing* is passive, whereas *listening* is active. Hearing voices in a crowd or a ringing telephone requires no analysis and no active involvement. We hear such sounds without choosing to listen to them—we have no choice but to hear them. Listening, however, requires actively focusing on a speaker, interpreting the message, and assessing its worth. Listening also requires that you consider the **context** of messages and the differences in meaning that may be the result of differences in the speaker's and the listener's occupation, education, culture, sex, race, or other factors. See also **biased language, connotation / denotation, English as a second language**, and **global communication**.

Active Listening

To become an active listener, you need to take the following steps:

Step 1: Make a Conscious Decision.   The first step to active listening is simply making up your mind to listen. Active listening requires a conscious effort, something that does not come naturally. The well-known precept offers good advice: "Seek first to understand and *then* to be understood."*

Step 2: Define Your Purpose.   Knowing why you are listening can go a long way toward managing the most common listening problems: drifting attention, formulating your response while the speaker is still talking, and interrupting the speaker. To help you define your purpose for listening, ask yourself these questions:

- What kind of information do I hope to get from this exchange, and how will I use it?
- What kind of message do I want to send while I am listening? (Do I want to portray understanding, determination, flexibility, competence, or patience?)
- What factors—boredom, daydreaming, anger, impatience—might interfere with listening during the interaction? How can I keep these factors from placing a barrier between the speaker and me?

Step 3: Take Specific Actions.   Becoming an active listener requires a willingness to become a responder rather than a reactor. A *responder*

---

*Stephen R. Covey, *The 7 Habits of Highly Effective People: Powerful Lessons in Personal Change*, 15th ed. (New York: Free Press, 2004).

is a listener who slows down the communication to be certain that he or she is accurately receiving the message sent by the speaker. A *reactor* simply says the first thing that comes to mind, without checking to make sure that he or she accurately understands the message. Take the following actions to help you become a responder and not a reactor.

- Make a conscious effort to be impartial when evaluating a message. For example, do not dismiss a message because you dislike the speaker or are distracted by the speaker's appearance, mannerisms, or accent.

- Slow down the communication by asking for more information or by **paraphrasing** the message received before you offer your thoughts. Paraphrasing lets the speaker know you are listening, gives the speaker an opportunity to clear up any misunderstanding, and keeps you focused.

- Listen with empathy by putting yourself in the speaker's position. When people feel they are being listened to empathetically, they tend to respond with appreciation and cooperation, thereby improving the communication.

- Take notes, when possible, to help you stay focused on what a speaker is saying. **Note-taking** not only communicates your attentiveness to the speaker but also reinforces the message and helps you remember it.

Step 4: Adapt to the Situation.   The requirements of active listening differ from one situation to another. For example, when you are listening to a lecture, you may be listening only for specific information. However, if you are on a team project that depends on everyone's contribution, you need to listen at the highest level so that you can gather information as well as pick up on nuances the other speakers may be communicating. See also **collaborative writing**.

lists

Vertically stacked lists of words, **phrases,** and other items that are often highlighted with bullets, numbers, or letters can save readers time by allowing them to see at a glance specific items or key points. Lists also help readers by breaking up complex statements and by focusing on such information as steps in sequence, materials or parts needed, questions or concluding points, and recommendations, as shown in Figure L–6.

Before we agree to hold the regional sales conference at the Brent Hotel, we need to make sure the hotel can provide the following resources:

- Business center with state-of-the-art digital and printing services
- Main exhibit area that can accommodate thirty 8-foot-by-15-foot booths
- Eight meeting rooms, each with a podium or table and seating for 25 people
- Wi-Fi Internet access and digital projection in each room
- Ballroom dining facilities for 250 people with a dais for four speakers

To confirm that the Brent Hotel is our best choice, we should tour the facilities during our stay in Kansas City.

FIGURE L–6. Bulleted List in a Paragraph

As Figure L–6 also shows, you should provide **context** for a list with an introductory sentence followed by a **colon** (or no punctuation for an incomplete sentence). Ensure **coherence** by following the list with some reference to the list or the statement that introduced it.

WRITER'S CHECKLIST   Using Lists

Follow the practices of your organization or use these guidelines for consistency and formatting.

CONSISTENCY

✔ Do not overuse lists or create extended lists or **presentation** slides that are dense with lists.

✔ List only comparable items, such as tasks or equipment, that are balanced in importance (as in Figure L–6).

✔ Begin each listed item in the same way — whether with **nouns**, **verbs**, or other **parts of speech** — and maintain **parallel structure** throughout.

FORMATTING

✔ Capitalize the first word in each listed item, unless doing so is visually awkward.

(continued)

WRITER'S CHECKLIST   Using Lists *(continued)*

✔ Use **periods** or other ending **punctuation** when the listed items are complete sentences.

✔ Avoid **commas** or **semicolons** following items and do not use the **conjunction** *and* before the last item in a list.

✔ Use numbers to indicate sequence or rank.

✔ Follow each number with a period and start the item with a capital letter.

✔ Use bullets (round, square, arrow) when you do not wish to indicate rank or sequence.

✔ List bulleted items in a logical order, keeping your **audience** and **purpose** in mind. See also **methods of development** and **persuasion**.

✔ When lists need subdivisions, use letters with numbers (see **outlining**).

L

logic errors

Logic is the study of the principles of reasoning. In most writing, especially in writing intended to persuade an **audience**, logic is essential to demonstrating that your conclusions are valid. This entry describes typical errors in logic that can undermine the point you are trying to communicate and your credibility. See also **persuasion**.

❖ ETHICS NOTE Many of the following errors in logic, when used to mislead **readers**, are unethical as well as illogical. See also **ethics in writing**. ❖

Lack of Reason

When a statement is contrary to the reader's common sense, that statement is not reasonable. If, for example, you stated, "New York City is a small town," your reader might immediately question your statement. However, if you stated, "Although New York City's population is over eight million, it is composed of neighborhoods that function as small towns," your reader could probably accept the statement as reasonable.

Sweeping Generalizations

Sweeping generalizations are statements that are too broad or all-inclusive to be supportable; they generally enlarge an observation about a small group to refer to an entire population. A flat statement such as "Management is never concerned about employees" ignores evidence that many managers are in fact concerned for their employees. Using such generalizations weakens your credibility.

Non Sequiturs

A non sequitur is a statement that does not logically follow a previous statement.

▶ I cleared off my desk, and the report is due today.

The missing link in these statements is that the writer cleared his or her desk to make space for materials to help finish the report that is due today. In your own writing, be careful that you do not allow gaps in logic to produce non sequiturs.

False Cause

A false cause (also called *post hoc, ergo propter hoc*) refers to the logical fallacy that because one event followed another event, the first somehow caused the second.

▶ I didn't bring my umbrella today. No wonder it is now raining.

▶ Because we now have our board meetings at the Education Center, our management turnover rate has declined.

Such errors in reasoning can happen when the writer hastily concludes that two events are related without examining whether a causal connection between them, in fact, exists.

Biased or Suppressed Evidence

A conclusion reached as a result of biased or suppressed evidence — self-serving data, questionable sources, purposely omitted or incomplete facts — is both illogical and unethical. Suppose you are preparing a report on the acceptance of a new policy among employees. If you distribute **questionnaires** only to those who think the policy is effective, the resulting evidence will be biased. Intentionally ignoring relevant data that might not support your position not only produces inaccurate results but also is unethical.

Fact Versus Opinion

Distinguish between fact and opinion. Facts include verifiable data or statements, whereas opinions are personal conclusions that may or may not be based on facts. For example, it is verifiable that distilled water boils at 100°C; that it tastes better or worse than tap water is an opinion.

Distinguish the facts from your opinions in your writing so that your readers can draw their own conclusions.

Loaded Arguments

When you include an opinion in a statement and then reach conclusions that are based on that statement, you are loading the argument. Consider the following opening for a memo:

▶ I have several suggestions to improve the poorly written policy manual. First, we should change . . .

Unless everyone agrees that the manual is poorly written, readers may reject a writer's entire message because they disagree with this loaded premise. Conclusions reached with loaded statements are weak and can produce negative reactions in readers who detect the loading.

WEB LINK	Avoiding Logical Fallacies
Stephen Downes of the University of Alberta provides a guide to logical fallacies ("Stephen's Guide to the Logical Fallacies") that offers advice on spotting and correcting fallacies in arguments. See *bedfordstmartins.com/alred* and select *Links for Handbook Entries*.	

loose / lose

Loose is an **adjective** meaning "not fastened" or "unrestrained." ("He discovered a *loose* wire.") *Lose* is a **verb** meaning "be deprived of" or "fail to win." ("I hope we do not *lose* the contract.")

malapropisms

A malapropism is a word that sounds similar to the one intended but is ludicrously wrong in the **context**.

> INCORRECT   Our employees are less *sedimentary* now that we have a fitness center.

> CORRECT   Our employees are less *sedentary* now that we have a fitness center.

Intentional malapropisms are sometimes used in humorous writing; unintentional malapropisms can confuse readers and embarrass a writer. See also **figures of speech**.

maps

M

Maps are often used to show specific geographic areas and features (roads, mountains, rivers, and the like). They can also illustrate geographic distributions of populations, climate patterns, corporate branch offices, and so forth. The map in Figure M–1, from an environmental assessment, shows the overlapping geographic areas served by three electric utilities in Missouri, Iowa, and Illinois. Note that the map contains a figure number and title, scale of distances, key (or legend), compass, and distinctive highlighting for emphasis. Maps are often used in **reports**, **proposals**, **brochures**, and other documents in which readers need to know the location or geographic orientation of buildings and other facilities.

WRITER'S CHECKLIST   Creating and Using Maps

✔ Follow the general guidelines discussed in **visuals** for placement of maps.

✔ Label each map clearly, and assign each map a figure number if it is one of a number of illustrations.

✔ Clearly identify all boundaries in the map. Eliminate unnecessary boundaries.

(continued)

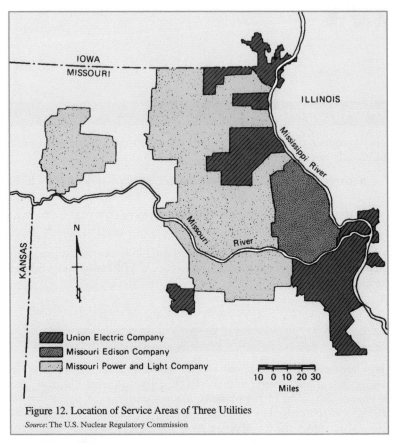

Figure 12. Location of Service Areas of Three Utilities

Source: The U.S. Nuclear Regulatory Commission

FIGURE M–1. Map

WRITER'S CHECKLIST Creating and Using Maps (*continued*)

✔ Eliminate unnecessary information that may clutter a map. For example, if the purpose of the map is to show population centers, do not include mountain elevations, rivers, or other physical features.

✔ Include a scale of miles/kilometers or feet/meters to give your readers an indication of the map's proportions.

✔ Indicate which direction is north with an arrow or a compass symbol.

✔ Emphasize key features by using color, shading, dots, crosshatching, or other appropriate symbols.

✔ Include a key, or legend, that explains what the different colors, shadings, or symbols represent.

WEB LINK	Maps and Mapping Information

The University of Texas Libraries offer a useful site with links to online maps and other types of mapping and cartographic resources. See *bedfordstmartins.com/alred* and select *Links for Handbook Entries.*

maybe / may be

Maybe (one word) is an **adverb** meaning "perhaps." ("*Maybe* the legal staff can resolve this issue.") *May be* (two words) is a **verb** phrase. ("It *may be* necessary to hire a specialist.")

media / medium

Media is the plural of *medium* and should always be used with a plural **verb**.

▶ Many communication *media are* available today.

▶ The Internet *is* a multifaceted *medium*.

M

meetings

Meetings allow people to share information and collaborate to produce better results than exchanges of **e-mail** messages or other means would allow. Like a **presentation**, a successful meeting requires planning and preparation. See also **selecting the medium**.

Planning a Meeting

Begin by determining the focus of the meeting, deciding who should attend, and choosing the best time and place to hold it. Prepare an agenda for the meeting and determine who should take the minutes.

Determine the Purpose of the Meeting.   The first step in planning a meeting is to focus on the desired outcome by asking questions to help you determine the meeting's **purpose**: What should participants know, believe, do, or be able to do as a result of attending the meeting?

Once you have your desired outcome in focus, use the information to write a purpose statement for the meeting that answers the questions *what* and *why*.

▶ The purpose of this meeting is to gather ideas from the sales force [*what*] in order to create a successful sales campaign for our new security scanner [*why*].

Decide Who Should Attend.   Determine first the key people who need to attend the meeting. If a meeting must be held without some key participants, ask those people for their contributions prior to the meeting or invite them to participate by speakerphone, videoconference, or such remote methods as described in *Digital Tip: Conducting Online Meetings* on page 339. Of course, the meeting minutes should be distributed to everyone, including appropriate nonattendees.

DIGITAL TIP

Scheduling Meetings Online

If you are responsible for scheduling meetings, you can simplify the process by using the advanced features of your organization's calendar application or using one of several free online scheduling tools. For a list of these tools and tips for scheduling meetings more effectively, go to *bedfordstmartins.com/alred* and select *Digital Tips*, "Scheduling Meetings Online."

Choose the Meeting Time.   Schedule a meeting for a time when all or most of the key people can be present. Consider as well other factors, such as time of day and the length of the meeting, that can influence its outcome:

• Monday morning is often a time people use to prepare for the coming week's work.

• Friday afternoon is often when people focus on completing the current week's tasks.

• Long meetings may need to include breaks to allow participants to respond to messages and refresh themselves.

- Meetings held during the last 15 minutes of the day will be quick, but few people will remember what happened.
- Remote participants may need consideration for their time zones.

Choose the Meeting Location. Having a meeting at your own location can give you an advantage: You feel more comfortable while your guests are new to the surroundings. Holding the meeting on someone else's premises, however, can signal cooperation. For balance, especially when people are meeting for the first time or are discussing sensitive issues, meet at a neutral site where no one gains an advantage and attendees may feel freer to participate.

DIGITAL TIP

Conducting Online Meetings

When participants cannot meet face to face, consider holding an online videoconference. In such meetings, the participants use an application on their computers to connect with other computers running the same application. Many of these applications are free or inexpensive, but all participants will need computers with high-speed Internet connections and webcams. For a list of software programs that support videoconferencing and tips for running a successful videoconference, see *bedfordstmartins.com/alred* and select *Digital Tips*, "Conducting Online Meetings."

M

Establish the Agenda. A tool for focusing the group, the agenda is an outline of what the meeting will address. Figure M–2 shows a typical agenda. Always prepare an agenda for a meeting, even if it is only an informal list of main topics. Ideally, the agenda should be distributed to attendees a day or two before the meeting. For a longer meeting in which participants are required to make a presentation, try to distribute the agenda a week or more in advance.

The agenda should list the attendees, the meeting time and place, and the topics you plan to discuss. If the meeting includes presentations, list the time allotted for each speaker. Finally, indicate an approximate length for the meeting so that participants can plan the rest of their day.

Sales Meeting Agenda

Purpose:	To get input for a sales campaign for the CZX software
Date:	Wednesday, May 16, 2012
Place:	Conference Room E
Time:	9:30 a.m.–11:00 a.m.
Attendees:	Advertising Manager, Sales Manager and Reps, Customer Service Manager

Topic	Presenter	Time
CZX Software	Bob Arbuckle	9:30–9:45
The Campaign	Maria Lopez	9:45–10:00
The Sales Strategy	Mary Winifred	10:00–10:15
Discussion	Led by Dave Grimes	10:15–11:00

FIGURE M–2. Meeting Agenda

If the agenda is distributed in advance of the meeting, it should be accompanied by a **cover letter** or message informing people of the following:

- The purpose of the meeting
- The date and place of the meeting
- The meeting start and stop times
- The names of the people invited
- Instructions on how to prepare

Figure M–3 shows a cover message to accompany an agenda.

Assign the Minute-Taking.   Delegate the minute-taking to someone other than the leader. The minute-taker should record major decisions made and tasks assigned. To avoid misunderstandings, the minute-taker needs to record each assignment, the person responsible for it, and the date on which it is due.

For a standing committee, it is best to rotate the responsibility of taking minutes. See also **minutes of meetings** and **note-taking**.

Conducting the Meeting

Assign someone to write on a board or project a computer image of information that needs to be viewed by everyone present.

During the meeting, keep to your agenda; however, create a productive environment by allowing room for differing views and fostering an environment in which participants listen respectfully to one another.

From: "S. McLaughlin" <smc@mscan.com>
To: "M. Lopez" <mlop@mscan.com>; "M. Winifred"
              <wini@mscan.com>; "B. Arbuckle" <arbu@mscan.com>;
              "D. Grimes" <dgri@mscan.com>; "Sales Reps"
              <sales-all@mscan.com>
Sent: Fri, 11 May 2012 13:30:12 EST
Subject: Sales Meeting (May 16 at 9:30 a.m.)

Attachments: Sales Meeting Agenda.doc (29 KB)

Purpose of the Meeting

The purpose of this meeting is to get your ideas for the upcoming
introduction and sales campaign for our new CZX software.

Date, Time, and Location

Date: Wednesday, May 16, 2012
Time: 9:30 a.m.–11:00 a.m.
Place: Conference Room E (go to the ground floor, take a right off the
       elevator, third door on the left)

Attendees

Those addressed above to attend.

Meeting Preparation

Everyone should be prepared to offer suggestions on the following topics:

- Sales features of the new software
- Techniques for selling the software
- Customer profile of potential buyers
- FAQs — questions customers may ask
- Anticipated support services

Agenda

Please see the attached document.

FIGURE M–3. E-mail to Accompany an Agenda

M

- Consider the feelings, thoughts, ideas, and needs of others — do not let your own agenda blind you to other points of view.
- Help other participants feel valued and respected by **listening** to them and responding to what they say.
- Respond positively to the comments of others whenever possible.
- Consider communication styles and approaches that are different from your own, particularly those from other cultures. See also **global communication**.

Deal with Conflict.   Despite your best efforts, conflict is inevitable. However, conflict is potentially valuable; when managed positively, it can stimulate creative thinking by challenging complacency and showing ways to achieve goals more efficiently or economically. See **collaborative writing**.

Members of any group are likely to vary in their personalities and attitudes, and you may encounter people who approach meetings differently. Consider the following tactics for the interruptive, negative, rambling, overly quiet, and territorial personality types.

- The *interruptive person* rarely lets anyone finish a sentence and may intimidate the group's quieter members. Tell that person in a firm but nonhostile tone to let the others finish in the interest of getting everyone's input. By addressing the issue directly, you signal to the group the importance of putting common goals first.

- The *negative person* has difficulty accepting change and often considers a new idea or project from a negative point of view. Such negativity, if left unchecked, can demoralize the group and suppress enthusiasm for new ideas. If the negative person brings up a valid point, however, ask for the group's suggestions to remedy the issue being raised. If the negative person's reactions are not valid or are outside the agenda, state the necessity of staying focused on the agenda and perhaps recommend a separate meeting to address those issues.

- The *rambling person* cannot collect his or her thoughts quickly enough to verbalize them succinctly. Restate or clarify this person's ideas. Try to strike a balance between providing your own interpretation and drawing out the person's intended meaning.

- The *overly quiet person* may be timid or may just be deep in thought. Ask for this person's thoughts, being careful not to embarrass the person. In some cases, you can have a quiet person jot down his or her thoughts and give them to you later.

- The *territorial person* fiercely defends his or her group against real or perceived threats and may refuse to cooperate with members of other departments, companies, and so on. Point out that although such concerns may be valid, everyone is working toward the same overall goal and that goal should take precedence.

Close the Meeting.   Just before closing the meeting, review all decisions and assignments. Paraphrase each to help the group focus on what individual participants have agreed to do and to ensure that the minutes will be complete and accurate. Now is the time to raise questions and clarify any misunderstandings. Set a date by which everyone at the meeting can expect to receive copies of the minutes. Finally, thank everyone for participating, and close the meeting on a positive note.

WRITER'S CHECKLIST   Planning and Conducting Meetings

✔ Develop a purpose statement for the meeting to focus your planning.

✔ Invite only those essential to fulfilling the purpose of the meeting.

✔ Select a time and place convenient to all those attending.

✔ Create an agenda and distribute it at least a day or two before the meeting.

✔ Assign someone to take meeting minutes.

✔ Ensure that the minutes record key decisions; assignments; due dates; and the date, time, and location of any follow-up meeting.

✔ Follow the agenda to keep everyone focused.

✔ Respect the views of others and how they are expressed.

✔ Use the strategies in this entry for handling conflict and attendees whose style of expression may prevent getting everyone's best thinking.

✔ Close the meeting by reviewing key decisions and assignments.

M

memos

Memos are documents that use a standard form (*To:*, *From:*, *Date:*, *Subject:*) whether sent on paper or as an attachment to an **e-mail**. They may be used within organizations for routine correspondence, short reports, proposals, and other internal documents.

Even in organizations where e-mail messages have largely taken the function of memos, a printed or an attached memo with organizational letterhead can communicate with formality and authority in addition to offering the full range of word-processing features. Paper memos are also useful in manufacturing and service industries, as well as in other businesses where employees do not have easy access to e-mail. For a discussion of writing strategies for memos, e-mail, and **letters**, see **correspondence**. See also **selecting the medium**.

Memo Format

The memo shown in Figure M–4 illustrates a typical memo format. As this example illustrates, the use of **headings** and **lists** often fosters **clarity** and provides **emphasis** in memos. For a discussion of subject lines, see pages 122–23.

Professional Publishing Services

MEMORANDUM

TO: Barbara Smith, Publications Manager

FROM: Hannah Kaufman, Vice President   *HK*

DATE: April 11, 2012

SUBJECT: Schedule for ACM Electronics Brochures

ACM Electronics has asked us to prepare a comprehensive set of brochures for its Milwaukee office by August 10, 2012. We have worked with similar firms in the past, so this job should be relatively easy to prepare. I estimate that the job will take nearly two months. Ted Harris has requested time and cost estimates for the project. Fred Moore in production will prepare the cost estimates, and I would like you to prepare a tentative schedule for the project.

Additional Personnel
In preparing the schedule, check the status of the following:
- Production schedule for all staff writers
- Availability of freelance writers
- Availability of dependable graphic designers

Ordinarily, we would not need to depend on outside personnel; however, because our bid for the *Wall Street Journal* special project is still under consideration, we could be short of staff in June and July. Further, we have to consider vacations that have already been approved.

Time Estimates
Please give me time estimates by April 17. A successful job done on time will give us a good chance to obtain the contract to do ACM Electronics' annual report for its stockholders' meeting this fall.

I have enclosed several brochures that may be helpful.

cc: Ted Harris, President
      Fred Moore, Production Editor

Enclosures: Sample Brochures

M

FIGURE M–4. Typical Memo Format (Printed with Sender's Handwritten Initials)

◀ PROFESSIONALISM NOTE As with e-mail, be alert to the practices of addressing and distributing memos in your organization. Consider who should receive or needs to be copied on a memo and in what order—senior managers, for example, take precedence over junior managers. If rank does not apply, alphabetizing recipients by last name is safe. ▶

Some organizations ask writers to initial or sign printed memos to verify that the writer accepts responsibility for a memo's content. Electronic copies of memos do not include simulated initials.

Additional Pages

When memos require more than one page, use a second-page header and always carry at least two lines of the body text over to that page. The header should include either the recipient's name or an abbreviated subject line (if there are too many names to fit), the page number, and the date. Place the header in the upper left-hand corner or across the page, as shown in Figure M–5.

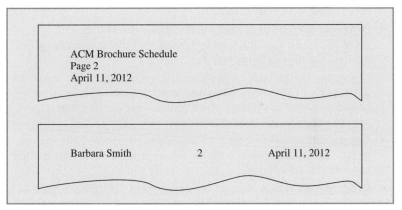

M

FIGURE M–5. Alternative Headers for the Second Page of Memos

WEB LINK	Writing Memos
For links to articles about when to write memos and tips for following organization protocol, see *bedfordstmartins.com/alred* and select *Links for Handbook Entries*.	

methods of development

A logical method of development satisfies the readers' need for shape and structure in a document, whether it is an **e-mail**, a **report**, or a Web page. It helps you as a writer move smoothly and logically from the **introduction** to a **conclusion**.

Choose the method or, as is often the case, a combination of methods that best suits your subject, **audience**, and **purpose**. Following are the most common methods, each of which is discussed in further detail in its own entry.

- **Cause-and-effect method of development** begins with either the cause or the effect of an event. This approach can be used to develop a report that offers a solution to a problem, beginning with the problem and moving on to the solution or vice versa.

- **Chronological method of development** emphasizes the time element of a sequence, as in a **trouble report** that traces events as they occurred in time.

- **Comparison method of development** is useful when writing about a new topic that is in many ways similar to another topic that is more familiar to your readers.

- **Definition method of development** extends definitions with additional details, examples, comparisons, or other explanatory devices. See also **defining terms**.

- **Division-and-classification method of development** either separates a whole into component parts and discusses each part separately (*division*) or groups parts into categories that clarify the relationship of the parts (*classification*).

- **General and specific methods of development** proceed either from general information to specific details or from specific information to a general conclusion.

- **Order-of-importance method of development** presents information in either decreasing order of importance, as in a **proposal** that begins with the most important point, or increasing order of importance, as in a **presentation** that ends with the most important point.

- **Sequential method of development** emphasizes the order of elements in a process and is particularly useful when writing step-by-step **instructions**.

- **Spatial method of development** describes the physical appearance of an object or area from top to bottom, inside to outside, front to back, and so on.

M

Rarely does a writer rely on only one of these methods. Documents often blend methods of development. For example, in a report that describes the organization of a company, you might use elements from three methods of development. You could divide the larger topic (the company) into operations (division and classification), arrange the operations according to what you see as their impact within the company (order of importance), and present their manufacturing operations in the order they occur (sequential). As this example illustrates, when outlining a document, you may base your major division on one primary method of development appropriate to your purpose and then subordinate other methods to it.

minutes of meetings

Organizations and committees refer to official records of their **meetings** as *minutes*. Because minutes are often used to record decisions and to settle disputes, they must be accurate, complete, and clear. When approved, minutes of meetings are official and can be used as evidence in legal proceedings. A section from the minutes of a meeting is shown in Figure M–6.

M

NORTH TAMPA MEDICAL CENTER

Minutes of the Monthly Meeting
Medical Audit Committee

DATE: June 25, 2012

PRESENT: G. Miller (Chair), C. Bloom, J. Dades, K. Gilley,
             D. Ingoglia (Secretary), S. Ramirez

ABSENT: D. Rowan, C. Tsien, C. Voronski, R. Fautier, R. Wolf

Dr. Gail Miller called the meeting to order at 12:45 p.m. Dr. David Ingoglia made a motion that the June 4, 2012, minutes be approved as distributed. The motion was seconded and passed.

The committee discussed and took action on the following topics.

(1) TOPIC: Meeting Time

  Discussion: The most convenient time for the committee to meet.
  Action taken: The committee decided to meet on the fourth Tuesday of every month, at 12:30 p.m.

FIGURE M–6. Minutes of a Meeting (Partial Section)

Keep your minutes brief and to the point. Except for recording formally presented motions, which must be transcribed word for word, summarize what occurs and paraphrase discussions. To keep the minutes concise, follow a set format, and use **headings** for each major point discussed. See also **note-taking**.

Avoid abstractions and generalities; always be specific. Refer to everyone in the same way—a lack of consistency in titles or names may suggest a deference to one person at the expense of another. Avoid **adjectives** and **adverbs** that suggest good or bad qualities, as in "Mr. Sturgess's *capable* assistant read the *comprehensive* report to the subcommittee." Minutes should be objective and impartial.

If a member of the committee is to follow up on something and report back to the committee at its next meeting, clearly state the person's name and the responsibility he or she has accepted.

WRITER'S CHECKLIST   Items to Include in Minutes of Meetings

- ✔ The name of the group or committee holding the meeting
- ✔ The topic of the meeting
- ✔ The kind of meeting (a regular meeting or a special meeting called to discuss a specific subject or problem)
- ✔ The number of members present and, for committees or boards of ten or fewer members, the names of those present and absent
- ✔ The place, time, and date of the meeting
- ✔ A statement that the chair and the secretary were present or the names of any substitutes
- ✔ A statement that the minutes of the previous meeting were approved or revised
- ✔ A list of any reports that were read and approved
- ✔ All the main motions that were made, with statements as to whether they were carried, defeated, or tabled (vote postponed), and the names of those who made and seconded the motions (motions that were withdrawn are not mentioned)
- ✔ A full description of resolutions that were adopted and a simple statement of any that were rejected
- ✔ A record of all ballots with the number of votes cast for and against resolutions
- ✔ The time the meeting was adjourned (officially ended) and the place, time, and date of the next meeting
- ✔ The recording secretary's signature and typed name and, if desired, the signature of the chairperson

mission statements

A mission statement articulates an organization's unique reason for being and attempts to motivate its stakeholders (employees, customers, and stockholders) to pursue common goals. (See **audience**.) A good mission statement can achieve a focused allocation of organizational resources by answering such tough questions as, Why do we exist? What is our business? What are we trying to accomplish? A good mission statement can be an important factor in the success of an organization.

Mission statements can be distributed in an organization's **annual report**, framed for display, published in a pamphlet, or posted on an organization's Web site. Figure M–7 shows a typical mission statement.

Writing a Mission Statement

Most mission statements have certain elements in common, such as a statement of purpose, a description of the organization's line of business, and an acknowledgment of such stakeholders as customers, employees, and stockholders. Following is a list of various goals that mission statements may be aimed to achieve. Some, or indeed all, may apply to a particular organization. Mission statements can do the following:

- Reflect an organization's purpose, function, and primary reason for existing.
- Guide the development and execution of organizational strategies.
- Offer benchmarks toward which long-range goals can be targeted and against which progress can be measured.
- Build and communicate company values over periods of time, thus providing an organization and its employees with a sense of identity.
- Distinguish an organization from others of the same type, and identify the scope of the organization's operations in product and market terms.

Before beginning to write a mission statement, get approval of your general approach from top management. Then determine who will write the draft. In a small organization, the top person normally writes it. In a large organization, it is often written by a committee that includes representatives from key stakeholders.

Gather as much information as possible about your organization and its goals by interviewing top management and researching annual reports and other company documents. If you have a committee to help you, use **brainstorming** to answer the following questions that will help you understand the **context** of the mission statement:

M

M

BARTLETT BANKARD MISSION STATEMENT

Mission

The strategic mission of Bartlett Bankard Corporation is to build high-performance, full-service community banks where people matter.

We offer and deliver competitive product lines that meet targeted customer needs and expectations while maintaining asset quality, capital strength, and earnings performance. We provide those products only when we are able to deliver them with the service and quality our customers deserve. For the Corporation to continue to fulfill these goals, we must be able to guarantee that the four cornerstones of our success — our customers, our employees, our communities, and our shareholders — are always firmly in place.

We must respond to:

Our customers: They are our business. We will provide them with the products they want and need.

Our employees: They are The Bank. Our customers know them as The Bank. We will provide them with the training, the working environment, and the recognition that encourage and promote growth.

Our communities: Their success is our success. As a corporation and personally as individuals, we will meet the financial and public service needs of our communities.

Our shareholders: They are the owners of the Corporation, and, as our shareholders, they are entitled to a fair return on their investment.

FIGURE M–7. Mission Statement

- Why was our organization established?
- Who are our customers and clients? What needs do we meet?
- What image do we want our products and services to project?

- What message do we want to send the community, customers, stockholders, and employees about the organization?
- Where do we see our organization in five or ten years?
- What does our organizational culture need to be to get us there?

When you have answered these questions, create an outline (see **outlining**) and then **write a draft**. As you write, try to find words and phrases that capture the essence of the organization's purpose and goals, and avoid **jargon, buzzwords**, platitudes, meaningless superlatives, and overuse of the word *quality*. If you overload your mission statement with platitudes and superlatives, you will move readers to cynicism. A mission to "Be the best computer manufacturer in the world" sounds good, but "To develop products that adapt to the ever-changing needs of our customers!" is a good deal more definable, measurable, and action-able—and it is motivational. To test the appropriateness of an assertion in your mission statement, ask whether anyone could reasonably dis-agree with it. If not, it is probably a platitude. Can you imagine anyone disagreeing with "To provide the best value for the money"?

When you are satisfied with your draft, circulate it to selected re-viewers (involving as many employees, customers, and stockholders as possible, in order to give everyone a sense of ownership). Then revise the draft based on the feedback you receive.

Format and Length

The format and the length of a mission statement should be determined by what the organization wants to say about itself and how it wants to say it. The length may vary from a pithy one-sentence statement, such as a pet-food company's concise "To enhance the well-being of dogs and cats," to multiple pages that begin with a mission statement and continue with a statement of the company's vision, values, philosophy, objectives, and strategies. Avoid letting the mission statement get too long, however, because readers will more readily remember a relatively short statement and incorporate its values into their daily business ac-tivities and planning. You can find mission statements at organizational Web sites as well as at general sites, such as *www.missionstatements .com/contact.html*. See also **business plans**.

mixed constructions

A mixed construction is a sentence in which the elements do not sensi-bly fit together. The problem may be a **grammar** error, a **logic error**, or both.

▶ Because the copier wouldn't start‚ ~~explains why~~ we called
a technician.

The original sentence mixes a subordinate **clause** (*Because the copier
wouldn't start*) with a **verb** (*explains*) that attempts to incorrectly
use the subordinate clause as its subject. The revision correctly uses
the **pronoun** *we* as the subject of the main clause. See also **sentence
construction**.

modifiers

Modifiers are words, phrases, or clauses that expand, limit, or make
otherwise more specific the meaning of other elements in a sentence.
Although we can create sentences without modifiers, we often need the
detail and clarification they provide.

> **WITHOUT MODIFIERS**   Production decreased.
>
> **WITH MODIFIERS**   *Glucose* production decreased *rapidly*.

Most modifiers function as **adjectives** or **adverbs**. Adjectives describe
qualities or impose boundaries on the words they modify.

▶ *noisy* machinery, *ten* files, *this* printer, *a* workstation

An adverb modifies an adjective, another adverb, a **verb**, or an entire
clause.

▶ Under test conditions, the brake pad showed *much* less wear than
it did under actual conditions.
[The adverb *much* modifies the adjective *less*.]

▶ The redesigned brake pad lasted *much* longer.
[The adverb *much* modifies another adverb, *longer*.]

▶ The wrecking ball hit the wall of the building *hard*.
[The adverb *hard* modifies the verb *hit*.]

▶ *Surprisingly*, the motor failed even after all the durability and performance tests it had passed.
[The adverb *surprisingly* modifies an entire clause.]

Adverbs are **intensifiers** when they increase the impact of adjectives
(*very* fine, *too* high) or adverbs (*very* slowly, *rather* quickly). Be cau-
tious using intensifiers; their overuse can lead to vagueness and a resulting lack of precision.

Stacked (Jammed) Modifiers

Stacked (or *jammed*) modifiers are strings of modifiers preceding **nouns** that make writing unclear or difficult to read.

▶ Your *staffing-level authorization reassessment* plan should result in a major improvement.

The noun *plan* is preceded by three long modifiers, a string that forces the reader to slow down to interpret its meaning. Stacked modifiers often result from a tendency to overuse **buzzwords** or **jargon**. See how breaking up the stacked modifiers makes the example easier to read.

▶ Your plan for reassessing the staffing-level authorizations should result in a major improvement.

Misplaced Modifiers

A modifier is misplaced when it modifies the wrong word or phrase. A misplaced modifier can cause **ambiguity**.

▶ We *almost* lost all of the files.
   [The files were *almost* lost but were not.]

▶ We lost *almost* all of the files.
   [Most of the files were in fact lost.]

To avoid ambiguity, place modifiers as close as possible to the words they are intended to modify. Note the two meanings possible when the phrase is shifted in the following sentences:

▶ The equipment *without the accessories* sold the best.
   [Different types of equipment were available, some with and some without accessories.]

▶ The equipment sold the best *without the accessories*.
   [One type of equipment was available, and the accessories were optional.]

Place clauses as close as possible to the words they modify.

REMOTE   We sent the brochure to several local firms *that had four-color art*.

CLOSE   We sent the brochure *that had four-color art* to several local firms.

Squinting Modifiers

A squinting modifier is one that can be interpreted as modifying either of two sentence elements simultaneously, thereby confusing readers about which is intended. See also **dangling modifiers**.

▶ We agreed *on the next day* to make the adjustments.
[Did they agree *to make the adjustments* on the next day? Or *on the next day*, did they agree to make the adjustments?]

A squinting modifier can sometimes be corrected simply by changing its position, but often it is better to rewrite the sentence.

▶ We agreed that *on the next day* we would make the adjustments.
[The adjustments were to be made *on the next day*.]

▶ *On the next day*, we agreed that we would make the adjustments.
[The agreement was made *on the next day*.]

mood

The grammatical term *mood* refers to the **verb** functions that indicate whether the verb is intended to make a statement, ask a question, give a command, or express a hypothetical possibility.

The *indicative mood* states a fact, gives an opinion, or asks a question.

▶ The setting *is* correct.

▶ *Is* the setting correct?

The *imperative mood* expresses a command, suggestion, request, or plea. In the imperative mood, the implied subject *you* is not expressed. ("*Install* the system today.")

The *subjunctive mood* expresses something that is contrary to fact or that is conditional, hypothetical, or purely imaginative; it can also express a wish, a doubt, or a possibility. In the subjunctive mood, *were* is used instead of *was* in clauses that speculate about the present or future, and the base form (*be*) is used following certain verbs, such as *propose*, *request*, or *insist*. See also progressive **tense**.

▶ If we *were* to close the sale today, we would meet our monthly goal.

▶ The senior partner insisted that she [I, you, we, they] *be* the project leader.

The most common use of the subjunctive mood is to express clearly that the writer considers a condition to be contrary to fact. If the condition is not considered to be contrary to fact, use the indicative mood.

SUBJUNCTIVE   If I *were* president of the firm, I would change several hiring policies.

INDICATIVE   Although I *am* president of the firm, I don't control every aspect of its policies.

ESL TIPS for Determining Mood

In written and especially in spoken English, the tendency increasingly is to use the indicative mood where the subjunctive traditionally has been used. Note the differences between traditional and contemporary usage in the following examples.

Traditional (formal) use of the subjunctive mood

► I wish he *were* here now.

► If I *were* going to the conference, I would travel with him.

► I requested that she *show* up on time.

Contemporary (informal) use of the indicative mood

► I wish he *was* here now.

► If I *was* going to the conference, I would travel with him.

► I requested that she *shows* up on time.

In professional writing, it is better to use the more traditional expressions.

M

Ms. / Miss / Mrs.

Ms. is used in business and public life to address or refer to a woman. Traditionally, *Miss* is used to refer to an unmarried woman, and *Mrs.* is used to refer to a married woman. Some women may indicate a preference for *Ms.*, *Miss*, or *Mrs.*, which you should honor. If a woman has an academic or a professional title, use the appropriate form of address (*Doctor*, *Professor*, *Captain*) instead of *Ms.*, *Miss*, or *Mrs.* See also **biased language**.

mutual / common

Common is used when two or more persons (or things) share something or possess it jointly.

▶ We have a *common* desire to make the program succeed.

▶ Our departments have *common* office space.

Mutual may also mean "shared" (*mutual* friend, of *mutual* benefit), but it usually implies something given and received reciprocally and is used with reference to only two persons or parties.

▶ Melek respects Roth, and from my observations the respect is *mutual*.
[Roth also respects Melek.]

M

N

narration

Narration is the presentation of a series of events in a prescribed (often chronological) sequence. Much narrative writing explains how something happened: a laboratory study, a site visit, an accident, the decisions in an important meeting. See also **chronological method of development**, **trip reports**, and **trouble reports**.

Effective narration rests on two key writing techniques: the careful, accurate sequencing of events and a consistent **point of view** on the part of the narrator. Narrative sequence and essential shifts in the sequence are signaled in three ways: chronology (clock and calendar time), transitional words pertaining to time (*before, after, next, first, while, then*), and verb tenses that indicate whether something has happened (past **tense**) or is under way (present tense). The point of view indicates the writer's relation to the information being narrated as reflected in the use of **person**. Narration usually expresses a first- or third-person point of view. First-person narration indicates that the writer is a participant, and third-person narration indicates that the writer is writing about what happened to someone or something else.

The narrative shown in Figure N–1 reconstructs the chronology of an early-morning accident of Chicago Transit Authority Green Line train run 2. This train struck two signal maintainers who were working near a tower on the section of the Chicago Loop that is above the intersection of Lake and Wells Streets. The Loop is elevated, and one maintainer fell from the structure. The investigators needed to "tell the story" in detail so that any lessons learned could be used to improve safety. To do that, they recount and sequence events as precisely as possible. The verb tenses throughout indicate past action: *approached, continued, heard, removed, stopped.*

Although narration often exists in combination with other forms of discourse (**description**, **exposition**, **persuasion**), avoid interrupting a narrative with lengthy explanations or analyses. Explain only what is necessary for readers to follow the events. See **audience**.

N

The Accident*

On the morning of the accident, two night-shift signal maintainers were repairing a switch at tower 18. Between 4:00 and 4:30 a.m., two day-shift maintainers joined them.[1] As the two crews conferred about the progress of the repair, Green Line train run 1 approached the tower. A trainee was operating the train, and a train operator/line instructor[2] was observing. Both crew members on the train later stated that they had not heard the control center's radioed advisory that workers were on the track structure at tower 18. The line instructor said that as the train approached the tower with a *proceed* (green) signal, he observed way-side maintenance personnel from about 150 feet away and told the trainee to stop the train, which he did. One of the maintainers gave the train a hand signal to proceed, and the train continued on its way. Shortly after the train left, the night-shift maintainers also left.

The day-shift maintainers continued to work. Just before the accident, they removed a defective part and started to install a replacement. According to both men, they were squatting over the switch machine. One was facing the center of the track and attaching wires, while the other was facing the Loop with his back to the normal direction of train movements. He was shining a flashlight on the work area.

The accident train approached the tower on the *proceed* signal. One maintainer later said that he remembered being hit by the train, while the other said that he was hit by "something." A train operator/line instructor was operating the train, and a trainee was observing. Both later said that they had not seen any wayside workers. They said that they had heard noise that the student described as a "thump" in the vicinity of the accident and caught a "glimpse" of something.

Both maintainers later stated that they had not seen or heard the train as it approached. After being struck, one of the maintainers fell from the structure. The other fell to the deck of the platform on the outside of the structure. He used his radio to tell the control center that he and another maintainer had been "hit by the train." Emergency medical personnel were dispatched to the scene, and an ambulance took both men to a local hospital.

In the meantime, the accident train continued past the tower and stopped at the next station, Clark and Lake, where the crew members inspected the train from the platform and found no damage. They continued on their way until they heard the radio report that workers had been struck by a train. They stopped their train at the next station and reported to a supervisor.

According to the operator of the accident train, nothing had distracted her from her duties, and she had been facing forward and watching the track before the train arrived at tower 18. The trainee supported her account. Both crew members said that they had not heard the control center's radioed advisory that workers were on the track structure at tower 18.

[1] All times referred to in this report are central standard time.
[2] Line instructors are working train operators who provide on-the-job training to operator trainees.

Source: National Transportation Safety Board, "Railroad Accident Brief: Chicago Transit Authority, DCA-02-FR-005, Chicago, Illinois, February 26, 2002." www.ntsb.gov/publictn/2003/RAB0304.htm

FIGURE N–1. Narration from an Accident Report

nature

Nature, when used to mean "kind" or "sort," is vague. Avoid this usage in your writing. Say exactly what you mean.

> *exclusionary clause in*
> ► The ~~nature of~~ the contract caused the problem.
>   ^

needless to say

The phrase *needless to say* sometimes occurs in speech and writing. Eliminate the phrase or replace it with a more descriptive **word choice**.

> *Service logs indicate that*
> ► ~~Needless to say,~~ staff reductions have decreased customer loyalty.
>   ^

newsletter articles

If your organization publishes a **newsletter,** you may be asked to contribute an article on a subject in your area of expertise. In fact, an article is a good way to promote your work or your department.

Before you begin to write, consider the traditional *who, what, where, when,* and *why* of journalism (*Who* did it? *What* was done? *Where* was it done? *When* was it done? *Why* was it done?) and then add *how,* which may be of as much interest to your colleagues as any of the five *w*'s. Next, determine whether the company has an official policy or position on your subject. If it does, adhere to it as you prepare your article. If there is no company policy, determine your management's attitude toward your subject. See also **audience** and **context.**

Gather several fairly recent issues of the newsletter and study the **style** and **tone** of the writing and the approach used for various kinds of subjects. Understand those perspectives before you begin to work on your own article. Ask yourself the following questions about your subject: What is its significance to the organization? What is its significance to my coworkers? The answers to those questions should help you establish the style, tone, and approach for your article and also heavily influence your conclusion.

Research for a newsletter article frequently consists of **interviewing for information.** Interview key personnel concerned with your subject. Get all available information and all points of view. Be sure to give maximum credit to the maximum number of people by quoting statements from those involved in projects and naming those who have developed initiatives. See also **quotations.**

Figure N–2 shows an article written for *Connection*, a newsletter produced by Ken Cook Company and distributed to current and prospective clients. This article describes how the company employed a third-party expert to perform an audit of the company's Quality Management System (designed to comply with ISO 9001:2000 standards). Notice the inset quotation, which draws **readers** to the article as well as

What Does ISO 9001:2000 Mean to the Supply Chain?

You may have noticed that some companies promote their goods and services as ISO 9001:2000 certified. But what does that mean to the supply chain? If you're responsible for making the purchasing decisions at your company, you're looking for a supplier that provides consistent, conforming, quality products and/or services.

According to the International Organization for Standardization (ISO) website, "The objective of ISO 9001:2000 is to provide a set of requirements that, if they are effectively implemented, will provide you with confidence that your supplier can consistently provide goods and services that meet your needs and expectations and comply with applicable regulations."

ISO 9001:2000 is a recognized international standard that sets the criteria for an organization's Quality Management System (QMS). Those companies that are ISO certified have a QMS meeting the requirements of ISO 9001:2000, the only standard in the ISO 9000 family that can be used for the purpose of conformity assessment.

To provide its clients with the highest level of confidence in its products and services, and to meet all stated requirements and applicable regulatory requirements, Ken Cook Co. pursues continuous improvement and the highest level of a Quality Management System in order to comply with ISO 9001:2000.

In 2003, Ken Cook Co. sought out an accredited, impartial third-party certification body to perform an audit of its QMS. Ken Cook Co. chose an accredited organization in order to verify the certifying body's independence and competence to carry out the certification process.

The certification body selected was accredited by ANAB (formerly ANSI-RAB), the accreditation body of the American National Standards Institute (ANSI) and the American Society for Quality (ASQ). As a result, Ken Cook Co.'s QMS was assessed and certified as meeting the requirements of ISO 9001:2000.

> **Ken Cook Co.'s internal audit process documentation indicates excellent methodology for system monitoring. This is a best practice system.**
> *- Wayne Uttke, lead auditor, Verisys Registrars*

As a purchaser, this information should provide you with confidence in Ken Cook Co.'s ability to provide consistent, conforming goods and services. ISO 9001:2000 requires Ken Cook Co. to monitor the levels of satisfaction of its customers and to provide feedback in order to improve the effectiveness of its QMS.

Ken Cook Co. has maintained ISO certification since 2003 and successfully renewed certification in July 2006. The

certifying body deemed several internal activities as best practices—including management planning and review and Ken Cook Co.'s internal auditing system.

Regarding the internal auditing system, Wayne Uttke, lead auditor for Verisys Registrars, noted, "Ken Cook Co.'s internal audit process documentation indicates excellent methodology for system monitoring. This is a best practice system."

Ken Cook Co. is pleased to have incorporated these, and other high standards into every aspect of day-to-day business. Robert T. Haukohl, Executive Vice President overseeing production operations, confirmed, "ISO 9001:2000 is now working seamlessly within Ken Cook Co. and has been fully integrated into our business model. This is exactly what we have been striving for and takes us to a new level of quality management."

ISO 9001:2000 is a useful basis for organizations to be able to demonstrate that they are managing their business to achieve consistent quality goods and services. As a supply chain tool, this ISO standard can provide you with the confidence that your supplier understands what you expect from them and the peace of mind that its Quality Management System has been recognized as superior. Ken Cook Co. is your partner in product documentation and demonstrates its commitment to quality through successful attainment of ISO 9001:2000 and continuous improvement.

World Class Owner's Manuals at IBEX (continued from page 2)

At the trade show, Ken Cook Co. is offering a coupon that entitles the bearer one free evaluation of their current boat owner's manual, a $250 value. The evaluation will report on compliance with the ABYC T-24 elements, ISO/DIS 10240 elements and a CE certification checklist.

Come to IBEX 2006 for the Ken Cook Co. presentation of "World Class Owner Manuals" Workshop. The workshop is free to attendees at IBEX 2006, but seating is limited—so come early! Renowned professionals in the boatbuilding industry will discuss how you can advance your business, gain a

clear understanding of the evolving government and industry regulations worldwide and hear about new processes being used in boatbuilding today. While you're there, also visit Ken Cook Co. at Booth 1118.

N

FIGURE N–2. Newsletter Article

giving them a sense of the article's content. By describing this process, the article aims to demonstrate Ken Cook Company's "commitment to quality."

WRITER'S CHECKLIST   Writing Newsletter Articles

- ✔ Write an intriguing <u>title</u> to catch the audience's attention; <u>rhetorical questions</u> often work well.
- ✔ Include as many eye-catching <u>photographs</u> or <u>visuals</u> as appropriate to entice your audience to read the lead <u>paragraph</u> of your <u>introduction</u>. See also <u>layout and design</u>.
- ✔ Fashion a lead, or first paragraph, that will encourage further reading. The first paragraph generally makes the <u>transition</u> from the title to the body of the article.
- ✔ Offer a well-developed presentation of your subject to hold the readers' interest all the way to the end of the article.
- ✔ Write a <u>conclusion</u> that emphasizes the significance of your subject to your audience and stresses the points you want your readers to retain. See <u>emphasis</u>.
- ✔ Follow the steps listed in the "Checklist of the Writing Process" on pages xxiii–xxiv as you prepare your newsletter article.

N

newsletters

Newsletters are designed to inform and to create and sustain interest and membership in an organization. They can also be used to sell products and services. The two main types of newsletters are organizational newsletters and subscription newsletters.

Types of Newsletters

Organizational newsletters like the one shown in Figure N–3 are sent to employees, clients, or members of an association to keep them informed about issues regarding their company or group, such as the development of new products or policies or the accomplishments of individuals or teams. Stories in organizational newsletters can both enhance the image and foster pride among employees of the organization's products or services. For example, Figure N–3 shows how Ken Cook Company partners with cutting-edge companies to produce high-quality training materials.

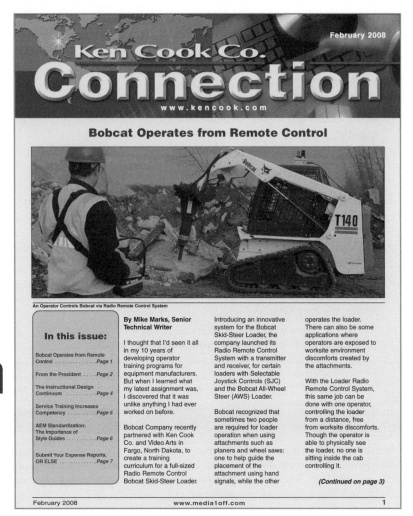

FIGURE N–3. Company Newsletter (Front Page)

Subscription newsletters are designed to attract and build a readership interested in buying specific products or services or in learning more about a specific subject. Subscribers are buying information, and they expect value for their money. For example, a person with experience in the stock market could create a financial newsletter and charge subscribers a monthly fee for the investing advice in that newsletter; a person who collects movie memorabilia could create an online newsletter that includes stories about ways to find and sell rare movie posters.

Developing Newsletters

Before you begin to develop a newsletter, decide on its specific **purpose** and the specific **audience** you will be targeting; then make sure the newsletter's appearance and editorial choices create a sense of identification among the readership. Newsletters often involve **collaborative writing** in which different individuals work on design, content, and project management. See also **persuasion** and **promotional writing**. If you are asked to contribute an article to a newsletter, see **newsletter articles**.

You will need to acquire a mailing list (names and addresses of your readers) and decide on the most strategic way to get the newsletter to these readers (whether through postal mail, interoffice mail, e-mail, or Web posting). Because it can be time-consuming and technically problematic to send out hundreds or thousands of online newsletters by yourself, you may also need to subscribe to a list-hosting service.*

◀ PROFESSIONALISM NOTE Update your subscriber lists regularly to be sure you are contacting only those who wish to continue receiving your newsletter. You risk damaging your reputation and that of your company if you badger former customers or current clients with unwanted mail. Include an opt-out waiver with each newsletter sent to afford subscribers the opportunity to remove themselves from your mailing list. ▶

Your **research** should include trade journals, business and technology magazines, the Web, and other sources to find specific angles for the articles that will appeal to your select audience. Attempt to provide content that your readers will not find elsewhere, for example, by interviewing and profiling customers, association members, or employees. Check your facts meticulously—newsletter readers are often specialists in their fields. Because newsletters are often distributed to branches and clients abroad, see **global communication** and **global graphics**. See also **interviewing for information**.

As shown in Figures N–2 and N–3, a newsletter's format should be simple and consistent, yet visually appealing to your readership. Use the active **voice** and a conversational **tone**. Use **headings** and bullets to break up the text and make the newsletter easy to read. Keep your sentences simple and paragraphs short. See **conciseness** and **layout and design**.

Using word-processing, desktop-publishing, or Web-development software, create newspaper columns and one or two **visuals** per page that complement the text. On the front page, identify the organization and include the date, volume and issue numbers, and a contents box.

*E-mail list-hosting services have their own servers and provide commercial delivery of premium e-mail that often contains graphic and other digital forms used for advertising.

For Web newsletters, follow the principles of good Web design. See also **layout and design**, **photographs**, and **writing for the Web**.

nominalizations

A nominalization is a **noun** form of a **verb** that is often combined with vague and general (or "weak") verbs like *make*, *do*, *give*, *perform*, and *provide*. Avoid nominalizations when you can use specific verbs that communicate the same idea more directly and concisely.

> *indicate*
> ▶ The scan will ~~give an indication~~ if the virus is present.

> *evaluate*
> ▶ The staff should ~~perform an evaluation of~~ the new software.

If you use nominalizations solely to make your writing sound more formal, the result will be **affectation**. You may occasionally have an appropriate use for a nominalization. For example, you might use a nominalization to slow the **pace** of your writing. See also **business writing style**, **conciseness**, **plain language**, and **voice**.

N

none

None can be either a singular or a plural **pronoun**, depending on the context. See also **agreement**.

> ▶ *None* of the material *has* been ordered.
> [Always use a singular **verb** with a singular **noun**, in this case, "material."]

> ▶ *None* of the clients *has* been called yet.
> [Use a singular verb even with a plural noun (*clients*) if the intended emphasis is on the idea of *not one*.]

> ▶ *None* of the clients *have* been called yet.
> [Use a plural verb if you intend *none* to refer to all clients.]

For **emphasis**, substitute *no one* or *not one* for *none* and use a singular verb.

> *not one*
> ▶ We paid the retail price for three of the machines, ~~none~~ of which was worth the money.

nor / or

Nor always follows *neither* in sentences with continuing negation. ("They will *neither* support *nor* approve the plan.") Likewise, *or* follows *either* in sentences. ("The firm will accept *either* a short-term *or* a long-term loan.")

Two or more singular subjects joined by *or* or *nor* usually take a singular **verb**. However, when one subject is singular and one is plural, the verb agrees with the subject nearer to it. See also **conjunctions** and **parallel structure**.

SINGULAR	Neither the *architect* nor the *client was* happy with the design.
PLURAL	Neither the *architect* nor the *clients were* happy with the design.
SINGULAR	Neither the *architects* nor the *client was* happy with the design.

note-taking

The purpose of note-taking is to summarize and record information you extract during **research**. The challenge in taking notes is to condense someone else's thoughts into your own words without distorting the original thinking. As you extract information, let your knowledge of the **audience** and the **purpose** of your writing guide you. For taking notes at a meeting, see **minutes of meetings**.

❖ ETHICS NOTE Resist copying your source word for word as you take notes; instead, paraphrase the author's idea or concept. If you only change a few words from a source and incorporate that text into your document, you will be guilty of **plagiarism**. See also **paraphrasing**. ❖

On occasion, when an expert source states something that is especially precise, striking, noteworthy, or that reinforces your point, you can justifiably quote the source directly and incorporate it into your document. If you use a direct quote, enclose the material in **quotation marks** in your notes. In your finished writing, document the source of your quotation. Normally, you will rarely need to quote anything longer than a paragraph. See also **documenting sources** and **quotations**.

When taking notes on abstract ideas, as opposed to factual data, do not sacrifice **clarity** for brevity—notes expressing concepts can lose their meaning if they are too brief. The critical test is whether you can understand the note a week later and recall the significant ideas of the passage. Consider the information in the following paragraph:

Long before the existence of bacteria was suspected, techniques were in use for combating their influence in, for instance, the decomposition of meat. Salt and heat were known to be effective, and these do in fact kill bacteria or prevent them from multiplying. Salt acts by the osmotic effect of extracting water from the bacterial cell fluid. Bacteria are less easily destroyed by osmotic action than are animal cells because their cell walls are constructed in a totally different way, which makes them much less permeable.

The paragraph says essentially three things:

1. Before the discovery of bacteria, salt and heat were used to combat the effects of bacteria.
2. Salt kills bacteria by extracting water from their cells by osmosis, hence its use in curing meat.
3. Bacteria are less affected by the osmotic effect of salt than are animal cells, because bacterial cell walls are less permeable.

If your readers' needs and your objective involve tracing the origin of the bacterial theory of disease, you might want to note that salt was traditionally used to kill bacteria long before people realized what caused meat to spoil. It might not be necessary to your topic to say anything about the relative permeability of bacterial cell walls.

You should record notes in a way you find efficient. Some find various shareware note and index programs useful. However, jotting notes on 3×5-inch index cards is often more flexible, and the cards are especially useful for **outlining** complex and long-term projects.

N

| **WRITER'S CHECKLIST** | **Taking Notes** |

✔ Ask yourself the following questions: What information do I need to fulfill my purpose? What are the needs of my audience?

✔ Record only the most important ideas and concepts. Be sure to record all vital names, dates, and definitions.

✔ When in doubt about whether to take a note, consider the difficulty of finding the source again should you want it later.

✔ Use direct or indirect quotations when sources state something that is precise, striking, or noteworthy or that succinctly reinforces a point you are making.

✔ Give proper credit. Record the author; title; publisher; place; page number; URL; and date of publication, posting, or retrieval. (On subsequent notes from the same source, include only the author and page number or URL.)

WRITER'S CHECKLIST   Taking Notes (*continued*)

✔ Use your own shorthand and record notes in a way that you find efficient, whether in an electronic document or on index cards.

✔ Photocopy or download pages and highlight passages that you intend to quote.

✔ Check your notes for accuracy against the original material before moving on to another source.

nouns

DIRECTORY

A noun is a **part of speech** that names a person, place, thing, concept, action, or quality.

Types of Nouns

The two basic types of nouns are proper nouns and common nouns. *Proper nouns*, which are capitalized, name specific people, places, and things (*H. G. Wells, Boston, United Nations, Nobel Prize*). See also **capitalization**.

Common nouns, which are not capitalized unless they begin sentences or appear in **titles**, name general classes or categories of persons, places, things, concepts, actions, and qualities (*writer, city, organization, award*). Common nouns include collective nouns, concrete nouns, abstract nouns, count nouns, and mass nouns.

Collective nouns are common nouns that indicate a group or collection. They are plural in meaning but singular in form (*audience, jury, brigade, staff, committee*). (See the subsection Collective Nouns on page 368 for advice on using singular or plural forms with collective nouns.)

Concrete nouns are common nouns used to identify those things that can be discerned by the five senses (*paper, keyboard, glue, nail, grease*).

Abstract nouns are common nouns that name ideas, qualities, or concepts that cannot be discerned by the five senses (*loyalty, pride, valor, peace, devotion*).

Count nouns are concrete nouns that identify things that can be separated into countable units (*desks, envelopes, printers, pencils, books*).

Mass nouns are concrete nouns that identify things that cannot be separated into countable units (*water, air, electricity, oil, cement*). See also **English as a second language**.

Noun Functions

Nouns function as subjects of **verbs**, direct and indirect objects of verbs and **prepositions**, subjective and objective **complements**, or **appositives**.

▶ The *metal* failed during the test. [subject]

▶ The bricklayer cemented the *blocks* efficiently.
[direct object of a verb]

▶ The state presented our *department* a safety award.
[indirect object]

▶ The event occurred within the *year*. [object of a preposition]

▶ A dynamo is a *generator*. [subjective complement]

▶ The regional manager was appointed *chairperson*.
[objective complement]

▶ Philip Garcia, the *treasurer*, gave his report last. [appositive]

Words normally used as nouns can also be used as **adjectives** and **adverbs**.

▶ It is *company* policy. [adjective]

▶ He went *home*. [adverb]

Collective Nouns

When a collective noun refers to a group as a whole, it takes a singular verb and pronoun.

▶ The staff *was* divided on the issue and could not reach *its* decision until May 15.

When a collective noun refers to individuals within a group, it takes a plural verb and pronoun.

▶ The staff *have returned* to *their* offices after the conference.

A better way to emphasize the individuals on the staff would be to use the phrase *the staff members*.

▶ The staff members *have returned* to *their* offices after the conference.

Treat organization names and titles as singular.

► LRM Associates *has* grown 30 percent in the last three years; *it* will move to a new facility in January.

Plural Nouns

Most nouns form the plural by adding *-s* (*dolphin/dolphins*, *pencil/pencils*). Nouns ending in *ch*, *s*, *sh*, *x*, and *z* form the plural by adding *-es*.

► *search/searches*, *glass/glasses*, *wish/wishes*, *six/sixes*, *buzz/buzzes*

Nouns that end in a consonant plus *y* form the plural by changing the *y* to *ies* (*delivery/deliveries*). Some nouns ending in *o* add *-es* to form the plural, but others add only *-s* (*tomato/tomatoes*, *dynamo/dynamos*). Some nouns ending in *f* or *fe* add *-s* to form the plural; others change the *f* or *fe* to *ves*.

► cliff/cliffs, cafe/cafes, hoof/hooves, knife/knives

Some nouns require an internal change to form the plural.

► woman/women, man/men, mouse/mice, goose/geese

Some nouns do not change in the plural form.

► many *fish*, several *deer*, fifty *sheep*

Some nouns remain in the plural form whether singular or plural.

► headquarters, means, series, crossroads

Hyphenated and open compound nouns form the plural in the main word.

► sons-in-law, high schools, editors in chief

Compound nouns written as one word add *-s* to the end (two *tablespoonfuls*).

If you are unsure of the proper usage, check a dictionary. See **possessive case** for a discussion of how nouns form possessives.

number (grammar)

Number is the grammatical property of **nouns**, **pronouns**, and **verbs** that signifies whether one thing (singular) or more than one (*plural*) is being referred to. (See also **agreement**.) Nouns normally form the plural by simply adding *-s* or *-es* to their singular forms.

▶ *Partners* in successful *businesses* are not always personal friends.

Some nouns require an internal change to form the plural.

▶ woman/women, man/men, goose/geese, mouse/mice

All pronouns except *you* change internally to form the plural.

▶ I/we, he/they, she/they, it/they

By adding *-s* or *-es*, most verbs show the singular of the third **person**, present **tense**, indicative **mood**.

▶ he *stands*, she *works*, it *goes*

The verb *be* normally changes form to indicate the plural.

SINGULAR   I *am* ready to begin work.

PLURAL   We *are* ready to begin work.

See also **agreement**.

numbers

The standards for using numbers vary; however, unless you are following an organizational or a professional style manual, observe the following guidelines.

Numerals or Words

Write numbers from zero through ten as words, and write numbers above ten as numerals.

▶ I rehearsed my presentation *three* times.

▶ The association added *152* new members.

Spell out numbers that begin a sentence, however, even if they would otherwise be written as numerals.

▶ *One hundred and fifty-two* new members joined the association.

If spelling out such a number seems awkward, rewrite the sentence so that the number does not appear at the beginning ("We added *152* new members").

Spell out approximate and round numbers.

▶ We've had *more than a thousand* requests this month.

In most writing, spell out small ordinal numbers, which express degree or sequence (*first, second*; but *27th, 42nd*), when they are single words (*our nineteenth year*), or when they modify a century (*the twenty-first century*). However, avoid ordinal numbers in **dates** (use *March 30* or *30 March*, not *March 30th*).

Plurals

Indicate the plural of numerals by adding *-s* (*7s, the late 1990s*). Form the plural of a written number (like any noun) by adding *-s* or *-es* or by dropping the *y* and adding *-ies* (*elevens, sixes, twenties*). See also **apostrophes**.

Measurements

Express units of measurement as numerals (*3 miles, 45 cubic feet, 9 meters*). When numbers run together in the same phrase, write one as a numeral and the other as a word.

        12 six-foot tables.
▶ The order was for ~~12 6-foot tables.~~

Generally give percentages as numerals and write out the word *percent*. ("Approximately *85 percent* of the land has been sold.") However, in a **table,** use a numeral followed by the percent symbol (*85%*).

Fractions

Express fractions as numerals when they are written with whole numbers (*27$^1/_2$ inches, 4$^1/_4$ miles*). Spell out fractions when they are expressed without a whole number (*one-fourth, seven-eighths*). Always write decimal numbers as numerals (*5.21 meters*).

Money

In general, use numerals to express exact or approximate amounts of money.

▸ We need to charge *$28.95* per unit.

▸ The new system costs *$60,000.*

Use words to express indefinite amounts of money.

▸ The printing system may cost *several thousand dollars.*

Use numerals and words for rounded amounts of money over one million dollars.

▸ The contract is worth *$6.8 million.*

Use numerals for more complex or exact amounts.

▸ The corporation paid *$2,452,500* in taxes last year.

For amounts under a dollar, ordinarily use numerals and the word *cents* ("The pens cost *75 cents* each"), unless other numerals that require dollar signs appear in the same sentence.

▸ The business-card holders cost *$10.49* each, the pens cost *$.75* each, and the pencil-cup holders cost *$6.49* each.

ESL TIPS for Punctuating Numbers

Some rules for punctuating numbers in English are summarized as follows:

Use a comma to separate numbers with four or more digits into groups of three, starting from the right (*5,289,112,001 atoms*).

Do not use a comma in years, house numbers, ZIP Codes, and page numbers.

▸ June *2012*

▸ *92401* East Alameda Drive

▸ The ZIP Code is *91601-1243.*

▸ Page *1204*

Use a period to represent the decimal point (*4.2 percent,* *$3,742,097.43*). See also **global communication** and **global graphics**.

Time

Divide hours and minutes with **colons** when *a.m.* or *p.m.* follows (*7:30 a.m., 11:30 p.m.*). Do not use colons with the 24-hour system (*0730, 2330*). Spelled-out time is not followed by *a.m.* or *p.m.* (*seven o'clock in the evening*).

Dates

In the United States dates are usually written in a month-day-year sequence (*August 11, 2012*). Never use the strictly numerical form for dates (*8/11/12*) because the date is not immediately clear, especially in <u>international correspondence</u>.

Addresses

Spell out numbered streets from one through ten unless space is at a premium (*East Tenth Street*). Write building numbers as numerals. The only exception is the building number *one* (*One East Monument Street*). Write highway numbers as numerals (*U.S. 40, Ohio 271, I-94*).

Documents

Page numbers are written as numerals in manuscripts (*page 37*). Chapter and volume numbers may appear as numerals or words (*Chapter 2* or *Chapter Two, Volume 1* or *Volume One*), but be consistent. Express figure and table numbers as numerals (*Figure 4, Table 3*).

Do not follow a word representing a number with a numeral in parentheses that represents the same number. Doing so is redundant.

▶ Send five ~~(5)~~ copies of the report.

N

O

objects

Objects are **nouns** or noun equivalents: **pronouns**, **verbals**, and noun **phrases** or **clauses**. The three kinds of objects are direct objects, indirect objects, and objects of **prepositions**. See also **complements**.

A *direct object* answers the question *what?* or *whom?* about a **verb** and its **subject**.

▶ We sent a *full report*.
[We sent *what?*]

▶ Michelle e-mailed the *client*.
[Michelle e-mailed *whom?*]

An *indirect object* is a noun or noun equivalent that occurs with a direct object after certain kinds of transitive verbs, such as *give*, *wish*, *cause*, and *tell*. The indirect object answers the question *to whom or what?* or *for whom or what?* The indirect object always precedes the direct object.

▶ We sent the *general manager* a full report.
[*Report* is the direct object; the indirect object, *general manager*, answers the question, "We sent a full report *to whom?*"]

The *object of a preposition* is a noun or pronoun that is introduced by a preposition, forming a prepositional phrase.

▶ At the *meeting*, the district managers approved the contract.
[*Meeting* is the object, and *at the meeting* is the prepositional phrase.]

OK / okay

The expression *okay* (also spelled *OK*) is common in informal writing, but it should be avoided in most business writing.

▶ Mr. Sturgess ~~gave his okay to~~ the project.
  ^approved^

on / onto / upon

On is normally used as a **preposition** meaning "attached to" or "located at." ("Install the shelf *on* the north wall.") *On* also stresses a position of rest. ("The victim lay *on* the stretcher.") *Onto* implies movement to a position on or movement up and on. ("The commuters surged *onto* the platform.") *Upon* emphasizes movement or a condition. ("The report is due *upon* completion of the project.")

one

When used as an indefinite **pronoun,** *one* may help you avoid repeating a **noun.** ("We need a new plan, not an old *one.*") *One* is often redundant in phrases in which it restates the noun, and it may take the proper emphasis away from the **adjective.**

> ▶ The training program was not a̶ u̶n̶i̶q̶u̶e̶ o̶n̶e̶. *unique.*

One can also be used in place of a noun or personal pronoun in a statement. ("*One* cannot ignore *one's* physical condition.") Using *one* in that way is formal and impersonal; in any but the most formal writing, you should address your reader directly and personally as *you.* ("*You* cannot ignore *your* physical condition.") See also **point of view.**

one of those . . . who

A dependent **clause** beginning with *who* or *that* and preceded by *one of those* takes a plural **verb.**

> ▶ She is *one of those* managers *who are* concerned about their writing.

> ▶ This is *one of those* policies *that make* no sense when you examine them closely.

In those two examples, *who* and *that* refer to plural antecedents (*managers* and *policies*) and thus take plural verbs (*are* and *make*). See also **agreement.**

If the phrase *one of those* is preceded by *the only,* however, the verb should be singular.

▶ She is *the only one of those* managers *who is* concerned about her writing.
[The verb is singular because its subject, *who*, refers to a singular antecedent, *one*. If the sentence were reversed, it would read, "Of those managers, she is *the only one who is* concerned about her writing."]

▶ This is *the only one of those* policies *that makes* no sense when you examine it closely.
[If the sentence were reversed, it would read, "Of those policies, this is *the only one that makes* no sense when you examine it closely."]

only

The word *only* should be placed immediately before the word or phrase it modifies. See also **modifiers**.

▶ We ~~only~~ lack ^only^ financial backing.

Be careful with the placement of *only* because it can change the meaning of a sentence.

▶ *Only* he said that he was tired.
[He alone said that he was tired.]

▶ He *only* said that he was tired.
[He actually was not tired, although he said he was.]

▶ He said *only* that he was tired.
[He said nothing except that he was tired.]

▶ He said that he was *only* tired.
[He said that he was nothing except tired.]

order-of-importance method of development

The order-of-importance **method of development** is a particularly effective and common organizing strategy. This method can use one of two ordering strategies—decreasing order (Figure O–1), which is often best for written documents, and increasing order (Figure O–2), which is especially effective for oral **presentations**.

Memorandum

To: Tawana Shaw, Director, Human Resources Department

From: Frank W. Nemitz, Chief, Claims Department   *FWN*

Date: November 20, 2012

Subject: Selection of Chief of the Claims Processing Section

I have assessed the candidates for Chief of the Claims Processing Section as you requested, and the following are my evaluations.

Top-Ranked Candidate
The most-qualified candidate is Michelle Bryant, acting chief of that section. In her 12 years in the Claims Department, Ms. Bryant has gained wide experience in all facets of its operations. She has maintained a consistently high production record and has demonstrated the skills and knowledge required for the supervisory duties she is now handling. She has continually been rated "outstanding" in all categories in her job-performance appraisals. However, her supervisory experience is limited to her present three-month tenure as acting chief of the section, and she lacks the college degree required by the job description.

Second-Ranked Candidate
Michael Bastick, Claims Coordinator, my second choice, also has strong potential for the position. An able administrator, he has been with the company for seven years. Further, he is enrolled in a management-training course at Metro State University's downtown campus. I have ranked him second because he lacks supervisory experience and because his most recent work has been with the department's maintenance and supply components. He would be the best person to take over many of Michelle Bryant's responsibilities if she were made full-time Chief of the Claims Processing Section.

Third-Ranked Candidate
Jane Fine, my third-ranked candidate, has shown herself to be a skilled administrator in her three years with the Claims Processing Section. Despite her obvious potential, she does not yet have the breadth of experience in claims processing that is required to manage the Claims Processing Section. Jane Fine also lacks on-the-job supervisory experience.

O

FIGURE O–1. Decreasing Order-of-Importance Method of Development

To: Sun-Hee Kim <kim@appliedsciences.com>
From: Harry Mathews <mathews@appliedsciences.com>
Sent: Friday, May 25, 2012 9:29 AM
Subject: Recruiting Qualified Data Input Operators

As our company continues to expand, and with the planned opening of the Lakeland Facility late next year, we need to increase and refocus our recruiting program to keep our company staffed with qualified data input operators. Below is my analysis of possible recruiting options.

Business School Recruitment
Over the past three years, we have relied on our in-house internship program and on local and regional business school graduates to fill these positions. Although our in-house internship program provides a qualified pool of potential employees, business school enrollments in the area have in the past provided candidates who are already trained. Each year, however, fewer business school graduates are being produced, and even the most vigorous Career Day recruiting has yielded disappointing results.

Military Veteran Recruitment
In the past, we relied heavily on the recruitment of skilled veterans from all branches of the military. This source of qualified applicants all but disappeared when the military offered attractive reenlistment bonuses for skilled operators in uniform. As a result, we need to become aggressive in our attempts to reach this group through advertising. I would like to meet with you soon to discuss the details of a more dynamic recruiting program for skilled operators leaving the military.

I am certain that with the right recruitment campaign, we can find the skilled employees essential to our expanding role in electronics products and consulting.

O

FIGURE O–2. Increasing Order-of-Importance Method of Development

Decreasing Order

Decreasing order begins with the most important fact or point, then moves to the next most important, and so on, ending with the least important. This order is especially appropriate for a **memo** or other **correspondence** addressed to a busy decision-maker (see Figure O–1), who may be able to reach a decision after considering only the most important points. In a **report** addressed to various **readers**, some of whom may be interested in only the major points and others who may need all the information, decreasing order may be ideal for your **purpose**.

The advantages of decreasing order are that (1) it gets the reader's attention immediately by presenting the most important point first, (2) it makes a strong initial impression, and (3) it ensures that even the most hurried reader will not miss the most important point.

Increasing Order

Increasing order begins from the least important point or fact, then progresses to the next more important, and builds finally to the most important or strongest point.

Increasing order of importance is effective for writing in which (1) you want to save your strongest points until the end or (2) you need to build the ideas point by point to an important **conclusion** (see Figure O–2). Many oral presentations benefit especially from increasing order because it leaves the **audience** with the strongest points freshest in their minds. The disadvantage of increasing order, especially for written documents, is that it begins weakly, and the reader or listener may become impatient or distracted before reaching your main point. In the example given in Figure O–2, the writer begins with the least productive source of applicants and builds up to the most productive source.

O

organization

Organization is essential to the success of any writing project, from a **formal report** to a Web page or an effective **presentation**. Good organization is achieved by **outlining** and by using a logical and an appropriate **method of development** that suits your subject, your **audience**, and your **purpose**.

During the organization stage of the writing process, you must consider a **layout and design** that will be helpful to your reader and a **format** appropriate to your subject and purpose. If you intend to include **visuals** with your writing, consider them as you create your outline, especially if they need to be prepared by someone else while you are writing and revising the draft. See also "Five Steps to Successful Writing" on page xv.

organizational charts

An organizational chart shows how the various divisions or units of an organization are related to one another. This type of **visual** is useful when you want to give **readers** an overview of an organization or to display the lines of authority within it, as in Figure O–3.

The title of each organizational component (office, section, division) is placed in a separate box. The boxes are then linked to a central authority. If readers need the information, include the name of the person and position title in each box. As with all visuals, place the organizational chart as close as possible to but not preceding the text that refers to it.

outlining

An outline is the skeleton of the document you are going to write; at the least, it should list the main topics and subtopics of your subject in a logical **method of development**.

O

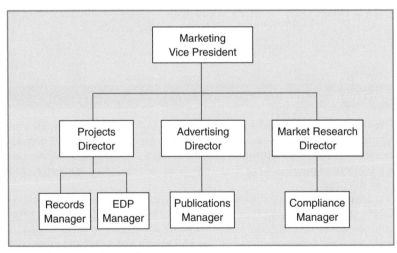

FIGURE O–3. Organizational Chart

Advantages of Outlining

An outline provides structure to your writing by ensuring that it has a beginning (**introduction**), a middle (main body), and an end (**conclusion**). Using an outline offers many other benefits.

- Larger and more complex subjects are easier to handle because an outline breaks them into manageable parts.

- Like a road map, an outline indicates a starting point and keeps you moving logically so that you do not lose your way before you arrive at your conclusion.

- Parts of an outline are easily moved around so that you can select the most effective arrangement of your ideas.

- Creating a good outline frees you from concerns of **organization** while you are **writing a draft**.

- An outline enables you to provide **coherence** and **transition** so that one part flows smoothly into the next without omitting important details.

- **Logic errors** are much easier to detect and correct in an outline than in a draft.

- An outline helps with **collaborative writing** because it enables a team to refine a project's **scope**, divide responsibilities, and maintain focus.

Types of Outlines

Two types of outlines are most common: short topic outlines and lengthy sentence outlines. A *topic outline* consists of short phrases arranged to reflect your primary method of development. A topic outline is especially useful for short documents such as **e-mails, letters**, or **memos**. See also **correspondence**.

For a large writing project, create a topic outline first, and then use it as a basis for creating a sentence outline. A *sentence outline* summarizes each idea in a complete sentence that may become the topic sentence for a paragraph in the rough draft. If most of your notes can be shaped into topic sentences for paragraphs in your rough draft, you can be relatively sure that your document will be well organized. See also **note-taking** and **research**.

Creating an Outline

When you are outlining large and complex subjects with many pieces of information, the first step is to group related notes into categories. Sort the notes by major and minor division headings. Use an appropriate method of development to arrange items and label them with Roman numerals. For example, the major divisions for this discussion of outlining could be as follows:

> I. Advantages of outlining
> II. Types of outlines
> III. Creating an outline

The second step is to establish your minor divisions within each major division. Arrange your minor points using a method of development under their major division and label them with capital letters.

> II. Types of outlines
>   A. Topic outlines ⎤
>   B. Sentence outlines ⎦ Division and Classification
> III. Creating an outline
>   A. Establish major and minor divisions. ⎤
>   B. Sort notes by major and minor divisions. ⎥ Sequential
>   C. Complete the sentence outline. ⎦

You will sometimes need more than two levels of headings. If your subject is complicated, you may need three or four levels of headings to better organize all your ideas in proper relationship to one another. In that event, use the following numbering scheme:

> I. First-level heading
>   A. Second-level heading
>   1. Third-level heading
>   a. Fourth-level heading

The third step is to mark each of your notes with the appropriate Roman numeral and capital letter. Arrange the notes logically within each minor heading, and mark each with the appropriate, sequential Arabic number. As you do, make sure your organization is logical and your headings have **parallel structure**. For example, all the second-level headings under "III. Creating an outline" are complete sentences in the active **voice**.

Treat **visuals** as an integral part of your outline, and plan approximately where each should appear. Either include a rough sketch of the visual or write "illustration of . . ." at each place. As with other information in an outline, freely move, delete, or add visuals as needed.

The outline samples shown earlier use a combination of numbers and letters to differentiate the various levels of information. You could also use a decimal numbering system, such as the following, for your outline.

1. FIRST-LEVEL HEADING
  1.1 Second-level heading
  1.2 Second-level heading
    1.2.1 Third-level heading
    1.2.2 Third-level heading
      1.2.2.1 Fourth-level heading
      1.2.2.2 Fourth-level heading
  1.3 Second-level heading
2. FIRST-LEVEL HEADING

This system should not go beyond the fourth level because the numbers get too cumbersome beyond that point. In many documents, such as **policies and procedures,** the decimal numbering system is carried over from the outline to the final version of the document for ease of cross-referencing sections.

Create your draft by converting your notes into complete sentences and **paragraphs.** If you have a sentence outline, the most difficult part of the writing job is over. However, whether you have a topic or a sentence outline, remember that an outline is flexible; it may need to change as you write the draft, but it should always be your point of departure and return.

DIGITAL TIP

Creating an Outline

Using the outline feature of your word-processing software allows you to create and quickly modify a structured outline in your document. You can choose an alphanumeric, Roman numeral, decimal, or bulleted style, and you can rearrange and reformat your outline as you write and revise. For step-by-step instructions on using outlines, go to *bedfordstmartins.com/alred* and select *Digital Tips,* "Creating an Outline."

O

---

outside [of]

In the phrase *outside of,* the word *of* is redundant.

  ► Place the equipment outside ~~of~~ the meeting room.

Do not use *outside of* to mean "aside from" or "except for."

    Except for
  ► ~~Outside of~~ his frequent absences, Jim has a good work record.

over [with]

In the expression *over with*, the word *with* is redundant; such words as *completed* or *finished* often better express the thought.

▶ The conference room is available when the managers' meeting is

   over ~~with.~~

▶ The conference room is available when the managers' meeting is
   finished.
   ~~over with.~~

O

P

Pace is the speed at which you present ideas to the reader. Your goal should be to achieve a pace that fits your **audience**, **purpose**, and **context**. The more knowledgeable the reader is about the subject, the faster your pace can be. Be careful, though, not to lose control of the pace. In the first version of the following passage, facts are piled on top of each other at a rapid pace. In the second version, the same facts are presented in two more easily assimilated sentences. In addition, the second version achieves a different and more desirable **emphasis**.

RAPID
: The corporate records database (CRD) contains every employee's full name, home address, social security number, and current job classification and is intended to help individual departments and offices process records for every one of the 21,000 employees worldwide.

CONTROLLED
: The corporate records database (CRD) contains identifying information for every one of the 21,000 employees worldwide. The CRD enables individual departments and offices to process employee records, and it contains every employee's full name, home address, social security number, and current job classification.

P

paragraphs

A paragraph performs three functions: (1) It develops the unit of thought stated in the topic sentence; (2) it provides a logical break in the material; and (3) it creates a visual break on the page, which signals a new topic.

Topic Sentence

A topic sentence states the paragraph's main idea; the rest of the paragraph supports and develops that statement with related details. The topic sentence is often the first sentence because it tells the reader what the paragraph is about.

> ▶ *The cost of training new employees is high.* In addition to the cost of classroom facilities and instructors, an organization must pay employees their regular salary while they sit in the classroom. For the companies to break even on this investment in their professional employees, those employees must stay in the job for which they have been trained for at least one year.

The topic sentence is usually most effective early in the paragraph, but a paragraph can lead to the topic sentence, which is sometimes done to achieve **emphasis**.

> ▶ Energy does far more than simply make our daily lives more comfortable and convenient. Suppose someone wanted to stop—and reverse—the economic progress of this nation. What would be the surest and quickest way to do it? Simply block the nation's ability to produce energy! The nation would face a devastating economic crisis. *Our economy, in short, is energy-based.*

On rare occasions, the topic sentence may logically fall in the middle of a paragraph.

> ▶ . . . [It] is time to insist that science does not progress by carefully designed steps called "experiments," each of which has a well-defined beginning and end. *Science is a continuous and often a disorderly and accidental process.* We shall not do the young psychologist any favor if we agree to reconstruct our practices to fit the pattern demanded by current scientific methodology.
> —B. F. Skinner, "A Case History in Scientific Method"

Paragraph Length

A paragraph should be just long enough to deal adequately with the subject of its topic sentence. A new paragraph should begin whenever the subject changes significantly. A series of short, undeveloped paragraphs can indicate poor **organization** and sacrifice unity by breaking a single idea into several pieces. A series of long paragraphs, however, can fail to provide the reader with manageable subdivisions of thought. Paragraph length should aid the reader's understanding of ideas.

Occasionally, a one-sentence paragraph is acceptable if it is used as a **transition** between longer paragraphs or as a one-sentence **introduction** or **conclusion** in **correspondence**.

Writing Paragraphs

Careful paragraphing reflects the writer's logical organization and helps the reader follow the writer's thoughts. A good working outline makes it easy to group ideas into appropriate paragraphs. (See also **outlining**.) The following partial topic outline plots the course of the subsequent paragraphs:

TOPIC OUTLINE (PARTIAL)

I. Advantages of Chicago as location for new facility
   A. Transport infrastructure
      1. Rail
      2. Air
      3. Truck
      4. Sea (except in winter)
   B. Labor supply
      1. Engineering and scientific personnel
         a. Similar companies in area
         b. Major universities
      2. Technical and manufacturing personnel
         a. Community college programs
         b. Custom programs

RESULTING PARAGRAPHS

Probably the greatest advantage of Chicago as a location for our new facility is its excellent transport facilities. The city is served by three major railroads. Both domestic and international air-cargo service are available at O'Hare International Airport; Midway Airport's convenient location adds flexibility for domestic air-cargo service. Chicago is a major hub of the trucking industry, and most of the nation's large freight carriers have terminals there. Finally, except in the winter months when the Great Lakes are frozen, Chicago is a seaport, accessible through the St. Lawrence Seaway.

Chicago's second advantage is its abundant labor force. An ample supply of engineering and scientific staff is assured not only by the presence of many companies engaged in activities similar to ours but also by the presence of several major universities in the metropolitan area. Similarly, technicians and manufacturing personnel are in abundant supply. The colleges in the Chicago City College system, as well as half a dozen other two-year colleges in the outlying areas, produce graduates with associate's degrees in a wide variety of technical specialties appropriate to our needs. Moreover, three of the outlying colleges have expressed an interest in developing off-campus courses attuned specifically to our requirements.

P

Paragraph Unity and Coherence

A good paragraph has **unity** and **coherence** as well as adequate development. *Unity* is singleness of purpose, based on a topic sentence that states the core idea of the paragraph. When every sentence in the paragraph develops the core idea, the paragraph has unity. *Coherence* is holding to one point of view, one attitude, one tense; it is the joining of sentences into a logical pattern. A careful choice of transitional words ties ideas together and thus contributes to coherence in a paragraph. Notice how the boldfaced italicized words tie together the ideas in the following paragraph.

> **TOPIC SENTENCE** *Over the past several months, I have heard complaints about the Merit Award Program.* **Specifically,** many employees feel that this program should be linked to annual *salary increases.* They believe that *salary increases* would provide a much better incentive than the current $500 to $700 cash awards for exceptional service. *In addition,* these *employees believe* that their supervisors consider the cash awards a satisfactory alternative to salary increases. Although I don't think this practice is widespread, the fact that the *employees believe* that it is justifies a reevaluation of the Merit Award Program.

Simple enumeration (*first, second, then, next,* and so on) also provides effective transition within paragraphs. Notice how the boldfaced italicized words and phrases give coherence to the following paragraph.

> ▶ Most adjustable office chairs have nylon tubes that hold metal spindle rods. To keep the chair operational, lubricate the spindle rods occasionally. *First,* loosen the set screw in the adjustable bell. *Then* lift the chair from the base. *Next,* apply the lubricant to the spindle rod and the nylon washer. *When you have finished,* replace the chair and tighten the set screw.

parallel structure

Parallel structure requires that sentence elements that are alike in function be alike in grammatical form as well. This structure achieves an economy of words, clarifies meaning, expresses the equality of the ideas, and achieves **emphasis**. Parallel structure assists **readers** because it allows them to anticipate the meaning of a sentence element on the basis of its construction.

Parallel structure can be achieved with words, **phrases**, or **clauses**.

► If you want to benefit from the jobs training program, you must be *punctual, courteous*, and *conscientious.* [parallel words]

► If you want to excel at customer service, you must recognize the importance *of punctuality, of courtesy*, and *of conscientiousness.* [parallel phrases]

► If you want to excel at customer service, *you must arrive punctually, you must behave courteously*, and *you must respond conscientiously.* [parallel clauses]

Correlative **conjunctions** (*either . . . or, neither . . . nor, not only . . . but also*) should always join elements that use parallel structure. Both parts of the pairs should be followed immediately by the same grammatical form: two similar words, two similar phrases, or two similar clauses.

► Viruses carry either *DNA* or *RNA*, never both. [parallel words]

► Clearly, neither *serological tests* nor *virus isolation studies* alone would have been adequate. [parallel phrases]

► Either *we must increase our production efficiency* or *we must decrease our production goals.* [parallel clauses]

To make a parallel construction clear and effective, it is often best to repeat an **article**, a **pronoun**, a helping **verb**, a **preposition**, a subordinating conjunction, or the mark of an infinitive (*to*).

► The association has *a* mission statement and *a* code of ethics. [article]

► The software is popular *because* it is compatible across platforms and *because* it is easily customized. [subordinating conjunction]

Parallel structure is especially important in creating **lists,** outlines, **tables of contents,** and **headings** because it lets readers know the relative value of each item in a table of contents and each heading in the body of a document. See also **outlining**.

Faulty Parallelism

Faulty parallelism results when joined elements are intended to serve equal grammatical functions but do not have equal grammatical form.

Faulty parallelism sometimes occurs because a writer tries to compare items that are not comparable.

NOT PARALLEL   The company offers special college training to help hourly employees move into professional careers like engineering management, software development,

> service technicians, and sales trainees. [Notice faulty comparison of occupations—*engineering management* and *software development*—to people—*service technicians* and *sales trainees*.]

To avoid faulty parallelism, make certain that each element in a series is similar in form and structure to all others in the same series.

PARALLEL The company offers special college training to help hourly employees move into professional careers like *engineering management, software development, technical services,* and *sales.*

paraphrasing

Paraphrasing is restating or rewriting in your own words the essential ideas of another writer. The following example is an original passage explaining the concept of *object blur*. The paraphrased version restates the essential information of the passage in a form appropriate for a **report**.

ORIGINAL One of the major visual cues used by pilots in maintaining precision ground reference during low-level flight is that of object blur. We are acquainted with the object-blur phenomenon experienced when driving an automobile. Objects in the foreground appear to be rushing toward us, while objects in the background appear to recede slightly.
—Wesley E. Woodson and Donald W. Conover, *Human Engineering Guide for Equipment Designers*

PARAPHRASED Object blur refers to the phenomenon by which observers in a moving vehicle report that foreground objects appear to rush at them, while background objects appear to recede slightly (Woodson & Conover, 1964).

❖ ETHICS NOTE Because paraphrasing does not quote a source word for word, **quotation marks** are not used. However, paraphrased material should be credited because the *ideas* are taken from someone else. See also **ethics in writing**, **note-taking**, **plagiarism**, and **quotations**. ❖

parentheses

Parentheses are used to enclose explanatory or digressive words, phrases, or sentences. Material in parentheses often clarifies or defines the preceding text without altering its meaning.

> ► She severely bruised her tibia (or shinbone) in the accident.

Parenthetical information may not be essential to a sentence (in fact, parentheses deemphasize the enclosed material), but it may be helpful to some readers.

Parenthetical material does not affect the punctuation of a sentence, and any punctuation (such as a **comma** or **period**) should appear following the closing parenthesis.

> ► She could not fully extend her knee because of a torn meniscus (or cartilage), and she suffered pain from a severely bruised tibia (or shinbone).

When a complete sentence within parentheses stands independently, the ending punctuation is placed inside the final parenthesis.

> ► The project director listed the problems her staff faced. (This was the third time she had complained to the board.)

For some constructions, however, you should consider using **subordination** rather than parentheses.

> ► The early tests showed little damage (the attending physician was pleased), but later scans revealed abdominal trauma.

, which pleased the attending physician,

Parentheses also are used to enclose numerals or letters that indicate sequence.

> ► The following sections deal with (1) preparation, (2) research, (3) organization, (4) writing, and (5) revision.

Do not follow spelled-out **numbers** with numerals in parentheses representing the same numbers.

> ► Send five (5) copies of the report.

Use **brackets** to set off a parenthetical item that is already within parentheses.

P

► We should be sure to give Emanuel Foose (and his brother Emilio [1912–1982]) credit for his part in founding the institute.

See also **documenting sources** and **quotations**.

parts of speech

The term *parts of speech* describes the class of words to which a particular word belongs, according to its function in a sentence.

PART OF SPEECH	FUNCTION
noun, **pronoun**	naming / referring
verb	acting / asserting
adjective, **adverb**	describing / modifying
conjunction, **preposition**	joining / linking
interjection	exclaiming

Many words can function as more than one part of speech. See also **functional shift**.

party

In legal language, *party* refers to an individual, a group, or an organization. ("The injured *party* sued my client.") The term *party* is inappropriate in all but legal writing; when you are referring to a person, use the word *person*.

P

  person
► The ~~party~~ whose file you requested is here now.

Party is, of course, appropriate when it refers to a group. ("Jim arranged a tour of the facility for the members of our *party*.")

per

When *per* is used to mean "for each," "by means of," "through," or "on account of," it is appropriate (*per annum, per capita, per diem, per head*). When used to mean "according to" (*per your request, per your order*), the expression is **jargon** and should be avoided.

  we discussed,
► As ~~per our discussion,~~ I will send revised instructions.

percent / percentage

Percent is normally used instead of the symbol % ("only 15 *percent*"), except in **tables**, where space is at a premium. *Percentage*, which is never used with **numbers**, indicates a general size ("only a small *percentage*").

periods

A period is a mark of **punctuation** that usually indicates the end of a declarative or an imperative sentence. Periods also link when used as leaders (as in rows of periods in **tables of contents**) and indicate omissions when used as **ellipses**. Periods are also used to end questions that are actually polite requests, or instructions to which an affirmative response is assumed. ("Will you call me as soon as he arrives.") See also **sentence construction**.

Periods in Quotations

Use a **comma**, not a period, after a declarative sentence that is quoted in the context of another sentence.

▶ "There is every chance of success," she stated.

A period is placed inside **quotation marks**. See also **quotations**.

▶ He stated clearly, "My vote is yes."

Periods with Parentheses

Place a period outside the final parenthesis when a parenthetical element ends a sentence.

▶ The institute was founded by Harry Denman (1902–1972).

Place a period inside the final parenthesis when a complete sentence stands independently within **parentheses**.

▶ The project director listed the problems her staff faced. (This was the third time she had complained to the board.)

Other Uses of Periods

Use periods following the numerals in a numbered **list** and following complete sentences in a list.

P

> 1. Enter your name and PIN.
> 2. Enter your address with ZIP Code.
> 3. Enter your home telephone number.

Use periods after initials in names (*Wilma T. Grant, J. P. Morgan*). Use periods as decimal points with **numbers** (*27.3 degrees Celsius, $540.26, 6.9 percent*). Use periods to indicate certain **abbreviations** (*Ms., Dr., Inc.*). When a sentence ends with an abbreviation that ends with a period, do not add another period. ("Please meet me at 3:30 p.m.")

Period Faults

The incorrect use of a period is sometimes referred to as a *period fault*. When a period is inserted prematurely, the result is a **sentence fragment**.

FRAGMENT   After a long day at the office during which we finished the quarterly report. We left hurriedly for home.

SENTENCE   After a long day at the office, during which we finished the quarterly report, we left hurriedly for home.

When two independent clauses are joined without any punctuation, the result is a *fused*, or *run-on*, *sentence*. Adding a period between the clauses is one way to correct a run-on sentence.

RUN-ON   Bill was late for ten days in a row Ms. Sturgess had to dismiss him.

CORRECT   Bill was late for ten days in a row. Ms. Sturgess had to dismiss him.

P

Other options are to add a comma and a coordinating **conjunction** (*and, but, for, or, nor, so, yet*) between the clauses, to add a **semicolon**, or to add a semicolon with a conjunctive **adverb**, such as *therefore* or *however*.

person

Person refers to the form of a personal **pronoun** that indicates whether the pronoun represents the speaker, the person spoken to, or the person or thing spoken about. A pronoun representing the speaker is in the *first* person. ("*I* could not find the answer in the manual.") A pronoun that represents the person or people spoken to is in the *second* person. ("*You* will be a good manager.") A pronoun that represents the person or people spoken about is in the *third* person. ("*They* received the news quietly.") The following list shows first-, second-, and third-person pronouns. See also **case, number,** and **one.**

PERSON	SINGULAR	PLURAL
First	I, me, my, mine	we, us, our, ours
Second	you, your, yours	you, your, yours
Third	he, him, his, she, her, hers, it, its	they, them, their, theirs

personal / personnel

Personal is an **adjective** meaning "of or pertaining to an individual person" (*a personal problem*). *Personnel* is a **noun** meaning "a group of people engaged in a common job" (*military personnel*). Be careful not to use *personnel* when the word you need is *persons, people,* or a more descriptive word.

▶ The remaining ~~personnel~~ *employees* will be moved next Thursday.

persons / people

The word *persons* is used to refer to a specific category or number of people, often in legal or official contexts. ("Admittance is limited to *persons* age 18 and over.") In all other contexts, use *people.* ("We need more qualified *people* to fill the vacant positions.")

P

persuasion

Persuasive writing attempts to convince an **audience** to adopt the writer's point of view or take a particular action. Workplace writing often uses persuasion to reinforce ideas that readers already have, to convince readers to change their current ideas, or to lobby for a particular suggestion or policy (as in Figure P–1). You may find yourself advocating for safer working conditions, justifying the expense of a new program, or writing a **proposal** for a large purchase. See also **context** and **purpose.**

  In persuasive writing, the way you present your ideas is as important as the ideas themselves. You must support your appeal with logic

Interoffice Memo

TO: Marketing Staff

FROM: Harold Kawenski, MIS Administrator   *HK*

DATE: April 23, 2012

SUBJECT: Plans for the Changeover to the NRT/R4 System

As you all know, the merger with Datacom has resulted in dramatic growth in our workload—a 30-percent increase in our customer support services during the last several months. To cope with this expansion, we will soon install the NRT/R4 server and QCS Enterprise software with Web-based applications.

Let me briefly describe the benefits of this system and the ways we plan to help you cope with the changeover.

The QCS system will help us access up-to-date marketing and product information when we need it. This system will speed processing dramatically and give us access to all relevant company-wide databases. Because we anticipate that our workload will increase another 30 percent in the next several months, we need to get the QCS system online and working smoothly as soon as possible.

The changeover to this system, understandably, will cause some disruption at first. We will need to transfer many of our legacy programs and software applications to the new system. In addition, all of us will need to learn to navigate in the R4 and QCS environments. Once we have made these adjustments, however, I believe we will welcome the changes.

To help everyone adapt to the changeover, we will offer training sessions that will begin next week. I have attached a sign-up form with specific class times. We will also provide a technical support hotline at extension 4040, which will be available during business hours; e-mail support at qcs-support@conco.com; and online help documentation.

I would like to urge you to help us make a smooth transition to the QCS system. Please e-mail me with your suggestions or questions about the impact of the changeover on your department. I look forward to working with you to make this system a success.

Enclosure: Training Session Schedule

P

FIGURE P–1. Persuasive Memo

and a sound presentation of facts, statistics, and examples. See also **logic errors**.

A writer also gains credibility, and thus persuasiveness, through the readers' impressions of the document's appearance. For this reason, consider carefully a document's **layout and design**. See also **résumés**.

❖ ETHICS NOTE Avoid ambiguity. Do not wander from your main point and, above all, never make false claims. You should also acknowledge any real or potentially conflicting opinions; doing so allows you to anticipate and overcome objections and builds your credibility. See also **ethics in writing** and **promotional writing**. ❖

The **memo** shown in Figure P–1 was written to persuade the marketing staff to accept and participate in a change to a new computer system. Notice that not everything in this memo is presented in a positive light. Change brings disruption, and the writer acknowledges that fact.

A persuasive technique that places the focus on your reader's interest and perspective is discussed in the entry **"you" viewpoint**. See also **correspondence**.

phenomenon / phenomena

A *phenomenon* is an observable thing, fact, or occurrence ("a natural *phenomenon*"). Its plural form is *phenomena*.

photographs

Photographs are effective in catching the readers' attention and adding personal relevance to **brochures**, **newsletters**, **annual reports**, and other **promotional writing**. Photographs are also an effective way to illustrate products in a printed catalog or on a Web site. They are often used for instructions to show the appearance of an object, although they cannot depict the internal workings of a mechanism or below-the-surface details of objects or structures. Such details are better represented in **drawings**. See also **readers**.

Figure P–2 shows a photograph from an interactive Web presentation for buyers of corporate aircraft. This photograph is one in a series that simulates a pilot's "walk-around"—a procedure in which pilots visually examine an aircraft in a 360-degree safety inspection prior to takeoff. In this photo, the stair steps are lowered to show the relative size of the aircraft.

For **reports**, treat photographs as you do other **visuals**, giving them figure numbers, call-outs (labels) to identify key features, and captions, if

FIGURE P–2. Photo (of Aircraft Door). (Photo courtesy of Ken Cook Company.)

needed. Position the figure number and caption so that readers can view them and the photograph from the same orientation.

❖ ETHICS NOTE Be careful to avoid **plagiarism** by appropriately **documenting sources** for photographs and by obtaining permission from the **copyright** holder if you plan to publish photographs that you do not take yourself. If you do take your own photographs, be sure to get the full name, contact information, and permission of any persons featured before publishing. ❖

phrases

A phrase is a meaningful group of words that cannot make a complete statement because it does not contain both a subject and a predicate, as **clauses** do. Phrases, which are based on **nouns**, nonfinite **verb** forms, or verb combinations, provide context within a clause or sentence in which they appear. See also **sentence construction**.

> ► She reassured her staff *by her calm confidence.* [phrase]

A phrase may function as an **adjective**, an **adverb**, a noun, or a verb.

> ► The subjects *on the agenda* were all discussed. [adjective]

> ► We discussed the project *with great enthusiasm.* [adverb]

> ► *Working hard* is her way of life. [noun]

> ► The human resources director *should have been notified.* [verb]

Even though phrases function as adjectives, adverbs, nouns, or verbs, they are normally named for the kind of word around which they are constructed—**preposition**, participle, infinitive, gerund, verb, or noun. A phrase that begins with a preposition is a *prepositional phrase*, a phrase that begins with a participle is a *participial phrase*, and so on. For typical verb phrases and prepositional phrases that can cause difficulty for speakers of **English as a second language**, see **idioms**.

Prepositional Phrases

A preposition is a word that shows relationship and combines with a noun or **pronoun** (its **object**) to form a modifying phrase. A prepositional phrase, then, consists of a preposition plus its object and the object's modifiers.

> ► *After the meeting,* the district managers adjourned *to the cafeteria.*

Prepositional phrases, because they normally modify nouns or verbs, usually function as adjectives or adverbs. A prepositional phrase may function as an adverb of motion ("Turn the dial four degrees *to the left*") or an adverb of manner ("Answer customers' questions *in a courteous fashion*"). A prepositional phrase may function as an adverb of place and may appear in different places in the sentence.

> ► *In home and office computer systems,* security is essential.

> ► Security is essential *in home and office computer systems.*

Prepositional phrases may function as adjectives; when they do, they follow the nouns they modify.

> ► Food waste *with a high protein content* can be processed into animal food.

Be careful when you use prepositional phrases because separating a prepositional phrase from the noun it modifies can cause **ambiguity**.

AMBIGUOUS   *The woman* standing by the security guard *in the gray suit* is our division manager.

CLEAR   *The woman in the gray suit* who is standing by the security guard is our division manager.

Watch as well for the overuse of prepositional phrases where **modifiers** would be more economical.

OVERUSED   The man *with gray hair in the blue suit with pin-stripes* is the former president *of the company*.

ECONOMICAL   The *gray-haired* man in the *blue pin-striped* suit is the former *company* president.

Participial Phrases

A participle is any form of a verb that is used as an adjective. A participial phrase consists of a participle plus its object and its modifiers.

▶ The division *having the largest sales increase* will win the award.

The relationship between a participial phrase and the rest of the sentence must be clear to the reader. For that reason, every sentence containing a participial phrase must have a noun or pronoun that the participial phrase modifies; if it does not, the result is a dangling participial phrase.

Dangling Participial Phrases.   A dangling participial phrase occurs when the noun or pronoun that the participial phrase is meant to modify is not stated but only implied in the sentence. See also **dangling modifiers**.

DANGLING   *Being unhappy with the job*, his efficiency suffered. [His efficiency was not unhappy with the job; what the participial phrase really modifies—*he*—is not stated but merely implied.]

CORRECT   *Being unhappy with the job*, he grew less efficient. [In this version, what that participial phrase modifies—*he*—is explicitly stated.]

Misplaced Participial Phrases.   A participial phrase is misplaced when it is too far from the noun or pronoun it is meant to modify and so appears to modify something else. Such an error can make the writer look ridiculous.

MISPLACED	We saw a large warehouse *driving down the highway.*
CORRECT	*Driving down the highway,* we saw a large warehouse.

Infinitive Phrases

An infinitive is the basic form of a verb (*go, run, talk*) without the restrictions imposed by **person** and **number**. An infinitive is generally preceded by the word *to* (which is usually a preposition but in this use is called the *sign*, or *mark*, of the infinitive). An infinitive phrase consists of the word *to* plus an infinitive and any objects or modifiers.

▶ *To improve as a writer,* you must be willing *to accept criticism.*

Do not confuse a prepositional phrase beginning with *to* with an infinitive phrase. In an infinitive phrase, *to* is followed by a verb; in a prepositional phrase, *to* is followed by a noun or pronoun.

PREPOSITIONAL PHRASE	We went *to the building site.*
INFINITIVE PHRASE	Our firm tries *to provide a comprehensive training program.*

The implied subject of an introductory infinitive phrase should be the same as the subject of the sentence. If it is not, the phrase is a dangling modifier. In the following example, the implied subject of the infinitive is *you* or *one*, not *practice*.

▶ To learn a new language, ~~practice is needed.~~ *you must practice.*

Gerund Phrases

A gerund is a **verbal** ending in *-ing* that is used as a noun. A gerund phrase consists of a gerund plus any objects or modifiers and always functions as a noun.

SUBJECT	*Preparing an annual report* is a difficult task.
DIRECT OBJECT	She liked *chairing the committee.*

Verb Phrases

A verb phrase consists of a main verb and its helping verb.

▶ He *is* [helping verb] *working* [main verb] hard this summer.

Words can appear between the helping verb and the main verb of a verb phrase. ("He *is* always *working.*") The main verb is always the last verb in a verb phrase.

Questions often begin with a verb phrase. (*"Will* he *audit* their account?") The adverb *not* may be appended to a helping verb in a verb phrase. ("He *did not work* today.")

Noun Phrases

A noun phrase consists of a noun and its modifiers. ("Have *the two new employees* fill out *these forms.*")

plagiarism

Plagiarism is the use of someone else's unique ideas without acknowledgment or the use of someone else's exact words without **quotation marks** and appropriate credit. Plagiarism is considered to be the theft of someone else's creative and intellectual property and is not accepted in business, science, journalism, academia, or any other field. See also **ethics in writing** and **research**.

Citing Sources

Quoting a passage—including cutting and pasting a passage from an Internet source into your work—is permissible only if you enclose the passage in quotation marks and properly cite the source. For detailed guidance on quoting correctly, see **quotations**. If you intend to publish, reproduce, or distribute material that includes quotations from published works, including Web sites, you may need to obtain written permission from the **copyright** holders of those works.

Even Web sites that grant permission to copy, distribute, or modify material under the "copyleft" principle, such as Wikipedia, nonetheless caution that you must give appropriate credit to the source from which material is taken (see *http://en.wikipedia.org/wiki/Wikipedia :Citing_Wikipedia*).

Paraphrasing the words and ideas of another *also requires that you cite your source*, even though you do not enclose paraphrased ideas or materials in quotation marks. (See also **documenting sources**.) Paraphrasing a passage without citing the source is permissible only when the information paraphrased is common knowledge.

Common Knowledge

Common knowledge generally refers to information that is widely known and readily available in handbooks, manuals, atlases, and other references. For example, the "law of supply and demand" is common knowledge and is found in virtually every economics and business textbook.

Common knowledge also refers to information within a specific field that is generally known and understood by most others in that field—even though it is not widely known by those outside the field. For examples, see the Web Link at the end of this entry.

An indication that something is common knowledge is its appearance in multiple sources without citation. However, when in doubt, cite the source.

❖ ETHICS NOTE In the workplace, employees often borrow material freely from in-house manuals, reports, and other company documents. Using or **repurposing** such material is neither plagiarism nor a violation of copyright. For information on the use of public domain and government material, see **copyright**. ❖

WEB LINK	Avoiding Plagiarism
For a tutorial on using sources correctly, see *bedfordstmartins.com/ alred* and select *Try a tutorial*, "On avoiding plagiarism." For links to other resources, select *Links for Handbook Entries*.	

plain language

Plain language means writing that is logically organized and understandable on the first reading. Many states have created "plain-language" laws, which require that documents be written in clear, understandable language. The federal government also requires that all its regulations be written in plain language. Plain language is also enhanced by using principles of **layout and design** that promote **clarity**. Cross-references to entries that describe plain-language principles in more detail appear throughout this entry.

Strive to communicate with your audience in language that is both uncomplicated and accurate. Assess your **audience** carefully to ensure that your language connects with their level of knowledge. Replace **jargon** and complex legal wording with familiar, concise words or terms when possible. See also **conciseness** and **gobbledygook**.

COMPLICATED   The systems integration specialist must be able to visually perceive the entire directional response module.

PLAIN LANGUAGE	The operator must be able to see the entire control panel.

If you are a health-care provider, for example, use the appropriate plain-language equivalent for medical terminology with patients in conversations and written guidelines: *bleeding* instead of *hemorrhaging*; *heart attack* instead of *myocardial infarction*; *cast* instead of *splint*; *stitches* instead of *sutures*. If a plain-language alternative does not exist, define or explain a technical term on its first use.

Avoid the tendency to create jargon or **acronyms and initialisms** unique to your subject. Unfamiliar acronyms may save a few words but they force readers to take more time and effort to understand your content. Of course, if acronyms, initialisms, and other **abbreviations** are familiar to your readers, use them (BTU, HTML, NASDAQ, USPS). And use consistent terminology for the same thing (*car*, *vehicle*, *automobile*—choose one). See also **affectation**.

Use appropriate **sentence construction** that produces coherent sentences and eliminates unnecessary words. See also **garbled sentences**.

BEFORE	The following executive summary is intended primarily to highlight the causes of the accident as outlined elsewhere in this investigative report.
AFTER	This summary highlights the causes of the accident investigated in this report.

Use the active **voice**. It is more direct, often more concise, and easier for readers to understand—all devices that promote plain language. Importantly, it identifies the doer of the action described ("we" in the following).

PASSIVE	The malfunctioning transmission was redesigned.
ACTIVE	We redesigned the malfunctioning transmission.

Avoid stating positive information as though it were negative. See also **positive writing**.

NEGATIVE	Persons other than the primary beneficiary may not receive these dividends.
POSITIVE	Only the primary beneficiary may receive these dividends.

Plain-language principles are especially useful when writing **international correspondence**. For format and visual elements that promote **clarity**, see **layout and design**, **lists**, and **visuals**. See also **English as a second language**.

WRITER'S CHECKLIST Using Plain Language

✔ Identify your average reader's level of technical knowledge.

✔ Avoid unnecessary jargon and legal language.

✔ Avoid confusing terms and constructions.

- Define necessary abbreviations and acronyms.
- Use the same words consistently for the same things.
- Do not give an obscure meaning to a word.

✔ Use the active voice for directness and to identify doers of actions.

✔ Use the second **person** (*you / your*) or imperative **mood** to write directly to the reader and to make the writing relevant to the reader.

✔ Write coherent sentences.

- Aim for one message in each sentence.
- Break up complex information into smaller, easier-to-understand units.
- Use positive writing and simple present **tense** as much as possible.

✔ Select word placement carefully.

- Keep subjects and **objects** close to their **verbs**.
- Put *only, always,* and other conditional words next to the words they modify.

WEB LINK	Plain Language
For links to sites that provide information about plain-language laws and practices, go to *bedfordstmartins.com/alred* and select *Links for Handbook Entries*.	

P

point of view

Point of view is the writer's relation to the information presented, as reflected in the use of grammatical **person**. The writer usually expresses point of view in first-, second-, or third-person personal **pronouns**. Use of first person indicates that the writer is a participant or an observer. Use of second or third person indicates that the writer is giving directions,

instructions, or advice, or is writing about other people or something impersonal.

FIRST PERSON	*I* scrolled down to find the settings option.
SECOND PERSON	*You* need to scroll down to find the settings option.
	[*You* is explicitly stated.]
	Scroll down to find the settings option.
	[*You* is understood in such an instruction.]
THIRD PERSON	*He* scrolled down to find the settings option.

Consider the following sentence, revised from an impersonal to a more personal point of view. Although the meaning of the sentence does not change, the revision indicates that people are involved in the communication.

> *I regret* ~~It is regrettable~~ that the equipment shipped on *we cannot accept*
>
> Friday ~~is unacceptable.~~

Some people think they should avoid the pronoun *I* in business writing. Such practice, however, often leads to awkward sentences, with people referring to themselves in the third person as *one* or as *the writer* instead of as *I*.

> *I believe* ~~The writer believes~~ that this project will be completed by July.

However, do not use the personal point of view when an impersonal point of view would be more appropriate or more effective because you need to emphasize the subject matter over the writer or the reader. In the following example, it does not help to personalize the situation; in fact, the impersonal version may be more tactful.

PERSONAL	I received objections to my proposal from several of your managers.
IMPERSONAL	Several managers have raised objections to the proposal.

Whether you adopt a personal or an impersonal point of view depends on the **purpose** and the **audience** of the document. For example, in an informal **e-mail** to an associate, you would most likely adopt a personal point of view. However, in a **report** to a large group, you would probably emphasize the subject by using an impersonal point of view. See also **plain language**.

❖ ETHICS NOTE In company **correspondence**, use of the pronoun *we* may be interpreted as reflecting company policy, whereas *I* clearly reflects personal opinion. Which pronoun to use should be decided according to whether you are speaking for yourself (*I*) or for the company (*we*).

▶ *I* understand your frustration with the price increase, but *we* must now add the import tax to the sales price. ❖

ESL TIPS for Stating an Opinion

In some cultures, stating an opinion in writing is considered impolite or unnecessary, but in the United States, readers expect to see a writer's opinion stated clearly and explicitly. The opinion should be followed by specific examples to help the reader understand the writer's point of view.

---

policies and procedures

A *policy* states an organization's position on a subject; a *procedure* may describe the steps or provide **instructions** for carrying out the policy. Policies and procedures are often written at the same time, usually by top or middle managers. Policies and procedures are subjected to a careful review process, often by legal staff. Writing these documents requires careful thought and planning as well as precise language and **word choice** so that the policies and procedures are clear and understandable. See also **plain language**.

P

Policies

A statement of policy may be preceded by an explanation of the policy's purpose or rationale. Specific details then follow in numbered sections as in the following company policy regarding tuition refunds.

   1. TUITION REIMBURSEMENT POLICY
      1.1 The Tuition Reimbursement Plan is available only to full-time staff.
      1.2 To receive a reimbursement, an individual must be employed by the company at the time of enrollment and at the time of completion of the course. Should an individual's employment be terminated because of a reduction

of staff, fees will be refunded for approved courses upon their satisfactory completion.

1.3 Satisfactory completion means that the employee has completed the course work and has achieved a grade at least one level above passing. If a course is not satisfactorily completed, reimbursement may be deferred if the employee, upon completion of the degree, attains a cumulative grade average of at least C (B for most graduate-degree programs).

Policies may be kept in loose-leaf binders or posted on an organization's internal Web site so that they can be easily referred to and updated.

Procedures

Procedures provide a step-by-step explanation of how to carry out a policy. They often provide instructions not only for employees but also for managers who must ensure that the company's policy is properly implemented.

To prepare for writing procedures, keep track of who must do what. An easy and effective way is to create a chart, as shown in Figure P–3. Draw a vertical line down a page. Label the left column "Actor" and the right "Directions." Under "Actor," list who must perform the action in each step; under "Directions," describe each step of the procedure fully and in the correct sequence. In effect, the list serves as an outline for the procedure you will write. The draft created from the chart in Figure P–3 might look like the following example:

P

Actor	Directions
Employee	Determines his or her eligibility for academic work, gains manager's approval, and submits request to Human Resources (HR)
Human Resources Department	Reviews request and, if reason is not obvious, asks manager to justify, in writing, the benefits of approving the academic work
Employee	Completes Sections I and II of Form F-6970
Human Resources Department	Sends form to employee's supervisor and department head for approval
Employee	Submits proof of course enrollment and fee payment to HR for reimbursement

FIGURE P–3. Procedures Chart

1. PROCEDURES
   1.1 Tuition Reimbursement Approval
      1.1.1 An employee who meets school requirements and is interested in receiving tuition reimbursement should gain the approval of his or her manager and submit the request to the Human Resources (HR) Department. Human Resources may ask the manager to justify, in writing, the benefits of the academic work, if the reason is not obvious.
      1.1.2 After reaching an agreement, the employee should complete Sections I and II of Form F-6970. After HR has obtained two levels of management approval — from the employee's supervisor and the head of the department — it approves the employee's enrollment in the course or degree program.
      1.1.3 The employee who has been granted approval must submit to HR proof of enrollment and payment of appropriate fees to receive tuition reimbursement.

positive writing

Presenting positive information as though it were negative is confusing to **readers**.

NEGATIVE   If the error does *not* involve data transmission, the backup function will *not* be used.

In this sentence, the reader must reverse two negatives to understand the exception that is being stated. (See also **double negatives**.) The following sentence presents the exception in a positive and straightforward manner. See also **plain language**.

POSITIVE   The backup function is used only when the error involves data transmission.

❖ ETHICS NOTE   Negative facts or conclusions, however, should be stated negatively; stating a negative fact or conclusion positively is deceptive because it can mislead the reader.

DECEPTIVE   In the first quarter of this year, employee exposure to airborne lead averaged within 10 percent of acceptable state health standards.

ACCURATE   In the first quarter of this year, employee exposure to airborne lead averaged 10 percent below acceptable state health standards.

See also **ethics in writing**. ❖

Even if what you are saying is negative, do not state it more negatively than necessary.

NEGATIVE   We are withholding your shipment because we have not received your payment.

POSITIVE   We will forward your shipment as soon as we receive your payment.

See also **correspondence** and **"you" viewpoint**.

possessive case

A **noun** or **pronoun** is in the possessive case when it represents a person, place, or thing that possesses something. Possession is generally expressed with an **apostrophe** and an *s* ("the *report's* title"), with a prepositional **phrase** using *of* ("the title *of the report*"), or with the possessive form of a pronoun ("*our* report").

Practices vary for some possessive forms, but the following guidelines are widely used. Above all, be consistent.

Singular Nouns

Most singular nouns show the possessive case with *'s*.

▶ the *hospital's* medical staff   the *witness's* testimony
an *employee's* paycheck   the *bus's* schedule

When pronunciation with *'s* is difficult or when a multisyllable noun ends in a *z* sound, you may use only an apostrophe.

▶ *New Orleans'* convention hotels

Plural Nouns

Plural nouns that end in *-s* or *-es* show the possessive case with only an apostrophe.

▶ the *managers'* reports   the *companies'* joint project
the *employees'* paychecks   the *witnesses'* testimony

Plural nouns that do not end in -s show the possessive with 's.

- *children's* clothing, *women's* resources, *men's* room

Apostrophes are not always used in official names ("*Consumers Union*") or for words that may appear to be possessive nouns but function as **adjectives** ("a *computer peripherals* supplier").

Compound Nouns

Compound words form the possessive with 's following the final letter.

- the *attorney general's* decision, the *editor-in-chief's* desk, the *pipeline's* diameter

Plurals of some compound expressions are often best expressed with a prepositional phrase ("presentations *of the editors in chief*").

Coordinate Nouns

Coordinate nouns show joint possession with 's following the last noun.

- *Fischer and Goulet's* partnership was the foundation of their business.

Coordinate nouns show individual possession with 's following each noun.

- The difference between *Barker's* and *Washburne's* test results was not statistically significant.

Possessive Pronouns

The possessive pronouns (*its, whose, his, her, our, your, my, their*) are also used to show possession and do not require apostrophes. ("Even good systems have *their* flaws.") Only the possessive form of a pronoun should be used with a gerund (a noun formed from an -*ing* **verb**).

- The safety officer insisted on *our* wearing protective clothing. [*Wearing* is the gerund.]

Possessive pronouns are also used to replace nouns. ("The responsibility was *theirs*.") See also **its / it's**.

Indefinite Pronouns

Some indefinite pronouns (*all, any, each, few, most, none, some*) form the possessive case with the **preposition** *of*.

► We tested both packages and found bacteria on the surface *of each*.

Other indefinite pronouns (*everyone, someone, anyone, no one*), however, use *'s*.

► *Everyone's* contribution is welcome.

prefixes

A prefix is a letter or group of letters placed in front of a root word that changes the meaning of the root word. When a prefix ends with a vowel and the root word begins with a vowel, the prefix is often separated from the root word with a **hyphen** (*re-enter, pro-active, anti-inflammatory*). Some words with the double vowel are written without a hyphen (*cooperate*) and others with or without a hyphen (*re-elect* or *reelect*).

Prefixes, such as *neo-* (derived from a Greek word meaning "new"), are often hyphenated when used with a proper **noun** (*neo-Keynesian*). Such prefixes are not normally hyphenated when used with common nouns, unless the base word begins with the same vowel (*neonatal, neo-orthodoxy*).

A hyphen may be necessary to clarify the meaning of a prefix; for example, *reform* means "correct" or "improve," and *re-form* means "change the shape of." When in doubt, check a current **dictionary**.

P

preparation

The preparation stage of the writing process is essential. By determining the needs of your **audience**, your **purpose**, the **context**, and the **scope** of coverage, you understand the information you will need to gather during **research**. See also **collaborative writing** and "Five Steps to Successful Writing" on page xv.

WRITER'S CHECKLIST   **Preparing to Write**

✔ Determine who your readers are and learn certain key facts about them — their knowledge, attitudes, and needs relative to your subject.

✔ Determine the document's primary purpose: What exactly do you want your readers to know, to believe, or to be able to do when they have finished reading your document?

✔ Consider the context of your message and how it should affect your writing.

✔ Establish the scope of your document — the type and amount of detail you must include — not only by understanding your readers' needs and purpose but also by considering any external constraints, such as word limits for trade journal articles or the space limitations of Web pages. See also **writing for the Web**.

✔ Select the medium appropriate to your readers and purpose. See also **selecting the medium**.

prepositions

A preposition is a word that links a **noun** or **pronoun** to another sentence element by expressing such relationships as direction (*to, into, across, toward*), location (*at, in, on, under, over, beside, among, by, between, through*), time (*before, after, during, until, since*), or position (*for, against, with*). Together, the preposition, its **object** (the noun or pronoun), and the object's **modifiers** form a prepositional **phrase** that acts as a modifier.

▶ Answer help-line questions *in a courteous manner*.
[The prepositional phrase *in a courteous manner* modifies the **verb** *answer*.]

The object of a preposition (the word or phrase following the preposition) is always in the objective **case**. When the object is a compound, both nouns and pronouns should be in the objective case. For example, the phrase "between you and *me*" is frequently and incorrectly written as "between you and *I*." *Me* is the objective form of the pronoun, and *I* is the subjective form.

Many words that function as prepositions also function as **adverbs**. If the word takes an object and functions as a connective, it is a preposition; if it has no object and functions as a modifier, it is an adverb.

PREPOSITIONS	The manager sat *behind* the desk *in* her office.
ADVERBS	The customer lagged *behind*; then he came *in* and sat down.

P

Certain verbs, adverbs, and adjectives are normally used with certain prepositions (interested *in*, aware *of*, equated *with*, adhere *to*, capable *of*, object *to*, infer *from*). See also **idioms**.

Prepositions at the End of a Sentence

A preposition at the end of a sentence can be an indication that the sentence is awkwardly constructed.

> *She was at the* •
> ► ~~The~~ branch office ~~is where she was at.~~
>   ^   ^

However, if a preposition falls naturally at the end of a sentence, leave it there. ("I don't remember which file name I saved it *under*.")

Prepositions in Titles

Capitalize prepositions in **titles** when they are the first or last words, or when they contain five or more letters (unless you are following a style that recommends otherwise). See also **capitalization**.

> ► The newspaper column "*In* My Opinion" included a review of the article "New Concerns *About* Distance Education."

Preposition Errors

Do not use redundant prepositions, such as "off *of*," "in back *of*," "inside *of*," and "at *about*."

EXACT	The client will arrive at ~~about~~ four o'clock.
APPROXIMATE	The client will arrive ~~at~~ about four o'clock.

Avoid unnecessarily adding the preposition *up* to verbs.

> *to*
> ► Call ~~up and~~ see if he is in his office.
>   ^

Do not omit necessary prepositions.

> *to*
> ► He was oblivious and not distracted by the view from his office window.
>   ^

See also **conciseness** and **English as a second language**.

presentations

The steps required to prepare an effective presentation parallel the steps you follow to write a document. As with writing a document, determine your **purpose** and analyze your **audience**. Then gather the facts that will support your point of view or proposal and logically organize that information. Presentations do, however, differ from written documents in a number of important ways. They are intended for listeners, not readers. Because you are speaking, your manner of delivery, the way you organize the material, and your supporting **visuals** require as much attention as your content.

Determining Your Purpose

Every presentation is given for a purpose, even if it is only to share information. To determine the primary purpose of your presentation, use the following question as a guide: What do I want the audience to know, to believe, or to do when I have finished the presentation? Based on the answer to that question, write a purpose statement that answers the *what?* and *why?* questions.

▶ The purpose of my presentation is to convince my company's chief information officer of the need to improve the appearance, content, and customer use of our company's Web site [*what*] so that she will be persuaded to allocate additional funds for site-development work in the next fiscal year [*why*].

Analyzing Your Audience

Once you have determined the desired end result of the presentation, analyze your audience so that you can tailor your presentation to their needs. Ask yourself these questions about your audience:

- What is your audience's level of experience or knowledge about your topic?
- What is the general educational level and age of your audience?
- What is your audience's attitude toward the topic you are speaking about, and—based on that attitude—what concerns, fears, or objections might your audience have?
- Do any subgroups in the audience have different concerns or needs?
- What questions might your audience ask about this topic?

Gathering Information

Once you have focused the presentation, you need to find the facts and arguments that support your point of view or the action you propose. As you gather information, keep in mind that you should give the audience only what will accomplish your goals; too much detail will overwhelm them, and too little will not adequately inform your listeners or support your recommendations. For detailed guidance about gathering information, see **research**.

Structuring the Presentation

When structuring the presentation, focus on your audience. Listeners are freshest at the outset and refocus their attention near the end. Take advantage of that pattern. Give your audience a brief overview of your presentation at the beginning, use the body to develop your ideas, and end with a summary of what you covered and, if appropriate, a call to action. See also **methods of development**.

The Introduction. Include in the **introduction** an opening that focuses your audience's attention, as in the following examples:

▶ [*Definition of a problem*] "You have to write an important report, but you'd like to incorporate lengthy handwritten notes from several meetings you attended. Your scanner will not read these notes, and you will have to type many pages. You groan because that seems an incredible waste of time. Have I got a solution for you!"

▶ [*An attention-getting statement*] "As many as 50 million Americans have high blood pressure."

▶ [*A rhetorical question*] "Would you be interested in a full-sized computer keyboard that is waterproof, is noiseless, and can be rolled up like a rubber mat?"

▶ [*A personal experience*] "As I sat at my computer one morning, deleting my eighth spam message of the day, I decided that it was time to take action to eliminate this time-waster."

▶ [*An appropriate quotation*] "According to researchers at the Massachusetts Institute of Technology, 'Garlic and its cousin, the onion, confer major health benefits—including fighting cancer, infections, and heart disease.'"

Following your opening, use the introduction to set the stage for your audience by providing an overview of the presentation. Such an overview can include general or background information that will be needed to understand the detailed information in the body of your presentation. It can also show how you have organized the material.

▶ This presentation analyzes three high-volume, on-demand printers for us to consider purchasing. Based on a comparison of all three, I will recommend the one I believe best meets our needs. To do so, I'll discuss the following five points:

   1. Why we need a high-volume printer [*the problem*]

   2. The basics of on-demand technology [*general information*]

   3. The criteria I used to compare the three printer models [*comparison*]

   4. The printer models I compared and why [*possible solutions*]

   5. The printer I propose we buy [*proposed solution*]

The Body.   If your goal is **persuasion**, present the evidence that will persuade the audience to agree with your conclusions and act on them. If you are discussing a problem, demonstrate that it exists and offer a solution or range of possible solutions. For example, if your introduction stated that the problem is low profits, high costs, outdated technology, or high employee absenteeism, you could use the following approach.

   1. Prove your point.
      • Strategically organize the facts and data you need.
      • Present the information using easy-to-understand visuals.
   2. Offer solutions.
      • Increase profits by lowering production costs.
      • Cut overhead to reduce costs, or abolish specific programs or product lines.
      • Replace outdated technology, or upgrade existing technology.
      • Offer employees more flexibility in their work schedules or offer them other incentives.

3. Anticipate questions ("How much will it cost?") and objections ("We're too busy now—when would we have time to learn the new software?") and incorporate the answers into your presentation.

The Closing.   Fulfill the goals of your presentation in the closing. If your purpose is to motivate the listeners to take action, ask them to do what you want them to do; if your purpose is to get your audience to think about something, summarize what you want them to think about. Many presenters make the mistake of not actually closing—they simply quit talking, shuffle papers, and then walk away.

Because your closing is what your audience is most likely to remember, use that time to be strong and persuasive. Consider the following typical closing.

▶ Based on all the data, I believe that the Worthington TechLine 5510 Production Printer best suits our needs. It produces 40 pages per minute more than its closest competitor and provides modular systems that can be upgraded to support new applications. The Worthington is also compatible with our current computer network, and staff training at our site is included with our purchase. Although the initial cost is higher than that for the other two models, the additional capabilities, compatibility with most standard environments, lower maintenance costs, and strong customer support services make it a better value.

I recommend we allocate the funds necessary for this printer by the fifteenth of this month in order to be well prepared for the production of next quarter's customer publications.

This closing brings the presentation full circle and asks the audience to fulfill the purpose of the presentation—exactly what a **conclusion** should do.

Transitions.   Planned **transitions** should appear between the introduction and the body, between major points in the body, and between the body and the closing. Transitions are simply a sentence or two to let the audience know that you are moving from one topic to the next. They also prevent a choppy presentation and provide the audience with assurance that you know where you are going and how to get there.

▶ Before getting into the specifics of each printer I compared, I'd like to present the benefits of networked, on-demand printers in general. That information will provide you with the background you'll need to compare the differences among the printers and their capabilities discussed in this presentation.

It is also a good idea to pause for a moment after you have delivered a transition between topics to let your listeners shift gears with you. Remember, they do not know your plan.

Using Visuals

Well-planned **visuals** not only add interest and emphasis to your presentation but also clarify and simplify your message because they communicate clearly, quickly, and vividly. Charts, graphs, and illustrations can greatly increase audience understanding and retention of information, especially for complex issues and technical information that could otherwise be misunderstood or overlooked.

❖ ETHICS NOTE Be sure to provide credit for any visual taken from a print or an online source. You can include a citation either on an individual visual (such as a slide) or in a list of references or works cited that you distribute to your audience. For information on citing visuals from print or Web sources, see **documenting sources**. ❖

You can create and present the visual components of your presentation by using a variety of media — flip charts, whiteboard or chalkboard, overhead transparencies, slides, or computer presentation software. See also **layout and design**.

Flip Charts. Flip charts are ideal for smaller groups in a conference room or classroom and are also ideal for **brainstorming** with your audience.

Whiteboard or Chalkboard. The whiteboard or chalkboard common to classrooms is convenient for creating sketches and for jotting notes during your presentation. If your presentation requires extensive notes or complex **drawings**, however, prepare handouts on which the audience can jot notes and which they can keep for future reference.

Overhead Transparencies. With transparencies you can create a series of overlays to explain a complex device or system, adding (or removing) the overlays one at a time. You can also lay a sheet of paper over a list of items on a transparency, uncovering one item at a time as you discuss it, to focus audience attention on each point in the sequence.

Presentation Software. Presentation software, such as Microsoft PowerPoint, Corel Presentations, and OpenOffice.org Impress, lets you create your presentation on your computer. You can develop charts and graphs with data from spreadsheet software or locate visuals on the Web, and then import those files into your presentation. This software also offers standard templates and other features that help you design effective visuals and integrated text. Enhancements include a selection of typefaces, highlighting devices, background textures and colors, and clip-art images. Images can also be printed out for use as overhead transparencies or handouts. However, avoid using too many enhancements, which may distract viewers from your message. Figure P–4 shows well-balanced slides for a presentation based on the sample formal report in Figure F–6.

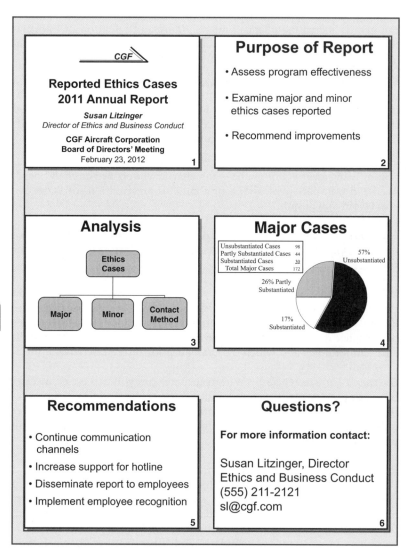

FIGURE P–4. Slides for a Presentation

◀ PROFESSIONALISM NOTE Rehearse your presentation using your electronic slides, and practice your transitions from slide to slide. Also practice loading your presentation and anticipate any technical difficulties that might arise. Should you encounter a technical snag during the presentation, stay calm and give yourself time to solve the problem. If you cannot solve the problem, move on without the technology. As a backup, carry a printout of your electronic presentation and copies for your audience as well as an extra electronic copy on a storage medium. ▶

WRITER'S CHECKLIST   Using Visuals in a Presentation

✔ Use text sparingly in visuals. Use bulleted or numbered lists, keeping them in **parallel structure** and with balanced content. Use numbers if the sequence is important and bullets if it is not.

✔ Limit the number of bulleted or numbered items to no more than five or six per visual.

✔ Limit each visual to no more than 40 to 45 words. Any more will clutter the visual and force you to use a smaller font, which could impair the audience's ability to read it.

✔ Make your visuals consistent in type style, size, and spacing.

✔ Use a type size visible to members of the audience at the back of the room. Type should be boldface and no smaller than 30 points. For headings, 45- or 50-point type works even better.

✔ Use graphs and charts to show data trends. Use only one or two illustrations per visual to avoid clutter and confusion.

✔ Avoid using sound or visual effects presentation software that tends to undermine the professionalism of your presentation and distract from the content.

✔ Make the contrast between your text and the background sharp. Use light backgrounds with dark lettering and avoid textured or decorated backgrounds.

✔ Use no more than 12 visuals per presentation. Any more will tax the audience's concentration.

✔ Match your delivery of the content to your visuals. Do not put one visual on the screen and talk about the previous visual or, even worse, the next one.

✔ Do not read the text on your visual word for word. Your audience can read the visuals; they look to you to provide the key points in detail.

P

WEB LINK	Preparing Presentation Slides

For a helpful tutorial on creating effective slides, see *bedfordstmartins.com/alred* and select *Try a tutorial*, "On preparing presentation slides." For links to additional information and tutorials for using presentation software, see *bedfordstmartins.com/alred* and select *Links for Handbook Entries*.

Delivering a Presentation

Once you have outlined and drafted your presentation and prepared your visuals, you are ready to practice your presentation and delivery techniques.

Practice. Familiarize yourself with the sequence of the material—major topics, notes, and visuals—in your outline. Once you feel comfortable with the content, you are ready to practice the presentation (in front of others if possible).

PRACTICE ON YOUR FEET AND OUT LOUD. Try to practice in the room where you will give the presentation. Practicing on-site helps you get the feel of the room: the lighting, the arrangement of the chairs, the position of electrical outlets and switches, and so forth. Practice out loud to gauge the length of your presentation, to uncover problems such as awkward transitions, and to eliminate verbal tics (such as "um," "you know," and "like").

PRACTICE WITH YOUR VISUALS AND TEXT. Integrate your visuals into your practice sessions to help your presentation go more smoothly. Operate the equipment (computer, slide projector, or overhead projector) until you are comfortable with it. Decide if you want to use a remote control or wireless mouse or if you want to have someone else advance your slides. Even if things go wrong, being prepared and practiced will give you the confidence and poise to continue.

Delivery Techniques That Work. Your delivery is both audible and visual. In addition to your words and message, your nonverbal communication affects your audience. Be animated—your words have impact and staying power when they are delivered with physical and vocal animation. If you want listeners to share your point of view, show enthusiasm for your topic. The most common delivery techniques include making eye contact; using movement and gestures; and varying voice inflection, projection, and pace.

EYE CONTACT.   The best way to establish rapport with your audience is through eye contact. In a large audience, directly address those people who seem most responsive to you in different parts of the room. Doing that helps you establish rapport with your listeners by holding their attention and gives you important visual cues that let you know how your message is being received. Do the listeners seem engaged and actively listening? Based on your observations, you may need to adjust the pace of your presentation.

MOVEMENT.   Animate the presentation with physical movement. Take a step or two to one side after you have been talking for a minute or so. That type of movement is most effective at transitional points in your presentation between major topics or after pauses or emphases. Too much movement, however, can be distracting, so try not to pace.

Another way to integrate movement into your presentation is to walk to the screen and point to the visual as you discuss it. Touch the screen with the pointer and then turn back to the audience before beginning to speak (remember the three *t*'s: touch, turn, and talk).

GESTURES.   Gestures both animate your presentation and help communicate your message. Most people gesture naturally when they talk; nervousness, however, can inhibit gesturing during a presentation. Keep one hand free and use that hand to gesture.

VOICE.   Your voice can be an effective tool in communicating your sincerity, enthusiasm, and command of your topic. Use it to your advantage to project your credibility. *Vocal inflection* is the rise and fall of your voice at different times, such as the way your voice naturally rises at the end of a question ("You want it *when?*"). A conversational delivery and eye contact promote the feeling among members of the audience that you are addressing them directly. Use vocal inflection to highlight differences between key and subordinate points in your presentation.

PROJECTION.   Most presenters think they are speaking louder than they are. Remember that your presentation is ineffective for anyone in the audience who cannot hear you. If listeners must strain to hear you, they may give up trying to listen. Correct projection problems by practicing out loud with someone listening from the back of the room.

PACE.   Be aware of the speed at which you deliver your presentation. If you speak too fast, your words will run together, making it difficult for your audience to follow. If you speak too slowly, your listeners will become impatient and distracted.

Presentation Anxiety. Everyone experiences nervousness before a presentation. Survey after survey reveals that for most people dread of public speaking ranks among their top five fears. Instead of letting fear inhibit you, focus on channeling your nervous energy into a helpful stimulant. Practice will help you, but the best way to master anxiety is to know your topic thoroughly—knowing what you are going to say and how you are going to say it will help you gain confidence and re-duce anxiety as you become immersed in your subject.

WRITER'S CHECKLIST   Preparing for and Delivering a Presentation

✔ Prepare a set of notes that will trigger your memory during the presentation.

✔ Make as much eye contact as possible with your audience to establish rapport and maximize opportunities for audience feedback.

✔ Animate your delivery by integrating movement, gestures, and vocal inflection into your presentation. However, keep your movements and speech patterns natural.

✔ Speak loudly and slowly enough to be heard and understood.

✔ Review the earlier checklist on using visuals as well as advice on delivery in this entry.

For information and tips on communicating with cross-cultural audiences, see **global communication**, **global graphics**, and **international correspondence**.

P

press releases

Companies and organizations write press releases (or *news releases*) to announce new products and services, new policies, special events (such as branch openings, company anniversaries, mergers, and grand open-ings), management changes, and sponsorship of social-action and cul-tural programs. The purpose of a press release is both to inform the public about the company and its products and services and to promote a favorable image. Even the announcement of what might be regarded as an unfavorable event, such as the closing of a division, can put a company in a good light by demonstrating candor, the ability to act effectively in a crisis, or the potential long-term benefits of a change. Large corporations and institutions usually have their own public rela-tions staffs or use outside agencies. However, if you work for a small company without public relations resources, you may be called on to write a press release.

The press release should be clear, concise, and written with particular attention to the five *w*'s: *who, what, where, when,* and *why.* Begin the first paragraph with the place and date of the announcement, as shown in Figure P–5.

News Release

BENTLEY PLASTICS
3535 Michigan Avenue ■ Chicago, IL 60653

Contact: Marjorie Kohls
E-mail: mkohls@bentley.com
Phone: (312) 712-1946
Fax: (312) 712-1950

FOR IMMEDIATE RELEASE

Mark Williams Joins Bentley Plastics as Vice President

Chicago, Illinois, May 22, 2012: Marketing expert and author Mark Williams has been appointed Vice President of Marketing at Bentley Plastics, a manufacturer of polymer tubing and coils. He will direct the Illinois and Indiana district sales offices and coordinate overseas distribution through the company's Singapore office. Williams will travel extensively throughout Southeast Asia while developing marketing channels for Bentley.

Formerly, Williams was director of services with International Marketing Associates, a consulting group in New York. While at IMA, he developed a computer-based marketing center that linked textile firms in the United States, Finland, and Great Britain. A graduate of the Columbia University Graduate School of Business, Williams is the author of *Marketing Dynamics*, an informal examination of psychological appeals to the buying public. The book has been used in marketing classrooms at several universities.

Bentley Plastics, headquartered in Chicago, has main plants in Skokie, Illinois, and Gary, Indiana. Since 1978, Bentley has also been producing tubing for French distribution through the firm of Jourdan and Sons, Paris.

# # #

FIGURE P–5. Press Release

Write the release using the decreasing **order-of-importance method of development**. Put all critical information in the first paragraph, information of the next level of importance in the second paragraph, and so on. Editors may need to make your release fit the space they have available; if they must cut your release, they will delete the last paragraph first, and then the next to last, and so on. Make sure your facts are accurate and be careful to define any unfamiliar terms.

Releases are usually sent to local newspapers, television and radio stations, and other special groups, such as trade publications or professional associations. Send the release to a specific person whenever possible. Otherwise, try to address the press release to a particular editor, such as to the business editor or the technology editor. See also **newsletter articles**.

WRITER'S CHECKLIST   Preparing Press Releases

- ✔ Print the release on company stationery with a minimum of one-inch margins on each side of the page.
- ✔ Provide contact information for the person who can supply further details.
- ✔ Use boldface type for the headlines and double-space text for easy reading and editing.
- ✔ Use "*-more-*" centered at the bottom of the page when you need to indicate that another page follows.
- ✔ Allow one blank line and center "# # #" or "*-30-*" or "*-End-*" to indicate where the press release ends.

P

WEB LINK	Press Releases

For links to Web sites that offer tips, samples, and resources for writing press releases, see *bedfordstmartins.com/alred* and select *Links for Handbook Entries*.

principal / principle

Principal, meaning "an amount of money on which interest is earned or paid" or "a chief official in a school or court proceeding," is sometimes confused with *principle*, which means "a basic truth or belief."

▶ The bank will pay 3.5 percent on the *principal*.

▶ He sent a letter to the *principal* of the high school.

▶ She is a person of unwavering *principles*.

Principal is also an adjective, meaning "main" or "primary." ("My *principal* objection is that it will be too expensive.")

process explanation

A process explanation may describe the steps in a process, an operation, or a procedure, such as the steps necessary to start a small business. The **introduction** often presents a brief overview of the process or lets **readers** know why it is important for them to become familiar with the process you are explaining. Be sure to define terms that readers might not understand and provide **visuals** to clarify the process. See also **defining terms** and **instructions**.

In describing a process, use transitional words and phrases to create unity within **paragraphs**, and select **headings** to provide **transition** from one step to the next. The example of a "Tuition Reimbursement Approval" on page 409 describes a step-by-step process.

progress and activity reports

Progress reports provide details on the tasks completed for major workplace projects, whereas *activity reports* focus on the ongoing work of individual employees. Both are sometimes called *status reports*. Although many organizations use standardized forms for these **reports**, the content and structure shown in Figures P–6 and P–7 are typical.

Progress Reports

A progress report provides information to decision-makers about the status of a project—whether it is on schedule and within budget. Progress reports are often submitted by a contracting company to a client company, as shown in Figure P–6. They are used mainly for projects that involve many steps over a period of time and are issued at regular intervals to describe what has been done and what remains to be done. Progress reports help projects run smoothly by helping managers assign work, adjust schedules, allocate budgets, and order supplies and

Hobard Construction Company

9032 Salem Avenue
Lubbock, TX 79409

www.hobardcc.com
(808) 769-0832
Fax: (808) 769-5327

August 15, 2012

Walter M. Wazuski
County Administrator
109 Grand Avenue
Manchester, NH 03103

Dear Mr. Wazuski:

Subject: Progress Report 8 for July 31, 2012

The renovation of the County Courthouse is progressing on schedule and within budget. Although the cost of certain materials is higher than our original bid indicated, we expect to complete the project without exceeding the estimated costs because the speed with which the project is being completed will reduce overall labor expenses.

Costs

Materials used to date have cost $178,600, and labor costs have been $293,000 (including some subcontracted plumbing). Our estimate for the remainder of the materials is $159,000; remaining labor costs should not exceed $400,000.

Work Completed

As of July 31, we finished the installation of the circuit-breaker panels and meters, the level-one service outlets, and all the subfloor wiring. The upgrading of the courtroom, the upgrading of the records-storage room, and the replacement of the air-conditioning units are in the preliminary stages.

Work Scheduled

We have scheduled the upgrading of the courtroom to take place from August 29 to October 9, the upgrading of the records-storage room from October 11 to November 16, and the replacement of the air-conditioning units from November 21 to December 17. We see no difficulty in having the job finished by the scheduled date of December 21.

Sincerely yours,

Tran Nuguélen

Tran Nuguélen
ntran@hobardcc.com

FIGURE P–6. Progress Report (Using Letter Format)

INTEROFFICE MEMO

Date: June 8, 2012

To: Kathryn Hunter, Director of IT

From: Wayne Tribinski, Manager, Applications Programs *WT*

Subject: Activity Report for May 2012

We are dealing with the following projects and problems, as of May 31.

Projects

1. For the *Software Training Mailing Campaign*, we anticipate producing a set of labels for mailing software training information to customers by June 13.
2. The *Search Project* is on hold until the PL/I training has been completed, probably by the end of June.
3. The project to provide a database for the *Information Management System* has been expanded in scope to provide a database for all training activities. We are rescheduling the project to take the new scope into account.

Problems

The *Information Management System* has been delayed. The original schedule was based on the assumption that a systems analyst who was familiar with the system would work on this project. Instead, the project was assigned to a newly hired systems analyst who was inexperienced and required much more learning time than expected.

Bill Michaels, whose activity report is attached, is correcting a problem in the *CNG Software*. This correction may take a week.

Plans for Next Month

- Complete the *Software Training Mailing Campaign*.
- Resume the *Search Project*.
- Restart the project to provide a database on information management with a schedule that reflects its new scope.
- Write a report to justify the addition of two software developers to my department.
- Congratulate publicly the recipients of Meritorious Achievement Awards: Bill Thomasson and Nancy O'Rourke.

Current Staffing Level

Current staff: 11
Open requisitions: 0

Attachment

FIGURE P–7. Activity Report (Using Printed Memo)

equipment. All progress reports for a particular project should have the same **format**.

The **introduction** to the first progress report should identify the project, methods used, necessary materials, expenditures, and completion date. Subsequent reports summarize the progress achieved since the preceding report and list the steps that remain to be taken. The body of the progress report should describe the project's status, including details such as schedules and costs, a statement of the work completed, and perhaps an estimate of future progress. The report ends with **conclusions** and recommendations about changes in the schedule, materials, techniques, and other information important to the project.

Activity Reports

Within an organization, employees often submit activity reports to managers on the status of ongoing projects. Managers may combine the activity reports of several individuals or teams into larger activity reports and, in turn, submit those larger reports to their own managers. The activity report shown in Figure P–7 was submitted by a manager (Wayne Tribinski) who supervises 11 employees; the reader of the report (Kathryn Hunter) is Tribinski's manager.

Because the activity report is issued periodically (usually monthly) and contains material familiar to its **readers**, it normally needs no introduction or conclusion, although it may need a brief opening to provide **context**. Although the format varies from company to company, the following sections are typical: Current Projects, Current Problems, Plans for the Next Period, and Current Staffing Level (for managers).

P

promotional writing

Promotional writing is vital to the success of any company or organization; high-quality, state-of-the-art products or services are of little value if customers and clients do not know they exist. Although you may not be a marketing or public relations specialist, you may be asked to prepare promotional (or marketing) materials, especially if you work for a small organization or are self-employed. Even at a large company, you may help prepare a brochure, a Web page, or a department newsletter. See also **collaborative writing**. Several elements are central to promotional writing:

- *Understanding your audience.* Analyzing the needs, interests, concerns, and makeup of your **audience** is crucial.

- *Understanding your product or service.* Conduct adequate **research**, especially by talking with those with firsthand knowledge of the product or service. (See **interviewing for information**.)

- *Understanding the principles of persuasion.* Good promotional writing uses **persuasion** to gain attention, build interest, reduce resistance, and motivate **readers** to act.

- *Making information both easy to find and visually appealing.* Make the most effective use of **organization**, **layout and design**, and appropriate **visuals** that are well integrated with the text.

- *Using good writing style.* Write with **clarity**, **coherence**, and **conciseness** to help your readers understand the message and to achieve your **purpose**.

❖ ETHICS NOTE Because readers are persuaded only if they believe the source is credible, be careful not to overstate claims and to avoid possible **logic errors**. See also **ethics in writing**. ❖

Specific types of promotional writing discussed in this book include **brochures**, **newsletters**, **press releases**, **proposals**, **sales letters**, and **writing for the Web**. Many other documents described in this book often include the additional or secondary purpose of promoting an organization. For example, **adjustment letters**, which are usually concerned with resolving a specific problem, offer opportunities to promote your organization. Likewise, **progress and activity reports** provide an opportunity to promote the value of your work in an organization.

WEB LINK	Writing Promotional Case Histories
One popular form of promotional writing is the *case history*, an informative story in a feature-article format that describes how a product or service solved a problem for a customer. Marketers use case histories to provide real-life examples of their products and services, adding credibility by mentioning real companies and references. For Web sites that provide advice on writing case studies, see *bedfordstmartins.com/ alred* and select *Links for Handbook Entries*.	

P

pronoun reference

A **pronoun** should refer clearly to a specific antecedent. Avoid vague and uncertain references.

► We got the account after we wrote the proposal. ~~It was a big one.~~

, which was a big one, (inserted after "account")

For **coherence**, place pronouns as close as possible to their antecedents—distance increases the likelihood of **ambiguity**.

► The office building next to City Hall ~~is praised for its architectural design.~~

, praised for its architectural design, is • (inserted)

A general (or broad) reference or one that has no real antecedent is a problem that often occurs when the word *this* is used by itself.

► He deals with personnel problems in his work. This *experience* helps him in his personal life.

Another common problem is a hidden reference, which has only an implied antecedent.

► A high-lipid, low-carbohydrate diet is "ketogenic" because it favors ~~their~~ *the* formation *of ketone bodies*.

Do not repeat an antecedent in parentheses following the pronoun. If you feel you must identify the pronoun's antecedent in that way, rewrite the sentence.

AWKWARD	The senior partner first met Bob Evans when he (Evans) was a trainee.
IMPROVED	Bob Evans was a trainee when the senior partner first met him.
IMPROVED	When the senior partner first met him, Bob Evans was a trainee.

For advice on avoiding pronoun-reference problems with gender, see **biased language**.

P

pronouns

DIRECTORY

A pronoun is a word that is used as a substitute for a **noun** (the noun for which a pronoun substitutes is called the *antecedent*). Using pronouns in place of nouns relieves the monotony of repeating the same noun over and over. See also **pronoun reference.**

Personal pronouns refer to the person or people speaking (*I, me, my, mine; we, us, our, ours*); the person or people spoken to (*you, your, yours*); or the person, people, or thing(s) spoken of (*he, him, his; she, her, hers; it, its; they, them, their, theirs*). See also **person** and **point of view.**

▶ If *their* figures are correct, *ours* must be in error.

Demonstrative pronouns (*this, these, that, those*) indicate or point out the thing being referred to.

▶ *This* is my desk. *These* are my coworkers. *That* will be a difficult job. *Those* are incorrect figures.

Relative pronouns (*who, whom, which, that*) perform a dual function: (1) They take the place of nouns and (2) they connect and establish the relationship between a dependent **clause** and its main clause.

▶ The department manager decided *who* would be hired.

Interrogative pronouns (*who, whom, what, which*) are used to ask questions.

▶ *What* is the trouble?

Indefinite pronouns specify a class or group of persons or things rather than a particular person or thing (*all, another, any, anyone, anything, both, each, either, everybody, few, many, most, much, neither, nobody, none, several, some, such*).

▶ Not *everyone* liked the new procedures; *some* even refused to follow them.

A *reflexive pronoun*, which always ends with the suffix *-self* or *-selves*, indicates that the subject of the sentence acts upon itself. See also **sentence construction.**

▶ The electrician accidentally shocked *herself*.

The reflexive pronouns are *myself, yourself, himself, herself, itself, oneself, ourselves, yourselves,* and *themselves*. *Myself* is not a substitute for *I* or *me* as a personal pronoun.

▶ Victor and ~~myself~~ completed the report on time.
    I

P

> *me*
> ► The assignment was given to Ingrid and ~~myself~~.
>   ^

Intensive pronouns are identical in form to the reflexive pronouns, but they perform a different function: Intensive pronouns emphasize their antecedents.

> ► I *myself* asked the same question.

Reciprocal pronouns (*one another*, *each other*) indicate the relationship of one item to another. *Each other* is commonly used when referring to two persons or things and *one another* when referring to more than two.

> ► Lashell and Kara work well with *each other*.

> ► The crew members work well with *one another*.

Case

Pronouns have forms to show the subjective, objective, and possessive cases.

SINGULAR	SUBJECTIVE	OBJECTIVE	POSSESSIVE
First person	I	me	my, mine
Second person	you	you	your, yours
Third person	he, she, it	him, her, it	his, her, hers, its

PLURAL	SUBJECTIVE	OBJECTIVE	POSSESSIVE
First person	we	us	our, ours
Second person	you	you	your, yours
Third person	they	them	their, theirs

ESL TIPS for Using Possessive Pronouns

In many languages, possessive pronouns agree in number and gender with the nouns they modify. In English, however, possessive pronouns agree in number and gender with their antecedents. Check your writing carefully for agreement between a possessive pronoun and the word, phrase, or clause to which it refers.

> ► The *woman* brought *her* brother a cup of coffee.

> ► *Robert* sent *his* mother flowers on Mother's Day.

A pronoun that functions as the subject of a clause or sentence is in the subjective **case** (*I, we, he, she, it, you, they, who*). The subjective case is also used when the pronoun follows a linking **verb**.

- *She* is my boss.
- My boss is *she*.

A pronoun that functions as the object of a verb or **preposition** is in the objective case (*me, us, him, her, it, you, them, whom*).

- Ms. Davis hired Tom and *me*. [object of verb]
- Between *you* and *me*, she's wrong. [object of preposition]

A pronoun that expresses ownership is in the **possessive case** (*my, mine, our, ours, his, her, hers, its, your, yours, their, theirs, whose*).

- He took *his* notes with him on the business trip.
- We took *our* notes with us on the business trip.

A pronoun **appositive** takes the case of its antecedent.

- Two systems analysts, Joe and *I*, were selected to represent the company.
  [*Joe and I* is in apposition to the subject, *two systems analysts*, and must therefore be in the subjective case.]
- The manager selected two representatives—Joe and *me*.
  [*Joe and me* is in apposition to *two representatives*, which is the object of the verb, *selected*, and therefore must be in the objective case.]

If you have difficulty determining the case of a compound pronoun, try using the pronoun singly.

- In his letter, Eldon mentioned *him* and *me*.
  In his letter, Eldon mentioned *him*.
  In his letter, Eldon mentioned *me*.
- *They* and *we* must discuss the terms of the merger.
  They must discuss the terms of the merger.
  We must discuss the terms of the merger.

When a pronoun modifies a noun, try it without the noun to determine its case.

- [*We / Us*] pilots fly our own planes.
  We fly our own planes.
  [You would not write, "*Us* fly our own planes."]
- He addressed his remarks directly to [*we / us*] technicians.
  He addressed his remarks directly to *us*.
  [You would not write, "He addressed his remarks directly to *we*."]

P

Gender

A pronoun must agree in gender with its antecedent. A problem some-times occurs because the masculine pronoun has traditionally been used to refer to both sexes. To avoid the sexual bias implied in such usage, use *he or she* or the plural form of the pronoun, *they*.

> All   *they choose.*
> ► ~~Each~~ may stay or go as ~~he chooses.~~
>   ^   ^

As in this example, when the singular pronoun (*he*) changes to the plu-ral (*they*), the singular indefinite pronoun (*each*) must also change to its plural form (*all*). See also **biased language**.

Number

Number is a frequent problem with only a few indefinite pronouns (*each, either, neither,* and those ending with -*body* or -*one,* such as *any-body, anyone, everybody, everyone, nobody, no one, somebody, some-one*) that are normally singular and so require singular verbs and are referred to by singular pronouns.

> ► As *each member arrives* for the meeting, please hand *him or her* a copy of the confidential report. *Everyone* must return the copy before *he or she* leaves. *Everybody* on the committee *understands* that *neither* of our major competitors *is* aware of the new process we have developed.

Person

Third-person personal pronouns usually have antecedents.

> ► Gina presented the report to the members of the board of direc-tors. *She* [Gina] first summarized *it* [the report] for *them* [the direc-tors] and then asked for questions.

First- and second-person personal pronouns do not normally require antecedents.

> ► *I* like my job.

> ► *You* were on vacation at the time.

> ► *We* all worked hard on the project.

proofreaders' marks

Publishers have established symbols called *proofreaders' marks* that writers and editors use to communicate in the production of publications. Familiarity with those symbols makes it easy for you to communicate your changes to others. Figure P–8 lists standard proofreaders' marks. For using Comment and Track Changes in word-processing programs, see *Digital Tip: Incorporating Tracked Changes* on page 513.

MARK/SYMBOL	MEANING	EXAMPLE	CORRECTED TYPE
	Delete	the manager's report	the report
	Insert	the report	the manager's report
	Let stand	the manager's report	the manager's report
	Capitalize	the monday meeting	the Monday meeting
	Lowercase	the Monday Meeting	the Monday meeting
	Transpose	the cover lettre	the cover letter
	Close space	a loud speaker	a loudspeaker
	Insert space	a loudspeaker	a loud speaker
	Paragraph	...report. The meeting...	...report. / The meeting...
	Run in with previous line or paragraph	...report. / The meeting...	...report. The meeting...
	Italicize	the New York Times	the *New York Times*
	Boldface	Use boldface sparingly.	Use **boldface** sparingly.
	Insert period	I wrote the e-mail	I wrote the e-mail.
	Insert comma	However we cannot...	However, we cannot...
	Insert hyphen	clear cut decision	clear-cut decision
	Insert em dash	Our goal productivity	Our goal—productivity
	Insert colon	We need the following	We need the following:
	Insert semicolon	we finished we achieved	we finished; we achieved
	Insert quotation marks	He said, I agree.	He said, "I agree."
	Insert apostrophe	the managers report	the manager's report

FIGURE P–8. Proofreaders' Marks

proofreading

Proofreading is essential whether you are writing a brief **e-mail** or a **résumé**. Grammar checkers and spell checkers are important aids to proofreading, but they can make writers overconfident. If a typographical error results in a legitimate English word (for example, *coarse* instead of *course*), the spell checker will not flag the misspelling. You may find some of the tactics discussed in **revision** useful when proofreading; in fact, you may find passages during proofreading that will require further revision.

◀ PROFESSIONALISM NOTE Proofreading not only demonstrates that you respect readers (who can be distracted, irritated, or misled by errors in writing) but also reflects that you are professional in the way you approach all your work. ▶

Whether the material you proofread is your own writing or that of someone else, consider proofreading in several stages. Although you need to tailor the stages to the specific document and to your own problem areas, the following *Writer's Checklist* should provide a useful starting point for proofreading. Consider using standard **proofreaders' marks** for proofreading someone else's document.

P

> **WRITER'S CHECKLIST**   Proofreading in Stages
>
> FIRST-STAGE REVIEW
> ✔ Appropriate **format**, as for **reports** or **correspondence**
> ✔ Consistent style, including **headings**, terminology, spacing, and fonts
> ✔ Correct numbering of figures and **tables**
>
> SECOND-STAGE REVIEW
> ✔ Specific **grammar** and **usage** problems
> ✔ Appropriate **punctuation**
> ✔ Correct and consistent **abbreviations** and **capitalization**
> ✔ Correct **spelling** (especially names and places)
> ✔ Complete Web or **e-mail** addresses
> ✔ Accurate data in tables and **lists**
> ✔ Cut-and-paste errors; for example, a result of moved or deleted text and **numbers**

WRITER'S CHECKLIST Proofreading in Stages (*continued*)

FINAL-STAGE REVIEW

✔ Survey of your overall goals: <u>audience</u> needs and <u>purpose</u>

✔ Appearance of the document (see <u>layout and design</u>)

✔ Review by a trusted colleague, especially for crucial documents (see <u>collaborative writing</u>)

DIGITAL TIP

Proofreading for Format Consistency

To check your documents for consistency, you should use both a "macro" and a "micro" approach. Zooming out in your word-processing software will show you the general appearance of your document and help you spot any problems with layout or structure. Printing your document and examining it slowly and carefully will help you notice inconsistencies in the details of your document, such as typography, line spacing, and indentation. For more detailed advice about these two techniques for reviewing documents, go to *bedfordstmartins.com/alred* and select *Digital Tips*, "Proofreading for Format Consistency."

---

proposals

P

A proposal is a document written to persuade readers that what is proposed will benefit them by solving a problem or fulfilling a need. When you write a proposal, therefore, you must convince readers that they need what you are proposing, that it is practical and appropriate, and that you are the right person or organization to provide the proposed product or service. See also **persuasion** and **"you" viewpoint**.

Proposal Strategies

For any proposal, support your assertions with relevant facts, statistics, and examples. Your supporting evidence must lead logically to your proposed plan of action or solution. Cite relevant sources of information that provide strong credibility to your argument. Avoid ambiguity, do not wander from your main point, and never make false claims. See **ethics in writing**.

Audience and Purpose. Proposals often require more than one level of approval, so take into account all the readers in your **audience**. Consider especially their levels of technical knowledge of the subject. For example, if your primary reader is an expert on your subject but a supervisor who must also approve the proposal is not, provide an **executive summary** written in nontechnical language for the supervisor. You might also include a **glossary** of terms used in the body of the proposal or an **appendix** that explains highly detailed information in nontechnical language. If your primary reader is not an expert but a supervisor is, write the proposal with the nonexpert in mind and include an appendix that contains the technical details for experts.

Writing a persuasive proposal can be simplified by composing a concise statement of **purpose**—the exact problem or opportunity that your proposal is designed to address and how you plan to persuade your readers to accept what you propose. Composing a purpose statement before outlining and writing your proposal will also help you and any collaborators understand the direction, **scope**, and goals of your proposal.

Project Management. Proposal writers are often faced with writing high-quality, persuasive proposals under tight organizational deadlines. Dividing the task into manageable parts is the key to accomplishing your goals, especially when proposals involve substantial **collaborative writing**. For example, you might set deadlines for completing various proposal sections or stages of the writing process.*

---

*For help with project management, see JoAnn T. Hackos, *Information Development: Managing Your Documentation Projects, Portfolio, and People* (Indianapolis, IN: Wiley, 2007).

WEB LINK	Proposal Management Software

Proposal management software is becoming increasingly popular in companies that manage frequent and extensive proposal writing projects. Such software allows businesses to automate the more routine tasks while easily tracking multiple versions. For links to proposal management software, see *bedfordstmartins.com/alred* and select *Links for Handbook Entries.*

Proposal Context and Types

Proposals are written within a specific **context**. As that entry describes, understanding the context will help you determine the most appropriate writing strategy. In general, to persuade those within your organization to make a change or an improvement or perhaps to fund a project, you would write an *internal proposal.* To persuade those outside your company to agree to a plan or take a course of action, you would write an *external proposal.*

WRITER'S CHECKLIST   Writing Persuasive Proposals

✔ Analyze your audience carefully to determine how to best meet your readers' needs or requirements.

✔ Write a concise purpose statement at the outset to clarify your proposal's goals.

✔ Divide the writing task into manageable segments and develop a timeline for completing tasks.

✔ Review the descriptions of proposal contexts, structure, and types in this entry.

✔ Focus on the proposal's benefits to readers and anticipate their questions or objections.

✔ Incorporate evidence to support the claims of your proposal.

✔ Select an appropriate, visually appealing format. See **layout and design**.

✔ Use a confident, positive **tone** throughout the proposal.

P

Internal Proposals

The purpose of an internal proposal is to suggest a change or an improvement within the writer's organization. Often in memo format, it is addressed to a superior within the organization who has the authority to accept or reject the proposal. Internal proposals are typically reviewed by one or more departments for cost, practicality, and potential benefits, so take account of all relevant audience members. Two common types of internal proposals—informal and formal—are often distinguished from each other by the frequency with which they are written and by the degree of change they propose.

Informal Internal Proposals.   Informal internal proposals are the most common type of proposal and typically include small spending requests, requests for permission to hire new employees or increase salaries, and requests to attend conferences or purchase new equipment. In writing informal or routine proposals, highlight any key benefits to be realized.

WEB LINK	Internal Proposals
For examples of brief solicited and unsolicited proposals, see *bedfordstmartins.com/alred* and select *Model Documents Gallery*.	

Formal Internal Proposals.   Formal internal proposals usually involve requests to commit large sums of money. They are usually organized into sections that describe a problem, propose a solution, and offer to implement the suggested recommendation. The body, in turn, is further divided into sections to reflect the subject matter. The proposal may begin with a section describing the background or history of an issue and go on to discuss options for addressing the issue in separate sections.

The *introduction* of your internal proposal should establish that a problem exists and needs a solution. If the audience is not convinced that there is a problem, your proposal will not succeed. After you identify the problem, summarize your proposed solution and indicate its benefits and estimated total cost. Notice how the introduction in Figure P–9 states the problem directly and then summarizes the writer's proposed solution.

WEB LINK	Complete Internal Proposal
For a complete version of Figure P–9 with annotations, see *bedfordstmartins.com/alred* and select *Model Documents Gallery*.	

The *body* of your internal proposal should offer a practical solution to the problem and provide the details necessary to inform and persuade your readers. In the body, describe the problem for which you are

ABO, Inc.
Interoffice Memo

To: Joan Marlow, Director, Human Resources Division

From: Leslie Galusha, Chief   *ℒ𝒢*
             Employee Benefits Department

Date: June 15, 2012

Subject: Employee Fitness and Health-Care Costs

Health-care and workers' compensation insurance costs at ABO, Inc., have risen 100 percent over the last six years. In 2006, costs were $5,675 per employee per year; in 2012, they have reached $11,560 per employee per year. This doubling of costs mirrors a national trend, with health-care costs anticipated to continue to rise at the same rate for the next ten years. Controlling these escalating expenses will be essential. They are eating into ABO's profit margin because the company currently pays 70 percent of the costs for employee coverage.

Healthy employees bring direct financial benefits to companies in the form of lower employee insurance costs, lower absenteeism rates, and reduced turnover. Regular physical exercise promotes fit, healthy people by reducing the risk of coronary heart disease, diabetes, osteoporosis, hypertension, and stress-related problems. I propose that to promote regular, vigorous physical exercise for our employees, ABO implement a health-care program that focuses on employee fitness. . . .

Problem of Health-Care Costs
The U.S. Department of Health and Human Services (HHS) recently estimated that health-care costs in the United States will triple by the year 2020. Corporate expenses for health care are rising at such a fast rate that, if unchecked, in seven years they will significantly erode corporate profits.

According to HHS, people who do not participate in a regular and vigorous exercise program incur nearly double the health-care costs and are hospitalized 30 percent more days than people who exercise regularly. Nonexercisers are also 41 percent more likely to submit medical claims over $10,000 at some point during their careers than are those who exercise regularly.

These figures are further supported by data from independent studies. A model created by the National Institutes of Health (NIH) . . .

P

FIGURE P–9. Special-Purpose Internal Proposal (*continued*) (Introduction and Body)

Joan Marlow   2   June 15, 2012

Proposed Solutions for ABO
The benefits of regular, vigorous physical activity for employees and companies are compelling. To achieve these benefits at ABO, I propose that we choose from one of two possible options: Build in-house fitness centers at our warehouse facilities, or offer employees several options for membership at a national fitness club. The following analysis compares . . .

Recommendation and Conclusion
I recommend that ABO, Inc., participate in the corporate membership program at AeroFitness Clubs, Inc., by subsidizing employee memberships. By subsidizing memberships, ABO shows its commitment to the importance of a fit workforce. Club membership allows employees at all five ABO warehouses to participate in the program. The more employees who participate, the greater the long-term savings. . . .

Enrolling employees in the corporate program at AeroFitness would allow them to receive a one-month free trial membership. Those interested in continuing could then join the club and pay half of the one-time membership fee. . . .

Implementing this program will help ABO, Inc., reduce its health-care costs while building stronger employee relations by offering employees a desirable benefit. If this proposal is adopted, I have some additional thoughts about publicizing the program to encourage employee participation. I look forward to discussing the details of this proposal with you and answering any questions you may have.

P

FIGURE P–9. Special-Purpose Internal Proposal (*continued*) (Conclusion)

offering a solution; the methodology of your proposed solution; details about equipment, materials, and staff; cost breakdowns; and a comprehensive schedule. Figure P–9 provides a section from the body of an internal proposal.

The *conclusion* of your internal proposal should tie everything together, restate your recommendation, and close with a spirit of cooperation (offering to set up a meeting, supply additional information, or provide any other assistance that might be needed). Keep your conclusion brief, as in Figure P–9.

If your proposal cites information that you obtained through research, such as published reports, government statistics, or interviews, follow the conclusion with a list of works cited that provides complete publication information for each source.

External Proposals

External proposals are prepared for clients and customers outside your company. They are either submitted in response to a request for goods and services from another organization (a solicited proposal) or sent to them without a prior request (an unsolicited proposal). See also **grant proposals**.

Solicited Proposals. To find the best method of meeting their needs and the most-qualified company to help reach that goal, procuring organizations commonly issue a request for proposals (RFP) or an invitation for bids (IFB) that asks competing companies such as yours to bid for a job.

An RFP often defines a need or problem and allows those who respond to propose possible solutions. The procuring organization generally distributes an RFP to several predetermined vendors. The RFP usually outlines the specific requirements for the ideal solution. For example, if an organization needs a new accounting system, it may require the proposed system to create customized reports. The RFP also may contain specific formatting requirements, such as page length, font type and size, margin widths, **headings**, sections, and appendix items. When responding to RFPs, follow their requirements exactly—proposals that do not provide the required information, do not follow the required format, or miss the submittal deadline are usually considered "noncompliant" and immediately rejected.

In contrast to an RFP, an IFB (invitation for bids) is commonly issued by federal, state, and local government agencies to solicit bids on clearly defined products or services. An IFB is restrictive, binding the bidder to produce an item or a service that meets the exact requirements of the organization issuing the IFB. The goods or services are defined in the IFB by references to performance standards stated in technical specifications. Bidders must be prepared to prove that their product will meet all requirements of the specifications. The procuring organization generally publishes its IFB on its Web site or in a specialized venue, such as Federal Business Opportunities at *www.fbo.gov*. Like RFPs, IFBs usually have specific format requirements; proposals that do not follow the required format can be rejected without review.

Unsolicited Proposals. Unsolicited proposals are those submitted to a company without a prior request for a proposal. Companies often operate for years with a problem they have never recognized (unnecessarily high maintenance costs, for example, or poor inventory-control methods). Many unsolicited proposals are preceded by a letter of inquiry that specifies the problem or unmet need to determine whether there is any potential interest. If you receive a positive response, you would conduct a detailed study of the prospective client's needs to determine whether you can be of help and, if so, exactly how. You would then prepare a formal proposal on the basis of your study.

Sales Proposals. The sales proposal, a major marketing tool for business and industry, is a company's offer to provide specific goods or services to a potential buyer within a specified period of time and for a specified price. The primary purpose of a sales proposal is to demonstrate that the prospective customer's purchase of the seller's products or services will solve a problem, improve operations, or offer other benefits.

Sales proposals vary greatly in length and sophistication. Some are a page or two written by one person; others are many pages written collaboratively by several people; and still others are hundreds of pages written by a proposal-writing team. Many sales proposals note that the offer is valid for a limited period (often 90 days). See also **collaborative writing**.

❖ ETHICS NOTE Once submitted, a sales proposal is a legally binding document that promises to offer goods or services within a specified time and for a specified price. ❖

Simple sales proposals typically follow the introduction-body-conclusion pattern. Long sales proposals must accommodate a greater variety of information and are organized to include some or all of the following sections specified in the RFP:

• Cover, or transmittal, letter	• Training requirements
• Title page	• Statement of responsibilities
• Executive or project summary	• Description of vendor
• General description of products	• Organizational sales pitch
• Detailed solution or rationale	(optional)
• Cost analysis	• Conclusion (optional)
• Delivery schedule or work plan	• Appendixes (optional)
• Site-preparation description	

A long sales proposal begins with a cover letter that expresses your appreciation for the opportunity to submit your proposal and for any assistance you may have received in studying the customer's requirements. The letter should acknowledge any previous positive association with the customer. Then it should summarize the recommendations offered in the proposal and express your confidence that they will satisfy the customer's needs. Transmittal letters often list the physical documents attached or enclosed to help readers keep the associated documents together.

A title page and an **executive summary**—sometimes called a *project summary*—follow the cover letter. The title page contains the title of the proposal, the date of submission, the company to which it is being submitted, your company's name, and any symbol or logo that identifies your company. The executive summary is addressed to the decision-maker who will ultimately accept or reject the proposal and should summarize in nontechnical language how you plan to approach the work.

If your proposal offers products as well as services, it should include a general description of the products. In many cases, product descriptions will already exist as company boilerplate; be sure to check your company's files or server for such information before drafting a description from scratch.

❖ ETHICS NOTE In the workplace, employees often borrow material freely from in-house manuals, reports, and other company documents. Using such "boilerplate" is neither **plagiarism** nor a violation of **copyright**. See also **repurposing**. ❖

Following the executive summary and general description of products, explain exactly how you plan to do what you are proposing. This section, called the *detailed solution* or *rationale*, will be read by specialists who can understand and evaluate your plan. It usually begins with a statement of the customer's problem, follows with a statement of the solution, and concludes with a statement of the benefits to the customer. In some proposals, the headings "Problem" and "Solution" are used for this section.

A cost analysis itemizes the estimated cost of all the products and services that you are offering; the delivery schedule—also called a *work plan*—commits you to a specific timetable for providing those products and services.

If your recommendations include modifying your customer's physical facilities by moving walls, adding increased electrical capacity, and the like, include a site-preparation description that details the modifications required. In some proposals, the headings "Facilities" and "Equipment" are used for this section.

If the products and services you are proposing require training the customer's employees, specify the required training and its cost.

To prevent misunderstandings about what your and the customer's responsibilities will be, draw up a statement of responsibilities that explains in detail the tasks solely your responsibility and those solely the customer's responsibility. Toward the end of the proposal include a description-of-vendor section, which gives a profile of your company, its history, and its present position in the industry. The description-of-vendor section typically includes a list of people or subcontractors and

P

the duties they will perform. The **résumés** of key personnel may also be placed here or in an appendix.

An organizational sales pitch usually follows the description-of-vendor section and is designed to sell the company and its general capability in the field. The sales pitch promotes the company and concludes the proposal on an upbeat note.

Some long sales proposals include a **conclusions** section that summarizes the proposal's salient points, stresses your company's strengths, and includes information about whom the potential client can contact for further information. It may also end with a request for the date the work will begin should the proposal be accepted.

Some proposals include **appendixes** made up of statistical analyses, maps, charts, tables, and résumés of the principal staff assigned to the project. Appendixes to proposals should contain only supplemental information; the primary information should appear in the body of the proposal.

Figure P–10 shows sections from a major sales proposal (shown in full at the following Web link).

WEB LINK	Sample Sales Proposal
For a complete annotated version of Figure P–10, as well as additional sample proposals and the RFP to which Figure P–10 responded, see *bedfordstmartins.com/alred* and select *Links for Handbook Entries* or *Model Documents Gallery*.	

P

The Waters Corporation
17 North Waterloo Blvd.
Tampa, Florida 33607
Phone: (813) 919-1213   Fax: (813) 919-4411
www.waters.com

September 10, 2012

Mr. John Yeung, General Manager
Cookson's Retail Stores, Inc.
101 Longuer Street
Savannah, Georgia 31499

Dear Mr. Yeung:

The Waters Corporation appreciates the opportunity to respond to
Cookson's Request for Proposals dated July 20, 2012. We would
like to thank Mr. Becklight, Director of your Management Information Systems Department, for his invaluable contributions to the
study of your operations that we conducted before preparing our
proposal.

It has been Waters's privilege to provide Cookson's with retail
systems and equipment since your first store opened many years
ago. Therefore, we have become very familiar with your requirements as they have evolved during the expansion you have
experienced since that time. Waters's close working relationship
with Cookson's has resulted in a clear understanding of Cookson's
philosophy and needs.

Our proposal describes a Waters Interactive Terminal / Retail Processor System designed to meet Cookson's network and processing needs. It will provide all of your required capabilities, from
the point-of-sale operational requirements at the store terminals to
the host processor. The system uses the proven Retail III modular
software, with its point-of-sale applications, and the superior
Interactive Terminal, with its advanced capabilities and design.
This system is easily installed without extensive customer
reprogramming.

P

FIGURE P–10. Sales Proposal (*continued*) (Cover Letter)

Mr. J. Yeung
Page 2
September 10, 2012

The Waters Interactive Terminal / Retail Processor System, which is compatible with much of Cookson's present equipment, not only will meet your present requirements but will provide the flexibility to add new features and products in the future. The system's unique hardware modularity, efficient microprocessor design, and flexible programming capability greatly reduce the risk of obsolescence.

Thank you for the opportunity to present this proposal. You may be sure that we will use all the resources available to the Waters Corporation to ensure the successful implementation of the new system.

Sincerely yours,

Janet A. Curtain

Janet A. Curtain
Executive Account Manager
General Merchandise Systems
(jcurtain@waters.com)

Enclosure: Proposal

FIGURE P–10. Sales Proposal (*continued*) (Cover Letter)

The Waters Proposal   September 10, 2012

EXECUTIVE SUMMARY

The Waters 319 Interactive Terminal / 615 Retail Processor System will provide your management with the tools necessary to manage people and equipment more profitably with procedures that will yield more cost-effective business controls for Cookson's.

The equipment and applications proposed for Cookson's were selected through the combined effort of Waters and Cookson's Management Information Systems Director, Mr. Becklight. The architecture of the system will respond to your current requirements and allow for future expansion.

The features and hardware in the system were determined from data acquired through the comprehensive survey we conducted at your stores in July of this year. The total of 71 Interactive Terminals proposed to service your four store locations is based on the number of terminals currently in use and on the average number of transactions processed during normal and peak periods. The planned remodeling of all four stores was also considered, and the suggested terminal placement has been incorporated into the working floor plan. The proposed equipment configuration and software applications have been simulated to determine system performance based on the volumes and anticipated growth rates of the Cookson's stores.

The information from the survey was also used in the cost justification, which was checked and verified by your controller, Mr. Deitering. The cost-effectiveness of the Waters Interactive Terminal / Retail Processor System is apparent. Expected savings, such as the projected 46 percent reduction in sales audit expenses, are realistic projections based on Waters's experience with other installations of this type.

Waters has a proven track record of success in the manufacture, installation, and servicing of retail business information systems stretching over decades. We believe that the system we propose will extend and strengthen our successful and long-term partnership with Cookson's.

– 1 –

FIGURE P–10. Sales Proposal (*continued*) (Executive Summary)

GENERAL SYSTEM DESCRIPTION

The point-of-sale system that Waters is proposing for Cookson's includes two primary Waters products. These are the 319 Interactive
Terminal and the 615 Retail Processor.

Waters 319 Interactive Terminal
The primary component in the proposed retail system is the Interactive
Terminal. It contains a full microprocessor, which gives it the flexibility
that Cookson's has been looking for.

The 319 Interactive Terminal provides you with freedom in sequencing
a transaction. You are not limited to a preset list of available steps or
transactions. The terminal program can be adapted to provide unique
transaction sets, each designed with a logical sequence of entry and processing to accomplish required tasks. In addition to sales transactions recorded on the selling floor, specialized transactions such as theater-ticket
sales and payments can be designed for your customer-service area.

The 319 Interactive Terminal also functions as a credit authorization
device, either by using its own floor limits or by transmitting a credit
inquiry to the 615 Retail Processor for authorization.

Data-collection formats have been simplified so that transaction editing
and formatting are much more easily accomplished. The IS manager
has already been provided with documentation on these formats and has
outlined all data processing efforts that will be necessary to transmit the
data to your current systems. These projections have been considered
in the cost justification.

Waters 615 Retail Processor
The Waters 615 Retail Processor is a minicomputer system designed
to support the Waters family of retail terminals. The . . .

[*The proposal next describes the Waters 615 Retail Processor before
moving on to the detailed-solution section.*]

FIGURE P–10. Sales Proposal (*continued*) (General Description of Products)

PAYROLL APPLICATION

Current Procedure

Your current system of reporting time requires each hourly employee to sign a time sheet; the time sheet is reviewed by the department manager and sent to the Payroll Department on Friday evening. Because the week ends on Saturday, the employee must show the scheduled hours for Saturday and not the actual hours; therefore, the department manager must adjust the reported hours on the time sheet for employees who do not report on the scheduled Saturday or who do not work the number of hours scheduled.

The Payroll Department employs a supervisor and three full-time clerks. To meet deadlines caused by an unbalanced workflow, an additional part-time clerk is used for 20 to 30 hours per week. The average wage for this clerk is $13.00 per hour.

Advantage of Waters's System

The 319 Interactive Terminal can be programmed for entry of payroll data for each employee on Monday morning by department managers, with the data reflecting actual hours worked. This system would eliminate the need for manual batching, controlling, and data input. The Payroll Department estimates conservatively that this work consumes 40 hours per week.

Hours per week	40
Average wage (part-time clerk)	× 13.00
Weekly payroll cost	$520.00
Annual savings	$27,040

Elimination of the manual tasks of tabulating, batching, and controlling can save 0.25 hourly unit. Improved workflow resulting from timely data in the system without data-input processing will allow more efficient use of clerical hours. This would reduce payroll by the 0.50 hourly unit currently required to meet weekly check disbursement.

Eliminate manual tasks	0.25
Improve workflow	0.75
40-hour unit reduction	1.00
Hours per week	40
Average wage (full-time clerk)	15.00
Savings per week	$600.00
Annual savings	$31,200

TOTAL SAVINGS: $58,240

FIGURE P–10. Sales Proposal (*continued*) (Detailed Solution)

COST ANALYSIS

This section of our proposal provides detailed cost information for the Waters 319 Interactive Terminal and the Waters 615 Retail Processor. It then multiplies these major elements by the quantities required at each of your four locations.

319 Interactive Terminal

Equipment	Price	Maint. (1 yr.)
Terminal	$2,895	$167
Journal Printer	425	38
Receipt Printer	425	38
Forms Printer	525	38
Software	220	—
TOTALS	$4,490	$281

[*The cost section goes on to describe other costs to install the system before summarizing the costs.*]

The following table summarizes all costs.

Location	Hardware	Maint. (1 yr.)	Software
Store No. 1	$72,190	$4,975	$3,520
Store No. 2	89,190	6,099	4,400
Store No. 3	76,380	5,256	3,740
Store No. 4	80,650	5,537	3,960
Data Center	63,360	6,679	12,480
Subtotals	$381,770	$28,546	$28,100

TOTAL $438,416

DELIVERY SCHEDULE

Waters is normally able to deliver 319 Interactive Terminals and 615 Retail Processors within 30 days of the date of the contract. This can vary depending on the rate and size of incoming orders.

All the software recommended in this proposal is available for immediate delivery. We do not anticipate any difficulty in meeting your tentative delivery schedule.

FIGURE P–10. Sales Proposal (*continued*) (Cost Analysis and Delivery Schedule)

SITE PREPARATION

Waters will work closely with Cookson's to ensure that each site is properly prepared prior to system installation. You will receive a copy of Waters's installation and wiring procedures manual, which lists the physical dimensions, service clearance, and weight of the system components in addition to the power, logic, communications-cable, and environmental requirements. Cookson's is responsible for all building alterations and electrical facility changes, including the purchase and installation of communications cables, connecting blocks, and receptacles.

Wiring
For the purpose of future site considerations, Waters's in-house wiring specifications for the system call for two twisted-pair wires and twenty-two shielded gauges. The length of communications wires must not exceed 2,500 feet.

As a guide for the power supply, we suggest that Cookson's consider the following:

1. The branch circuit (limited to 20 amps) should service no equipment other than 319 Interactive Terminals.
2. Each 20-amp branch circuit should support a maximum of three Interactive Terminals.
3. Each branch circuit must have three equal-size conductors — one hot leg, one neutral, and one insulated isolated ground.
4. Hubbell IG 5362 duplex outlets or the equivalent should be used to supply power to each terminal.
5. Server-room wiring will have to be upgraded to support the 615 Retail Processor.

P

FIGURE P–10. Sales Proposal (*continued*) (Site Preparation Section)

TRAINING

To ensure a successful installation, Waters offers the following training course for your operators.

Interactive Terminal / Retail Processor Operations
Course number: 8256
Length: three days
Tuition: $500.00

This course provides the student with the skills, knowledge, and practice required to operate an Interactive Terminal / Retail Processor System. Online, clustered, and stand-alone environments are covered.

We recommend that students have a department-store background and that they have some knowledge of the system configuration with which they will be working.

P

FIGURE P–10. Sales Proposal (*continued*) (Training Section)

The Waters Proposal   September 10, 2012

RESPONSIBILITIES

On the basis of its years of experience in installing information-processing systems, Waters believes that a successful installation requires a clear understanding of certain responsibilities.

Waters's Responsibilities
Generally, it is Waters's responsibility to provide its users with needed assistance during the installation so that live processing can begin as soon thereafter as is practical. The following items describe our specific responsibilities:

- Provide operations documentation for each application that you acquire from Waters.
- Provide forms and other supplies as ordered.
- Provide specifications and technical guidance for proper site planning and installation.
- Provide adviser assistance in the conversion from your present system to the new system.

Cookson's Responsibilities
Cookson's will be responsible for the suggested improvements described earlier, as well as the following:

- Identify an installation coordinator and system operator.
- Provide supervisors and clerical personnel to perform conversion to the system.
- Establish reasonable time schedules for implementation.
- Ensure that the physical site requirements are met.
- Provide personnel to be trained as operators and ensure that other employees are trained as necessary.
- Assume the responsibility for implementing and operating the system.

P

– 11 –

FIGURE P–10. Sales Proposal (*continued*) (Statement of Responsibilities)

DESCRIPTION OF VENDOR

The Waters Corporation develops, manufactures, markets, installs, and services total business information-processing systems for selected markets. These markets are primarily in the retail, financial, commercial, industrial, health-care, education, and government sectors.

The Waters total-system concept encompasses one of the broadest hardware and software product lines in the industry. Waters computers range from small business systems to powerful general-purpose processors. Waters computers are supported by a complete spectrum of terminals, peripherals, and data-communication networks, as well as an extensive library of software products. Supplemental services and products include data centers, field service, systems engineering, and educational centers.

The Waters Corporation was founded in 1934 and presently has approximately 26,500 employees. The Waters headquarters is located at 17 North Waterloo Boulevard, Tampa, Florida, with district offices throughout the United States and Canada.

WHY WATERS?

Strong Commitment to the Retail Industry
Waters's commitment to the retail industry is stronger than ever. We are continually striving to provide leadership in the design and implementation of new retail systems and applications that will ensure our users of a logical growth pattern.

Dynamic Research and Development
Over the years, Waters has spent increasingly large sums on research-and-development efforts to ensure the availability of products and systems for the future. In 2011, our research-and-development expenditure for advanced systems design and technological innovations reached the $70-million level.

Leading Point-of-Sale Vendor
Waters is a leading point-of-sale vendor, having installed over 150,000 units. The knowledge and experience that Waters has gained over the years from these installations ensure well-coordinated and effective systems implementations.

FIGURE P–10. Sales Proposal (*continued*) (Vendor Description and Organizational Sales Pitch)

The Waters Proposal   September 10, 2012

CONCLUSION

Waters welcomes the opportunity to submit this proposal to Cookson's. The Waters Corporation is confident that we have offered the right solution at a competitive price. Based on the hands-on analysis we conducted, our proposal takes into account your current and projected workloads and your plans to expand your facilities and operations. Our proposal will also, we believe, enable Cookson's to minimize future employee costs and to enhance its accounting features.

Waters has a proven track record of success in the manufacture, installation, and servicing of retail business information systems stretching over many decades. We also have a demonstrated record of success in our past business associations with Cookson's. We believe that the system we propose will extend and strengthen this partnership.

Should you require additional information about any facet of this proposal, please contact Janet A. Curtain, who will meet with you or arrange for Waters's technical staff to meet with you or send you the information you need.

We look forward to your decision and to continued success in our working relationship with Cookson's.

P

FIGURE P–10. Sales Proposal (*continued*) (Conclusion)

pseudo- / quasi-

As a **prefix,** *pseudo-*, meaning "false or counterfeit," is joined to the root word without a **hyphen** unless the root word begins with a capital letter (*pseudo*science, *pseudo*-Keynesian). *Pseudo-* is sometimes confused with *quasi-*, meaning "somewhat" or "partial." Unlike *semi-*, *quasi-* means "resembling something" rather than "half." *Quasi-* is usually hyphenated in combinations (*quasi*-marketing initiatives). See also **bi- / semi-.**

punctuation

Punctuation helps **readers** understand the meaning and relationships of words, phrases, clauses, and sentences. Marks of punctuation link, separate, enclose, indicate omissions, terminate, and classify. Most punctuation marks can perform more than one function. See also **sentence construction.**

The use of punctuation is determined by grammatical conventions and the writer's intention. Understanding punctuation is essential for writers because it enables them to communicate with **clarity** and precision. See also **grammar.**

Detailed information on each mark of punctuation is given in its own entry. The following are the 13 marks of punctuation.

apostrophe	'	parentheses	( )
brackets	[ ]	period	.
colon	:	question mark	?
comma	,	quotation marks	" "
dash	—	semicolon	;
exclamation mark	!	slash	/
hyphen	-		

See also **abbreviations, capitalization, contractions, dates, ellipses, italics,** and **numbers.**

WEB LINK	Practicing Punctuation
For online exercises on punctuation, see *bedfordstmartins.com/alred* and select *Exercise Central*.	

purpose

What do you want your **readers** to know, to believe, or to do when they have read your document? When you answer that question about your **audience**, you have determined the primary purpose, or objective, of your document. Be careful not to state a purpose too broadly. A statement of purpose such as "to explain continuing-education standards" is too general to be helpful during the writing process. In contrast, "to explain to members of the American Association of Critical-Care Nurses how to determine if a continuing-education course meets the association's professional standards" is a specific purpose that will help you focus on what you need your document to accomplish. Often the **context** will help you focus your purpose.

The writer's primary purpose is often more complex than simply "to explain" something, as shown in the previous paragraph. To fully understand this complexity, you need to ask yourself not only *why* you are writing the document but *what* you want to influence your reader to believe or to do after reading it. Suppose a writer for a **newsletter** has been assigned to write an article about cardiopulmonary resuscitation (CPR). In answer to the question *what?* the writer could state the purpose as "to emphasize the importance of CPR." To the question *why?* the writer might respond, "to encourage employees to sign up for evening CPR classes." Putting the answers to the two questions together, the writer's purpose might be stated as, "To write a document that will emphasize the importance of CPR and encourage employees to sign up for evening CPR classes." Note that the primary purpose of this document is to persuade the readers of the importance of CPR, and the secondary goal is to motivate them to register for a class. Secondary goals often involve such abstract notions as to motivate, to persuade, to reassure, or to inspire your reader. See also **persuasion**.

If you answer the questions *what?* and *why?* and put the answers into writing as a stated purpose that includes both primary and secondary goals, you will simplify your writing task and more likely achieve your purpose. For a **collaborative writing** project, it is especially important to collectively write a statement of your purpose to ensure that the document achieves its goals. Do not lose sight of that purpose as you become engrossed in the other steps of the writing process. See also "Five Steps to Successful Writing" on page xv.

Q

question marks

The question mark (?) most often ends a sentence that is a direct question or request.

► Where did you put the tax report? [direct question]

► Will you e-mail me if your shipment does not arrive by June 10? [request]

Use a question mark to end a statement that has an interrogative meaning—a statement that is declarative in form but asks a question.

► The tax report is finished? [question in declarative form]

Question marks may follow a series of separate items within an interrogative sentence.

► Do you remember the date of the contract? Its terms? Whether you signed it?

Use a question mark to end an interrogative clause within a declarative sentence.

► It was not until July (or was it August?) that we submitted the report.

Retain the question mark in a title that is being cited, even though the sentence in which it appears has not ended.

► *Can Investments Be Protected?* is the title of her book.

Never use a question mark to end a sentence that is an indirect question.

► He asked me where I put the tax report.

When a question is a polite request or an instruction to which an affirmative response is assumed, a question mark is not necessary.

► Will you call me as soon as he arrives. [polite request]

When used with **quotations**, the placement of the question mark is important. When the writer is asking a question, the question mark belongs outside the **quotation marks**.

▶ Did she actually say, "I don't think the project should continue"?

If the quotation itself is a question, the question mark goes inside the quotation marks.

▶ She asked, "Do we have enough funding?"

If both cases apply—the writer is asking a question and the quotation itself is a question—use a single question mark inside the quotation marks.

▶ Did she ask, "Do we have enough funding?"

questionnaires

A questionnaire—a series of questions on a particular topic sent to a number of people—serves the same function as an interview but does so on paper, as an **e-mail** attachment, or as an online form. As you prepare a questionnaire, therefore, keep in mind your **purpose** and your intended **audience**. See also **interviewing for information** and **research**.

Questionnaires have several advantages over the personal interview as well as several disadvantages.

ADVANTAGES

- A questionnaire allows you to gather information from more people than you could by conducting personal interviews.
- A questionnaire enables you to obtain responses from people who are difficult to reach or who are in various geographic locations.
- When responding to a questionnaire, people have more time to think through their answers than when faced with the pressure of composing thoughtful and complete answers to an interviewer in person.
- The questionnaire may yield more objective data than an interview because it reduces the possibility that the interviewer's tone of voice, facial expressions, or mere presence might influence an answer.
- The cost of distributing and tabulating a questionnaire is lower than the cost of conducting numerous personal interviews.

Q

DISADVANTAGES

- The results of a questionnaire may be slanted in favor of those people who have strong opinions on a subject because they are more likely to respond than those with only moderate views.

- The questionnaire does not allow specific follow-up questions to answers; at best, it can be designed to let one question lead logically to another.

- Distributing questionnaires and waiting for replies may take considerably longer than conducting personal interviews.

The sample cover memo and questionnaire in Figure Q–1 were sent to employees in a large organization who had participated in a six-month program of flexible working hours.

Selecting the Recipients

Selecting the proper recipients for your questionnaire is crucial if you are to gather representative and usable data. If you wanted to survey the opinions of large groups in the general population—for example, all medical technologists working in private laboratories or all independent garage owners—your task would not be easy. Because you cannot include everybody in your survey, you need to choose a representative cross section. Depending on the topic, you may need to include people from different geographic areas, members of both genders, and people with different educational backgrounds. Only by using a representative sample of your target population can you make a generalized statement based on your findings from the sample. (The best sources of information on sampling techniques are market-research and statistics texts.)

WEB LINK	Online Surveys

Surveymonkey.com offers help for designing online surveys as well as for collecting and analyzing the results. For links to this site and more, see *bedfordstmartins.com/alred* and select *Links for Handbook Entries*.

Preparing the Questions

A key goal in designing the questionnaire is to keep it as brief as possible. The longer a questionnaire is, the less likely the recipient will be to complete and return it. Also, the questions should be easy to understand. A confusing question will yield confusing results, whereas a carefully worded question will be easy to answer. Ideally, recipients should be able to answer most questions with a "yes" or "no" or by checking or circling a choice among several options. Such answers are easy

Luxwear Products Corporation
MEMO

To: All Company Employees

From: Nelson Barrett, Director   *NB*
           Human Resources Department

Date: October 19, 2012

Subject: Review of Flexible Working Hours Program

Please complete and return the questionnaire enclosed regarding Luxwear's trial program of flexible working hours. Your answers will help us decide whether we should make the program permanent.

Return the completed questionnaire to Ken Rose, Mail Code 12B, by October 29. Your signature on the questionnaire is not necessary. All responses will be confidential and given serious consideration. Feel free to raise additional issues pertaining to the program.

If you want to discuss any item in the questionnaire, call Pam Peters in the Human Resources Department at extension 8812 or e-mail her at pp1@lpc.com.

Enclosure: Questionnaire

Q

FIGURE Q–1. Questionnaire (*continued*) (Printed Cover Memo)

Flexible Working Hours Program
Questionnaire

1. What is your job category?

    ☐ Supervisory
    ☐ Nonsupervisory

2. Indicate to the nearest quarter of an hour your starting time under flextime.

    ☐ 7:00 a.m.   ☐ 8:15 a.m.
    ☐ 7:15 a.m.   ☐ 8:30 a.m.
    ☐ 7:30 a.m.   ☐ 8:45 a.m.
    ☐ 7:45 a.m.   ☐ 9:00 a.m.
    ☐ 8:00 a.m.   ☐ Other (specify) _____

3. Where do you live?

    ☐ Talbot County   ☐ Greene County
    ☐ Montgomery County   ☐ Other (specify) _____

4. How do you usually travel to work?

    ☐ Drive alone   ☐ Walk
    ☐ Bus   ☐ Car pool
    ☐ Train   ☐ Motorcycle
    ☐ Bicycle   ☐ Other (specify) _____

5. Has flextime affected your commuting time?

    ☐ Increase: Approximate number of minutes _____
    ☐ Decrease: Approximate number of minutes _____
    ☐ No change

6. If you drive alone or in a car pool, has flextime increased or decreased the amount of time it takes you to find a parking space?

    ☐ Increased   ☐ Decreased   ☐ No change

7. Has flextime had an effect on your productivity?

    a. Quality of work
        ☐ Increased   ☐ Decreased   ☐ No change

    b. Accuracy of work
        ☐ Increased   ☐ Decreased   ☐ No change

    c. Quiet time for uninterrupted work
        ☐ Increased   ☐ Decreased   ☐ No change

FIGURE Q–1. Questionnaire (*continued*)

8. Have you had difficulty getting in touch with coworkers who are on different work schedules from yours?

☐ Yes   ☐ No

9. Have you had trouble scheduling meetings within flexible starting and quitting times?

☐ Yes   ☐ No

10. Has flextime affected the way you feel about your job?

☐ Yes   ☐ No

If yes, please answer (a) or (b):

a. Feel better about job
   ☐ Slightly   ☐ Considerably

b. Feel worse about job
   ☐ Slightly   ☐ Considerably

11. How important is it for you to have flexibility in your working hours?

☐ Very   ☐ Somewhat   ☐ Not at all

12. Has flextime allowed you more time to be with your family?

☐ Yes   ☐ No

13. If you are responsible for the care of a young child or children, has flextime made it easier or more difficult for you to obtain babysitting or day-care services?

☐ Easier   ☐ More difficult   ☐ No change

14. Do you recommend that the flextime program be made permanent?

☐ Yes   ☐ No

15. Please describe below or on an attached sheet any major changes you recommend for the program.

Thank you for your assistance.

FIGURE Q–1. Questionnaire (*continued*)

to tabulate and require minimum effort on the part of the respondent, thus increasing your chances of obtaining a response. See also **forms**.

► Do you recommend that the flextime program be made permanent?

☐ Yes   ☐ No   ☐ No opinion

If you need more information than such questions produce, provide an appropriate range of answers, as in the following example:

► How many hours of overtime would you be willing to work each week?

☐ 4 hours   ☐ 8 hours   ☐ More than 10 hours

☐ 6 hours   ☐ 10 hours   ☐ No overtime

❖ ETHICS NOTE Questions should be neutral; they should not be worded in such a way as to lead respondents to give a particular answer, which can result in inaccurate or skewed data.

SLANTED   Would you prefer the freedom of a four-day workweek?

NEUTRAL   Would you choose to work a four-day workweek, ten hours a day, with every Friday off? ❖

WRITER'S CHECKLIST   Designing a Questionnaire

✔ Prepare a **cover letter** (or a memo or an e-mail) explaining who you are, the questionnaire's purpose, the date by which you need a response, and how and where to send the completed questionnaire.

✔ Include a stamped, self-addressed envelope if you are using regular mail.

✔ Construct as many questions as possible for which the recipient does not have to compose an answer.

✔ Include a section on the questionnaire for additional comments where the recipient may clarify his or her overall attitude toward the subject.

✔ Include questions about the respondent's age, gender, education, occupation, and so on, only if such information will be of value in interpreting the answers.

✔ State whether the information provided as well as the recipient's identity will be kept confidential.

Designing a Questionnaire (*continued*)

✔ Include your contact information (mailing address, phone number, and e-mail address) and be sure to thank respondents for participating.

✔ Consider offering some tangible appreciation to those who answer the questionnaire by a specific date, such as a copy of the results or, for a customer questionnaire, a credit toward a future purchase.

quid pro quo

Quid pro quo, which is Latin for "one thing for another," suggests mutual cooperation or "tit for tat" in a relationship between two groups or individuals. The term may be appropriate to business and legal contexts if you are sure your **readers** understand its meaning. ("Before approving the plan, we insisted on a fair *quid pro quo*.") See also **foreign words in English**.

quotation marks

Quotation marks (" ") are used to enclose a direct quotation of spoken or written words. Quotation marks have other special uses, but they should not be used for **emphasis**.

Direct Quotations

Enclose in quotation marks anything that is quoted word for word (a direct quotation) from speech or written material.

▶ She said clearly, "I want the progress report by three o'clock."

Do not enclose indirect quotations—usually introduced by the word *that*—in quotation marks. Indirect quotations are paraphrases of a writer's or speaker's words or ideas. See also **paraphrasing**.

▶ She said that she wanted the progress report by three o'clock.

❖ ETHICS NOTE When you use quotation marks to indicate that you are quoting, do not make any changes or omissions inside the quoted material unless you clearly indicate what you have done. For further information on incorporating quoted material and inserting comments, see **plagiarism** and **quotations**. ❖

Use single quotation marks (' ') to enclose a quotation that appears within a quotation.

▶ John said, "Jane told me that she was going to 'stay with the project if it takes all year.'"

Words and Phrases

Use quotation marks to set off special words or terms only to point out that the term is used in context for a unique or special purpose (that is, in the sense of the term *so-called*).

▶ A remarkable chain of events caused the sinking of the "unsinkable" *Titanic* on its maiden voyage.

Slang, colloquial expressions, and attempts at humor, although infrequent in workplace writing, should seldom be set off by quotation marks.

▶ Our first six months amounted to a "shakedown cruise." *shakedown cruise.*

Titles of Works

Use quotation marks to enclose **titles** of reports, short stories, articles, essays, single episodes of radio and television programs, and short musical works (including songs). However, do not use quotation marks for titles of books and periodicals, which should appear in **italics**.

▶ His report, "Effects of Government Regulations on Motorcycle Safety," cited the article "No-Fault Insurance and Motorcycles," published in *American Motorcyclist* magazine.

Use quotation marks for parts of publications, such as chapters of books and articles or sections within periodicals.

▶ "Bad Writing," an article by Barbara Wallraff, appeared in the "On Language" column of the *New York Times*.

Some titles, by convention, are not set off by quotation marks, underlining, or italics, although they are capitalized.

▶ Professional Writing [college course title], the Bible, the Constitution, Lincoln's Gettysburg Address, the Lands' End Catalog

Punctuation

Commas and **periods** always go inside closing quotation marks.

▶ "Reading *Computer World* gives me the insider's view," he says, adding, "It's like a conversation with the top experts."

Semicolons and colons always go outside closing quotation marks.

▶ He said, "I will pay the full amount"; this statement surprised us.

All other punctuation follows the logic of the context: If the punctuation is part of the material quoted, it goes inside the quotation marks; if the punctuation is not part of the material quoted, it goes outside the quotation marks.

quotations

Using direct and indirect quotations is an effective way to make or support a point. However, avoid the temptation to overquote during the note-taking phase of your research; concentrate on summarizing what you read.

❖ ETHICS NOTE When you use a quotation (or an idea of another writer), cite your source properly. If you do not, you will be guilty of plagiarism. For specific details on citation systems, see documenting sources. ❖

Direct Quotations

A direct quotation is a word-for-word copy of the text of an original source. Choose direct quotations (which can be of a word, a phrase, a sentence, or, occasionally, a paragraph) carefully and use them sparingly. Enclose direct quotations in quotation marks and separate them from the rest of the sentence by a comma or colon. Use the initial capital letter of a quotation if the quoted material originally began with a capital letter.

▶ The economist stated, "Regulation cannot supply the dynamic stimulus that in other industries is supplied by competition."

When dividing a quotation, set off the material that interrupts the quotation with commas, and use quotation marks around each part of the quotation.

▶ "Regulation," the economist said in a recent interview, "cannot supply the dynamic stimulus that in other industries is supplied by competition."

Indirect Quotations

An indirect quotation is a paraphrased version of an original text. It is usually introduced by the word *that* and is not set off from the rest of the sentence by punctuation marks. See also paraphrasing.

Q

▶ In a recent interview, he said *that* regulation does not stimulate the industry as well as competition does.

Deletions or Omissions

Deletions or omissions from quoted material are indicated by three **ellipsis** points (. . .) within a sentence and a period plus three ellipsis points (. . . .) at the end of a sentence.

ORIGINAL	"Their touchstones, which to an outsider might appear as arbitrary and simplistic, were developed through highly specific research using both internal and outside expertise, distilled from a complex historical process of examining rhetorical variables, and documented as operational guidelines rather than narratives of processes or of theoretical models."
WITH ELLIPSES	"Their touchstones . . . were developed through highly specific research using both internal and outside expertise, distilled from a complex historical process of examining rhetorical variables, and documented as operational guidelines. . . ."

When a quoted passage begins in the middle of a sentence rather than at the beginning, ellipsis points are not necessary; the fact that the first letter of the quoted material is not capitalized tells the reader that the quotation begins in midsentence.

▶ Rivero goes on to conclude that "coordination may lessen competition within a region."

Inserting Material into Quotations

When it is necessary to insert a clarifying comment within quoted material, use **brackets**.

▶ "The industry is an integrated system that serves an extensive [geographic] area, with divisions existing as islands within the larger system's sphere of influence."

When quoted material contains an obvious error or might be questioned in some other way, insert the expression *sic* (Latin for "thus") in italic type and enclose it in brackets ([*sic*]) following the questionable material to indicate that the writer has quoted the material *exactly as it appeared in the original.*

▶ The company considers the Baker Foundation to be a "guilt-edged [*sic*] investment."

Incorporating Quotations into Text

Quote word for word only when a source with particular expertise states something that is especially precise, striking, or noteworthy, or that may reinforce a point you are making. Quotations must also logically, grammatically, and syntactically match the rest of the sentence and surrounding text. Notice in Figure Q–2 that the quotation blends with the content of the surrounding text, which uses **transition** to introduce and comment on the quotation.

Depending on the citation system, the style of incorporating quotations varies. For examples of three different styles, see **documenting sources**. Figure Q–2 shows APA style for a long quotation. At the end of the document, the following entry would appear in the APA-style list of references as the source of the quotation in Figure Q–2.

▶ Alred, G. J. (2006). Bridging cultures: The academy and the workplace. *Journal of Business Communication, 43,* 79–88.

Do not rely too heavily on the use of quotations in the final version of your document. Generally, avoid quoting anything that is longer than one paragraph.

According to Alred (2006), academics and workplace professionals might not value the same book or article because they do not share the same goals:

> Generally, the goals of workplace professionals demand that they think in specific, practical, and immediately applicable ways; those of us in the academy must think in terms that are more abstract, conceptual, and long-term. It is understandable, then, that works that might be highly valued by either practitioners or academics can seem entirely irrelevant to the other. (p. 82)

The works that seem irrelevant to practitioners, then, often do not give practical advice on accomplishing tasks. However, academics often find . . .

Q

FIGURE Q–2. Long Quotation (APA Style)

R

raise / rise

Both *raise* and *rise* mean "move to a higher position." However, *raise* is a transitive **verb** and always takes an **object** ("*raise* crops"), whereas *rise* is an intransitive verb and never takes an object ("heat *rises*").

readers

The first rule of effective writing is to *help your readers*. If you overlook this commitment, your writing will not achieve its **purpose**, either for you or for your business or organization. For meeting the needs of both individual and multiple readers, see **audience**.

really

Really is an **adverb** meaning "actually" or "in fact." Although both *really* and *actually* are often used as **intensifiers** for **emphasis** or sarcasm in speech, avoid such use in formal and professional writing.

► Did he ~~really~~ finish the report on time?

reason is [because]

Replace the redundant phrase *the reason is because* with *the reason is that* or simply *because*. See also **conciseness**.

reference letters

Writing a reference letter (or letter of recommendation) can range from completing an admission form for a prospective student to composing

CITY OF SPRINGFIELD
LEGISLATIVE REFERENCE BUREAU
200 EAST MAIN STREET
SPRINGFIELD, AK 99501
(414) 224-5555

January 12, 2012

Mr. Phillip Lester
Human Resources Director
Thompson Enterprises
201 State Street
St. Louis, MO 63102

Dear Mr. Lester:

How long writer has known applicant and the circumstances	As Kerry Hawkin's former employer, I am happy to have the opportunity to recommend her. I've known Kerry for five years, first as an intern in our office and for two years as a full-time research associate. This past year she has remained in contact as she completed graduate school.
	Our office is the official research arm for the Springfield City Council, so we approved Kerry as an intern not only because of her outstanding grades but also because the university internship coordinator reported that she possessed excellent re-
Outstanding characteristics of applicant	search skills. Kerry proved her worth in our office as an intern and was offered a full-time position as a research associate to work on projects under my supervision. I found Kerry not only to be a careful researcher but also to be capable of completing her assignments on schedule within tight deadlines. The material provided in her well-written reports unfailingly met the requirements for my work and more. During her time in our office, Kerry also proved herself to be a most valued colleague.
Recommendation and summary of qualifications	I strongly recommend Kerry for her ability to work independently, to organize her time efficiently, and to write clearly and articulately. I regret that we have no position to offer her at this time. Please do not hesitate to let me know if I can provide further information.

Sincerely yours,

Michelle Paul

Michelle Paul, Manager
mpaul@springfield.ak.gov

FIGURE R–1. Reference Letter (Printed on Letterhead Stationery)

a detailed description of professional accomplishments and personal characteristics for someone seeking employment. In Figure R–1 on page 475, a former employer has written a letter for someone who is seeking an advanced position as a researcher.

To write an effective letter of recommendation, you must be familiar enough with the applicant's abilities and performance to offer an evaluation, and you must keep in mind the following:

- Identify yourself by name, title or position, employer, and address.
- Respond directly to the inquiry, carefully addressing the specific questions asked.
- Describe specifically the applicant's skills, abilities, knowledge, and character, guided by the person's **résumé** when possible.
- Communicate truthfully and without embellishment.

You could begin, as in Figure R–1, by stating the circumstances of your acquaintance and how long you have known the person for whom you are writing the letter. Mention, with as much evidence as possible, one or two outstanding characteristics of the applicant. Organize the details in your letter using the decreasing **order-of-importance method of development**. Conclude with a brief summary of the applicant's qualifications and a clear statement of recommendation. See **correspondence** for letter format and general advice.

❖ ETHICS NOTE When you are asked to serve as a reference or to supply a letter of reference, be aware that applicants have a legal right to examine what you have written about them, unless they sign a waiver. ❖

refusal letters

A refusal delivers a negative message (or bad news) in the form of a **letter**, a **memo**, or an **e-mail**. The ideal refusal says "no" in such a way that you not only avoid antagonizing your reader but also maintain goodwill. See also **audience**.

When the stakes are high, you must convince your reader *before* you present the bad news that your reasons for refusing are logical or understandable. (See also **correspondence**.) Stating a negative message in your opening may cause your reader to react too quickly and dismiss your explanation. The following pattern, used in the message shown in Figure R–2, is an effective way to handle this problem:

1. Open with **context** for the message (often called a "buffer").
2. Review the facts or details leading to the refusal or bad news.
3. Give the negative message based on the facts or details.
4. Close by establishing or reestablishing a positive relationship.

From: Nancy Nygaard <nn@bank21.com>
To: Marsha Coleman <mc2@ntr.com>
Sent: Monday, February 27, 2012 10:47 AM
Subject: NTR Check Sorter

Dear Ms. Coleman:

Context

Thank you for your cooperation and your patience with us as we struggled to reach a decision. We believe our long involvement with your company indicates our confidence in your products.

Review of facts

Based on our research, we found that the Winton Check Sorter has all the features that your sorter offers and, in fact, has two additional features that your sorter does not. The more important one is a backup feature that retains totals in its memory, even if the power fails. The second additional feature is stacked pockets, which are less space-consuming than the linear pockets on your sorter. After much deliberation, therefore, **Refusal** we have decided to purchase the Winton Check Sorter.

Goodwill close

Although we did not select your sorter, we were very favorably impressed with your system and your people. Perhaps we will be able to use other NTR products in the future.

Sincerely,

Nancy Nygaard

FIGURE R–2. Refusal Letter (Sent as E-mail)

Your opening should provide an appropriate context and establish a professional **tone,** for example by expressing appreciation for a reader's time, effort, or interest.

▶ The Screening Procedures Committee appreciates the time and effort you spent on your proposal for a new security-clearance procedure.

Next, review the circumstances of the situation sympathetically by placing yourself in the reader's position. Clearly detail the reasons you cannot do what the reader wants—even though you have not yet said you cannot do it. A good explanation should ideally detail the reasons for your refusal so thoroughly that the reader will accept the negative message as a logical conclusion, as shown in the following example.

▶ We reviewed the potential effects of implementing your proposed security-clearance procedure company-wide. We not only asked the Security Systems Department to review the data but also surveyed industry practices, sought the views of senior management, and submitted the idea to our legal staff. As a result of this process, we have reached the following conclusions:
   • The cost savings you project are correct only if the procedure could be required throughout the company.
   • The components of your procedure are legal, but most are not widely accepted by our industry.
   • Based on our survey, some components could alienate employees who would perceive them as violating an individual's rights.
   • Enforcing company-wide use would prove costly and impractical.

Do not belabor the negative message—state your refusal quickly, clearly, and as positively as possible.

▶ For those reasons, the committee recommends that divisions continue their current security-screening procedures.

Close your message in a way that reestablishes goodwill—do not repeat the bad news. (Avoid writing "Again, we are sorry we cannot use your idea.") Ideally, provide an alternative, as in the following:

▶ Because some components of your procedure may apply in certain circumstances, we would like to feature your ideas in the next issue of *The Guardian*. I have asked the editor to contact you next week. On behalf of the committee, thank you for the thoughtful proposal.

If such an option is not possible or reasonable, offer a friendly remark that anticipates a positive future relationship, assure the reader of your high opinion of his or her product or service, or merely wish the reader success.

For responding to a complaint, see **adjustment letters**. For refusing a job offer, see **acceptance / refusal letters**.

regarding / with regard to

In *regards to* and *with regards to* are incorrect **idioms** for *in regard to* and *with regard to*. Both *as regards* and *regarding* are acceptable variants.

> *regard*
> ► In ~~regards~~ to your last question, I think a meeting is a good idea.

> *Regarding*
> ► ~~With regards to~~ your last question, I think a meeting is a good idea.

regardless

Always use *regardless* instead of the nonstandard *irregardless*, which expresses a double negative. The prefix *ir-* renders the base word negative, but *regardless* is already negative, meaning "unmindful."

repetition

The deliberate use of repetition to build a sustained effect or to emphasize a feeling or an idea can be a powerful device. See also **emphasis**.

> ► Similarly, atoms *come and go* in a molecule, but the molecule *remains*; molecules *come and go* in a cell, but the cell *remains*; cells *come and go* in a body, but the body *remains*; persons *come and go* in an organization, but the organization *remains*.
> —Kenneth Boulding, *Beyond Economics*

Repetition of keywords from a previous sentence or paragraph can also be used effectively to achieve **transition**.

> ► For many years, *oil* has been a major industrial energy source. However, *oil* supplies are limited, and other sources of energy must be developed.

Be consistent in the word or phrase you use to refer to something. In business writing, it is generally better to repeat a word or use a clear **pronoun reference** (so readers know that you mean the same thing) than to use **synonyms** to avoid repetition. See also **affectation**.

SYNONYMS	Several recent *analyses* support our conclusion. These *studies* cast doubt on the feasibility of long-range forecasting. The *reports*, however, are strictly theoretical.
CONSISTENT TERMS	Several recent *studies* support our conclusion. These *studies* cast doubt on the feasibility of long-range forecasting. *They* are, however, strictly theoretical.

Purposeless repetition, however, makes a sentence awkward and hides its key ideas. See also **conciseness**.

▶ She said that the customer ~~said that he~~ was canceling the order.

reports

A report is an organized presentation of factual information, often aimed at multiple **audiences** that may present the results of an investigation, a trip, or a research project. For any report—whether formal or informal—assessing the readers' needs is essential. Following is a list of report entries in this book:

feasibility reports	198	progress and activity reports	427
formal reports	209	trip reports	560
investigative reports	298	trouble reports	563

Formal reports often present the results of long-term projects or those that involve multiple participants. (See also **collaborative writing**.) Such projects may be done either for your own organization or as a contractual requirement for another organization. Formal reports generally follow a precise format and include such elements as **abstracts** and **executive summaries**. See also **proposals**.

Informal and short reports normally run from a few paragraphs to a few pages and ordinarily include only an **introduction**, a body, a **conclusion**, and (if necessary) recommendations. Because of their brevity, informal reports are customarily written as **correspondence**, including **letters** (if sent outside your organization), **memos**, and **e-mails**.

The introduction announces the subject of the report, states its **purpose**, and gives any essential background information. It may also summarize the conclusions, findings, or recommendations made in the report. The body presents a clearly organized account of the report's subject—the results of a test carried out, the status of a project, and other details readers may need. The amount of detail to include depends on your reader's knowledge, your **scope**, and the complexity of the subject.

The conclusion summarizes your findings and interprets their significance for readers. In some reports, a final, separate section gives recommendations; in others, the conclusions and the recommendations are combined into one section. This final section makes suggestions for a course of action based on the data you have presented. See also **persuasion**.

repurposing

Repurposing is the copying or converting of existing content, such as written text and **visuals**, from one document or medium into another for a different **purpose**.* For example, if you are preparing a promotional **brochure**, you may be able to reuse material from a product **description** that is currently published on your organization's Web site. The brochure may then be printed or even placed on the Web site where it can be downloaded. See also **selecting the medium**.

In the workplace, this process saves time because content that often requires substantial effort to develop need not be re-created for each new application. The process of repurposing may be as simple as copying and pasting content from one document into another or as complex as distributing content and updates through a system of content management. See also **form letters**.

Content can be repurposed exactly as it is written only if it fits the **scope**, **audience**, and purpose of the new document. If the content alters the focus of these areas, you must adapt the content to fit its new **context**, as described in the following sections.

Repurpose for the Context

Staying focused on the purpose of your new document is critical, especially when repurposing content between different media. If you are writing a sales **proposal**, for example, and you only need to describe the specifications for a product, it may be useful to repurpose the specification list from your organization's Web site. However, the purpose of the Web-site content may be *to inform* customers about your products, whereas the purpose of a proposal is *to persuade* customers to buy your products. To effectively use the repurposed content in your proposal, you may need to adapt the **tense**, **voice**, **tone**, **grammar**, and **point of view** to make the repurposed content more persuasive and fit within the context of a sales proposal.

Repurpose for the Medium

The proper **style** and **format** of content written for a specific medium, such as a brochure or fact sheet, may not work as effectively when repurposed for a different medium, such as a Web site. Solid blocks of text may be easy to read in a brochure, but Web readers often need

R

---

*The reuse of standard texts or content in technical publications is often referred to as "single-source publishing" or simply "single sourcing." See *www.stcsig.org/ss*. Traditionally, such reuse of standard texts has been referred to as "boilerplate."

blocks of text to be separated into bulleted **lists** or very short paragraphs because readers process information differently when reading on a computer monitor. Adapt the **layout and design** of the repurposed content as appropriate to accommodate your reader's needs for the medium. See also **writing for the Web**.

❖ ETHICS NOTE In the workplace, repurposing content within an organization does not violate **copyright** because an organization owns the information it creates and can share it across the company. Likewise, a writer in an organization may use and repurpose material in the public domain and, with some limitations, content that is licensed under Creative Commons (see *http://creativecommons.org/about*). See also **blogs and forums** and *Digital Tip: Using Collaborative Software* on page 83.

In the classroom, of course, the use of content or someone else's unique ideas without acknowledgment or the use of someone else's exact words without **quotation marks** and appropriate credit is **plagiarism**. ❖

research

R

Research is the process of investigation—the discovery of information. To be focused, research must be preceded by **preparation**, especially consideration of your **audience**, **purpose**, and **scope**. Effective **note-taking** is essential for a coherent **organization** that strategically integrates your own ideas, supporting facts, and any well-selected **quotations** into an effective draft and final document. See also **documenting sources**, **outlining**, and "Five Steps to Successful Writing" on page xv.

In an academic setting, your preparatory resources include not only the Internet but also conversations with your fellow students, instructors, and especially a reference librarian. On the job, your main resources are your own knowledge and experience and that of your colleagues. In business, the most important sources of information may also include market research, **questionnaires** and surveys, focus groups, shareholder meetings, and the like. In this setting, begin by **brainstorming** with colleagues about what sources will be most useful to your topic and how you can find them.

Primary Research

Primary research is the gathering of raw data from such sources as first-hand experience, interviews, direct observation, surveys and questionnaires, focus groups, **meetings**, and the like. In fact, direct observation and interaction are the only ways to obtain certain kinds of information, such as about human behavior and the functioning of organizations. You can also conduct primary research on the Internet by participating in discussion groups and newsgroups and by using **e-mail** to request information from specific audiences. See also **interviewing for information** and **listening**.

❖ ETHICS NOTE If you conduct research that involves observation or a questionnaire at your university or college, ask your instructor whether your methods or questions are appropriate and whether you may need to file an application with your school's institutional review board (IRB). For an observation, be sure to obtain permission in advance and remain as unobtrusive as possible during your observation. Keep accurate, complete records that indicate date, time of day, duration of the observation, and so on. Save interpretations of your observations for future analysis. ❖

Secondary Research

Secondary research is the gathering of information that has been previously analyzed, assessed, evaluated, compiled, or otherwise organized into accessible form. Sources include books and articles as well as **reports**, Web documents, audio and video recordings, podcasts, **correspondence**, **minutes of meetings**, **brochures**, **annual reports**, and so forth. The following two sections—Library Research Strategies and Internet Research Strategies—provide methods for finding secondary sources.

R

As you seek information, keep in mind that in most cases the more recent the information, the better. Recently published periodicals and newspapers—as well as academic (.edu), organizational (.org), and government (.gov) Web sites—can be good sources of current information and can include published interviews, articles, papers, and conference proceedings. See *Writer's Checklist: Evaluating Print and Online Sources* on page 489.

When a resource seems useful, read it carefully and take notes that include any additional questions about your topic. Some of your questions may eventually be answered in other sources; those that remain unanswered can guide you to further primary research. For example, you may discover that you need to interview an expert. Not only can someone skilled in a field answer many of your questions, but he or she can also suggest further sources of information. See **paraphrasing** and **plagiarism**.

Library Research Strategies

The library provides organized paths into scholarship and the Internet as well as specialized resources—such as licensed online databases, indexes, catalogs, and directories—that are not accessible through standard Web searches. The first step in using library resources, either in an academic institution or in a workplace, is to develop a search strategy appropriate to the information needed for your topic. You may want to begin by asking a reference librarian for help (in person, by phone, by live chat, or by e-mail) to find the best print or online resources for your topic—a brief conversation can focus your research and save you time. In addition, use your library's homepage for access to its catalogs, databases of articles, subject directories to the Web, and more.

Your search strategy depends on the kind of information you are seeking. For example, if you need the latest data offered by government research, check the Web, as described later in this entry. Likewise, if you need a current scholarly article on a topic, search an online database (such as EBSCOhost's Academic Search Premier) subscribed to by your library. For an overview of a subject, you might turn to an encyclopedia; for historical background, your best resources are books, journals, and primary documents (such as a labor contract).

R

DIGITAL TIP

Storing Search Results

Databases offer various ways to save your results. You may be able to save your searches and results within the database itself by creating a personal account, by sending selected references and full-text articles to an e-mail account, or by exporting them to citation-management software such as RefWorks, Endnote, or Zotero. These programs allow you to build your own database of references from multiple sources, sort them into folders, and generate bibliographies in the format of your choice. Database search tools will vary from library to library, so contact a reference librarian for usage guidance at your library.

Online Catalogs (Locating Books). An online catalog—accessed through library research terminals and through the Internet—allows you to search a library's licensed holdings, indicates an item's location and availability, and may allow you to arrange an interlibrary loan.

You can search a library's online catalog by author, title, keyword, or subject. The most common ways of searching for a specific topic are by subject or by keyword. If your search turns up too many results, you can usually narrow it by using the "limit search" or "advanced search" option.

Online Databases and Indexes (Locating Articles). Most libraries subscribe to online databases, such as the following, which are usually available through a library's Web site:

- *EBSCOhost's Academic Search Premier*: a large multidisciplinary database, providing full text for nearly 4,500 periodicals, including more than 3,700 peer-reviewed journals.

- *Expanded Academic ASAP*: a large database covering general-interest and scholarly journals plus business, law, and health-care publications (many in full text)

- *ERIC (Educational Resources Information Center)*: a U.S. Department of Education database providing access to journals and reports in education

- *JSTOR*: a full-text, archival collection of journals in humanities, social sciences, and sciences

- *Lexis/Nexis Academic*: a collection of databases that is particularly strong for news, business, legal, and corporate and financial information (most articles in full text) as well as congressional, statistical, and government resources

These databases, sometimes called *periodical indexes*, are excellent resources for articles published within the last 10 to 20 years. Many include descriptive abstracts and full texts of articles. To find older articles, you may need to consult a print index, such as the *Readers' Guide to Periodical Literature* and the *New York Times Index*, both of which have been digitized and may be available in some libraries.

R

Reference Works. In addition to articles, books, and Web sources, you may want to consult reference works such as encyclopedias, dictionaries, and manuals for a brief overview of your subject. Ask your reference librarian to recommend works and **bibliographies** that are most relevant to your topic. Many are available online and can be accessed through your library's homepage.

ENCYCLOPEDIAS. Encyclopedias are comprehensive, multivolume collections of articles arranged alphabetically. Some cover a wide range of subjects, while others—such as *The Encyclopedia of Careers and Vocational Guidance*, 15th ed. (Chicago: Ferguson, 2010)—focus on specific areas. The free online encyclopedia Wikipedia at *www.wikipedia .org* should be used only as a starting point for your research because users continuously update entries (with varying degrees of expert oversight).

DICTIONARIES. Specialized **dictionaries** define terms used in a particular field, such as business, computers, architecture, or consumer affairs, and they offer detailed definitions of field-specific terms, usually written in straightforward language.

HANDBOOKS AND MANUALS. Handbooks and manuals are typically one-volume compilations of frequently used information in a particular field. They offer brief definitions of terms or concepts, standards for presenting information, procedures for documenting sources, and **visuals** such as **graphs** and **tables**.

BIBLIOGRAPHIES. Bibliographies list books, periodicals, and other research materials published in areas such as business, medicine, the humanities, and the social sciences.

GENERAL GUIDES. The *Guide to Reference* at *www.guidetoreference .org* can help you locate reference books, indexes, and other research materials. Check your library's homepage or ask a reference librarian if your library subscribes to this or another particular index.

OTHER LIBRARY RESOURCES. Many libraries offer special kinds of research information. For example, a library may provide access to data that can be downloaded into statistical packages, such as SPSS (statistical package for the social sciences) for manipulation. Others offer GIS (geographic information systems) software that links data to spatial information, allowing the researcher to create detailed maps that show factors such as income, ethnicity, or purchasing habits.

Internet Research Strategies

The Web varies widely in its completeness and accuracy, so you need to evaluate Internet sources critically by following the advice in *Writer's Checklist: Evaluating Print and Online Sources* on page 489.

Search Engines. Search engines use words or combinations of words that you specify to locate the documents or files that contain one or more of these words in their titles, descriptions, or text. Common search engines include Google (*www.google.com*), BING (*www.bing .com*), and Yahoo! (*www.yahoo.com*).

As comprehensive as search engines and directories may seem, none is complete or objective and they carry only a preselected range of content. Some, for example, may not index Adobe PDF files or Usenet newsgroups, and many cannot index databases and other non–HTML-based content. Search engines rank the sites they believe will be relevant to your search based on a number of different strategies. Although search engines vary in what and how they search, you can use some basic strategies, described in the following *Writer's Checklist*.

WRITER'S CHECKLIST   Using Search Engines and Keywords

✔ Check any search tips available at the engine you use. For example, some engines allow you to use an advanced search that narrows your search by combining phrases with double quotation marks: "usability testing" will return only pages that have the full compound phrase.

✔ Enter keywords and phrases that are as specific to your topic as possible. For example, if you are looking for information about *nuclear power* and enter only the term *nuclear*, the search will also yield listings for *nuclear family, nuclear medicine,* and hundreds of others not related to your topic.

✔ Try several search engines to get more varied results and remember that search engines may sell high rankings to advertisers and therefore may not highlight the pages most relevant to your search.

✔ Consider using a metasearch engine, such as Dogpile (*www.dogpile .com*) and Metacrawler (*www.metacrawler.com*), if you are interested in obtaining as many hits as possible.

✔ Refine and narrow your terms as you evaluate the results of each search.

R

Web Subject Directories.   A subject directory (also known as an *index*) organizes information by broad subject categories (business, entertainment, health, sports) and related subtopics (marketing, finance, investing). One such directory is *http://directory.google.com*. A subject-directory search eventually produces a list of specific sites that contain information about the topics you request.

In addition to the subject directories offered by many search engines, the following directories will help you to conduct selective, scholarly research on the Web:

Infomine	*http://infomine.ucr.edu*
The Internet Public Library	*www.ipl.org*
The WWW Virtual Library	*www.vlib.org*

The Internet includes numerous directories and sites devoted to specific subject areas. Following are some suggested resources for researching a business topic.

CIO's Resource Centers	*www.cio.com/solutions/research-and -analysis*
GlobalEDGE	*http://globaledge.msu.edu*
Inc.com Articles by Topic	*www.inc.com* (use search function)
LSU Libraries Federal Agencies Directory	*www.lib.lsu.edu/gov/index.html*
FedStats	*www.fedstats.gov*

Some sites combine search engines with directories; for example, Google operates both a standard search engine and directory and a special contributor-generated directory referred to as an "Open Directory" (*http://dmoz.org*).

Evaluating Sources

The easiest way to ensure that information is valid is to obtain it from a reputable source. For Internet sources, be especially concerned about the validity of the information provided. Because anyone can publish on the Web, it is sometimes difficult to determine authorship of a document, and frequently a person's qualifications for speaking on a topic are absent or questionable. The Internet versions of established, reputable journals in medicine, management, engineering, computer software, and the like merit the same level of trust as the printed versions. Use the following domain abbreviations to help you determine an Internet site sponsor:

.aero	aerospace industry	.mil	U.S. military
.biz	business	.museum	museum
.com	company or individual	.name	individual
.coop	business cooperative	.net	network provider
.edu	college or university	.org	nonprofit organization
.gov	federal government	.int	international
.pro	professionals	.info	general use

As you move away from established, reputable sites, exercise more caution. Be especially wary of unmoderated, public Web forums. Collectively generated Web sites, such as Wikipedia, often make no guarantee of the validity of information on their sites (see *http://en.wikipedia.org/ wiki/Wikipedia:General_disclaimer*).

WRITER'S CHECKLIST   Evaluating Print and Online Sources

Keep in mind the following four criteria when evaluating Internet sources: authority, accuracy, bias, and currency.*

FOR ALL SOURCES

✔ Is the resource recent enough and relevant to your topic? Is it readily available?

✔ Who is the intended audience? Is it the mainstream public? A small group of professionals?

✔ Who is the author(s)? Is the author(s) an authority on the subject?

✔ Does the author(s) provide enough supporting evidence and document sources so that you can verify the information's accuracy?

✔ Is the information presented in an objective, unbiased way? Are any biases made clear? Are opinions clearly labeled? Are viewpoints balanced, or are opposing opinions acknowledged?

✔ Are the language, tone, and style appropriate and cogent?

FOR A BOOK

✔ Does the preface or introduction indicate the author's or book's purpose?

✔ Does the table of contents relate to your topic? Does the index contain terms related to your topic?

✔ Are the chapters useful? Skim through one chapter that seems related to your topic — notice especially the introduction, headings, and closing.

FOR AN ARTICLE

✔ Is the publisher of the magazine or other periodical well known?

✔ What is the article's purpose? For a journal article, read the abstract; for a newspaper article, read the headline and opening sentences.

✔ Does the article contain informative diagrams or other visuals that indicate its scope?

FOR A WEB SITE

✔ Does a reputable group or organization sponsor or maintain the site?

✔ Are the purpose and scope of the site clearly stated? Check the "Mission Statement" or "About Us" pages. Does the site carry any disclaimers?

(continued)

*For more details, see Leigh Ryan and Lisa Zimmereli, *The Bedford Guide for Writing Tutors*, 5th ed. (Boston: Bedford/St. Martin's, 2010).

WRITER'S CHECKLIST   **Evaluating Print and Online Sources** (*continued*)

✔ Is the site updated, thus current? Are the links functional and up to date?

✔ Is the documentation authoritative and credible? Check the links to other sources and cross-check facts at other reputable Web sites, such as academic ones.

✔ Is the site well designed? Is the material well written and error free?

WEB LINK	Evaluating Online Sources
For a tutorial on evaluating information online, see *bedfordstmartins .com/alred* and select *Try a tutorial*, "On evaluating online sources." For links to additional related resources, select *Links for Handbook Entries*.	

resignation letters

Resignation **letters** (or **memos**), as shown in Figures R–3 and R–4, should be as positive as possible, regardless of the reason you are leaving a job. You usually write a resignation letter to your supervisor or to an appropriate person in the Human Resources Department. Use the following guidelines:

- Start on a positive note, regardless of the circumstances under which you are leaving.
- Consider pointing out how you have benefited from working for the company or say something complimentary about the company.
- Comment on something positive about the people with whom you have been associated.
- Explain why you are leaving in an objective, factual tone.
- Avoid angry recriminations because your resignation will remain on file with the company and could haunt you in the future should you need references.

Your letter or memo should give enough notice to allow your employer time to find a replacement. It might be no more than two weeks or it might be enough time to enable you to train your replacement. Some organizations may ask for a notice equivalent to the number of weeks of vacation you receive. Check the policy of your employer before you begin your letter.

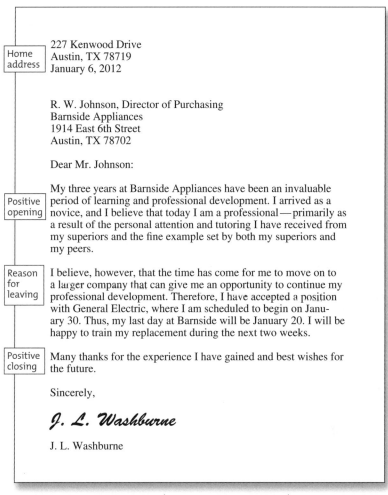

Home address

227 Kenwood Drive
Austin, TX 78719
January 6, 2012

R. W. Johnson, Director of Purchasing
Barnside Appliances
1914 East 6th Street
Austin, TX 78702

Dear Mr. Johnson:

Positive opening

My three years at Barnside Appliances have been an invaluable period of learning and professional development. I arrived as a novice, and I believe that today I am a professional — primarily as a result of the personal attention and tutoring I have received from my superiors and the fine example set by both my superiors and my peers.

Reason for leaving

I believe, however, that the time has come for me to move on to a larger company that can give me an opportunity to continue my professional development. Therefore, I have accepted a position with General Electric, where I am scheduled to begin on January 30. Thus, my last day at Barnside will be January 20. I will be happy to train my replacement during the next two weeks.

Positive closing

Many thanks for the experience I have gained and best wishes for the future.

Sincerely,

J. L. Washburne

J. L. Washburne

FIGURE R–3. Resignation Letter (to Accept a Better Position)

R

The sample resignation letter in Figure R–3 is from an employee who is leaving to take a job offering greater opportunities. The memo of resignation in Figure R–4 is written by an employee who is leaving because her position has been reclassified and her supervisor has not supported her advancement, but no personal conflict is mentioned. Notice that it opens and closes positively and that the reason for the resignation is stated without apparent anger or bitterness. For strategies concerning negative messages, see **correspondence** and **refusal letters**.

MEMORANDUM

To: T. W. Haney, Vice President, Administration

From: L. R. Rupp *LRR*

Date: February 13, 2012

Subject: Resignation from Winterhaven, effective
           March 2, 2012

Positive opening	My five-year stay with the Winterhaven Company has been a pleasant experience, and I believe that it has been mutually beneficial.
Reason for leaving	Because of the recent restructuring of my job, I have accepted a position with another company that I feel will offer me greater advancement opportunities. I am, therefore, submitting my resignation, to be effective on March 2, 2012.
Positive closing	I have enjoyed working with my coworkers at Winterhaven and wish the company success in the future.

FIGURE R–4. Resignation Memo (Under Negative Conditions)

respective / respectively

Respective is an **adjective** that means "pertaining to two or more things regarded individually." ("The committee members returned to their *respective* offices.") *Respectively* is the adverb form of *respective*, meaning "singly, in the order designated."

▶ The first, second, and third prizes in the sales contest were awarded to Maria Juarez, Dan Wesp, and Simone Luce, *respectively*.

Respective and *respectively* are unnecessary if the meaning of individuality is clear.

                Each   *member*   *a report.*
▶ ~~The~~ committee ~~members~~ prepared ~~their respective reports.~~

restrictive and nonrestrictive elements

Modifying **phrases** and **clauses** may be either restrictive or nonrestrictive. A *nonrestrictive phrase or clause* provides additional information about what it modifies, but it does not restrict the meaning of what it modifies. A nonrestrictive phrase or clause can be removed without changing the essential meaning of the sentence. It is a parenthetical element that is set off by **commas** to show its loose relationship with the rest of the sentence.

> NONRESTRICTIVE   The annual report, *which was distributed yesterday*, shows that sales increased 20 percent last year.

A *restrictive phrase or clause* limits, or restricts, the meaning of what it modifies. If it were removed, the essential meaning of the sentence would change. Because a restrictive phrase or clause is essential to the meaning of the sentence, it is never set off by commas.

> RESTRICTIVE   All employees *wishing to donate blood* may take Thursday afternoon off.

Writers need to distinguish between nonrestrictive and restrictive elements. The same sentence can take on two entirely different meanings, depending on whether a modifying element is set off by commas (because it is nonrestrictive) or is not (because it is restrictive). A slip by the writer can not only mislead **readers** but also embarrass the writer.

> MISLEADING   He gave a poor performance evaluation to the staff members who protested to the Human Resources Department.
> [This suggests that he gave the poor evaluation because the staff members had protested.]
>
> ACCURATE   He gave a poor performance evaluation to the staff members, who protested to the Human Resources Department.
> [This suggests that the staff members protested because of the poor evaluation.]

Use *which* to introduce nonrestrictive clauses and *that* to introduce restrictive clauses.

> NONRESTRICTIVE   After John left the restaurant, *which* is one of the finest in New York, he came directly to my office.
>
> RESTRICTIVE   Companies *that* diversify usually succeed.

résumés

A résumé is a document that serves as the key component of an effective **job search** and the foundation for your **application cover letter** (often referred to as a *cover letter*). The résumé is a snapshot of the professional attributes you will bring to a particular position: a summary of your professional experience, relevant accomplishments, and education. The length of your résumé will depend on your level of experience. Limit your résumé* to one page unless your credentials, skills, and abilities are significant and match those a prospective employer is seeking to fill a particular position. Prospective employers use the information in the résumé and application cover letter to screen applicants and select candidates for the interview process. During a job interview, the content of your résumé and application cover letter provide the interviewer with a guideline for developing specific questions. See also **interviewing for a job**.

R

The résumé is typically the first contact an employer has with a potential employee and will serve as your personal introduction. To ensure your résumé creates a positive first impression, make certain it is well organized, is carefully designed, is consistent in formatting, is free of errors, and generates interest in the reviewer. The content should

---

*A detailed résumé for someone in an academic or a scientific area is often called a *curriculum vitae* (also *vita* or *c.v.*). It may include education, publications, projects, grants, and awards as well as a full work history. Outside the United States, the term *curriculum vitae* is often used to mean *résumé*.

emphasize the key knowledge, skills, and attributes you possess and, when possible, mirror those the employer is looking for in a candidate. Use a format that highlights your strengths and portrays your value. The **layout and design** should be attractive, uncluttered, and easy to read. Uniformity in the design will ensure that the reviewer is able to identify your value during a brief visual scan, and the strategic use of bold print to highlight items of interest will help draw the eye down the page. **Consistency** in the presentation of information is especially important in a résumé. For example, use the same spacing, punctuation, and date format throughout (*2010–2012, 01/2012,* or *May 2012*). **Proofreading** is essential. Mistakes in an application cover letter or résumé may eliminate you from consideration. Verify that all information you have provided is accurate and have someone else review it. For hard-copy résumés, use a quality printer and high-grade paper.

❖ ETHICS NOTE Be truthful. The consequences of giving false information in your résumé are serious. In fact, the truthfulness of your résumé reflects not only on your own ethical stance but also on the integrity with which you would represent the organization. See also **ethics in writing**. ❖

Sample Résumés

The sample résumés in this entry will stimulate your thinking about how to tailor your résumé to your own job search. Today's word-processing programs provide nearly unlimited opportunities for candidates to express their creative talents and market their value on paper yet still retain the professionalism associated with best business practices. Before you design and write your résumé, look at as many samples as possible, and then organize and format your own to best highlight your strengths, present your professional goals, and make the most persuasive case to your target employers. See also **persuasion**.

- Figure R–5 presents a conventional student résumé in which the student is seeking an entry-level position.

- Figure R–6 shows a résumé with a variation in the design and placement of conventional headings to highlight professional credentials.

- Figure R–7 presents a student résumé with a format that is appropriately nonconventional for the purpose of demonstrating the student's skill in graphic design to a target audience. This résumé matches the letter in Figure A–9.

- Figure R–8 depicts a résumé that incorporates a tagline and focuses on the applicant's management experience. A tagline is a short quotation summarizing your reasons for seeking a certain position.

R

(Taglines are described in more detail on pages 506–7.) This résumé matches the letter in Figure A–10.

- Figure R–9 reflects the résumé of a candidate seeking to switch career fields. It uses a job title and immediately states a goal, followed by credentials.

- Figure R–10 focuses on how the applicant advanced and was promoted within a single company.

- Figure R–11 illustrates how an applicant can organize a résumé by combining functional and chronological elements.

WEB LINK	Annotated Sample Résumés

For more examples of résumés with helpful annotations, see *bedfordstmartins.com/alred* and select *Model Documents Gallery*.

Analyzing Your Background

In preparing to write your résumé, determine what kind of job you are seeking. There is rarely a one-size-fits-all résumé and as you progress in your career, you gain experience holding positions in a variety of diverse industries. Review your credentials and highlight the information that will best support your objective and be most important to a prospective employer. Consider the following as you gather information:

- Schools you attended, degrees you hold, your major field of study, academic honors you were awarded, your grade point average, particular academic projects that reflect your best work; continuing education; conferences or seminars you have attended

- Jobs you have held, your principal and secondary duties in each job, when and how long you held each job, promotions, skills you developed in your jobs that a potential employer may value and seek in the ideal candidate, and projects or accomplishments that reflect important contributions

- Other experiences and skills you have developed that would be of value in the kind of job you are seeking; extracurricular activities that have contributed to your learning experience; leadership assignments you have accepted; interpersonal and communication skills you have developed; speeches, public presentations, or classes you have given; collaborative work you have performed; publications you have contributed to; computer skills you have acquired or data-management programs you are proficient in using; languages you speak; notable awards or other types of recognition you have received

R

CAROL ANN WALKER

CAMPUS ADDRESS
148 University Drive
Bloomington, Indiana 47405
(812) 652-4781
caw2@iu.edu

HOME (after June 2012)
1436 West Schantz Avenue
Laurel, Pennsylvania 17322
(717) 399-2712
caw@yahoo.com

OBJECTIVE

Position in financial research, leading to management in corporate finance.

EDUCATION

Bachelor of Science in Business Administration, expected June 2012
Indiana University

Emphasis: Finance   Minor: Professional Writing
Grade Point Average: 3.88 out of possible 4.0
Senior Honor Society

FINANCIAL EXPERIENCE

FIRST BANK, INC., Bloomington, Indiana, 2011
Research Assistant, Summer and Fall Quarters
    Developed long-range planning models for the manager of corporate
    planning.

MARTIN FINANCIAL RESEARCH SERVICES, Bloomington, Indiana, 2010
Financial Audit Intern
    Created a design concept for in-house financial audits and provided
    research assistance to staff.
Associate Editor, *Martin Client Newsletter*, 2009–2010
    Wrote articles on financial planning with computer models; developed
    article ideas from survey of business periodicals; edited submissions.

COMPUTER PROFICIENCIES

Software: Microsoft Word, Excel, PowerPoint, InDesign, QuarkXPress
Hardware: Macintosh, IBM-PC
Languages: UNIX, JAVA, C++

VOLUNTEER ACTIVITY

Student Affiliate NAPFA: Weekend program to assist low-income elderly
with managing their financial obligations. 2010–2012

R

FIGURE R–5. Student Résumé (for an Entry-Level Position)

CHRIS RENAULT, RN

3785 Raleigh Court, #46 • Phoenix, AZ 67903
(555) 467-1115 • chris@resumepower.com

Qualifications

➢ *Recent Honors Graduate of Approved Nursing Program*
➢ *Current Arizona Nursing Licensure and BLS Certification*
➢ *Presently Completing Clinical Nurse Internship Program*

Education & Licensure

ARIZONA STATE UNIVERSITY Tempe, AZ **Bachelor of Science in Nursing (BSN)**, 2012 Graduated summa cum laude (GPA: 4.0)	MOHAVE COMMUNITY COLLEGE Kingman, AZ **Associate Degree in Nursing (AN)**, 2010 Graduated cum laude (GPA: 3.5)

Coursework Highlights: Family and Community Nursing, Health-Care Delivery Models, Health Assessment, Pathology, Microbiology, Nursing Research, Nursing of Older Adults, Health-Care Ethics

Arizona RN License, 2012
BLS Certification, 2012

Clinical Internship

CAMELBACK MEDICAL CENTER — Phoenix, AZ
Nurse Intern, 2011 to Present

- Accepted into new graduate RN training program and completing in-depth, eight-month rotation working under a trained preceptor.
- Gaining valuable clinical experience to assume the role of a professional nurse within an acute-care setting. Rotating through all medical center areas, including Postsurgical, Orthopedics, Pediatrics, Oncology, Emergency Department, Psychiatric Nursing, Cardiac Telemetry, and Critical Care.
- Developing speed and skill in the day-to-day functions of a staff nurse. Participating in patient assessment, treatment, medication disbursement, and surgical preparation as a member of the health-care team.
- Earned written commendations from preceptor for *"excellent ability to interact with patients and their families, showing a high degree of empathy, medical knowledge, and concern for quality and continuity of patient care."*

Community Involvement

Active Volunteer and Fundraising Coordinator, The American Cancer Society — Scottsdale, AZ, Chapter (2010 to Present)
Participant, Annual AIDS Walkathon (2007–2010) and "Find the Cure" Breast Cancer Awareness Marathon (2009, 2010)

FIGURE R–6. Résumé (Highlighting Professional Credentials). Prepared by Kim Isaacs, Advanced Career Systems, Inc.

OBJECTIVE

A position as a graphic designer with responsibilities in information design, packaging, and media presentations.

Joshua S. Goodman
222 Morewood Avenue
Pittsburgh, PA 15212
cell: 412-555-1212
jgoodman@aol.com

EDUCATION

Carnegie Mellon University, Pittsburgh, Pennsylvania BFA in Graphic Design — May 2012

Graphic Design
Corporate Identity
Industrial Design
Graphic Imaging Processes
Color Theory
Computer Graphics
Typography
Serigraphy
Photography
Video Production

GRAPHIC DESIGN EXPERIENCE

Assistant Designer • Dyer/Khan, Los Angeles, California Summer 2010, Summer 2011
Assistant Designer in a versatile design studio. Responsible for design, layout, comps, mechanicals, and project management.
Clients: Paramount Pictures, Mattel Electronics, and Motown Records.

Photo Editor • Paramount Pictures Corporation, Los Angeles, California Summer 2009
Photo Editor for merchandising department. Established art files for movie and television properties. Edited images used in merchandising. Maintained archive and database.

Production Assistant • Grafis, Los Angeles, California Summer 2008
Production assistant at fast-paced design firm. Assisted with comps, mechanicals, and miscellaneous studio work.
Clients: ABC Television, A&M Records, and Ortho Products Division.

COMPUTER PROFICIENCIES

XML, HTML, JavaScript, Forms, Macromedia Dreamweaver, Macromedia Flash Professional, Photoshop, Illustrator, Image Ready (Animated GIFs), CorelDRAW, DeepPaint, iGrafx Designer, MapEdit (Image Mapping), Scanning, Microsoft Access/Excel, QuarkXPress.

ACTIVITIES

Member, Pittsburgh Graphic
   Design Society
Member, The Design Group

R

FIGURE R–7. Student Résumé (for a Graphic Design Job)

ROBERT MANDILLO
7761 Shalamar Drive
Dayton, Ohio 45424
(937) 255-4137
mand@juno.com

| Tagline | "Seeking a management position in the aerospace industry with responsibility for developing new designs and products."

MANAGEMENT EXPERIENCE

MANAGER, EXHIBIT DESIGN LAB—May 2005–Present
Wright-Patterson Air Force Base, Dayton, Ohio

Supervise 11 technicians in support of engineering exhibit design and production. Develop, evaluate, and improve materials and equipment for the design and construction of exhibits. Write specifications, negotiate with vendors, and initiate procurement activities for exhibit design support.

SUPERVISOR, GRAPHICS ILLUSTRATORS—June 2002–April 2005
Henderson Advertising Agency, Cincinnati, Ohio

Supervised five illustrators and four drafting mechanics after promotion from Graphics Technician. Analyzed and approved work-order requirements. Selected appropriate media and techniques for orders. Rendered illustrations in pencil and ink. Converted department to CAD system.

EDUCATION

MASTER OF BUSINESS ADMINISTRATION, 2011
University of Dayton, Ohio

BACHELOR OF SCIENCE IN MECHANICAL ENGINEERING TECHNOLOGY, 2002
Edison State College, Wooster, Ohio

ASSOCIATE'S DEGREE IN MECHANICAL DRAFTING, 2000
Wooster Community College, Wooster, Ohio

PROFESSIONAL AFFILIATION

National Association of Mechanical Engineers

REFERENCES / WEB SITE

References, letters of recommendation, and a portfolio of original designs and drawings available online at www.juno.com/mand.

R

FIGURE R–8. Résumé (Applicant with Management Experience)

LINDA H. GRANGER

lhg.granger@email.com   942 Shower Lane Drive
(206) 577-8869 / (206) 656-3324   Sun Valley Heights, VA 20109

INFORMATION TECHNOLOGY / SECURITY SPECIALIST

Seeking to build an exciting career in law enforcement, with a focus on the application of Information Technology (IT) / Information Security (INFOSEC).

- Application Design / System Analysis
- Testing / Implementation / Integration
- Program / Project Development
- Business Policies / Procedures
- Customer / Client Service
- Dynamic Team Building / Leadership

ACADEMIC BACKGROUND

BACHELOR OF SCIENCE – INFORMATION TECHNOLOGY
Sun Valley University, VA, May 2011

INTERNSHIP / PROFESSIONAL EXPERIENCE

Federal Law Enforcement Training Center (FLETC), Arlington, VA   *June–Sept. 2011*
Volunteer — Computer, Financial, Intelligence Division

- Accepted into the highly selective, competitive FLETC College Intern Summer Program
- Analyzed, evaluated, assessed the performance or operating methodology of forensic software
- Assisted law enforcement staff and instructors with office support in efforts to advance the mission of the FLETC
- Participated in and observed basic training classes and activities designed to develop and promote the growth of future law enforcement candidates

Board of Education, Forrest Hills, VA   *Sept. 2009–June 2011*
Instructor / Substitute Teacher

- Helped provide an educational foundation designed to enable K–12 students to develop confidence, self-direction, and a lifelong interest in learning
- Fostered the development of communication, citizenship, and personal growth in the provision of curriculum through emotional and educational support, and guidance

AWARDS / RECOGNITION

SUPERB ADMINISTRATIVE SUPPORT – FORENSIC DATA HUB
Federal Law Enforcement Training Center

R

FIGURE R–9. Résumé (Experienced Applicant Seeking Career Change)

CAROL ANN WALKER
1436 West Schantz Avenue
Laurel, Pennsylvania 17322
(717) 399-2712
caw@yahoo.com

FINANCIAL EXPERIENCE

KERFHEIMER CORPORATION, Philadelphia, Pennsylvania

Senior Financial Analyst, June 2007–Present
Report to Senior Vice President for Corporate Financial Planning.
Develop manufacturing cost estimates totaling $30 million annually
for mining and construction equipment with Department of Defense.

Financial Analyst, November 2004–June 2007
Developed $50-million funding estimates for major Department of
Defense contracts for troop carriers and digging and earth-moving
machines. Researched funding options, resulting in savings of
$1.2 million.

FIRST BANK, INC., Bloomington, Indiana

Planning Analyst, September 1999–November 2004
Developed successful computer models for short- and long-range planning.

EDUCATION

Ph.D. in Finance: expected, June 2012
The Wharton School of the University of Pennsylvania

M.S. in Business Administration, 2003
University of Wisconsin–Milwaukee
"Executive Curriculum" for employees identified as promising by their
employers.

B.S. in Business Administration (*magna cum laude*), 1999
Indiana University
Emphasis: Finance　　　　　　Minor: Professional Writing

PUBLISHING AND MEMBERSHIP

Published "Developing Computer Models for Financial Planning,"
Midwest Finance Journal 34.2 (2009): 126–36.

Association for Corporate Financial Planning, Senior Member.

REFERENCES

References and a portfolio of financial plans are available on request.

FIGURE R–10. Advanced Résumé (Showing Promotion Within a Single Company)

─────────CAROL ANN WALKER─────────

1436 West Schantz Avenue • Laurel, PA 17322
(717) 399-2712 • caw@yahoo.com

Award-Winning Senior Financial Analyst

Astute senior analyst and corporate financial planner with 11 years of experience and proven success enhancing P&L scenarios by millions of dollars. Demonstrated ability to apply critical thinking and sound strategic/economic analysis to multidimensional business issues. Advanced computer skills include Hyperion, SQL, MS Office, and Crystal Reports.

Financial Analyst of the Year, 2010

Recipient of prestigious national award from the Association for Investment Management and Research (AIMR)

Areas of Expertise

- Financial Analysis & Planning
- Forecasting & Trend Projection
- Trend/Variance Analysis
- Comparative Analysis

- Expense Analysis
- Strategic Planning
- SEC & Financial Reporting
- Risk Assessment

Career Progression

KERFHEIMER CORPORATION—Philadelphia, PA   2004 to Present

Senior Financial Analyst, June 2007 to Present
Financial Analyst, November 2004 to June 2007

Rapidly promoted to lead team of 15 analysts in the management of financial/SEC reporting and analysis for publicly traded, $2.3-billion company. Develop financial/statistical models used to project and maximize corporate financial performance. Support nationwide sales team by providing financial metrics, trends, and forecasts.

Key Accomplishments:

- **Developed long-range funding requirements crucial to firm's subsequent capture of $1 billion** in government and military contracts.
- **Facilitated a 45% decrease in company's long-term debt** during several major building expansions through personally developed computer models for capital acquisition.
- **Jointly led large-scale systems conversion to Hyperion**, including personal upload of database in Essbase. Completed conversion without interrupting business operations.

R

FIGURE R–11. Advanced Résumé (Combining Functional and Chronological Elements). Prepared by Kim Isaacs, Advanced Career Systems, Inc. (*continued on next page*)

———————————CAROL ANN WALKER———————————

Résumé • Page Two

Career Progression (*continued*)

FIRST BANK, INC. — Bloomington, IN   1999 to 2004

Planning Analyst, September 1999 to November 2004
Compiled and distributed weekly, monthly, quarterly, and annual closings/
financial reports, analyzing information for presentation to senior management. Prepared depreciation forecasts, actual-vs.-projected financial statements, key-matrix reports, tax-reporting packages, auditor packages, and
balance-sheet reviews.

Key Accomplishments:

- **Devised strategies to acquire over $1 billion at 3% below market rate.**
- **Analyzed financial performance for consistency to plans and forecasts**, investigated trends and variances, and alerted senior management to areas requiring action.
- **Achieved an average 23% return on all personally recommended investments.** Applied critical thinking and sound financial and strategic analysis in all funding options research.

Education

THE WHARTON SCHOOL of the UNIVERSITY OF PENNSYLVANIA
(Philadelphia)

Ph.D. in Finance Candidate, Expected June 2012

UNIVERSITY OF WISCONSIN–MILWAUKEE

M.S. in Business Administration, May 2003

INDIANA UNIVERSITY (Bloomington)

B.S. in Business Administration, Emphasis in Finance
(*magna cum laude*), May 1999

Affiliations

- Association for Investment Management and Research (AIMR), Member, 2006 to Present
- Association for Corporate Financial Planning (ACFP), Senior Member, 2004 to Present

Portfolio of Financial Plans Available on Request
(717) 399-2712 • caw@yahoo.com

R

FIGURE R–11. Advanced Résumé (Combining Functional and Chronological
Elements) (*continued*)

Use this information to brainstorm further details and personal attributes. Then, based on all the details, decide which to include in your résumé and how you can most effectively present your qualifications.

Returning Job Seekers

If you are returning to the workplace after an absence, most career experts say that it is important to acknowledge the gap in your career. This is particularly true if, for example, you are reentering the workforce because you have devoted a full-time period to care for children or dependent adults. Do not undervalue such work. Although unpaid, it often provides experience that develops important time-management, problem-solving, organizational, and interpersonal skills. Although gaps in employment can be explained in the application cover letter, the following examples illustrate how you might reflect such experiences in a résumé. These samples would be especially appropriate for an applicant seeking employment in a field related to child or health care.

- ▶ **Primary Child-Care Provider, 2010–2012** Provided full-time care to three preschool children at home. Facilitated early learning activities; taught basic academic skills, nutrition, arts, and swimming. Organized schedules and events, managed the household, and served as Neighborhood-Watch Captain.

- ▶ **Home Caregiver, 2010–2012** Provided 60 hours per week in-home care for Alzheimer's patient. Coordinated health care and medical appointments, developed and supervised exercise programs, completed and processed complex medical forms, administered medications, organized and maintained budgets, and managed home environment.

If you have performed volunteer work during such a period, list that experience. Volunteer work often results in the same experience as does full-time, paid work, a fact that your résumé should reflect, as in the following example:

- ▶ **School Association Coordinator, 2010–2012** Managed special activities of the High School Parent-Teacher Association. Planned and coordinated meetings, scheduled events, and supervised fund-drive operations. Raised $70,000 toward refurbishing the school auditorium.

Organizing Your Résumé (Sections)

The following résumé sections and section headings are typical and, depending on the subject matter resource, may sometimes be represented with alternative terminology as indicated in the following list. The sections you choose to include in your résumé and the order in which you list them should depend on your experience, your goals, the employer's needs, and any standard practices in your profession.

- Heading (name and contact information)
- Job Objective (Job Title, Tagline)
- Qualifications Summary (Professional Profile, Key Attributes)
- Education (Academic Background, Certifications)
- Employment Experience (Career History, Career Chronology)
- Related Skills and Abilities (Professional Affiliations, Volunteer Work, Networking Assets)
- Honors and Activities (Awards, Recognition, Notable Contributions)
- Miscellaneous (to highlight other volunteer work, publications, or affiliations you believe the employer would find valuable)
- References and Portfolios

There really is no right or wrong way to organize your résumé and any number of organizational patterns can be effective. For example, whether you place "education" before "employment experience" depends on the job you are seeking. The use of strategy in how you present your information lies in selecting the credentials that will strengthen your résumé the most. A recent graduate without much work experience may decide to list education first. A candidate with many years of job experience, including jobs directly related to the target position, may decide to list employment experience first. When you list information in the education and employment sections, use a reverse chronological sequence: list the most-recent employer or credential first, the next most-recent experience second, and so on.

Heading. At the top of your résumé, include your name, address, telephone number (home or cell), and a professional **e-mail** address.* Make sure that your name stands out on the page. If you are in transition and have both a school address and a permanent home address, include both underneath your name (see Figure R–5).

Job Objective vs. Tagline. Job objectives and job titles or taglines introduce the material in a résumé and help the reader quickly understand your goal. The differences between these two are slight but should be considered when organizing your résumé. A tagline is a brief quotation

---

*Do not use a clever or unprofessional e-mail address in employment correspondence; e-mail addresses that are based on your last name work well.

that summarizes your vision in seeking a particular employment opportunity. Although your personal objective may not provoke interest in the reviewer or meet the needs of a potential employer, a job title, tagline, or combination of both will immediately reveal your goal. Weigh the benefits of using a job title or tagline versus stating your objective. The following examples illustrate the difference between stating an objective and the use of a job title or tagline combination.

SAMPLE OBJECTIVE STATEMENTS

- A full-time computer-science position aimed at solving engineering problems and contributing to a management team.
- A position involving meeting the concerns of women, such as family planning, career counseling, or crisis management.
- A summer research or programming position providing opportunities to use software-development and software-debugging skills.

SAMPLE JOB TITLE AND TAGLINE COMBINATIONS

- FINANCIAL SERVICES / BANKING PROFESSIONAL
  "Ensuring the Financial Success of Customers, Clients, and Communities"

- MECHANICAL ENGINEER
  "Developing Innovative, Efficient, Environmentally Friendly Energy Solutions"

- FIREFIGHTER / EMT
  "Prevention, Mitigation, Response" or "Protecting Life, Property, and the Environment"

◀ PROFESSIONALISM NOTE Although taglines might more readily address the needs of the employer over a personal job objective, they can be difficult to construct. Not everyone can create clever taglines; use them wisely and only when you are confident that one is warranted and well written. ▶

R

Qualifications Summary. You may wish to include a brief summary of your qualifications to persuade hiring managers to select you for an interview. Sometimes called a *professional profile, summary statement,* or *career summary,* a qualifications summary can include skills, achievements, experience, or personal qualities that make you especially well suited to the position. You may give this section a unique heading or simply use a job title as shown in Figure R–9 and Figure R–11.

Education. List the school(s) you have attended, the degree(s) you received and the dates you received them, your major field(s) of study, and any academic honors you have earned. Most career-development professionals recommend that you should only include your grade point average (GPA) if it is 3.0 or higher. List individual courses if they are unusually impressive, if they provide the opportunity to include key-words, or if your résumé is otherwise sparse (see Figures R–6 and R–7). Consider including any special skills developed or projects completed in your course work. Mention high school only if you do not possess higher education or if you want to call attention to special high school achievements, awards, projects, programs, internships, or study abroad.

Employment Experience. Organize your employment experience in reverse chronological order, starting with your most-recent job and working backward under a single heading. You can also organize your experience functionally by clustering similar types of jobs into several sections with specific section headings such as "Management," "Leadership," "Administration," or "Logistics."

Depending on the situation, one type of arrangement might be more persuasive than the other. For example, if you are applying for an accounting job but have no experience in accounting, simply list past and present jobs in chronological order (most to least recent). If you are applying for a supervisory position and have had three supervisory jobs in addition to two nonsupervisory positions, you might choose to create a section heading called "Supervisory Experience" and list the three supervisory jobs, followed by another section heading labeled "General Experience" to include the nonsupervisory jobs.

In general, consider the following guidelines when working on the "Experience" section of your résumé.

- Include jobs or internships when they relate directly to the position you are seeking. Including such experiences can make a résumé more persuasive if they have helped you develop relevant skills.

- Include extracurricular experiences, such as taking on a leadership position in a college organization or directing a community-service project, if they demonstrate the skills valued by a potential employer.

- Determining how to portray military service can be challenging because of the acquisition of multiple occupational specialties and the performance of service in multiple locations. List this service as a job; give the dates served, the duty specialty, and the rank at discharge. Discuss military duties if they relate to the job you are seeking.

- For each job or experience, list both the job and company titles. Throughout each section, consistently begin with either the job or the company name, depending on which will likely be more impressive to potential employers.

R

- Under each job or experience, provide a concise description of your accomplishments. By listing your accomplishments and quantifying them with numbers, percentages, or monetary value, you will let the employer know what separates you from the competition. That said, it's not a good idea to omit job duties entirely from your résumé; employers still want to see the scope of what you were responsible for. A good strategy for effectively organizing both is to create a brief paragraph outlining your responsibilities, followed by a bulleted list of your strongest accomplishments in the position.

- Focus as much as possible on your achievements in your work history. ("Increased employee retention rate by 16 percent by developing a training program.") Employers will picture themselves on the receiving end of your previous accomplishments.

- Use action verbs ("managed," "supervised," "developed," "facilitated," and "analyzed"). Be consistent when using past or present tense. Even though the résumé is about you, do not use "I" (for example, instead of "I was promoted to Section Leader," use "Promoted to Section Leader").

Related Knowledge, Skills, and Abilities. Employers are interested in hiring applicants with a variety of skills or the ability to learn new ones quickly. Depending on the position, you might list items such as fluency in foreign languages, writing and editing abilities, specialized technical knowledge, or computer skills (including knowledge of specific languages, software, and hardware).

Honors and Activities. List any honors and unique activities near the end of your résumé, unless they are exceptionally notable or would be more persuasive for a particular objective. Include items such as student or community activities, professional or club memberships, awards received, and published works. Do not duplicate information given in other categories, and include only information that supports your employment objective. Use a heading for this section that fits its contents, such as "Activities," "Honors," "Professional Affiliations," or "Publications and Memberships."

References and Portfolios. Avoid specifying on your résumé that references are available unless that is standard practice in your profession or your résumé is sparse. Employers assume that a well-prepared job seeker will provide a list of professional references. Create a separate list of references in the same format design and layout as your résumé, and be ready to provide this page to prospective employers during the interview process. Always seek permission from anyone you list as a reference and notify them in advance when you provide their information to a prospective employer.

A portfolio is a collection of samples in a binder or on the Internet of your most impressive work and accomplishments. The portfolio can include successful documents you have written, articles, letters of praise from employers, copies of awards and certificates, and a compact disk (CD) with links to samples of your work. If you have developed a portfolio, you can include the phrase "Portfolio available on request" in your résumé. If portfolios are standard in your profession, you might even include a small section that outlines the contents of your portfolio.

◖ PROFESSIONALISM NOTE Avoid listing the salary you desire in the application letter or résumé unless specifically requested to do so by an employer. See **salary negotiations**. ▶

Electronic Résumés

In addition to the traditional paper résumé, many resources offer the opportunity to post a Web-based résumé. Some employers may request you to submit a "scannable" plain-text résumé through e-mail or complete an online application form to be included in an organization's database. Technology continues to change. To ensure that you maintain a competitive edge in seeking employment opportunity, remain current with the automated forms, programs, and protocols that employers prefer by reviewing popular job-search sites, such as Monster.com at *www.monster.com* or CareerBuilder at *www.careerbuilder.com*.

Web Résumés. If you plan to post your résumé on your own Web site, keep the following points in mind:

- Follow the general advice for **writing for the Web**, and view your résumé on several browsers to see how it looks.

- Just below your name, you may wish to provide a series of internal page links to such important categories as "experience" and "education."

- Consider building a multipage site for displaying a work portfolio, publications, reference letters, and other related materials.

- To maintain privacy and protect your personal information, include a "contact link" in Web-based résumés so prospective employers and recruiters can reach you. This way, you will not have to include your e-mail address and phone number, or risk your safety by publishing your home address online.

The disadvantage of posting a résumé at your own Web site is that you must attract the attention of employers on your own. For that reason, commercial services may be a better option because they offer a variety of job-search resources and often work with multiple employers and recruiters.

Scannable and Plain-Text Résumés. A scannable résumé format is a paper document that you mail to the employer; after it is received, the document will be scanned into an automated program then downloaded into the company's searchable database. These résumés should not contain decorative fonts, underlining, shading, letters that touch each other, or other features that will not scan easily. Before sending, scan the résumé yourself to make sure that it is legible.

Some employers request ASCII or plain-text résumés via e-mail, which can be added directly into the résumé database without scanning. The ASCII résumés also allow employers to read the file no matter what type of software they are using. You can copy and paste such a résumé directly into the body of the e-mail message.

For résumés that will be downloaded into databases, it is better to use nouns than verbs to describe experience and skills (*designer* and *management* rather than *designed* and *managed*). Keywords, also called *descriptors*, allow potential employers to search the database for qualified candidates, so be sure to use keywords that mirror those used in job announcements or job descriptions that best match your interests and qualifications. This section can follow the main heading or appear near the end of your résumé.

E-mail–Attached Résumés. An employer may request, or you may prefer to submit, a résumé as an e-mail attachment. If the employer does not specify the file format (such as Word 2003 or Word 2007), consider using a relatively plain design and sending the résumé as a rich text format (.rtf) document. If the retention of formatting is important, send the résumé as a portable document format (PDF) file that will preserve the fonts, images, graphics, and layout. You can attach this file to an e-mail message that will then serve as your application cover letter.

R

revision

When you revise your draft, read and evaluate it primarily from the point of view of your **audience**. In fact, revising requires a different frame of mind than **writing a draft**. To achieve that frame of mind, experienced writers have developed the following tactics:

- Allow a "cooling period" between writing the draft and revision in order to evaluate the draft objectively.

- Print your draft and mark up the paper copy; it is often difficult to revise on-screen.
- Read your draft aloud—often, hearing the text will enable you to spot problems that need improvement.
- Revise in passes by reading through your draft several times, each time searching for and correcting a different set of problems.

When you can no longer spot improvements, you may wish to give the draft to a colleague for review—especially for projects that are crucial for you or your organization as well as for collaborative projects, as described in **collaborative writing**.

WRITER'S CHECKLIST   Revising Your Draft

✔ COMPLETENESS. Does the document achieve its primary **purpose**? Will it fulfill the readers' needs? Your writing should give readers exactly what they need but not overwhelm them.

✔ APPROPRIATE INTRODUCTION AND CONCLUSION. Check to see that your **introduction** frames the rest of the document and that your **conclusion** ties the main ideas together. Both should account for revisions to the content of the document.

✔ ACCURACY. Look for any inaccuracies that may have crept into your draft.

✔ UNITY AND COHERENCE. Check to see that sentences and ideas are closely tied together (**coherence**) and contribute directly to the main idea expressed in the topic sentence of each **paragraph** (see **unity**). Provide **transitions** where they are missing and strengthen those that are weak.

✔ CONSISTENCY. Make sure that **layout and design**, **visuals**, and use of language are consistent. Do not call the same item by one term on one page and by a different term on another page.

✔ CONCISENESS. Tighten your writing so that it says exactly what you mean. Prune unnecessary words, phrases, sentences, and even paragraphs. See **conciseness**.

✔ AWKWARDNESS. Look for **awkwardness** in **sentence construction** — especially any **garbled sentences**.

✔ ETHICAL WRITING. Check for **ethics in writing** and eliminate **biased language**.

✔ ACTIVE VOICE. Use the active **voice** unless the passive voice is more appropriate.

WRITER'S CHECKLIST   Revising Your Draft *(continued)*

✔ WORD CHOICE. Delete or replace **vague words** and unnecessary **intensifiers**. Check for **affectation** and unclear **pronoun references**. See also **word choice**.

✔ JARGON. If you have any doubt that all your readers will understand any **jargon** or special terms you have used, eliminate or define them.

✔ CLICHÉS. Replace **clichés** with fresh **figures of speech** or direct statements.

✔ GRAMMAR. Check your draft for grammatical errors. Because **grammar** checkers are not always accurate, treat the recommendations only as *suggestions*.

✔ TYPOGRAPHICAL ERRORS. Check your final draft for typographical errors both with your spell checker and with thorough **proofreading** because spell checkers do not catch all errors.

✔ WORDY PHRASES. Use the search-and-replace command to find and revise wordy phrases, such as *that is*, *there are*, *the fact that*, and *to be*, and unnecessary helping **verbs** such as *will*.

DIGITAL TIP

Incorporating Tracked Changes

When colleagues review your document, they can "track" changes and insert comments within the document itself. Tracking and commenting vary with types and versions of word-processing programs, but in most programs you can view the document with all reviewers' edits and comments highlighted, or see the document as it would look if you accepted any changes made. For more advice on this topic, go to *bedfordstmartins.com/alred* and select *Digital Tips*, "Incorporating Tracked Changes."

R

rhetorical questions

A rhetorical question does not require a specific answer because it is intended to make an **audience** think about the subject from a different perspective. The writer or speaker then answers the question in an article or a **presentation**. The answer to a rhetorical question such as "Is space exploration worth the cost?" may not be a simple yes or no;

it might be a detailed explanation of the pros and cons of the value of space exploration.

The rhetorical question can be used as an effective **title** or opening, especially in **newsletter articles**, **brochures**, **presentations**, or even **blogs**. However, it should be used judiciously in other, more-formal documents. A rhetorical question, for example, would not be appropriate for the title of a **report** or an **e-mail** addressed to a manager who needs to quickly understand the subject and purpose of the document or message.

run-on sentences

A run-on sentence, sometimes called a *fused sentence*, is two or more sentences without punctuation to separate them. The term is also sometimes applied to a pair of independent **clauses** separated by only a **comma**, although this variation is usually called a **comma splice**. See also **sentence construction** and **sentence faults**.

Run-on sentences can be corrected, as shown in the following examples, by (1) making two sentences, (2) joining the two clauses with a **semicolon** (if they are closely related), (3) joining the two clauses with a comma and a coordinating **conjunction**, or (4) subordinating one clause to the other.

▶ The client suggested several solutions *. Some* ~~some~~ are impractical. [1]

▶ The client suggested several solutions *;* some are impractical. [2]

▶ The client suggested several solutions *, but* some are impractical. [3]

▶ The client suggested several solutions *, although* some are impractical. [4]

R

S

salary negotiations

Salary negotiations usually take place either at the end of a job interview or after a formal job offer has been made. If possible, delay discussing salary until after you receive a formal written job offer because you will have more negotiating leverage at that point. See also **job search**.

Before **interviewing for a job**, prepare for possible salary negotiations by researching the following:

- The current range of salaries for the work you hope to do at your level (entry? intermediate? advanced?) in your region of the country. Check trade journals and organizations in your field, or ask a reference librarian for help in finding this information. Job listings that include salary can also be helpful.
- Salaries made by last year's graduates from your college or university at your level and in your line of work. Your campus career-development office should have these figures.
- Salaries made by people you know at your level and in your line of work. Attend local organizational meetings in your field or contact officers of local organizations who might have this information or steer you to useful contacts.

If a potential employer requests your salary requirements with your **résumé**, consider your options carefully. If you provide a salary that is too high, the company might never interview you; if you provide a salary that is too low, you may have no opportunity later in the hiring process to negotiate for a higher salary. However, if you fail to follow the potential employer's directions and omit the requested information, an employer may disqualify you on principle. If you choose to provide salary requirements, always do so in a range (for example, $35,000 to $40,000). See also **application cover letters**.

If an interviewer asks your salary requirements toward the end of the job interview, you can try the following strategies to delay salary negotiations:

- Say something like, "I am sure that this company pays a fair salary for a person with my level of experience and qualifications" or "I am ready to consider your best offer."

S

- Indicate that you would like to learn more details about the position before discussing salary; point out that your primary goal is to work in a stimulating environment with growth potential, not to earn a specific salary.
- Express your strong interest in the position and the organization without referring to the salary.
- Reemphasize your unique qualifications (or combination of skills) for the job and what you can do for the company that other candidates cannot.

If the interviewer or company demands to know your salary requirements during a job interview, provide a wide salary range that you know would be reasonable for someone at your level in your line of work in that region of the country. For example, you could say, "I would hope for a salary somewhere between $35,000 and $45,000, but of course this is negotiable."

WEB LINK	Salary Information Resources

Some employers may ask for a salary history, a document that lists the starting and ending salaries for each position held. This form gives the employer an idea of how earnings have changed over the course of your employment history and what you hope to earn as a starting salary in your new position. For links to Web sites offering salary-history samples and useful resources for salary negotiations, see *bedfordstmartins.com/alred* and select *Links for Handbook Entries*.

Once salary negotiations begin, resist the temptation to immediately accept the first salary offer you receive. If you have done thorough **research**, you will know if the first salary offer is at the low, middle, or high end of the salary range for your level of experience in your line of work. If you have little or no experience and receive an offer for a salary at the low end of the range, you will realize that the offer probably is fair and reasonable. However, if you receive the same low-end offer but bring considerable experience to the job, you can negotiate for a higher salary that is more reasonable for someone with your background and credentials in your line of work in your region of the country.

Never say that you are unable to accept a salary below a particular figure. To keep negotiations going, simply indicate that you would have trouble accepting the first offer because it was lower than you had expected.

Remember that you are negotiating a package and not just a starting salary. For example, consider the value of a chance for an early promotion, thus a higher salary, within a few years or a particular job title or special responsibilities that would provide you with impressive chances for career growth. If the starting salary seems low, consider negotiating for some of the following possible job perks, if they are not already provided:

- Tuition reimbursement for continued education
- Payment of relocation costs
- Paid personal leave or paid vacations
- Paid personal or sick days
- Overtime potential and compensation
- Flexible hours and work-from-home options
- Health, dental, optical or eye care, disability, and life insurance

- Retirement plans, such as 401(k) and pension plans
- Profit sharing; investment or stock options
- Bonuses or cost-of-living adjustments
- Commuting or parking-cost reimbursement
- Family leave
- Child-care or elder-care benefits
- Fitness or wellness benefits
- Discounts on company products and services

You might find it most comfortable to respond to an initial offer in writing and then meet later with the potential employer for further negotiation. If possible, indicate all your preferences and requirements at one time instead of continually asking for new and different benefits as you negotiate. Throughout this process, focus on what is most important to you (which might differ from what is most important to your friends) and on what you would find acceptable and comfortable.

sales letters

S

A sales letter—a printed or an electronic message that promotes a product, service, or business—requires both a thorough knowledge of the product or service and an understanding of the potential customer's needs.

An effective sales letter (1) catches readers' attention, (2) arouses their interest, (3) convinces them that your product or service will fulfill a need or desire, and (4) confidently asks them to take the course of action you suggest. See also **correspondence**, **persuasion**, **promotional writing**, and **tone**.

Your first task in writing a sales letter is to determine to whom your message should be sent. One good source of names is a list of your customers; people who have at some time purchased a product or service from you may do so again. Other sources are lists of people who may be interested in similar products or services. Companies that specialize in marketing techniques compile such lists from the membership rolls of professional associations, lists of trade-show attendees, and the like. Because outside lists may be expensive, select them with care.

Once you determine who is to receive your sales letter, learn as much as you can about your readers so that you can effectively tell them how your product or service will satisfy their needs. Knowledge of your **audience**—their gender, age, vocation, geographic location, educational level, financial status, and interests—will help determine your approach.

Analyze your product or service carefully to determine your strongest psychological sales points. Psychological selling involves stressing a product's benefits, which may be intangible, rather than its physical features. Select the most important psychological selling point about your product or service and build your sales message around it. Show how your product or service will make your readers' jobs easier, increase their status, make their personal lives more pleasant, and so on. Show how your product or service can satisfy your readers' needs or desires, which you identified in your opening. Then describe the physical features of your product in terms of their benefit to your readers. Help your readers imagine themselves using your product or service—and enjoying the benefits of doing so. See also **"you" viewpoint**.

❖ ETHICS NOTE Be certain that any claim you make in a sales message is valid. To claim that a product is safe guarantees its absolute safety; therefore, say that the product is safe "provided that normal safety precautions are taken." Further, do not exaggerate or speak negatively about a competitor. For further ethical and legal guidelines, visit the Direct Marketing Association Web site at *www.the-dma.org*. See also **ethics in writing**. ❖

| **WRITER'S CHECKLIST** | **Writing Sales Letters** |

S

✔ Attract your readers' attention and arouse their interest in the opening, for example, by describing a product's feature that would appeal strongly to their needs. See also **introductions**.

✔ Convince readers that your product or service is everything you say it is through case histories, free-trial use, money-back guarantee, or testimonials and endorsements.*

---

*For detailed advice, see the FTC guides concerning use of endorsements and testimonials in advertising at *www.ftc.gov/opa/2009/10/endortest.shtm*.

✔ Suggest ways readers can make immediate use of the product or service.

✔ Minimize the negative effect price can have on readers.

- Mention the price along with a reminder of the benefits of the product.

- State the price in terms of units rather than sets ($20 per item, not $600 per set).

- Identify the daily, monthly, or even yearly cost based on the estimated life of the product.

- Suggest a series of payments rather than one total payment.

- Compare the cost of your product with that of something readers accept readily. ("This entire package costs no more than a dinner and a concert.")

✔ Make it easy and worthwhile for customers to respond: Include a **brochure**, a discount coupon, instructions for phone-in orders, information about free delivery, or a Web address or link where customers can view special discounts and order online.

WEB LINK	Sales-Letter Resources
For links to advice on writing sales letters as well as samples, see *bedfordstmartins.com/alred* and select *Links for Handbook Entries*.	

scope

Scope is the depth and breadth of detail you include in a document as defined by your audience's needs, your **purpose**, and the **context**. (See also **audience**.) For example, if you write a **trip report** about a routine visit to a company facility, your readers may need to know only the basic details and any unusual findings. However, if you prepare a trip report about a visit to a division that has experienced problems and your purpose is to suggest ways to solve those problems, your report will contain many more details, observations, and even recommendations.

You should determine the scope of a document during the **preparation** stage of the writing process, even though you may refine it later. Defining your scope will expedite your **research** and can help determine team members' responsibilities in **collaborative writing**.

Your scope will also be affected by the type of document you are writing as well as the medium you select for your message. For example,

S

funding organizations often prescribe the general content and length for **grant proposals**, and some organizations set limits for the length of **memos** and **e-mails**. See **selecting the medium** and "Five Steps to Successful Writing" on page xv.

selecting the medium

With so many media and forms of communication available, selecting the most appropriate medium can be challenging. Which electronic or paper medium (or *channel*) is best depends on a wide range of factors related to your **audience**, your **purpose**, and the **context** of the communication. Those factors include the following:

- The audience's preferences and expectations
- Your own most effective communication style
- How widely information needs to be distributed
- What kind of record you need to keep
- The urgency of the communication
- The sensitivity or confidentiality required
- The technological resources available
- The organizational practices or regulations

As this list suggests, choosing the best medium may involve personal considerations or the essential functions of the medium. If you need to collaborate with someone to solve a problem, for example, you may find e-mail exchanges less effective than a phone call or face-to-face meeting. If you need precise wording or a record of a complex or sensitive message, however, using a written medium is often essential.

Keep in mind that many of the following media and forms of communication evolve and overlap as technology develops. Understanding their basic functions will help you select the most appropriate medium for your needs. See **adapting to new technologies** for advice on how to learn and make the best use of new technologies as they continue to evolve.

E-mail

E-mail (or *email*) functions in the workplace as a primary medium to communicate and share electronic files with colleagues, clients, and customers. Although e-mail may function as informal notes, e-mail messages should follow the writing strategy and style described in **cor-**

respondence. Because recipients can easily forward messages and attachments to others and because e-mail messages are subject to legal disclosure, e-mail requires writers to review their messages carefully before clicking the "Send" button.

Memos

Memos are appropriate for internal communication among members of the same organization; they use a standard header and are sent on paper or as attachments to e-mails. Organizations may use memos printed on organizational stationery when they need to communicate with the formality and authority of business letters. Memos may also be used in manufacturing or service industries, for example, where employees do not have easy access to e-mail. In such cases, memos can be used to instruct employees, announce policies, report results, disseminate information, and delegate responsibilities.

Letters

Business **letters** with handwritten signatures are often the most appropriate choice for formal communications with professional associates or customers outside an organization. Letters printed on organizational letterhead stationery communicate formality, respect, and authority. They may be especially effective for those people who receive a high volume of e-mail and other electronic correspondence. Letters are often used for job applications, for recommendations, and in other official and social contexts.

Faxes

A fax is used when the information—a drawing or signed contract, for example—must be viewed in its original form. Although scanning such documents and attaching them to e-mail is common, faxing is often used when scanning is not available or when a recipient prefers a faxed document. Fax machines in offices can be located in shared areas, so let the intended recipient know before you send confidential or sensitive messages. Consider using a cover sheet that says "confidential" and be sure to include the name of the person to whose attention the fax is being sent and number of pages in the document to ensure full receipt.

Instant Messaging

Instant messaging (IM) on a computer or handheld device may be an efficient way to communicate in real time with coworkers, suppliers, and customers—especially those at sites without access to e-mail. Instant messaging, like **text messaging**, often uses online slang and such shortened spellings as "u" for *you* to save time and screen space. Instant messaging may have limited application in the workplace because recipients must be ready and willing to participate in an online conversation. For ethical and security issues for both text and instant messaging, see pages 276–77.

Text Messaging

Text messaging, or *texting*, refers to the exchange of brief written messages between mobile phones over cellular networks. Text messaging is effective for simple messages communicated between people on the move or in nontraditional workplaces. For the real-time message exchanges of brief messages, use the telephone or instant messaging.

Telephone and Conference Calls

Telephone calls are best used for exchanges that require substantial interaction and the ability of participants to interpret each other's tone of voice. They are useful for discussing sensitive issues and resolving misunderstandings, although they do not provide the visual cues possible during face-to-face meetings. Cell (or *mobile*) phones are useful for communicating away from an office, but users should follow appropriate etiquette and organizational policies, such as speaking in an appropriate tone and turning off the phone or switching it to vibration mode during meetings.

A teleconference, or *conference call*, among three or more participants is a less-expensive alternative to face-to-face meetings requiring travel. Conference calls work best when the person coordinating the call works from an agenda shared by all the participants and directs the discussion as if chairing a meeting. Participants can use the Web during conference calls to share and view common documents. Conference calls in which decisions have been reached should be followed with written confirmation.

Voice-Mail Messages

Voice-mail messages should be clear and brief. ("I got your package, so you don't need to call the distributor.") If the message is complicated or contains numerous details, use another medium, such as e-mail. If you want to discuss a subject at length, let the recipient know the subject so that he or she can prepare a response before returning your call. When you leave a message, give your name and contact information as well as the date and time of the call (if you are unsure whether the message will be time-stamped).

Face-to-Face Meetings

In-person **meetings** are most appropriate for initial or early contacts with associates and clients with whom you intend to develop an important, long-term relationship or need to establish rapport. Meetings may also be best for brainstorming, negotiating, interviewing someone on a complex topic, solving a technical problem, or handling a controversial issue. For advice on how to record discussions and decisions, see **minutes of meetings**.

Videoconferences

Videoconferences are particularly useful for meetings when travel is impractical. Unlike telephone conference calls, videoconferences have the advantage of allowing participants to see as well as to hear one another. They work best with participants who are at ease in front of the camera and when the facilities offer good production quality.

Web Communication

The Web can encompass many of the media and forms of communication described in this entry; it can also include some other interactive capabilities.

Web Conferencing. The Web can be used to conduct meetings, which are often referred to as Web conferences. In such meetings, the participants' computers may be connected to those of other participants through a downloaded application on each of the attendees' computers. In such a conference, a moderator can control the cursor on the participants' computers. Various programs, like Skype with video or phone connections, can enrich these meetings.

Professional Networking. Using the model of social-networking sites, like Facebook.com, some professional organizations and businesses are creating their own networking sites to foster professional contacts. Other commercial networks, like LinkedIn.com, aim to connect professionals for business purposes. Many businesses place advertising on both professional and social-networking sites—and, if used with caution, both may be helpful for your professional advancement and **job search**.

Web-Site Postings. A public Internet or company intranet Web site is ideal for posting announcements or policies as well as for sharing or exchanging documents and files with others. Your Web site can serve not only as a home base for resources but also as a place where ideas can be developed through, for example, discussion boards, **blogs and forums**, and wikis. See also **collaborative writing**, **writing for the Web**, and *Digital Tip: Using Collaborative Software* on page 83.

DIGITAL TIP

Synchronizing Information

If you use multiple computers (for instance, one at your office and one at home) to work on the same files, synchronizing the data on all of your computers can save you time and eliminate the hassle of e-mailing or copying files from one computer to another. You can also synchronize data between your computer(s) and your mobile devices, which allows you access to your e-mail, contacts, and calendars when you are away from your computer. Numerous "cloud computing" (or off-site) applications offer free or inexpensive accounts for keeping your most important data synchronized. For a list of these applications and a comparison of their features, see *bedfordstmartins.com/alred* and select *Digital Tips*, "Synchronizing Information."

---

semicolons

The semicolon (;) links independent **clauses** or other sentence elements of equal weight and grammatical rank when they are not joined by a **comma** and a **conjunction**. The semicolon indicates a greater pause between clauses than does a comma but not as great a pause as a **period**.

Independent clauses joined by a semicolon should balance or contrast with each other, and the relationship between the two statements should be so clear that further explanation is not necessary.

► The new Web site was a success; every division reported increased online sales.

Do not use a semicolon between a dependent clause and its main clause.

► No one applied for the position; even though it was heavily advertised.

With Strong Connectives

In complicated sentences, a semicolon may be used before transitional words or **phrases** (*that is*, *for example*, *namely*) that introduce examples or further explanation. See also **transition**.

▶ The press understands Commissioner Curran's position on the issue; *that is*, local funds should not be used for the highway project.

A semicolon should also be used before conjunctive **adverbs** (*therefore, moreover, consequently, furthermore, indeed, in fact, however*) that connect independent clauses.

▶ The test results are not complete; *therefore*, I cannot make a recommendation.
[The semicolon in the example shows that *therefore* belongs to the second clause.]

For Clarity in Long Sentences

Use a semicolon between two independent clauses connected by a co-ordinating conjunction (*and, but, for, or, nor, so, yet*) if the clauses are long and contain other **punctuation**.

▶ In most cases, these individuals are executives, bankers, or lawyers; *but* they do not, as the press seems to believe, simply push the button of their economic power to affect local politics.

A semicolon may also be used if any items in a series contain commas.

▶ Among those present were John Howard, president of the Omega Paper Company; Carol Delgado, president of Environex Corporation; and Larry Stanley, president of Stanley Papers.

Use **parentheses** or **dashes**, not semicolons, to enclose a parenthetical element that contains commas.

▶ All affected job classifications *(*receptionist, secretary, transcriptionist, and clerk*)* will be upgraded this month.

Use a **colon**, not a semicolon, as a mark of anticipation or enumeration.

▶ Three decontamination methods are under consideration; a

zeolite-resin system, an evaporation system, and a filtration system.

The semicolon always appears outside closing **quotation marks**.

▶ The attorney said, "You must be accurate"; her client replied, "I will."

sentence construction

DIRECTORY

A sentence is the most fundamental and versatile tool available to writers. Sentences generally flow from a subject to a **verb** to any **objects**, **complements**, or **modifiers**, but they can be ordered in a variety of ways to achieve **emphasis**. When shifting word order for emphasis, however, be aware that word order can make a great difference in the meaning of a sentence.

> ► He was *only* the accountant. [suggests importance]

> ► He was the *only* accountant. [defines the number]

The most basic components of sentences are subjects and predicates.

Subjects

The *subject* of a sentence is a **noun** or **pronoun** (and its modifiers) about which the predicate of the sentence makes a statement. Although a subject may appear anywhere in a sentence, it most often appears at the beginning. ("*To increase sales* is our goal.") Grammatically, a subject must agree with its verb in **number**.

> ► *These departments have* much in common.

> ► *This department has* several functions.

The subject is the actor in sentences using the active **voice**.

> ► *The Webmaster reported* an increase in site visits for May.

A *compound subject* has two or more substantives (nouns or noun equivalents) as the subject of one verb.

> ► *The president* and *the treasurer* agreed to begin the audit.

ESL TIPS for Understanding the Subject of a Sentence

In English, every sentence, except commands, must have an explicit subject.

                  He established
▸ *Paul* worked fast. ~~Established~~ the parameters for the project.

In commands, the subject *you* is understood and is used only for emphasis.

▸ (*You*) Meet me at the airport at 6:30 tomorrow morning.

▸ (*You*) Do your homework, young man. [parent to child]

If you move the subject from its normal position (subject-verb-object), English often requires you to replace the subject with an expletive (*there, it*). In this construction, the verb agrees with the subject that follows it.

▸ *There are* two files on the desk.
   [The subject is *files*.]

▸ *It is* presumptuous for me to speak for Jim.
   [The subject is *to speak for Jim*.]

Time, distance, weather, temperature, and environmental expressions use *it* as their subject.

▸ *It* is ten o'clock.

▸ *It* is ten miles down the road.

▸ *It* seldom snows in Florida.

▸ *It* is very hot in Jorge's office.

Predicates

The *predicate* is the part of a sentence that makes an assertion about the subject and completes the thought of the sentence.

▸ Bill *has piloted the corporate jet.*

The *simple predicate* is the verb and any helping verbs (*has piloted*). The *complete predicate* is the verb and any modifiers, objects, or complements (*has piloted the corporate jet*). A *compound predicate* consists of two or more verbs with the same subject.

▸ The company *tried* but *did not succeed* in that field.

S

Such constructions help achieve **conciseness** in writing. A *predicate nominative* is a noun construction that follows a linking verb and renames the subject.

> ► She is my *attorney.* [noun]

> ► His excuse was *that he had been sick.* [noun clause]

Sentence Types

Sentences may be classified according to *structure* (simple, compound, complex, compound-complex); *intention* (declarative, interrogative, imperative, exclamatory); and *stylistic use* (loose, periodic, minor).

Structure.   A *simple sentence* consists of one independent clause. At its most basic, a simple sentence contains only a subject and a predicate.

> ► Profits [subject] rose [predicate].

A *compound sentence* consists of two or more independent clauses connected by a comma and a coordinating **conjunction**, by a **semicolon**, or by a semicolon and a conjunctive **adverb**.

> ► Drilling is the only way to collect samples of the layers of sediment below the ocean floor, *but* it is not the only way to gather information about these strata. [comma and coordinating conjunction]

> ► The chemical composition of seawater bears little resemblance to that of river water; the various elements are present in entirely different proportions. [semicolon]

> ► It was 500 miles to the site; *therefore*, we made arrangements to fly. [semicolon and conjunctive adverb]

A *complex sentence* contains one independent clause and at least one dependent clause that expresses a subordinate idea.

> ► The generator will shut off automatically [independent clause] if the temperature rises above a specified point [dependent clause].

A *compound-complex sentence* consists of two or more independent clauses plus at least one dependent clause.

> ► Productivity is central to controlling inflation [independent clause]; when productivity rises [dependent clause], employers can raise wages without raising prices [independent clause].

Intention.   A *declarative sentence* conveys information or makes a factual statement. ("The motor powers the conveyor belt.") An *interrogative sentence* asks a direct question. ("Does the conveyor belt run constantly?") An *imperative sentence* issues a command. ("Submit your résumé online.") An *exclamatory sentence* is an emphatic expression of feeling, fact, or opinion. It is a declarative sentence that is stated with great feeling. ("The files were deleted!")

Stylistic Use.   A *loose sentence* makes its major point at the beginning and then adds subordinate phrases and clauses that develop or modify that major point. A loose sentence could end at one or more points before it actually does end, as the periods in brackets illustrate in the following sentence:

► It went up[.], a great ball of fire about a mile in diameter[.], an elemental force freed from its bonds[.] after being chained for billions of years.

A *periodic sentence* delays its main ideas until the end by presenting subordinate ideas or modifiers first.

► During the last century, the attitude of the American citizen toward automation underwent a profound change.

A *minor sentence* is an incomplete sentence that makes sense in its context because the missing element is clearly implied by the preceding sentence.

► In view of these facts, is the service contract really useful? *Or economical?*

Constructing Effective Sentences

The subject-verb-object pattern is effective because it is most familiar to **readers**. In "The company increased profits," we know the subject (*company*) and the object (*profits*) by their positions relative to the verb (*increased*).

An *inverted sentence* places the elements in unexpected order, thus emphasizing the point by attracting the readers' attention.

► A better job I never had. [direct object-subject-verb]

► More optimistic I have never been. [subjective complement-subject-linking verb]

► A poor image we presented. [direct object-subject-verb]

Use uncomplicated sentences to state complex ideas. If readers have to cope with a complicated sentence in addition to a complex idea, they are likely to become confused. Just as simpler sentences make complex ideas more digestible, a complex sentence construction makes a series of simple ideas more smooth and less choppy.

S

Avoid loading sentences with a number of thoughts carelessly tacked together. Such sentences are monotonous and hard to read because all the ideas seem to be of equal importance. Rather, distinguish the relative importance of sentence elements with **subordination**. See also **garbled sentences**.

LOADED   We started the program three years ago, only three members were on the staff, and each member was responsible for a separate state, but it was not an efficient operation.

IMPROVED   When we started the program three years ago, only three members were on the staff, each responsible for a separate state; however, that arrangement was not efficient.

Express coordinate or equivalent ideas in similar form. The structure of the sentence helps readers grasp the similarity of its components, as illustrated in **parallel structure**.

ESL TIPS for Understanding the Requirements of a Sentence

- A sentence must start with a capital letter.
- A sentence must end with a period, a question mark, or an exclamation mark.
- A sentence must have a subject.
- A sentence must have a verb.
- A sentence must conform to subject-verb-object word order (or inverted word order for questions or emphasis).
- A sentence must express an idea that can stand on its own (called the *main*, or *independent*, *clause*).

S

sentence faults

A number of problems can create sentence faults, including faulty **subordination**, **clauses** with no subjects, rambling sentences, omitted **verbs**, and illogical assertions.

Faulty subordination occurs when a grammatically subordinate element contains the main idea of the sentence or when a subordinate element is so long or detailed that it obscures the main idea. Both of the following sentences are logical, depending on what the writer intends as the main idea and as the subordinate element.

▶ Although the new filing system saves money, many of the staff are unhappy with it.
[If the main point is that *many of the staff are unhappy*, this sentence is correct.]

▶ The new filing system saves money, although many of the staff are unhappy with it.
[If the main point is that *the new filing system saves money*, this sentence is correct.]

In the following example, the subordinate element overwhelms the main point.

FAULTY   Because the noise level in the assembly area on a typical shift is as loud as a smoke detector's alarm ten feet away, employees often develop hearing problems.

IMPROVED   Employees in the assembly area often develop hearing problems because the noise level on a typical shift is as loud as a smoke detector's alarm ten feet away.

Missing subjects occur when writers inappropriately assume a subject that they do not state in the clause. See also **sentence fragments**.

INCOMPLETE   Your application program can request to end the session after the next command.
[Your application program can request *who* or *what* to end the session?]

COMPLETE   Your application program can request *the host program* to end the session after the next command.

Rambling sentences contain more information than the reader can comfortably absorb. The obvious remedy for a rambling sentence is to divide it into two or more sentences. (See also **run-on sentences**.) When you do that, put the main message of the rambling sentence into the first of the revised sentences.

RAMBLING   The payment to which a subcontractor is entitled should be made promptly in order that in the event of a subsequent contractual dispute we, as general contractors, may not be held in default of our contract by virtue of nonpayment.

DIRECT   Pay subcontractors promptly. Then if a contractual dispute occurs, we cannot be held in default of our contract because of nonpayment.

S

Missing verbs produce some sentence faults.

> I never have$_\wedge$and probably never will write the annual report.
>
> *written*

Faulty logic results when a predicate makes an illogical assertion about its subject. "Mr. Wilson's *job* is a sales representative" is not logical, but "*Mr. Wilson* is a sales representative" is logical. "Jim's *height* is six feet tall" is not logical, but "*Jim* is six feet tall" is logical. See also **logic errors**.

sentence fragments

A sentence fragment is an incomplete grammatical unit that is punctuated as a sentence.

> FRAGMENT   And quit his job.
>
> SENTENCE   He quit his job.

A sentence fragment lacks either a subject or a **verb** or is a subordinate **clause** or **phrase**. Sentence fragments are often introduced by relative **pronouns** (*who, whom, which, that*) or subordinating **conjunctions** (such as *although, because, if, when,* and *while*).

> The new manager instituted several new procedures. ~~Although~~ she didn't clear them with Human Resources.
>
> *, although*

A sentence must contain a finite verb; **verbals** (nonfinite) do not function as verbs. The following sentence fragments use verbals (*providing, to work*) that cannot function as finite verbs.

> FRAGMENT   *Providing* all employees with disability insurance.
>
> SENTENCE   The company *provides* all employees with disability insurance.
>
> FRAGMENT   *To work* a 40-hour week.
>
> SENTENCE   Most of our employees *must work* a 40-hour week.

Explanatory phrases beginning with *such as, for example,* and similar terms often lead writers to create sentence fragments.

> The staff wants additional benefits. ~~For example,~~ the use of company cars.
>
> *, such as*

A hopelessly snarled fragment simply must be rewritten. To rewrite such a fragment, pull the main points out of the fragment, list them in the proper sequence, and then rewrite the sentence as illustrated in **garbled sentences**. See also **sentence construction** and **sentence faults**.

sentence variety

Sentences can vary in length, structure, and complexity. As you revise, vary your sentences so that they do not become tiresomely alike. See also **sentence construction**.

Sentence Length

A series of sentences of the same length is monotonous, so varying sentence length makes writing less tedious to the **reader**. For example, avoid stringing together a number of short independent **clauses**. Either connect them with subordinating connectives, thereby making some dependent clauses, or make some clauses into separate sentences.

STRING   The river is 63 miles long, and it averages 50 yards in width, and its depth averages 8 feet.

IMPROVED   The river, which is 63 miles long and averages 50 yards in width, has an average depth of 8 feet.

IMPROVED   The river is 63 miles long. It averages 50 yards in width and 8 feet in depth.

You can often effectively combine short sentences by converting **verbs** into **adjectives**.

    failed
▶ The digital shift indicator ~~failed. It~~ was pulled from the market.

Although too many short sentences make your writing sound choppy and immature, a short sentence can be effective following a long one.

▶ During the past two decades, many changes have occurred in American life—the extent, durability, and significance of which no one has yet measured. *No one can.*

In general, short sentences are good for emphatic, memorable statements. Long sentences are good for detailed explanations and support. Nothing is inherently wrong with a long sentence, or even with a complicated one, as long as its meaning is clear and direct. Sentence length becomes an element of style when varied for **emphasis** or contrast; a conspicuously short or long sentence can be used to good effect.

S

Word Order

When a series of sentences all begin in exactly the same way (usually with an **article** and a **noun**), the result is likely to be monotonous. You can make your sentences more interesting by occasionally starting with a modifying word, **phrase**, or clause.

▶ *To salvage the project*, she presented alternatives when existing policies failed to produce results. [modifying phrase]

However, overuse of this technique can itself be monotonous, so use it in moderation.

Inverted word order can be an effective way to achieve variety, but be careful not to create an awkward construction.

AWKWARD   So good sales have never been.

EFFECTIVE   Never have sales been so good.

For variety, you can alter normal sentence order by inserting a phrase or clause.

▶ Titanium fills the gap, *both in weight and in strength*, between aluminum and steel.

The technique of inserting a phrase or clause is good for achieving emphasis, providing detail, breaking monotony, and regulating **pace**.

Loose and Periodic Sentences

A loose sentence makes its major point at the beginning and then adds subordinate phrases and clauses that develop or modify the point. A loose sentence could end at one or more points before it actually ends, as the periods in brackets illustrate in the following example:

▶ It went up[.], a great ball of fire about a mile in diameter[.], an elemental force freed from its bonds[.] after being chained for billions of years.

A periodic sentence delays its main idea until the end by presenting modifiers or subordinate ideas first, thus holding the readers' interest until the end.

▶ During the last century, the attitude of Americans toward technology underwent a profound change.

Experiment with shifts from loose sentences to periodic sentences in your own writing, especially during **revision**. Avoid the monotony of a long series of loose sentences, particularly a series containing coordinate clauses joined by **conjunctions**. Using **subordination** not only provides emphasis but also makes your sentences more interesting.

sequential method of development

The sequential, or *step-by-step*, **method of development** is especially effective for explaining a process or describing a mechanism in operation. (See **process explanation**.) It is also the logical method for writing **instructions**, as shown in Figure S–1.

The main advantage of the sequential method of development is that it is easy to follow because the steps correspond to the process or operation being described. The disadvantages are that it can become monotonous and does not lend itself well to achieving **emphasis**.

From: Steven Scott <scott@techline.org>
To: All Hourly Employees <hourly@techline.org>
Sent: Friday, January 27, 2012 2:16 PM
Subject: Flextime Eligibility and Requests

Because Human Resources has received numerous calls about the approval process for using the new "flextime" working schedule, this message outlines the eligibility requirements and the procedure for requesting flextime.

First, determine if you are eligible to use a flextime schedule. You are eligible if your job does not require you to answer telephones or to be available to the public between the hours of 8:00 a.m. and 5:00 p.m. In addition, you must meet with your department manager to ensure that any necessary duties will be covered during those hours.

After you have established your eligibility, submit a copy of Form FT, signed by your department manager, to Human Resources. We will send the form to your division manager for his or her approval.

Human Resources will notify you when your request is approved or denied. If your request is approved, you may begin your new schedule on the first Monday thereafter. After three weeks, your manager must advise Human Resources in writing that your flextime schedule has not interfered with the smooth functioning of your department.

You may obtain copies of Form FT from Margaret Dienstein in Room 129. If you have any questions, please feel free to contact Margaret at ext. 5648 or mld@techline.org.

S

FIGURE S–1. Sequential Method of Development

Most methods of development have elements of sequence to a greater or lesser extent. The **chronological method of development**, for example, is also sequential: To describe a trip chronologically, from beginning to end, is also to describe it sequentially. The **cause-and-effect method of development** may contain certain elements of sequence. For example, a report of the causes leading to an accident (the effect) might describe those causes in the order they occurred (or their sequence).

service

When used as a **verb**, *service* means "keep up or maintain" as well as "repair." ("Our company will *service* your equipment.") If you mean "provide a more general benefit," use *serve*.

► Our company ~~services~~ the northwest area of the state.
       serves

set / sit

Sit is an intransitive **verb**; it does not, therefore, require an **object**. ("I *sit* by a window in the office.") Its past **tense** is *sat*. ("We *sat* around the conference table.") *Set* is usually a transitive verb, meaning "put or place," "establish," or "harden." Its past tense is *set*.

► Please *set* the supplies on the shelf.

► The jeweler *set* the stone carefully.

► Can we *set* a date for the meeting?

► The high temperature *sets* the epoxy quickly.

Set is occasionally an intransitive verb.

► The new adhesive *sets* in five minutes.

shall / will

Although traditionally *shall* was used to express the future **tense** with *I* and *we*, *will* is generally accepted with all persons. *Shall* is commonly used today only in questions requesting an opinion or a preference ("*Shall* we go?") rather than a prediction ("*Will* we go?"). It is also used in statements expressing determination ("I *shall* return!") or in formal regulations that express a requirement ("Applicants *shall* provide a proof of certification").

slashes

The slash (/)—also called *slant line*, *diagonal*, *virgule*, *bar*, and *solidus*—both separates and shows omission. The slash can indicate alternatives or combinations.

- ► David's telephone numbers are (800) 549-2278/2235.
- ► Check the on/off switch before you leave.

The slash often indicates omitted words and letters.

- ► miles/hour (miles per hour); w/o (without)

In fractions and mathematical expressions, the slash separates the numerator from the denominator (3/4 for three-fourths; x/y for x over y).

Although the slash is used informally with **dates** (*5/9/12*), avoid this form in business writing, especially in **international correspondence**.

The forward slash often separates items in URL (uniform resource locator) addresses for sites on the Internet (*bedfordstmartins.com/alred*). The backward slash is used to separate parts of file names (*c:\myfiles\ reports\annual12.doc*).

so / so that / such

Avoid *so* as a substitute for *because*. See also **as / because / since**.

▸ ~~She~~ reads faster, ~~so~~ she finished before I did.
   Because she (above "She")

Do not replace the phrase *so that* with *so* or *such that*.

▸ The report should be written ~~such that~~ it can be widely understood.
   so that (above "such that")

Such, an **adjective** meaning "of this or that kind," should never be used as a **pronoun**.

- ► Our company provides on-site child care, but I do not anticipate using ~~such~~.
   it. (above "such")

S

some / somewhat

When *some* functions as an indefinite **pronoun** for a plural count **noun** or as an indefinite **adjective** modifying a plural count noun, use a plural **verb**.

▸ *Some* of us *are* prepared to work overtime.

▸ *Some* people *are* more productive than others.

Some is singular, however, when used with mass nouns.

▸ *Some* sand *has* trickled through the crack.

When *some* is used as an adjective or a pronoun meaning "an undetermined quantity" or "certain unspecified persons," it should be replaced by the **adverb** *somewhat*, which means "to some extent."

▸ His writing has improved ~~some.~~ *somewhat.*

some time / sometime / sometimes

Some time refers to a duration of time. ("We waited for *some time* before making the decision.") *Sometime* refers to an unknown or unspecified time. ("We will visit with you *sometime*.") *Sometimes* refers to occasional occurrences at unspecified times. ("He *sometimes* visits the branch offices.")

spatial method of development

The spatial **method of development** describes an object or a process according to the physical arrangement of its features. Depending on the subject, you describe its features from bottom to top, side to side, east to west, outside to inside, and so on. Descriptions of this kind rely mainly on dimension (height, width, length), direction (up, down, north, south), shape (rectangular, square, semicircular), and proportion (one-half, two-thirds). Features are described in relation to one another or to their surroundings, as illustrated in Figure S–2, which might be written by a home inspector or crime-scene investigator. The description in Figure S–2 relies on a bottom-to-top, clockwise (south to west to north to east) sequence, beginning with the front door. Such descriptions often benefit from **visuals**, such as **drawings**, that can provide overviews and details.

S

DESCRIPTION

Interior of Two-Story, Six-Room House

Ground Floor

Front hall and stairwell. The front door faces south and opens into a hallway seven feet deep and ten feet wide. At the end of the hallway is a stairwell that begins on the right-hand (east) side of the hallway, rises five steps to a landing, and reverses direction at the left-hand (west) side of the hallway.

Dining room. To the left (west) of the hallway is the dining room, which measures 15 feet along its southern exposure and ten feet along its western exposure.

Kitchen. North of the dining room is the kitchen, which measures ten feet along its western exposure and 15 feet along its northern exposure.

Bathroom. East of the kitchen, along the northern side of the house, is a bathroom that measures ten feet (west to east) by five feet.

Living room. Parallel to the bathroom is a passageway the same size as the bathroom and leading from the kitchen to the living room. The living room (15 feet west to east by 20 feet north to south) occupies the entire eastern end of the floor.

Second Floor

Hallway. On the second floor, at the top of the stairs, is an L-shaped hallway, five feet wide. The base of the L, over the door, is 15 feet long. The vertical arm of the L is 13 feet long.

Southwest bedroom. To the west of the hall is the southwest bedroom, which measures ten feet along its southern exposure and eight feet along its western exposure.

Northwest bedroom. Directly to the north, over the kitchen, is the northwest bedroom, which measures 12 feet along its western exposure and ten feet along its northern exposure.

S

FIGURE S–2. Spatial Method of Development

The spatial method of development might be used for descriptions of warehouse inventory, **proposals** for landscape work, construction-site **progress and activity reports**, and, in combination with a step-by-step sequence, many types of **instructions**.

spelling

Because spelling errors in your documents can confuse readers and damage your credibility, careful **proofreading** is essential. The use of a spell checker is crucial; however, it will not catch all mistakes, especially those in personal and company names. It cannot detect a spelling error if the error results in a valid word; for example, if you mean *to* but inadvertently type *too*, the spell checker will not detect the error. If you are unsure about the spelling of a word, do not rely on guesswork or a spell checker—consult a print or an online **dictionary**.

style

A dictionary definition of *style* is "the way in which something is said or done, as distinguished from its substance." Writers' styles are determined by the way writers think and transfer their thoughts to paper—the way they use words, sentences, images, **figures of speech**, and so on.

A writer's style is the way his or her language functions in particular situations. For example, an **e-mail** to a friend would be relaxed, even chatty, in **tone**, whereas a job **application cover letter** would be more restrained and formal. Obviously, the style appropriate to one situation would not be appropriate to the other. In both situations, the **audience**, the **purpose**, and the **context** determine the manner or style the writer adopts. Beyond an individual's personal style, various kinds of writing have distinct stylistic traits, such as **business writing style**.

Standard English can be divided into two broad categories of style—formal and informal—according to how it functions in certain situations. Understanding the distinction between formal and informal writing styles helps writers use the appropriate style. We must recognize, however, that no clear-cut line divides the two categories and that some writing may call for a combination of the two. See also **English, varieties of**.

Formal Writing Style

A formal writing style can perhaps best be defined by pointing to certain material that is clearly formal, such as scholarly and scientific articles in professional journals, lectures read at meetings of professional societies, and legal documents. Material written in a formal style is usually the work of a specialist writing to other specialists or writing that embodies laws or regulations. As a result, the vocabulary is specialized and precise. The writer's tone is impersonal and objective because the subject matter looms larger in the writing than does the author's personality. (See **point of view**.) A formal writing style does not use **contractions**, slang, or dialect. Because the material generally examines complex ideas, the **sentence construction** may be elaborate.

Formal writing need not be dull and lifeless. By using such techniques as the active **voice** whenever possible, **sentence variety**, and **subordination**, a writer can make formal writing lively and interesting, especially if the subject matter is inherently interesting to **readers**. In the following conclusion to a historical study, a scholar reflects on the problem of jargon in business writing.

▶ Compared to some of the problems that afflict business and administrative writing—poor organization, obfuscation, and lack of consideration for the reader—phrases such as "as *per* your request" are a minor ill. It is my own view, however, that texts and teachers should continue to urge students to avoid jargon. People in organizations who face the same situation repeatedly will use similar language to different correspondents; however, the repeated language can be standard English that is friendly and that makes literal sense. Jargon that is not part of spoken English distances the writer from the reader; jargon that does not make literal sense devalues language as communication.

—Kitty O. Locker, "'As *Per* Your Request':
A History of Business Jargon,"
Journal of Business and Technical Communication 1.1

Whether you should use a formal style in a particular instance depends on your readers and purpose. When writers attempt to force a formal style when it should not be used, their writing is likely to fall victim to **affectation**, **awkwardness**, and **gobbledygook**.

Informal Writing Style

An informal writing style is a relaxed and colloquial way of writing standard English. It is the style found in most personal e-mail and in some business **correspondence**, nonfiction books of general interest, and mass-circulation magazines. There is less distance between the writer and the reader because the tone is more personal than in a formal writing style. Consider the following passage, written in an informal style, from a nonfiction book on business management.

▶ Business, like art and science, has been revealed and conceived through the intellect and imagination of people, and it develops or declines because of the intellect and imagination of people.

In fact, there is no business; there are only people. Business exists only among people and for people.

Seems simple enough, and it applies to every aspect of business, but not enough businesspeople seem to get it.

Reading the economic forecasts and the indicators and the ratios and the rates of this or that, someone from another planet might actually believe that there really are invisible hands at work in the marketplace.

It's easy to forget what the measurements are measuring. Every number—from productivity rates to salaries—is just a device contrived by people to measure the results of the enterprise of other people. For managers, the most important job is not measurement but motivation. And you can't motivate numbers.

—James A. Autry,
Love and Profit: The Art of Caring Leadership

As the example illustrates, the vocabulary of an informal writing style is made up of generally familiar rather than unfamiliar words and expressions, although slang and dialect are usually avoided. An informal style approximates the cadence and structure of spoken English while conforming to the grammatical conventions of written English.

◀ PROFESSIONALISM NOTE Writers who consciously attempt to create a distinctive style usually defeat their purpose. Attempting to impress readers with a flashy writing style can lead to affectation; attempting to impress them with scientific objectivity can produce a style that is dull and lifeless. Business writing need be neither affected nor dull. It can and should be simple, clear, direct, even interesting—the key is to master basic writing skills and always to keep your readers in mind. What will be both informative and interesting to your readers? When that question is uppermost in your mind as you apply the steps of the writing process, you will achieve an interesting and informative writing style. See "Five Steps to Successful Writing" on page xv. ▶

S

WRITER'S CHECKLIST   Developing an Effective Style

✔ Use the active voice — not exclusively but as much as possible without becoming awkward or illogical.

✔ Use **parallel structure** whenever a sentence or **list** presents two or more thoughts of equal importance.

✔ Vary sentence structure to avoid a monotonous style.

WRITER'S CHECKLIST   Developing an Effective Style (*continued*)

✔ Avoid stating positive thoughts in negative terms (write "40 percent responded" instead of "60 percent failed to respond"). See also **ethics in writing**, **plain language**, and **positive writing**.

✔ Concentrate on achieving the proper balance between **emphasis** and subordination.

WEB LINK	Style Guides

Style guides, such as *The Chicago Manual of Style* and the Associated Press *Stylebook and Briefing on Media Law*, provide specific and sometimes varied advice for handling issues of usage, style, and formats for citations, correspondence, and documents. For a selected list of such style guides, see *bedfordstmartins.com/alred* and select *Links for Handbook Entries*.

subordination

Use subordination to show, by the structure of a sentence, the appropriate relationship between ideas of unequal importance. Subordination allows you to emphasize your main idea by putting less-important ideas in subordinate **clauses** or **phrases**.

▶ Envirex Systems now employs 500 people. It was founded just three years ago.
  [The two ideas are equally important.]

▶ Envirex Systems, *which now employs 500 people*, was founded just three years ago.
  [The number of employees is subordinated; the founding date is emphasized.]

▶ Envirex Systems, *which was founded just three years ago*, now employs 500 people.
  [The founding date is subordinated; the number of employees is emphasized.]

Effective subordination can be used to achieve **conciseness**, **emphasis**, and **sentence variety**. For example, consider the following sentences.

DEPENDENT CLAUSE	The regional manager's report, *which covered five pages*, was carefully illustrated.
PHRASE	The regional manager's report, *covering five pages*, was carefully illustrated.

S

SINGLE MODIFIER   The regional manager's *five-page* report was carefully illustrated.

Subordinating **conjunctions** (*because, if, while, when, although*) achieve subordination effectively.

▶ An increase in local sales is unlikely *because* the local population has declined.

You may use a coordinating conjunction (*and, but, for, nor, or, so, yet*) to concede that an opposite or balancing fact is true; however, a subordinating conjunction can often make the point more smoothly.

▶ *Although* their bank has a lower interest rate on loans, ours provides a wider range of essential services.

The relationship between a conditional statement and a statement of consequences is clearer if the condition is expressed as a subordinate clause.

▶ *Because* the bill was incorrect, the customer was angry.

Relative **pronouns** (*who, whom, which, that*) can be used effectively to combine related ideas within sentences.

▶ OnlinePro, *which* protects computers from malicious programs, makes your system "invisible" to hackers.

Avoid overlapping subordinate constructions that depend on the preceding construction. Overlapping can make the relationship between a relative pronoun and its antecedent less clear.

OVERLAPPING   Shock, *which* often accompanies severe injuries and infections, is a failure of the circulation, *which* is marked by a fall in blood pressure *that* initially affects the skin (*which* explains pallor) and later the vital organs such as the kidneys and brain.

CLEAR   Shock often accompanies severe injuries and infections. Marked by a fall in blood pressure, it is a failure of the circulation, initially to the skin (thus producing pallor) and later to the vital organs like the kidneys and the brain.

S

suffixes

A suffix is a letter or letters added to the end of a word to change its meaning in some way. Suffixes can change the part of speech of a word.

NO SUFFIX   The proposal was *thorough*. [**adjective**]

SUFFIX   The *thoroughness* is obvious. [**noun**]

SUFFIX   The proposal *thoroughly* described the problem. [**adverb**]

The suffix *-like* is sometimes added to nouns to make them into adjectives. The resulting compound word is hyphenated only if it is unusual or might not immediately be clear (childlike, lifelike, *but* dictionary-like, Greenspan-like). See **hyphens**.

surveys (*see* questionnaires)

synonyms

A synonym is a word that means nearly the same thing as another word does (*seller, vendor, supplier*). The dictionary definitions of synonyms are similar, but the connotations may differ. For example, a *seller* may be the same thing as a *supplier*, but the term *supplier* does not suggest a retail transaction as strongly as *seller* does.

Do not try to impress your **readers** by finding fancy or obscure synonyms in a **thesaurus**; the result is likely to be **affectation**. See also **connotation / denotation** and **antonyms**.

syntax

Syntax refers to the way words, phrases, and clauses are combined to form sentences. In English, the most common structure is the subject-verb-object pattern. For more information about the word order of sentences, see **sentence construction**, **sentence faults**, **sentence fragments**, and **sentence variety**.

S

T

tables of contents

A table of contents is typically included in a document longer than ten pages. It previews what the work contains and how it is organized, and it allows **readers** looking for specific information to locate sections by page number quickly and easily.

When creating a table of contents, use the major **headings** and sub-headings of your document exactly as they appear in the text, as shown in the entry **formal reports**. (See the table of contents in Figure F–6 on page 218.) The table of contents is placed in the front matter following the title page and **abstract**, and precedes the list of tables or figures, the foreword, and the preface.

tables

A table organizes numerical and verbal data, such as statistics, into parallel rows and columns that allow **readers** to make precise item-to-item comparisons. Overall trends, however, are more easily conveyed in **graphs** and other **visuals**.

Table Elements

Tables typically include the elements shown in Figure T–1.

Table Number. Table numbers should be placed above tables and as-signed sequentially throughout the document.

Table Title. The title (or *caption*), which is normally placed just above the table, should describe concisely what the table represents.

Box Head. The box head contains the column headings, which should be brief but descriptive. Units of measurement should be either specified as part of the heading or enclosed in parentheses beneath it. Standard **abbreviations** and symbols are acceptable. Avoid vertical or diagonal lettering.

	Table 1. Estimated Emissions from Electric Power Generation (tons per gigawatthour)					
Fuel	Sulphur Dioxide	Nitrogen Oxides	Particulate Matter	Carbon Dioxide	Volatile Organic Compounds	
Eastern coal	1.74	2.90	0.10	1,000	0.06	
Western coal	0.81	2.20	0.06	1,039	0.09	
Gas	0.003	0.57	0.02	640	0.05	
Biomass	0.06	1.25	0.11	0*	0.61	
Oil	0.51	0.63	0.02	840	0.03	
Wind	0	0	0	0	0	
Geothermal	0	0	0	0	0	
Hydro	0	0	0	0	0	
Solar	0	0	0	0	0	
Nuclear	0	0	0	0	0	

*Net emissions.

Source: Department of Energy

Labels pointing to the table: Table number, Table title, Box head, Column headings, Stub, Body, Rule, Footnote, Source line

FIGURE T–1. Elements of a Table

Stub. The stub, the left vertical column of a table, lists the items about which information is given in the body of the table.

Body. The body comprises the data below the column headings and to the right of the stub. Within the body, arrange columns so that the items to be compared appear in adjacent rows and columns. Align the numerical data in columns for ease of comparison, as shown in Figure T–1. Where no information exists for a specific item, substitute a row of dots or a dash to acknowledge the gap.

Rules. Rules are the lines (or *borders*) that separate the table into its various parts. Tables should include top and bottom borders. Tables often include right and left borders, although they may be open at the sides, as shown in Figure T–1. Generally, include a horizontal rule between the column headings and the body of the table. Separate the columns with vertical rules within a table only when they aid clarity.

Footnotes. Footnotes are used for explanations of individual items in the table. Symbols (such as * and †) or lowercase letters (sometimes in parentheses) rather than numbers are ordinarily used to key table footnotes because numbers might be mistaken for numerical data or could be confused with the numbering system for text footnotes. See also **documenting sources**.

Source Line. The source line identifies where the data originated. When a source line is appropriate, it appears below the table. Many or-

Dear Customer:
To order replacement parts, use the following part numbers and prices:

Part	Part Number	Price ($)
Diverter valve	2-912	12.50
Gasket kit	2-776	0.95
Adapter	3-212	0.90

FIGURE T–2. Informal Table

ganizations place the source line below the footnotes. See also **copyright** and **plagiarism**.

Continuing Tables.   When a table must be divided so that it can be continued on another page, repeat the column headings and the table number and title on the new page with a "continued" label (for example, "Table 3. [title], *continued*").

Informal Tables

To list relatively few items that would be easier for the reader to grasp in tabular form, you can use an informal table, as long as you introduce it properly. Although informal tables do not need titles or table numbers to identify them, they do require column headings that accurately describe the information listed, as shown in Figure T–2.

telegraphic style

Telegraphic style condenses writing by omitting **articles**, **pronouns**, **conjunctions**, and **transitions**. Although **conciseness** is important, especially in **instructions**, writers sometimes try to achieve conciseness by omitting necessary words and thus producing misunderstandings. Compare the following two passages and notice how much easier the revised version reads (the added words are italicized).

TELEGRAPHIC   Per 5/21 e-mail, 12 instruction booklets/questionnaire enclosed. Report can be complete when above materials received. July filling quickly, so let's set date. Please advise.

CLEAR *As promised in my May 21* e-mail, enclosed *are* 12 *copies of the* instruction booklet *and the* questionnaire. *We* can complete *the* report when *we* receive *the questionnaires. Our* July *calendar is* filling quickly, so please *call me to* set *a meeting* date *as soon as possible.*

Telegraphic style can also produce __ambiguity__, as the following example demonstrates.

AMBIGUOUS The director wants report written by New York office. [Does the director want a report that the New York office *wrote in the past*, or does the director want the New York office *to write a report in the future*?]

CLEAR The director wants the report *that was* written by the New York office.

CLEAR The director wants the report *to be* written by the New York office.

◀ PROFESSIONALISM NOTE Although you may save yourself work by writing telegraphically, your readers will have to work that much harder to decipher your meaning. Professional courtesy requires that you help your __reader__. ▶

tenant / tenet

A *tenant* is a person who holds or temporarily occupies a property owned by another person. ("The *tenant* was upset by the rent increase.") A *tenet* is an opinion or principle held by a person, an organization, or a system. ("Competition is a central *tenet* of capitalism.")

tense

T

Tense is the grammatical term for <u>verb</u> forms that indicate time distinctions. The six tenses in English are past, past perfect, present, present perfect, future, and future perfect. Each tense also has a corresponding progressive form.

TENSE	BASIC FORM	PROGRESSIVE FORM
Past	I began	I was beginning
Past perfect	I had begun	I had been beginning
Present	I begin	I am beginning
Present perfect	I have begun	I have been beginning
Future	I will begin	I will be beginning
Future perfect	I will have begun	I will have been beginning

Perfect tenses allow you to express a prior action or condition that continues in a present, past, or future time.

PRESENT PERFECT   I *have begun* to write the annual report and will continue for the rest of the month.

PAST PERFECT   I *had begun* to read the manual when the fire alarm sounded.

FUTURE PERFECT   I *will have begun* this project by the time funds are allocated.

Progressive tenses allow you to describe some ongoing action or condition in the present, past, or future.

PRESENT PROGRESSIVE   I *am beginning* to be concerned that we will not meet the deadline.

PAST PROGRESSIVE   I *was beginning* to think we would not finish by the deadline.

FUTURE PROGRESSIVE   I *will be requesting* a leave of absence when this project is finished.

Past Tense

The simple past tense indicates that an action took place in its entirety in the past. The past tense is usually formed by adding *-d* or *-ed* to the root form of the verb. ("We *closed* the office early yesterday.")

Past Perfect Tense

The past perfect tense (also called *pluperfect*) indicates that one past event preceded another. It is formed by combining the helping verb *had* with the past-participle form of the main verb. ("He *had finished* by the time I arrived.")

Present Tense

The simple present tense represents action occurring in the present, without any indication of time duration. ("I *ride* the train.")

A general truth is always expressed in the present tense. ("Time *heals* all wounds.") The present tense can be used to present actions or conditions that have no time restrictions. ("Water *boils* at 212 degrees Fahrenheit.") Similarly, the present tense can be used to indicate habitual action. ("I *pass* the coffee shop every day.") The present tense is also used for the "historical present," as in newspaper headlines ("Dow Jones *Reaches* a High for the Year") or as in references to an author's opinion or a work's contents—even though it was written in the past and the author is no longer living.

> ▶ In *Post-Capitalist Society*, Peter Drucker argues that the educated person will need "to live and work simultaneously in two cultures—that of the 'intellectual,' who focuses on words and ideas, and that of the 'manager,' who focuses on people and work" (215).

Present Perfect Tense

The present perfect tense describes something from the recent past that has a bearing on the present—a period of time before the present but after the simple past. The present perfect tense is formed by combining a form of the helping verb *have* with the past-participle form of the main verb. ("We *have finished* the draft and can now revise it.")

Future Tense

The simple future tense indicates a time that will occur after the present. It uses the helping verb *will* (or *shall*) plus the main verb. ("I *will finish* the job tomorrow.") Do not use the future tense needlessly; doing so merely adds complexity.

> ▶ This system ~~will be~~ *is* explained on page 3.

> ▶ When you press this button, the feeder ~~will move~~ *moves* the paper into position.

Future Perfect Tense

The future perfect tense indicates action that will have been completed at the time of or before another future action. It combines *will have* and the past participle of the main verb. ("She *will have driven* 1,400 miles by the time she returns.")

Shift in Tense

Be consistent in your use of tense. The only legitimate shift in tense records a real change in time. Illogical shifts in tense will only confuse your <u>readers</u>.

▶ Before he visited the facility, the manager ~~meets~~ *met* with the staff.

ESL TIPS for Using the Progressive Form

The progressive form of the verb is composed of two features: a form of the helping verb *be* and the *-ing* form of the base verb.

PRESENT PROGRESSIVE	I *am updating* the Web site.
PAST PROGRESSIVE	I *was updating* the Web site last week.
FUTURE PROGRESSIVE	I *will be updating* the Web site regularly.

The present progressive is used in three ways:

1. To refer to an action that is in progress at the moment of speaking or writing:

   ▶ The technician *is repairing* the copier.

2. To highlight that a state or an action is not permanent:

   ▶ The office temp *is helping* us for a few weeks.

3. To express future plans:

   ▶ The summer intern *is leaving* to return to school this Friday.

The past progressive is used to refer to a continuing action or condition in the past, usually with specified limits.

▶ I *was failing* calculus until I got a tutor.

The future progressive is used to refer to a continuous action or condition in the future.

▶ We *will be monitoring* his condition all night.

Verbs that express mental activity (*believe*, *know*, *see*, and so on) are generally not used in the progressive.

▶ I ~~am believing~~ *believe* the defendant's testimony.

text messaging

Text messaging, or *texting*, refers to the exchange of brief written messages between mobile phones over cellular networks. Text messaging is effective for simple messages communicated between people on the move or in nontraditional workplaces. Although text messaging is similar to **e-mail**, the screen and device size means that text messages are short. ("Client's backup servers down.") Like e-mail, text messages can also include photographs, video, and other digital files. Keep in mind that because texting can be less secure than other media, various policies often limit its use, especially in highly regulated industries like financial services. For the real-time exchange of brief messages, use the phone or **instant messaging**.

◀ PROFESSIONALISM NOTE Avoid using text messages to communicate complicated or vital information. The abbreviated format does not allow for the transmittal of complex or detailed information, and as the sender, you cannot always be certain the text message has been viewed or even received. See **selecting the medium**. ▶

that / which / who

Use *which*, not *that*, with nonrestrictive clauses (clauses that do not change the meaning of the basic sentence). See also **restrictive and nonrestrictive elements**.

NONRESTRICTIVE	After John left the law firm, *which* is the largest in the region, he started a private practice.
RESTRICTIVE	Companies *that* diversify usually succeed.

That and *which* should refer to animals and things; *who* should refer to people. See also **who / whom**.

▶ Dr. Cynthia Winter, *who* recently joined the clinic, treated a dog *that* was severely burned.

The word *that* is often overused and can foster wordiness.

▶ ~~I think that when~~ this project is finished, ~~that~~ you should publish the results.
  (*When* ... *I think*)

However, include *that* in a sentence if it avoids **ambiguity** or improves the **pace**. See also **conciseness**.

T

> *that*
> ► Some designers fail to appreciate̖the workers who operate equipment constitute an important safety system.

there / their / they're

There is an **expletive** (a word that fills the position of another word, phrase, or clause) or an **adverb**.

> EXPLETIVE　*There* were more than 1,500 people at the conference.
>
> ADVERB　More than 1,500 people were *there*.

Their is the **possessive case** form of *they*. ("Managers check *their* e-mail regularly.") *They're* is a **contraction** of *they are*. ("Clients tell us *they're* pleased with our services.")

thesaurus

A thesaurus lists **synonyms** and **antonyms** that are arranged alphabetically or retrievable by categories. Thoughtfully used, a thesaurus can help you with **word choice** during the **revision** phase of the writing process. However, the variety of words it offers may tempt you to choose an inappropriate word for the **context** or to use an obscure synonym. Do not use a thesaurus to impress your **readers**. (See also **affectation**.) Never use a word unless you are sure of its meanings; its **connotations** might be unknown to you and could mislead your readers.

titles

Titles are important because many **readers** use them to decide whether to read documents such as **e-mails**, **memos**, **reports**, and **newsletter articles**. Titles are also crucial for filing and retrieving documents. This entry discusses both creating titles and referring to them in your writing. For advice on titles for figures and tables, see **visuals**.

Reports and Long Documents

Titles for reports, **proposals**, articles, and similar documents should identify the document's topic, reflect its **tone**, and indicate its **scope** and **purpose** as in the following title of an academic article.

> ▶ "Using Chaos Theory to Evaluate Small Business Growth Management"

Such titles should be concise but not so short that they are not specific. For example, the title "Chaos Theory and Small Businesses" announces the topic and might be appropriate for a book, but it does not answer important questions that readers of an article would expect, such as "What does the article say about the relationship of chaos theory and small businesses?" and "What aspect of small businesses is related to chaos theory?"

Avoid titles with such redundancies as "Notes on," "Studies on," or "A Report on." However, works like **annual reports** or **feasibility reports** should be identified as such in the title because this information specifies the purpose and scope of the report. For titles of **progress and activity reports**, indicate the dates in a subtitle ("Quarterly Report on Hospital Admission Rates: January–March 2012"). Avoid using technical shorthand, such as chemical formulas, and other **abbreviations** in your title unless the work is addressed exclusively to specialists in the field. For multivolume publications, repeat the title on each volume and include the subtitle and number of each volume.

Titles should not use the sentence form, except for titles of articles in **newsletters** and magazines that ask a **rhetorical question**.

> ▶ "Is Online Learning Right for You?"

Memos, E-mail, and Internet Postings

Subject lines of memos, e-mails, and Internet postings function as titles and should concisely and accurately describe the topic of the message. Because recipients often use subject-line titles to prioritize and sort their **correspondence**, such titles must be specific.

VAGUE	Subject: Tuition Reimbursement
SPECIFIC	Subject: Tuition Reimbursement for Time-Management Seminar

Although the title in the subject line announces your topic, you should still develop an opening that provides **context** for the message.

Formatting Titles

Capitalization. Capitalize the initial letters of the first and last words of a title as well as all major words in the title. Do not capitalize articles (*a, an, the*), coordinating conjunctions (*and, but*), or short prepositions (*at, in, on, of*) unless they begin or end the title (*The Lives of a Cell*). Capitalize prepositions in titles if they contain five or more letters (*Between, Since, Until, After*), unless you are following a style that recommends otherwise.

Italics.   Use **italics** or underlining when referring to titles of separately published works, such as books, periodicals, newspapers, pamphlets, brochures, legal cases, movies, television programs, and Web sites.

▶ *Turning Workplace Conflict into Collaboration* [book] by Joyce Richards was reviewed in the *New York Times* [newspaper].

▶ We will include a link to *The Weather Channel* (*www.weather.com*).

Abbreviations of such titles are italicized if their spelled-out forms would be italicized.

▶ *NEJM* stands for the *New England Journal of Medicine.*

Italicize the titles of compact and digital video discs, videotapes, plays, long poems, paintings, sculptures, and long musical works.

CD-ROM	*Computer Security Tutorial* (CD-ROM edition)
PLAY	Arthur Miller's *Death of a Salesman*
LONG POEM	T. S. Eliot's *The Wasteland*
PAINTING	M. C. Escher's *Drawing Hands*
SCULPTURE	Auguste Rodin's *The Thinker*
MUSICAL WORK	Gershwin's *Porgy and Bess*

Quotation Marks.   Use **quotation marks** when referring to parts of publications, such as chapters of books and articles or sections within periodicals.

▶ Her chapter titled "Effects of Government Regulations on Motorcycle Safety" in the book *Government Regulation and the Economy* was cited in a recent article, "No-Fault Insurance and Motorcycles," published in *American Motorcyclist* magazine.

Titles of reports, essays, short poems, short musical works (including songs), short stories, and single episodes of radio and television programs are also enclosed in quotation marks.

REPORT	"Analysis of Ethics Cases at CGF Corporation"
ESSAY	Ralph Waldo Emerson's "The American Scholar"
SHORT POEM	Robert Frost's "The Road Not Taken"
SONG	Bob Dylan's "Like a Rolling Stone"
SHORT STORY	Nathaniel Hawthorne's "The Birthmark"
TV PROGRAM	"In Depth: Ray Kurzweil" on C-Span (episode of *In Depth*)

Special Cases.   Some titles, by convention, are not set off by quotation marks, underlining, or italics. Such titles follow standard practice for capitalization and the practice of the organization.

▶ Business Writing [college course title], Old Testament, Magna Carta, the Constitution, Lincoln's Gettysburg Address, the Lands' End Catalog

For citing titles in references and works cited, see **documenting sources**.

to / too / two

To, *too*, and *two* are frequently confused because they sound alike. *To* is used as a **preposition** or to mark an infinitive. See **verbs**.

▶ Send the report *to* the district manager. [preposition]

▶ I do not wish *to* attend. [mark of the infinitive]

Too is an **adverb** meaning "excessively" or "also."

▶ The price was *too* high. [excessively]

▶ I, *too*, thought it was high. [also]

Two is a **number** (*two* buildings, *two* concepts).

tone ·

Tone is the attitude a writer expresses toward the subject and his or her readers. In workplace writing, tone may range widely—depending on the **purpose**, situation, **context**, **audience**, and even the medium of a communication. For example, in an **e-mail** message to be read only by an associate who is also a friend, your tone might be casual.

▶ Your proposal to Smith and Kline is super. We'll just need to hammer out the schedule. If we get the contract, I owe you lunch!

In a message to your manager or superior, however, your tone might be more formal and respectful.

▶ I think your proposal to Smith and Kline is excellent. I have marked a couple of places where I'm concerned that we are committing ourselves to a schedule that we might not be able to keep. If I can help in any other way, please let me know.

T

In a message that serves as a **report** to numerous readers, the tone would be professional, without the more personal **style** that you would use with an individual reader.

> ▶ The Smith and Kline proposal appears complete and thorough, based on our department's evaluation. Several small revisions, however, would ensure that the company is not committing itself to an unrealistic schedule. These revisions are marked on the copy of the report attached to this message.

The **word choice**, the **introduction**, and even the **title** contribute to the overall tone of your document. For instance, a title such as "Ecological Consequences of Diminishing Water Resources in California" clearly sets a different tone from "What Happens When We've Drained California Dry?" The first title would be appropriate for a report; the second title would be more appropriate for a popular magazine or **newsletter article**. See also **correspondence** and **business writing style**.

transition

Transition is the means of achieving a smooth flow of ideas from sentence to sentence, **paragraph** to paragraph, and subject to subject. Transition is a two-way indicator of what has been said and what will be said; it provides **readers** with guideposts for linking ideas and clarifying the relationship between them.

Transition can be obvious.

> ▶ *Having considered* the benefits of a new facility, *we move next* to the question of adequate staffing.

Transition can be subtle.

> ▶ *Even if* this facility can be built at a reasonable cost, there *still remains* the issue of adequate staffing.

Either way, you now have your readers' attention fastened on the problem of adequate staffing, exactly what you set out to do.

Methods of Transition

Transition can be achieved in many ways: (1) using transitional words and phrases, (2) repeating keywords or key ideas, (3) using **pronouns** with clear antecedents, (4) using enumeration (1, 2, 3, or first, second, third), (5) summarizing a previous paragraph, (6) asking a question, and (7) using a transitional paragraph.

Certain words and phrases are inherently transitional. Consider the following terms and their functions:

FUNCTION	TERMS
Result	therefore, as a result, consequently, thus, hence
Example	for example, for instance, specifically, as an illustration
Comparison	similarly, likewise, in comparison
Contrast	but, yet, still, however, nevertheless, on the other hand
Addition	moreover, furthermore, also, too, besides, in addition
Time	now, later, meanwhile, since then, after that, before that time
Sequence	first, second, third, initially, then, next, finally

Within a paragraph, such transitional expressions clarify and smooth the movement from idea to idea. Conversely, the lack of transitional devices can make for disjointed reading. See also **telegraphic style**.

Transition Between Sentences

You can achieve effective transition between sentences by repeating keywords or key ideas from preceding sentences and by using pronouns that refer to antecedents in previous sentences. Consider the following short paragraph, which uses both of those means.

> ► Representative of many American university towns is Middletown. *This midwestern town*, formerly *a sleepy farming community*, is today the home of a large and vibrant *academic community*. Attracting students from all over the Midwest, *this university town* has grown very rapidly in the last ten years.

Enumeration is another device for achieving transition.

> ► The recommendation rests on *two conditions*. *First*, the department staff must be expanded to handle the increased workload. *Second*, sufficient time must be provided for training the new staff.

Transition Between Paragraphs

The means discussed so far for achieving transition between sentences can also be effective for achieving transition between paragraphs. For paragraphs, however, longer transitional elements are often required. One technique is to use an opening sentence that summarizes the preceding paragraph and then moves on to a new paragraph.

> ► One property of material considered for manufacturing processes is hardness. Hardness is the internal resistance of the material to

T

the forcing apart or closing together of its molecules. Another property is ductility, the characteristic of material that permits it to be drawn into a wire. Material also may possess malleability, the property that makes it capable of being rolled or hammered into thin sheets of various shapes. Purchasing managers must consider these properties before selecting manufacturing materials for use in production.

The requirements of hardness, ductility, and malleability account for the high cost of such materials. . . .

Another technique is to ask a question at the end of one paragraph and answer it at the beginning of the next.

▶ New technology has always been feared because it has at times displaced some jobs. However, it invariably creates many more jobs than it eliminates. Almost always, the jobs eliminated by technological advances have been menial, unskilled jobs, and workers who have been displaced have been forced to increase their skills, which resulted in better and higher-paying jobs for them. *In view of this history, should we now uncritically embrace new technology?*

Certainly technology has given us unparalleled access to information and created many new roles for employees. . . .

A purely transitional paragraph may be inserted to aid readability.

▶ The problem of poor management was a key factor that caused the weak performance of the company.

Two other setbacks to the company's fortunes also marked the company's decline: the loss of many skilled workers through the early retirement program and the increased rate of employee turnover.

The early retirement program resulted in engineering staff . . .

If you provide logical **organization** and have prepared an outline, your transitional needs will easily be satisfied and your writing will have **unity** and **coherence**. During **revision**, look for places where transition is missing and add it. Look for places where it is weak and strengthen it.

T

trip reports

A trip report provides a permanent record of a business trip and its accomplishments. It provides managers with essential information about the results of the trip and can enable other staff members to benefit from the information. See also **reports**.

A trip report is normally written as a **memo** or an **e-mail** and addressed to an immediate superior, as shown in Figure T–3. The subject line identifies the destination and dates of the trip. The body of the report explains why you made the trip, whom you visited, and what you accomplished. The report should devote a brief section to each major activity and may include a **heading** for each section. You need not give

From:	James D. Kerson <jdkerson@psys.com>
To:	Roberto Camacho <rcamacho@psys.com>
Sent:	Wed, 11 Jan 2012 12:16:30 EST
Subject:	Trip to Smith Electric Co., Huntington, West Virginia, January 5–6, 2012
Attachments:	📄 Expense Report.xls (25 KB)

I visited the Smith Electric Company in Huntington, West Virginia, to determine the cause of a recurring failure in a Model 247 printer.

Problem
The printer stopped printing periodically for no apparent reason. Repeated efforts to bring it back online eventually succeeded, but the problem recurred at irregular intervals. Neither customer personnel operating the printer nor the local maintenance specialist was able to solve the problem.

Action
On January 5, I met with Ms. Ruth Bernardi, the office manager, who explained the problem. My troubleshooting did not reveal the cause of the problem then or on January 6.

Only when I tested the logic cable did I find that it contained a broken wire. I replaced the logic cable and then ran all the normal printer test patterns to make sure no other problems existed. All patterns were positive, so I turned the printer over to the customer.

Conclusion
There are over 12,000 of these printers in the field, and to my knowledge this is the first occurrence of a bad cable. I believe the logic cable problem found at Smith Electric Company reflects the recurring failures during 2011.

```
==================================
James D. Kerson, Product Analyst
Printer Systems, Inc.
1366 Federal St., Allentown, PA 18101
(610) 747-9955 Fax: (610) 747-9956
jdkerson@psys.com
www.psys.com
==================================
```

T

FIGURE T–3. Trip Report Sent as E-mail (with Attachment)

equal space to each activity—instead, elaborate on the more important ones. Follow the body of the report with the appropriate **conclusions** and recommendations. Finally, if required, attach a record of expenses to the trip report.

trouble reports

The trouble report is used to analyze such events as accidents, equipment failures, or health emergencies. For example, the report shown in Figure T–4 describes a workplace accident involving personal injury. The report assesses the causes of the problem and suggests changes necessary to prevent its recurrence. Because it is usually an internal document, the trouble report normally follows the **memo** format.

In the subject line of the memo, state the precise problem you are reporting. Then, in the body of the report, provide a detailed, precise description of the problem. What happened? Where and when did the problem occur? Was anybody hurt? Was there any property damage? Was there a work stoppage?

In your **conclusion**, state what has been or will be done to correct the conditions that led to the problem. That may include, for example, recommendations for training in safety practices, using improved equipment, and wearing protective clothing. See also **reports**.

❖ ETHICS NOTE Because insurance claims, workers'-compensation awards, and even lawsuits may hinge on the information contained in a trouble report, be sure to include precise times, dates, locations, treatment of injuries, names of any witnesses, and any other crucial information. (Notice the careful use of language and factual detail in Figure T–4.) Be thorough and accurate in your analysis of the problem and support any judgments or conclusions with facts. Be objective: Always use a neutral **tone** and avoid assigning blame. If you speculate about the cause of the problem, make it clear to your **readers** that you are speculating. See also **ethics in writing**. ❖

T

try to

The phrase *try and* is colloquial for *try to*. For business writing, use *try to*.

▶ Please try ~~and~~ finish the report by next week.
   ^to

Consolidated Energy, Inc.

To: Marvin Lundquist, Vice President
           Administrative Services

From: Kalo Katarlan, Safety Officer *KK*
           Field Service Operations

Date: August 20, 2012

Subject: Field Service Employee Accident on August 6, 2012

The following is an initial report of an accident that occurred on Monday,
August 6, 2012, involving John Markley, and that resulted in two days of
lost time.

Accident Summary
John Markley stopped by a rewiring job on German Road. Chico Ruiz
was working there, stringing new wire, and John was checking with
Chico about the materials he wanted for framing a pole. Some tree
trimming had been done in the area, and John offered to help remove
some of the debris by loading it into the pickup truck he was driving.
While John was loading branches into the bed of the truck, a piece
broke off in his right hand and struck his right eye.

Accident Details
1. John's right eye was struck by a piece of tree branch. John had just
   undergone laser surgery on his right eye on Friday, August 3, to
   reattach his retina.
2. John immediately covered his right eye with his hand, and Chico
   Ruiz gave him a paper towel with ice to cover his eye and help ease
   the pain.

7. On Thursday, August 9, John returned to his eye surgeon. Although
   bruised, his eye was not damaged, and the surgically reattached
   retina was still in place.

Recommendations
To prevent a recurrence of such an accident, the Safety Department will
require the following actions in the future:

- When working around and moving debris such as tree limbs or
  branches, all service crew employees must wear safety eyewear with
  side shields.
- All service crew employees must always consider the possibility of
  shock for an injured employee. If crew members cannot leave the job
  site to care for the injured employee, someone on the crew must
  call for assistance from the Service Center. The Service Center
  phone number is printed in each service crew member's handbook.

T

FIGURE T–4. Trouble Report (Using Printed Memo)

U

unity

Unity is singleness of **purpose** and focus; a unified **paragraph** or document has a central idea and does not digress into unrelated topics.

The logical sequence provided through **outlining** is essential to achieving unity. An outline enables you to lay out the most direct route from **introduction** to **conclusion**, and it enables you to build each paragraph around a topic sentence that expresses a single idea. Effective **transition** helps build unity, as well as **coherence**, because transitional terms clarify the relationship of each part to what precedes it.

up

Adding the word *up* to **verbs** often creates a redundant phrase. See also **conciseness**.

- ▶ He quickly wrote ~~up~~ the report.

usage

Usage describes the choices we make among the various words and expressions available in our language. The lines between standard English and nonstandard English and between formal and informal English are determined by those choices. Your guideline in any situation requiring such choices should be appropriateness: Is the word or expression you use appropriate to your **audience** and your subject? When it is, you are practicing good usage.

This book contains many entries on specific usage questions. For a complete list of the usage entries in this book, see "Commonly Misused Words and Phrases" on pages 639–40. Usage entries are also distinguished by italicized section titles (for example, see **utilize**). An up-to-date **dictionary** is also an invaluable aid in your selection of the right word.

U

WEB LINK	Online Usage and Style Guides

Bartleby.com provides classic reference books online, including the *American Heritage Book of English Usage*. For this and additional useful links, see *bedfordstmartins.com/alred* and select *Links for Handbook Entries*.

utilize

Do not use *utilize* as a long variant of *use*, which is the general word for "employ for some purpose." *Use* will almost always be clearer and less pretentious. See **affectation** and **plain language**.

U

V

vague words

A vague word is one that is imprecise in the context in which it is used. Some words encompass such a broad range of meanings that there is no focus for their definition. Words such as *real, nice, important, good, bad, contact, thing,* and *fine* are often called "omnibus words" because they can have so many meanings and interpretations. In speech, our vocal inflections help make the meanings of such words clear. Because you cannot rely on vocal inflections when you are writing, avoid using vague words. Be concrete and specific. See also **abstract / concrete words** and **word choice**.

VAGUE   It was a *good* meeting.
         [Why was it good?]

SPECIFIC The meeting resolved three questions: pay scales, fringe benefits, and workloads.

verbals

Verbals are derived from **verbs** but function as **nouns**, **adjectives**, and **adverbs**. The three types of verbals are gerunds, infinitives, and participles.

Gerunds

A gerund is a verbal ending in *-ing* that is used as a noun. A gerund can be used as a subject, a direct **object**, the object of a **preposition**, a subjective **complement**, or an **appositive**.

► *Budgeting* is a useful managerial skill. [subject]

► I find *budgeting* difficult. [direct object]

► We were unprepared for their *coming*. [object of preposition]

► Seeing is *believing*. [subjective complement]

► My primary departmental function, *programming*, occupies about two-thirds of my time on the job. [appositive]

Only the possessive form of a noun or **pronoun** should precede a gerund.

▶ *John's* working has not affected his grades.

▶ *His* working has not affected his grades.

Infinitives

An infinitive is the bare, or uninflected, form of a verb (for example, *go*, *run*, *fall*, *talk*, *dress*, *shout*) without the restrictions imposed by **person** and **number**. Along with the gerund and the participle, it is one of the nonfinite verb forms. The infinitive is generally preceded by the word *to*, which, although not an inherent part of the infinitive, is considered to be the sign of an infinitive. An infinitive is a verbal and can function as a noun, an adjective, or an adverb.

▶ *To expand* is not the only objective. [noun]

▶ These are the instructions *to follow*. [adjective]

▶ The company struggled *to survive*. [adverb]

The infinitive can reflect two **tenses**: the present and (with a helping verb) the present perfect.

▶ to go [present tense]

▶ to have gone [present perfect tense]

The most common mistake made with infinitives is using the present perfect tense when the simple present tense is sufficient.

▶ I should not have tried to ~~have gone~~ _{go} so early.

Infinitives formed with the root form of transitive verbs can express both active and (with a helping verb) passive **voice**.

▶ to hit [present tense, active voice]

▶ to have hit [present perfect tense, active voice]

▶ to be hit [present tense, passive voice]

▶ to have been hit [present perfect tense, passive voice]

A split infinitive is one in which an adverb is placed between the sign of the infinitive, *to*, and the infinitive itself. Because they make up a grammatical unit, the infinitive and its sign are better left intact than separated by an intervening adverb.

▶ To ~~initially~~ build a client base, experts recommend networking with friends and family.

However, it may occasionally be better to split an infinitive than to allow a sentence to become awkward, ambiguous, or incoherent.

AMBIGUOUS   She agreed immediately *to deliver* the specimen to the lab.
[This sentence could be interpreted to mean that she agreed immediately.]

CLEAR   She agreed *to* immediately *deliver* the specimen to the lab.
[This sentence is no longer ambiguous.]

Participles

A participle is a verb form that functions as an adjective. Present participles end in *-ing*.

▶ *Declining* sales forced us to close one branch office.

Past participles end in *-ed*, *-t*, *-en*, *-n*, or *-d*.

▶ What are the *estimated* costs?

▶ Repair the *bent* lever.

▶ Return the *broken* part.

▶ What are the metal's *known* properties?

▶ The story, *told* many times before, was still interesting.

The perfect participle is formed with the present participle of the helping verb *have* plus the past participle of the main verb.

▶ *Having gotten* [perfect participle] a large bonus, the *smiling* [present participle], *contented* [past participle] sales representative worked harder than ever.

A participle cannot be used as the verb of a sentence. Inexperienced writers sometimes make that mistake, and the result is a **sentence fragment**.

▶ The committee chair was responsible. His vote being the decisive one.   *, his*

▶ The committee chair was responsible. His vote being the decisive one.   *was*

For information on participial and infinitive phrases, see **phrases**.

V

verbs

A verb is a word or group of words that describes an action ("The copier *jammed* at the beginning of the job"), states how something or someone is affected by an action ("He *was disappointed* that the proposal was rejected"), or affirms a state of existence ("She *is* a district manager now").

Types of Verbs

Verbs are either transitive or intransitive. A *transitive verb* requires a direct **object** to complete its meaning.

▶ They *laid* the foundation on October 24.
[*Foundation* is the direct object of the transitive verb *laid*.]

▶ Rosalie Anderson *wrote* the treasurer a memo.
[*Memo* is the direct object of the transitive verb *wrote*.]

An *intransitive verb* does not require an object to complete its meaning. It makes a full assertion about the subject without assistance (although it may have **modifiers**).

▶ The engine *ran*.

▶ The engine *ran* smoothly and quietly.

A *linking verb* is an intransitive verb that links a **complement** to the subject.

▶ The carpet *is* stained.
[*Is* is a linking verb; *stained* is a subjective complement.]

Some intransitive verbs, such as *be*, *become*, *seem*, and *appear*, are almost always linking verbs. A number of others, such as *look*, *sound*, *taste*, *smell*, and *feel*, can function as either linking verbs or simple intransitive or transitive verbs. If you are unsure about whether one of those verbs is a linking verb, try substituting *seem*; if the sentence still makes sense, the verb is probably a linking verb.

▶ Their antennae *feel* delicate.
   [*Seem* can be substituted for *feel*—thus *feel* is a linking verb.]

▶ Their antennae *feel* delicately for their prey.
   [*Seem* cannot be substituted for *feel*; in this case, *feel* is a simple
   intransitive verb.]

Forms of Verbs

Verbs are described as being either finite or nonfinite.

Finite Verbs.   A finite verb is the main verb of a **clause** or sentence. It
makes an assertion about its subject and often serves as the only verb
in its clause or sentence. ("The telephone *rang*, and the receptionist *answered* it.") See also **sentence construction**.

A helping verb (sometimes called an *auxiliary verb*) is used in a
verb **phrase** to help indicate **mood**, **tense**, and **voice**. ("The phone *had*
rung.") Phrases that function as helping verbs are often made up of combinations with the sign of the infinitive, *to* (for example, *am going to*,
is about to, *has to*, and *ought to*). The helping verb always precedes the
main verb, although other words may intervene. ("Machines *will* never
completely *replace* people.")

Nonfinite Verbs.   Nonfinite verbs are **verbals**—verb forms that function as **nouns**, **adjectives**, or **adverbs**.

A *gerund* is a noun that is derived from the *-ing* form of a verb.
("*Seeing* is *believing*.") An *infinitive*, which uses the root form of a
verb (usually preceded by *to*), can function as a noun, an adverb, or an
adjective.

▶ He hates *to complain*. [noun, direct object of *hates*]

▶ The valve closes *to stop* the flow. [adverb, modifies *closes*]

▶ This is the proposal *to consider*. [adjective, modifies *proposal*]

A *participle* is a verb form that can function as an adjective.

▶ The *rejected* proposal may be resubmitted when the concerns are
   addressed.
   [*Rejected* is a verb form that is used as an adjective modifying
   proposal.]

Properties of Verbs

Verbs must (1) agree in **person** with personal pronouns functioning as
subjects, (2) agree in tense and **number** with their subjects, and (3) be in
the appropriate voice.

ESL TIPS for Avoiding Shifts in Voice, Mood, or Tense

To achieve clarity in your writing, you must maintain consistency and avoid shifts. A shift is an abrupt change in voice, mood, or tense. Pay special attention when you edit your writing to check for the following types of shifts.

VOICE

> The captain permits his crew to go ashore, but ~~they are not~~ *he does not permit them* ~~permitted~~ to go downtown.
> [The entire sentence is now in the active voice.]

MOOD

> Reboot your computer, and ~~you should~~ empty the cache.
> [The entire sentence is now in the imperative mood.]

TENSE

> I was working quickly, and suddenly a box ~~falls~~ *fell* off the conveyor belt and ~~breaks~~ *broke* my foot.
> [The entire sentence is now in the past tense.]

Person is the term for the form of a personal pronoun that indicates whether the pronoun refers to the speaker, the person spoken to, or the person (or thing) spoken about. Verbs change their forms to agree in person with their subjects.

> I *see* [first person] a yellow tint, but she *sees* [third person] a yellow-green hue.

Tense refers to verb forms that indicate time distinctions. The six tenses are past, past perfect, present, present perfect, future, and future perfect.

Number refers to the two forms of a verb that indicate whether the subject of a verb is singular ("The copier *was* repaired") or plural ("The copiers *were* repaired").

Most verbs show the singular of the present tense by adding *-s* or *-es* (he *stands*, she *works*, it *goes*), and they show the plural without *-s* or *-es* (they *stand*, we *work*, they *go*). The verb *to be*, however, normally changes form to indicate the singular ("I *am* ready") or plural ("We *are* ready").

Voice refers to the two forms of a verb that indicate whether the subject of the verb acts or receives the action. The verb is in the *active voice* if the subject of the verb acts ("The bacteria *grow*"); the verb is in the *passive voice* if it receives the action ("The bacteria *are grown* in a petri dish").

WEB LINK	Conjugation of Verbs

The conjugation of a verb arranges all forms of the verb so that the differences caused by the changing of the person, tense, number, and voice are readily apparent. For a chart showing the full conjugation of the verb *drive*, see *bedfordstmartins.com/alred* and select *Links for Handbook Entries*.

---

very

The use of **intensifiers** like *very* is tempting, but the word can usually be deleted.

▶ The board was ~~very~~ worried about a possible product recall.

When you do use intensifiers, clarify their meaning.

▶ Web sales were *very* strong; they were up 43 percent this month.

via

Via is Latin for "by way of." The term should be used only in routing instructions.

▶ The package was shipped *via* FedEx.

▶ Her project was funded ~~via~~ the recent legislation.
   as a result of

V

visuals

Visuals can express ideas or convey information in ways that words alone cannot by making abstract concepts and relationships concrete. Visuals can show how things look (drawings, photographs, maps), represent numbers and quantities (graphs, tables), depict processes or relationships (flowcharts, Gantt charts, schematic diagrams), and show hierarchical relationships (organizational charts). They also highlight important information and emphasize key concepts succinctly and clearly.

Many of the qualities of good writing—simplicity, clarity, conciseness, directness—are equally important when creating and using visuals. Presented with clarity and consistency, visuals can help **readers** focus on key portions of your document, presentation, or Web site. Be aware, though, that even the best visual will not be effective without **context**—and most often context is provided by the text that introduces the visual and clarifies its purpose.

The following entries in this book are related to specific visuals and their use in printed and online documents, as well as in **presentations** (see that entry for presentation graphics).

Selecting Visuals

Consider your **audience** and your **purpose** carefully in selecting visuals. You would need different illustrations for an automobile owner's manual or an auto dealer's Web site, for example, than you would for a technician's diagnostic guide. Figure V–1 can help you select the most appropriate visuals, based on their purposes and special features. Jot down visual options when you are considering your **scope** and **organization**.

❖ ETHICS NOTE Visuals have the potential of misleading readers when data are selectively omitted or distorted. For example, Figure G–6 shows a graph that gives a misleading impression of investment returns because the scale is compressed, with some of the years selectively omitted. Visuals that mislead readers call the credibility of you and your organization into question at the least—and they are unethical. The use of misleading visuals can even subject you and your organization to lawsuits. ❖

CHOOSING APPROPRIATE VISUALS

TO SHOW OBJECTS AND SPATIAL RELATIONSHIPS

DRAWINGS CAN . . .

- Depict real objects difficult to photograph
- Depict imaginary objects
- Highlight only parts viewers need to see
- Show internal parts of equipment in cutaway views
- Show how equipment parts fit together in exploded views

PHOTOGRAPHS CAN . . .

- Show actual physical images of subjects
- Record an event in process
- Record the development of phenomena over time
- Record the as-found condition of a situation for an investigation

TO DISPLAY GEOGRAPHIC INFORMATION

MAPS CAN . . .

- Show specific geographic features of an area
- Show distance, routes, or locations of sites
- Show the geographic distribution of information (e.g., populations by region)

TO SHOW NUMERICAL AND OTHER RELATIONSHIPS

TABLES CAN . . .

Divisions	Employees
Research	1,050
Marketing	2,782
Automotive	13,251
Consumer Products	2,227

- Organize information systematically in rows and columns
- Present large numerical quantities concisely
- Facilitate item-to-item comparisons
- Clarify trends and other graphical information with precise data

BAR & COLUMN GRAPHS CAN . . .

- Depict data in vertical or horizontal bars and columns for comparison
- Show quantities that make up a whole
- Track status of projects from start to finish
- Visually represent data shown in tables

V

FIGURE V–1. Chart for Choosing Appropriate Visuals

LINE GRAPHS CAN . . .

- Show trends over time in amounts, sizes, rates, and other measurements
- Give an at-a-glance impression of trends, forecasts, and extrapolations of data
- Compare more than one kind of data over the same time period
- Visually represent data shown in tables

PICTURE GRAPHS CAN . . .

- Use recognizable images to represent specific quantities
- Help nonexpert readers grasp the information
- Visually represent data shown in tables

PIE GRAPHS CAN . . .

- Show quantities that make up a whole
- Give an immediate visual impression of the parts and their significance
- Visually represent data shown in tables or lists

TO SHOW STEPS IN A PROCESS OR RELATIONSHIPS IN A SYSTEM

FLOWCHARTS CAN . . .

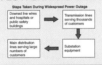

- Show how the parts or steps in a process or system interact
- Show the stages of an actual or a hypothetical process in the correct direction, including recursive steps

TO SHOW RELATIONSHIPS IN A HIERARCHY

ORGANIZATIONAL CHARTS CAN . . .

- Give an overview of an organization's departmental components
- Show how the components relate to one another
- Depict lines of authority within an organization

TO SUPPLEMENT OR REPLACE WORDS

SYMBOLS OR ICONS CAN . . .

- Convey ideas without words
- Save space and add visual appeal
- Transcend individual languages to communicate ideas effectively for international readers

V

FIGURE V–1. Chart for Choosing Appropriate Visuals (*continued*)

Integrating Visuals with Text

After selecting your visuals, carefully integrate them with your text. The following guidelines will improve the effectiveness of your visuals by describing how to position and identify them consistently and uniformly.

Begin by considering the best locations for visuals during the **outlining** stage of your draft. At appropriate points in your outline, either make a rough sketch of the visual, if you can, or write "illustration of . . . ," noting the source of the visual and enclosing each suggestion in a text box. You may also include sketches of visuals in your thumbnail pages, as discussed in **layout and design**. When **writing a draft**, place visuals as close as possible to the text where they are discussed—in fact, no visual should precede its first text mention. Refer to graphics (such as drawings and photographs) as "figures" and to tables as "tables." Clarify for readers why each visual is included in the text. The amount of description you should provide will vary, depending on your readers' backgrounds. For example, nonexperts may require lengthier explanations than experts need.

❖ ETHICS NOTE Obtain written permission to use copyrighted visuals—including images and multimedia material from Web sites—and acknowledge borrowed material in a source line below the caption for a figure and in a footnote at the bottom of a table. Use a site's "Contact Us" page to request approval. Acknowledge your use of any material from the public domain (thus uncopyrighted), such as demographic or economic data from government publications and Web sites, with a source line. See also **copyright**, **documenting sources**, and **plagiarism**. ❖

WRITER'S CHECKLIST   Creating and Integrating Visuals

CREATING VISUALS

✔ Keep visuals simple. Include only information needed for discussion in the text and eliminate unneeded labels, arrows, boxes, and lines.

✔ Position the lettering of any explanatory text or labels horizontally; allow adequate white space within and around the visual.

✔ Specify the units of measurement used, make sure relative sizes are clear, and indicate distance with a scale when appropriate.

✔ Use consistent terminology; for example, do not refer to the same information as a "proportion" in the text and a "percentage" in the visual.

Creating and Integrating Visuals (*continued*)

✔ Define <u>abbreviations</u> the first time they appear in the text and in figures and tables. If any symbols are not self-explanatory, include a key, as in Figure G–11.

✔ Give each visual a caption or concise <u>title</u> that clearly describes its content, and assign figure and table numbers if your document contains more than one illustration or table.

✔ Refer to visuals in the text of your document by their figure or table numbers.

✔ Review <u>global graphics</u> before preparing visuals for an international audience.

INTEGRATING VISUALS

✔ Clarify for readers why each visual is included in the text and provide an appropriate description.

✔ Place visuals as close as possible to the text where they are discussed but always after their first text mention.

✔ Allow adequate white space on the written or Web page around and within each illustration.

✔ Refer to visuals in the text of your document as "figures" or "tables" and by their figure or table numbers.

✔ Consider placing lengthy or detailed visuals in an <u>appendix</u>, which you refer to in the body of your document.

✔ In documents with more than five illustrations or tables, include a section following the <u>table of contents</u> titled "List of Figures" or "List of Tables" that identifies each by number, title, and page number.

✔ Check the editorial guidelines or recommended style manual when preparing visuals for a publication.

voice

In grammar, *voice* indicates the relation of the subject to the action of the <u>verb</u>. When the verb is in the *active voice*, the subject acts; when it is in the *passive voice*, the subject is acted upon.

ACTIVE David Cohen *wrote* the newsletter article.
[The subject, *David Cohen*, performs the action; the verb, *wrote*, describes the action.]

PASSIVE   The newsletter article *was written* by David Cohen.
[The subject, *the newsletter article*, is acted upon; the verb, *was written*, describes the action.]

The two sentences say the same thing, but each has a different emphasis: The first emphasizes *David Cohen*; the second emphasizes *the newsletter article*. In business writing, it is often important to emphasize who or what performs an action. Further, the passive-voice version is indirect because it places the performer of the action behind the verb instead of in front of it. Because the active voice is generally more direct, more concise, and easier for **readers** to understand, use the active voice unless the passive voice is more appropriate, as described on page 579. Whether you use the active voice or the passive voice, be careful not to shift voices in a sentence.

▶ David Cohen corrected the inaccuracy as soon as ~~it was identified~~
                                                identified it
~~by~~ the editor.

Using the Active Voice

Improving Clarity.   The active voice improves **clarity** and avoids confusion, especially in **instructions** and **policies and procedures**.

PASSIVE   Sections B and C *should be checked* for errors.
[Are they already checked?]

ACTIVE   *Check* sections B and C for errors.
[The performer of the action, *you*, is understood: (You) *Check* the sections.]

Active voice can also help avoid **dangling modifiers**.

PASSIVE   Hurrying to complete the work, the cables *were connected* improperly.
[*Who* was hurrying? The implication is the cables were hurrying!]

ACTIVE   Hurrying to complete the work, the technician *connected* the cables improperly.
[Here, *hurrying to complete the work* properly modifies the performer of the action: *the technician*.]

V

Highlighting Subjects.   One difficulty with passive sentences is that they can bury the performer of the action within **expletives** and prepositional **phrases**.

PASSIVE	It *was reported by* the testing staff that the new model is defective.
ACTIVE	The testing staff *reported* that the new model is defective.

Sometimes writers using the passive voice fail to name the performer—information that might be missed.

PASSIVE	The problem *was discovered* yesterday.
ACTIVE	The attending physician *discovered* the problem yesterday.

Achieving Conciseness. The active voice helps achieve **conciseness** because it eliminates the need for an additional helping verb as well as an extra **preposition** to identify the performer of the action.

PASSIVE	Arbitrary changes in policy *are resented by* employees.
ACTIVE	Employees *resent* arbitrary changes in policy.

The active-voice version takes one verb (*resent*); the passive-voice version takes two verbs (*are resented*) and an extra preposition (*by*).

Using the Passive Voice

The passive voice is sometimes effective or even necessary. Indeed, for reasons of tact and diplomacy, you might need to use the passive voice to avoid accusing others.

ACTIVE	Your staff *did not meet* the sales quota last month.
PASSIVE	The sales quota *was not met* last month.

❖ ETHICS NOTE Be careful not to use the passive voice to evade responsibility or to obscure an issue or information that readers should know.

► Several mistakes *were made*.
  [*Who* made the mistakes?]

► It *has been decided*.
  [*Who* has decided?]

See also **ethics in writing**. ❖

When the performer of the action is either unknown or unimportant, of course, use the passive voice. ("The copper mine *was discovered* in 1929.") When the performer of the action is less important than the receiver of that action, the passive voice is sometimes more appropriate. ("Ann Bryant *was presented* with an award by the president.")

When you are explaining an operation in which the reader is not actively involved or when you are explaining a process or a procedure, the passive voice may be more appropriate. In the following example, anyone—it really does not matter who—could be the performer of the action.

> ▶ Area strip mining *is used* in regions of flat to gently rolling terrain, like that found in the Midwest. Depending on applicable reclamation laws, the topsoil *may be removed* from the area *to be mined*, *stored*, and later *reapplied* as surface material during reclamation of the mined land. After the removal of the topsoil, a trench *is cut* through the overburden to expose the upper surface of the coal to be mined. The overburden from the first cut *is placed* on the unmined land adjacent to the cut. After the first cut *has been completed*, the coal *is removed*.

Do not, however, simply assume that any such explanation should be in the passive voice; in fact, as in the following example, the active voice is often more effective.

> ▶ In the operation of an internal combustion engine, an explosion in the combustion chamber *forces* the pistons down in the cylinders. The movement of the pistons in the cylinders *turns* the crankshaft.

Ask yourself, "Would it be of any advantage to the reader to know the performer of the action?" If the answer is yes, use the active voice, as in the previous example.

ESL TIPS for Choosing Voice

Different languages place different values on active-voice and passive-voice constructions. In some languages, the passive is used frequently; in others, hardly at all. As a nonnative speaker of English, you may have a tendency to follow the pattern of your native language. But remember, even though business writing may sometimes require the passive voice, active verbs are highly valued in English.

V

W

wait for / wait on

Wait on should be restricted in writing to the activities of hospitality and service employees. ("We need extra staff to *wait on* customers.") Otherwise, use *wait for*. ("Be sure to *wait for* Ms. Garcia's approval.") See also **idioms**.

Web design (*see* writing for the Web)

when / where / that

When and if (or *if and when*) is a colloquial expression that should not be used in writing.

▶ When ~~and if~~ funding is approved, you will get the position.

If
▶ ~~When and if~~ funding is approved, you will get the position.
  ^

In phrases using the *where . . . at* construction, *at* is unnecessary and should be omitted.

▶ Where is his office ~~at~~?

Do not substitute *where* for *that* to anticipate an idea or fact to follow.

that
▶ I read in the newsletter ~~where~~ sales increased last quarter.
  ^

whether

Whether communicates the notion of a choice. The use of *whether or not* to indicate a choice between alternatives is redundant.

▶ The client asked whether ~~or not~~ the proposal was finished.

W

The phrase *as to whether* is clumsy and redundant. Either use *whether* alone or omit it altogether.

> *We have decided to*
> ▸ ~~As to whether we will~~ commit to a long-term ~~contract, we have~~ *contract.*
> ~~decided to do so.~~

while

While, meaning "during an interval of time," is sometimes substituted for connectives like *and*, *but*, *although*, and *whereas*. Used as a connective in that way, *while* often causes ambiguity.

> *and*
> ▸ Ian Evans is a media director, ~~while~~ Joan Thomas is a vice president for research.

Do not use *while* to mean *although* or *whereas*.

> *Although*
> ▸ ~~While~~ Ryan Sims is retired, he serves as our financial consultant.

Restrict *while* to its meaning of "during the time that."

> ▸ I'll have to catch up on my reading *while* I am on vacation.

who / whom

Who is a subjective case pronoun, and *whom* is the objective case form of *who*. When in doubt about which form to use, substitute a personal pronoun to see which one fits. If *he*, *she*, or *they* fits, use *who*.

> ▸ *Who* is the training coordinator?
> [You would say, "*She* is the training coordinator."]

If *him*, *her*, or *them* fits, use *whom*.

> ▸ It depends on *whom*?
> [You would say, "It depends on *them*."]

W

who's / whose / of which

Who's is the contraction of *who is*. ("*Who's* scheduled today?") *Whose* is the possessive case of *who*. ("Consider *whose* budget should be cut.")

Normally, *whose* is used with persons, and *of which* is used with inanimate objects.

▶ The employee *whose* car had been towed away was angry.

▶ The report recommended over 100 changes, more than half *of which* the client approved.

If *of which* causes a sentence to sound awkward, *whose* may be used with inanimate objects. (Compare: "The business the profits *of which* steadily declined" versus "The business *whose* profits steadily declined.")

-wise

Although the **suffix** *-wise* often seems to provide a tempting shortcut in writing, it leads more often to **affectation** than to economical expression. It is better to rephrase the sentence.

▶ Our department ~~rates~~ high ~~efficiencywise.~~
              has a   *efficiency rating.*

The *-wise* suffix is appropriate, however, in instructions that indicate certain space or directional requirements (*lengthwise, clockwise*).

word choice

Mark Twain once said, "The difference between the right word and almost the right word is the difference between 'lightning' and 'lightning bug.'" The most important goal in choosing the right word in business writing is the preciseness implied by Twain's comment. Vague words and abstract words defeat preciseness because they do not convey the writer's meaning directly and clearly.

VAGUE   It was a *productive* meeting.

PRECISE   The meeting resulted in the approval of the health-care benefits package.

In the first sentence, *productive* sounds specific but conveys little information; the revised sentence says specifically what made the meeting

W

584 writing a draft

"productive." Although **abstract words** may at times be appropriate to your topic, using them unnecessarily will make your writing difficult to understand.

Being aware of the **connotations** and denotations of words will help you anticipate reactions of your audience to the words you choose. Understanding **antonyms** (*fresh/stale*) and **synonyms** (*notorious/infamous*) will increase your ability to choose the proper word. Make other **usage** decisions carefully, especially in technical contexts, such as **average / median / mean** and **biannual / biennial**.

Although many entries throughout this book will help you improve your word choices and avoid impreciseness, the following entries should be particularly helpful:

affectation	24	**euphemisms**	192
biased language	54	**idioms**	269
buzzwords	69	**jargon**	302
clichés	82	**logic errors**	332
conciseness	104	**vague words**	566

A key to choosing the correct and precise word is to keep current in your reading and to be aware of new words in your profession and in the language. In your quest for the right word, an up-to-date **dictionary** is essential. See also **English as a second language**.

WEB LINK | Wise Word Choices

For online exercises on word choice, see *bedfordstmartins.com/alred* and select *Exercise Central.*

---

writing a draft

You are well prepared to write a rough draft when you have established your **purpose** and reader's needs, considered the **context**, defined your **scope**, completed adequate **research**, and prepared an outline (whether rough or developed). (See also **audience** and **outlining**.) Writing a draft is simply transcribing and expanding the notes from your outline into **paragraphs**, without worrying about **grammar**, refinements of language, or **spelling**. Refinement will come with **revision** and **proofreading**. See also "Five Steps to Successful Writing" on page xv.

Writing and revising are different activities. Do not let worrying about a good opening slow you down. Instead, concentrate on getting your ideas on paper—now is not the time to polish or revise. Do not wait for inspiration—treat writing a draft as you would any other on-the-job task.

W

WRITER'S CHECKLIST   Writing a Rough Draft

- ✔ Set up your writing area with whatever supplies you need (laptop, notepads, reference material, and so on). Avoid distractions.
- ✔ Resist the temptation of writing first drafts without planning.
- ✔ Use an outline (rough or developed) as a springboard to start and to write quickly.
- ✔ Give yourself a set time in which you write continuously, regardless of how good or bad your writing seems to be. But don't stop if you are rolling along easily — keep your momentum.
- ✔ Start with the section that seems easiest. Your readers will neither know nor care that the middle section of the document was the first section you wrote.
- ✔ Keep in mind your readers' needs, expectations, and knowledge of the subject. Doing so will help you write directly to your readers and suggest which ideas need further development.
- ✔ When you come to something difficult to explain, try to relate the new concept to something with which the readers are familiar, as discussed in **figures of speech**.
- ✔ Routinely save to your hard drive and create a backup copy of your documents on separate disks or on the company network.
- ✔ Give yourself a small reward — a short walk, a soft drink, a brief chat with a friend, an easy task — after you have finished a section.
- ✔ Reread what you have written when you return to your writing. Seeing what you have already written can return you to a productive frame of mind.

---

writing for the Web

With the importance and pervasiveness of Web technology in the workplace, you may be asked to contribute content for your company or organization Web site. See also **blogs and forums**, **FAQs**, and **questionnaires**.*

---

*For questions about the appropriateness of content you plan to post on the Web, check with your Webmaster or manager to determine if your content complies with your organization's Web policy. On campus, consult your instructor or campus computer support staff about standards for posting Web content.

Crafting Content for Web Pages

Most **readers** scan Web pages for specific information, so state your important points first before providing detailed supporting information. Keep your writing **style** simple and straightforward and, when possible, use **plain language**. Use the following techniques to make your content more accessible to your audience.

Chunking Content. Break up dense blocks of text by dividing them into short **paragraphs** so that they stand out and can be quickly scanned and absorbed. Focus each passage on one facet of your topic. Where necessary, include links to more detailed secondary information.

Headings. Use informative topic **headings** for paragraphs or sections to help readers decide at a glance whether to read a passage. Headings also clarify text by highlighting structure and organization. They signal breaks in coverage from one topic to the next as well as mark **transitions** between topics. Set off headings in boldface or another text style, such as color, on a separate line either directly above or in the left margin, directly across from the text they describe.

Lists. Use bulleted and numbered **lists** to break up dense paragraphs, reduce text length, and highlight important content. Do not overuse lists, however. Lists without supporting explanatory text lack **coherence**.

Keywords. To help search engines and your audience find your site, use terms that highlight content in the first 50 or so words of text for each new topic.

WITHOUT KEYWORDS	We are proud to introduce a new commemorative coin honoring our bank's founder and president. The item will be available on this Web site after December 3, 2011, which is the hundredth anniversary of our first deposit.
WITH KEYWORDS	The new *Reynolds* commemorative coin features a portrait of *George G. Reynolds*, the founder and president of *Reynolds Bank*. The coin can be purchased after December 3, 2011, in honor of the hundredth anniversary of *Reynolds* first deposit.

Directional Cues. Avoid navigational cues that make sense on the printed page but not on a Web screen, such as "as shown in the example below" or "in the graph at the top of this page." Instead, position links so that they are tied directly to the content to which they pertain, such as the *Back to Top* links at sites that are several screens long.

W

Graphics.   Graphics provide information that text alone cannot, as well as visual relief. Use only **visuals** that are appropriate for your audience and **purpose**, however. Avoid overusing complex graphs and animation that can clutter or slow access to your site. Work with the site Webmaster to optimize all graphics for speed of access. Ask about the preferred file-compression format for your visuals. Also consider giving visitors a graphics-free option for quicker access to your content.

Hyperlinks.   Use *internal hyperlinks* to help readers navigate the information at your site. If text is longer than two or three screens, create a table of contents of hyperlinks for it at the top of the Web page and link each item to the relevant content further down the page. Use *external hyperlinks* to enrich coverage of your topic with information outside your site and to help reduce content on your page. When you do, consider placing an icon or a text label next to the hyperlink to inform users that they are leaving the host site. Avoid too many hyperlinks within text paragraphs because they can distract readers, make scanning the text difficult, and tempt readers to leave your site before reaching the end of your page.

Fonts.   Font sizes and styles affect screen legibility. Because computer screens display fonts at lower resolutions compared to printed text, sans serif fonts often work better for online text passages. Do not use ALL CAPITAL LETTERS or **boldface type** for blocks of text because they slow the reader. For content that contains special characters (such as mathematical or chemical content), consult your Webmaster about the best way to submit the files for HTML (hypertext markup language) coding or post them as PDF (portable document format) files. See **layout and design** for a discussion of typography.

Line Length.   Line length also affects readability; short line lengths reduce the amount of eye movement necessary to scan text. Optimal line length is approximately half the width of the screen. To achieve this optimal length, draft text that is between 50 and 70 characters (or between 10 and 12 words) to a line.

❖ ETHICS NOTE   Document sources of information—text, images, **tables**, streaming video, and other multimedia material—or of help received. Seek prior approval from the **copyright** holder before using any such information. Documenting your sources not only is required legally and ethically but also bolsters the credibility of your site. To document your sources, either provide links to your source or use a citation, as described in **documenting sources**. See also **plagiarism**. ❖

W

Linking to Reputable Sites

Links to outside sites can expand your content. However, review such sites carefully before linking to them. Is the site's author or sponsoring organization reputable? Is its content accurate, current, and unbiased? Does the site date-stamp its content with notices such as "This page was last updated on January 1, 2011"? (For more advice on evaluating Web sites, see **research**.) Link directly to the page or specific area of an outside site that is relevant to your users, and be sure that you provide a clear **context** for why you are sending your readers there.

Posting an Existing Document

If you post existing documents to a Web site, try to retain the original sequence and layout of the documents. If, for example, you shorten or revise an existing document for posting to the Web, add a notice informing readers how it differs from the original.

Before posting the document publicly, review it offline to ensure that it is the correct version and that all links work and go to the right places. Consider creating a "single-file version" of the content (a version formatted as a single, long Web page) for readers who will print the content to read offline. See also **proofreading** and **repurposing**.

Protecting User Privacy

Ensure that your content is consistent with your site's privacy policies for site users. A site's privacy statement informs visitors about how the site sponsor handles solicited and unsolicited information, its policy on the use of cookies,* and legal action it takes against hackers.

Writing for a Global Audience

When you write for public access sites, eliminate expressions and references that make sense only to someone familiar with American English. Express **dates**, clock times, and measurements consistent with international practices. For visuals, choose symbols and icons, colors, representations of human beings, and captions that can be easily understood, as described in **global communication** and **global graphics**. See also **biased language** and **English as a second language**.

W

* "Cookies" are small files that are downloaded to your computer when you browse certain Web pages. Cookies hold information, such as your user name and password, so you do not need to reenter it each time you visit the site.

DIGITAL TIP

Using PDF Files

Convert documents such as reports, flyers, and brochures to PDF files to make sure your electronic documents look identical to your printed documents. Readers can view a PDF file online, download it, or print it in whole or in part. Using specialized PDF software, you can create sophisticated forms, add signatures and watermarks to documents, and password-protect sensitive files. For more tips on this topic, go to *bedfordstmartins.com/alred* and select *Digital Tips*, "Using PDF Files."

WEB LINK	Web Design Resources

For a helpful overview of the process and principles of designing Web sites, see *bedfordstmartins.com/alred* and select *Try a Tutorial*, "On Web design." For links to related sites that include advice for improving accessibility for people with disabilities, select *Links for Handbook Entries*.

W

"you" viewpoint

The "you" viewpoint places the reader's interest and perspective foremost. It is based on the principle that most readers are naturally more concerned about their own needs than they are about those of a writer or a writer's organization. See **audience**.

The "you" viewpoint often, but not always, means using the words *you* and *your* rather than *we, our, I,* and *mine.* Consider the following sentence that focuses on the needs of the writer and organization (*we*) rather than on those of the reader.

> ▶ *We must receive* your signed invoice before *we can process* your payment.

Even though the sentence uses *your* twice, the words in italics suggest that the **point of view** centers on the writer's need to receive the invoice in order to process the payment. Consider the following revision, written with the "you" viewpoint.

> ▶ *So you can receive* your payment promptly, please send your signed invoice.

Because the benefit to the reader is stressed, the writer is more likely to motivate the reader to act. See also **persuasion**.

In some instances, as suggested earlier, you may need to avoid using the **pronouns** *you* and *your* to achieve a positive **tone** and maintain goodwill. Notice how the first of the following examples (with *your*) seems to accuse the reader. But the second (without *your*) uses **positive writing** to emphasize a goal that reader and writer share—meeting a client's needs.

ACCUSATORY   *Your* budget makes no allowance for setup costs.

POSITIVE   The budget should include an allowance for setup costs to meet all the concerns of our client.

As this example illustrates, the "you" viewpoint means more than using the pronouns *you* and *your* or adopting a particular writing **style**. By genuinely considering the readers' interests as you write, you can achieve your **purpose** not only in **correspondence** but also in **proposals**, many **reports**, and **presentations**.

your / you're

Your is a possessive **pronoun** ("*your* wallet"); *you're* is the contraction of *you are* ("*You're* late for the meeting"). If you tend to confuse *your* with *you're*, use the search function to review both terms during **proofreading**.

Y

Acknowledgments (continued)

Figure D–10. Conventional Line Drawing Showing Custom Features. Reprinted with the permission of the DeSantis Collection.

Figure D–11. Exploded-View Drawing. From Xerox Corporation, *WorkCentre XD Series User Guide*, page 6. Copyright © Xerox Corporation. Used with permission.

Figure F–6. Formal Report. Reprinted with the permission of Susan Litzinger, a student at Pennsylvania State University, Altoona.

Figure F–8. Online Form with Typical Components. Copyright © Facebook, Inc. Reprinted with permission.

Figure G–4. International Organization for Standardization Symbols. From "Graphical Symbols to Address Consumer Needs" by John Perry, in the *ISO Bulletin* page, March 2003. Copyright © 2003 by ISO. Reprinted with permission.

Figure N–2. Newsletter Article. "What Does ISO 9001:2000 Mean to the Supply Chain?" From *Connection* (October–November 2006): 6. Reprinted with the permission of Ken Cook Company.

Figure N–3. Company Newsletter (Front Page). From *Connection* (February 2008). Reprinted with the permission of Ken Cook Company.

Figure P–2. Photo (of Control Device). Copyright © July 2007 by Ken Cook Company. Reprinted with the permission of Ken Cook Company.

Figure R–6. Résumé (Highlighting Professional Credentials). Prepared by Kim Isaacs, Advanced Career Systems, Inc. Reprinted with permission.

Figure R–11. Advanced Résumé (Combining Functional and Chronological Elements). Prepared by Kim Isaacs, Advanced Career Systems, Inc. Reprinted with permission.

Index

Words and phrases in **bold type** indicate main alphabetical entries. Usage terms appear in *italic type*.

Commonly Misused Words and Phrases

Model Documents and Figures by Topic

Use the following list as a quick reference for finding selected samples of business writing and visuals by topic. See also the complete Contents by Topic on the inside front cover of this book. For additional model documents, see the companion Web site at *bedfordstmartins.com/alred*.

Design and Visuals

Presentations and Meetings

Research and Documentation

Organization, Writing, and Revision